# The
# HUMAN
# RECORD

## Volume II

*The*

# HUMAN
# RECORD

## SOURCES OF GLOBAL HISTORY

FOURTH EDITION / Volume II: Since 1500

### Alfred J. Andrea

*University of Vermont*

### James H. Overfield

*University of Vermont*

HOUGHTON MIFFLIN COMPANY    BOSTON   NEW YORK

Editor-in-Chief: Jean L. Woy
Sponsoring Editor: Nancy Blaine
Associate Editor: Julie Dunn
Project Editor: Tracy Patruno
Senior Manufacturing Coordinator: Priscilla J. Bailey
Senior Marketing Manager: Sandra McGuire

Cover image: The Fitzwilliam Museum, University of Cambridge, England

Source credits appear on pages 539–543, which constitute an extension of the copyright page.

Printed in the U.S.A.

Library of Congress Catalog Card Number: 00-133868

ISBN: 0-618-04247-4

56789-QF-05 04 03 02 01

*As always, our love and thanks to*
*Juanita B. Andrea and Susan L. Overfield*

# Contents

# Geographic Contents

# Topical Contents

## Politics and Government

### *Authority and Leadership*

### *Nationalism*

### *Revolution*

## Women

## Religions and Ethical Systems

### *Christianity*

### *Confucianism*

# Preface

The fourth edition of *The Human Record: Sources of Global History* follows the pedagogical goals and academic principles that guided the first three editions. Foremost among these is our continuing commitment to the proposition that all students of history must meet the challenge of analyzing primary sources, thereby becoming active inquirers into the past. Involvement with primary-source evidence enables students to see that historical scholarship is primarily the intellectual process of drawing inferences and discovering patterns from clues yielded by the past, not of memorizing someone else's conclusions. Moreover, such analysis motivates students to learn by stimulating curiosity and imagination and helps them become critical thinkers who are comfortable with the complex challenges and ambiguities of life.

## Themes and Structure

We have compiled a source collection that traces the intricate course of human history from the rise of the earliest civilizations to the present. Volume I follows the evolution of those cultures that most significantly influenced the history of the world from around 3500 B.C.E. to 1700 C.E., with emphasis on the development of the major religious, social, intellectual, and political traditions of the societies that flourished on that supercontinent known as the *Afro-Eurasian World.* Although our primary focus in Volume I is on the Eastern Hemisphere, we do not neglect the Americas. This first volume also concurrently develops the theme of the growing links and increasingly important exchanges among the world's cultures down to the early modern era. Volume II picks up this theme of growing human interconnectedness by tracing the gradual establishment of Western global hegemony; the simultaneous historical developments in other civilizations and societies around the world; the anti-Western, anticolonial movements of the twentieth century; and the emergence of today's integrated but still often bitterly divided world.

To address these themes in both the depth and breadth they deserve, we have chosen and fit into place selections that combine to present an overview of global history in mosaic form. Each source, in essence, serves two functions: It presents an intimate glimpse into some meaningful aspect of the human past and simultaneously contributes to the creation of a single large composition — an integrated history of the world. With this dual purpose in mind, we have been careful to avoid isolated sources that provide a taste of some culture or age but, by their dissociation, shed no light on patterns of cultural creation, continuity, change, and interchange — the essential components of world history.

In selecting and arranging the various pieces of our mosaic, we have sought to create a balanced picture of human history and to craft a book that reveals the contributions of the world's major cultures. We also have attempted to give our readers a collection of sources representing a wide variety of perspectives and experiences. Believing that the study of history properly concerns every aspect of past human activity and thought, we have sought sources that mirror the practices and concerns of a wide variety of representative persons and groups.

Our pursuit of historical balance has also led us into the arena of artifactual evidence. Although most historians center their research on documents, the discipline requires us to consider all of the clues surrendered by the past, and these include its artifacts. Moreover, we have discovered that students enjoy analyzing artifacts and seem to remember vividly the conclusions they draw from them. For these reasons, we have included a number of illustrations of works of art and other artifacts, such as seals and coins, that users of this book can analyze as historical sources.

## New to This Edition

We have been gratified with the positive response from colleagues and students to the first three editions of *The Human Record.* Many have taken the trouble to write or otherwise contact us to express their satisfaction. Because, however, no textbook is perfect, these correspondents have been equally generous in sharing their perceptions of how we might improve our book and meet more fully the needs of its readers. In response to such suggestions, we engaged in a major restructuring of Volume II in the second edition and an equally radical restructuring of Volume I in the third edition. Despite our overall satisfaction with these revisions, we believe that the changes incorporated in this fourth edition will make both volumes more interesting and useful to students and professors alike.

As difficult as it is to let go of sources that have proved valuable and important for us and our students (and our classroom has always been the laboratory in which we test and refine *The Human Record*), we are always searching for sources that enable us and our students to explore more fully and deeply the rich heritage of world history. For this reason, about a quarter of the sources that appear in the fourth edition are new. In Volume I, for example, we added an early Chinese text on medicine, *The Yellow Emperor's Classic of Medicine,* so students can make comparisons with Hippocrates' *On the Sacred Disease,* and two texts on visits to the Underworld, one from Virgil's *Aeneid,* and one from Muhammad ibn Ishaq's *The Life of the Messenger of God,* which balance similar visits in two other sources, *The Epic of Gilgamesh* and Homer's *Odyssey.* To illustrate major shifts in Chinese thought in the era of the Song Dynasty, we have included excerpts from the seminal Neo-Confucian writings of Zhu Xi. A new section in Chapter 12 illustrates the world as seen from China in the thirteenth century, from Europe in the fourteenth century, and from Korea in the fifteenth century. In Volume II, we have added, among others, new selections on Ming Era Confucianism *(Meritorious Deeds at No Cost);* the colonial experience in Africa and India (G. V. Joshi, "The Economic Results of Free Trade and Railway Extension"; Charlotte Maxeke, "Social Conditions among Bantu Women and Girls"; and Kabaka Daudi Chwa, "Education, Civilization, and 'Foreignization' in Buganda"); the coming of the American and French revolutions (Thomas Paine, *Common Sense,* and excerpts from a prerevolutionary *cahiers*); the Zionist movement (Hayyim Nahman Bialik, Speech at the Inauguration of the Hebrew University of Jerusalem); the decision to drop atomic bombs on Japan (the Franck Report and Secretary of War Henry L. Stimson's "The Decision to Use the Atomic Bomb"); and the origins of the Cold War (George Kennan's Long Telegram and Nikolai Novikov's Telegram of September 27, 1946). Numerous sources carried over from earlier editions have been revised and reconfigured. These include the selections from the Qur'an, the *Analects* of Confucius, Gunther of Pairis's *Constantinopolitan History,* and Marco Polo's descriptions of his travels in Asia in Volume I; and the writings of Martin Luther, Lenin, Mao Zedong, Adam Smith, Jahangir, and Mustafa Kemal in Volume II. In keeping with our goal of providing students a rich array of artifactual sources, we have added new artwork to both volumes. To Volume I we have added examples of fifth-century B.C.E. Hellenic art, second-century C.E. Roman imperial funerary sculptures, a sixth-century Byzantine ivory, and an early fifteenth-century Korean map; and to Volume II, another woodcut from the Reformation Era. In both volumes we have attempted to reflect the most up-to-date scholarly discoveries and controversies in our work. With that in mind we have extensively revised many of our commentaries and notes. As a result, more than one-third of the pages of each volume are essentially new.

## *Learning Aids*

Source analysis initially can be a daunting challenge for any student. With this in mind, we have labored to make these selected sources as accessible as possible by providing the student-user with a variety of aids. First there is the *Prologue,* in which we explain, initially in a theoretical manner and then through concrete examples, how a student of history interprets written and artifactual sources. Next we offer *part, chapter, section, and individual source introductions* — all to help the reader place each selection into a meaningful context and understand each source's historical significance. Because we consider *The Human Record* to be an interpretive overview of global history and therefore a survey of the major patterns of global history that stands on its own as a text, our introductions are significantly fuller than what one normally encounters in a book of sources.

Suggested *Questions for Analysis* precede each source; their purpose is to help the student make sense of each piece of evidence and wrest from it as much insight as possible. The questions are presented in a three-tiered format designed to resemble the historian's approach to source analysis and to help students make historical comparisons on a global scale. The first several questions are usually quite specific and ask the reader to pick out important pieces of information. These initial questions require the student to address two issues: What does this document or artifact say, and what meaningful facts can I garner from it? Addressing concrete questions of this sort prepares the student researcher for the next, more significant level of critical thinking and analysis: drawing inferences. Questions that demand inferential conclusions follow the fact-oriented questions. Finally, whenever possible, we offer a third tier of questions that challenge the student to compare the individual or society that produced a particular source with an individual, group, or culture encountered earlier in the volume. We believe such comparisons help students fix more firmly in their minds the distinguishing cultural characteristics of the various societies they encounter in their survey of world history. Beyond that, this underscores the fact that global history is, at least on one level, comparative history.

Another form of help we offer is to *gloss the sources,* explaining fully words and allusions that first-year college students cannot reasonably be expected to know. To facilitate reading and to encourage reference, the notes appear at the bottom of the page on which they are cited. A few documents also contain *interlinear notes* that serve as transitions or provide needed information.

Some instructors might use *The Human Record* as their sole textbook. Most, however, will probably use it as a supplement to a standard narrative textbook, and many of these professors might decide not to require their students to analyze every entry. To assist instructors (and students) in selecting sources that best suit their interests and needs, we have prepared *two analytical tables of contents* for each volume. The first lists readings and artifacts by geographic and cultural area, and the second by topic. The two tables of contents suggest to professor and student alike the rich variety of material available within these pages, particularly for essays in comparative history.

In summary, our goal in crafting *The Human Record* has been to do our best to prepare the student-reader for success — *success* being defined as comfort with historical analysis, proficiency in critical thinking, learning to view history on a global scale, and a deepened awareness of the rich cultural varieties, as well as shared characteristics, of the human family.

## *Using* The Human Record: *Suggestions from the Editors*

Specific suggestions for assignments and classroom activities appear in the manual entitled *Using* The Human Record: *Suggestions from the Editors.* In it we explain why we have chosen the sources that appear in this book and what insights we believe students should be capable of drawing from them. We also describe classroom tactics for encouraging student thought and discussion on the various sources. The advice we present is the fruit of our own use of these sources in the classroom.

## *Feedback*

As suggested above, we are always interested in receiving comments from professors and students who are using this book. Comments on the Prologue (which appears in each volume) and Volume I should be addressed to A. J. Andrea, whose e-mail address is <aandrea@zoo.uvm.edu>; comments on

Volume II should be addressed to J. H. Overfield at <joverfie@zoo.uvm.edu>. The fact that our university's computer center decided to give the faculty an e-mail address that contains the designation "zoo" opens a line of speculation into which we dare not venture.

## *Acknowledgments*

We are in debt to the many professionals who offered their expert advice and assistance during the various incarnations of *The Human Record*. Scholars and friends at the University of Vermont who generously shared their expertise with us over the years as we crafted these four editions include Doris Bergen, Robert V. Daniels, Carolyn Elliott, Shirley Gedeon, Eric Gilbert, William Haviland, Walter Hawthorn, Richard Horowitz, David Massell, Kristin M. Peterson-Ishaq, Abubaker Saad, Wolfe W. Schmokel, Peter Seybolt, John W. Seyller, Sean Stilwell, Mark Stoler, Marshall True, Diane Villemaire, and Denise Youngblood. We are also in debt to the many reference librarians at the University of Vermont, who have cheerfully helped us in countless ways through all four editions. Additionally, Tara Coram of the Freer and Sackler museums of the Smithsonian Institution deserves special thanks for the assistance she rendered A. J. Andrea in his exploration into the Asian art holdings of the two museums.

We wish also to acknowledge the following instructors who read and commented on portions of this edition in its earliest stages of revision: Blake Beattie, University of Louisville; Frank A. Gerome, James Madison University; Matthew Gordon, Miami University; Joseph Kirklighter, Auburn University; Robert V. Kubicek, University of British Columbia.

Finally, our debt to our beloved spouses is beyond payment, but the dedication to them of each edition of this book reflects in some small way how deeply we appreciate their constant support and good-humored tolerance.

A. J. A.
J. H. O.

# *The* HUMAN RECORD

Volume II

# Prologue

▼▼▼

## *Primary Sources and How We Read Them*

### *What Is History?*

Many students believe that the study of history involves nothing more than memorizing dates, names, battles, treaties, and endless numbers of similar, often uninteresting facts with no apparent relevance to their lives and concerns. After all, so they think, the past is over and done with. Historians know what has happened, and all students have to do is absorb this body of knowledge.

But these notions are wrong. *History involves discovery and interpretation, and its content is vitally relevant to our lives.* Our understanding of history is constantly changing and deepening as historians learn more about the past by discovering new evidence as well as by re-examining old evidence with new questions and methods of analysis. Furthermore, each person who studies the past brings to it a unique perspective and raises questions that are meaningful to that individual. The drive to understand what has gone before us is innately human and springs from our need to know who we are. History serves this function of self-discovery in a special way because of its universality. In short, *the study of history deals with all aspects of past human activity and belief, for there is no subject or concern that lacks a history.* Therefore, each of us can and should explore the origins and historical evolution of whatever is most important to us. Beyond that, history exposes us to new interests, new ways of perceiving reality, and new vistas as we study cultures and times that once were quite unknown to us but which, through our study of the human past, become quite familiar to us.

Regardless of what our questions and interests, old or new, might be, the study and interpretation of our historical heritage involves coming to grips with the dynamics of the historical process. It means exploring how human societies reacted to challenges, threats, and opportunities and how they sought to reshape themselves and the world about them to meet their needs. It means exploring the complex interplay of geography, technology, religion, social structures, and a myriad of other historical factors. It means exploring the ways societies change and the ways they resist change. It means exploring the traditions that have imprinted themselves upon a culture and the ways those traditions have provided continuity over long periods of time. It means exploring the roles of individuals in shaping the course of history and the ways individuals have been shaped by historical circumstances. Indeed, the questions we ask of the past are limited only by our imaginations; the answers we arrive at are limited only by the evidence and our ability to use that evidence thoroughly and creatively.

This collection of sources will help you discover some of the major lines of global historical development and understand many of the major cultural traditions and forces that have shaped history around the world. The word *history,* which is Greek in origin, means "learning through inquiry," and that is precisely what historians do. They discover and interpret the past by asking questions and conducting research. Their inquiry revolves around an examination of evidence left by the past. For lack of a better term, historians call that evidence *primary source material.*

## Primary Sources: Their Value and Limitations

*Primary sources are records that for the most part have been passed on in written form, thereby preserving the memory of past events.* These written sources include, but are not limited to, official records, law codes, private correspondence, literature, religious texts, merchants' account books, memoirs, and the list goes on and on. No source by itself contains unadulterated truth or the whole picture. Each gives us only a glimpse of reality, and it is the historian's task to fit these fragments of the past into a coherent picture.

Imagine for a moment that a mid-twenty-first-century historian decides to write a history of your college class. Think about the primary sources this researcher would use: the school catalogue, class lists, academic transcripts, and similar official documents; class lecture notes, course syllabi, examinations, term papers, and possibly even textbooks; diaries and private letters; the school newspaper, yearbooks, and sports programs; handbills, posters, and even photographs of graffiti; recollections written down or otherwise recorded by some of your classmates long after they graduated. With a bit of thought you could add other items to the list, among them some unwritten sources, such as recordings of popular music and photographs and videotapes of student life and activity. But let us confine ourselves, for the moment, to written records. What do all these documentary sources have in common?

Even this imposing list of sources does not present the past in its entirety. Where do we see the evidence that never made it into any written record, including long telephone calls home, e-mail notes to friends and professors, all-night study groups, afternoons spent at the student union, complaints shared among classmates about professors and courses? Someone possibly recorded memories of some of these events and opinions, but how complete and trustworthy is such evidence? Also consider that all the documents available to this future historian will be fortunate survivors. They will represent only a small percentage of the vast bulk of written material generated during your college career. Thanks to the wastebasket, the "delete" key, the disintegration of materials, and the inevitable loss of life's memorabilia as years slip by, the evidence available to any future historian will be fragmentary. This is always the case with historical evidence. We cannot preserve the records of the past in their totality. Clearly, the more remote the past, the more fragmentary our documentary evidence will be. Imagine the feeble chance any particular document from the twelfth century had of surviving the wars, worms, and wastebaskets of the past eight hundred years.

Now let us consider the many individual pieces of surviving documentary evidence relating to your class's history. As we review the list, we see that no single primary source gives us a complete or totally unbiased picture. Each has its perspective, value, and limitations. Imagine that the personal essays submitted by applicants for admission were a historian's only sources of information about the student body. Would it not then be reasonable for this researcher to conclude that the school attracted only the most gifted and interesting people imaginable?

Despite their flaws, however, essays composed by applicants for admission are still important pieces of historical evidence — when used judiciously. They certainly reflect the would-be students' perceptions of the school's cultural values and the types of people it hopes to attract, and usually the applicants are right on the mark because they have read the school's catalogue — itself an exercise in creative advertising. That catalogue, of course, presents an idealized picture of campus life. But it has value for the careful researcher because it reflects the values of the faculty and administrators who composed it. It also provides useful information regarding rules and regulations, courses, instructors, school organizations, and similar items. That factual information, however, is the raw material of history, not history itself, and certainly it does not reflect the full historical reality of your class's collective experience.

What is true of the catalogue is equally true of the student newspaper and every other piece of evidence pertinent to your class. Each primary source is a part of a larger whole, but as we have already seen, we do not have all the pieces. Think of historical evidence in terms of a jigsaw puzzle. Many of the pieces are missing, but it is possible to put most, though probably not all, of the remaining pieces together in a reasonable fashion to form a fairly accurate and coherent picture. The picture that emerges might not be complete (it never is), but it is useful and valid. The keys to fitting these pieces together are hard work and imagination. Each is absolutely necessary.

## Examining the Sources

Hard work speaks for itself, but students are often unaware that the historian also needs imagination to reconstruct the past. After all, many students ask, doesn't history consist of strictly defined and irrefutable dates, names, and facts? Where does imagination enter into the process of learning these facts?

Again, let us consider your class's history and its documentary sources. Many of those documents provide factual data — dates, names, grades, statistics. While these data are important, individually and collectively they have no historical meaning until they have been *interpreted.* Your college class is more than a collection of statistics and facts. It is a group of individuals who, despite their differences, share and help mold a collective experience. It is a community evolving within a particular time and place. Influenced by its environment, it is, in turn, an influence on that environment. Any valid or useful history must reach beyond dates, names, and facts and interpret the historical characteristics and role of your class. What were its values? How did it change and why? What impact did it have? These are some of the important questions a historian asks of the evidence. The answers the historian achieves help us gain insight into ourselves, our society, and our human nature.

To arrive at answers, the historian must examine each and every piece of relevant evidence in its full context and wring from that evidence as many *inferences* as possible. Facts are the foundation stones of history, but inferences are its edifices. *An inference is a logical conclusion drawn from evidence, and it is the heart and soul of historical inquiry.*

Every American schoolchild learns that "In fourteen hundred and ninety-two, Columbus sailed the ocean blue." That fact is worthless, however, unless the individual understands the motives, causes, and significance of this late-fifteenth-century voyage. Certainly a historian must know when Columbus sailed west. After all, time is history's framework. *Yet the questions historians ask go far beyond simple chronology.* Why did Columbus sail west? What factors made possible Spain's engagement in such enterprises at this time? Why were Europeans willing and able to exploit, as they did, the so-called New World? What were the short- and long-term consequences of the European presence in the Americas? These are some of the significant questions to which historians seek inferential answers, and those answers can only be found in the evidence.

One noted historian, Robin Winks, has written a book titled *The Historian as Detective,* and the image is appropriate although inexact. Like the detective, the historian examines clues in order to reconstruct events. The detective, however, is essentially interested in discovering what happened, who did it, and why, whereas the historian goes one step beyond and asks what it all means. *In addressing the question of meaning, the historian transforms simple curiosity about past events into a humanistic discipline.*

As a humanist, the historian seeks insight into the human condition, but that insight cannot be based on theories spun out of fantasy, wishful thinking, or preconceived notions. It must be based on a methodical and probing investigation of the evidence. Like a detective interrogating witnesses, the historian also must carefully examine the testimony of sources. First and foremost, the historian must evaluate the *validity* of the source. Is it what it purports to be? Artful forgeries have misled many historians. Even if the source is authentic (and most are), it still can be misleading. The possibility always exists that the source's author lied or deliberately misrepresented reality. Even if this is not the case, the historian can easily be led astray by not fully understanding the *perspective* reflected in the document. As any detective who has examined a number of eyewitnesses to an event knows, witnesses' reports often differ radically. The detective has the opportunity to re-examine witnesses and offer them the opportunity to change their testimony in the light of new evidence and deeper reflection. The historian is usually not so fortunate. Even when the historian compares a piece of documentary evidence with other evidence in order to uncover its flaws, there is no way to cross-examine it. Given this fact, it is absolutely necessary for the historian to understand as fully as possible the source's perspective. Thus, the historian must ask several key questions — all of which share the letter W. *What* kind of document is this? *Who* wrote it? *For whom* and *why?* *Where* was it composed and *when?*

The *what* is important because understanding the nature of a particular source can save the historian a great deal of frustration. Many historical sources simply do not address the questions a historian would like to ask of them. That future historian would be foolish to try to learn much about the academic quality of your school's courses from a study of the registrar's class lists and grade sheets. Student and faculty class notes, copies of syllabi, examinations, papers, and textbooks would be far more useful sources.

*Who, for whom,* and *why* are equally important questions. The school catalogue undoubtedly addresses some issues pertaining to student social life. But should this document — designed to attract potential students and to place the school in the best possible light — be read and accepted uncritically? Obviously not. It must be tested against student testimony, which is discovered in such sources as private letters, memoirs, posters, the student newspaper, and the yearbook.

*Where* and *when* are also important questions to ask of any primary source. As a rule, distance in space and time from an event colors perceptions and can diminish the validity of a source's testimony. The recollections of a person celebrating a twenty-fifth class reunion could be insightful and valuable. Conceivably this graduate now has a perspective and information that he or she lacked a quarter of a century earlier. Just as conceivably, however, that person's memory might be playing tricks. A source can be so close to or so distant from the event it deals with that its view is distorted or totally erroneous. Even so, the source is not necessarily worthless. Often the blind spots and misinformation within a source reveal to the researcher important insights into the author's attitudes and sources of information.

The historical detective's task is difficult. In addition to constantly questioning the validity and particular perspectives of available sources, the historical researcher must often use whatever evidence is available in imaginative ways. The researcher must interpret these fragmentary and flawed glimpses of the past and piece together the resultant inferences and insights as well as possible. While recognizing that a complete picture of the past is impossible, the historian assumes the responsibility of recreating a past that is valid and has meaning for the present.

## You and the Sources

*This book will actively involve you in the work of historical inquiry by asking you to draw inferences based on your analysis of primary source evidence. This is* not an easy task, especially at first, but it is well within your capability. Moreover, your professor and we, the authors, will be helping you all along the way.

You realize by now that historians do not base their conclusions on analysis of a single isolated source. Historical research consists of laborious sifting through mountains of documents. We have already done much of this work for you by selecting, paring down, and annotating important sources that individually allow you to gain some significant insight into a particular issue or moment in the long and complex history of our global community. In doing this for you, we do not relieve you of the responsibility of recognizing that no single source, no matter how rich it might appear, offers a complete picture of the individual or culture that produced it. Each source that appears in this book is a piece of valuable evidence, but you should not forget that it is only partial evidence.

*You will analyze two types of evidence: documents and artifacts.* Each source will be authentic, so you do not have to worry about validating it. We will also supply you with the information necessary to place each piece of evidence into its proper context and will suggest questions you legitimately can and should ask of each source. If you carefully read the introductions and notes, the suggested Questions for Analysis, and, most important of all, the sources themselves — and think about what you are doing — solid inferences will follow.

To illustrate how you should go about this task and what is expected of you, we will take you through a sample exercise, step by step. We will analyze two sources: a document from the pen of Christopher Columbus and an early sixteenth-century woodcut. By the end of this exercise, if you have worked closely with us, you should be ready to begin interpreting sources on your own.

Let us now look at the document. We present it just as it would appear in any chapter of this book: first an introduction, then suggested Questions for Analysis, and finally the source itself, with explanatory notes. Because we want to give you a full introduction to the art of documentary source analysis, this excerpt is longer than most documents in this book. Also, to help you refer back to the letter as we analyze it, we have numbered each fifth line. No other sources in this book will have numbered lines. Our notes that comment on the text are probably fuller than necessary, but we prefer to err on the side of providing too much information and help rather than too little. But do not let the length of the document or its many notes intimidate you. Once you get into the source, you should find it fairly easy going.

Your first step in analyzing any source in this book is to read the introduction and the Questions for Analysis. The former places the source into context; the latter provide direction when it comes time to analyze the source. One important point to keep in mind is that every historian approaches a source with at least one question, even though it might be vaguely formulated. Like the detective, the historian wants to discover some particular truth or shed light on an issue. This requires asking specific questions of the witnesses or, in the historian's case, of the evidence. These questions should not be prejudgments. One of the worst errors a historian can make is setting out to prove a point or to defend an ideological position. Questions are simply starting points, nothing else, but they are essential. Therefore, as you approach a source, have your question or questions fixed in your mind and constantly remind yourself as you work your way through a source what issue or issues you are investigating. We have provided you with a number of suggested questions for each source. Perhaps you or your professor will want to ask other questions. Whatever the case, keep focused on these questions and issues, and take notes as you read each source. Never rely on unaided memory; it will almost inevitably lead you astray.

*Above all else, you must be honest and thorough as you study a source.* Read each explanatory footnote carefully, lest you misunderstand a word or an allusion. Try to understand exactly what the source is saying and what its author's perspective is. Be careful not to wrench items, words, or ideas out of context, thereby distorting them. Above all, read the entire source so that you understand as fully as possible what it says and, just as important, what it does not say.

This is not as difficult as it sounds. It just takes concentration and a bit of work. To illustrate the point, let us read and analyze Christopher Columbus's letter and, in the process, try to answer the core question: What evidence is there in this document that allows us to judge Columbus's reliability as a reporter? By addressing this issue, we will actually answer questions 1–5 and 8.

# "With the Royal Standard Unfurled"
▼▼▼

▼ *Christopher Columbus,*
## *A LETTER CONCERNING RECENTLY DISCOVERED ISLANDS*

Sixteenth-century Spain's emergence as the dominant power in the Americas is forever associated with the name of a single mariner — Christopher Columbus (1451–1506). Sponsored by King Ferdinand II of Aragon and Queen Isabella I of Castile, this Genoese sea captain sailed west into the Atlantic seeking a new route to the empires of East Asia described by John Mandeville (Volume I, Chapter 12, source 102), Marco Polo (Volume I, Chapter 12, source 105), and other travel writers he had avidly read. On October 12, 1492, his fleet of three ships dropped anchor at a small Bahamian island, which Columbus claimed for Spain, naming it San Salvador. The fleet then sailed to two larger islands, which he named Juana and Española (today known as Cuba and Hispaniola).

After exploring these two islands and establishing on Española the fort of Navidad del Señor, Columbus departed for Spain in January 1493. On his way home, the admiral prepared a preliminary account of his expedition to the "Indies" for Luis de Santángel, a counselor to King Ferdinand and one of Columbus's enthusiastic supporters. In composing the letter, Columbus borrowed heavily from his official ship's log, often lifting passages verbatim. When he landed in Lisbon in early March, Columbus dispatched the letter overland, expecting it to precede him to the Spanish royal court in faraway Barcelona, where Santángel would communicate its contents to the two monarchs. The admiral was not disappointed. His triumphal reception at the court in April was proof that the letter had served its purpose.

As you analyze the document, be aware of several facts. The admiral was returning with only two of his vessels. He had lost his flagship, the *Santa María,* when it was wrecked on a reef off present-day Haiti on Christmas Day. Also, many of Columbus's facts and figures reflect more his enthusiasm than dispassionate analysis. His estimates of the dimensions of the two main islands he explored grossly exaggerate their sizes, and his optimistic report of the wide availability of such riches as gold, spices, cotton, and mastic was not borne out by subsequent explorations and colonization. Although he obtained items of gold and received plenty of reports of nearby gold mines, the metal was rare in the islands. Moreover, the only indigenous spice proved to be the fiery chili pepper; the wild cotton was excellent but not plentiful; and mastic, an eastern Mediterranean aromatic gum, did not exist in the Caribbean.

---

## QUESTIONS FOR ANALYSIS

1. What does Columbus's description of the physical attributes of the islands suggest about the motives for his voyage?
2. Often the eyes only see what the mind prepares them to see. Is there any evidence that Columbus saw what he wanted to see and discovered what he expected to discover?
3. Is there any evidence that Columbus's letter was a carefully crafted piece of self-promotion by a person determined to prove he had reached the Indies?
4. Is there any evidence that Columbus attempted to present an objective and fairly accurate account of what he had seen and experienced?
5. In light of your answers to questions 3 and 4, to what extent, if at all, can we trust Columbus's account?
6. What do the admiral's admitted actions regarding the natives and the ways in which he describes these people allow us to conclude about his attitudes toward these "Indians" and his plans for them?
7. What does this letter tell us about the culture of the Tainos on the eve of European expansion into their world? Is there anything that Columbus tells us about these people that does not seem to ring totally true?
8. How, if at all, does this letter illustrate that a single historical source read in isolation can mislead the researcher?

1 Sir, as I know that you will be pleased at the great victory with which Our Lord has crowned my voyage, I write this to you, from which you will learn how in thirty-three days, I passed from
5 the Canary Islands to the Indies[1] with the fleet which the most illustrious king and queen, our sovereigns, gave to me. And there I found very many islands filled with people[2] innumerable, and of them all I have taken possession for their
10 highnesses, by proclamation made and with the royal standard unfurled, and no opposition was offered to me. To the first island which I found, I gave the name *San Salvador*,[3] in remembrance of the Divine Majesty, Who has marvelously be-
15 stowed all this; the Indians call it "Guanahani." To the second, I gave the name *Isla de Santa Maria de Concepción;*[4] to the third, *Fernandina;* to the fourth, *Isabella;* to the fifth, *Isla Juana,*[5] and so to each one I gave a new name.
20 When I reached Juana, I followed its coast to the westward, and I found it to be so extensive that I thought that it must be the mainland, the province of Catayo.[6] And since there were neither towns nor villages on the seashore, but only
25 small hamlets, with the people of which I could not have speech, because they all fled immediately, I went forward on the same course, thinking that I should not fail to find great cities and towns. And, at the end of many leagues,[7] seeing
30 that there was no change and that the coast was bearing me northwards, which I wished to avoid, since winter was already beginning, . . . [I] retraced my path as far as a certain harbor known to me. And from that point, I sent two men in-
35 land to learn if there were a king or great cities. They traveled three days' journey and found an infinity of small hamlets and people without number, but nothing of importance. For this reason, they returned.

I understood sufficiently from other Indians, 40 whom I had already taken,[8] that this land was nothing but an island. And therefore I followed its coast eastwards for one hundred and seven leagues to the point where it ended. And from that cape, I saw another island, distant eighteen 45 leagues from the former, to the east, to which I at once gave the name "Española." And I went there and followed its northern coast, as I had in the case of Juana, to the eastward for one hundred and eighty-eight great leagues in a straight 50 line. This island and all the others are very fertile to a limitless degree, and this island is extremely so. In it there are many harbors on the coast of the sea, beyond comparison with others which I know in Christendom, and many rivers, 55 good and large, which is marvelous. Its lands are high, and there are in it very many sierras and very lofty mountains, beyond comparison with the island of Teneriffe.[9] All are most beautiful, of a thousand shapes, and all are accessible and 60 filled with trees of a thousand kinds and tall, and they seem to touch the sky. And I am told that they never lose their foliage, as I can understand, for I saw them as green and as lovely as they are in Spain in May, and some of them were 65 flowering, some bearing fruit, and some in another stage, according to their nature. And the nightingale was singing and other birds of a thousand kinds in the month of November there where I went. There are six or eight kinds of 70 palm, which are a wonder to behold on account of their beautiful variety, but so are the other

---

[1]An inexact term that referred to the entire area of the Indian Ocean and East Asia.
[2]Tainos. See Volume I, Chapter 11, source 98.
[3]"Holy Savior," Jesus Christ.
[4]"The Island of Holy Mary of the Immaculate Conception." Catholics believe that Mary, the mother of Jesus, was absolutely sinless, to the point that she was conceived without the stain of Original Sin (the sin of Adam and Eve) on her soul.
[5]Named for Prince Juan, heir apparent of Castile.

[6]The Spanish term for *Cathay,* which technically was only northern China. Columbus, however, used the term to refer to the entire Chinese Empire of the Great Khan (see note 20).
[7]A league is three miles.
[8]Columbus took seven Tainos on board at San Salvador to instruct them in Spanish and use them as guides and interpreters.
[9]One of the Canary Islands.

trees and fruits and plants. In it are marvelous pine groves, and there are very large tracts of cultivable lands, and there is honey, and there are birds of many kinds and fruits in great diversity. In the interior are mines of metals, and the population is without number. Española is a marvel.

The sierras and mountains, the plains and arable lands and pastures, are so lovely and rich for planting and sowing, for breeding cattle of every kind, for building towns and villages. The harbors of the sea here are such as cannot be believed to exist unless they have been seen, and so with the rivers, many and great, and good waters, the majority of which contain gold. In the trees and fruits and plants, there is a great difference from those of Juana. In this island, there are many spices and great mines of gold and of other metals.

The people of this island, and of all the other islands which I have found and of which I have information, all go naked, men and women, as their mothers bore them,[10] although some women cover a single place with the leaf of a plant or with a net of cotton which they make for the purpose. They have no iron or steel or weapons, nor are they fitted to use them, not because they are not well built men and of handsome stature, but because they are very marvelously timorous. They have no other arms than weapons made of canes, cut in seeding time, to the ends of which they fix a small sharpened stick. And they do not dare to make use of these, for many times it has happened that I have sent ashore two or three men to some town to have speech, and countless people have come out to them, and as soon as they have seen my men approaching they have fled, even a father not waiting for his son. And this, not because ill has been done to anyone; on the contrary, at every point where I have been and have been able to have speech, I have given to them of all that I had, such as cloth and many other things, without receiving anything for it; but so they are, incurably timid. It is true that, after they have been reassured and have lost their fear, they are so guileless and so generous with all they possess, that no one would believe it who has not seen it. They never refuse anything which they possess, if it be asked of them; on the contrary, they invite anyone to share it, and display as much love as if they would give their hearts, and whether the thing be of value or whether it be of small price, at once with whatever trifle of whatever kind it may be that is given to them, with that they are content.[11] I forbade that they should be given things so worthless as fragments of broken crockery and scraps of broken glass, and ends of straps, although when they were able to get them, they fancied that they possessed the best jewel in the world. So it was found that a sailor for a strap received gold to the weight of two and a half *castellanos,*[12] and others much more for other things which were worth much less. As for new *blancas,*[13] for them they would give everything which they had, although it might be two or three *castellanos'* weight of gold or an *arroba*[14] or two of spun cotton. . . . They took even the pieces of the broken hoops of the wine barrels and, like savages, gave what they had, so that it seemed to me to be wrong and I forbade it. And I gave a thousand handsome good things, which I had brought, in order that they might conceive affection, and more than that, might become Christians and be inclined to the love and service of their highnesses and of the whole Castilian nation, and strive to aid us and to give

[10]Marco Polo described a number of islanders in South Asia who went naked. Compare also Columbus's description of this nudity with John Mandeville's account of the people of Sumatra in Volume I, Chapter 12, source 102.

[11]Compare this with Mandeville's description of the people of Sumatra's attitude toward possessions (Volume I, Chapter 12, source 102).

[12]A gold coin of considerable value that bore the seal of Castile.

[13]The smallest and least valuable Spanish coin, it was worth about one-sixtieth of a castellano. Composed of billon, a mixture of copper and silver, it had a whitish hue, hence the name *blanca,* or white.

[14]The equivalent of about sixteen skeins, or balls, of spun textile.

us of the things which they have in abundance and which are necessary to us. And they do not know any creed and are not idolaters;[15] only they all believe that power and good are in the heavens, and they are very firmly convinced that I, with these ships and men, came from the heavens, and in this belief they everywhere received me, after they had overcome their fear. And this does not come because they are ignorant; on the contrary, they are of a very acute intelligence and are men who navigate all those seas, so that it is amazing how good an account they give of everything, but it is because they have never seen people clothed or ships of such a kind.

And as soon as I arrived in the Indies, in the first island which I found, I took by force some of them, in order that they might learn and give me information of that which there is in those parts, and so it was that they soon understood us, and we them, either by speech or signs, and they have been very serviceable. I still take them with me, and they are always assured that I come from Heaven, for all the intercourse which they have had with me; and they were the first to announce this wherever I went, and the others went running from house to house and to the neighboring towns, with loud cries of, "Come! Come to see the people from Heaven!" So all, men and women alike, when their minds were set at rest concerning us, came, so that not one, great or small, remained behind, and all brought something to eat and drink, which they gave with extraordinary affection. In all the island, they have very many canoes, like rowing *fustas,*[16] some larger, some smaller, and some are larger than a *fusta* of eighteen benches. They are not so broad, because they are made of a single log of wood, but a *fusta* would not keep up with them in rowing, since their speed is a thing incredible. And in these they navigate among all those islands, which are innumerable, and carry their goods. One of these canoes I have seen with seventy and eighty men in her, and each one with his oar.

In all these islands, I saw no great diversity in the appearance of the people or in their manners and language. On the contrary, they all understand one another,[17] which is a very curious thing, on account of which I hope that their highnesses will determine upon their conversion to our holy faith, towards which they are very inclined.

I have already said how I have gone one hundred and seven leagues in a straight line from west to east along the seashore of the island Juana, and as a result of that voyage, I can say that this island is larger than England and Scotland together, for, beyond these one hundred and seven leagues, there remain to the westward two provinces to which I have not gone. One of these provinces they call "Avan,"[18] and there the people are born with tails;[19] and these provinces cannot have a length of less than fifty or sixty leagues, as I could understand from those Indians whom I have and who know all the islands.

The other, Española, has a circumference greater than all Spain, . . . since I voyaged along one side one hundred and eighty-eight great leagues in a straight line from west to east. It is a land to be desired and, seen, it is never to be left. And . . . I have taken possession for their highnesses . . . in this Española, in [a] situation

---

[15]Normally the term *idolater* means anyone who worships idols, or sacred statues, but it is unclear exactly what Columbus means here. The Tainos worshipped a variety of deities and spirits known as *cemis,* whom they represented in stone statues and other handcrafted images, also known as cemis. For further information on Taino cemis see Volume I, Chapter 11, source 98. It is hard to imagine Columbus's not having seen carved cemis, which filled the Tainos' villages. To compound the problem of what Columbus meant by their not being idolaters, consider lines 297–299 of this letter, where the admiral refers to idolaters who will be enslaved.

[16]A small oared boat, often having one or two masts.

[17]This is not totally accurate. Columbus's Taino interpreters knew only a little of the language of the Ciguayos whom the admiral encountered on Española in January 1493 (see note 27).

[18]Which the Spaniards transformed into La Habana, or Havana.

[19]Marco Polo reported the existence of tailed humans in the islands of Southeast Asia. In his description of the various fantastic people who supposedly inhabited the islands of Southeast Asia, John Mandeville listed hairy persons who walked on all fours and climbed trees.

most convenient and in the best position for the mines of gold and for all intercourse as well with the mainland . . . belonging to the Grand Khan,[20] where will be great trade and gain. I have taken possession of a large town, to which I gave the name *Villa de Navidad*,[21] and in it I have made fortifications and a fort, which now will by this time be entirely finished, and I have left in it sufficient men for such a purpose with arms and artillery and provisions for more than a year, and a *fusta*, and one, a master of all seacraft, to build others, and great friendship with the king of that land, so much so, that he was proud to call me, and to treat me as a brother. And even if he were to change his attitude to one of hostility towards these men, he and his do not know what arms are and they go naked, as I have already said, and are the most timorous people that there are in the world, so that the men whom I have left there alone would suffice to destroy all that land, and the island is without danger for their persons, if they know how to govern themselves.[22]

In all these islands, it seems to me that all men are content with one woman, and to their chief or king they give as many as twenty.[23] It appears to me that the women work more than the men. And I have not been able to learn if they hold private property; what seemed to me to appear was that, in that which one had, all took a share, especially of eatable things.[24]

In these islands I have so far found no human monstrosities, as many expected,[25] but on the contrary the whole population is very well-formed, nor are they negroes as in Guinea,[26] but their hair is flowing, and they are not born where there is intense force in the rays of the sun; it is true that the sun has there great power, . . .

As I have found no monsters, so I have had no report of any, except in an island "Quaris," the second at the coming into the Indies, which is inhabited by a people who are regarded in all the islands as very fierce and who eat human flesh. They have many canoes with which they range through all the islands of India and pillage and take as much as they can.[27] They are no more malformed than the others, except that they have the custom of wearing their hair long like women, and they use bows and arrows of the same cane stems, with a small piece of wood at the end, owing to lack of iron which they do not possess. They are ferocious among these other people who are cowardly to an excessive degree, but I make no more account of them than of the rest. These are those who have intercourse with the women of "Matinino," which is the first island met on the way from Spain to the Indies,

---

[20]The Mongol emperor of Cathay. Columbus did not know that the Mongol khans had been expelled from power in China in 1368.

[21]"Village of the Nativity" (of the Lord). The destruction of the *Santa Maria* off the coast of Española on Christmas Day (Navidad del Señor) forced Columbus to leave behind thirty-nine sailors at the village garrison, which he named after the day of the incident.

[22]When Columbus returned to Española in November 1493, he discovered the fortification burned to the ground and all thirty-nine men dead. Almost as soon as Columbus had sailed away, the Spaniards began fighting among themselves and split into factions, with only eleven remaining to garrison the fort. The widely scattered groups of Spaniards were wiped out by Tainos led by a chief named Caonabó. Guacanagarí, the king to whom Columbus refers, apparently was wounded trying to defend the Spaniards.

[23]Generally only chiefs could afford large numbers of wives because of the substantial bride prices that were paid, in goods or services, to the families of the women. Notwithstanding, many commoners could and did have two or three wives.

[24]See note 11.

[25]Europeans were prepared to find various races of monstrous humans and semi-humans in the Indies. Accepted accounts of the wonders of the East, such as the travelogue of John Mandeville, told of dog-headed people and a species of individuals who, lacking heads, had an eye on each shoulder. These stories had been inherited from ancient Greek, Roman, and Arabic ethnographies.

[26]Sub-Saharan West Africa (see Volume I, Chapter 12, source 111).

[27]These were the Caribs, who shortly before the arrival of Columbus began to displace the Arawak peoples of the Lesser Antilles, the archipelago to the east and south of Hispaniola. Sixteenth-century Spanish writers unanimously agreed that the Caribs were fierce warriors and cannibalistic. On January 13, 1493, Columbus and his men had a short skirmish on Española with some previously unknown natives, who the admiral incorrectly assumed were Caribs. They were actually Ciguayos, who were less peaceful than the Tainos.

275 in which there is not a man. The women engage in no feminine occupation, but use bows and arrows of cane, like those already mentioned, and they arm and protect themselves with plates of copper, of which they have 280 much.[28]

In another island, which they assure me is larger than Española, the people have no hair.[29] In it, there is gold incalculable, and from it and from the other islands, I bring with me Indians 285 as evidence.[30]

In conclusion, to speak only of that which has been accomplished on this voyage, which was so hasty, their highnesses can see that I will give them as much gold as they may need, if their 290 highnesses will render me very slight assistance; moreover, spice and cotton, as much as their highnesses shall command; and mastic,[31] as much as they shall order to be shipped and which, up to now, has been found only in Greece, in the island 295 of Chios,[32] and the Seignory[33] sells it for what it pleases; and aloe wood, as much as they shall order to be shipped, and slaves, as many as they shall order to be shipped and who will be from the idolaters.[34] And I believe that I have found 300 rhubarb and cinnamon,[35] and I shall find a thousand other things of value, which the people whom I have left there will have discovered, for I have not delayed at any point, so far as the wind allowed me to sail, except in the town of Navidad, 305 in order to leave it secured and well established, and in truth, I should have done much more, if the ships had served me, as reason demanded.

This is enough . . . and the eternal God, our Lord, Who gives to all those who walk in His way triumph over things which appear to be impos- 310 sible, and this was notably one; for, although men have talked or have written of these lands, all was conjectural, without suggestion of ocular evidence, but amounted only to this, that those who heard for the most part listened and judged 315 it to be rather a fable than as having any vestige of truth. So that, since Our Redeemer[36] has given this victory to our most illustrious king and queen, and to their renowned kingdoms, in so great a matter, for this all Christendom ought to 320 feel delight and make great feasts and give solemn thanks to the Holy Trinity[37] with many solemn prayers for the great exaltation which they shall have, in the turning of so many people to our holy faith, and afterwards for temporal 325 benefits,[38] for not only Spain but all Christians will have hence refreshment and gain.

---

[28]The same account appears in Columbus's log. Father Ramón Pane, who composed an ethnographic study of Taino culture during Columbus's second voyage of 1493–1494 (see Volume I, Chapter 11, source 98), also related in great detail the legend of the island of Matinino, where only women resided. The story, as reported by Pane, however, contains no hint that they were warlike women. Apparently Columbus took this Taino legend and combined it with the Greco-Roman myth of the warrior Amazons (see Volume I, Chapter 4, source 31). Mandeville wrote of the land of Amazonia, populated totally by warrior women, and Marco Polo described two Asian islands, one inhabited solely by women and another exclusively by men. There is no evidence that this female society reported by Columbus and Pane ever existed in the Caribbean. The Tainos, however, who were essentially a stone-age people, did import from South America an alloy of copper and gold, which they used for ornaments.

[29]John Mandeville described people with little body hair, and Marco Polo told of Buddhist monks whose heads and faces were shaved.

[30]Columbus brought seven Tainos back to Spain, where they were baptized, with King Ferdinand and Prince Juan acting as godparents. One remained at the Spanish court, where he died, and the others returned with Columbus on his second voyage of 1493.

[31]Columbus and his men wrongly identified a native gumbo-limbo tree, which contains an aromatic resin, with the rare mastic tree, whose costly resin was a profitable trade item for Genoa (see note 33).

[32]An island in the eastern Mediterranean.

[33]The ruling body of Genoa, an Italian city-state. Chios was a possession of Genoa, whose merchants controlled the mastic trade.

[34]Church law forbade the enslavement of Christians, except in the most exceptional circumstances.

[35]Actually, when members of the crew showed Columbus what they thought were aloe, mastic, and cinnamon, the admiral accepted the aloe and mastic as genuine but rejected the supposed cinnamon. One of his lieutenants reported seeing rhubarb while on a scouting expedition.

[36]Jesus Christ.

[37]The Christian belief of three divine persons — Father, Son, and Holy Spirit — contained in a single divine essence.

[38]Benefits that are of this world and last only for a time, as opposed to eternal, or heavenly, rewards.

This in accordance with that which has been accomplished, thus briefly.

330   Done in the caravel,[39] off the Canary Islands,

on the fifteenth of February, in the year one thousand four hundred and ninety-three.

At your orders.          El Almirante.[40]          333

---

[39]A Spanish ocean-going ship.

[40]The Admiral.

### Interpreting Columbus's Letter

Columbus's letter contains a number of interesting facts. For example, the natives Columbus encountered constructed seaworthy canoes and communicated with one another through inter-island travel (lines 181–191). Yet as fascinating and important as such facts are, reading a source with an eye toward garnering tidbits of information is not historical analysis in its fullest sense. *True historical analysis consists of drawing inferential insights from a source and trying to answer, at least in part, the central question of historical study: What does it all mean?* This document allows us to do just that.

*Historians use no secret method or magic formula to draw historical insights from their evidence. All they need are attention to detail, thoroughness, common sense, and a willingness to enter imaginatively into the mind of the source's author as fully and honestly as possible, while trying to set aside personal values and perspectives.* Anyone who is willing to work at it can profitably interpret primary sources.

The researcher always has to evaluate the worth of each source, which means understanding its point of view and reliability. In this letter several things are obvious. Columbus believed he had reached Asian islands (lines 5–23). Marco Polo, John Mandeville, and other writers had provided a number of reference points by which to recognize the Orient (notes 10, 11, 19, 25, 28, and 29), and Columbus believed he had found many of them. Equally obvious is that Columbus tried to present his discoveries in the best light possible. He sent this letter ahead to the court of Ferdinand and Isabella to ensure that when he arrived he would be received with due honor.

Certainly there is exaggeration, self-puffery, error, and possibly even deliberate distortion in this account. As the introduction to the letter informs us, he overestimated the size of several islands (lines 199–206 and 212–215) and, except for chilies, the spices he claimed to have discovered (lines 89, 291, and 299–300) were not there. The admiral also failed to mention that the *Santa Maria* had been lost. Columbus could not escape informing his royal patrons of this unhappy incident, but presumably he wanted to wait until he was at the court, where he could put his own spin on the facts surrounding the incident. Also not mentioned is a skirmish that he and his men had on January 13, 1493, with some hostile strangers, whom he incorrectly assumed were Caribs (note 27). Perhaps that incident, if reported without explanation, would weaken the admiral's implied claim that Spain could easily subjugate these timid Indians (lines 97–110 and 232–240). Generally, however, despite Columbus's enthusiasm and understandable tendency to exaggerate, to conveniently neglect to mention anything negative, and to see what he wanted to see, the admiral *seems* to have wanted to present an essentially factual account.

One indication of this is how Columbus described the people of these islands. His reading of popular travel accounts had prepared him to encounter every sort of human monstrosity (note 25), and undoubtedly he would have enjoyed reporting such contacts. But he honestly reported that all the natives he encountered were quite unmonstrous in appearance and temperament (lines 249–252). Of course, he reported stories of people with tails, cannibals, and warlike women who lived apart from men (lines 206–211 and 256–282), but it is unlikely that the admiral was deliberately misleading anyone on this issue. The Carib cannibals were real enough. Rumors of tailed people and latter-day Amazons conceivably were nothing more than the natives trying to please Columbus or simply the result of poor communication. It is not difficult to imagine that the admiral inquired after the locations of the various human curiosities whom Mandeville, Polo, and others had placed in the islands of the Indian Ocean, and the Tainos, not knowing what he was asking, agreeably pointed across the waters to other islands.

In fact, this raises one issue that has long vexed us and which goes straight to the heart of the question of this source's overall reliability. *How well was Columbus able to communicate with these people?* Columbus insisted that through gestures and learned words the Spaniards and Tainos were able to communicate with one another (lines 163–169), and he certainly learned enough of the Tainos' language to report that they called the island on which he initially landed *Guanahani* (line 15). Nevertheless, we suspect that, despite Columbus's use of captive interpreters, only the most primitive forms of communication were possible between the Europeans and the Native Americans in 1492–1493. Therefore, we should have a healthy skepticism about anything that Columbus reports about the Tainos' beliefs and cosmological perspectives (for example, lines 150–156 and 169–176).

Still, all things considered, it seems reasonable to conclude that Columbus's letter can be accepted as a generally honest, if not totally accurate, account of his discoveries and experiences. That basic honesty, compromised to an extent by an understandable enthusiasm to present his accomplishments positively, comes through in his attempt to describe the islands' physical qualities and the people he encountered. The picture that emerges tells us a great deal about the complex motives that underlay his great adventure.

We notice that Columbus had taken possession of the lands in the names of the Spanish monarchs and even renamed the islands, without once giving thought to the claims of anyone else (lines 7–19). He also thought nothing of seizing some natives as soon as he arrived (lines 40–41 and 163–169) and of bringing several Indians back to Spain (lines 284–285). Moreover, he noted toward the end of his letter that the monarchs of Spain could obtain as many *slaves* as they desired from among the islands' *idolaters* (lines 297–299). At the same time (and this might strike the modern student as curious), Columbus claimed that he had acted generously and protectively toward the native people (lines 111–115 and 127–132), and his letter conveys a tone of admiration and even affection for the people whom he had encountered. Indeed, the admiral expressed a deep interest in winning over the native people of the Indies in an avowed hope that they might become Catholic Christians and loyal subjects of Ferdinand and Isabella (lines 143–150), and he even claimed that they were strongly inclined toward religious conversion (lines 194–198). Yet the very qualities that, as Columbus implied, made the Tainos prime candidates for conversion — intelligence, timidity, naiveté, generosity, ignorance, technological backwardness, lack of an articulated religious creed, an ability to communicate freely among themselves, and a sense of wonder at the Europeans — also made them ripe for subjugation.

The tone of this letter suggests that Columbus was concerned with these people as humans and was genuinely interested in helping them achieve salvation through conversion. It is equally clear, however, that Columbus believed he and Catholic Spain had a right and duty to subjugate and exploit these same people. Such tension continued throughout the Spanish colonial experience in the Americas.

Subjugation of the Indians and their lands involved more than just a sense of divine mission and Christian altruism — as real as those motives were. Columbus, his royal patrons, and most others who joined overseas adventures expected to gain in earthly wealth as well (see especially lines 317–327). Even a superficial reading of his letter reveals the admiral's preoccupation with the riches of the islands — riches that it seems he knowingly exaggerated (note 35). Gold, spices, cotton, aromatic mastic, and, of course, slaves were the material rewards that awaited Christian Europeans, and Columbus was fully interested in them and wanted Ferdinand and Isabella to underwrite future trips so that he could discover them in abundance (lines 286–307). So exaggeration can be found in this account, but it seems to be exaggeration based on conviction.

Was Columbus being cynical, hypocritical, or deliberately ironic when in his closing words he claimed that Jesus Christ had provided this great victory to the Spanish monarchs (and indeed to all Christendom) and from that victory would flow the dual benefits of the conversion of so many people and worldly riches (lines 317–327)? Cynicism, hypocrisy, and conscious irony are not likely explanations. It seems more likely that these closing remarks reveal the mind of a man who saw no contradiction between spreading the faith and benefiting materially from that action, even if doing so meant exploiting the converts.

Please note that in presenting this insight, we have tried to avoid moral judgments. This does not mean that we accept slavery as justifiable or believe it is proper to dispossess people of their lands and cultures. What it does mean is that we are trying to understand Columbus and his world view and not to sit in judgment of a man whose values in some respects were radically different from our own. Passing moral judgment on a distant society's values and the actions that resulted from them might be emotionally satisfying, but it will not change what has happened. Doing so also could conceivably blind the judge to the historical context in which those actions took place. As suggested earlier, *we study the past in order to gain insight and wisdom regarding the human condition. If that insight is to have any validity whatsoever, it must be based on as dispassionate a study of the evidence as possible.*

Another point merits mention. Perhaps you disagree with our conclusion that Columbus's letter is basically an honest and valuable source, despite its shortcomings. Well, if you do, you are in excellent company. Two eminent historians — William D. Phillips, Jr., and Carla Rahn Phillips, in their book *The Worlds of Christopher Columbus* — characterize this letter as "a tissue of exaggerations, misconceptions, and outright lies." We obviously disagree in our interpretation of the degree, nature, and extent of the letter's misstatements. No historian is infallible, and certainly we do not claim that distinction. Moreover, no source is so clear in all respects that it lacks areas of potential disagreement for historians. That, in fact, is one of the exciting aspects of historical research. Despite all the facts and conclusions that historians generally agree on, there are numerous areas in which they carry on spirited debate. *The very nature of history's fragmentary, flawed evidence makes debate inevitable.*

What is more, no historian can possibly see everything there is to be seen in every source. What this means, so far as you are concerned, is that *there is plenty of latitude in the sources that appear in this book for you to arrive at valid insights that are unique to you.* In so doing, however, you must at all times attempt to divorce yourself of present-mindedness and to enter imaginatively into the world of the author whose work you are analyzing. You will note that, as is the case with this letter from Columbus, throughout this book we have endeavored to help you do this by means of suggested Questions for Analysis. Use these questions for guidance, but do not be constrained by them. If you find a question inappropriate, misleading, or wrong-headed in its assumptions, feel free to follow your own mind. Just be ready to defend the questions you have chosen to ask along with the conclusions you have reached in answering them.

We can ask many other questions of Columbus's letter and garner other insights from it. Certainly it tells us a lot about Taino culture. Despite his cultural blinders, his naiveté, his tendency to see what he wanted to see, and his probably exaggerated belief in his ability to communicate with these people, Columbus seems to be a reasonably accurate and perceptive observer. Thus anyone interested in Caribbean cultures before the Europeans had much of a chance to influence them must necessarily look to this and similar accounts of first contacts. In fact, it would be good practice for you, right now, to try to answer question 7, which we have deliberately left unanswered. You will be surprised at how much you can learn about the Tainos from this brief description. As you do this exercise, however, do not forget to ask yourself constantly: How reliable does Columbus appear to be on this specific point, and what is the basis for my conclusion?

After you have tested your own powers of historical analysis in this exercise, it would be wise to put the letter aside for the present. We trust that by now you have a good idea of how to examine and mine a documentary source. Now let us consider artifacts.

### Unwritten Sources

Historians distinguish between the prehistorical and historical past, with the chief defining feature of any historical culture being that it provides written records from which we can reconstruct its past. Without a large volume and variety of documentary sources, it is impossible to write any society's history in detail. This is not to say that the unwritten relics of the past are worthless. Archeology proves their value, and even historians use such sources. As a rule, however, no matter how extensive a culture's physical remains might be, if it has not left us records we can read, its history largely remains a closed book.

Given the central role documents play in our reconstruction of the past, it should surprise no one to learn that most historians concentrate their research almost exclusively on written sources. Yet historians would be foolish to overlook *any* piece of evidence from the past. As suggested earlier, photographs could be a rich source for anyone researching the history of your class. That future historian might also want to study all of the extant souvenirs and supplies sold in your school's bookstore. Examined properly they could help fill in some gaps in the story of your class's cultural history.

Artifacts can be illuminating, particularly when used in conjunction with written records. Coins can tell us a lot about a society's ideals or its leaders' programs. Art in its many forms can reveal the interests, attitudes, and perceptions of various segments of society, from the elites to the masses. More down-to-earth items, such as domestic utensils and tools, allow us to infer quite a bit about the lives of common individuals. In this book we concentrate largely on written sources, for reasons already outlined. It would be wrong, however, if we totally overlooked artifacts. So, scattered throughout these chapters you will find important pieces of unwritten evidence. Let us look at an example and proceed to interpret it.

# The Family Dinner
▼▼▼
## ▼ *AN ANONYMOUS WOODCUT OF 1511*

Columbus arrived in Barcelona in April 1493 to learn not only had his letter arrived, but it had already been published and publicly circulated. Within months the letter was translated into several languages; the Latin translation alone went through nine editions, several of which were lavishly illustrated, before the end of 1494. Printers discovered that educated Europeans had an almost insatiable

desire to learn about the peoples and lands Columbus and other explorers were discovering, and they catered to that interest. Their clientele wanted not only to read about the fascinating peoples, plants, and animals of these lands — they wanted also to see them. Consequently, as books on the new explorations proliferated, so did the number of printed illustrations. Many are fanciful and tell us more about the Europeans who created them than the peoples and regions they supposedly portrayed. The woodcut print we have chosen appeared in a popular English pamphlet of 1511.

---

## QUESTIONS FOR ANALYSIS

1. What scene has the artist set? What has the artist placed to the immediate right of the standing man, and what function does it have in this scene?

2. What do each person's actions, dress, and demeanor tell us about her or him?
3. What does this illustration tell us about popular European notions concerning the natives of the New World?

## Interpreting the Woodcut

What a charming, even idyllic domestic scene! An attractive mother nurses an infant at her breast while amusing an older child with a feather. A well-muscled, equally attractive, and proud father stands nearby, holding the tools of his trade while next to him the family's dinner is slowly cooking. Dinner, of course, may strike us as macabre, as these are cannibals, and it looks like roast European is on the menu. The tools of the father's trade are weapons. Both children are naked, and the parents are virtually nude, save for what appear to be leaves that cover their loins, decorative necklaces, armbands and anklets of some indeterminate material, and feathers in their long and unkempt hair.

What is the message? What we have is a reprise of the image provided by Columbus in his letter of 1493: the *noble savage.* These are fully human beings with human bonds and affections. Yet they are still savages, as their clothing (or lack of it), decorations, hair styles, weapons, and choice of food would have suggested to most sixteenth-century Europeans. Here, as Columbus and many of those who followed agreed, were a people who could become Christians but who also, by virtue of their backwardness, were to be subjugated. There is something appealing about their innocent savagery, but what of that poor fellow whose severed leg and head are slowly roasting?

Have we read too much into the woodcut? It is arguable that we may have. The historian always faces this problem when trying to analyze an isolated piece of evidence, particularly a nonverbal source. Yet this artifact is not completely isolated, for we brought to its analysis insight gained from documentary evidence — Columbus's letter. That is how we generally read the artifacts of historical cultures. We attempt to place them in the context of what we have already learned or inferred from documentary sources. Documents illuminate artifacts, and artifacts make more vivid and tangible the often shadowy world of words.

As you attempt to interpret the unwritten sources in this book, keep in mind what you have learned from the documents you have already read, your textbook, and class lectures. Remember that we have chosen these artifacts to illustrate broad themes and general trends. You should not find their messages overly subtle. As with the documents, always try to place each piece of nonverbal evidence into its proper context, and in that regard, read the introductions and Questions for Analysis very carefully. We will do our best to provide you with all the information and clues you need.

Good luck and have fun!

# Part One

⌄⌄⌄

## *The World in the Era of Europeanean Expansion: 1500–1650*

A new era in world history began in 1419 when two Portuguese ships left Lagos harbor, at the southwest corner of the Iberian peninsula, and sailed into the ocean waters off Africa's northwest coast. Sailing some six hundred miles, they reached Porto Santo, an uninhabited island that was part of the Madeiras and some four hundred miles west of Morocco, then returned home. In 1420, the first Portuguese settlers arrived in the Madeiras with a charter from Prince Henry the Navigator (1394–1460), the third son of the Portuguese King João I and the driving force behind the 1419 expedition and those that followed. Within a decade the settlers had introduced grapevines from Crete and sugar cane from Sicily, and were reaping handsome profits from the export of wine, high-quality wood, and especially sugar to Europe.

The significance of these events is indisputable: They launched the era of European exploration, expansion, and colonization. During the fifteenth century the Portuguese pushed farther south, claiming and colonizing the Cape Verde Islands and the islands of São Thomé and Principe, establishing fortified trading posts on Africa's coast, and learning more about wind patterns, ocean currents, commercial opportunities, and the peoples of Africa. In 1488 Bartholomeu Dias rounded the Cape of Good Hope, and in 1498, a fleet of four ships under the command of Vasco da Gama sailed around the cape and reached Calicut, on India's west coast. From India the Portuguese pushed on, reaching the Malay Coast in 1511, China in 1513, and Japan in 1542. They soon established regular commercial routes to Asia and began to reap huge profits from the sale of African ivory, pepper, and slaves and Asian spices, silks, and dyes.

Even before da Gama had reached India, other Europeans were seeking new ocean routes to Asia. Columbus's voyage of 1492 was the first of dozens of expeditions that established a vast Spanish empire not in Asia but the Americas. Northern European rulers, mariners, and merchants soon joined the competition. The French, Dutch, English, Danes, and Swedes struck claims to lands in the Americas and the Caribbean, and the French, Dutch, and English challenged the Portuguese in Asia. That modest Portuguese expedition of 1419 thus initiated two centuries of European exploration, conquest, and commercial expansion, the consequences of which were so momentous that no other development in the era rivals its importance.

Early European expansion had its greatest impact on Mexico and Central and South America, where Spanish and Portuguese conquests, accompanied by economic exploitation and the introduction of Old World diseases, killed millions of Amerindians and destroyed much of their ancient culture. The indigenous people north of Mexico faced similar threats only after 1600, when European settlers arrived on North America's east coast and soon began their slow but relentless expansion into the continent's interior. Here, the Native Americans' loss of territory and identity was not as sudden or dramatic, but the process was no less painful, and the results no less disastrous.

Africa too was deeply affected by European expansion, even though Europeans remained on the coast and relied on Africans to bring them items for trade. In addition to ivory, gold, and pepper, these items included slaves, who at first were shipped by the Portuguese to the Canary Islands and the Azores, then to Europe, and finally, in ever greater numbers, to the New World.

Asia underwent important changes during the 1500s and 1600s but they had little to do with the Europeans' arrival. In Southwest Asia the Ottoman Turks conquered and consolidated an empire that was centered in Anatolia, Syria-Palestine, and the Arabian Peninsula but also included territory in northern Africa and southeastern Europe. Farther east two new states, the Safavid Empire in Persia and the Mughal Empire in India, took shape. In Southeast Asia the continued expansion of Islam was the most notable development. In Japan, a century of civil war ended in 1603, when the Tokugawa clan established a new regime that kept Japan unified and stable for nearly three centuries. In China, Manchu invaders from the north displaced the declining Ming Dynasty in 1644, and established China's last imperial dynasty, the Qing. By 1650, only the Philippine Islands, conquered by Spain; Siberia, conquered by Russia; and parts of Indonesia, controlled by the Dutch, were under direct European rule.

Europeans, although successful in extending their influence around the world, experienced wrenching changes and bitter conflicts at home. Overseas trade and the influx of gold and silver from the Americas fueled economic growth, but its impact was uneven. Inflation caused hardship for individuals and governments alike, and some regions such as Italy declined as commerce began to shift from the Mediterranean to the Atlantic coast. Knowledge of new lands and peoples added to the intellectual ferment fueled by Renaissance humanism, Protestantism, new scientific discoveries, and the invention in the 1450s of printing by movable type by the German goldsmith Johannes Gutenberg. Wars, religious controversy, and revolts were endemic, and some states such as France came close to disintegrating. By 1650, however, Europeans had resolved many of their conflicts. European society had not just survived a century and a half of rapid change but had gathered strength from it. Europe's emergence as a world power had begun.

# Chapter 1

▼▼▼

# Europe in an Age of Conflict and Expansion

The early modern period in European history, traditionally dated from 1500 to 1650, was a time of contrasts and contradictions. Religious bigotry and intolerance were rife, and tens of thousands of individuals from across the religious spectrum were persecuted because of their convictions. But the era also produced Europe's first advocates of religious toleration, and a few societies actually implemented their ideas. Spectacular advances were made in astronomy, physics, and mathematics, and a solid foundation was laid for one of Europe's most enduring achievements — experimental, mathematics-based science. Yet the same society that produced Copernicus, Kepler, and Descartes was terrorized by witchcraft, and the resulting witch hunts and witch trials resulted in the execution of tens of thousands of individuals, most of whom were women who confessed after agonizing torture. Tons of gold and silver poured into Europe from mines in the Americas, and some merchants and investors amassed huge fortunes from Asian and transatlantic trade. But mounting inflation caused hardship for many sixteenth-century Europeans, and around 1600, plague, famine, war, and economic contraction caused a decline in the overall standard of living. Similar contrasts existed in politics. Advocates of centralized monarchy contended with defenders of local autonomy, divine right absolutists faced believers in regicide, and kings battled parliaments.

The origins of these conflicts and contradictions are rooted in the disasters that struck Europe in the fourteenth and fifteenth centuries — papal exile and schism, the Black Death, war, and economic dislocation. They were the backdrop for even more jarring changes initiated in the early 1500s. Within just a few decades Europeans faced a host of disconcerting new realities — overseas discoveries, the rapid spread of print culture, Copernicus's rejection of ancient astronomy, Ottoman Turkish conquests in Hungary and Austria, and massive peasant revolts in Germany. Overshadowing everything else was the onset of the Protestant Reformation, sparked by Martin Luther's attack on the Roman Catholic Church in 1517. The Protestant revolt shattered Europe's religious unity and destroyed the defining characteristic of medieval society — its allegiance to Catholic Christianity as defined by the Roman papacy. In addition, the religious conflicts spawned by the Reformation heightened social and political tensions and contributed to the wars, revolts, and social conflicts that marred the age.

Expansionist Europe was not, as one might expect, a stable, cohesive, and self-confident society. Its success in developing the military potential of gunpowder weapons, in particular the ability to mount guns on ocean-going ships, enabled Europeans to extend their political and economic power to the Americas, Africa, and Asia. But these accomplishments, rightly deemed significant by historians, gave scant comfort to the majority of Europeans, who faced a troubled present and anticipated the future with more foreboding than hope.

▼▼▼

# Protestant Revolt and Catholic Response

During the High Middle Ages (ca. 1000–1300), the "age of faith," the esteem and devotion accorded the Catholic Church resulted in part from the clergy's moral example and leadership and in part from the Church's promise that its doctrines and practices, if followed, assured eternal salvation. During the fourteenth and fifteenth centuries, however, the Church was rocked by schism, scandal, financial deficits, political challenges, and uninspired and corrupt leadership. Anger over abuses intensified, especially in northern Europe, and many Europeans began to question the Church's ability to "deliver" the salvation they fervently sought. This doubt and alienation goes far in explaining the success of the Protestant Reformation, begun in 1517 when a German friar, Martin Luther, openly challenged certain Catholic teachings, especially the doctrine that people could escape punishment for their sins by purchasing indulgences. By 1650, Protestants dominated northern Germany, Scandinavia, England, Scotland, the Netherlands, and major Swiss cities, and comprised a significant minority in France and central Europe.

No area of European life was unaffected by the Protestant Reformation. Education expanded throughout Europe because of the need of competing churches for educated leadership, and especially among Protestants because of their belief in the importance of Bible reading by the laity. The distinction between clergy and laity was narrowed because of the Protestant doctrine that devout Christian laypersons were just as pleasing to God as priests and members of religious orders. Literacy among women increased as a result of Protestant educational efforts, and in the view of some historians, the Protestant affirmation of clerical marriage fostered a more positive view of women. Conversely, Protestant women saw no appreciable gains in their legal or economic status and were just as likely as their Catholic sisters to be victims of witch hunts and witch trials.

The religious struggles of the Reformation era also profoundly affected politics. With religious passions exacerbating dynastic rivalries and internal conflicts, Europe endured a century of religious wars, some of which were civil wars and some wars between states. They began with warfare between Protestant and Catholic factions in Switzerland in 1531 and ended with the Thirty Years' War (1618–1648), Europe's most deadly and devastating military conflict until the twentieth century.

The most significant result of the Reformation era was its contribution to the ongoing secularization of European politics, culture, and thought. In the short run, the emergence of Protestantism intensified religious feeling and thrust religion into the forefront of European life. Largely as a result of its struggles with Protestantism, the Catholic Church itself regained much of its spiritual focus and vitality. In the long run, however, the proliferation of competing faiths divided and weakened Europe's churches, and the interminable years of religious intolerance and warfare discredited religion in the eyes of many. The gradual acceptance of religious diversity within individual states and Europe as a whole was a sign that religion was being taken less seriously. Paradoxically, the very intensity of the era's religious passions helped undermine the role of religion in European life and thought.

# Luther's Views of Christianity and Society
▼▼▼

## 1 ▼ Martin Luther, TABLE TALK

The Protestant Reformation had many voices, but its first prophet was Martin Luther (1483–1546), whose Ninety-Five Theses initiated the momentous anti-Catholic rebellion in 1517. Born into the family of a German miner and educated at the University of Erfurt, the young Luther was preparing for a career as a lawyer when suddenly in 1505 he abandoned his plans and became an Augustinian friar. Luther's decision resulted from dissatisfaction over his relationship with God and doubts about his personal salvation. He hoped that life as an Augustinian would protect him from temptation and give him the opportunity to win God's favor by devoting himself to prayer, study, and the sacraments. His spiritual anxieties soon returned, however. Overwhelmed by his perceived inadequacies and failings, he became convinced that he could never "earn" his salvation by living up to the high standards of selflessness, charity, and purity required by

Jesus of his followers. Certain he could never satisfy an angry, judging God, he was terrorized by the prospect of eternal damnation.

During the 1510s, however, while teaching theology at the University of Wittenberg, Luther found spiritual peace through his reflections on the scriptures, especially Paul's letter to the Romans. He concluded that human beings, burdened as they were by weakness and sin, could never *earn* salvation by leading blameless lives and performing in the proper spirit the pious acts enjoined by the Catholic Church. Rather, salvation was an unmerited divine gift, resulting from God-implanted faith in Jesus, especially the redemptive power of His death and resurrection. This fundamental Protestant doctrine of *justification by faith alone* inspired Luther's Ninety-Five Theses, in which he attacked Catholic teaching on indulgences, by which people could atone for their sins and ensure their own and loved ones' salvation by contributing money to the Church. Within five years Luther was the recognized leader of a religious movement — Protestantism — that broke with the Catholic Church over the question of salvation and a host of other issues concerning Christianity and the Christian life.

As the Reformation spread from Germany to other parts of Europe, leadership of Protestantism passed to younger people such as John Calvin in Geneva and John Knox in Scotland. Luther remained at Wittenberg, and as pastor and professor wrote hundreds of sermons and treatises in defense of his religious vision. He and his wife, Katharina, a former nun, made their home in the Augustinian convent in Wittenberg where Luther had lived as a friar. Here they raised a family and entertained scores of religious leaders and students with whom the talkative Luther loved to discourse on the issues of the day. From 1522 to 1546 some of these guests recorded Luther's most notable sayings as they remembered them, and from their journals we have what is known as Luther's *Tischreden,* or *Table Talk.*

## QUESTIONS FOR ANALYSIS

1. According to Luther, what is the importance of the Bible in a Christian's life? How in his view had the Roman Catholic Church obscured the meaning and message of the Bible?
2. How does Luther define faith? Why is it superior to external acts of devotion?
3. What are Luther's objections to the pope and other officials of the Catholic Church?
4. How does Luther view marriage, in particular women's role in marriage?
5. What perspective does Luther have on the Turkish threat to European society? How is his perspective affected by his religious beliefs?

## SALVATION

Because as the everlasting, merciful God, through his Word[1] and Sacraments,[2] talks and deals with us, all other creatures excluded, not of temporal things which pertain to this vanishing life, and which in the beginning he provided richly for us, but as to where we shall go when we depart from here, and gives unto us his Son for a Savior, delivering us from sin and death, and purchasing for us everlasting righteousness, life, and salvation, therefore it is most certain, that we do not die away like the beasts that have no understanding; but so many of us . . . shall through him be raised again to life everlasting at the last day, and the ungodly to everlasting destruction.

▾ ▾ ▾

## FAITH VERSUS GOOD WORKS

He that goes from the gospel to the law,[3] thinking to be saved by good works,[4] falls as uneasily as he who falls from the true service of God to idolatry; for, without Christ, all is idolatry and fictitious imaginings of God, whether of the Turkish Qur'an, of the pope's decrees, or Moses' laws; if a man think thereby to be justified and saved before God, he is undone.

▾ ▾ ▾

The gospel preaches nothing of the merit of works; he that says the gospel requires works for salvation, I say, flat and plain, is a liar.

Nothing that is properly good proceeds out of the works of the law, unless grace be present; for what we are forced to do, goes not from the heart, nor is acceptable.

▾ ▾ ▾

A Capuchin[5] says: wear a grey coat and a hood, a rope round thy body, and sandals on thy feet. A Cordelier says: put on a black hood; an ordinary papist says: do this or that work, hear mass, pray, fast, give alms, etc. But a true Christian says: I am justified and saved only by faith in Christ, without any works or merits of my own; compare these together, and judge which is the true righteousness.

▾ ▾ ▾

I have often been resolved to live uprightly, and to lead a true godly life, and to set everything aside that would hinder this, but it was far from being put in execution; even as it was with Peter,[6] when he swore he would lay down his life for Christ.

▾ ▾ ▾

I will not lie or dissemble before my God, but will freely confess, I am not able to effect that good which I intend, but await the happy hour when God shall be pleased to meet me with his grace.

▾ ▾ ▾

A Christian's worshiping is not the external, hypocritical mask that our friars wear, when they

---

[1]The *Word* is God's message, especially as revealed through Jesus' life.

[2]Sacraments are rites that are outward visible signs of an inward spiritual grace. Of the seven Catholic sacraments, Luther retained two: baptism and the eucharist.

[3]By *law* Luther meant religious rules and regulations; he believed that futile human efforts to live strictly according to the dictates of the law undermined true faith.

[4]All the ceremonies and pious activities such as pilgrimages, relic veneration, and attendance at Mass that the Catholic Church promoted as vehicles of God's grace and eternal salvation.

[5]The Capuchins and Cordeliers were both branches of the Franciscan order noted for their austerity and strict poverty. A distinctive feature of the Capuchins' dress was their peaked hood, or *capuche*.

[6]One of Jesus' twelve apostles; following Jesus' arrest by Roman soldiers before his crucifixion, Peter three times denied any relationship with Jesus, despite having vowed shortly before to lay down his life for his teacher. Eventually, Peter died a martyr in Rome.

chastise their bodies, torment and make themselves faint, with ostentatious fasting, watching, singing, wearing hair shirts, scourging themselves, etc. Such worshiping God does not desire.

## THE BIBLE

Great is the strength of the divine Word. In the epistle to the Hebrews,[7] it is called "a two-edged sword." But we have neglected and scorned the pure and clear Word, and have drunk not of the fresh and cool spring; we are gone from the clear fountain to the foul puddle, and drunk its filthy water; that is, we have sedulously read old writers and teachers, who went about with speculative reasonings, like the monks and friars.

▼ ▼ ▼

The ungodly papists prefer the authority of the church far above God's Word; a blasphemy abominable and not to be endured; void of all shame and piety, they spit in God's face. Truly, God's patience is exceeding great, in that they are not destroyed; but so it always has been.

## THE PAPACY AND THE CLERGY

How does it happen that the popes pretend that they form the Church, when, all the while, they are bitter enemies of the Church, and have no knowledge, certainly no comprehension, of the holy gospel? Pope, cardinals, bishops, not a soul of them has read the Bible; it is a book unknown to them. They are a pack of guzzling, gluttonous wretches, rich, wallowing in wealth and laziness, resting secure in their power, and never, for a moment, thinking of accomplishing God's will.

▼ ▼ ▼

Kings and princes coin money only out of metals, but the pope coins money out of everything — indulgences, ceremonies, dispensations, pardons; all fish come to his net. . . .

▼ ▼ ▼

A gentleman being at the point of death, a monk from the next convent came to see what he could pick up, and said to the gentleman: Sir, will you give so and so to our monastery? The dying man, unable to speak, replied by a nod of the head, whereupon the monk, turning to the gentleman's son, said: You see, your father makes us this bequest. The son said to the father: Sir, is it your pleasure that I kick this monk down the stairs? The dying man nodded as before, and the son immediately drove the monk out of doors.

▼ ▼ ▼

The papists took the invocation of saints from the pagans, who divided God into numberless images and idols, and ordained to each its particular office and work. . . .

The invocation of saints is a most abominable blindness and heresy; yet the papists will not give it up. The pope's greatest profit arises from the dead; for the calling on dead saints brings him infinite sums of money and riches, far more than he gets from the living. . . .

▼ ▼ ▼

In Popedom they make priests, not to preach and teach God's Word, but only to celebrate mass, and to roam about with the sacrament. For, when a bishop ordains a man, he says: Take the power to celebrate mass, and to offer it for the living and the dead. But we ordain priests according to the command of Christ and St. Paul, namely, to preach the pure gospel and God's Word. The papists in their ordinations make no mention of preaching and teaching God's Word, therefore their consecrating and ordaining is false and wrong, for all worshiping which is not ordained

---

[7]Paul's Letter to the Hebrews, a part of the Christian Bible, or New Testament.

of God, or erected by God's Word and command, is worthless, yea, mere idolatry.

## THE REFORM OF THE CHURCH

The pope and his crew can in no way endure the idea of reformation; the mere word creates more alarm at Rome than thunderbolts from heaven or the day of judgment. A cardinal said the other day: Let them eat, and drink, and do what they will; but as to reforming us, we think that is a vain idea; we will not endure it. Neither will we Protestants be satisfied, though they administer the sacrament in both kinds, and permit priests to marry;[8] we will also have the doctrine of the faith pure and unfalsified, and the righteousness that justifies and saves before God, and which expels and drives away all idolatry and false-worshiping; with these gone and banished, the foundation on which Popedom is built also falls.

▼ ▼ ▼

The chief cause that I fell out with the pope was this: the pope boasted that he was the head of the church, and condemned all that would not be under his power and authority; . . . Further, he took upon him power, rule, and authority over the Christian church, and over the Holy Scriptures, the Word of God; no man must presume to expound the Scriptures, but only he, and according to his ridiculous conceits; this was not to be endured. They who, against God's word, boast of the church's authority, are mere idiots.

## MARRIAGE AND CELIBACY

Who can sufficiently admire the state of conjugal union, which God has instituted and founded, and from which all human creatures, indeed, all states proceed. Where would we be if it did not exist? But neither God's ordinance, nor the gra-cious presence of children, the fruit of matrimony, moves the ungodly world, which sees only the temporal difficulties and troubles of matrimony, but sees not the great treasure that is hidden in it. We were all born of women — emperors, kings, princes, yea, Christ himself, the Son of God, did not disdain to be born of a virgin. Let the scoffers and rejecters of matrimony go hang, . . . and the papists, who reject married life, and yet have mistresses; if they need to scoff at matrimony, let them be consistent, and keep no concubines.

▼ ▼ ▼

Marrying cannot be without women, nor can the world subsist without them. To marry is medicine against unchastity. A woman is, or at least should be, a friendly, courteous, and merry companion in life; this is why they are named house-honors, the honor and ornament of the house, and inclined to tenderness; for this reason are they chiefly created, to bear children, and be the pleasure, joy, and solace of their husbands.

## THE TURKISH THREAT

The 21st of December, 1536, George, marquis of Brandenburg came to Wittenberg, and announced that the Turks had obtained a great victory over the Germans,[9] whose fine army had been betrayed and massacred; he said that many princes and brave captains had perished, and that such Christians as remained prisoners, had been treated with extreme cruelty, their noses being slit, and themselves used most scornfully. Luther said: We, Germans, must consider hereupon that God's anger is at our gates, that we should hasten to repentance while there is yet time. . . .

▼ ▼ ▼

---

[8]Two of the many changes that Protestants demanded were allowing all Christians to receive the sacrament of the eucharist in the forms of bread and wine (in medieval Roman Catholic practice, only the priest drank the eucharistic wine) and allowing priests to marry. The principle behind both changes was Luther's teaching that all Christians are priests — that is, responsible for their own religious faith.
[9]It is unclear what battle the marquis is describing.

Luther complained of the emperor Charles's[10] negligence, who, taken up with other wars, suffered the Turk to capture one place after another. It is with the Turks as previously it was with the Romans, every subject is a soldier, as long as he is able to bear arms, so they have always a disciplined army ready for the field; whereas we gather together ephemeral bodies of vagabonds, untried wretches, upon whom is no dependence. My fear is, that the papists will unite with the Turks to exterminate us.[11] Please God, may my anticipation not come true, but certain it is, that the desperate creatures will do their best to deliver us over to the Turks.

---

[10]Holy Roman Emperor Charles V, also known as Charles I as king of Spain, a devout Roman Catholic.

[11]The German Lutherans.

# A Blueprint for Catholic Revival

▼▼▼

## 2 ▼ *DECREES OF THE COUNCIL OF TRENT*

The reform and revival of the Roman Catholic Church in the sixteenth century had many dimensions — the foundation of new religious orders such as the Society of Jesus; reforms initiated by dedicated popes, bishops, and leaders of religious orders; the political and military victories of arch-Catholic Spain; the emotional appeal of Baroque art and architecture; and the renewed religious dedication on the part of countless individual Catholic men and women. Nothing, however, had more impact than the Council of Trent, an assembly of Catholic churchmen that met on and off for almost twenty years between 1545 and 1563. Out of its debates and decisions there emerged a new Catholic Church more confident of its doctrines, clearer in its mission, and better prepared to meet the challenge of Protestantism.

Many times in the past, popes had convened Church councils to give bishops, archbishops, leaders of religious orders, and theologians an opportunity to debate and resolve fundamental theological and policy issues. In the 1520s, the main supporter of convening a Church council was the Holy Roman Emperor, Charles V. He hoped that such a gathering, attended by both Protestants and Catholics, would encourage Protestants to return to the Catholic fold by ending abuses and working out compromises on divisive theological issues. Such a strategy was at first opposed by many Catholics, including Pope Clement VII (1523–1534), who feared that a council would undermine the papacy's fiscal base and authority.

Clement's successor, Paul III (1534–1549), who fully understood the gravity of the Church's situation and faced continuing pressure from Charles V, concluded that convening a Church council was necessary. Agreeing on a time, place, and agenda was difficult, however, and as a result, the long-awaited council did not begin until 1545 in the small city of Trent, on the southern slope of the Austrian Alps. With its deliberations and votes gradually coming under the control of the papacy and the numerically ascendant Italian bishops, the council continued to meet until 1563, during which time it clarified numerous theological issues and approved a broad program of reform and renewal for the Church.

For those hoping for reconciliation between Protestants and Catholics, the Council of Trent was a disappointment. Few Protestants attended, and in any case by the time the council met, theological disagreements had hardened to the point that meaningful compromises were unlikely. Instead of a vehicle for reconciliation, the Council of Trent affirmed traditional Catholic teachings and girded the Church for its struggle with Protestantism during the era of religious wars.

## QUESTIONS FOR ANALYSIS

1. The council's declarations on justification affirm the importance of God's freely given grace as the beginning of the process of salvation. What else is required of the believer to gain salvation?
2. What do the "Rules Concerning Prohibited Books" reveal about the Church's attitudes toward the printed book?
3. How openly do the council's statements admit that abuses existed among the clergy? What steps are proposed concerning clerical performance and behavior?
4. If Luther or one of his followers had been given the opportunity to comment on the decisions of the Council of Trent represented in this assignment, what would they have said about the following issues: individual salvation; the Bible; the nature of the priesthood; saints; indulgences?

## CONCERNING JUSTIFICATION[1]

If anyone says that man can be justified before God by his own works, whether done by his own natural powers or through the teaching of the law, without divine grace through Jesus Christ, let him be an anathema.[2] . . .

If anyone says that the sinner is justified by faith alone, meaning that nothing else is required . . . in order to obtain the grace of justification, and that it is not in any way necessary that he be prepared and disposed by the action of his own will, let him be anathema. . . .

If anyone says that the commandments of God are, even for one that is justified and constituted in grace, impossible to observe, let him be anathema. . . .

If anyone says that the justice received is not preserved and also not increased before God through good works, but that those works are merely the fruits and signs of justification obtained, but not the cause of its increase, let him be anathema. . . .

## CONCERNING PROHIBITED BOOKS

Since it is clear from experience that if the Sacred Books[3] are permitted everywhere and without discrimination in the vernacular, there will . . . arise . . . more harm than good, the matter is . . . left to the judgement of the bishop or inquisitor;[4] who may . . . permit the reading of the

---

[1]The process by which a person is freed from the penalty of his or her sin and is accepted by God as worthy of being saved.

[2]Refers to a person made subject to excommunication and extreme condemnation by an official ecclesiastical authority.

[3]The Bible.

[4]An official approved by the Church to discover and suppress heresy, an opinion at variance with the authorized teaching of the Church.

Sacred Books translated into the vernacular by Catholic authors to those who they know will derive from such reading no harm but rather an increase of faith and piety, which permission they must have in writing. Those, however, who presume to read or possess them without such permission may not receive absolution from their sins till they have handed them over to the ordinary.[5] Bookdealers who sell or in any other way supply Bibles written in the vernacular to anyone who has not this permission, shall lose the price of the books, which is applied by the bishop to pious purposes, and . . . they shall be subject to other penalties which are left to the judgement of the same bishop. . . .

All book-dealers and venders of books shall have in their libraries a list of books which they have for sale subscribed by the said persons, and without the permission of the same appointed persons they may not under penalties of confiscation of the books and other penalties, . . . possess or sell or . . . supply other books. . . .

Finally, all the faithful are commanded not to presume to read or possess any books contrary to the prescriptions of these rules or the prohibition of this list. And if anyone should read or possess books by heretics . . . , he incurs immediately the sentence of excommunication.[6]

## ON THE FOUNDING OF SEMINARIES

Since the age of youth, . . . unless educated from its tender years in piety and religion before the habits of vice take possession of the whole man, will never perfectly and without the greatest and well-nigh extraordinary help of Almighty God persevere in ecclesiastical discipline, the holy council decrees that all cathedral and metropolitan churches[7] and churches greater than these shall be bound, . . . to provide for, to educate in religion, and to train in ecclesiastical discipline, a certain number of boys of their city and diocese, . . . in a college located near the said churches or in some other suitable place. . . . Into this college shall be received such as are at least twelve years of age, are born of lawful wedlock, who know how to read and write competently, and whose character and inclination justify the hope that they will dedicate themselves forever to the ecclesiastical ministry. . . . And that they may be better trained in . . . ecclesiastical discipline, they shall . . . always wear the tonsure[8] and the clerical garb; they shall study grammar, singing, ecclesiastical computation,[9] and other useful arts; shall be instructed in Sacred Scripture, ecclesiastical books, the homilies of the saints, the manner of administering the sacraments, especially those things that seem adapted to the hearing of confessions, and the rites and ceremonies. The bishop shall see to it that they are present every day at the sacrifice of the mass, confess their sins at least once a month, receive the body of our Lord Jesus Christ[10] in accordance with the directions of their confessor, and on festival days serve in the cathedral and other churches of the locality. . . .

## ON CLERICAL CONDUCT

Since therefore the more these things contribute usefulness and honor in the Church of God, so the more zealously must they be observed, the holy council ordains that those things which have in the past been frequently and wholesomely enacted by the supreme pontiffs and holy coun-

---

[5]Church official with jurisdiction in a certain area of Church life.

[6]An ecclesiastical censure that excludes a person from communion with the faithful and prevents him or her from partaking in the sacraments of the Church.

[7]A cathedral church is the home church of a bishop; a metropolitan church is the church of an archbishop.

[8]The rite by which a layman becomes a member of the

clergy; during the rite a small circular area is shaved on the top of the candidate's head.

[9]The process of determining the dates of Holy Days, especially Easter.

[10]In other words, to receive the consecrated communion wafer, believed by Catholics to have been transformed into the body of Christ.

cils concerning adherence to the life, conduct, dress, and learning of clerics, as also the avoidance of luxury, feastings, dances, gambling, sports, and all sorts of crime and secular pursuits shall in the future be observed under the same or greater penalties. . . .

It is to be desired that those who assume the episcopal office know what are their duties, and understand that they have been called not for their own convenience, not for riches or luxury, but to labors and cares for the glory of God. . . . Wherefore, it commands not only that bishops be content with modest furniture and a frugal table, but also that they take heed that in the rest of their manner of living and in their whole house, nothing appears that is at variance with this holy ordinance, or that does not manifest simplicity, zeal for God and a contempt for vanities. But above all does it forbid them to attempt to enrich their relations or domestics from the revenues of the Church. . . . And what has been said of bishops is to hold ecclesiastical benefices,[11]. . . but it decrees that it applies also to the cardinals[12] of the holy Roman Church.

How shameful and how unworthy it is of the name of clerics . . . to live in the filth of impurity and unclean cohabitation,[13] the thing itself sufficiently testifies by the common scandal of all the faithful and the supreme disgraces on the clerical order. Wherefore, that the ministers of the Church may be brought back to the continency and purity of life which is proper to them, . . . the holy council forbids all clerics whatsoever to presume to keep concubines or other women concerning whom suspicion can be had in their house or elsewhere, or to presume to have any association with them; . . .

## ON INDULGENCES

Since the power of granting indulgences[14] was conferred by Christ on the Church, . . . the holy council teaches and commands that the use of indulgences, . . . is to be retained in the Church, and it condemns . . . those who assert that they are useless or deny that there is in the Church the power of granting them. In granting them, however, it desires that . . . moderation be observed, lest by too great facility ecclesiastical discipline be weakened. But desiring that the abuses which have become connected with them . . . be amended and corrected, it ordains . . . that all evil traffic in them, which has been a most prolific source of abuses among the Christian people, be absolutely abolished. . . .

## ON THE VENERATION OF SAINTS AND SACRED IMAGES

The holy council commands all bishops and others who hold the office of teaching and have charges of the [care of souls], that they instruct the faithful diligently, teaching them that the saints who reign together with Christ offer up their prayers to God for men, that it is good and beneficial . . . to invoke them and to have recourse to their prayers, assistance and support in order to obtain favors from God through His Son, Jesus Christ our Lord. . . . [Also,] those who maintain that veneration and honor are not due to the relics of the saints, or that these and other memorials are honored by the faithful without profit, and that the places dedicated to the memory of the saints for the purpose of obtaining their aid are visited in vain, are to be utterly

[11]An ecclesiastical office to which a permanent source of income or revenue is attached.
[12]High Church officials who served as counselors and assistants of the pope and, as members of the College of Cardinals, elected new popes.
[13]Living with a woman.
[14]Connected with the sacrament of penance, an indulgence was originally a grant by the Church that exempted a person from the temporal penalties (the "acts of penance")

imposed by a priest after confession. Crusaders were given a plenary (full) indulgence for their participation in the Holy War against the Muslims. By the early sixteenth century indulgences could be purchased for one's own benefit and for the benefit of souls believed to be in Purgatory. Indulgence trafficking became a major source of revenue for the Church, and many Christians came to believe the claims of indulgence preachers that salvation could be purchased through indulgences.

condemned. . . . Moreover, that the images of Christ, of the Virgin Mother of God, and of the other saints are to be placed and retained especially in the churches, and that due honor and veneration is to be given them.

# Art as Protestant Propaganda
▼▼▼

## 3 ▼ *Lucas Cranach the Younger,* TWO KINDS OF PREACHING: EVANGELICAL AND PAPAL, *and* Mattias Gerung, THE CHARIOT OF THE POPE AND THE TURK

Some seventy years before Luther posted his Ninety-Five Theses in Wittenberg, in Mainz another German, Johannes Gutenberg (ca. 1395–1468) perfected a new method of printing books through movable metal type. Printing shops soon were established in hundreds of European towns and cities, and by the mid sixteenth century many millions of books and pamphlets had been published. Many of these publications played a key role in determining the dynamics and outcome of the Reformation era's religious struggles.

The Ninety-Five Theses, intended by Luther to spark academic debate at the University of Wittenberg, instead rocketed him to national prominence when they were translated into German and made available in cheap printed editions. Subsequently, Luther and his followers used the printed page to advance their ideas in Latin treatises for learned audiences and, more tellingly, in thousands of German books and pamphlets for the general population. Many of these works contained woodcuts and engravings to illustrate key points and make Protestant ideas accessible even to the illiterate. Catholics were slower to utilize the new technology, thus putting themselves at a disadvantage in the competition for the public's religious allegiance.

Both woodcuts in this section were produced by Lutheran artists in the 1540s. The first, *Two Kinds of Preaching: Evangelical and Papal,* is the work of Lucas Cranach the Younger (1515–1586), a lifelong resident of Wittenberg and a friend of Luther. The second, *The Chariot of the Pope and the Turk,* was executed by Mattias Gerung (ca. 1500–1569), a painter and woodcutter from western Germany; in the 1530s and 1540s he received a number of commissions from a German prince, Count Palatine Otthenreich, who introduced Lutheranism into his territories in 1542.

*Two Kinds of Preaching,* printed in 1547, was distributed as a broadsheet, a large single printed sheet sold by booksellers for a few cents and designed to reach a wide audience. We have produced the broadsheet on two pages, although in its original form it is undivided. Facing left from a central pulpit is Luther, whose left hand rests on a Bible. On the pulpit itself are words from the New Testament Book of Acts, "All prophets attest to this, that there is no other name in heaven than that of Christ." Above Luther is a dove, representing the Holy Spirit, the third person of the Trinity, whose major functions are inspiration, solace, and sanctification. Luther points to images of the Paschal Lamb (a symbol of the risen Christ), the risen Christ himself, and finally to God the Father, who holds an orb symbolizing his dominion over creation. Christ directs the following words toward God: "Holy Father, save them. I have sacrificed myself for them with my wounds." Below Christ is written, "If we sin we have an advocate before God, so let us turn in consolation to this means of grace." In the center and lower left are depicted the two Lutheran sacraments, baptism and the eucharist. It is noteworthy that in the celebration of the eucharist, both the bread and wine are offered to the laity, as opposed to the Catholic practice of restricting the drinking of the wine to the priest.

The right side of the woodcut is a Lutheran version of how the Roman Church perverted Christianity. The preaching friar is inspired by an imp-like demon blowing air into his ear. Directed to an audience mostly of clergy, his message, according to the words above his head, is that the practices going on about him offer an easy path to salvation. In the upper right corner an angry God rains down thunderbolts while Francis of Assisi, the founder of the Franciscan order, shows the uselessness of saints as mediators between man and God by attempting in vain to intercede on behalf of humanity. In the lower right corner indulgences are being sold by the pope, who holds a sign reading, "Because the coin rings, the soul to heaven springs." But the message on the money bag reads, "This is shame and vice, squeezed from your donations." Just behind the pope is a priest celebrating a private mass and an altar being consecrated by a bird-like demon. Still deeper in the background is a dying man having his hair clipped to resemble a monk and having a monk's hood placed on his head, steps that supposedly would ensure his salvation. The attending nun sprinkles the man with holy water and holds a banner reading, "May the cowl, the tonsure, and the water aid you." To the right of this scene a bishop consecrates a bell. In the far background two pilgrims stride toward a chapel surrounded by a procession in honor of the saint depicted on the banner.

Mattias Gerung's *The Chariot of the Pope and Turk* was one of more than fifty woodcuts that were to accompany a printed version of a commentary on the New Testament Book of Revelations. In many of them the pope and the Ottoman Turkish sultan are portrayed together as the two greatest enemies of Christendom: The pope threatened true religion, while the sultan, with his recent conquests in southeastern Europe, threatened military disaster for Europe and the triumph of Islam. In this woodcut, a chariot blocks a narrow passage through which a ship is attempting to pass to a placid body of water in the background. This strange chariot, which is being pulled in two directions, may refer to the German proverb, "A wagon with horses hitched at both ends will not likely move." From the chariot the sultan urges on his soldiers on the left, while the pope exhorts his followers, armed with banners of processions and indulgence proclamations, on the right. From the clouds above emerges God's hand holding the sword of divine punishment.

*(See page 19 for Questions for Analysis.)*

*Lucas Cranach the Younger,* Two Kinds of Preaching: Evangelical

*Lucas Cranach the Younger,* Two Kinds of Preaching: Papal

*Mattias Gerung,* The Chariot of the Pope and the Turk

*QUESTIONS FOR ANALYSIS*

1. What differences in the makeup of the crowds surrounding the pulpit do you see in the two sides of Cranach's picture? What point is Cranach trying to make?
2. Note the figures in the right side of Cranach's picture who are members of religious orders (identifiable by their tonsure, or shaven crown). How do their garb and general appearance confirm Lutheran beliefs about the hypocrisy of monks?
3. Compare the two preachers. What messages is Cranach trying to communicate in their gestures and in his depiction of the pulpits from which they are preaching?
4. In both sides of Cranach's picture the eucharist is being celebrated. What differences do you see, and what is their significance?
5. Cranach's woodcut depicts the Catholic Church as full of abuses. What are some of these abuses, and how are they illustrated?
6. Cranach depicts Lutheranism as an expression of true Christianity. What specific details from the left side of the woodcut convey this message?
7. In the Gerung woodcut what in your opinion is the symbolism of the ships?
8. Compare the "weapons" being held by the followers of the pope and sultan in the Gerung woodcut. What message do they communicate about the Turks and the Catholics?

▼▼▼

# Spanish Perspectives on the New World

Europeans were surprised and intrigued by what their mariners and merchants encountered in Africa and Asia, but nothing prepared them for their explorers' astounding discoveries across the Atlantic. No one knew what to make of two vast continents populated not only by "savages" with unsophisticated tools and crude weapons but also by others who lived in large cities, had powerful, complex governments, and enjoyed great wealth. Were the Indians, as they came to be known, truly human? Did they have souls and the gift of reason? How should they be treated? These questions gained urgency when the Europeans realized that their superior weaponry and the devastating effect of epidemic disease made it difficult for the native people to resist European aggression. Did their very weakness justify exploitation and enslavement? Or did it oblige the Europeans not just to convert these people to Christianity but to educate them and make them partners in the use of European tools, livestock, crops, and medicines?

The Spaniards were the first Europeans to seriously discuss such questions. Churchmen, soldiers, royal officials, colonists, kings, and queens searched their souls and exercised their minds to find policies that satisfied both their quest for gain and their religious principles. The controversy in Spain reached a climax in 1550 when, at the command of King Charles I (also known as the Holy Roman Emperor, Charles V), two intellectuals, Juan Ginés de Sepúlveda and Bartolomé de Las Casas, debated Spain's Indian policy before a panel of judges at Valladolid for an entire week. The judges never came to a decision, and both Las Casas, who defended the Indians' rights, and Sepúlveda, who justified their enslavement, claimed victory.

# The Uncivilized
# Have Been Justly Conquered
▼▼▼

## 4 ▼ *Juan Ginés de Sepúlveda,*
## *DEMOCRATES SECUNDUS, OR*
## *THE JUST CAUSES OF WAR*
## *AGAINST THE INDIANS*

Juan Ginés de Sepúlveda was born in 1490 into a Spanish aristocratic family and studied ancient literature and philosophy at the University of Alcalá in Spain. With ambitions for a scholarly career, he moved to Italy, the center of Renaissance Aristotelianism, where he studied and taught for twenty years. He later served as chaplain and official historian for King Charles I of Spain and later for his son, Philip II. Although best known for his commentaries on Aristotle, Sepúlveda also wrote a number of original philosophical and theological works. His view that superior peoples had the right to enslave inferiors was an elaboration of an argument found in Aristotle. He first expounded his theory in 1547 in his *Democrates Secundus, or the Just Causes of War against the Indians,* a dialogue between fictitious Democrates, who expresses the author's views, and Leopoldo, who serves as his foil. The arguments he advanced in 1550 against Las Casas were based on this work. Sepúlveda died in 1573, embittered by the controversies that had clouded his old age.

---

## QUESTIONS FOR ANALYSIS

1. How does Sepúlveda justify the enslavement of inferior peoples by their superiors?
2. For Sepúlveda, what qualities of the Spaniards make them superior?
3. How does he "prove" the inferiority of the Indians?
4. What is there about the fate of the Aztecs that reinforces Sepúlveda's general views of the Indians?
5. If, for the sake of argument, one were to accept Sepúlveda's premises concerning the Indians' inferiority, would one be forced to accept his conclusions?
6. What might the judges at Valladolid have found convincing in Sepúlveda's arguments? What weaknesses might they have discerned?

It is established then, in accordance with the authority of the most eminent thinkers, that the dominion of prudent, good, and humane men over those of contrary disposition is just and natural. Nothing else justified the legitimate empire of the Romans over other peoples, according to the testimony of St. Thomas[1] in his work on the rule of the prince. St. Thomas here followed St. Augustine, who, in referring to the empire of the Romans in the fifth book of *The City of God,* wrote: "God conceded to the Romans a very extensive and glorious empire in order to keep grave evils from spreading among many peoples who, in search of glory, coveted riches and many other vices." In other words God gave the Romans their empire so that, with the good legislation that they instituted and the virtue in which they excelled, they might change the customs and suppress and correct the vices of many barbarian peoples. . . .

Turning then to our topic, whether it is proper and just that those who are superior and who excel in nature, customs, and laws rule over their inferiors, you can easily understand . . . if you are familiar with the character and moral code of the two peoples, that it is with perfect right that the Spaniards exercise their dominion over those barbarians of the New World and its adjacent islands. For in prudence, talent, and every kind of virtue and human sentiment they are as inferior to the Spaniards as children are to adults, or women to men, or the cruel and inhumane to the very gentle, or the excessively intemperate to the continent and moderate.

But I do not think that you expect me to speak of the prudence and talent of the Spaniards, for you have, I think, read Lucan, Silius Italicus, the two Senecas, and among later figures St. Isidore, who is inferior to none in theology, and Averroës and Avempace who are excellent in philosophy, and in astronomy King Alfonso,[2] not to mention others whom it would take too long to enumerate. And who is ignorant of the Spaniards' other virtues: courage, humanity, justice, and religion? I refer simply to the princes and to those whose aid and skill they utilize to govern the state, to those, in short, who have received a liberal education. And what shall I say of their moderation in rejecting gluttony and lasciviousness, inasmuch as no nation or very few nations of Europe can compare with the frugality and sobriety of the Spaniards? I admit that I have observed in these most recent times that through contact with foreigners luxury has invaded the tables of our nobles. Still, since this is reproved by good men among the people, it is to be hoped that in a short while they may return to the traditional and innate sobriety of our native custom.

As for the Christian religion, I have witnessed many clear proofs of the firm roots it has in the hearts of Spaniards, even those dedicated to the military. The best proof of all has seemed to me to be the fact that in the great plague that followed the sack of Rome, in the Pontificate of Clement VII, not a single Spaniard among those who died in the epidemic failed to request in his will that all the goods stolen from the citizens be restored to them.[3] And I, who was following the army and was in the city observing it all diligently, was a witness to it. . . . What shall I say of the Spanish soldiers' gentleness and humanitarian sentiments? Their only and greatest solicitude and care in the battles, after the winning

[1]The theologian St. Thomas Aquinas (1225–1274) was a member of the Dominican religious order; his views were accepted as authoritative by the Catholic Church in the sixteenth century. St. Augustine of Hippo (354–430) was a convert to Christianity whose discussions of salvation, the Church, human nature, and the sacraments exerted enormous influence on Christian thought.

[2]All eight of these men were born in Spain. Lucan (65–39 B.C.E.) and Silius Italicus (100–26 B.C.E.) were poets; Seneca the Elder (55 B.C.E.–39 C.E.) wrote a book on Roman rhetoricians; Seneca the Younger (4 B.C.E.–65 C.E.) was a statesman, philosopher, and tragedian; Isidore of Seville (560–636) was a historian and theologian; Averroës (1126–1198) and Avempace (d. 1138) were Spanish Muslim philosophers; and King Alfonso X (1221–1284) was a famous patron of learning and literature.

[3]The Sack of Rome occurred in 1527 during the Italian Wars (1494–1559) when troops loyal to Emperor Charles V (as king of Spain, Charles I), frustrated over back pay owed them, went on a protracted rampage.

of the victory, is to save the greatest possible number of vanquished and free them from the cruelty of their allies. Now compare these qualities of prudence, skill, magnanimity, moderation, humanity, and religion with those of those little men of America in whom one can scarcely find any remnants of humanity. They not only lack culture but do not even use or know about writing or preserve records of their history — save for some obscure memory of certain deeds contained in painting. They lack written laws and their institutions and customs are barbaric. And as for their virtues, if you wish to be informed of their moderation and mildness, what can be expected of men committed to all kinds of passion and nefarious lewdness and of whom not a few are given to the eating of human flesh. Do not believe that their life before the coming of the Spaniards was one of Saturnine[4] peace, of the kind that poets sang about. On the contrary, they made war with each other almost continuously, and with such fury that they considered a victory to be empty if they could not satisfy their prodigious hunger with the flesh of their enemies. This form of cruelty is especially prodigious among these people, remote as they are from the invincible ferocity of the Scythians,[5] who also ate human bodies. But in other respects they are so cowardly and timid that they can scarcely offer any resistance to the hostile presence of our side, and many times thousands and thousands of them have been dispersed and have fled like women on being defeated by a small Spanish force scarcely amounting to one hundred.

So as not to detain you longer in this matter, consider the nature of those people in one single instance and example, that of the Mexicans, who are regarded as the most prudent and courageous.[6] Their king was Moctezuma, whose empire extended the length and breadth of those regions and who inhabited the city of Mexico, a city situated in a vast lake, and a very well defended city both on account of the nature of its location and on account of its fortifications. . . . Informed of the arrival of Cortés and of his victories and his intention to go to Mexico under pretext of a conference, Moctezuma sought all possible means to divert him from his plan. Failing in this, terrorized and filled with fear, he received him in the city with about three hundred Spaniards. Cortés for his part, after taking possession of the city, held the people's cowardliness, ineptitude, and rudeness in such contempt that he not only compelled the king and his principal subjects, through terror, to receive the yoke and rule of the king of Spain, but also imprisoned King Moctezuma himself, because of his suspicion that a plot was on foot to kill some Spaniards in a certain province. This he could do because of the stupor and inertia of the people, who were indifferent to the situation and preoccupied with other things than the taking up of arms to liberate their king. . . . Could there be a better or clearer testimony of the superiority that some men have over others in talent, skill, strength of spirit, and virtue? Is it not proof that they are slaves by nature? For the fact that some of them appear to have a talent for certain manual tasks is no argument for their greater human prudence. We see that certain insects, such as the bees and the spiders, produce works that no human skill can imitate. And as for the civil life of the inhabitants of New Spain and the province of Mexico, I have already said that the people are considered to be the most civilized of all. They themselves boast of their public institutions as if it were not a sufficient proof of their industry and civilization that they have rationally constructed cities, and kings appointed by popular suffrage rather than by hereditary right and age, and a commerce like that of civilized people. But see how they deceive themselves and how differ-

---

[4]Refers to the idea of a golden age.
[5]Originally from central Asia, the Scythians were nomads who moved into southern Russia in the eighth and seventh centuries B.C.E. Ancient Greek and Roman historians described them as wild and cruel savages.

[6]On the capitulation of the Aztecs to Cortés, see source 16).

ent is my opinion from theirs, since for me the foremost proof of the rudeness and barbarism and innate servitude of those people lies precisely in their public institutions, nearly all of which are servile and barbarous. They do have houses, and some rational mode of common life, and such commerce as natural necessity demands, but what does this prove other than that they are not bears or monkeys completely lacking in reason?

I have made reference to the customs and character of the barbarians. What shall I say now of the impious religion and wicked sacrifices of such people, who, in venerating the devil as if he were God, believed that the best sacrifice that they could placate him with was to offer him human hearts?[7] . . . Opening up the human breasts they pulled out the hearts and offered them on their heinous altars. And believing that they had made a ritual sacrifice with which to placate their gods, they themselves ate the flesh of the victims. These are crimes that are considered by the philoso-phers to be among the most ferocious and abominable perversions, exceeding all human iniquity. . . .

How can we doubt that these people — so uncivilized, so barbaric, contaminated with so many impieties and obscenities — have been justly conquered by a nation excellent in every kind of virtue, with the best law and best benefit for the barbarians? Prior to the arrival of the Christians they had the nature, customs, religion, and practice of evil sacrifice as we have explained. Now, on receiving with our rule our writing, laws, and morality, imbued with the Christian religion, having shown themselves to be docile to the missionaries that we have sent them, as many have done, they are as different from their primitive condition as civilized people are from barbarians, or as those with sight from the blind, as the inhuman from the meek, as the pious from the impious, or to put it in a single phrase, in effect, as men from beasts.

---

[7]Huitzilopochtli, a sun and war god, was worshipped daily with offerings of blood and hearts torn from the bodies of sacrificed victims.

# "They Are Our Brothers"
▼▼▼

## 5 ▼ Bartolomé de Las Casas, *IN DEFENSE OF THE INDIANS*

Bartolomé de Las Casas was born into the family of a Spanish merchant in 1474. After abandoning his academic studies for a career of soldiering, he embarked for Hispaniola in 1502 in the entourage of the new governor of the island, Nicolas de Ovando. Las Casas received grants of land from the governor and participated in the conquest of Cuba between 1511 and 1515. In 1515 he renounced his property and rights in the Americas and returned to Spain, where he began to lobby Spanish officials on behalf of the Amerindians. In 1519, with royal approval, he established a cooperative Spanish-Amerindian farming community in Venezuela, but it generated little enthusiasm and the experiment failed. He then joined the Dominican religious order and continued to write and work on behalf of the American Indians while living in Spanish America and traveling regularly back to Spain. His denunciations of alleged Spanish cruelties so struck the conscience of Charles I that the king arranged the debate between Las Casas and Sepúlveda in 1550. After the debate Las Casas remained in Spain, where he died in 1566.

The following selection is an excerpt from Las Casas's response to Sepúlveda at the Valladolid debate. Given the title *In Defense of the Indians,* it existed in several Latin manuscript copies but was not published until the twentieth century.

*QUESTIONS FOR ANALYSIS*

1. Why, according to Las Casas, is it significant that the Indians established effective governments?
2. What is Las Casas's definition of *barbarian?* How does it differ from Sepúlveda's definition?
3. How do Las Casas's historical arguments and views of the Spaniards differ from those of Sepúlveda?
4. What, according to Las Casas, are the implications of Sepúlveda's arguments for international relations?
5. The judges could not decide a winner in the debate. What might explain this?
6. Put yourself in the place of one of the Valladolid judges and write an explanation of why you chose Las Casas or Sepúlveda as the winner of the debate.

However, he admits, and proves, that the barbarians he deals with . . . have a lawful, just, and natural government. Even though they lack the art and use of writing, they are not wanting in the capacity and skill to rule and govern themselves, both publicly and privately. Thus they have kingdoms, communities, and cities that they govern wisely according to their laws and customs. Thus their government is legitimate and natural, even though it has some resemblance to tyranny. From these statements we have no choice but to conclude that the rulers of such nations enjoy the use of reason and that their people and the inhabitants of their provinces do not lack peace and justice. Otherwise they could not be established or preserved as political entities for long. This is made clear by the Philosopher and Augustine.[1] Therefore not all barbarians are irrational or natural slaves or unfit for government. Some barbarians, then, in accord with justice and nature, have kingdoms, royal dignities, jurisdiction, and good laws, and there is among them lawful government.

Now if we shall have shown that among our Indians of the western and southern shores (granting that we call them barbarians and that they are barbarians) there are important kingdoms, large numbers of people who live settled lives in a society, great cities, kings, judges and laws, persons who engage in commerce, buying, selling, lending, and the other contracts of the law of nations, will it not stand proved that the Reverend Doctor Sepúlveda has spoken wrongly and viciously against peoples like these, either out of malice or ignorance of Aristotle's teaching, and, therefore, has falsely and perhaps irreparably slandered them before the entire world? From the fact that the Indians are barbarians it does not necessarily follow that they are incapable of government and have to be ruled by others, except to be taught about the Catholic faith and to be admitted to the holy sacraments.

---

[1]The term *Philosopher* refers to Aristotle; on *Augustine,* see source 4, footnote 1.

They are not ignorant, inhuman, or bestial. Rather, long before they had heard the word Spaniard they had properly organized states, wisely ordered by excellent laws, religion, and custom. They cultivated friendship and, bound together in common fellowship, lived in populous cities in which they wisely administered the affairs of both peace and war justly and equitably, truly governed by laws that at very many points surpass ours, and could have won the admiration of the sages of Athens, as I will show in the second part of this *Defense*.

Now if they are to be subjugated by war because they are ignorant of polished literature, let Sepúlveda hear Trogus Pompey:[2]

> Nor could the Spaniards submit to the yoke of a conquered province until Caesar Augustus, after he had conquered the world, turned his victorious armies against them and organized that barbaric and wild people as a province, once he had led them by law to a more civilized way of life.

Now see how he called the Spanish people barbaric and wild. I would like to hear Sepúlveda, in his cleverness, answer this question: Does he think that the war of the Romans against the Spanish was justified in order to free them from barbarism? And this question also: Did the Spanish wage an unjust war when they vigorously defended themselves against them?

Next, I call the Spaniards who plunder that unhappy people torturers. Do you think that the Romans, once they had subjugated the wild and barbaric peoples of Spain, could with secure right divide all of you among themselves, handing over so many head of both males and females as allotments to individuals? And do you then conclude

that the Romans could have stripped your rulers of their authority and consigned all of you, after you have been deprived of your liberty, to wretched labors, especially in searching for gold and silver lodes and mining and refining the metals? And if the Romans finally did that, as is evident from Diodorus,[3] [would you not judge] that you also have the right to defend your freedom, indeed your very life, by war? Sepúlveda, would you have permitted Saint James[4] to evangelize your own people of Córdoba in that way? For God's sake and man's faith in him, is this the way to impose the yoke of Christ on Christian men? Is this the way to remove wild barbarism from the minds of barbarians? Is it not, rather, to act like thieves, cut-throats, and cruel plunderers and to drive the gentlest of people headlong into despair? The Indian race is not that barbaric, nor are they dull witted or stupid, but they are easy to teach and very talented in learning all the liberal arts, and very ready to accept, honor, and observe the Christian religion and correct their sins (as experience has taught) once priests have introduced them to the sacred mysteries and taught them the word of God. They have been endowed with excellent conduct, and before the coming of the Spaniards, as we have said, they had political states that were well founded on beneficial laws.

Furthermore, they are so skilled in every mechanical art that with every right they should be set ahead of all the nations of the known world on this score, so very beautiful in their skill and artistry are the things this people produces in the grace of its architecture, its painting, and its needlework. . . .

In the liberal arts that they have been taught up to now, such as grammar and logic, they are

---

[2] A Roman historian of the first century B.C.E.; only fragments of his ambitious history of Assyria, Persia, Greece, Rome, Gaul, and Spain survive.

[3] A Greek historian of the first century B.C.E.

[4] James, son of Zebedee, was one of the original twelve apostles, or closest followers of Jesus, and suffered martyrdom for his faith in 43 C.E. According to legend, his body

was carried to Spain, where, as St. James "the Moor-Slayer," he became the patron saint of the Christian Reconquest of the Iberian peninsula from Islam. The church of Santiago de Compostela in northwest Spain, believed to be the site of his relics, became one of the most popular pilgrimage destinations in all of Europe from the late ninth century onward.

remarkably adept. With every kind of music they charm the ears of their audience with wonderful sweetness. They write skillfully and quite elegantly, so that most often we are at a loss to know whether the characters are handwritten or printed. . . .

From this it is clear that the basis for Sepúlveda's teaching that these people are uncivilized and ignorant is worse than false. Yet even if we were to grant that this race has no keenness of mind or artistic ability, certainly they are not, in consequence, obliged to submit themselves to those who are more intelligent and to adopt their ways, so that, if they refuse, they may be subdued by having war waged against them and be enslaved, as happens today. . . . We are bound by the natural law to embrace virtue and imitate the uprightness of good men. . . .

Therefore, not even a truly wise man may force an ignorant barbarian to submit to him, especially by yielding his liberty, without doing him an injustice. This the poor Indians suffer, with extreme injustice, against all the laws of God and of men and against the law of nature itself. For evil must not be done that good may come of it, for example, if someone were to castrate another against his will. For although eunuchs are freed from the lust that drives human minds forward in its mad rush, yet he who castrates another is most severely punished. . . .

Now if, on the basis of this utterly absurd argument, war against the Indians were lawful, one nation might rise up against another and one man against another man, and on the pretext of superior wisdom, might strive to bring the other into subjection. On this basis the Turks, and the Moors — the truly barbaric scum of the nations — with complete right and in accord with the law of nature could carry on war, which, as it seems to some, is permitted to us by a lawful decree of the state. If we admit this, will not everything high and low, divine and human, be thrown into confusion? What can be proposed more contrary to the eternal law than what Sepúlveda often declares? What plague deserves more to be loathed? . . .

Hence every nation, no matter how barbaric, has the right to defend itself against a more civilized one that wants to conquer it and take away its freedom. And, moreover, it can lawfully punish with death the more civilized as a savage and cruel aggressor against the law of nature. And this war is certainly more just than the one that, under pretext of wisdom, is waged against them. . . .

Again, if we want to be sons of Christ and followers of the truth of the gospel, we should consider that, even though these peoples may be completely barbaric, they are nevertheless created in God's image. They are not so forsaken by divine providence that they are incapable of attaining Christ's kingdom. They are our brothers, redeemed by Christ's most precious blood, no less than the wisest and most learned men in the whole world. Finally, we must consider it possible that some of them are predestined to become renowned and glorious in Christ's kingdom. Consequently, to these men who are wild and ignorant in their barbarism we owe the right which is theirs, that is, brotherly kindness and Christian love, according to Paul: "I owe a duty to Greeks just as much as to barbarians, to the educated just as much as to the uneducated, and it is this that makes me want to bring the Good News to you too in Rome."[5] Christ wanted love to be called his single commandment. This we owe to all men. Nobody is excepted. "There is no room for distinction between Greek and Jew, between the circumcised and the uncircumcised, or between barbarian and Scythian, slave and free man. There is only Christ: he is everything and he is in everything."[6]

---

[5]From Paul's Letter to the Romans, 1:14, 15.

[6]From Paul's Letter to the Colossians, 3:17.

▼▼▼

# Women's Roles in Early Modern Europe

The popular assumption that Europe's transition from the Middle Ages to the Renaissance and early modern period was marked by general progress is contradicted by the experiences of most European women. Although medieval women were far from having equality with men, they enjoyed more freedom and higher status than in antiquity and the postmedieval period. Aristocratic women in the Middle Ages owned land and managed their family's estates when their husbands were on military campaigns. Urban women joined guilds, were apprenticed to learn craft skills, and in some cities monopolized whole professions, such as leatherworking, brewing, and especially textile weaving and finishing. Religious women were admired for their charity and piety, and some achieved distinction as models of spirituality.

During the fourteenth and fifteenth centuries, however, the era that saw the decline of medieval civilization and the flowering of the Renaissance in Italy, women's economic and social prospects began to deteriorate, and continued to do so in the early modern period. In cities guilds excluded women from membership, and municipal councils barred women from receiving payment for work as physicians and apothecaries. For city women work increasingly meant domestic service, spinning, shopkeeping, or prostitution, all poorly paid jobs with low status. In the countryside women's work was crucial to the peasant household's economic survival, as it had been throughout the Middle Ages. Women tended gardens, raised poultry, helped with planting and harvesting, cooked, preserved food, and cared for children and the elderly. Many also worked for wages as servants or laborers.

Irrespective of a woman's social status, there was universal agreement that her main purpose was to marry and have children. Moralists and religious leaders agreed that matrimony was the foundation of a sound, God-fearing society and offered men and women the best opportunity for fulfillment and happiness. This was especially true among Protestant writers, whose enthusiasm for marriage was linked to their rejection of the Catholic doctrine of clerical celibacy.

During the sixteenth century, however, many writers on the topic were convinced that the institution of marriage was threatened. The age of first marriage in northern and northwestern Europe steadily rose, and the proportion of unmarried individuals throughout Europe grew. Estimates of the number of single European women throughout the 1500s and early 1600s range from 20 to 40 percent, equally divided between spinsters and widows. For those who were married, one gains the impression from contemporary writers and preachers that more and more husbands and wives were unhappy. Writers on the topic agreed that a strong marriage depended on mutual affection and clearly defined responsibilities and rights between spouses, but laws made wives subservient to husbands, and the endless written commentaries on unhappy marriages, abusive husbands, and disobedient wives suggests that such ideal marriages were far from universal.

Throughout the early modern period learned opinion (generated of course by educated men) continued to emphasize women's intellectual, spiritual, and moral inferiority to men. Although Protestantism encouraged female literacy because it emphasized each Christian's need to read the Bible and the mother's role in teaching religious lessons to her children, Catholic and Protestant universities remained exclusively male, thus effectively barring women from scholarly careers and the learned professions. The deadliest result of women's low status and perceived inferiority was early modern Europe's persecution of witches. Witchcraft was considered a uniquely female crime, and 80 percent or more of those accused and executed as witches were women.

The sources in this section provide insights into several topics relating to women in early modern Europe: marriage, work, and perceptions of their character and social role. All the sources were produced by men. Because of the disparity between male and female literacy and the difficulties women faced in publishing their ideas, few women were able to contribute to the literary discussion of women's roles and capabilities. Nonetheless, in the selections that follow we can get some sense of women's perspectives and expectations.

# A Woman of Virtue and Piety

▼▼▼

## 6 ▼ John Mayer, "A PATTERN FOR WOMEN"

In the early 1600s an Englishwoman, Lucy Thornton, died, leaving behind a husband and several young children. John Mayer, an Anglican priest, delivered her eulogy, which was later published as a pamphlet titled "A Pattern for Women." It provides numerous insights into what was expected of Protestant wives and mothers in the patriarchal society of early seventeenth-century England. Mayer opened his eulogy by praising Lucy Thornton's religious zeal and then goes on to describe her other virtues.

---

### QUESTIONS FOR ANALYSIS

1. What are the qualities of Lucy Thornton's life that make her in Mayer's view a "pattern for women"?
2. In what ways did Thornton show her human weaknesses and shortcomings?
3. In what ways is Mayer's praise for Thornton indirect criticism of most other women?
4. What does Mayer's eulogy reveal about the subservience of women in the family and in society in general?

She was anointed with wisdom, as Abigail,[1] who is said to be of excellent understanding. . . . Such was her understanding as that she could readily recite fit texts of Scripture for any purpose and find them out; and for harder places, by singular labor she attained good skill herein. . . .

She was anointed with true love, causing in her plenty of good works; as in Dorcas,[2] her love was exceeding great both towards God and towards her neighbor. Of God, her love was so great that she burnt with the fire of earnest zeal for his glory, stoutly (even beyond the strength of her sex) opposing sin and maintaining virtue in those that were about her. . . . For the love of God, she kept a continual watch over her ways, lest she should offend against his holy will; no child is more afraid of offending the father or master than she of offending God. Because that, notwithstanding all watches, sin cannot altogether be kept out, she was not a little troubled for her frailties and falls, being always glad when the Lord took the matter into his own hands by chastising her with sickness; for then, and in health time also, she did much complain of her sins and forgetfulness for which it was necessary to be corrected. . . .

Of her neighbor she had also a true love, not in word but in deed. She had love of almsdeeds which she plentifully performed to the poor. . . . From her youth up, the poor were nourished up with her; their lives blessed her, for that they were kept warm with her fleeces. Whilst she lived, the hungry could not go unfed, the naked unclothed, the sick unvisited. . . . She showed love by admonishing the disorderly, instructing the ignorant, and exhorting the backward in religion, by all means provoking to love and good works.

She was anointed with humility, as Mary the blessed mother of Christ who, being so highly graced by God, yet acknowledgeth herself his humble handmaiden. . . . She despised the ornaments of vanity, which other women so much delight in; her outward habit did show the inward lowliness and modesty of her mind. She strove against the sharpness of her natural disposition, and by striving did attain a great measure of meekness and gentleness. . . .

She was anointed with due subjection to her own husband, as Sarah,[3] who reverenced her husband, whose example is most earnestly commended by St. Peter[4] to all wives. . . . promising that thus they become the daughters of Sarah, not being terrified with any fear. Wherefore, having this virtue also added, she was doubtless without fear steadfast in the faith of her salvation.

Unruly wives . . . have such a mist or dark cloud of black sins before their eyes as that they cannot see this salvation. They may have hope indeed, but their hope is presumption, the end of which is damnation.

Now as this elect servant of God was beautified with these graces in her health, so they remained in her without being dimmed in her last sickness.

For heavenly zeal, she gave a sure instance hereof in the beginning of this sickness by commanding her servants not to trouble her with any worldly affairs, for now she would wholly be settled to heaven. And indeed she lay in her sickbed as in heaven, full of heavenly speeches and of heavenly comfort. Now all her practice was praying, confessing of sins, singing Psalms, and godly conference.

For wisdom, when strength of body failed her, this was strong yet in her even unto the end;

---

[1]One of the wives of King David (?1010–970 B.C.E.), the second king of Israel and the reputed author of many of the *Psalms.*

[2]Dorcas, also known as Tabitha, was an early Christian convert mentioned in the New Testament Book of Acts. She was noted for her good works and charity.

[3]The wife of the biblical patriarch Abraham; she represents loyalty, hope, and God's promise to His people.

[4]Peter was the most prominent of Jesus' disciples. The two Epistles of Peter in the New Testament are ascribed to him, although the attribution is questioned. The reference to wives can be found in I Peter 3:16.

most wisely she spoke to everything, with much understanding producing sundry places of the holy Scriptures. Being much troubled for her sins and buffeted by the temptations of Satan, she said that she had yet much assurance because that "Come unto me," saith the Lord, "all you that are weary and heavy laden, and I will refresh you."

## Two Sixteenth-Century Images of Women
▼▼▼

### 7 ▼ *Anton Woensam,*
### *ALLEGORY OF A WISE WOMAN;*
### *Erhard Schön, NO MORE PRECIOUS*
### *TREASURE IS ON THE EARTH THAN A*
### *GENTLE WIFE WHO LONGS FOR HONOR*

Hundreds of thousands of sixteenth-century Europeans were introduced to the new technology of printing, not through books but through the broadsheet. Printed on a single sheet and usually consisting of a woodcut illustration and a brief text, these inexpensive publications were designed for the mass market. As seen earlier in the chapter, such broadsheets were used as instruments of propaganda in the Reformation, especially by Protestants. But broadsheets were not limited to religious issues. They were also instruments of satire, social commentary, and moral instruction, and a way of communicating news about murders, witchcraft trials, astronomical portents, monsters, strange births, and countless other events and phenomena.

The following broadsheets, both produced in Germany, address the issue of female virtue and relations between husbands and wives. The first is by Anton Woensam (ca. 1500–1541), a Catholic painter and woodblock carver from Cologne, whose *Allegory of a Wise Woman* appeared in 1525. The second is the work of Erhard Schön (ca. 1491–1550), a Protestant from Nuremberg, who produced hundreds of woodcuts for book illustrations and broadsheets. His woodcut, *No More Precious Treasure Is on the Earth Than a Gentle Wife Who Longs for Honor,* appeared in 1531. In neither case is the author of the text known.

Each of these woodcuts is simple and straightforward. The "wise woman" in Woensam's woodcut explains in the text the significance of her various attributes and of the objects she is holding or are attached to her. In Schön's woodcut one sees from left to right the husband (pulling a cart that is carrying a laundry tub, probably filled with diapers), the wife, a young man, his sweetheart, an old woman wearing a fool's cap, and finally an old man. In the text, they present their views on marriage.

---

### QUESTIONS FOR ANALYSIS

1. What is the meaning of the various objects (the lock, key, mirror, bird, snakes, pillow, vessel) included in Woensam's woodcut?

2. How do the horse's hooves in Woensam's work shed light on the woodcut's portrayal of women?
3. What meaning do you see in the posture, dress, and facial expression of the woman in Woensam's print?
4. What are the most important qualities of a "wise woman" according to Woensam?
5. What qualities of his wife does the husband in Schön's woodcut (p. 33) most bitterly complain about?
6. What is the significance of the britches, purse, and sword that the wife holds in Schön's print?
7. According to Schön, how does the wife justify her actions and behavior? How do her justifications compare to the expectations about marriage set forth by the young girl?
8. Compare and contrast the arguments for and against marriage presented by the old man and the female fool in Schön's print. To what extent do the comments of the old man confirm the fears about marriage expressed by the young man?
9. Taking the two woodcuts together, describe all they say about sixteenth-century views of women and men and their roles in society.

## ALLEGORY OF A WISE WOMAN

Contemplate this figure which signifies a wise
   woman;
a woman who behaves like her protects her honor
   well.

*Eyes*
I see as keenly as a hawk
And discern the pious ones from the scoundrels.
I guard myself both day and night
From one who plots against my honor.

*Ears*
I will not be discouraged
From opening my ears
So that they can hear God's word.
Which keeps the pious on their guard.

*Right Hand*
Pride I will despise
And behold myself in the mirror of Christ,
Through whom God has redeemed us.

*Mouth*
I wear a lock of gold upon my lips
All hours of the day and night
So that they say no harmful words
Or wound another's honor.

*Breast*
Also I keep a steady heart
Similar to what a turtledove does.
And to the one who will be my husband
I will be true no matter what his faults.

*Waist*
With serpents I gird my body.
This an upright woman should do
Who wants to protect herself from
Poisonous scandal, evil love and shameful play.

*Left Hand*
I shall gladly serve the poor
And thereby earn eternal life.
For I cannot find anything else
To do differently to bring this about.

*Feet*
On horses' hoofs shall I go about
So I can stand firm in honor.
On this I will not fall into sin
Which is sweet, but turns as bitter as gall.

Any woman who has such morals
Will never damage her honor
And surely merit from God
An eternal kingdom in heaven.

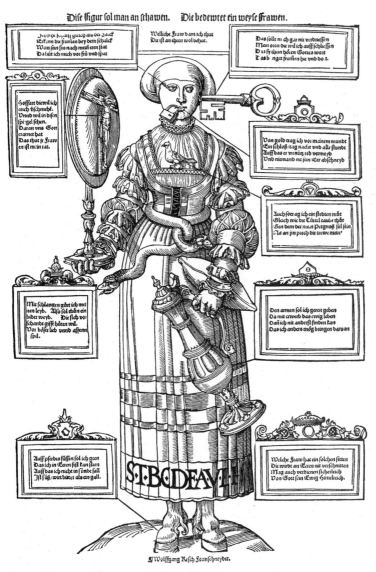

*Anton Woensam,* Allegory of a Wise Woman

## NO MORE PRECIOUS TREASURE

*The Wretched Idol {the Husband}*
Oh woe, oh woe to me, wretched fool,
With what difficulty I pull this cart
To which point marriage has brought me.
I wish I had never thought of it!
A shrewish scold has come into my house
and has taken my sword, pants and purse.
Night and day I have no peace
And no good word from her.
My fidelity does not please her;
My words provoke hostility from her.
Thus is the fate of many a man
Who has, knows and can do nothing,
And yet in time must have a wife.

*The Wife Speaks*

Hey, beloved mate, but is this really true?
Be quiet! Or I will pull you by the hair.
If you want a nice and gentle wife
Who will always be subservient to you
Then stay at home in your own house
And stop your carousing.
Naked I go running around to peddle things,
Suffering from hunger and quaffing water.
It's difficult for a nice young wife
To maintain her wifely honor.
If you won't work to support me,
Then you have to wash, spin and pull the cart
And must let your back be bared.

*The Journeyman*

What do you say about this, young lady?
Would you like to be like her
And yourself hold sword, pants, purse and authority?
With words bite, rasp and cut?

That I should and would never suffer.
Should I fight and brawl with you,
Then perhaps I would end up
Pulling a cart like this poor man,
Who has lost all joy and pleasure.
Should I waste my life of freedom
With spinning, washing, cooking and carting?
I would rather swear off from taking up marriage.

*The Girl*

Boy, believe me on my honor.
I don't wish for such power.
If you want to fight over rank,
Then you will be the man in all things.
What a wife deserves,
To love, to experience hardship together and honor,
I will demand nothing besides this.
You should have no doubt about it.
I will devote my life to serving you

*Erhard Schön,* No More Precious Treasure Is on the Earth Than a Gentle Wife Who Longs for Honor

And love you in constant friendship.
And you won't be scolded by a single word.

*The Woman Fool*

Watch yourself, young man.
I, a poor fool speak the truth.
Much good is said about marriage
But it means more correctly "Woe."
You must suffer 'til you die
Much anxiety, uncertainty, worry and want.
From this no married person is spared.
Now when you see a pretty girl,
She will gladly do what you want
For a bottle of wine.
Afterwards you can let her go
And take on another.
A wife you have forever.

*The Wise Man*

Young man I will teach you better.
Do not listen to this woman fool.
Beware of the tricks of whores,
Who are always there to deceive you.
Take a young lady into marriage.
God will guide your lives.
Stay with her in love and pain
And always be patient.
If you experience aggravation,
Consider it to be God's will.
Provide for your wife by the sweat of your brow,
As God commands in the Book of Genesis.
Patience and suffering make a door
Through which we arrive at that place
Where the angels have their home.

# Midwives and Their Duties

▼▼▼

## 8 ▼ *NUREMBERG ORDINANCES CONCERNING MIDWIVES, 1522, 1579*

Among the hundreds of occupations of early modern European women, only one was considered absolutely essential to the well-being of society. This was the woman's role as midwife. Although male apothecaries, barber-surgeons, and university-trained physicians in the early modern period had worked hard and successfully to exclude women from most health-related careers, they were more than happy to leave the physically and emotionally demanding job of providing prenatal care and delivering babies to female midwives and their assistants. Although physicians and barber-surgeons might be called upon to perform caesarean sections or attend a woman dying in childbirth, what we call today the fields of gynecology and obstetrics were exclusive female specialties.

So essential were midwives that municipal governments in many parts of Europe took steps to ensure the quality of obstetrical care by regulating the apprenticeship, recruitment, licensing, and practices of midwives. In Germany many cities also appointed a special board to oversee the activities of midwives and adjudicate disputes. Usually drawn from upper-class families, board members were known as "honorable women," or *Ehrbare Frauen.* City governments also provided modest stipends for midwives (two to eight *gulden* a year, compared to ten to twenty-five gulden paid to barber-surgeons), which could be augmented by fees collected from patients.

The following excerpts are drawn from an ordinance concerning midwives issued by the Nuremberg city council in 1522 and an addendum to that ordinance from 1579. Nuremberg was a prosperous Lutheran city in south central Germany with a population of approximately forty thousand during the early modern period. The number of practicing midwives in the city ranged between eight and twenty-two, with the most experienced of them attending three to five births a week. The excerpts provide insights into the responsibilities of midwives, the perceived abuses connected with their activities, and the penchant of municipal governments to minutely regulate the activities of their citizens.

## QUESTIONS FOR ANALYSIS

1. What specific information does the source provide concerning the duties of midwives and their training?
2. What are the main concerns of the members of the Nuremberg city council relating to midwives and their practices?
3. On the basis of these documents what can be inferred about the social background of midwives in Nuremberg and their status?
4. What does the source reveal about contemporary attitudes toward illegitimate births?
5. What attitudes toward the welfare and capabilities of women are revealed in these documents?

Every midwife should give her oath and swear she will conscientiously care for and stand by every expectant mother in her time of need to whom she is called, whether she is rich or poor, to the best of her abilities and understanding. She should proceed to whomever she is called first, immediately and without objection, and make absolutely no excuses or delays, as has often been the case, but faithfully stand by her. Also no woman is to be hurried or forced to deliver before the proper time; she should wait and hold out until the appropriate time.

If the thing [the delivery] looks like it will be dangerous, she should call one or two of the women who are responsible for this[1] and proceed with the emergency according to their advice. In no case is she to wait or delay to call them until the need is so great they cannot handle it, or she will warrant serious punishment.

If it happens that the birth takes so long and the first midwife has a pressing need to rest or sleep for a while, she should call another sworn midwife and not an apprentice, who will then be just as responsible to appear immediately without opposition. She should then steadfastly and helpfully care for the woman in labor just as if she had been called at first. . . .

If any midwives show themselves to be disobedient or disagreeable, the council will not only remove them from office, but will also punish them severely, so that all will know to shape up and watch their behavior. . . .

From now on no midwife will be allowed to take on an apprentice who has begun with a different midwife and left her without justifiable cause, but every apprentice shall stay with the woman with whom she started. Justifiable and legitimate cause for leaving may be proven to the council or to those appointed by it. In such cases, the apprentice will not be forbidden to complete her training years with another sworn midwife. In this case, the woman that caused the

---

[1]The "honorable women," or *Ehrbare Frauen.*

apprentice to leave through her unfairness and unreasonableness will not be allowed to take on another apprentice until the end of the training years of the first.

They should not take on any flighty, young apprentices, as it so often happens that they marry during the course of their training and that all sorts of injuries result from their inexperience. They should rather take on apprentices well advanced in years and preferably living alone, from whom one expects more diligence than from younger ones.

They should also not allow themselves to drink wine in excess, as all kinds of injury and harm have been inflicted on the pregnant women because of this. The council has decided to punish severely any who break this restriction.

The honorable council has discovered that the midwives often send their maids (that have not completed their instruction or that have just completed it and have no experience yet) alone to women who are giving birth for the first time, through which these women are often neglected and deplorably injured. Therefore the honorable council orders that from now on no maid, whether she has half-completed her training or not, is to attend alone any woman bearing her first or second child, whether she goes with the knowledge of her instructor or not. After the passing of the normal years of training, the apprentice shall carry out her first birth in the presence of her instructor. . . .

The high honorable council has also had enough of midwives taking their proper salary for poor women not only from the established overseer of the charity[2] but also from the women themselves, and therefore receive double payment. This gives the honorable council great displeasure. Because of this the midwives are to swear that when they receive their proper salary from the overseer for caring for a poor woman, they are not to demand or want anything more, but let themselves be completely satisfied with their established salary. All of this is liable to punishment which the high honorable council will set each time according to the crime and opportunities of the case.

Recently evil cases have taken place, that those women who live in sin and adultery have illegitimate children, and during birth or before purposefully attempt to kill them by taking harmful, abortion-causing drugs, or through other notorious means. Some of these cases never come to the attention of the authorities, and proper punishment for them cannot be carried out. This the high honorable council, because of the God-given authority it carries, can no longer tolerate. Therefore they have made the recommendation that the midwives' oath be added to. They are to swear yearly, that when one of them is called to deliver a baby for such a woman, one who is carrying an illegitimate child, she [the midwife] is obliged to ask what the name of the child's mother is, and who the child's father is. As soon as she has brought the child into the world, she is to report to the Lord Mayor whether the child is alive or dead, who its mother and father are, and where the mother is lying in bed. Also no dead illegitimate children are to be carried to the grave before she gives her report to the Lord Mayor. At least three or four female persons are to go with the child to the grave. If one or more of the midwives act against this, and will not comply with what has been sent forth above, the high honorable council will deal with them as perjurers with corporal punishment. Then they will finally know to conform to this.

▾ ▾ ▾

On the request of the sworn midwives to the high honorable council to improve their ordinance in several various points this further pronouncement is to be published, to bring the following improvements to their ordinances. . . .

---

[2]The city council had established a special fund, the *Arme Kindbetter Almosen,* for poor expectant mothers.

The midwives have sworn in their oaths not to send or use an apprentice during her normal training years to a woman having her first baby, but have requested to have this limited to only the first quarter-year. The high honorable council believes this to be much too short a time, and will set the limit at one year. Therefore from now on no midwife should send a maid to a woman having her first child unless she has completed one year of her training program. . . .

Some women have allowed their little children to be carried to holy baptism by strange people when the midwife was too busy, although such small children are easily harmed and injured. Therefore, the high honorable council orders that from now on all new-born children are to be carried to holy baptism by their sworn midwife or her apprentice. Any midwife will be fined . . . if she breaks this ordinance.

No midwife is to take on a maid-apprentice without the knowledge of the *Ehrbare Frauen.* No maid-apprentice is to be accepted who is married or has her own household, but only those who are single or widowed, so that these persons are not called away from their instructors to their private business or housework, and will always

be available. They should not live in the midwife's house, but in the neighborhood, and should keep themselves occupied at all times.

The high honorable council has discovered that some of the midwives are taking all or half of the tips that have been given to their maid-apprentices by people, which leads to all sorts of lack of diligence and care among the maids. In order to prevent this, the high honorable council has decided that from now on all that a maid receives for herself from a child's mother, father, relatives or others, that has been given willingly above the normal payments, should remain the maid's and she is not to be required to give any to her mistress. . . .

The high honorable council has also discovered that some midwives have no maid-apprentices, with the result that when the old midwives die no qualified people may be appointed to their posts. In order to improve this the high honorable council seriously asks all midwives who have completed the training period with one or more maids to take on another capable one in their place a quarter or at longest a half year later.

▼▼▼

# An Expanding Intellectual Universe

Although European intellectuals during the Middle Ages and Renaissance had many disagreements and controversies, all but a few shared a number of basic beliefs and assumptions. They believed that Christianity, as interpreted by the Roman Catholic Church, provided a complete revelation of God's purposes and true and perfect guidelines for human conduct. All of them revered antiquity. They looked to the Greeks for guidance in logic, philosophy, and natural science and to the Romans for inspiration in literature, government, and law. All believed that the earth was the center of the universe, and that on earth Catholic Christians came closest to realizing God's design for humanity.

During the sixteenth century European thinkers were forced to re-evaluate every one of these assumptions. The secularism of the Renaissance, the religious divisions caused by the Reformation, new scientific discoveries, and surprising encounters with Africans, Asians, and Amerindians all challenged Europe's intellectual assumptions. As one revered authority after another was questioned, intellectuals' reactions ranged from dogmatism to skepticism to bewilderment.

No serious European thinker was immune from the unsettling new ideas and events of the age.

This section begins with an essay by the sixteenth-century French writer Michel de Montaigne, whose personal experiences, studies, and observations led him to question facile generalizations and unexamined assumptions. The section concludes with a letter by Galileo Galilei, one of the scientific giants of the age. His career came to symbolize conflict between science and religion, which in his case reached a climax in his famous controversy with the Roman Catholic Church in the 1620s and 1630s. Thus both authors were products of the intellectual tensions of the age and contributed to them.

# Who Is the True Barbarian?
▼▼▼

## 9 ▼ *Michel de Montaigne, "ON CANNIBALS"*

Michel de Montaigne (1533–1592), one of the most influential figures in all of European literature, was the son of a Bordeaux merchant who had recently purchased both a title of nobility and a rural estate. After studying law at the University of Toulouse and serving as a counselor for several courts of law in the province of Bordeaux, Montaigne retired after his father's death in 1568 to his family estate where he planned to read, meditate, and write. He successfully followed his plan, interrupting it only for travel, occasional forays into politics, and brief entanglements in the French Wars of Religions, which persisted through most of his adult life. Although he died a Catholic, he belonged to the faction known as the *politiques,* whose members believed that religious toleration and strong princely rule provided the only means of saving France from destructive religious and factional rivalries.

Montaigne invented the essay as a literary genre. To Montaigne the essay was, as it is today, a short prose composition that treats a given subject in a personal and informal way. The English term is derived from the French word *essai,* meaning an attempt, trial, or experiment. An essay, therefore, offered Montaigne an opportunity to test and explore his ideas rather than transmit absolute truths. It was the perfect genre for a man who distrusted dogmatism and believed that truth needed continuing reassessment. Montaigne published three books of essays, which contained a total of 107 chapters. "On Cannibals," published in his first book of essays, was written sometime between 1578 and 1580.

### QUESTIONS FOR ANALYSIS

1. What is Montaigne's definition of barbarism?
2. In what sense do the people of Brazil and the Europeans fulfill this definition?
3. How does Montaigne's description of the Brazilians' reactions to European customs fit into the overall theme of the essay?

4. If Montaigne had been given an opportunity to examine the arguments of Las Casas and Sepúlveda, would he have agreed with either of them? Explain your answer.
5. What implications does Montaigne's essay have for Christianity, especially Christian ethical doctrine?

I had with me for a long time a man who had lived for ten or twelve years in that other world which has been discovered in our century, in the place where Villegaignon landed, and which he called Antarctic France.[1] This discovery of a boundless country seems worthy of consideration. . . .

This man I had was a simple, crude fellow — a character fit to bear true witness; for clever people observe more things and more curiously, but they interpret them; and to lend weight and conviction to their interpretation, they cannot help altering history a little. . . . Such was my man; and besides this, he at various times brought sailors and merchants, whom he had known on that trip, to see me. So I content myself with his information, without inquiring what the cosmographers say about it. . . .

Now, to return to my subject, I think there is nothing barbarous and savage in that nation, from what I have been told, except that each man calls barbarism whatever is not his own practice; for indeed it seems we have no other test of truth and reason than the example and pattern of the opinions and customs of the country we live in. *There* is always the perfect religion, the perfect government, the perfect and accomplished manners in all things. Those people are wild, just as we call wild the fruits that Nature has produced by herself and in her normal course; whereas really it is those that we have changed artificially and led astray from the common order, that we should rather call wild. The former retain alive and vigorous their genuine, their most useful and natural, virtues and properties, which we have

debased in the latter in adapting them to gratify our corrupted taste. . . .

These nations, then, seem to me barbarous in this sense, that they have been fashioned very little by the human mind, and are still very close to their original naturalness. The laws of nature still rule them, very little corrupted by ours; and they are in such a state of purity that I am sometimes vexed that they were unknown earlier, in the days when there were men able to judge them better than we. . . .

Their buildings are very long, with a capacity of two or three hundred souls; they are covered with the bark of great trees, the strips reaching to the ground at one end and supporting and leaning on one another at the top, in the manner of some of our barns, whose covering hangs down to the ground and acts as a side. They have wood so hard that they cut with it and make of it their swords and grills to cook their food. Their beds are of a cotton weave, hung from the roof like those in our ships, each man having his own; for the wives sleep apart from their husbands.

They get up with the sun, and eat immediately upon rising, to last them through the day; for they take no other meal than that one. . . . Their drink is made of some root, and is of the color of our claret wines. They drink it only lukewarm. . . . In place of bread they use a certain white substance like preserved coriander. I have tried it; it tastes sweet and a little flat.

The whole day is spent in dancing. The younger men go to hunt animals with bows. Some of the women busy themselves meanwhile with warming their drink, which is their chief

---

[1]Antarctic France was a term that referred to the area of modern Brazil. *Antarctic* is used in the sense of "opposite of the Arctic," or "toward the south," that is, this region lay south of the kingdom of France.

duty. Some one of the old men, in the morning before they begin to eat, preaches to the whole barnful in common, walking from one end to the other, and repeating one single sentence several times until he has completed the circuit (for the buildings are fully a hundred paces long). He recommends to them only two things: valor against the enemy and love for their wives. . . .

They have some sort of priests and prophets, but they rarely appear before the people, having their home in the mountains. On their arrival there is a great feast and solemn assembly of several villages — each barn, as I have described it, makes up a village, and they are about one French league from each other. The prophet speaks to them in public, exhorting them to virtue and their duty; but their whole ethical science contains only these two articles: resoluteness in war and affection for their wives. . . .

They have their wars with the nations beyond the mountains, further inland, to which they go quite naked, with no other arms than bows or wooden swords ending in a sharp point, in the manner of the tongues of our boar spears. It is astonishing what firmness they show in their combats, which never end but in slaughter and bloodshed; for as to routs and terror, they know nothing of either.

Each man brings back as his trophy the head of the enemy he has killed, and sets it up at the entrance to his dwelling. After they have treated their prisoners well for a long time with all the hospitality they can think of, each man who has a prisoner calls a great assembly of his acquaintances. He ties a rope to one of the prisoner's arms, by the end of which he holds him, a few steps away, for fear of being hurt, and gives his dearest friend the other arm to hold in the same way; and these two, in the presence of the whole assembly, kill him with their swords. This done, they roast him and eat him in common and send some pieces to their absent friends. . . .

I am not sorry that we notice the barbarous horror of such acts, but I am heartily sorry that,

judging their faults rightly, we should be so blind to our own. I think there is more barbarity in eating a man alive than in eating him dead; and in tearing by tortures and the rack a body still full of feeling, in roasting a man bit by bit, in having him bitten and mangled by dogs and swine (as we have not only read but seen within fresh memory, not among ancient enemies, but among neighbors and fellow citizens, and what is worse, on the pretext of piety and religion), than in roasting and eating him after he is dead. . . .

So we may well call these people barbarians, in respect to the rules of reason, but not in respect to ourselves, who surpass them in every kind of barbarity. . . .

Three of these men, ignorant of the price they will pay some day, in loss of repose and happiness, for gaining knowledge of the corruptions of this side of the ocean; ignorant also of the fact that of this intercourse will come their ruin (which I suppose is already well advanced: poor wretches, to let themselves be tricked by the desire for new things, and to have left the serenity of their own sky to come and see ours!) — three of these men were at Rouen, at the time the late King Charles IX[2] was there. The king talked to them for a long time; they were shown our ways, our splendor, the aspect of a fine city. After that, someone asked their opinion, and wanted to know what they had found most amazing. They mentioned three things, of which I have forgotten the third, and I am very sorry for it; but I still remember two of them. They said that in the first place they thought it very strange that so many grown men, bearded, strong, and armed, who were around the king (it is likely that they were talking about the Swiss of his guard) should submit to obey a child, and that one of them was not chosen to command instead. Second (they have a way in their language of speaking of men as halves of one another), they had noticed that there were among us men full and gorged with all sorts of good things, and

----

[2]Charles IX was ten years old when he became king in 1570. He died in 1574.

that their other halves were beggars at their doors, emaciated with hunger and poverty; and they thought it strange that these needy halves could endure such an injustice, and did not take the others by the throat, or set fire to their houses.

I had a very long talk with one of them; but I had an interpreter who followed my meaning so badly, and who was so hindered by his stupidity in taking in my ideas, that I could get hardly any satisfaction from the man. When I asked him what profit he gained from his superior position among his people (for he was a captain, and our sailors called him king), he told me that it was to march foremost in war. How many men followed him? He pointed to a piece of ground, to signify as many as such a space could hold; it might have been four or five thousand men. Did all his authority expire with the war? He said that this much remained, that when he visited the villages dependent on him, they made paths for him through the underbrush by which he might pass quite comfortably.

All this is not too bad — but what's the use? They don't wear breeches.

# Science and the Claims of Religion
▼▼▼

## 10 ▼ *Galileo Galilei,*
## *LETTER TO THE*
## *GRAND DUCHESS CHRISTINA*

The greatest European scientist in the early 1600s was the Italian physicist and astronomer Galileo Galilei (1564–1642). His most important work was in mechanics, in which he developed the theory of inertia and described the laws that dictate the movement of falling bodies. In astronomy he pioneered the use of the telescope and defended the theory of a sun-centered universe, advanced by the Polish astronomer Nicholas Copernicus in 1543. His public support of Copernicus disturbed Catholic clergymen and theologians, who were convinced it threatened correct belief and the authority of the Church.

In 1615 Galileo, a devout Catholic, defended his approach to science in a published letter addressed to Christina, the grand duchess of Tuscany. In the short run Galileo lost his case. The Church officially condemned Copernican theory in 1616 and forced Galileo to renounce many of his ideas in 1632. His works continued to be read, however, and in the long run his writings contributed to the acceptance of Copernican theory and the new methodology of science.

## QUESTIONS FOR ANALYSIS

1. How does Galileo characterize the motives of his enemies? Why in his view do they use religious arguments against him?
2. According to Galileo, why is it dangerous to apply passages of scripture to science?
3. To Galileo, how does nature differ from the Bible as a source of truth?
4. In Galileo's view, what is the proper relationship between science and religion?

Some years ago, as Your Serene Highness well knows, I discovered in the heavens many things that had not been seen before our own age. The novelty of these things, as well as some consequences which followed from them in contradiction to the physical notions commonly held among academic philosophers, stirred up against me no small number of professors — as if I had placed these things in the sky with my own hands in order to upset nature and overturn the sciences. They seemed to forget that the increase of known truths stimulates the investigation, establishment, and growth of the arts; not their diminution or destruction.

Showing a greater fondness for their own opinions than for truth, they sought to deny and disprove the new things which, if they had cared to look for themselves, their own senses would have demonstrated to them. To this end they hurled various charges and published numerous writings filled with vain arguments, and they made the grave mistake of sprinkling these with passages taken from places in the Bible which they had failed to understand properly, and which were ill suited to their purposes.

Persisting in their original resolve to destroy me and everything mine by any means they can think of, these men are aware of my views in astronomy and philosophy. They know that as to the arrangement of the parts of the universe, I hold the sun to be situated motionless in the center of the revolution of the celestial orbs while the earth rotates on its axis and revolves about the sun. They know also that I support this position not only by refuting the arguments of Ptolemy[1] and Aristotle, but by producing many counter-arguments; in particular, some which relate to physical effects whose causes can perhaps be assigned in no other way. In addition there are astronomical arguments derived from

many things in my new celestial discoveries that plainly confute the Ptolemaic system while admirably agreeing with and confirming the contrary hypothesis. Possibly because they are disturbed by the known truth of other propositions of mine which differ from those commonly held, and therefore mistrusting their defense so long as they confine themselves to the field of philosophy, these men have resolved to fabricate a shield for their fallacies out of the mantle of pretended religion and the authority of the Bible. These they apply, with little judgment, to the refutation of arguments that they do not understand and have not even listened to.

First they have endeavored to spread the opinion that such propositions in general are contrary to the Bible and are consequently damnable and heretical. . . . Next, becoming bolder, and hoping (though vainly) that this seed which first took root in their hypocritical minds would send out branches and ascend to heaven, they began scattering rumors among the people that before long this doctrine would be condemned by the supreme authority.[2] They know, too, that official condemnation would not only suppress the two propositions which I have mentioned, but would render damnable all other astronomical and physical statements and observations that have any necessary relation or connection with these. . . .

To this end they make a shield of their hypocritical zeal for religion. They go about invoking the Bible, which they would have minister to their deceitful purposes. Contrary to the sense of the Bible and the intention of the holy Fathers, if I am not mistaken, they would extend such authorities until even in purely physical matters — where faith is not involved — they would have us altogether abandon reason and the evidence of our senses in favor of some biblical

---

[1]Ptolemy (ca. 100 to 170 C.E.) spent most of his life in Alexandria, Egypt, and was the Greek astronomer who propounded key aspects of the geocentric planetary system that prevailed in Europe until the time of Copernicus.

[2]The pope.

passage, though under the surface meaning of its words this passage may contain a different sense.

I hope to show that I proceed with much greater piety than they do, when I argue not against condemning this book, but against condemning it in the way they suggest — that is, without understanding it, weighing it, or so much as reading it. . . .

The reason produced for condemning the opinion that the earth moves and the sun stands still is that in many places in the Bible one may read that the sun moves and the earth stands still. Since the Bible cannot err, it follows as a necessary consequence that anyone takes an erroneous and heretical position who maintains that the sun is inherently motionless and the earth movable.

With regard to this argument, I think in the first place that it is very pious to say and prudent to affirm that the holy Bible can never speak untruth — whenever its true meaning is understood. But I believe nobody will deny that it is often very abstruse, and may say things which are quite different from what its bare words signify. Hence in expounding the Bible if one were always to confine oneself to the unadorned grammatical meaning, one might fall into error. Not only contradictions and propositions far from true might thus be made to appear in the Bible, but even grave heresies and follies. Thus it would be necessary to assign to God feet, hands, and eyes, as well as corporeal and human affections, such as anger, repentance, hatred, and sometimes even the forgetting of things past and ignorance of those to come. These propositions uttered by the Holy Ghost were set down in that manner by the sacred scribes[3] in order to accommodate them to the capacities of the common people, who are rude and unlearned. . . .

This being granted, I think that in discussions of physical problems we ought to begin not from the authority of scriptural passages but from sense-experiences and necessary demonstrations; for the holy Bible and the phenomena of nature proceed alike from the divine Word, the former as the dictate of the Holy Ghost and the latter as the observant executrix of God's commands. It is necessary for the Bible, in order to be accommodated to the understanding of every man, to speak many things which appear to differ from the absolute truth so far as the bare meaning of the words is concerned. But Nature, on the other hand, is inexorable and immutable; she never transgresses the laws imposed upon her, or cares a whit whether her abstruse reasons and methods of operation are understandable to men. For that reason it appears that nothing physical which sense-experience sets before our eyes, or which necessary demonstrations prove to us, ought to be called in question (much less condemned) upon the testimony of biblical passages which may have some different meaning beneath their words. For the Bible is not chained in every expression to conditions as strict as those which govern all physical effects; nor is God any less excellently revealed in Nature's actions than in the sacred statements of the Bible.

---

[3]The Holy Ghost is the third divine person of the Trinity (God the Father, God the Son, God the Holy Ghost), who sanctifies and inspires humankind. Christians believe the authors of the Bible wrote under the sacred and infallible inspiration of the Holy Ghost.

# Chapter 2

### ▼▼▼

# Africa and the Americas

Between the fifteenth and seventeenth centuries Africa and the Americas became the first areas of the world to experience significant consequences from early modern Europe's expansion. On both sides of the Atlantic the arrival of Europeans resulted in demographic and biological changes, political disruption, and the introduction of new weapons, trade patterns, and religions. But the magnitude of Europe's impact on the two regions was far different — Africa was affected by the Europeans' arrival, but the Americas were transformed.

The European presence in Africa primarily meant trade — in gold, ivory, and spices, and a mounting number of human beings. By the 1500s slaves had become the most lucrative commodity for European traders on Africa's west coast. In the eighteenth century, more than six million enslaved Africans were transported to the New World. Even then, most of the rest of the continent was still unaffected by the European presence, and in central West Africa, where slaving was most intense, Europeans stayed on the coast, content to have Africans bring them slaves for purchase and transport to the Americas. European colonization of sub-Saharan Africa did not begin until 1652, when Dutch farmers began to settle on the southernmost tip of the continent. As a result of all these factors, the arrival of Europeans in Africa had relatively little effect on the continent's politics, culture, and religious life.

In the Americas, however, the Europeans' appearance was catastrophic for the indigenous peoples. By 1650 Spaniards and Portuguese ruled and exploited Mexico and Central and South America, and the English, French, Dutch, and other Europeans had begun to settle North America's Atlantic coast and the St. Lawrence River basin. Throughout the Western Hemisphere Native American political structures disintegrated, millions of Amerindians died from Old World diseases, and traditional patterns of life and belief managed only a tenuous survival.

Why were the experiences of Africa and the Americas so different? In the case of Africa, two factors that discouraged deeper European involvement were diseases such as yellow fever and malaria and the absence of easily navigable rivers from the seacoast to the continent's interior. More significant was the fact that Portugal, which led the way in African exploration and trade, was a small country with limited fiscal resources and during the sixteenth century concentrated its energies on Asia, the source of the ceramics, silks, and spices coveted by Europeans. Later, in the seventeenth and eighteenth centuries, when England, France, and the Netherlands began to trade in Africa, the Africans had firearms and were able to resist European political encroachment.

Europeans faced a far different situation in the Americas. They soon discovered that the region contained easily exploitable sources of wealth such as gold, silver, and furs and was capable of producing profitable agricultural products such as tobacco and sugar. All these things were more or less theirs for the taking, not only in the thinly populated regions of North America and eastern and southern South America, but also in the more populous regions of Mexico, Peru, and the Caribbean.

The ease of the Europeans' conquest of the Americas can be attributed only in part to the initial military advantages afforded by their guns, steel swords, and horses. A more important factor was disease. In Mexico, for example, under normal circumstances several hundred Spaniards, even with their Indian allies, artillery, and arquebuses, would have been no match for thousands of Aztec warriors with arrows, clubs, lances, and spears. But in the midst of their struggle against the Spaniards, the Aztecs were struck by an epidemic of smallpox, a disease contracted from the Spaniards. It was a sorely weakened and demoralized Aztec empire that succumbed to the Spaniards and their Amerindian allies in 1521.

Like the Aztecs all Amerindians had to contend with the bacteria, viruses, and parasites Europeans and Africans carried in their bodies from across the Atlantic. Because of their long isolation they lacked immunity to Old World diseases such as diphtheria, measles, chicken pox, whooping cough, yellow fever, influenza, dysentery, and smallpox. Thus the arrival of Europeans and Africans had immediate and devastating consequences. On the island of Hispaniola, where Columbus established the first Spanish settlement in the New World, the indigenous population plummeted from one million to only a few thousand by 1530. Within fifty years after the arrival of the Spaniards in Mexico, the region's estimated population fell by 90 percent. No part of the Americas was untouched.

Such human devastation made it relatively easy for the Europeans to conquer or displace the Native Americans. It also led to the enslavement of Africans in the New World. The epidemics created labor shortages that plantation and mine owners sought to overcome by importing enslaved Africans. Before the transatlantic slave trade ended, as many as eleven million Africans were sold into slavery in the Americas and millions more died in slave raids and the holds of slave ships. These Africans too were indirect victims of the bacilli, viruses, and parasites introduced to the New World in the early years of European expansion.

▼▼▼

# The Diversity of African Societies

Africa's vast size and the wide variety of its climate and topography largely explain the diversity of African societies, especially those south of the Sahara. Although scholars discern certain continentwide commonalities in areas of life such as politics, music, art, and agriculture, Africa lacked any broadly shared cultural tradition of the type that gave unity to Confucian China, Hindu India, and Muslim Southwest Asia.

Thus in the 1500s and 1600s, as had been true for centuries, African governments included large empires, smaller kingdoms, chieftainships, and self-governing city-states. Millions of Africans also lived in stateless societies in which custom and clan leaders provided alternatives to formal government. Most Africans supported themselves economically through agriculture or raising livestock. But Africa's population also included a small number of hunters and gatherers, many skilled artisans, and numerous merchants, some of whom were parts of trade networks that linked Africa commercially to many parts of Eurasia. In religion most Africans were animists who believed in a high creator-god, local divinities, and ancestral spirits. But Africans in Ethiopia were Christians, and many inhabitants of Mediterranean Africa, the Sudan, and the east coast were Muslims. Africans spoke approximately two thousand different languages.

Because traditional non-Christian and non-Muslim African societies left no written records, information about their histories is sparse. Historians have utilized oral traditions, linguistic analysis, and insights from archaeologists, anthropologists, and art historians to reconstruct some of Africa's past but have been unable to sketch the outlines of Africa's early political and cultural development with any precision. Knowledge of Africa increases after the arrival of Europeans, whose letters, diaries, memoirs, and books provide rich sources of information about the societies they encountered.

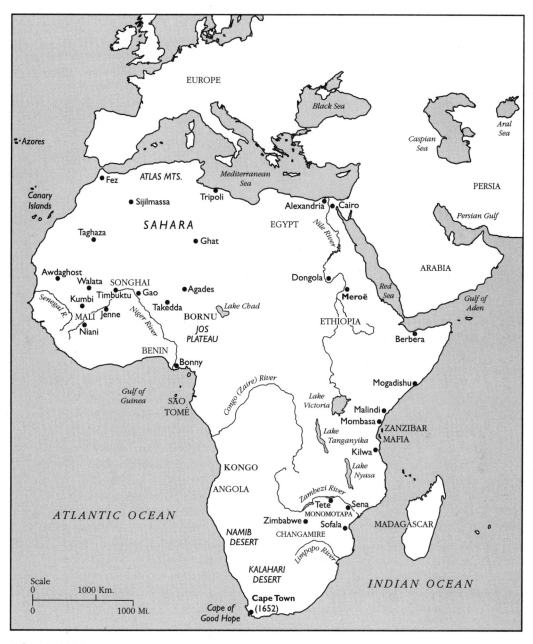

*Africa in 1500*

The two selections in this section include one account of Africa written by a European and one written by an African who lived part of his life in Europe. They describe societies in two different parts of the continent — several kingdoms in the Sudan, the region south of the Sahara; and various states and cities on Africa's east coast. They provide a small sample of Africa's rich political, religious, and social diversity.

# Africa's Sudanic Kingdoms
▼▼▼

## 11 ▼ *Leo Africanus,*
### *HISTORY AND DESCRIPTION OF AFRICA*

Al-Hassan ibn-Muhammad al-Wazzan al-Fasi, better known as Leo Africanus, was probably born in the 1460s in Granada, the last Muslim toehold in Spain, but was raised in Fez (in modern Morocco), where his family migrated in the face of mounting Spanish military pressure. Educated in Islamic law, he entered the service of the sultan of Fez, who sent him on a number of commercial and diplomatic missions, including two trips across sub-Saharan West Africa. Captured by Christian pirates and brought to Rome in 1518, he was presented as a slave to Pope Leo X, who persuaded him to accept Christianity and a new name, Giovanni Leone (John Leo).

While in Rome in 1526 John Leo completed in Italian his *History and Description of Africa,* probably based on an earlier Arabic version. It recounts his observations during his travels in Africa north of the equator and became a principal source of European knowledge of the region. Because of this work he became known as Leo Africanus, Latin for Leo the African. Little is known about the rest of his life except that sometime after 1530 he returned to Africa and died a Muslim in Tunis around 1554.

In the following excerpts, Leo describes several states he visited in the western part of the Sudan, the extensive grass-covered plain that stretches across Africa south of the Sahara. The western Sudan, known as the Sahel, for centuries had been the center of important historical developments, including the rise and fall of several large, impressive states. When Leo visited the region in the early 1500s, the Songhai Empire had replaced the Kingdom of Mali as the dominant state in the region. Its two most important cities were Gao, the capital, and Timbuktu, which was ruled by a governor in the name of the emperor. To the east of Songhai was the Kingdom of Bornu, situated on the shores of Lake Chad.

## QUESTIONS FOR ANALYSIS

1. What do Leo's observations reveal about the economic activities of this region of Africa?
2. How did one become a slave in these Sudanic societies? How were slaves utilized?

3. What generalizations can be made about the intellectual, religious, and cultural life in these Sudanic kingdoms?
4. What similarities and differences were there among the various rulers described by Leo? What was the basis of their authority and power?
5. Consider the powers exercised by the king of Timbuktu, who was a vassal of the Songhai emperor in Gao. What does the king's wealth and authority reveal about the government of the Songhai Empire?

## THE KINGDOM OF MALI

In this kingdom there is a large and ample village containing more than six thousand families, and named Mali, which is also the name of the whole kingdom. Here the king has his residence. The region itself yields great abundance of wheat, meat and cotton. Here are many craftsmen and merchants in all places: and yet the king honorably entertains all strangers. The inhabitants are rich and have plenty of merchandise. Here is a great number of temples, clergymen, and teachers, who read their lectures in the mosques because they have no colleges at all. The people of the region excel all other Negroes in wit, civility, and industry, and were the first that embraced the law of Muhammad.[1] . . .

## THE CITY OF TIMBUKTU

All its houses are . . . cottages, built of mud and covered with thatch. However, there is a most stately mosque to be seen, whose walls are made of stone and lime, and a princely palace also constructed by the highly skilled craftsmen of Granada.[2] Here there are many shops of artisans and merchants, especially of those who weave linen and cotton, and here Barbary[3] merchants bring European cloth. The inhabitants, and especially resident aliens, are exceedingly rich,

since the present king[4] married both of his daughters to rich merchants. This region yields great quantities of grain, cattle, milk, and butter, but salt is very scarce here, for it is brought here by land from Tegaza, which is five hundred miles away. When I was there, I saw one camel-load of salt sold for eighty ducats.[5]

The rich king of Timbuktu has many plates and scepters of gold, some of which weigh 1,300 pounds, and he keeps a magnificent and well-furnished court. When he travels anywhere, he rides upon a camel, which is led by some of his noblemen. He does so likewise when going to war, and all his soldiers ride upon horses. Whoever wishes to speak to this king must first of all fall down before his feet and then taking up earth must sprinkle it on his own head and shoulders. . . . [The king] always has under arms 3,000 horsemen and a great number of foot soldiers who shoot poisoned arrows. They often skirmish with those who refuse to pay tribute and whomever they capture they sell to the merchants of Timbuktu. Here very few horses are bred. . . . Their best horses are brought out of North Africa. . . .

Here are great numbers of religious teachers, judges, scholars and other learned persons, who are bountifully maintained at the king's expense. Here too are brought various manuscripts or written books from Barbary, which are sold for more money than any other merchandise.

---

[1]In fact, the establishment of Islam in western Africa preceded the rise of Mali in the mid thirteenth century. The rulers of Ghana (ca. 990–ca. 1180), the first major empire in the region, probably accepted Islam shortly after 1100.
[2]A region of southern Spain which had had a large Muslim population.

[3]The northern region of Africa from the Atlantic to the Egyptian border.
[4]The king of Timbuktu, a vassal of the Songhai emperor, as governor exercised a good deal of local power.
[5]An Italian coin.

The coin of Timbuktu is gold, without any stamp or inscription, but in matters of small value they use certain shells from the Kingdom of Persia. Four hundred of these are worth a ducat, and six pieces of Timbuktu's golden coin weigh two-thirds of an ounce.

The inhabitants are gentle and cheerful and spend a great part of the night in singing and dancing throughout the city streets. They keep large numbers of male and female slaves, and their town is greatly vulnerable to fire. . . .

## THE TOWN AND KINGDOM OF GAO

Here are very rich merchants and to here journey continually large numbers of Negroes who purchase here cloth from Barbary and Europe. The town abounds in grain and meat but lacks wine, trees and fruits. However, there are plenty of melons, lemons and rice. Here there are many wells, which also contain very sweet and wholesome water. Here also is a certain place where slaves are sold, especially upon those days when merchants assemble. A young slave of fifteen years of age is sold for six ducats, and children are also sold.

The king of this region has a certain private palace in which he keeps a large number of concubines and slaves, who are watched by eunuchs. To guard his person he maintains a sufficient troop of horsemen and foot soldiers. Between the first gate of the palace and the inner part, there is a walled enclosure wherein the king personally decides all of his subjects' controversies. Although the king is most diligent in this regard and conducts all business in these matters, he has in his company counsellors and such other officers as his secretaries, treasurers, stewards and auditors.

It is a wonder to see the quality of merchandise that is daily brought here and how costly and sumptuous everything is. Horses purchased in Europe for ten ducats are sold here for forty and sometimes fifty ducats apiece. There is not European cloth so coarse as to sell for less than four ducats an ell.[6] If it is anywhere near fine quality, they will give fifteen ducats for an ell, and an ell of the scarlet of Venice or of Turkish cloth is here worth thirty ducats. A sword is here valued at three or four crowns,[7] and likewise are spears, bridles and similar commodities, and spices are all sold at a high rate. However, of all other items, salt is the most expensive.

The rest of this kingdom contains nothing but villages and hamlets inhabited by herdsmen and shepherds, who in winter cover their bodies with the skins of animals, but in summer they go naked, save for their private parts. . . . They are an ignorant and rude people, and you will scarcely find one learned person in the square of a hundred miles. They are continually burdened by heavy taxes; to the point that they scarcely have anything left on which to live.

## THE KINGDOM OF BORNU

They have a most powerful prince. . . . He has in readiness as many as three thousand horsemen and a huge number of foot soldiers; for all his subjects are so . . . obedient to him, that whenever he commands them, they will arm themselves and will follow him wherever he leads them. They pay him no tribute except tithes on their grain; neither does the king have any revenues to support his state except the spoils he gets from his enemies by frequent invasions and assaults. He is in a state of perpetual hostility with a certain people who live beyond the desert of Seu, who in times past marching with a huge army of footsoldiers over the said desert, devastated a great part of the Kingdom of Bornu. Whereupon the king sent for the merchants of Barbary and ordered them to bring him a great store of horses: for in this country they exchange horses for slaves, and sometimes give fifteen or twenty slaves for a horse. And by this means there were a great many horses bought although the

---

[6]A measurement of length, approximately forty-five inches.

[7]A gold coin, worth substantially more than a ducat.

merchants were forced to stay for their slaves until the king returned home as a conqueror with a great number of captives, and satisfied his creditors for his horses. Frequently it happens that the merchants must stay three months before the king returned from the wars. . . . Sometimes he does not bring home enough slaves to satisfy the merchants and sometimes they are forced to wait a whole year. . . . And yet the king seems marvelously rich, because his spurs, bridles, platters, dishes, pots and other vessels are made of gold. The king is extremely covetous and would rather pay his debts in slaves rather than gold.

# Africa's Cosmopolitan East Coast
▼▼▼

## 12 ▼ *Duarte Barbosa,*
## *AN ACCOUNT OF THE COUNTRIES BORDERING THE INDIAN OCEAN*

Duarte Barbosa (ca. 1480–1521) was a native of Lisbon who as a government official participated in a number of Portuguese commercial enterprises on the east African coast and in India. When passed over for a promotion, he resigned to take a position with the Spanish government. He died in 1521 in the Philippines. Before his resignation, he collected information about the societies he visited, compiling it as a book.

### QUESTIONS FOR ANALYSIS

1. What can you gather from Barbosa's account about the characteristics of the east African coast in the areas of (a) trade, (b) types of government, (c) religion, and (d) language?
2. What impresses Barbosa about the cities he is describing?
3. On the basis of his account, what can you infer about the impact of the Portuguese in this region?
4. What is there in Barbosa's account that may explain why most east coast Africans had little success defending themselves against the Portuguese?

### SOFALA

Going forward in the direction of India there is a river of no great size upon which up the stream is a town of the Moors[1] which they call Sofala, close to which the King our Lord[2] possesses a fort. These Moors have dwelt there for a long time by reason of the great traffic which they carried on with the heathen of the mainland. The Moors of this place speak Arabic and have a king over them who is subject to the King our Lord.

And the manner of their traffic was this: they came in small vessels named *zambucos*[3] from the kingdoms of Kilwa, Mombasa, and Malindi, bringing many cotton cloths, some spotted and others white and blue, also some of silk, and many

---

[1]African Muslims.
[2]The king of Portugal, Manuel I.

[3]Derived from the Arabic word *zambuc,* meaning small sailing vessel with a single mast.

small beads, grey, red, and yellow, which things come to the said kingdoms from the great kingdom of Cambay[4] in other greater ships. And these wares the said Moors who came from Malindi and Mombasa paid for in gold at such a price that those merchants departed well pleased. . . .

The Moors of Sofala kept these wares and sold them afterward to the heathen of the Kingdom of Monomotapa, who came there laden with gold which they gave in exchange for the said cloths without weighing it. These Moors collect also a great store of ivory which they find all around Sofala and this also they sell in the Kingdom of Cambay at five or six cruzados[5] the quintal.[6] They also sell some amber which is brought to them, . . . and is exceeding good. These Moors are black, and some of them tawny; some of them speak Arabic, but the greater part use the language of the country. They clothe themselves from the waist down with cotton and silk cloths, and other cloths they wear over their shoulders like capes, and turbans on their heads. . . . In this same Sofala now of late they make great store of cotton and weave it, and from it they make much white cloth, and as they know not how to dye it, or have not the needed dyes, they take the Cambay cloths, blue or otherwise colored, and unravel them and make them up again, so that it becomes a new thing. With this thread and their own white they make much colored cloth, and from it they gain much gold. . . .

## KILWA

Going along the coast, . . . there is an island hard by the mainland which is called Kilwa, in which is a Moorish town with many fair houses of stone and mortar, with many windows after our fashion, very well arranged in streets, with many flat roofs. The doors are of wood, well carved, with excellent joinery. Around it are streams and orchards and fruit-gardens with many channels of sweet water. It has a Moorish king over it. From this place they trade with Sofala, from which they bring back gold, and from here they spread all over Arabia. . . . Before the King our Lord sent out his expedition to discover India the Moors of Sofala, Cuama, Angoya and Mozambique were all subject to the King of Kilwa, who was the mightiest king among them. And in this town was an abundance of gold, as no ships passed toward Sofala without first coming to this island. Of the Moors there are some fair and some black, they are finely clad in many rich garments of gold and silk and cotton, and the women as well; also with much gold and silver in chains and bracelets, which they wear on their legs and arms, and many jeweled earrings in their ears. . . .

This town was taken by force from its king by the Portuguese, as, moved by arrogance, he refused to obey the King our Lord. There they took many prisoners and the king fled from the island, and His Highness ordered that a fort should be built there, and kept it under his rule and governance. . . .

## MOMBASA

Further on, an advance along the coast toward India, there is an island hard by the mainland, on which is a town called Mombasa. It is a very fair place, with lofty stone and mortar houses, well aligned in streets after the fashion of Kilwa. The wood is well-fitted with excellent joiner's work. It has its own king, himself a Moor. The men are in color either tawny, black or white and also their women go very bravely attired with many fine garments of silk and gold in abundance. This is a place of great trade, and has a good harbor, in which are always moored craft of many kinds and also great ships, both of those which come from Sofala and those which go there, and others which come from the great kingdom of Cambay and from Malindi; others which sail to the islands of Zanzibar, and yet others of which I shall speak later.

---

[4]A region of northwest coastal India, named after its major city, an important international port.

[5]A Portuguese unit of money.
[6]A unit of weight, roughly 100 to 130 pounds.

This Mombasa is a land very full of food. Here are found many very fine sheep with round tails, cows and other cattle in great plenty, and many fowls, all of which are exceeding fat. There is much millet and rice, sweet and bitter oranges, lemons, pomegranates, Indian figs, vegetables of diverse kinds, and much sweet water. The men are oft-times at war . . . but at peace with those of the mainland, and they carry on trade with them, obtaining great amounts of honey, wax, and ivory.

The king of this city refused to obey the commands of the King our Lord, and through this arrogance he lost it, and our Portuguese took it from him by force. He fled away, and they slew many of his people and also took captive many, both men and women, in such sort that it was left ruined and plundered and burnt. Of gold and silver great booty was taken here, bangles, bracelets, earrings and gold beads, also great store of copper with other rich wares in great quantity, and the town was left in ruins.

## MALINDI

Leaving Mombasa, and journeying along the coast toward India, there is a fair town on the mainland lying along a strand, which is named Malindi. It belongs to the Moors and has a Moorish king over it; the place has many fair stone and mortar houses of many stories, with great plenty of windows and flat roofs, after our fashion. The place is well laid out in streets. The folk are both black and white; they go naked, covering only their private parts with cotton and silk cloths. Others of them wear cloths folded like cloaks and waist-bands, and turbans of many rich stuffs on their heads.

They are great barterers, and deal in cloth, gold, ivory, and diverse other wares with the Moors and heathen of the great kingdom of Cambay; and to their harbor come every year many ships with cargoes of merchandise, from which they get great store of gold, ivory, and wax. In this traffic the Cambay merchants make great profits, and thus, on one side and the other,

they earn much money. There is plenty of food in this city (rice, millet, and some wheat which they bring from Cambay), and diverse sorts of fruit, inasmuch as there is here abundance of fruit-gardens and orchards. Here too are plenty of round-tailed sheep, cows, and other cattle and great store of oranges, also of hens.

The king and people of this place ever were and are friends of the King of Portugal, and the Portuguese always find in them great comfort and friendship and perfect peace, and there the ships, when they chance to pass that way, obtain supplies in plenty. . . .

## MAFIA, ZANZIBAR, AND PEMBA

Between this island of San Lorenzo and the continent, not very far from it, are three islands, which are called one Mafia, another Zanzibar, and the other Pemba; these are inhabited by Moors; they are very fertile islands, with plenty of provisions, rice, millet, and flesh, and abundant oranges, lemons, and citrons. All the mountains are full of them; they produce many sugar canes, but do not know how to make sugar. These islands have their kings. The inhabitants trade with the mainland with their provisions and fruits; they have small vessels, very loosely and badly made, without decks, and with a single mast; all their planks are sewn together with cords of reed or matting, and the sails are of palm mats. They are very feeble people, with very few and despicable weapons. In these islands they live in great luxury, and abundance; they dress in very good cloths of silk and cotton, which they buy in Mombasa of the merchants from Cambay, who reside there. Their wives adorn themselves with many jewels of gold from Sofala, and silver, in chains, earrings, bracelets, and ankle rings, and are dressed in silk stuffs: and they have many mosques. . . .

## OF THE CITY OF BRAVA

It has no king, but is ruled by elders, and ancients of the land, who are the persons held in the highest esteem, and who have the chief dealings in merchandise of diverse kinds. And this place was destroyed by the Portuguese, who slew many of its people and carried many into captivity, and took great spoil of gold and silver and goods. Thenceforth many of them fled away toward the inland country, forsaking the town; yet after it had been destroyed the Portuguese again settled and peopled it, so that now it is as prosperous as it was before.

▼▼▼

# The Portuguese in Africa

By the time the news of Columbus's voyage to "the Indies" began to ripple through Europe in the spring of 1493, the Portuguese had more than seventy years' experience exploring and trading in Africa. By the early 1480s, having established a line of fortified coastal trading posts as far as Benin on the Guinea Coast, they were generating profits from trade in gold, ivory, and slaves. Then in 1482, under King João II, the Portuguese embarked on a more ambitious and daring campaign to reach India by sailing around Africa. In 1488 Bartholomeu Dias rounded the Cape of Good Hope, and in 1498 Vasco da Gama sailed around Africa all the way to Calicut on India's west coast. During the early sixteenth century the Portuguese annexed east African coastal cities, defeated Arab and Persian navies, and established control of a direct sea route to India and beyond. Africa became a link in a Portuguese commercial empire stretching from Europe to China and, for a time, Japan.

Early Portuguese merchants and missionaries presented themselves to the Africans as friendly traders and potential allies. Government officials proclaimed idealistic aims of educating the Africans and converting them to Christianity. On the whole, however, Portuguese involvement in Africa was self-serving and disastrous for the Africans. The Portuguese became engaged in the slave trade in the 1450s, and by 1500 they were shipping better than a thousand slaves a year to Europe and to the islands off the African coast, where they had established sugar plantations. In the sixteenth century indiscriminate Portuguese slaving contributed to the disintegration of the Kingdom of Kongo and led to long decades of war against the Kingdom of Ndongo, to the south. The heavy-handed Portuguese conquest of Africa's prosperous east coast disrupted the region's commerce and resulted in the looting and destruction of numerous cities. But the Africans were capable of mounting spirited and effective resistance against the Portuguese, who, despite their artillery and arquebuses, did not always have their way.

# An African Voice of Protest

▼▼▼

## 13 ▼ Nzinga Mbemba (Afonso I), *LETTERS TO THE KING OF PORTUGAL*

The largest state in central West Africa around 1500 was the Kingdom of Kongo, stretching along the estuary of the Congo River in territory that today lies within Angola and Zaire. In 1483 the Portuguese navigator Diogo Cão made contact with Kongo and several years later visited its inland capital. When he sailed home he was accompanied by Kongo emissaries, whom King Nzinga a Kuwu dispatched to Lisbon to learn European ways. They returned in 1491, along with Portuguese priests, artisans, and soldiers who brought numerous European goods, including a printing press. In the same year, the king and his son, Nzinga Mbemba, were baptized as Catholics.

Around 1506 Nzinga Mbemba, who took the name Afonso after his baptism, succeeded his father and ruled until about 1543. Afonso promoted the introduction of European culture in his kingdom by proclaiming Christianity the state religion (a step that affected few of his subjects), imitating the etiquette of Portuguese royalty, and using the Portuguese language in state business. His son Henrique was educated in Portugal and returned to serve as the region's Roman Catholic bishop. European firearms, horses, and cattle were introduced, and Afonso dreamed of achieving a powerful and prosperous state through cooperation with the Europeans. By the time of his death, however, his kingdom verged on disintegration, in no small measure because of the Portuguese. As many later African rulers were to discover, the introduction of European products and customs caused dissension and social instability. Worse, Portuguese involvement in the slave trade undermined Afonso's authority and made his subjects restive. In 1526 the king wrote the following three letters to King João III of Portugal, urging him to control his rapacious subjects. The documents are part of a collection of twenty-four letters that Afonso and his Portuguese-educated, native secretaries dispatched to the kings of Portugal on a variety of issues.

---

## QUESTIONS FOR ANALYSIS

1. According to Afonso, what have been the detrimental effects of the Portuguese presence in his kingdom?
2. What do the letters reveal about the workings of the slave trade in the kingdom? Who participated in it?
3. What do the letters reveal about Afonso's attitude toward slavery? Explain whether he opposes the practice as such or only certain aspects of it.
4. What steps had the king taken to deal with the problems caused by the Portuguese? What do the letters suggest about the effectiveness of these steps?

5. How would you characterize Afonso's attitude toward the power and authority of the king of Portugal? Does he consider himself inferior to the Portuguese king or his equal?
6. How would you characterize King Afonso's conception of the ideal relationship between the Portuguese and his kingdom?

Sir, Your Highness should know how our Kingdom is being lost in so many ways that it is convenient to provide for the necessary remedy, since this is caused by the excessive freedom given by your agents and officials to the men and merchants who are allowed to come to this Kingdom to set up shops with goods and many things which have been prohibited by us, and which they spread throughout our Kingdoms and Domains in such an abundance that many of our vassals, whom we had in obedience, do not comply because they have the things in greater abundance than we ourselves; and it was with these things that we had them content and subjected under our vassalage and jurisdiction, so it is doing a great harm not only to the service of God, but the security and peace of our Kingdoms and State as well.

And we cannot reckon how great the damage is, since the mentioned merchants are taking every day our natives, sons of the land and the sons of our noblemen and vassals and our relatives, because the thieves and men of bad conscience grab them wishing to have the things and wares of this Kingdom which they are ambitious of; they grab them and get them to be sold; and so great, Sir, is the corruption and licentiousness that our country is being completely depopulated, and Your Highness should not agree with this nor accept it as in your service. And to avoid it we need from those (your) Kingdoms no more than some priests and a few people to teach in schools, and no other goods except wine and flour for the holy sacrament. That is why we beg of Your Highness to help and assist us in this matter, commanding your factors that they should not send here either merchants or

wares, because it is *our will that in these Kingdoms there should not be any trade of slaves nor outlet for them.*[1] Concerning what is referred [to] above, again we beg of Your Highness to agree with it, since otherwise we cannot remedy such an obvious damage. Pray Our Lord in His mercy to have Your Highness under His guard and let you do forever the things of His service. I kiss your hands many times.

*At our town of Kongo, written on the sixth day of July, João Teixeira*[2] *did it in 1526.*
*The King. Dom*[3] *Afonso.*
    {*On the back of this letter the following can be read:*
    *To the most powerful and excellent prince Dom João, King our Brother.*}

▼ ▼ ▼

Moreover, Sir, in our Kingdoms there is another great inconvenience which is of little service to God, and this is that many of our people, keenly desirous as they are of the wares and things of your Kingdoms, which are brought here by your people, and in order to satisfy their voracious appetite, seize many of our people, freed and exempt men, and very often it happens that they kidnap even noblemen and the sons of noblemen, and our relatives, and take them to be sold to the white men who are in our Kingdoms; and for this purpose they have concealed them; and others are brought during the night so that they might not be recognized.

And as soon as they are taken by the white men they are immediately ironed and branded with fire, and when they are carried to be embarked, if they are caught by our guards' men the whites allege that they have bought them

---

[1]Emphasis appears in original letter.
[2]One of Afonso's secretaries.

[3]Portuguese for "lord."

but they cannot say from whom, so that it is our duty to do justice and to restore to the freemen their freedom, but it cannot be done if your subjects feel offended, as they claim to be.

And to avoid such a great evil we passed a law so that any white man living in our Kingdoms and wanting to purchase goods in any way should first inform three of our noblemen and officials of our court whom we rely upon in this matter, and these are Dom Pedro Manipanza and Dom Manuel Manissaba, our chief usher, and Gonçalo Pires our chief freighter, who should investigate if the mentioned goods are captives or free men, and if cleared by them there will be no further doubt nor embargo for them to be taken and embarked. But if the white men do not comply with it they will lose the aforementioned goods. And if we do them this favor and concession it is for the part Your Highness has in it, since we know that it is in your service too that these goods are taken from our Kingdom, otherwise we should not consent to this. . . .

▼ ▼ ▼

Sir, Your Highness has been kind enough to write to us saying that we should ask in our letters for anything we need, and that we shall be provided with everything, and as the peace and the health of our Kingdom depend on us, and as there are among us old folks and people who have lived for many days, it happens that we have continuously many and different diseases which put us very often in such a weakness that we reach almost the last extreme; and the same happens to our children, relatives and natives owing to the lack in this country of physicians and surgeons who might know how to cure properly such diseases. And as we have got neither dispensaries nor drugs which might help us in this forlornness, many of those who had been already confirmed and instructed in the holy faith of Our Lord Jesus Christ perish and die; and the rest of the people in their majority cure themselves with herbs and breads and other ancient methods, so that they put all their faith in the mentioned herbs and ceremonies if they live, and believe that they are saved if they die; and this is not much in the service of God.

And to avoid such a great error and inconvenience, since it is from God in the first place and then from your Kingdoms and from Your Highness that all the good and drugs and medicines have come to save us, we beg of you to be agreeable and kind enough to send us two physicians and two apothecaries and one surgeon, so that they may come with their drugstores and all the necessary things to stay in our kingdoms, because we are in extreme need of them all and each of them. We shall do them all good and shall benefit them by all means, since they are sent by Your Highness, whom we thank for your work in their coming. We beg of Your Highness as a great favor to do this for us, because besides being good in itself it is in the service of God as we have said above.

*{Extracts from letter of King Afonso to the King of Portugal dated Oct. 18, 1526. By hand of Dom João Teixeira.}*

# The Zimba and the Portuguese
▼▼▼
## 14 ▼ *João dos Santos, EASTERN ETHIOPIA*

An example of African response to the Portuguese disruption of traditional trade patterns is provided by the military campaigns launched by the people known as the Zimba in the late sixteenth century. The *Zimba,* a term used by the Portuguese to describe any and all marauders from north of the Zambezi River, were in fact warriors of the Mang'aja tribe, whose attacks on the Portuguese and other African peoples to their east were ordered by their Lundu, or chief, in the late

1580s in response to disruption of their traditional trade. During the sixteenth century the market for Mang'aja ivory was ruined when the gold-obsessed Portuguese took over the coastal cities with which the Mang'aja had traded. The Zimba's military campaigns were intended to force the reopening of these markets. The Portuguese efforts to suppress the Zimba's attacks failed spectacularly. The Mang'aja continued their attacks until the early 1600s, but they never succeeded in re-establishing the traditional market for their ivory.

The following excerpt is from *Eastern Ethiopia* by João dos Santos, about whom little is known except that he was a Catholic clergyman who traveled along the east African coast and resided for a time in Sofala during the late sixteenth century. He uses the term *eastern Ethiopia* to include all of Africa's east coast from the Cape of Good Hope to the Red Sea.

## QUESTIONS FOR ANALYSIS

1. According to dos Santos's account, why do the Portuguese decide to resist the Zimba?
2. What seems to have been the attitude of the Zimba toward the Portuguese?
3. How would you characterize the attitude of the African allies of the Portuguese toward the Zimba? How dedicated were the allies to the Portuguese themselves?
4. How great an advantage did Portuguese firearms give them over their enemy?
5. What tactics of the Zimba were most effective in the conflict with the Portuguese and their allies? What purposes did cannibalism play in their overall strategy?
6. What hints does dos Santos's account provide about the motives of the Zimba's military campaign?

Opposite the fort of Sena, on the other side of the river, live some Kaffirs,[1] lords of those lands, good neighbors and friends of the Portuguese, and always most loyal to them. It so happened at the time I was there that the Zimba Kaffirs, . . . who eat human flesh, invaded this territory and made war upon one of these friendly Kaffirs, and by force of arms took from him the kraal[2] in which he resided and a great part of his land, besides which they killed and ate a number of his people. The Kaffir, seeing himself thus routed

and his power destroyed, proceeded to Sena[3] to lay his trouble before the captain, who was then André de Santiago, and to beg for assistance in driving out of his house the enemy who had taken possession of it. The captain, upon hearing his pitiful request, determined to assist him, both because he was very friendly to us and because he did not wish to have so near to Sena a neighbor as wicked as the Zimba.

Therefore, having made all necessary preparations for this war, he set out, taking with him a

---

[1]Based on the Arab word *kafir,* meaning "black," Kaffir was used to refer to the Bantu-speaking peoples of southeastern Africa and more generally to non-Muslim black Africans. Today in South Africa it is a derogatory term used by some whites for all blacks.

[2]Based on the Portuguese word *curral,* an enclosed pen for cattle, kraal refers to the enclosed area surrounding a royal residence.

[3]Sena and Tete were towns on the Zambesi River where the Portuguese had established trading posts.

great number of the Portuguese of Sena with their guns and two pieces of heavy cannon from the fort. On arriving at the place where the Zimba were, they found them within a strong double palisade of wood, with its ramparts and loopholes for arrows, surrounded by a very deep and wide trench, within which the enemy were most defiant. André de Santiago, seeing that the enterprise was much more formidable than he had anticipated and that he had brought with him but few men to attack so strong an enemy and his fortress, fixed his camp on the bank of a rivulet which ran by the place, and sent a message to the captain of Tete, Pedro Fernandes de Chaves, to come to his assistance with the Portuguese of Tete and as many Kaffir vassals of his fort as he could bring.

Pedro Fernandes de Chaves immediately prepared to go to the assistance of André de Santiago, and assembled more than a hundred men with their guns, Portuguese and half-castes,[4] and the eleven vassal chiefs. They all crossed to the other side of the river and proceeded by land until they were near the place where the Zimba had fortified themselves. These had information of their approach, and greatly feared their arrival. For this reason they sent out spies secretly upon the road, that when they approached they might see them, and report concerning the men who were coming. And learning from these spies that the Portuguese were in front of the Kaffirs in palanquins[5] and hammocks and not disposed in order of battle, they sallied out of their fortress by night secretly, without being heard by André de Santiago, and proceeded to conceal themselves in a dense thicket at about half a league's distance, through which the men of Tete would have to pass. When they were thus stationed the Portuguese came up nearly half a league in advance of the Kaffirs of their company, quite unsuspicious of what might befall them in the thicket. Just as they were entering it the Zimba fell upon

them suddenly with such violence that in a short time they were all killed, not one surviving, and when they were dead the Zimba cut off their legs and arms, which they carried away on their backs with all the baggage and arms they had brought with them, after which they returned secretly to their fortress. When the chiefs reached the thicket and found all the Portuguese and their captain dead, they immediately turned back from the place and retreated to Tete, where they related the lamentable event that had occurred.

At the time that preparations for this war were being made there was a friar of St. Dominic preaching at Tete, named Nicolau do Rosario, . . . a man who had reached perfection in many virtues. . . . In the ambush he was severely wounded, and seizing him yet alive the Zimba carried him away with them to put him to death more cruelly afterwards, which they did upon arriving at their fortress, where they bound him hand and foot to a tree and killed him with their arrows in the most cruel manner. This they did to him rather than to others because he was a priest and head of the Christians, as they called him, laying all the blame for the war upon him and saying that Christians did nothing without the leave and counsel of their cacis.[6] . . .

After the Zimba had put Father Nicolau to death they rested during the remainder of that sad day, and on the night that followed they celebrated their victory and success, playing upon many cornets and drums, and the next day at dawn they all sallied out of their fortress, the chief clothed in the chasuble[7] that the father had brought with him to say mass, carrying the golden chalice in his left hand and an assagai[8] in his right, all the other Zimba carrying on their backs the limbs of the Portuguese, with the head of the captain of Tete on the point of a long lance, and beating a drum they had taken from him. In this manner, with loud shouts and cries they came within sight of André de Santiago and all the

---

[4]People of mixed Portuguese/African ancestry.
[5]Covered litters or couches that were mounted on long horizontal poles so they could be carried about.
[6]Religious leaders.

[7]A chasuble is one of the vestments worn by a Catholic priest while celebrating mass.
[8]A spear.

Portuguese who were with him, and showed them all these things. After this they retired within their fortress, saying that what they had done to the men of Tete who had come to help their enemies, they would do to them, and that it was the flesh of those men that they were about to eat.

André de Santiago . . . was greatly shocked, as also were all the other Portuguese, at this most horrible and pitiful spectacle, for which reason they decided to retreat as soon as night came on. In carrying this decision into execution they were in so great a hurry to reach the other side of the river that they were heard by the Zimba, who sallied out of their fortress and falling upon them with great violence killed many of them on the bank of the river. Among the slain was André de Santiago, who died as the valiant man he was. . . .

Thus these robbers and fierce Zimba killed one hundred and thirty Portuguese and half-castes of Tete and Sena and the two captains of these forts. This they accomplished with very little loss on their side, with their usual cunning, as they always took the Portuguese unawares, when they were unable to fight. This took place in the year 1592.

Great sorrow was felt at the death of Father Nicolau, whom all looked upon as a saint, and for all the Portuguese who lost their lives in this most disastrous war, both because some of them were married and left wives and children at these rivers, and because the Zimba were victorious, more insolent than before, and were within fortifications close to Sena, where with greater audacity they might in the future do much damage to the Portuguese who passed up and down these rivers with their merchandise. For these reasons Dom Pedro de Sousa, captain of Mozambique, determined to chastise these Zimba, conquer them, and drive them from the vicinity of Sena. . . .

After obtaining information of the condition of the Zimba, he commanded all the necessary preparations to be made for this war, and assembled nearly two hundred Portuguese and fif-

teen hundred Kaffirs, with whom he crossed to the other side of the Zambesi and proceeded by land to the fortress of the Zimba, where he formed a camp at the same place that André de Santiago had formed his. Then he commanded that the various pieces of artillery which he had taken with him for the purpose should be fired against the wall of the fortress, but this had no effect upon it, as it was made of large wood, strengthened within by a strong and wide rampart which the Zimba had constructed with the earth from the trench.

Dom Pedro, seeing that his artillery had no effect upon the enemy's wall, determined to enter the fortress and take it by assault, and for this purpose he commanded part of the trench to be filled up, which was done with great difficulty and danger to our men, as the Zimba from the top of the wall wounded and killed some of them with arrows. When this part of the trench was filled up, a number of men crossed over with axes in their hands to the foot of the palisade, which they began to cut down, but the Zimba from the top of the wall poured so great a quantity of boiling fat and water upon them that nearly all were scalded and badly wounded, especially the naked Kaffirs, so that no one dared go near the palisade, because they were afraid of the boiling fat and through fear of certain iron hooks similar to long harpoons, which the Zimba thrust through the loopholes in the wall and with which they wounded and caught hold of all who came near and pulled from within with such force that they drew them to the apertures, where they wounded them mortally. For this reason the captain commanded all the men to be recalled to the camp to rest, and the remainder of that day was spent in tending the wounded and the scalded.

The following day the captain commanded a quantity of wood and branches of trees to be collected, with which huge wicker-work frames were made, as high as and higher than the enemy's palisade, and he commanded them to be placed in front of the wall and filled with earth that the soldiers might fight on them with their guns, and the Zimba would not dare to appear on the wall or be able to pour boiling fat upon the men cutting down the palisade. When this stratagem of war was almost in readiness, another peaceful or cowardly device was planned in the following manner. The war had lasted two months, for which reason the residents of these rivers, who were there rather by force than of their own free will, being away from their homes and trade, which is their profession, and not war, pretended to have received letters from their wives in Sena relating the danger they were in from a rebel Kaffir who they said was coming with a number of men to rob Sena, knowing that the Portuguese were absent, for which reason they ought immediately to return home. This false information was spread through the camp, and the residents of Sena went to the captain and begged him to abandon the siege of the Zimba and attend to what was of greater importance, as otherwise they would be compelled to return to their homes and leave him.

Dom Pedro, seeing their determination and believing the information said to be given in the letters to be true, abandoned the siege and commanded the men to pass by night to the other side of the river and return to Sena, but this retreat could not be effected with such secrecy as to be unknown to the Zimba, who sallied out of their fortress with great cries, fell upon the camp, killed some men who were still there, and seized the greater part of the baggage and artillery, that had not been taken away.

With this defeat and disappointment the captain returned to Sena, and thence to Mozambique, without accomplishing what he desired; and the Zimba's position was improved and he became more insolent than before. . . .

## Images of Europeans in the Art of Benin
▼▼▼

## 15 ▾ *A BENIN-PORTUGUESE SALTCELLAR and A BENIN WALL PLAQUE*

Over many centuries sub-Saharan Africans have produced some of the world's most impressive artworks, especially sculpture. Since at least 500 B.C.E., sculptors used clay, wood, ivory, and bronze to create a wide variety of works — masks, animal figures, ceremonial weapons, images of rulers, and religious objects — that were of central importance to African society, politics, and religion. In some regions bronze casting and ivory carving were royal monopolies carried on by highly trained professionals.

Such was the case in Benin, a kingdom located on the west coast of tropical Africa in an area that today is part of Nigeria. The kingdom took shape in the 1200s and 1300s when a number of agricultural villages accepted the authority of an *oba,* or divine king, who ruled with a hierarchy of chiefs from the capital, Benin City. By the time the Portuguese arrived in 1485, Benin was a formidable military and commercial power and a center of state-sponsored artistic activity. Ivory carvers and bronze casters were organized into hereditary guilds and resided in their own neighborhoods in Benin City. They produced bronze heads, animal and human figures, pendants, plaques, musical instruments, drinking vessels, and armlets that were sold for a profit or utilized for ceremonial purposes.

The arrival of the Portuguese affected Benin's artistic development in two important ways. First, Portuguese merchants, prevented by the oba from establishing Benin as a major source of slaves, turned to other commodities, including artworks, as objects of trade. Benin ivory carvers received numerous commissions from Portuguese merchants to produce condiment sets, utensils, and hunting horns for sale in Europe. Second, the Portuguese stimulated the production of artworks for use in Benin itself by purchasing African goods with copper, the major component of the alloys used by Benin artists to create their plaques and sculptures.

The two works included in this section provide opportunities to appreciate the skills of Benin artists and to gain insights into Benin attitudes toward Europeans. The first work, an ivory carving, was crafted in the sixteenth or early seventeenth century and is usually identified as a *salario,* or saltcellar. It depicts two Portuguese officials, flanked by two assistants. Above them is a Portuguese ship, with a man peering out of a crow's nest.

The second work is a sixteenth-century bronze plaque, approximately eighteen inches high, designed to be hung on a wall in the oba's palace in Benin City. One can see the holes on the top and bottom of the plaque where it was attached. The central figure is the oba, shown holding a spear and shield. On each of his sides are represented three subordinate chiefs. The one on the left is holding a bent iron bar, used as currency in trade; the figure next to him is holding a ceremonial sword; the figure on the far right is playing a flute-like musical instrument. The two figures in the background, on each side of the oba's head, represent the Portuguese. In one hand each figure holds a rectangular object, perhaps a glass mirror, and in the other hand what appears to be a goblet. Experts believe these objects represent items the Portuguese offered in trade for Benin goods.

---

## QUESTIONS FOR ANALYSIS

1. In the saltcellar, notice what hangs around the standing figure's neck, what he holds in his hands, and his facial expression. What is the sculptor trying to communicate about this figure?
2. Why might this image of the Portuguese official have appealed to the European purchasers for which the carving was intended?
3. What distinguishes the oba from the other figures in the plaque? What details illustrate the oba's power and perhaps his divinity?
4. How does the representation of the Portuguese in the plaque differ from that of the saltcellar?
5. What might you infer from these works about Portuguese-Benin relations and attitudes of the Benin people toward the Portuguese?

*A Benin-Portuguese Saltcellar*

*A Benin Wall Plaque*

# Encounters in the Americas

For many millennia, perhaps beginning as early as 40,000 B.C.E., hunters from Asia crossed the land bridge linking northeast Siberia with the area of modern Alaska. Then after 10,000 B.C.E., as the Ice Age ended and the world's oceans rose, this single link between Eurasia and the Americas was submerged under the Bering Sea, and the peoples of the Americas were cut off from the rest of the world. This isolation ended in the years following Columbus's voyage to the New World in 1492, when Europeans and Africans, along with their animals, plants, and pathogens, began to arrive.

First in the West Indies, then in Mexico and Peru, and ultimately throughout the Americas, Native Americans after 1492 faced the decision to resist or cooperate with the Europeans. Cooperation most commonly took the form of trade in which Amerindians exchanged dyes, foodstuffs, and furs for hardware, firearms, trinkets, and alcoholic beverages. Cooperation also took the form of military alliances. In Mexico, thousands of Amerindians fought on Cortés's side against their hated enemy, the Aztecs, while in North America, the Hurons allied with the French and the Iroquois with the Dutch and later the English in a long series of major and minor wars.

Many Amerindians chose to resist the European invaders. In Mexico and South America, however, military defeat for the Native Americans came early with the conquests of the Aztec Empire by Cortés between 1519 and 1521 and the overthrow of the Inca Empire by Pizarro between 1531 and 1533. In North America, Indian raids inflicted considerable casualties and damage on the early European settlements in New England, the middle colonies, and the Chesapeake region. But the colonists' reprisals were equally bloody and destructive to the Indians, and in larger-scale conflicts such as the Pequot War (1637) in Connecticut and the Algonquin-Dutch wars (1643–1645) in modern New York and New Jersey, the Amerindians were routed and massacred. The long-term outcome of the Amerindians' resistance was never in doubt. The single-mindedness, weaponry, and devastating biological effect of the Europeans made their dominance of the Americans inevitable.

# The Battle for Tenochtitlán
▼▼▼

## 16 ▼ *Bernardino de Sahagún,*
## *GENERAL HISTORY OF THE*
## *THINGS OF NEW SPAIN*

Bernardino de Sahagún (ca. 1499–1590), a member of the Franciscan religious order, was one of the earliest Spanish missionaries in Mexico, arriving in 1529. He soon developed a keen interest in the culture of the Amerindians of Mexico, for whom he had deep affection and respect. Having mastered the Nahuatl language, spoken by the Aztecs and other central Mexican peoples, around 1545 he began a systematic collection of oral and pictorial information about the culture of the native Mexicans. The result was his *General History of the Things of New Spain,* our principal source of information about Mexican culture at the time of the Spanish conquest. Many Spaniards considered Sahagún's work dangerous because they believed his efforts to preserve the memory of native culture threatened their plan to exploit and Christianize the Amerindians. As a result, in 1578 his writings and notes were confiscated by royal decree and sent back to Spain, where they gathered dust in an archive until rediscovered and published in the nineteenth century.

The following selection comes from the twelfth and last book of the *General History.* Based on interviews Sahagún and his Amerindian assistants had with Aztecs who had lived through the conquest some twenty-five years earlier, Book Twelve, which exists in both Nahuatl and Spanish versions, recounts the conquest of Mexico from the time Cortés arrived on the Mexican coast in April 1519 until the days following the Aztecs' capitulation in August 1521. Although the exact role of Sahagún and his assistants in composing and organizing Book Twelve has been hotly debated by scholars, most agree that it accurately portrays Aztec views and perceptions of the events that unfolded between 1519 and 1521.

The following excerpt picks up the story in November 1519. By then the Spaniards had gained as allies the Tlaxcalans, the Aztecs' bitter enemies, and were leaving Cholula, an ancient city that the Spaniards and their allies had sacked and looted because of its leaders' lack of cooperation. They were on their way to Tenochtitlán, the splendid Aztec capital on Lake Texcoco, for an anticipated meeting with Emperor Moctezuma.

---

## QUESTIONS FOR ANALYSIS

1. What does the source reveal about the motives of the Spaniards and their Indian allies for their attack on the Aztecs?
2. What was Moctezuma's strategy to deal with the Spaniards? Why did it fail?
3. Aside from their firearms, what other military advantages did the Spaniards have over their opponents?
4. On several occasions the Aztecs routed the Spaniards. What explains these Aztec victories?
5. How did the Aztec view of war differ from that of the Spaniards?
6. What does the source reveal about Aztec religious beliefs and values?
7. What similarities and differences do you see between the Aztec-Spanish conflict and the armed clashes between the Zimba and the Portuguese (see source 14)?

And after the dying in Cholula, the Spaniards set off on their way to Mexico,[1] coming gathered and bunched, raising dust. . . .

Thereupon Moteuccoma[2] named and sent noblemen and a great many other agents of his . . . to go meet [Cortés] . . . at Quauhtechcac. They gave [the Spaniards] golden banners of precious feathers, and golden necklaces.

And when they had given the things to them, they seemed to smile, to rejoice and to be very happy. Like monkeys they grabbed the gold. It was as though their hearts were put to rest, brightened, freshened. For gold was what they greatly thirsted for; they were gluttonous for it, starved for it, piggishly wanting it. They came lifting up the golden banners, waving them from side to side, showing them to each other. They seemed to babble; what they said to each other was in a babbling tongue. . . .

Another group of messengers — rainmakers, witches, and priests — had also gone out for an encounter, but nowhere were they able to do anything or to get sight of [the Spaniards]; they did not hit their target, they did not find the people they were looking for, they were not sufficient. . . .

---

▷　Cortés and his entourage continue their march.

---

Then they set out in this direction, about to enter Mexico here. Then they all dressed and equipped themselves for war. They girded themselves, tying their battle gear tightly on themselves and then on their horses. Then they arranged themselves in rows, files, ranks.

Four horsemen came ahead going first, staying ahead, leading. . . .

Also the dogs, their dogs, came ahead, sniffing at things and constantly panting.

By himself came marching ahead, all alone, the one who bore the standard on his shoulder. He came waving it about, making it spin, tossing it here and there. . . .

Following him came those with iron swords. Their iron swords came bare and gleaming. On their shoulders they bore their shields, of wood or leather.

The second contingent and file were horses carrying people, each with his cotton cuirass,[3] his leather shield, his iron lance, and his iron sword hanging down from the horse's neck. They came with bells on, jingling or rattling. The horses, the deer,[4] neighed, there was much neighing, and they would sweat a great deal; water seemed to fall from them. And their flecks of foam splatted on the ground, like soapsuds splatting. . . .

The third file were those with iron crossbows, the crossbowmen. Their quivers went hanging at their sides, passed under their armpits, well filled, packed with arrows, with iron bolts. . . .

The fourth file were likewise horsemen; their outfits were the same as has been said.

The fifth group were those with harquebuses,[5] the harquebusiers, shouldering their harquebuses; some held them [level]. And when they went into the great palace, the residence of the ruler, they repeatedly shot off their harquebuses. They exploded, sputtered, discharged, thundered, disgorged. Smoke spread, it grew dark with smoke, everyplace filled with smoke. The fetid smell made people dizzy and faint.

Then all those from the various altepetl[6] on the other side of the mountains, the Tlaxcalans, the people of Tliliuhquitepec, of Huexotzinco,

---

[1]*Mexico* throughout the text refers to Tenochtitlán, the capital of the Aztec empire. *Mexica* (pronounced Mezh ee´ ka) refers to the people of Tenochtitlán and Tlatelolco, a large suburb of Tenochtitlán.

[2]One of several spellings of the Aztec emperor's name, including Montezuma and Moctezuma.

[3]A piece of armor covering the body from neck to waist.

[4]Having never seen horses, some Aztecs considered them to be large deer.

[5]A heavy matchlock gun that was portable but capable of being fired only with a support.

[6]The Nahuatl term for any sovereign state, especially for the local ethnic states of central Mexico.

came following behind. They came outfitted for war with their cotton upper armor, shields, and bows, their quivers full and packed with feathered arrows, some barbed, some blunted, some with obsidian[7] points. They went crouching, hitting their mouths with their hands yelling, singing, . . . whistling, shaking their heads.

Some bore burdens and provisions on their backs; some used tump[8] lines for their forehead, some bands around their chests, some carrying frames, some board cages, some deep baskets. Some made bundles, perhaps putting the bundles on their backs. Some dragged the large cannons, which went resting on wooden wheels, making a clamor as they came.

---

▷    Cortés and his army entered Tenochtitlán in November 1519 and were amicably received by Moctezuma, who was nonetheless taken captive by the Spaniards. Cortés's army was allowed to remain in a palace compound, but tensions grew the following spring. Pedro de Alvarado, in command while Cortés left to deal with a threat to his authority from the governor of Cuba, became concerned for the Spaniards' safety as the Aztecs prepared to celebrate the annual festival in honor of the god Huitzilopochtli.

---

And when it had dawned and was already the day of his festivity, very early in the morning those who had made vows to him[9] unveiled his face. Forming a single row before him they offered him incense; each in his place laid down before him offerings of food for fasting and rolled amaranth dough. And it was as though all the youthful warriors had gathered together and had hit on the idea of holding and observing the festivity in order to show the Spaniards something, to make them marvel and instruct them. . . .

When things were already going on, when the festivity was being observed and there was dancing and singing, with voices raised in song, the

singing was like the noise of waves breaking against the rocks.

When it was time, when the moment had come for the Spaniards to do the killing, they came out equipped for battle. They came and closed off each of the places where people went in and out. . . . Then they surrounded those who were dancing, going among the cylindrical drums. They struck a drummer's arms; both of his hands were severed. Then they struck his neck; his head landed far away. Then they stabbed everyone with iron lances and struck them with iron swords. They struck some in the belly, and then their entrails came spilling out. They split open the heads of some, they really cut their skulls to pieces, their skulls were cut up into little bits. And if someone still tried to run it was useless; he just dragged his intestines along. There was a stench as if of sulfur. Those who tried to escape could go nowhere. When anyone tried to go out, at the entryways they struck and stabbed him.

And when it became known what was happening, everyone cried out, "Mexica warriors, come running, get outfitted with devices, shields, and arrows, hurry, come running, the warriors are dying; they have died, perished, been annihilated, O Mexica warriors!" Thereupon there were war cries, shouting, and beating of hands against lips. The warriors quickly came outfitted, bunched together, carrying arrows and shields. Then the fighting began; they shot at them with barbed darts, spears, and tridents, and they hurled darts with broad obsidian points at them.

---

▷    The fighting that ensued drove the Spaniards and their allies back to the palace enclave. Without a reliable supply of food and water, in July 1520, Cortés, who had returned with his power intact, led his followers on a desperate nocturnal escape from the city, but they were

---

[7]A volcanic glass, generally black.
[8]A strap or sling passed around the chest or forehead to help support a pack being carried on a person's back.

[9]The reference is to the god Huitzilopochtli. An image of the god, made from amaranth seed flour and the blood of recently sacrificed victims, played a central role in the festival.

discovered and suffered heavy losses as they fled. They retreated to the other side of the lake, and the Aztecs believed the Spanish threat had passed.

---

Before the Spanish appeared to us, first an epidemic broke out, a sickness of pustules.[10] . . . Large bumps spread on people; some were entirely covered. They spread everywhere, on the face, the head, the chest, etc. The disease brought great desolation; a great many died of it. They could no longer walk about, but lay in their dwellings and sleeping places, no longer able to move or stir. They were unable to change position, to stretch out on their sides or face down, or raise their heads. And when they made a motion, they called out loudly. The pustules that covered people caused great desolation; very many people died of them, and many just starved to death; starvation reigned, and no one took care of others any longer.

On some people, the pustules appeared only far apart, and they did not suffer greatly, nor did many of them die of it. But many people's faces were spoiled by it, their faces and noses were made rough. Some lost an eye or were blinded.

This disease of pustules lasted a full sixty days; after sixty days it abated and ended. When people were convalescing and reviving, the pustules disease began to move in the direction of the Chalco.[11] And many were disabled or paralyzed by it, but they were not disabled forever. . . . The Mexica warriors were greatly weakened by it.

And when things were in this state, the Spaniards came, moving toward us from Tetzcoco. . . .

---

▷ Having resupplied his Spanish/Tlaxcalan army and having constructed a dozen cannon-carrying brigantines for use on the lake, Cortés resumed his offensive late in 1520. In April 1521 he reached Tenochtitlán and placed the city under a blockade.

---

When their twelve boats had come from Tetzcoco, at first they were all assembled at Acachinanco, and then the Marqués[12] moved to Acachinanco. He went about searching where the boats could enter, where the canals were straight, whether they were deep or not, so that they would not be grounded somewhere. But the canals were winding and bent back and forth, and they could not get them in. They did get two boats in; they forced them down the road coming straight from Xoloco. . . .

The Tlatelolca fought in Çoquipan, in war boats. And in Xoloco the Spaniards came to a place where there was a wall in the middle of the road, blocking it. They fired the big guns at it. At the first shot it did not give way, but the second time it began to crumble. The third time, at last parts of it fell to the ground, and the fourth time finally the wall went to the ground once and for all. . . .

Once they got two of their boats into the canal at Xocotitlan. When they had beached them, then they went looking into the house sites of the people of Xocotitlan. But Tzilacatzin and some other warriors who saw the Spaniards immediately came out to face them; they came running after them, throwing stones at them, and they scattered the Spaniards into the water. . . .

When they got to Tlilhuacan, the warriors crouched far down and hid themselves, hugging the ground, waiting for the war cry, when there would be shouting and cries of encouragement. When the cry went up, "O Mexica, up and at them!" the Tlappanecatl Ecatzin, a warrior of Otomi[13] rank, faced the Spaniards and threw himself at them, saying, "O Tlatelolca warriors, up and at them, who are these barbarians? Come running!" Then he went and threw a Spaniard down, knocking him to the ground; the one he threw down was the one who came first, who came leading them. And when he had thrown him down, he dragged the Spaniard off.

---

[10] The disease was smallpox.
[11] A city on the southeast corner of Lake Texcoco.

[12] Cortés.
[13] Elite warriors bound by oath never to retreat.

And at this point they let loose with all the warriors who had been crouching there; they came out and chased the Spaniards in the passageways, and when the Spaniards saw it the Mexica seemed to be intoxicated. The captives were taken. Many Tlaxcalans, and people of Acolhuacan, Chalco, Xochimilco, etc., were captured. A great abundance were captured and killed. . . .

Then they took the captives to Yacacolco, hurrying them along, going along herding their captives together. Some went weeping, some singing, some went shouting while hitting their hands against their mouths. When they got them to Yacacolco, they lined them all up. Each one went to the altar platform where the sacrifice was performed.[14] The Spaniards went first, going in the lead; the people of the different altepetl just followed, coming last. And when the sacrifice was over, they strung the Spaniards' heads on poles on skull racks; they also strung up the horses' heads. They placed them below, and the Spaniards' heads were above them, strung up facing east. . . .

▷    Despite this victory, the Aztecs could not overcome the problems of shortages of food, water, and warriors. In mid July 1521 the Spaniards and their allies resumed their assault, and in early August the Aztecs decided to send into battle a quetzal-owl warrior, whose success or failure, it was believed, would reveal if the gods wished the Aztecs to continue fighting.

And all the common people suffered greatly. There was famine; many died of hunger. They no longer drank good, pure water, but the water they drank was salty. Many people died of it, and because of it many got dysentery and died. Everything was eaten: lizards, swallows, maize, straw, grass that grows on salt flats. And they chewed at wood, glue flowers, plaster, leather, and deerskin, which they roasted, baked, and toasted so that they could eat them, and they ground up medicinal herbs and adobe bricks. There had never been the like of such suffering. The siege was frightening, and great numbers died of hunger. . . .

And . . . the ruler Quauhtemoctzin[15] and the warriors Coyohuehuetzin, Temilotzin, Topantemoctzin, the Mixcoatlailotlac Ahuelitoctzin, Tlacotzin, and Petlauhtzin took a great warrior named Tlapaltecatl Opochtzin . . . and outfitted him, dressing him in a quetzal-owl costume. . . . When they put it on him he looked very frightening and splendid. . . . They gave him the darts of the devil,[16] darts of wooden rods with flint tips. And the reason they did this was that it was as though the fate of the rulers of the Mexica were being determined.

When our enemies saw him, it was as though a mountain had fallen. Every one of the Spaniards was frightened; he intimidated them, they seemed to respect him a great deal. Then the quetzal-owl climbed up on the roof. But when some of our enemies had taken a good look at him they rose and turned him back, pursuing him. Then the quetzal-owl turned them again and pursued them. Then he snatched up the precious feathers and gold and dropped down off the roof. He did not die, and our enemies did not carry him off. Also three of our enemies were captured. At that the war stopped for good. There was silence, nothing more happened. Then our enemies went away. It was silent and nothing more happened until it got dark.

And the next day nothing more happened at all, no one made a sound. The common people just lay collapsed. The Spaniards did nothing more either, but lay still, looking at the people. Nothing was going on, they just lay still. . . .

▷    Two weeks passed before the Aztecs capitulated on August 13, 1521.

---

[14]Traditionally the sacrifice consisted of cutting the heart out of the victim.

[15]Quauhtemoctzin was now the Aztec emperor.
[16]Darts sacred to Huitzilopochtli.

# Amerindian Perspectives on French Civilization
▼▼▼

## 17 ▼ *A MI'KMAQ ELDER'S SPEECH TO FRENCH SETTLERS*

When the first European explorers arrived in eastern Canada, the regions of Nova Scotia, Prince Edward Island, and parts of Quebec, Newfoundland, and New Brunswick were populated by the Mi'kmaqs (Micmacs), Algonquian speakers who had migrated from around the Great Lakes centuries earlier. Hunters and gatherers, the Mi'kmaqs lived on the coastline from spring to early fall, where they had a diet of fish, shellfish, eels, and birds, then during the winter moved inland where they hunted moose, beaver, bear, and caribou. The arrival of French traders quickly undermined this traditional way of life, as more and more Mi'kmaqs turned to the fur trade, exchanging beaver and bear pelts for the copper kettles, alcoholic beverages, and metal knives and axes offered by the French.

Although successful in drawing the Mi'kmaqs into their commercial endeavors, the French found it difficult to wean them from traditional beliefs and customs. From the beginning of their involvement in Canada the French had dreamed of turning the Native Americans into French-speaking Catholics who lived in farming settlements just as the French did in Europe and the St. Lawrence River valley. The first French missionaries assigned to the task of transforming the native peoples into French Catholics were the Recollets, members of the Franciscan order who began their work in New France in 1615. They soon were joined by Ursuline nuns, who were given the task of converting and "civilizing" Amerindian girls, and the wealthy and powerful Society of Jesus, which originally worked with the Recollets, but was given a monopoly for work in Canadian missions between 1632 and 1670. The French missionaries learned native languages, built schools and hospitals, and endured great hardships, but early results were discouraging. In the 1660s, an Ursuline nun admitted that of a hundred Native girls "that have passed through our hands, we have scarcely civilized one."

Some of the reasons for the missionaries' difficulties are revealed in the following speech, delivered by a Mi'kmaq elder to a group of French settlers and missionaries around 1670. It was recorded by Chrétien LeClerq, a Recollet father who had mastered the Mi'kmaq language. In 1691 he published his *New Relation of Gaspesia,* a book describing his experiences with the Mi'kmaqs on the Gaspé Peninsula, a rugged area of eastern Quebec that projects into the Gulf of St. Lawrence between Chaleur Bay and the mouth of the St. Lawrence River. The speech was in response to persistent French appeals that the Mi'kmaqs abandon their birch bark wigwams and begin living in permanent wooden homes. Such a step, it was hoped, would help "civilize" the Mi'kmaqs and make them better candidates for religious conversion by discouraging their seasonal migration.

## QUESTIONS FOR ANALYSIS

1. What information about the Mi'kmaq way of life does the speech provide?
2. How much knowledge of France and French society does the Mi'kmaq speaker seem to have? What are his reasons for his belief in the inferiority of French ways?
3. What can be inferred from the elder's speech about French attitudes toward the Mi'kmaqs?
4. What can be inferred from the speech about the dealings between the French and the Mi'kmaqs and about the impact of the French on Mi'kmaq society?
5. How do views of Native Americans expressed in LeClerq's commentary on the speech compare with those of Montaigne in his essay, "On Cannibals" (Chapter 1, source 9)?
6. If given the opportunity to read the speech and LeClerq's commentary on it, what would have been the reactions of Las Casas and Sepúlveda (Chapter 1, sources 4 and 5)?

I pass without mention several other methods of camping which are in use among our Gaspesians,[1] because . . . they are all equally mean and miserable. But however that may be, the Indians esteem their camps as much as, and even more than, they do the most superb and commodious of our houses. To this they testified one day to some of our gentlemen . . . who, having asked me to serve them as interpreter in a visit which they wished to make to these Indians in order to make the latter understand that it would be much more advantageous for them to live and to build in our fashion, were extremely surprised when the leading Indian, who had listened with great patience to everything I had said to him on behalf of these gentlemen, answered me in these words: "I am greatly astonished that the French have so little cleverness, as they seem to exhibit in the matter of which you have just told me on their behalf, in the effort to persuade us to convert our poles, our barks, and our wigwams into those houses of stone and of wood which are tall and lofty, according to their account, as these trees. Very well! But why now," he continued, "do men of five to six feet in height need houses which are sixty to eighty? For, in fact, as you know very well yourself — do we not find in our own all the conveniences and the advantages that you have with yours, such as resting, drinking, sleeping, eating, and amusing ourselves with our friends when we wish? This is not all," he said, addressing himself to one of our captains, "my brother, have you as much ingenuity and cleverness as the Indians, who carry their houses and their wigwams with them so that they may lodge wherever they please, independently of any lord whatsoever? You are not as bold nor as stout as we, because when you go on a voyage you cannot carry upon your shoulders your buildings and your edifices. Therefore it is necessary that you prepare as many lodgings as you make changes of residence, or else you live in a hired house which does not belong to you. As for us, we find ourselves secure from all these inconveniences, and we can always say, more truly than you, that we are at home everywhere, because we set up our wigwams with ease wherever we go, and without asking permission of anybody. You

---

[1]The term LeClerq used for the Mi'kmaqs who lived on the Gaspé Peninsula.

reproach us, very inappropriately, that our country is a little hell in contrast with France, which you compare to a terrestrial paradise, inasmuch as it yields you, so you say, every kind of provision in abundance. You say to us also that we are the most miserable and most unhappy of all men, living without religion, without manners, without honor, without social order, and, in a word, without any rules, like the beasts in our woods and our forests, lacking bread, wine, and a thousand other comforts which you have in abundance in Europe. Well, my brother, if you do not yet know the real feelings which our Indians have towards your country and towards all your nation, it is proper that I inform you at once. I beg you now to believe that, as miserable as we seem in your eyes, we consider ourselves nevertheless much happier than you in this, that we are very content with the little that we have; and believe also once for all, I pray, that you deceive yourself greatly if you think to persuade us that your country is better than ours. For if France, as you say, is a little terrestrial paradise, are you reasonable to leave it? And why abandon wives, children, relatives, and friends? Why risk your life and your property every year, and why put yourself at risk, in any season whatsoever, to the storms and tempests of the sea in order to come to a strange and barbarous country which you consider the poorest and least fortunate of the world? Besides, since we are wholly convinced of the contrary, we scarcely take the trouble to go to France, because we fear, with good reason, lest we find little satisfaction there, seeing, in our own experience, that those who are natives thereof leave it every year in order to enrich themselves on our shores. We believe, further, that you are also incomparably poorer than we, and that you are not only simple journeymen, valets, servants, and slaves, all masters and grand captains though you may appear, seeing that you glory in our old rags and in our miserable suits of beaver which can no longer be of use to us, and that you find among us, in the fishery for cod which you make in these parts, the means to comfort your misery and the

poverty which oppresses you. As to us, we find all our riches and all our conveniences among ourselves, without trouble and without exposing our lives to the dangers in which you find yourselves constantly through your long voyages. And, while feeling compassion for you in the sweetness of our repose, we wonder at the anxieties and cares which you give yourselves night and day in order to load your ship. We see also that all your people live, as a rule, only upon cod which you catch among us. It is everlastingly nothing but cod — cod in the morning, cod at midday, cod at evening, and always cod, until things come to such a pass that if you wish some good morsels, it is at our expense; and you are obliged to depend on the Indians, whom you despise so much, and to beg them to go a-hunting that you may feast. Now tell me this one little thing, if you have any sense: Which of these two is the wiser and happier — he who labors without ceasing and only obtains, and that with great trouble, enough to live on, or he who rests in comfort and finds all that he needs in the pleasure of hunting and fishing? It is true," he added, "that we have not always had the use of bread and of wine which your France produces; but, in fact, before the arrival of the French in these parts, did not the Gaspesians live much longer than now? And if we have not any longer among us any of those old men of a hundred and thirty to forty years, it is only because we are gradually adopting your manner of living, for experience is making it very plain that those of us live longest who, despising your bread, your wine, and your brandy, are content with their natural food of beaver, of moose, of waterfowl, and fish, in accord with the custom of our ancestors and of all the Gaspesian nation. Learn now, my brother, once for all, because I must open to you my heart: there is no Indian who does not consider himself infinitely happier and more powerful than the French." He finished his speech by the following last words, saying that an Indian could find his living everywhere, and that he could call himself the lord and the sovereign of his country, because he could reside there just as freely as it pleased him, with every kind of rights of hunting and fishing, without any anxiety, more content a thousand times in the woods and in his wigwam than if he were in palaces and at the tables of the greatest princes of the earth.

No matter what can be said of this reasoning, I assert, for my part, that I should consider these Indians incomparably more fortunate than ourselves, and that the life of these barbarians would even be capable of inspiring envy, if they had the instructions, the understanding, and the same means for their salvation which God has given us that we may save ourselves by preference over so many poor pagans, and as a result of His pity;

for, after all, their lives are not vexed by a thousand annoyances as are ours. . . . Possessing nothing of their own, they are consequently free from trickery and legal proceedings in connection with inheritances from their relatives. . . . All their ambition centers in surprising and killing quantities of beavers, moose, seals, and other wild beasts in order to obtain their meat for food and their skins for clothing. They live in great harmony, never quarreling and never beating one another except in drunkenness. On the contrary, they mutually aid one another in their needs with much charity and without self-seeking. There is continual joy in their wigwams. . . .

▼▼▼

## Land and Labor in Spanish America

Throughout its more than three centuries of existence the Spanish Empire in the Americas was based on the economic exploitation of Native Americans. This was already evident as early as the 1490s when Columbus sought to found a permanent Spanish settlement on Hispaniola, the island he had discovered on his first voyage in 1492. The island's first Spanish settlers were determined that their new life across the Atlantic would make them wealthy, and this spelled disaster for the island's native Arawaks, who were robbed of their food, drafted to work in the Spaniards' homes, fields, and mines, and in some cases enslaved. In 1497 Columbus attempted to impose some discipline on the rapaciousness of his countrymen by allocating specific groups of Arawaks to his followers, who could demand tribute and labor from these Indians and these Indians alone. This system brought prosperity to a rapidly growing Spanish population, but it was short-lived. By the mid sixteenth century slaves imported from Africa were doing much of the Spaniards' work on Hispaniola. Victims of agricultural disruption, harsh labor, and epidemics, the Arawaks, who numbered one million in 1492, no longer existed.

Elsewhere in Spain's colonial empire the effects of forced labor on the native peoples were less catastrophic, but economic realities were no different than on Hispaniola. Clearly, the New World would yield no income to the monarchy, nor would colonists be willing to settle in the Americas unless the Amerindians were forced to work for the Spaniards, pay them tribute, or both. This rarely meant slavery. As a result of royal legislation, enslavement of Native Americans was tolerated only in peripheral areas of the empire such as Chile and Argentina, where persistent native resistance to Spanish authority seemed to justify it. Although not slaves, Indians might be assigned to work for an individual Spanish landowner, or *encomendero;* required to pay tribute to individuals or the state;

subjected to state-controlled labor drafts; or forced in the open market to accept pittance wages for their work.

This need for Indian labor raised perplexing and hotly debated questions among Spanish landowners, clergy, and royal officials. Through what mechanisms should the Indians be compelled to work for the Spaniards? What kind of work could they reasonably be asked to do? When did Indian labor cross the line from reasonable work to the kind of brutal exploitation that contributed to the demise of the Arawaks? Most fundamentally, how was it possible to reconcile the need to compel Indians to work with the need to convert them to Christianity, civilize them, and treat them as fellow human beings? The Spaniards never found satisfactory answers to questions such as these, even after more than three hundred years of colonial rule.

# Exploitation versus Amerindian Rights in the Encomienda System

▼▼▼

## 18 ▾ ENCOMIENDA REGULATIONS IN PARAGUAY, 1556

In 1503 the Spanish government sought to regulate and refine the utilization of Arawak labor on Hispaniola by giving the island's governor, Nicholas de Ovando, authority to gather the Arawaks into villages where they would be placed under the authority of a Spanish trustee, or *encomendero*. The encomendero received the right to extract tribute and labor from the Arawaks, but he also assumed responsibility for their material and spiritual welfare. This was the beginnings of the *encomienda* system, a method of forced Indian labor that soon spread to Mexico and South America, and still existed in parts of Spanish America at the close of the colonial era.

The subject of frequent royal legislation and countless court cases, the encomienda system varied from place to place and over time. Grants of Indians might be as small as one hundred, or, as was the case with the encomienda of Cortés in Mexico, as large as one hundred thousand. In the Caribbean islands Indians held by encomenderos were required to make tribute payments and provide labor in agriculture, gold mining, domestic service, and construction projects. In Mexico, however, demands were limited to tribute payments in agricultural products, textiles, or cash. In Venezuela and Paraguay, mainly labor was required.

In most of the Spanish Empire the encomienda system was short-lived. It disappeared in the 1540s in the Caribbean as a result of depopulation, and several decades later in Mexico and Peru as a result of unprofitability and royal legislation designed to suppress a labor system too easily abused by holders of encomiendas. The encomienda system lasted longest in peripheral regions of the empire such as Paraguay, Chile, and northern Argentina, where Spanish administrators often were negligent in enforcing laws and Spaniards would have been unwilling to settle without access to forced Indian labor.

From its beginnings the encomienda system represented an effort by Spanish officials to balance the need to utilize cheap Indian labor and their sense of obligation to Christianize the Indians and protect them from blatant exploitation and cruelty. Such concerns are revealed in the following set of rules concerning encomiendas in Paraguay issued by the territory's first governor, Domingo Martinez de Irala, in 1556. Note that the regulations deal largely with labor exactions. No tribute was demanded, because it was believed that the Guana and Guarani peoples who populated the region produced nothing of value to the Spaniards.

## QUESTIONS FOR ANALYSIS

1. According to these regulations, what specific demands can the encomenderos make on the Indians allocated to them?
2. What specific provisions are made to protect the interests and well-being of the Indians held in encomienda?
3. What can you infer from these regulations about the motives of Spanish officials in their efforts to protect the Indians from abuses?
4. What provisions have been made to ensure the enforcement of these regulations? In your opinion, how adequate are these provisions in protecting the Indians from abuse?

First we order and command that all the Indians that have been allocated and commended . . . shall be obliged to obey the *principales*[1] and headmen that they may have or may be placed over them; and they shall not move, go, or absent themselves from their homes and *pueblos*[2] to other *pueblos* and houses or any other places, living and remaining there all the time that God leaves them life; and if their *principales* or headmen should move to another place or seat as an improvement, then all of them shall also move with him; and the persons to whom they are commended shall compel and force them to do this and carry it out under penalties established at the will of the judicial authorities; . . .

Also, we order and command that with regard to the persons to whom the said Indians belong or may be commended, it is prohibited for them to obtain, ask for, or procure through trade any Indian woman from the Indians . . . under pain

of the suspension of the service of the said Indians for the time of one year.

Also, we order and command that because the said Indians are so few, and because it would encourage the growth and settlement of the country not to give them excessive labor . . . the persons to whom they belong and may be granted in *encomienda* are prohibited, without the express consent of the said Indians, from giving or loaning them to other persons for any labor or service, or from receiving any payment for this; and when it might happen that such labor was agreed to both by the *encomendero* and the said Indians, it can be done when both parties thus agree to it and not in any other manner for a job in which the work is suitable and bearable, and the payment shall be received and enjoyed by the said Indians for themselves. . . .

Also, we order and command that the said Indians will be and are obligated to serve the

---

[1]Spanish for the Indians' *chieftains.*

[2]Spanish for *villages.*

persons to whom they are commended in building and repairing their houses, in farming, stock raising, hunting, fishing, and other enterprises that may be carried on in the country, and they shall obey him and carry out his orders under the penalties that may be imposed at the will of the judge, and so that the work of building and cultivating may be moderated and assessed, we prohibit such persons from building houses or clearing fields to sell beyond those they need to live in and support themselves. . . .

Also, we order and command that the persons to whom the said Indians belong and are commended, as was said, shall be obliged to treat them very well and to favor and support them in everything possible, giving them moderate rather than excessive labor in accord with the intention of His Majesty . . . , treating them like relatives, instructing and indoctrinating them in the things of our Holy Catholic faith, as well as possible considering the land and the time, reprimanding them and weaning them from their vices and evil customs, so that their souls can be saved by means of divine grace and mercy; and the persons who take on this work shall be especially deserving with God, and we make this a charge on the conscience of these persons, and not on those of His Majesty or ours in his Royal name.

Also we order and command that no one be permitted to employ in his service more than the fourth part of the Indians granted to him in *encomienda* at the same time, so that they will not make them abandon their houses, and only in case of clear and recognized necessity can they order up to one half to serve as this may occur, but this will seldom be necessary; the penalty for violation shall be the said three thousand *maravedis*.[3] . . .

Also, we order and command that whenever these persons may go to visit the Indians that

belong and are commended to them, when they go to their houses and villages, they shall not make bold to do them any injury or to allow the people of the land or the *criados*[4] they take with them to do them any; nor shall they beg, demand, take, or obtain in trade any of the things they may have inside or outside of their houses, since they are only allowed to ask for and the Indians are only obliged to give them three days' worth of their normal food supplies, without having to give them chickens or pigs they may have, unless they wish to do so of their own will in return for a moderate payment; and the chickens, livestock, and other things they may have there cannot be touched, taken, or consumed by the *encomenderos* without the permission of their owners; and if they should be consumed for some necessity, [the *encomenderos*] shall be obliged to pay for them. . . .

Also, we order and command that the said Indian *principales* be obliged, whenever a message is sent them with an Indian, to order Indians to go and do what they are commanded to, and also to send the Indians needed to live in the houses of their *encomenderos* during the times or months of the year they are required, serving and doing what they may be ordered, on condition that their *encomenderos* feed them and care for them when ill, indoctrinate them as stated, help them to die well, and teach them the best order and manner of living they can; . . .

Also, we order and command that these persons [the *encomenderos*] try to have two or three children of ten years or less from their *encomiendas* in their houses, so that they can learn to live as Christians and see and understand the things of God and His Holy Church and the proper manner of living, so that when they reach the age of twelve or thirteen years they can return to their homes and teach and instruct their parents, brothers, and other relatives; . . .

---

[3]Thirty-four *maravedis* equaled one *real;* eight reales equaled one *peso.* An ordinance issued in Paraguay in 1541 stated that one maravedi was worth one fishhook in value, and twenty-five maravedis were worth one large knife.

[4]Spanish for *servants.*

Also, we order and command that if the said Indians, either *principales* or ordinary Indians, should come to make just complaint over ill treatment, violence, injuries, or excessive labor, they should be heard by the judicial authorities and [their rights] maintained and protected, and if some person or persons should mistreat or punish them for this, they shall incur the penalties stated in the preceding ordinance;[5] and with regard to this and the violence, injury, and other crimes that may be committed, the testimony of the Indians shall be accepted, as long as it is supported and the Indians are not suborned or induced. . . .

Also, we order and command that every year after the said Indians are allocated to serve and pay tribute to their *encomenderos, visitadores* shall be sent out through all of the country and its districts with solemn judicial authority, a notary, and an interpreter, receiving authority and instructions from the person governing in addition to being obliged for the carrying out of these ordinances, in order that they may carry out a visitation of the country and the Indians and collect testimony concerning the acts of violence, injuries, and other crimes committed, and to arrest the Christians and Indians implicated and bring them as prisoners to this city, so that justice may be done in everything and the relief, welfare, benefit, conservation, and pacification of the Indians may be obtained as His Majesty has ordered and charged. . . .

Also we order and command that . . . [if any Indians] should rebel and refuse to serve and pay tribute to their *encomenderos,* with the license and authority of the person governing, [men] can go to pacify, settle, and reduce these Indians to the service of His Majesty with the *caudillo*[7] or captain appointed for them and with the help of the obedient Indians, and the persons who hold *encomiendas* of Indians in these provinces, shall be obliged to go personally on foot or horseback with their arms at their own cost, or to send others in their place if there is some just impediment or illness that prevents them from going. . . .

And we command that these ordinances and each and every one of them be communicated and explained to all the Indians, when . . . there may be sufficient interpreters, so that it may come to the attention of all of them, and of [Indians in] other, separate villages that have not been granted in *encomienda,* so that they may understand, see, and recognize their condition and advantage and the manner in which they should live in order to be saved. Also, we command that these ordinances be read, affixed, and made public in this city so that they may come to the attention of all and no one can pretend ignorance of any part of them. . . .

---

[5]The reference is to the fine of three thousand *maravedis.*
[6]Spanish for *visitors;* judges or other officials sent out to investigate conditions of encomiendas.

[7]Spanish for *military commander.*

# The "Mountain of Silver" and the Mita System

▼▼▼

## 19 ▼ Antonio Vazquez de Espinosa, COMPENDIUM AND DESCRIPTION OF THE WEST INDIES

In 1545 an Indian herder lost his footing on a mountain in the eastern range of the Andes while chasing a llama. To keep from falling he grabbed a bush, which he uprooted to reveal a rich vein of silver. This is the most popular story of how the world learned of the world's richest silver mine, at Potosí, in modern Bolivia. Located two miles above sea level in a cold, desolate region, Potosí became the site of the Western Hemisphere's first mining boom town. By the late 1500s Potosí had a racially mixed population of 160,000, making it the largest, wildest, gaudiest city in the New World. With one-fifth of its extracted silver going to the Spanish crown, Potosí was a major reason why Spanish kings were able to carry on their massive military campaigns against Protestants in Europe and Muslims in the Mediterranean.

The backbone of the Potosí operation was a system of government-controlled draft labor known as the *repartimiento* ("distribution") system and widely practiced throughout Spanish America. In Peru it was known as the *mita* (Quechua for "time" or "distribution") system, a term used by the Incas for their own preconquest system of required state labor. In the repartimiento and mita systems native communities were ordered to supply a proportion of their population at fixed intervals for assignment to particular tasks. In their original form these labor drafts may well have been less burdensome than what was required in the encomienda system. Required work was distributed more evenly throughout the community, and an individual might go months or even years without being called for labor service. But as revealed in the following document, the mita system still caused hardship and disruption for Indian communities.

The following description of the mita system is provided by Antonio Vazquez de Espinosa (d. 1630), a Spanish Carmelite friar who abandoned an academic career to perform priestly work in the Americas. During his retirement in the 1620s, he wrote a half a dozen books on Spanish America and his experiences as a priest. His best-known work is his *Compendium and Description of the West Indies,* a summary of his observations of conditions in Mexico and Spanish South America. In this excerpt he describes the mercury mines and facilities at Huancavelica and then Potosí itself.

---

## QUESTIONS FOR ANALYSIS

1. What was the range of annual wages for each laborer at Huancavelica? How did this amount of money compare with the annual salary of the royal hospital chaplain? How did the annual sum of the workers' wages compare with the cost of tallow candles at Potosí? Compare the wages of the mita

workers at Potosí with the wages paid those Amerindians who freely hired themselves out. What do you conclude from all these figures?

2. What were the major hazards connected with the extraction and production of gold and silver?

3. What evidence does this source provide of Spanish concern for the welfare of the Indian workers? What evidence of indifference does it provide? Where does the weight of the evidence seem to lie?

4. What appears to have been the impact of the mita system on native Peruvian society?

## HUANCAVELICA

. . . It contains 400 Spanish residents, as well as many temporary shops of dealers in merchandise and groceries, heads of trading houses, and transients, for the town has a lively commerce. It has a parish church with vicar and curate,[1] a Dominican convent, and a Royal Hospital under the Brethren of San Juan de Diós for the care of the sick, especially Indians on the range; it has a chaplain with a salary of 800 pesos[2] contributed by His Majesty; he is curate of the parish of San Sebastian de Indios, for the Indians who have come to work in the mines and who have settled down there. . . .

Every two months His Majesty sends by the regular courier from Lima[3] 60,000 pesos to pay for the mita of the Indians, for the crews are changed every two months, so that merely for the Indian mita payment (in my understanding of it) 360,000 pesos are sent from Lima every year, not to speak of much besides, which all crosses at his risk that cold and desolate mountain country which is the puna[4] and has nothing on it but llama ranches.

Up on the range there are 3,000 or 4,000 Indians working in the mine; it is colder up there than in the town, since it is higher. The mine where the mercury is located is a large layer which they keep following downward. When I was in that town [in 1616] I went up on the range and down into the mine, which at that time was considerably more than 130 stades[5] deep. The ore was very rich black flint, and the excavation so extensive that it held more than 3,000 Indians working away hard with picks and hammers, breaking up that flint ore; and when they have filled their little sacks, the poor fellows, loaded down with ore, climb up those ladders or rigging, some like masts and others like cables, and so trying and distressing that a man empty-handed can hardly get up them. That is the way they work in this mine, with many lights and the loud noise of the pounding and great confusion. Nor is that the greatest evil and difficulty; that is due to thievish and undisciplined superintendents. As that great vein of ore keeps going down deeper and they follow its rich trail, in order to make sure that no section of that ore shall drop on top of them, they keep leaving supports or pillars of the ore itself, even if of the richest quality, and they necessarily help to sustain and insure each section with less risk. This being so, there are men so heartless that for the sake of stealing a little rich ore, they go down out of hours and deprive the innocent Indians of this protection by hollowing into these pillars to steal the rich ore in them, and then a great

---

[1]A parish priest and his assistant priest.
[2]A standard Spanish coin worth eight *reals* (note 9).
[3]Lima was the capital city of the viceroyalty of Peru, one of the two major administrative units of Spanish America, covering all of South America except part of the Caribbean coast. Appointed by the crown, the viceroy was the chief military and civil administrator.
[4]A high, cold plateau.
[5]A stade was a measure of length, approximately an eighth of a mile.

section is apt to fall in and kill all the Indians, and sometimes the unscrupulous and grasping superintendents themselves, as happened when I was in that locality; and much of this is kept quiet so that it shall not come to the notice of the manager and cause the punishment of the accomplices. . . .

## POTOSÍ

According to His Majesty's warrant, the mine owners on this massive range have a right to the mita of 13,300 Indians in the working and exploitation of the mines, both those which have been discovered, those now discovered, and those which shall be discovered. It is the duty of the Corregidor[6] of Potosí to have them rounded up and to see that they come in from all the provinces between Cuzco over the whole of El Collao and as far as the frontiers of Tarija and Tomina;[7] this Potosí Corregidor has power and authority over all the Corregidors in those provinces mentioned; for if they do not fill the Indian mita allotment assigned each of them in accordance with the capacity of their provinces as indicated to them, he can send them, and does, salaried inspectors to report upon it, and when the remissness is great or remarkable, he can suspend them, notifying the Viceroy of the fact.

These Indians are sent out every year under a captain whom they choose in each village or tribe, for him to take them and oversee them for the year each has to serve; every year they have a new election, for as some go out, others come in. This works out very badly, with great losses and gaps in the quotas of Indians, the villages being depopulated; and this gives rise to great extortions and abuses on the part of the inspectors toward the poor Indians, ruining them and thus depriving the . . . chief Indians of their property and carrying them off in chains because they do not fill out the mita assignment, which they cannot

do, for the reason given and for others which I do not bring forward.

These 13,300 are divided up every 4 months into 3 mitas, each consisting of 4,433 Indians, to work in the mines on the range and in the 120 smelters in the Potosí and Tarapaya areas; it is a good league[8] between the two. These mita Indians earn each day, or there is paid each one for his labor, 4 reals.[9] Besides these there are others not under obligation, who are mingados or hire themselves out voluntarily: these each get from 12 to 16 reals, and some up to 24, according to their reputation of wielding the pick and knowing how to get the ore out. These mingados will be over 4,000 in number. They and the mita Indians go up every Monday morning to the locality of Guayna Potosí which is at the foot of the range; the Corregidor arrives with all the provincial captains or chiefs who have charge of the Indians assigned them, and he there checks off and reports to each mine and smelter owner the number of Indians assigned him for his mine or smelter; that keeps him busy till 1 p.m., by which time the Indians are already turned over to these mine and smelter owners.

After each has eaten his ration, they climb up the hill, each to his mine, and go in, staying there from that hour until Saturday evening without coming out of the mine; their wives bring them food, but they stay constantly underground, excavating and carrying out the ore from which they get the silver. They all have tallow candles, lighted day and night; that is the light they work with, for as they are underground, they have need of it all the time. The mere cost of these candles used in the mines on this range will amount every year to more than 300,000 pesos, even though tallow is cheap in that country, being abundant; but this is a very great expense, and it is almost incredible, how much is spent for candles in the operation of breaking down and getting out the ore.

---

[6]A district military officer.
[7]This region consisted of approximately 139 villages.

[8]Approximately three miles.
[9]A Spanish silver coin (see note 2).

These Indians have different functions in the handling of the silver ore; some break it up with bar or pick, and dig down in, following the vein in the mine; others bring it up; others up above keep separating the good and the poor in piles; others are occupied in taking it down from the range to the mills on herds of llamas; every day they bring up more than 8,000 of these native beasts of burden for this task. These teamsters who carry the metal do not belong to the mita, but are mingados — hired.

So huge is the wealth which has been taken out of this range since the year 1545, when it was discovered, up to the present year of 1628, which makes 83 years that they have been working and reducing its ores, that merely from the registered mines, as appears from an examination of most of the accounts in the royal records, 326,000,000 assay[10] pesos have been taken out. At the beginning when the ore was richer and easier to get out, for then there were no mita Indians and no mercury process, in the 40 years between 1545 and 1585, they took out 111,000,000 of assay silver. From the year 1585 up to 1628, 43 years, although the mines are harder to work, for they are deeper down, with the assistance of 13,300 Indians whom His Majesty has granted to the mine owners on that range, and of other hired Indians, who come there freely and voluntarily to work at day's wages, and with the great advantage of the mercury process, in which none of the ore or the silver is wasted, and with the better knowledge of the technique which the miners now have, they have taken out 215,000,000 assay pesos. That, plus the 111 extracted in the 40 years previous to 1585, makes 326,000,000 assay pesos, not counting the great amount of silver secretly taken from these mines . . . to Spain, paying no 20 percent or registry fee, and to other countries outside Spain; and to the Philippines and China, which is beyond all reckoning; but I should venture to imagine and even assert that what has been taken from the Potosí range must be as much again as what paid the 20 percent royal impost.[11]

Over and above that, such great treasure and riches have come from the Indies in gold and silver from all the other mines in New Spain and Peru, Honduras, the New Kingdom of Granada, Chile, New Galicia, New Vizcaya,[12] and other quarters since the discovery of the Indies, that they exceed 1,800 millions.

---

[10]Measured so that silver content met official standards.
[11]The "20 percent royal impost" was the one-fifth of all New World silver owed to the Spanish crown.

[12]New Galicia and New Vizcaya were regions and administrative jurisdictions in New Spain located in north-central and northwestern Mexico.

# The Evils of Cochineal
▼▼▼
## 20 ▼ *DELIBERATIONS OF THE TLAXCALAN MUNICIPAL COUNCIL, MARCH 1553*

Accounts of the Native Americans' postconquest experience justifiably center on themes of decline, destruction, and demoralization, but this is not a totally accurate picture. In the economic sphere, despite Spanish demands for tribute and labor, Indians in Mexico and elsewhere in the sixteenth century maintained much of their traditional agricultural way of life while simultaneously taking advantage of new opportunities provided by the arrival of the Spaniards. Evidence of such economic adjustments and their consequences in Tlaxcala, a Mexican province to the east of Tenochtitlán/Mexico City, is provided in the following document.

The single province in preconquest central Mexico to maintain its independence from the Aztecs, Tlaxcala was defeated by Cortés in September 1519 and then became Cortés's ally in his campaign against the Aztecs and later conquests in southern Mexico and Central America. With the establishment of Spanish authority, the Tlaxcalans, like other Mexican peoples, were subject to labor conscription and tribute payments, but in some ways they received preferential treatment because of their alliance with Cortés. Spanish civilians were prevented from permanently residing in Tlaxcala until the seventeenth century; Tlaxcalan communal property rights were protected; and the encomienda system was never imposed. In addition, the political powers and privileges of Tlaxcalan noblemen were preserved. The main institution through which the nobles exercised their political authority was the Tlaxcalan *cabildo,* or municipal council, made up of twenty-one officials chosen from a list of approximately 220 noblemen who also served as electors. The cabildo interacted with Spanish officials, collected tribute, oversaw religious festivals, and maintained churches, municipal buildings, and roads. And, as revealed in the following document, it also petitioned Spanish authorities for legislative action to address perceived problems in the Tlaxcalan community.

In this instance the problem was cochineal, a brilliant red dye produced from the dried bodies of female cochineal insects, a species that thrives on the nopal cactus of central and southern Mexico. The market for cochineal expanded to all of Europe after the Spanish conquest, and many Indians were quick to take advantage of the increased demand. In the eyes of the noblemen on the Tlaxcalan cabildo, this was not without its negative results.

---

## QUESTIONS FOR ANALYSIS

1. What does this document reveal about the relative political authority of the Tlaxcalan municipal council and the Spanish colonial administration?
2. How, according to this document, has the booming cochineal trade affected religion and morality among the Tlaxcalan people?
3. What role is played by women in getting cochineal to the market? Why do the members of the municipal council find their role disturbing?
4. To what degree does the Tlaxcalan trade in cochineal provide evidence of Spanish involvement in the region's economy?
5. According to the members of the municipal council, how has the boom in cochineal affected social relationships and attitudes? In their analysis of these changes, how do the council members reveal their bias as noblemen?

They deliberated about how the cochineal cactus, from which cochineal comes, is being planted all over Tlaxcala. Everyone does nothing but take care of cochineal cactus; no longer is care taken that maize and other edibles are planted. For food — maize, chilis, and beans — and other things that people need were once not expensive in Tlaxcala. It is because of this neglect, the cabildo members considered, that all the foods are becoming expensive. The owners of cochineal cactus merely buy maize, chilis, etc., and are very occupied only with their cochineal, by which their money, cacao beans,[1] and cloth are acquired. They no longer want to cultivate their fields, but idly neglect them. Because of this, now many fields are going to grass, and famine truly impends. Things are no longer as they were long ago, for the cochineal cactus is making people lazy. And it is excessive how sins are committed against our Lord God. These cochineal owners devote themselves to their cochineal on Sundays and holy days; no longer do they go to church to hear mass as the holy church commands us, but look only to getting their sustenance and their cacao, which makes them proud. And then later they buy pulque[2] and then get drunk; all of the cochineal owners gather together. If they buy a turkey, they give it away for less than its price, and pulque, too; they lightly give away their money and cacao. Not remembering how our lord God mercifully granted them whatever wealth is theirs, they vainly squander it. And he who belonged to someone no longer respects whoever was his lord and master, because he is seen to have gold and cacao. That makes them proud and swells them up, whereby it is fully evident that they esteem themselves only through wealth. And also the cochineal dealers, some of them noblemen, some commoners, and some women,

line up here in the Tlaxcala marketplace and there await the cochineal. When they are not collecting cochineal quickly, then they go to the various homes of the cochineal owners, entering the houses. And there many things happen; they make the women drunk there, and there some commit sins. They go entering the homes of anyone who has cochineal plants; they already know those from whom they customarily buy dye, and sometimes they also go on Sundays and holy days, whereby they miss attending mass and hearing the sermon, but go only wanting to get drunk. And these cochineal dealers act as if the women who gather dye have been made their relatives.[3] Some of the men hire themselves out to Spaniards to gather dye for them, and they give them money and cacao. And later they distribute the women to them, making them like their relatives; to some they assign seven or eight (women), or thereabouts, to gather dye for them. Because of this many improper things are done. And of those who hire themselves out, many are likewise ruined, because some act as slaves in the hands of the Spaniards. If it were not for cochineal, they would not become such. And both the cactus owners and the cochineal dealers so act that for little reason they begin to pair with each other,[4] or take another as cogodparents, or just feed one another, gathering and collecting together with their wives. They feed one another, however many of them there are; they give one another a great deal of food, and the chocolate they drink is very thick, with plenty of cacao in it. When they find the chocolate just a little watery, then it is not to their liking and they do not want to drink it. Some pour it on the ground, whereby whoever has given his very good cacao to someone is affronted, but they imagine themselves very grand because

---

[1]In addition to being the main ingredient in chocolate, the cacao bean was a unit of money. Two hundred cacao beans equaled one tomine; eight tomines made one peso.
[2]A fermented beverage made from the maguey plant; the most widely consumed intoxicating beverage in colonial Mexico.

[3]By this is meant that the women perform limitless labor for the cochineal dealers in much the same way that people related by blood would selflessly serve one another.
[4]The meaning of this Nahuatl phrase is unclear; it may simply mean that dealers and growers become close friends and cooperate with one another.

of it. And also then they buy pulque or Castilian wine,[5] even though it is very expensive, they pay no heed, but give the price to the person selling it. And then they become entirely inebriated and senseless, together with their wives; they fall down one at a time where they are congregated, entirely drunk. Many sins are committed there, and it all comes from cochineal. Also these cochineal dealers no longer want to cultivate the soil; though some of them own fields, they no longer want to cultivate; they do nothing but look for cochineal. And both the cactus owners and the cochineal dealers, some of them, sleep on cotton mats, and their wives wear great skirts, and they have much money, cacao, and clothing. The wealth they have only makes them proud and swaggering. For before cochineal was known and everyone planted cochineal cactus, it was not this way. There were some people of whom it was clearly evident that they lived in knowledge of their humility, but just because of the cochineal now there is much drunkenness and swaggering; it is very clear that cochineal has been making people idle in the last eight or nine years. But in the old days there was a time of much care in cultivation and planting; everyone cultivated the soil and planted. Because of this, the cabildo members said it is necessary that the cochineal cactus decrease and not so much be planted, since it causes idleness. It is greatly urged that everyone cultivate and plant; let much maize, chili beans, and all edible plants be grown, because if our lord God should wish that famine come, and if there are in people's possession much money, cacao, and cloth, will those things be eaten? Will there be salvation through them? It cannot be. Money, cacao, and cloth do not fill one. But if people have much food, through it they will save themselves, since no one will starve; no one will die being wealthy. Therefore two or three times the lord viceroy who presides in Mexico City, don Luis de Velasco, has been told and it has been brought to his attention how the dye brings affliction, and he has been informed of all the harm done. And after that the lord viceroy gave orders in reply, ordering the lord corregidor that in his presence there be consultation here in the cabildo to approve how many plantings of cochineal cactus are to be kept by each person; it is to be a definite number, and no longer will there be planting at whim. And in consulting, some of the cabildo members said that five plantings of cochineal cactus should be kept (by each person), and others said that fifteen should be kept. But when the discussion was complete, everyone approved keeping ten plantings of cactus, and the lord corregidor also approved it. No one is to exceed (the number). And the women who gather dye in the marketplace are to gather dye no more. Nevertheless, it is first to be put before the lord viceroy; what he should order in reply will then be made public. Then in the cabildo were appointed those who will go to Mexico City to set before the lord viceroy what was discussed as said above.

---

[5]Spanish wine from the province of Castile.

# Chapter 3

▼▼▼

# The Islamic Heartland and India

In the early thirteenth century Mongol warriors under the legendary conqueror Chinggis Khan descended on Southwest Asia. After overrunning Persia, defeating the Seljuk Turks in 1243 in Asia Minor, and obliterating the enfeebled Abbasid Empire in 1258, the Mongols incorporated much of the region into their vast empire that stretched from Hungary to Korea. As Mongol political authority declined in the fourteenth century, Southwest Asia became a battleground for local dynasties, religious sects, nomad armies, and military adventurers, the most notable of whom was Timur the Lame, the Turko-Mongol conqueror whose large but short-lived empire collapsed after his death in 1405. Although India was spared the Mongol onslaught, its political history, especially in the north, was as chaotic and turbulent as Southwest Asia's. In the fourteenth century it was nominally ruled by the sultanate of Delhi, but the regime had already been undermined by revolt and warfare by the time Timur the Lame's devastating raid into northern India dealt it a death blow in 1398. Following the sultanate's demise India fractured into hundreds of states of varying sizes and degrees of effectiveness.

Following these years of conquest and upheaval, three dominant empires emerged in South and Southwest Asia between the mid fifteenth and early sixteenth centuries. The first empire to take shape was that of the Ottoman Turks, a seminomadic people who migrated to Anatolia in the 1200s and almost immediately embarked on conquests that expanded their state in Anatolia and extended it into southeastern Europe. In 1453 they conquered the last remnant of the Byzantine Empire when they captured the imperial city, Constantinople, and, as Istanbul, made it the seat of their sultan's expanding state. During the 1500s the Ottomans ruled an empire that included Egypt, Anatolia, Syria, and lands in

North Africa, and the western coast of the Arabian Peninsula, and southeastern Europe. Meanwhile, on the Ottoman Empire's eastern flank in the early sixteenth century, Ismail I created the Safavid Empire in Persia, distinguished by its rulers' fervent devotion to Shi'ite Islam. Finally, during the 1500s, the Mughal Empire emerged in India as a result of the conquests of Babur (1483–1530), a military adventurer from central Asia who won control of northwest India, and his grandson, Akbar (1542–1605), who extended Mughal authority to the east and south.

In addition to their leaders' common allegiance to Islam, these three empires resembled one another in several respects. Each was established through military conquest, each was ruled by an all-powerful emperor, and each was a formidable military power. In each, the arts and literature flourished. Each at first rested on a strong economic foundation, and each experienced the weakening of that foundation by inflation, high taxation, bureaucratic corruption, and broad changes in the world economy.

Differences among the three empires were most pronounced in the sphere of religion. The intense devotion of the Safavids to Shi'ism antagonized the Sunni Ottomans, and led to frequent Ottoman-Safavid wars. Furthermore, Safavid Persia was unique in that it lacked a substantial non-Muslim population. In contrast, the Ottomans' subjects in Europe were overwhelmingly Christian, and a smaller number of Christians and Jews was scattered throughout the rest of their empire. Most of the Mughals' subjects were Hindus.

The three empires also had different experiences with Europeans during the sixteenth and seventeenth centuries. The Ottomans and Europeans were archrivals, each representing to the other a despised religion, and, moreover, a threat to their territory and commerce. European and Ottoman fleets clashed over supremacy in the Mediterranean, and their armies fought for control of southeastern Europe. Nonetheless, European merchants continued to trade and even reside in Ottoman cities, and European powers such as France forged military alliances with Christendom's enemy when it suited their purposes.

Relations between Europeans and Safavid Persia, on the other hand, were more cordial. Shah Abbas I (r. 1587–1629) relied on European military advisers and sent two missions to Europe in 1599 and 1608 to explore the possibility of joint action against the Ottoman Turks.

In India the Portuguese quickly capitalized on the success of Vasco da Gama's voyage around Africa to Calicut in 1498. They undercut the monopoly of Arab merchants in the spice trade on the west Indian coast and established a base of operations on the island of Goa, which they forcibly annexed from the local Muslim ruler. The Dutch, English, and French became seriously involved in India only after 1600. They, too, established commercial operations on the coast, but only after having gained the permission of a local ruler or a Mughal official. Emperors Akbar and Jahangir were interested in European art and religion, but overall the Mughals viewed Europe neither as a threat nor a potential trading partner or ally of any significance.

By the mid seventeenth century all three Islamic empires were beginning to decline. The Mughal and Safavid empires disappeared in the eighteenth century, and the Ottoman Empire, although it survived until after World War I, gradually became a symbol of decrepitude and decay. Yet in the 1500s and 1600s, few other societies, if any, could rival these three empires' wealth, cultural sophistication, and military strength.

▼▼▼

# Rulers and Their Challenges in the Ottoman, Safavid, and Mughal Empires

Many factors — resources, wealth, technological development, social coherence, cultural unity, and military strength — contribute to the rise and fall of states. But as the histories of the Ottoman, Safavid, and Mughal empires confirm, quality of rule is also significant, especially when authority is exercised by a single all-powerful ruler. Each of these empires flourished under strong, energetic rulers who quashed dissent, maintained bureaucratic rigor, acted decisively, and provided effective military leadership. But gradually the quality of rulers declined, and this, along with other factors, contributed to economic stagnation, territorial loss, and military decay.

The emergence of all three empires confirms the importance of leadership, especially on the battlefield. The Ottoman state resulted from the conquests of three men — Mehmet II (r. 1451–1481), who directed the siege of Constantinople in 1453; Selim I (r. 1512–1520), who conquered Egypt, Syria, Palestine, and parts of southern and western Arabia; and Suleiman I (r. 1520–1566), who added Hungary, the Mediterranean island of Rhodes, and some Persian territory to Ottoman domains. The Safavid Empire was forged through the exploits of Shaykh Ismail (r. 1501–1524), a military and religious leader whose original power base was Azerbaijan in northern Persia. Believed by his followers to be a descendant of the

Prophet Muhammad's son-in-law, Ali, he conquered Persia and in 1501 assumed the title *shah,* or emperor. Babur, the founder of the Mughal Empire in India, was a military adventurer of Mongol-Turkish ancestry who invaded India after having lost his original kingdom in Afghanistan. In 1526 he led an army of twelve thousand troops into northern India and, with superior tactics and firepower, defeated the much larger army of the ruling Muslim Lodi Dynasty.

The cultural achievements of these Islamic empires also depended on the interests and patronage of individual rulers. Akbar (r. 1556–1605), a brilliant military commander whose conquests substantially expanded the Mughal Empire, patronized painters, poets, historians, and religious thinkers. Under his free-spending successors, Jahangir (r. 1605–1627) and Shah Jahan (r. 1627–1658), Mughal culture reached new heights. The Taj Mahal, one of the world's most beautiful buildings, is only one of many masterpieces they planned and paid for. Under Shah Abbas I (r. 1587–1629) the Safavid capital, Isfahan, was transformed through the construction of hundreds of mosques, formal gardens, palaces, royal tombs, and public squares. Similarly, the early Ottoman sultans, following the precedent of Mehmet II, who had the Greek Orthodox church of Hagia Sophia converted into an impressive mosque, all sought to leave their mark on Istanbul and Islamic culture by sponsoring ambitious building programs and the work of scholars, poets, and artists.

The sources in this section provide insights into the personalities and policies of three of the most renowned Islamic rulers of the sixteenth and seventeenth centuries — Suleiman I, Jahangir, and Abbas I. They allow us to analyze their styles of leadership and the strengths and weaknesses of their regimes.

# A European Diplomat's Impressions of Suleiman I

▼▼▼

## 21 ▼ *Ogier Ghiselin de Busbecq, TURKISH LETTERS*

Suleiman I, known to Europeans as *Suleiman the Magnificent,* is remembered largely for his military conquests, but his accomplishments go beyond battlefield exploits. He was a patron of history and literature, oversaw the codification of Ottoman law (hence his honorific title *the Lawgiver*), and contributed to the architectural grandeur of Istanbul. He was one of the outstanding rulers of the age.

The following description and analysis of Suleiman and his reign was written by Ogier Ghiselin de Busbecq (1522–1590), a Flemish nobleman who spent most of his life in the service of the Hapsburgs, in particular Ferdinand I, the archduke of Austria, king of Hungary and Bohemia, and, from 1558 to 1564, Holy Roman Emperor. In 1555 Ferdinand sent Busbecq to Suleiman's court in Istanbul to represent his interests in a dispute over Transylvania, a region that had been part of Hungary and today is in Romania. After six years of discussions, the two sides agreed on a compromise by which Transylvania became an autonomous state in theory but paid an annual tribute to the sultan.

During his six years in Ottoman lands Busbecq recorded his observations and impressions and sent them in the form of four long letters to a friend and fellow diplomat, Nicholas Michault. All four letters were published in Paris in 1589. Subsequently appearing in numerous Latin versions and translated into the major European languages, Busbecq's letters provide a wealth of information about Ottoman society.

The following excerpt begins with a description of Busbecq's first meeting with Suleiman I in 1555. It then goes on to comment on the Ottoman military. It concludes with a summary of the events surrounding the murder of Suleiman's oldest son and most likely successor, Mustafa, in 1553. As Busbecq explains, Mustafa's interests clashed with the ambitions of Roxelana, Suleiman's Russian-born wife and the mother of two sons and a daughter by Suleiman. To ensure that her elder son, Selim, would become sultan after Suleiman's death, she convinced her aging husband that Mustafa was plotting against him and that he and his son must be killed. With power passing on to one of the ruler's sons, but not necessarily the eldest, such incidents were not uncommon in all three Islamic empires.

---

## QUESTIONS FOR ANALYSIS

1. What does Busbecq's first meeting with Suleiman reveal about the sultan's attitudes toward Europeans? What further insights into his attitudes are provided later in the excerpt?
2. What does Busbecq see as the main difference between Ottoman and European attitudes toward social privilege and inherited status? How do these attitudes affect Ottoman government?
3. What insights do Busbecq's observations provide about the sources of Ottoman military power?
4. What does the episode of Mustafa's assassination reveal about the power and influence of Roxelana? About Ottoman attitudes toward the imperial succession? About Suleiman's character?
5. What advantages and disadvantages were there in the Ottoman practice of not making the eldest son the automatic heir of the reigning sultan?
6. Shortly after Suleiman's reign the Ottoman Empire began to decline. What in Busbecq's account points to future problems for the Ottoman state?

## FIRST IMPRESSIONS

On our arrival . . . we were taken to call on Achmet Pasha (the chief Vizier) and the other pashas[1] — for the Sultan himself was not then in the town — and commenced our negotiations with them touching the business entrusted to us by King Ferdinand. The pashas . . . told us that the whole matter depended on the Sultan's pleasure. On his arrival we were admitted to an

---

[1] *Pasha* was an honorary title for a high-ranking military or government official; the *grand vizier* was the sultan's chief advisor and head of the Ottoman administration.

audience; but the manner and spirit in which he . . . listened to our address, our arguments, and our message was by no means favorable. . . .

On entering we were separately conducted into the royal presence by the chamberlains, who grasped our arms. . . . After having gone through a pretense of kissing his [Suleiman's] hand, we were conducted backwards to the wall opposite his seat, care being taken that we should never turn our backs on him. The Sultan then listened to what I had to say; but the language I used was not at all to his taste, for the demands of his Majesty[2] breathed a spirit of independence and dignity, which was by no means acceptable to one who deemed that his wish was law; and so he made no answer beyond saying in an impatient way, "Giusel, giusel," i.e. well, well. After this we were dismissed to our quartets.

The Sultan's hall was crowded with people, among whom were several officers of high rank. Besides these there were all the troopers of the Imperial guard, and a large force of Janissaries,[3] but there was not in all that great assembly a single man who owed his position to anything save his valor and his merit. No distinction is attached to birth among the Turks; the respect to be paid to a man is measured by the position he holds in the public service. There is no fighting for precedence; a man's place is marked out by the duties he discharges. . . . It is by merit that men rise in the service, a system which ensures that posts should only be assigned to the competent. . . . Those who receive the highest offices from the Sultan are for the most part the sons of shepherds or herdsmen, and so far from being ashamed of their parentage, they actually glory in it, and consider it a matter of boasting that they owe nothing to the accident of birth; for they do not believe that high qualities are either natural or hereditary, nor do they think that they can be handed down from father to son, but that they are partly the gift of God, and partly

the result of good training, great industry, and unwearied zeal. . . . Among the Turks, therefore, honors, high posts, and judgeships are the rewards of great ability and good service.

## OTTOMAN MILITARY STRENGTH

Against us stands Suleiman, that foe whom his own and his ancestors' exploits have made so terrible; he tramples the soil of Hungary with 200,000 horses, he is at the very gates of Austria, threatens the rest of Germany, and brings in his train all the nations that extend from our borders to those of Persia. The army he leads is equipped with the wealth of many kingdoms. Of the three regions, into which the world is divided,[4] there is not one that does not contribute its share towards our destruction. . . .

▼ ▼ ▼

The Turkish monarch going to war takes with him over 40,000 camels and nearly as many baggage mules, of which a great part, when he is invading Persia, are loaded with rice and other kinds of grain. These mules and camels also serve to carry tents and armor, and likewise tools and munitions for the campaign. The territories, which bear the name of Persia, . . . are less fertile than our country, and even such crops as they bear are laid waste by the inhabitants in time of invasion in hopes of starving out the enemy, so that it is very dangerous for an army to invade Persia if it is not furnished with abundant supplies. . . .

▼ ▼ ▼

After dinner I practice the Turkish bow, in the use of which weapon people here are marvelously expert. From the eighth, or even the seventh, year of their age they begin to shoot at a mark, and practice archery ten or twelve years. This constant exercise strengthens the muscles of their

---

[2]Archduke Ferdinand, Busbecq's employer.
[3]An elite military force in the service of the sultan. Its ranks were filled originally by young Christian boys who were converted to Islam and given over to military training. They

lived by a strict code of absolute obedience, austerity, religious observance, celibacy, and confinement to barracks.
[4]Asia, Europe, and Africa.

arms, and gives them such skill that they can hit the smallest marks with their arrows. . . . So sure is their aim that in battle they can hit a man in the eye or in any other exposed part they choose.

▼ ▼ ▼

No nation in the world has shown greater readiness than the Turks to avail themselves of the useful inventions of foreigners, as is proved by their employment of cannons and mortars, and many other things invented by Christians. . . . The Turks are much afraid of carbines and pistols, such as are used on horseback. The same, I hear, is the case with the Persians, on which account someone advised Rustem,[5] when he was setting out with the Sultan on a campaign against them, to raise from his household servants a troop of 200 horsemen and arm them with firearms, as they would cause much alarm . . . in the ranks of the enemy. Rustem, in accordance with this advice, raised a troop of dragoons,[6] furnished them with firearms, and had them drilled. But they had not completed half the journey when their guns began to get out of order. Every day some essential part of their weapons was lost or broken, and it was not often that armorers could be found capable of repairing them. So, a large part of the firearms having been rendered unserviceable, the men took a dislike to the weapon; and this prejudice was increased by the dirt which its use entailed, the Turks being a very cleanly people; for the dragoons had their hands and clothes begrimed with gunpowder, and moreover presented such a sorry appearance, with their ugly boxes and pouches hanging about them, that their comrades laughed at them and called them apothecaries. So, . . . they gathered around Rustem and showing him their broken and useless firearms, asked what advantage he hoped to gain from them when they met the enemy, and demanded that he should relieve them of them, and give them their old arms again. Rustem, af-

ter considering their request carefully, thought there was no reason for refusing to comply with it, and so they got permission to resume their bows and arrows.

## PROBLEMS OF THE SUCCESSION

Suleiman had a son by a concubine who came from the Crimea. . . . His name was Mustafa, and at the time of which I am speaking he was young, vigorous, and of high repute as a soldier. But Suleiman had also several other children, by a Russian woman.[7] . . . To the latter he was so much attached that he placed her in the position of wife, and assigned her a dowry. . . .

Mustafa's high qualities and matured years marked him out to the soldiers who loved him, and the people who supported him, as the successor of his father, who was now in the decline of life. On the other hand, his step-mother [Roxelana], by throwing the claim of a lawful wife onto the balance, was doing her utmost to counterbalance his personal merits and his rights as eldest son, with a view to obtaining the throne for her own children. In this intrigue, she received the advice and assistance of Rustem, whose fortunes were inseparably linked with hers by his marriage with a daughter she had had by Suleiman. . . .

Inasmuch as Rustem was chief Vizier, . . . he had no difficulty . . . in influencing his master's mind. The Turks, accordingly, are convinced that it was by the calumnies of Rustem and the spells of Roxelana, who was in ill repute as a practitioner of sorcery, that the Sultan was so estranged from his son as to entertain the design of getting rid of him. A few believe that Mustafa, being aware of the plans, . . . decided to anticipate them, and thus engaged in designs against his father's throne and person. The sons of Turkish Sultans are in the most wretched position in the world, for, as soon as one of them succeeds his

---

[5]Pasha Rustem, the grand vizier, was also Suleiman's son-in-law. He married the daughter of Suleiman and Roxelana, originally a Russian slave girl in the sultan's harem.

[6]Heavily armed mounted troops.
[7]The reference is to Roxelana.

father, the rest are doomed to certain death. The Turk can endure no rival to the throne, and, indeed, the conduct of the Janissaries renders it impossible for the new Sultan to spare his brothers; for if one of them survives, the Janissaries are forever asking generous favors. If these are refused, the cry is heard, "Long live the brother!" "God preserve the brother!" — a tolerably broad hint that they intend to place him on the throne. So that the Turkish Sultans are compelled to celebrate their succession by staining their hands with the blood of their nearest relatives. . . .

Being at war with Shah Tahmasp, Shah of the Persians, he [Suleiman] had sent Rustem against him as a commander-in-chief of his armies. Just as he was about to enter Persian territory, Rustem suddenly halted, and hurried off dispatches to Suleiman, informing him that affairs were in a very critical state; that treason was rife; . . . that the soldiers had been tampered with, and cared for no one but Mustafa; . . . and he must come at once if he wished to preserve his throne. Suleiman was seriously alarmed by these dispatches. He immediately hurried to the army, sent a letter to summon Mustafa to his presence, inviting him to clear himself of those crimes of which he was suspected. . . .

There was great uneasiness among the soldiers, when Mustafa arrived. . . . He was brought to his father's tent, and there everything betokened peace. . . . But there were in the tent certain mutes — . . . strong and sturdy fellows, who had been appointed as his executioners. As soon as he entered the inner tent, they threw themselves upon him, and endeavored to put the fatal noose around his neck. Mustafa, being a man of considerable strength, made a stout defense and fought — there being no doubt that if he escaped . . . and threw himself among the Janissaries, the news of this outrage on their beloved prince would cause such pity and indignation, that they would not only protect him, but also proclaim him Sultan. Suleiman felt how critical the matter was, being only separated by the linen hangings of his tent from the stage on which this tragedy was being enacted. When he found that there was an unexpected delay in the execution of his scheme, he thrust out his head from the chamber of his tent, and glared on the mutes with fierce and threatening eyes; at the same time, with signs full of hideous meaning, he sternly rebuked their slackness. Hereon the mutes, gaining fresh strength from the terror he inspired, threw Mustafa down, got the bowstring round his neck, and strangled him. Shortly afterwards they laid his body on a rug in front of the tent, that the Janissaries might see the man they had desired as their Sultan. . . .

Meanwhile, Roxelana, not content with removing Mustafa from her path, . . . did not consider that she and her children were free from danger, so long as his offspring survived. Some pretext, however, she thought necessary, in order to furnish a reason for the murder, but this was not hard to find. Information was brought to Suleiman that, whenever his grandson appeared in public, the boys of Ghemlik[8] — where he was being educated — shouted out, "God save the Prince, and may he long survive his father;" and that the meaning of these cries was to point him out as his grandsire's future successor, and his father's avenger. Moreover, he was bidden to remember that the Janissaries would be sure to support the son of Mustafa, so that the father's death had in no way secured the peace of the throne and realm. . . .

Suleiman was easily convinced by these arguments to sign the death-warrant of his grandson. He commissioned Ibrahim Pasha to go to the Ghemlik with all speed, and put the innocent child to death.[9]

---

[8]A town in northwest Turkey.
[9]The assassination was carried out by a eunuch hired by Ibrahim Pasha, who had succeeded Rustem Pasha as grand vizier.

# A Carmelite Friar's View of Shah Abbas I

▼▼▼

## 22 ▼ *Father Paul Simon, REPORT TO POPE PAUL V*

When Shah Abbas I ascended the Safavid throne in 1587 after the forced abdication of his father, he inherited an empire on the brink of disintegration. He faced a rebellion from Turkoman tribal leaders and invasions by the Ottomans from the west and the Uzbeks from the east. Within fifteen years he crushed the rebels and routed the Uzbeks and Ottomans. Subsequently, Abbas defeated the Mughals in 1621, taking Kandahar, seized the Persian Gulf island of Bahrain in 1622, and in the same year with English help expelled the Portuguese from their trading post at Ormuz. In addition to his military exploits, Abbas encouraged foreign and domestic trade, lent his support to manufacturing enterprises, and presided over a glorious era in Persian culture.

Part of Abbas's strategy to make Persia strong and prosperous was the cultivation of useful contacts with foreigners, especially Europeans. Two English brothers, Anthony and Robert Sherley, helped the shah enlarge and modernize his army and used their contacts to increase Persian trade with the English and Dutch. Abbas also sought alliances with European states against his enemy, the Ottomans. To that end he sent two embassies to Europe in 1599 and 1608 and tolerated the activities of Catholic missionaries, who were encouraged to think he might convert.

Such was the background for the negotiations between the envoys of Abbas I and Pope Clement VIII in 1600 that led to the dispatch of three Carmelite friars to Isfahan in 1604 to explore opportunities for missionary work. After an arduous journey through Russia and Poland, the three friars reached Isfahan in 1605 and remained in Persia six months. One of three, Father Paul Simon of Jesus Mary (1576–1643), a Genoese who became a Carmelite in 1595, traveled extensively during his visit. After a hair-raising return journey on foot through Ottoman territory, Father Simon presented a detailed report on Persia to the new pope, Paul V. Paul then dispatched Father Simon to Spain to discuss with King Philip III the complaints of Abbas I concerning the activities of Portuguese merchants in Ormuz, an important port city in the shah's territory, which the Portuguese (now subjects of the King of Spain) had controlled since 1507. Until his death in 1643 he held a number of administrative posts within his order. His report to Paul V remained in the Vatican archives until it was found and translated into English by a historian of the Carmelites.

---

## QUESTIONS FOR ANALYSIS

1. What sort of impression does Abbas attempt to make on his subjects? What strategies does he use to make this impression?
2. What methods has Abbas used to suppress the powerful descendants of the Kizilbash who helped Ismail I (r. 1501–1524) establish the Safavid state (referred to by Father Simon as "the old nobles of Persia")?

3. What impresses Father Simon about Abbas's army? How do his comments and observations resemble Busbecq's characterization of Suleiman's troops (source 21)?
4. On the basis of Father Simon's account, what conclusions can be drawn about Abbas's religious views?
5. What factors seem to have shaped Abbas's policies toward the European Christians?
6. Despite the impressive strength of Persia under Abbas, the Persian state quickly declined after his death. What underlying weaknesses do you see in the Persian state during Abbas's rule?

## PERSONALITY AND POLICIES

The king . . . is sturdy and healthy, accustomed to much exercise and toil: many times he goes about on foot, and recently he had been forty days on pilgrimage, which he made on foot the whole time. He has extraordinary strength, and with his scimitar[1] can cut a man in two and a sheep with its wool on at a single blow — and the Persian sheep are of large size. . . . In his food he is frugal, as also in his dress, and this to set an example to his subjects; and so in public he eats little else than rice, and that cooked in water only. His usual dress is of linen, and very plain: similarly the nobles and others in his realm follow suit, whereas formerly they used to go out dressed in brocade with jewels and other fopperies: and if he sees anyone who is overdressed, he takes him to task, especially if it be a soldier. But in private he eats what he likes.

He is sagacious in mind, likes fame and to be esteemed: he is courteous in dealing with everyone and at the same time very serious. For he will go through the public streets, eat from what they are selling there and other things, speak at ease freely with the lower classes, cause his subjects to remain sitting while he himself is standing, or will sit down beside this man and that. He says that is how to be a king, and that the king of Spain and other Christians do not get any pleasure out of ruling, because they are obliged to comport themselves with so much pomp and majesty. . . .

He is very strict in executing justice and pays no regard to his own favorites in this respect; but rather is the stricter with them in order to serve an example for others. So he has no private friends, nor anyone who has influence with him. . . . While we were at Court, he caused the bellies of two of his favorites to be ripped open, because they behaved improperly to an ordinary woman. . . .

He is very speedy in dispatching business: when he gives audience, which he does at the gate of his palace, . . . he finishes off all the cases that are brought to him. The parties stand present before him, the officers of justice and his own council, with whom he consults when it pleases him. The sentence which he gives is final and is immediately executed. If the guilty party deserves death, they kill him at once: to this end, when he gives audience, twelve men and twelve dogs who devour men alive, are kept ready: he keeps them in order to use the greater severity. Apart from the officials, once the sentence is given, it is not permitted to anyone to make any reply: for the person is at once driven off with blows of the sticks of some 30 to 40 royal guards, who stand ready to do this. When he wants to stop giving audience, he causes it to be proclaimed that no one, on pain of death, may bring him petitions, and, when he wants to go

---

[1]A curved steel saber.

out of doors unaccompanied, that no one should follow him. . . .

There are four councilors of the king — Allah Virdi Khan, his general; 'Ata Baig his vizier; the Qurchi Bashi; and one who was his "governor" and preceptor. The three last are always with the Shah, and when he gives audience are standing next to him. He has to be obeyed absolutely: anyone failing in the slightest will pay for it with his head. And so he has had most of the old nobles of Persia killed off and put in their stead low-bred persons whom he has aggrandized. In the whole of Persia there are only two of the old-time governors. . . . Because of the great obedience they pay him, when he wills to have one of the nobles killed, he dispatches one of his men to fetch the noble's head: the man goes off to the grandee, and says to him: "The Shah wants your head." The noble replies: "Very well," and lets himself be decapitated — otherwise he would lose it and, with it, all his family would become extinct. But, when they [the nobles] allow themselves to be decapitated, he aggrandizes the children.

The Shah of Persia is very rich, because, besides having the treasure of his predecessors, he has seized those of the princes of Lar and of Gilan,[2] who were powerful and rich princes, and others. He has many sources of income and is master over the property of his subjects. . . .

## MILITARY STRENGTH

He is very valiant and has a great liking for warfare and weapons of war, which he has constantly in his hands: we have been eye-witnesses of this because, whenever we were with him, he was adjusting scimitars, testing arquebuses,[3] etc.: and to make him a present that will give him pleasure is to give him some good pieces of arms. This is the great experience which he has obtained of warfare over so many years, that he

makes it in person and from the first it has made him a fine soldier and very skilled, and his men so dexterous that they are little behind our men in Europe. He has introduced into his militia the use of and esteem for arquebuses and muskets, in which they are very practiced. Therefore it is that his realm has been so much extended on all sides. . . .

His militia is divided into three kinds of troops: one of the Georgians,[4] who will be about 25,000 and are mounted; . . . this is the old-time militia of the kings of Persia for the guarding of their persons. The present king has introduced the second force, which is made up of slaves of various races, many of them Christian renegades; their number will be as many again, and they are more esteemed than the first cited, both because they are servants of the king, and he assigns posts to them and promotes them. . . . The third body consists of soldiers whom the great governors of Persia are obliged to maintain and pay the whole year; they will be about 50,000. . . . When they [the governors] accomplish something signal in war, he gives them a governorship which produces greater revenue and sometimes the territory they capture is left to them. All the above-mentioned soldiers, who will total some 100,000, receive pay for the whole year. Then, according to the campaign and enterprise the king wishes to undertake, he enlists others, and, when it is necessary to make a great effort, he has it proclaimed throughout his country that whosoever is his well-wisher should follow him. Then everyone takes up arms.

## THE SHAH'S FAMILY

The Shah has three sons: the eldest aged 22 years; . . . His mother was a Christian, and he is friendly toward Christians and not so quick-tempered as his father. The second son, 12 years old, has a temperament similar to that of his father. The

---

[2]Lar was a Persian province on the Persian Gulf; Gilan was a province in northwest Persia.
[3]A portable matchlock gun invented in the fifteenth century and usually fired from a support.

[4]A Christian people inhabiting a region between the Caspian and Black seas.

third is aged 5 or 6. He has several daughters. His predecessors were wont to kill off their daughters because there were no neighboring monarchs of equal rank to whom to marry them, and they did not like giving them in marriage to nobles of the country, for fear of the latter rebelling. In order to eliminate such cruel procedure this present Shah marries them to men of lowly position, as he did when we were there, giving one daughter to a camp commandant, the other to a captain. The eldest son born to the Shah inherits the throne even though he be by a slave woman.

## HIS RELIGIOUS VIEWS

Regarding the religion of the king I think that no one knows what he believes: he does not observe the Muslim law in many things, nor is he a Christian. Six or seven years ago he displayed many signs of not being averse to our Faith. . . .

It is true that when the Augustinian Fathers[5] went to Persia the king showed himself extraordinarily affectionate with them, and gave many signs of being well disposed toward the Christian Faith and of wanting to embrace it. . . . In notifying the king the objects of their mission, the Augustinian Fathers told him that they came to show him the True Faith, and to baptize him. He answered that he would discuss that at more length when he had the opportunity. Almost always he kept them near him. . . . He gave them 2,000 scudi[6] yearly for their subsistence, and entertained them several times at banquets, always making them sit near him, and he took one of them into the harem of his women, which was an exceptional mark of favor, since he did not even allow his own son to enter it; he made some of them [the women] dance. When the Fathers proposed to him [that he should adopt] our Faith, he made show to agree to everything. He gave them, sealed with his small seal, and also by the

prince his son and three of his councilors who alone were present at this, a writing in which he promised to construct a church with bells in every town he should capture from the Turks, to allow the Gospel to be preached, if the King of Spain kept to that which he promised him by the same Fathers, i.e. to take up arms against the Turks, and to send him artillery and engineers, which up till now has not been fulfilled. As evidence that he still had the mind to fulfil what he was promising, he said that on the following day he would go to their church — as in fact he did. . . . [We were] told that the king wanted to make a great bell and a church for the Fathers in Isfahan, asked the Fathers for relics and a piece of the wood of the Cross, and that they gave it to him. . . .

---

▷ By the time Father Simon arrived in Persia in 1607, Abbas's views of European Christians, especially the Portuguese Augustinians, had changed. As Father Simon states, this change was caused by two things: the efforts of the Augustinians to turn the shah's newly conquered Armenian Christian subjects into Roman Catholics and the failure of the King of Spain, who at this point also ruled Portugal, to attack the Ottoman Empire.

---

In Tabriz it was told the king that the Augustinian Fathers had put up a bell in their church in Isfahan and that for this reason there were many people sick in that town. The Shah bit his finger, muttering two or three times: "Church with a bell! church with a bell!"; and gave orders that they should immediately take it down, as they did. In many other actions he demonstrated the small goodwill he had for Christians; and this increased to such an extent that, when we arrived in the city of Isfahan, he had given instructions for publication of an edict to the effect that all 'Frankish'[7] Christians and

---

[5]Members of the Augustinian religious order, which traces its spiritual lineage to St. Augustine (354–430). The Augustinians in question were Portuguese.

[6]A gold or silver coin minted in Italy.

the Augustinian Fathers should quit his realm. . . .

. . . The cause of so great a change . . . God alone knows; the Augustinian Fathers say that in the beginning the king was merely pretending and that those demonstrations of affection and goodwill did not come from his heart. Other people attribute it to the many causes for annoyance the officials of his Catholic Majesty in Ormuz[8] have given him; to the Christian princes, His Holiness, the Emperor, the king of Spain not having kept the word they had given to various ambassadors that they would make war on the Turks, when they exhorted him himself to do the same, as he in fact has done; to many of the Franks, who had gone to his country, having committed a great many follies; and, more recently still, to the Emperor having agreed to a treaty[9] of peace between himself and the Turks, without giving him notice. . . . Certain it is that the mullahs[10] — this the name they give in their tongue to the learned men of their belief — went to the Shah, and told him to reflect on what he was doing — that he knew very well that the [Ottoman] Sultan was the head of the Muslim belief; if he should bring about the destruction of the latter in this warfare, the Christians would do the same to him, and to all of their belief. For they observed what poor sort of friends they were, when even their kings did not keep their word to him, while, the Franks who came to his country, what scant respect they paid him. It would be better to make peace with the Turkish Sultan, and then both of them together to attack the Christians. . . .

[All this left Father Simon at a loss about Abbas's true religious convictions.] . . . In his seraglio he has many Christian Armenian, Georgian, and Circassian woman.[11] I think that he lets them live as they wish, because when I enquired what the Shah did with so many holy pictures that were presented to him as gifts and some relics of the Saints, for which he asked, the answer was that he used to give them to the women in his seraglio. Besides that he is well informed regarding the mysteries of our holy Faith and discourses on the mystery of the most holy Trinity: he knows many examples and allusions which the Saints give in order to prove it, and discourses about the other mysteries . . . if he does not discourse about the women in his seraglio or about some demon or other. On account of the many disappointments which he asserts the Christians have caused him all this fervor has cooled. With all that he does not detest them, for he converses and eats with them, he suffers us to say frankly what we believe about our Faith and his own: sometimes he asks us about this. To us he has given a house: he knows that we say Mass publicly, he allows whoever may wish among the Persians to come to it, and we can teach them freely regarding our holy Faith, whenever they make inquiries about it. . . . Till now none of them has been converted: I think they are waiting for one of the nobles or of their mullahs to break the ice. . . .

---

[7]"Frankish" was a term for European.

[8]Ormuz, a port city on the Persian Gulf, had been taken by the Portuguese in 1507; between 1580 and 1640 Portugal was ruled by the king of Spain.

[9]The reference is to the Treaty of Sitvatorok, signed on November 11, 1606.

[10]A Muslim religious leader trained in law and doctrine.

[11]Like the Georgians, the Circassians were a Christian people living between the Caspian and Black seas.

# A Self-Portrait of Jahangir

▼▼▼

## 23 ▾ *Jahangir,* MEMOIRS

Jahangir, Mughal emperor from 1605 to 1627, modestly increased the size of the empire through conquest, snuffed out a half dozen rebellions, and on the whole continued the policies of his illustrious father, Akbar (r. 1556–1605). The lands he ruled provided him the wealth to indulge his tastes for formal gardens, entertaining, ceremony, sports, literature, and finely crafted books. In addition to subsidizing the work of hundreds of painters and writers, Jahangir himself contributed to the literature of his age by writing a memoir. Intended to glorify himself and instruct his heirs, it covered the first thirteen years of his reign, before his addiction to alcohol and opium sapped his energy and effectiveness.

---

## QUESTIONS FOR ANALYSIS

1. Other than to glorify the person of the emperor, what political purposes might have been served by Jahangir's elaborate coronation ceremony?
2. What do the "twelve special regulations" issued at the beginning of Jahangir's reign reveal about his priorities as emperor?
3. How does Jahangir view his Hindu subjects? What are his reasons for allowing them to practice their religion?
4. What does the episode of the Afghan bandits reveal about Jahangir's view of the emperor's responsibilities?
5. What similarities and differences do you see in the authority and leadership style of Suleiman I, Abbas I (sources 21 and 22), and Jahangir?

## JAHANGIR'S CORONATION

On the eighth of the latter month of Jammaudy, of the year of the Hegira one thousand and fourteen,[1] in the metropolis of Agrah, and in the forenoon of the day, being then at the age of thirty-eight, I became Emperor, and under the most felicitous auspices, took my seat on the throne of my wishes. . . . As at the very instant that I seated myself on the throne the sun rose from the horizon, I accepted this as the omen of victory, and as indicating a reign of unvarying prosperity. Hence I assumed the titles of Jahangir

Padshah, and Jahangir Shah: the world-subduing emperor; the world-subduing king. I ordained that the following legend should be stamped on the coinage of the empire: "Stricken at Agrah by that . . . safeguard of the world; the sovereign splendor of the faith, Jahangir, son of the imperial Akbar."

On this occasion I made use of the throne prepared by my father, and enriched at an expense without parallel, for the celebration of the festival of the new year. . . . In the fabrication of the throne a sum not far short of ten krours of ashrefies[2] was expended in jewels alone. . . .

---

[1]October 10, 1605. Jahangir uses the Muslim calendar, dated from the Hegira, Muhammad's flight from Mecca to Medina.

[2]A *krour* is a measurement of weight, and an *ashrefy* is a unit of money. Although it is impossible to determine the exact value of ten "krours of ashrefies," it is an enormous sum.

. . . The legs and body of the throne were at the same time loaded with fifty maunds of ambergris,[3] so that wherever it might be found expedient to put it together, no further perfumes were necessary for an assemblage of whatever magnitude.

Having thus seated myself on the throne of my expectation and wishes, I caused also the imperial crown, which my father had caused to be made after the manner of that which was worn by the great kings of Persia, to be brought before me, and then, in the presence of the whole assembled Emirs,[4] having placed it on my brows, as an omen auspicious to the stability and happiness of my reign, kept it there for the space of a full . . . hour. On each of the twelve points of this crown was a single diamond . . . the whole purchased by my father with the resources of his own government, not from anything accruing to him by inheritance from his predecessors. At the point in the center of the top part of the crown was a single pearl . . . and on different parts of the same were set altogether two hundred rubies. . . .

For forty days and forty nights I caused the . . . great imperial state drum to strike up, without ceasing, the strains of joy and triumph; and . . . around my throne, the ground was spread by my directions with the most costly brocades and gold embroidered carpets. Censers[5] of gold and silver were disposed in different directions for the purpose of burning fragrant drugs, and nearly three thousand camphorated wax lights, . . . in branches of gold and silver perfumed with ambergris, illuminated the scene from night till morning. Numbers of blooming youth, . . . clad in dresses of the most costly materials, woven in silk and gold, with . . . amulets sparkling with the lustre of the diamond, the emerald, the sapphire, and the ruby, awaited my commends, rank after rank, and in attitude most respectful. And finally, the Emirs of the empire, . . . stood round in brilliant array, also waiting for the commands of their sovereign. . . .

## THE EMPEROR'S DECREES

The very first ordinance that issued from me . . . related to the chain of justice, one end of which I caused to be fastened to the battlements of the royal tower of the castle of Agrah, and the other to a stone post near the bed of the river Jumnah; to the end that whenever those charged with administering the courts were slack in dispensing justice to the downtrodden, he who had suffered injustice by applying his hand to the chain would find himself in the way of obtaining speedy redress.[6] . . . I ordered a chain of pure gold, sixty ells[7] in length, with sixty bells. It weighs four Hindustani maunds.[8] . . .

I issued twelve special regulations to be implemented and observed in all the realm.

1. I canceled the *tamgha,* the *mirabari,*[9] and all other imposts the *jagirdars*[10] of every province and district had imposed for their own profit.
2. I ordered that when a district lay wasted by thieves and highway bandits or was destitute of inhabitants, that towns should be built, . . . and every effort made to protect the subjects from injury. I directed the jagirdars in such deserted places to erect mosques and caravansaries, or places for the

---

[3]A *maund* was a unit of weight, which could vary from as little as 10 pounds to as much as 160; *ambergris,* a waxy substance secreted by sperm whales and found floating in tropical seas, is used as a perfume.
[4]High government officials.
[5]A container for burning incense.
[6]Presumably pulling the chain would be the first step in bringing the perceived injustice to the emperor's attention.
[7]An *ell* was a unit of length, equal to approximately forty-five inches.

[8]A *Hindustani maund* equaled just over ten pounds.
[9]The *tamgha* and *mirabari* were both customs duties.
[10]A *jagir* was a grant of land by the emperor that entitled the holder to the income from the land. The income was to be used mainly to finance the maintenance of troops. A *jagirdar* was the holder of a jagir.

accommodation of travelers, in order to render the district once more an inhabited country, and that men might again be able to travel back and forth safely. . . .

3. Merchants travelling through the country were not to have their bales or packs opened without their consent.

4. When a person shall die and leave children, whether he is an infidel[11] or Muslim, no man was to interfere a pin's point in his property; but when he has no children or direct and unquestionable heirs his inheritance is to be spent on approved expenditures such as construction of mosques and caravansaries, repair of bridges, and the creation of watertanks and wells.

5. No person was permitted either to make or to sell wine or any other intoxicating liquor. I undertook to institute this regulation, although it is sufficiently well known that I myself have the strongest inclination for wine, in which from the age of sixteen I have liberally indulged. . . .

6. No official was permitted to take up his abode in the house of any subject of my realm. On the contrary, when individuals serving in the state armies come to any town, and can rent a place to live, it would be commendable; otherwise they were to pitch their tents outside the town and prepare abodes for themselves.

7. No person was to suffer, for any offence, the cutting off of a nose or ear. For theft, the offender was to be scourged with thorns, or deterred from further transgressions by an oath on the Qur'an.

8. I decreed that superintendents of royal lands and jagirdars were prohibited from seizing the lands of their subjects or cultivating the lands themselves for their own benefit; neither was any jagirdar to exercise any authority beyond the limits of his own. . . .

On the contrary, his attention was to be wholly and exclusively devoted to the cultivation and improvement of the district allotted to him.

9. The tax collectors of royal lands and jagirdars may not intermarry with the people of the districts in which they reside without my permission.[12]

10. Governors in all the large cities were directed to establish infirmaries and hospitals with physicians appointed to treat the sick. Expenses are to be covered by income from royal lands.

11. During the month of my birth there could be no slaughter of animals in my realm. . . . In every week also, on Thursday, that being the day of my accession, and Sunday, my father's birthday, . . . and also because it is the day attributed to the sun and the day on which the creation of the world was begun. It was unjustifiable to deprive any animal of life on such a day.

12. I issued a decree confirming the dignitaries and jagirs of my father's government in all that they had enjoyed while he was living; and where I found sufficient merit, I conferred an advance of rank in various gradations. . . .

I told Miran Sadr-i-Jahan, who is one of the *sayyids*[13] of true lineage in Hundustan and long held the glorious post of comptroller for my father, that every day the deserving poor should be brought before me. I set free . . . all criminals who had long been imprisoned in fortresses and jails.

## POLICY TOWARD THE HINDUS

I am here led to relate that at the city of Banaras[14] a temple had been erected [in which] . . . the principal idol . . . had on its head a tiara or cap, enriched with jewels. . . . [Also] placed in this

---

[11]A Hindu.
[12]This was to prevent any tax collector or jagirdar from gaining a vested interest in the fortunes of a particular region or family.

[13]A *sayyid* is considered to be a lineal descendant of the Prophet Muhammad.
[14]A city on the Ganges River.

temple, moreover, as the associates and ministering servants of the principal idol, [were] four other images of solid gold, each crowned with a tiara, in the like manner enriched with precious stones. It was the belief of these non-believers that a dead Hindu, provided when alive he had been a worshiper, when laid before this idol would be restored to life. As I could not possibly give credit to such a pretense, I employed a confidential person to ascertain the truth; and, as I justly supposed, the whole was detected to be an impudent fraud. . . .

On this subject I must however acknowledge, that having on one occasion asked my father the reason why he had forbidden anyone to prevent or interfere with the building of these haunts of idolatry, his reply was in the following terms: "My dear child," said he, "I find myself a powerful monarch, the shadow of God upon earth. I have seen that he bestows the blessing of his gracious providence upon all his creatures without distinction. . . . With all of the human race, with all of God's creatures, I am at peace: why then should I permit myself, under any consideration, to be the cause of molestation or aggression to any one? Besides, are not five parts in six . . . either Hindus or aliens to the faith; and were I to be governed by motives of the kind suggested in your inquiry, what alternative can I have but to put them all to death! I have thought it therefore my wisest plan to let these men alone. Neither is it to be forgotten, that the class of whom we are speaking . . . are usefully engaged, either in the pursuits of science or the arts, or of improvements for the benefit of mankind, and have in numerous instances arrived at the highest distinctions in the state, there being, indeed, to be found in this city men of every description, and of every religion on the face of the earth." . . .

▾ ▾ ▾

In the practice of being burnt on the funeral pyre of their husbands[15] as sometimes exhibited among the widows of the Hindus, I had previously directed that no woman who was the mother of children should be thus made a sacrifice, however willing to die; and I now further ordained, that in no case was the practice to be permitted, when compulsion was in the slightest degree employed, whatever might be the opinions of the people. In other respects they were in no way to be molested in the duties of their religion, nor exposed to oppression or violence in any manner whatever. . . .

## THE DUTIES OF THE EMPEROR

. . . It had been made known to me that the roads about Kandahar[16] were grievously infested by the Afghans, who by their vexatious exactions rendered the communications in that quarter extremely unsafe for travelers of every description. . . .

Lushker Khan . . . was despatched by my orders toward Kabul for the purpose of clearing the roads in that direction, which had been rendered unsafe by the outrages of licentious bandits. It so happened that when this commander had nearly reached the point for which he was destined he found opposed to him a body of mountaineers . . . , who had assembled to the number of forty thousand, horse and foot and musketeers, had shut up the approaches against him, and prevented his further advance. . . . A conflict began, which continued . . . from dawn of day until nearly sunset. The enemy were however finally defeated, with the loss of seventeen thousand killed, a number taken prisoners, and a still greater proportion escaping to their hiding-places among the mountains. The prisoners were conducted to my presence yoked together, with the heads of the seventeen thousand slain in the battle suspended from their necks. After some deliberation as to the destiny of these captives, I resolved that their lives should be

---

[15]A woman who burned herself in this way was known as *sati* (Sanskrit for "virtuous woman"). The word *sati* also is used to describe the burning itself.

[16]A city in Afghanistan.

spared, and that they should be employed in bringing forage for my elephants.

. . . The shedding of so much human blood must ever be extremely painful; but until some other resource is discovered, it is unavoidable. Unhappily the functions of government cannot be carried on without severity, and occasional extinction of human life: for without something of the kind, some species of coercion and chas-

tisement, the world would soon exhibit the horrible spectacle of mankind, like wild beasts, worrying each other to death with no other motive than rapacity and revenge. God is witness that there is no repose for crowned heads. There is no pain or anxiety equal to that which attends the possession of sovereign power, for to the possessor there is not in this world a moment's rest. . . .

▼▼▼

# Religion and Society in South and Southwest Asia

Although many major religions — Hinduism, Buddhism, Zoroastrianism, Judaism, Islam, and Christianity — originated in South and Southwest Asia, by the sixteenth century, the region was dominated by two faiths. They were Islam, ascendant everywhere except India, and Hinduism, the Indian subcontinent's ancient religion that endured despite centuries of competition from Buddhism, Jainism, and Islam.

At first glance, one is struck by the many differences between Islam — with its uncompromising monotheism, its reliance on its holy book, the Qur'an, and its origin in the prophecies of a single human being, Muhammad — and Hinduism — with its thousands of gods, its slow and continuous evolution, and its lack of a single creed or holy book. Yet on a deeper level, a fundamental similarity exists in the religions. Both reject any separation between a person's religious and secular life. Islam and Hinduism not only guide each believer's spiritual development but also define that believer's role as a parent, spouse, subject, and man or woman. Secularism as such does not exist in either religious tradition.

Islam originated in the seventh century C.E. and was based on the prophecies of Muhammad (ca. 570–632 C.E.), whose revelations about Allah (Arabic for God) were recorded in Islam's most holy book, the Qur'an. *Islam* in Arabic means "submission," and a Muslim is one who submits to God's will. Islam's basic creed is the statement that every follower must utter daily: "There is no God but God, and Muhammad is the Prophet of God." All Muslims are expected to accept the Qur'an as the word of God, perform works of charity, fast during the holy month of Ramadan, say daily prayers, and, if possible, make a pilgrimage to Mecca, the city on the Arabian peninsula where Muhammad received Allah's revelation. Islam teaches that at death each person will be judged by Allah, with the faithful rewarded by Heaven and the unfaithful damned to an eternity in Hell.

Hinduism, which evolved over many centuries, has no single creed, set of rituals, holy book, or organized church. Unlike Judaism, Christianity, and Islam, which affirm the existence of only one God, Hinduism includes many thousands of deities in its pantheon, although all are believed to be manifestations of the Divine Essence or Absolute Reality, called Brahman. Hindus believe many paths can lead to enlightenment, and Hinduism thus encompasses a wide range of beliefs and rituals.

All Hindus are part of the caste system, a religiously sanctioned order of social relationships that goes back to the beginnings of Indian civilization between 1500 and 1000 B.C.E. A person's caste, into which he or she is born for life, determines social and legal status, restricts marriage partners to other caste members, limits an individual to certain professions, and, in effect, minimizes contacts with members of other castes. The English word *caste* is derived from the Portuguese word *casta,* meaning "pure." Hindus use two different words for caste: *varna* (color) and *jati* (birth). *Varna* refers only to the four most ancient and fundamental social-religious divisions: *Brahmins* (priests and teachers), *Kshatriyas* (warriors, nobles, and rulers), *Vaisyas* (landowners, merchants, and artisans), and *Sudras* (peasants and laborers). Outside the caste system and at the bottom of the Hindu hierarchy are the "untouchables," who are relegated to such despised tasks as gathering manure, sweeping streets, and butchering animals. Each of the four major castes is further divided into *jatis,* local hereditary occupational groups that during the 1500s and 1600s numbered around three thousand.

The caste system is related to belief in the transmigration of souls, or reincarnation. This is the belief that each individual soul, or *atman,* a dislocated piece of the Universal Soul, or Brahman, strives through successive births to reunite with Brahman and win release from the chains of material existence and the cycle of death and rebirth. Reincarnation is based on one's *karma,* the fruit of one's actions, or the soul's destiny, which is decided by how well or poorly a person has conformed to *dharma,* a Hindu concept connected with the caste system. *Dharma* is the duty to be performed by members of each *jati* and *varna.* If a person fulfills his or her *dharma,* in the next incarnation he or she will move up the cosmic ladder, closer to ultimate reunion with the One.

# Sunni versus Shi'ite in the Early Sixteenth Century
▼▼▼

## 24 ▼ *Sultan Selim I,* LETTER TO SHAH ISMAIL OF PERSIA

The following letter, written by the Ottoman Sultan Selim I (r. 1512–1520) to the founder of the Persian Safavid Empire, Ismail I (r. 1501–1524), is an example of the enduring bitterness between Shi'ite and Sunni Muslims. Selim, who in the Ottoman tradition was a Sunni, was deeply disturbed by the emergence of a Shi'ite state in Persia under Ismail. Ismail, believed by his followers to have descended from Ali, the Prophet Muhammad's son-in-law, had many supporters among the Turks of eastern Anatolia and had aided Selim's brother and rival, Ahmed, in the succession conflict following Sultan Bayezid's death in 1512. When Ismail invaded eastern Ottoman territory in 1513, war seemed inevitable. Nonetheless, Selim wrote the following letter to Ismail in early 1514 threatening to destroy him militarily unless he embraced Sunni Islam and relinquished his recent conquests. Ismail did neither, and later in the year, Selim's armies defeated Ismail's forces at the battle of Chaldiran, on the border of the two empires. Despite this loss, Persia remained under Ismail's control and thus committed to Shi'ism. The battle of Chaldiran was only the first act in a long and bitter struggle between the two Islamic empires.

## QUESTIONS FOR ANALYSIS

1. Even though Selim's letter is designed to malign Shi'ism, not define Islam, it contains many references to essential Muslim beliefs. Which ones can you find?
2. What does Selim's letter reveal about the differences between Sunnis and Shi'ites?
3. How does Selim perceive himself within the Islamic world?
4. Selim must have realized that the deeply religious Ismail was unlikely to abandon Shi'ism. Why might he have written the letter, despite the likelihood that its appeal would fall on deaf ears?

The Supreme Being who is at once the sovereign arbiter of the destinies of men and the source of all light and knowledge, declares in the holy book[1] that the true faith is that of the Muslims, and that whoever professes another religion, far from being hearkened to and saved, will on the contrary be cast out among the rejected on the great day of the Last Judgment; He says further, this God of truth, that His designs and decrees are unalterable, that all human acts are perforce reported to Him, and that he who abandons the good way will be condemned to hell-fire and eternal torments. Place yourself, O Prince, among the true believers, those who walk in the path of salvation, and who turn aside with care from vice and infidelity. May the purest and holiest blessings be upon Muhammad, the master of the two worlds, the prince of prophets, as well as upon his descendants and all who follow his Law!

I, sovereign chief of the Ottomans, master of the heroes of the age; . . . I, the exterminator of idolators, destroyer of the enemies of the true faith, the terror of the tyrants and pharaohs of the age; I, before whom proud and unjust kings have humbled themselves, and whose hand breaks the strongest sceptres; I, the great Sultan-Khan, son of Sultan Bayezid-Khan, son of Sultan Muhammad-Khan, son of Sultan Murad-Khan, I address myself graciously to you, Amir Isma'il, chief of the troops of Persia, comparable in tyranny to Sohak and Afrasiab,[2] and predestined to perish . . . in order to make known to you that the works emanating from the Almighty are not the fragile products of caprice or folly, but make up an infinity of mysteries impenetrable to the human mind. The Lord Himself says in his holy book: "We have not created the heavens and the earth in order to play a game" [Qur'an, 21:16]. Man, who is the noblest of the creatures and the summary of the marvels of God, is in consequence on earth the living image of the Creator. It is He who has set up Caliphs[3] on

---

[1]The Qur'an.
[2]Legendary kings of central Asia.

[3]Deputies, or successors, of the Prophet Muhammad who lead the Muslim community on earth.

earth, because, joining faculties of soul with perfection of body, man is the only being who can comprehend the attributes of the divinity and adore its sublime beauties; but he possesses this rare intelligence, he attains this divine knowledge only in our religion and by observing the precepts of the prince of prophets, the Caliph of Caliphs, the right arm of the God of Mercy; it is then only by practicing the true religion that man will prosper in this world and merit eternal life in the other. As to you, Amir Isma'il, such a recompense will not be your lot; because you have denied the sanctity of the divine laws; because you have deserted the path of salvation and the sacred commandments; because you have impaired the purity of the dogmas of Islam; because you have dishonored, soiled, and destroyed the altars of the Lord, usurped the sceptre of the East by unlawful and tyrannical means; because coming forth from the dust, you have raised yourself by odious devices to a place shining with splendor and magnificence; because you have opened to Muslims the gates of tyranny and oppression; because you have joined iniquity, perjury, and blasphemy to your sectarian impiety; because under the cloak of the hypocrite, you have sowed everywhere trouble and sedition; because you have raised the standard of irreligion and heresy; because yielding to the impulse of your evil passions, and giving yourself up without rein to the most infamous disorders, you have dared to throw off the control of Muslim laws and to permit lust and rape, the massacre of the most virtuous and respectable men, the destruction of pulpits and temples, the profanation of tombs, the ill-treatment of the *ulama,* the doctors and amirs[4] descended from the Prophet, the repudiation of the Qur'an, the cursing of the legitimate Caliphs. Now as the first duty of a Muslim and above all of a pious prince is to obey the commandment, "O, you faithful who believe,

be the executors of the decrees of God!" the *ulama* and our doctors have pronounced sentence of death against you, perjurer and blasphemer, and have imposed on every Muslim the sacred obligation to arm in defense of religion and destroy heresy and impiety in your person and that of all your partisans.

Animated by the spirit of this *fetwa,*[5] conforming to the Qur'an, the code of divine laws, and wishing on one side to strengthen Islam, on the other to liberate the lands and peoples who writhe under your yoke, we have resolved to lay aside our imperial robes in order to put on the shield and coat of mail, to raise our ever victorious banner, to assemble our invincible armies, to take up the gauntlet of the avenger, to march with our soldiers, whose sword strikes mortal blows, and whose point will pierce the enemy even to the constellation of Sagittarius. In pursuit of this noble resolution, we have entered upon the campaign, and guided by the hand of the Almighty, we hope soon to strike down your tyrannous arm, blow away the clouds of glory and grandeur which trouble your head and cause your fatal blindness, release from your despotism your trembling subjects, smother you in the end in the very mass of flames which your infernal *jinn*[6] raises everywhere along your passage, accomplishing in this way on you the maxim which says: "He who sows discord can only reap evils and afflictions." However, anxious to conform to the spirit of the law of the Prophet, we come, before commencing war, to set out before you the words of the Qur'an, in place of the sword, and to exhort you to embrace the true faith; this is why we address this letter to you.

We all have a different nature, and the human race resembles mines of gold and silver. Among some, vice is deeply rooted; these are incorrigible, and one could no more draw them to virtue than one could whiten a Negro's skin; among others,

---

[4]*Ulama* were bodies of religious teachers and interpreters of Muslim law; *doctors* here means teachers; *amirs* were military commanders and princes.

[5]Religious decree.
[6]Supernatural spirit.

vice has not become second nature; they retract their errors when they wish, by a serious return, to mortify their senses and repress their passions. The most efficacious means of remedying evil is to search the conscience deeply, to open one's eyes to faults, and to ask pardon of the God of Mercy with true sorrow and repentance. We urge you to look into yourself, to renounce your errors, and to march towards the good with a firm and courageous step; we ask further that you give up possession of the territory violently seized from our state and to which you have only illegitimate pretensions, that you deliver it back into the hands of our lieutenants and officers; and if you value your safety and repose, this should be done without delay.

But if, to your misfortune, you persist in your past conduct, puffed up with the idea of your power and your foolish bravado, you wish to pursue the course of your iniquities, you will see in a few days your plains covered with our tents and inundated with our battalions. Then prodigies of valor will be done, and we shall see the decrees of the Almighty, Who is the God of Armies, and sovereign judge of the actions of men, accomplished. For the rest, victory to him who follows the path of salvation!

# A Muslim's Description of Hindu Beliefs and Practices
▼▼▼

## 25 ▼ Abu'l Fazl, AKBARNAMA

As Akbar, Mughal emperor from 1556 to 1605, extended and strengthened his state, at his side was Abu'l Fazl, his close friend and chief advisor from 1579 until his assassination in 1602. Abu'l Fazl is best known today as the author of the *Akbarnama,* a long laudatory history of Akbar's reign full of information about the emperor's personality and exploits. At the time of Abu'l Fazl's assassination, instigated by the future Emperor Jahangir, his history had covered only the first forty-six years of Akbar's life, but that was enough to ensure his work's standing as one of the masterpieces of Mughal literature.

One reason for the great length of the *Akbarnama* is that in addition to chronicling Akbar's life, it contains numerous descriptions of Indian society such as the passage on Hinduism that follows. Abu'l Fazl, who shared the tolerant religious views of the emperor, was interested in presenting Hinduism favorably to his Islamic readers, many of whom were uncomfortable with the religious freedom Akbar offered his Hindu subjects. Even more disturbing to many Muslims was Akbar's genuine interest not just in Hinduism but also Christianity, Jainism, and Zoroastrianism, religions from which he borrowed to found a new religious cult, *Din Illahi,* or Divine Faith. Abu'l Fazl sought to address concerns of orthodox Muslims that Hindus were guilty of the two greatest sins against the majesty and oneness of God — idolatry (the worship of idols) and polytheism (a belief in many gods). He also explained the religious basis of the Hindu caste system, the rigid hierarchies of which were far removed from the Muslim belief in the equality of all believers before Allah.

## QUESTIONS FOR ANALYSIS

1. How does Abu'l Fazl counter the charge that Hindus are polytheists? Do you find his arguments convincing? Why?
2. How does Abu'l Fazl address the charge that Hindus are idol worshipers?
3. In what ways do caste and karma provide Hindus a moral understanding of the universe?
4. What do the dharmas of the castes reveal about Hindu social values?
5. Where do women fit into the structure of the ladder of reincarnation? What does this suggest about their status in Hindu society?
6. Abu'l Fazl is attempting to make Hinduism more acceptable to Muslims, but this does not necessarily invalidate what he writes. If you accept what he says as basically true, what conclusions can you reach about the ways Hindus perceive and relate to Divine Reality?

They one and all believe in the unity of God, and as to the reverence they pay to images of stone and wood and the like, which simpletons regard as idolatry, it is not so. The writer of these has exhaustively discussed the subject with many enlightened and upright men, and it became evident that these images . . . are fashioned as aids to fix the mind and keep the thoughts from wandering, while the worship of God alone is required as indispensable. In all their ceremonial observances and usage they ever implore the favor of the world-illumining sun and regard the pure essence of the Supreme Being as transcending the idea of power in operation.

Brahma . . . they hold to be the Creator; Vishnu, the Nourisher and Preserver; and Rudra,[1] called also Mahadeva, the Destroyer. Some maintain that God who is without equal, manifested himself under these three divine forms, without thereby sullying the garment of His inviolate sanctity, as the Nazarenes hold of the Messiah.[2] Others assert that these were human creatures exalted to these dignities through perfectness of

worship, probity of thought and righteousness of deed. The godliness and self-discipline of this people is such as is rarely to be found in other lands.

They hold that the world had a beginning, and some are of opinion that it will have an end. . . . They allow of no existence external to God. The world is a delusive appearance, and as a man in sleep sees fanciful shapes, and is affected by a thousand joys and sorrows, so are its seeming realities. . . .

Brahman is the Supreme Being; and is essential existence and wisdom and also bliss. . . .

Since according to their belief, the Supreme Deity can assume an elemental form without defiling the skirt of the robe of omnipotence, they first make various idols of gold and other substances to represent this ideal and gradually withdrawing the mind from this material worship, they become meditatively absorbed in the ocean of His mysterious Being. . . .

They believe that the Supreme Being in the wisdom of His counsel, assumes an elementary form of a special character[3] for the good of the

---

[1]Also known as Shiva.

[2]Abu'l Fazl draws two comparisons here. He compares this Hindu trinity with both the Christian Trinity (three divine and full separate persons in one God) and with the incarnation of Jesus Christ, the Second Person of the Holy

Trinity. His Muslim readers would have known basic Christian beliefs.

[3]That is, the Hindu Supreme Being assumes various bodies. These incarnations are known as *avataras*.

creation, and many of the wisest of the Hindus accept this doctrine. . . .

## CASTE

The Hindu philosophers reckon four states of auspiciousness which they term *varna*. 1. *Brahmin*. 2. *Kshatriya*. 3. *Vaisya*. 4. *Sudra*. Other than these are termed *Mlechchha*.[4] At the creation of the world the first of these classes was produced from the mouth of Brahma, a brief account of whom has already been given: the second, from his arms; the third, from his thigh and the fourth from his feet; the fifth from the cow *Kamadhenu*, the name of Mlechchha being employed to designate them.

The *Brahmins* have six recognized duties. 1. The study of the Vedas[5] and other sciences. 2. The instruction of others (in the sacred texts). 3. The performance of the *Jag*, that is oblation of money and kind to the Devatas.[6] 4. Inciting others to the same. 5. Giving presents. 6. Receiving presents.

Of these six the *Kshatriya* must perform three. 1. Perusing the holy texts. 2. The performance of the Jag. 3. Giving presents. Further they must, 1. Minister to Brahmins. 2. Control the administration of worldly government and receive the reward thereof. 3. Protect religion. 4. Exact fines for delinquency and observe adequate measure therein. 5. Punish in proportion to the offense. 6. Amass wealth and duly expend it. 7. Supervise the management of elephants, horses, and cattle and the functions of ministerial subordinates. 8. Levy war on due occasion. 9. Never ask for alms. 10. Favor the meritorious and the like.

The *Vaisya* also must perform the same three duties of the Brahmin, and in addition must occupy himself in: 1. Service. 2. Agriculture. 3. Trade. 4. The care of cattle. 5. The carrying of loads. . . .

The Sudra is incapable of any other privilege than to serve these three castes, wear their cast-off garments and eat their leavings. He may be a painter, goldsmith, blacksmith, carpenter, and trade in salt, honey, milk, butter-milk, clarified butter and grain.

Those of the fifth class, are reckoned as beyond the pale of religion, like infidels, Jews, and the like.[7] By the inter-marriages of these, sixteen other classes are formed. The son of Brahmin parents is acknowledged as a Brahmin. If the mother be a Kshatriya (the father being a Brahmin), the progeny is called *Murdhavasikta*. If the mother be a Vaisya, the son is named *Ambastha*, and if a Sudra girl, *Nishada*. If the father and mother are both Kshatriya, the progeny is Kshatriya. If the mother be a Brahmin (and the father a Kshatriya), the son is called *Suta*. If the mother be a Vaisya, the son is *Mahisya*. If the mother be a Sudra, the progeny is *Ugra*. If both parents be Vaisya, the progeny is Vaisya. If the mother be a Brahmin (which is illicit), the progeny is *Vaideha* but if she be a Kshatriya, which also is regarded as improper, he is *Magadha*. From the Vaisya by a Sudra mother is produced a *Karana*. When both parents are Sudra, the progeny is Sudra. If the mother be a Brahmin, the progeny is *Chandala*. If she be a Kshatriya, it is called *Chatta*. From a Sudra by a Vaisya girl is produced the *Ayogava*.

In the same way still further ramifications are formed, each with different customs and modes of worship and each with infinite distinctions of habitation, profession, and rank of ancestry that defy computation. . . .

## KARMA

Or the ripening of actions. This is a system of knowledge of an amazing and extraordinary character, in which the learned of Hindustan concur

---

[4]The outcastes of Hindu society.
[5]The four collections of ancient poetry that are essential sacred texts among Hindus.
[6]Hindu deities.

[7]Abu'l Fazl is drawing an analogy for his Muslim readers. Just as Muslims consider all nonbelievers to be outside the community of God, so Hindus regard the Mlechchha as outside their community.

without dissenting opinion. It reveals the particular class of actions performed in a former birth which have occasioned the events that befall men in this present life, and prescribes the special expiation of each sin, one by one. It is of four kinds.

The first kind discloses the particular action which has brought a man into existence in one of the five classes into which mankind is divided, and the action which occasions the assumption of a male or female form. A *Kshatriya* who lives continently, will, in his next birth, be born a *Brahmin*. A *Vaisya* who hazards his transient life to protect a Brahmin, will become a *Kshatriya*. A *Sudra* who lends money without interest and does not defile his tongue by demanding repayment, will be born a *Vaisya*. A *Mlechchha* who serves a *Brahmin* and eats food from his house till his death, will become a *Sudra*. A *Brahmin* who undertakes the profession of a *Kshatriya* will become a *Kshatriya,* and thus a *Kshatriya* will become a *Vaisya,* and a *Vaisya* a *Sudra,* and a *Sudra* a *Mlechchha.* Whosoever accepts in alms . . . the bed on which a man has died[8] . . . will, in the next birth, from a man become a woman. Any woman or *Mlechchha,* who in the temple . . . sees the form of *Narayana,*[9] and worships him with certain incantations, will in the next birth, if a woman, become a man, and if a *Mlechchha,* a *Brahmin. . . .*

The second kind shows the strange effects of actions on health of body and in the production of manifold diseases.

Madness is the punishment of disobedience to father and mother. . . .

Pain in the eyes arises from having looked upon another's wife. . . .

Dumbness is the consequence of killing a sister. . . .

Colic results from having eaten with an impious person or a liar. . . .

Consumption is the punishment of killing a *Brahmin. . . .*

The third kind indicates the class for actions which have caused sterility and names suitable remedies. . . .

A woman who does not menstruate, in a former existence . . . roughly drove away the children of her neighbors who had come as usual to play at her house. . . .

A woman who gives birth to only daughters is thus punished for having contemptuously regarded her husband from pride. . . .

A woman who has given birth to a son that dies and to a daughter that lives, has, in her former existence, taken animal life. Some say that she had killed goats. . . .

The fourth kind treats of riches and poverty, and the like. Whoever distributes alms at auspicious times, as during eclipses of the moon and sun, will become rich and bountiful (in his next existence). Whoso at these times, visits any place of pilgrimage . . . and there dies, will possess great wealth, but will be avaricious and of a surly disposition. Whosoever when hungry and with food before him, hears the supplication of a poor man and bestows it all upon him, will be rich and liberal. But whosoever has been deprived of these three opportunities, will be empty-handed and poor in his present life.

---

[8]An "unclean" object.
[9]The personification of solar and cosmic energy underlying creation.

# Women in Ottoman Society

▼▼▼

## 26 ▼ *Ogier Ghiselin de Busbecq, TURKISH LETTERS*

Many of Muhammad's teachings were favorable to women. He taught the spiritual equality between men and women in God's eyes, and in his own treatment of his wives and daughters he exemplified his teachings about the moral and ethical dimensions of marriage. Women were among his earliest and most important followers and sometimes fought alongside men on the battlefield. For reasons that are not well understood, as Islam expanded and developed, women's position changed markedly. Women, especially from the upper classes, were secluded in their homes and required to wear veils in public. Their role in religious affairs disappeared, and vocational and educational opportunities declined. Some came to believe that Heaven itself was closed to females.

As the Ottomans and other Turkic peoples moved into Southwest Asia and became Muslims, they accepted the norms of the people they encountered in regard to the status of women. To Ogier de Busbecq (1522–1590), the European diplomat who resided in sixteenth-century Istanbul for six years, the role of women was one of many extraordinary aspects of Ottoman culture. (For more on Busbecq, see introduction to source 21.)

---

## QUESTIONS FOR ANALYSIS

1. According to Busbecq, why do the Ottomans practice the seclusion of women?
2. What are the distinctions between a man's lawful wife and his concubines?
3. Busbecq's account reveals that despite policies such as seclusion and the veil, Turkish women were not without rights and authority in certain areas. What were some of these rights and powers?
4. What does the Ottoman custom of divorce reveal about the status of women?
5. As a distinguished diplomat, Busbecq was in a position mainly to observe the practices of well-to-do and privileged families. Do you think that he would have seen similar customs in poor and rural families?

The Turks are the most careful people in the world of the modesty of their wives, and therefore keep them shut up at home and hide them away, so that they scarce see the light of day. But if they have to go into the streets, they are sent out so covered and wrapped up in veils that they seem to those who meet them mere gliding ghosts. They have the means of seeing men through their linen or silken veils, while no part of their own body is exposed to men's view. For it is a received opinion among them, that no woman who is distinguished in the very smallest degree by her figure or youth can be seen by a man without his desiring her, and therefore without her receiving some contamination; and so it is the universal practice to confine the women to the harem. Their brothers are allowed to see them, but not their brothers-in-law. Men of the richer classes, or of higher rank, make it a condition when they marry, that their wives shall never set foot outside the threshold, and that no man or woman shall be admitted to see them for any reason whatever, not even their nearest relations, except their fathers and mothers, who are allowed to pay a visit to their daughters at the Turkish Easter.[1]

On the other hand, if the wife has a father of high rank, or has brought a larger dowry than usual, the husband promises on his part that he will take no concubine, but will keep to her alone. Otherwise, the Turks are not forbidden by any law to have as many concubines as they please in addition to their lawful wives. Between the children of wives and those of concubines there is no distinction, and they are considered to have equal rights. As for concubines they either buy them for themselves or win them in war; when they are tired of them there is nothing to prevent their bringing them to market and selling them; but they are entitled to their freedom if they have

borne children to their master. . . . A wife who has a portion settled on her[2] is mistress of her husband's house, and all the other women have to obey her orders. The husband, however, may choose which of them shall spend the night with him. He makes known his wishes to the wife, and she sends to him the slave he has selected. . . . Only Friday night, which is their Sabbath,[3] is supposed to belong to the wife; and she grumbles if her husband deprives her of it. On all the other nights he may do so as he pleases.

Divorces are granted among them for many reasons which it is easy for the husbands to invent. The divorced wife receives back her dowry, unless the divorce has been caused by some fault on her part. There is more difficulty in a woman's getting a divorce from her husband.

---

[1]Busbecq apparently is referring to the festival of Bairam, which follows Ramadan, the Muslim month of fasting from sunup to sundown. He equated Ramadan with the Christian practice of Lent, so the identification of Bairam with Easter is logical but lacking in theological merit.

[2]Brings a dowry to the marriage.
[3]Like Sundays in Christian lands, Fridays (actually beginning at sunset on Thursdays) in the Muslim world were days of rest, given over to religious acts and rituals.

## The Beginnings of Sikhism in India
▼▼▼

## 27 ▼ Nanak,
### SACRED HYMNS FROM THE ADI-GRANTH

The Mughal emperor Akbar (r. 1556–1605) was not the only person in sixteenth-century India who dreamed of combining elements of Hinduism and Islam into a new religious faith. Such a process was going on during his reign and resulted in the founding of Sikhism, a religion that now has approximately ten million followers, mostly in the northwest Indian state of East Punjab. The founder of Sikhism and its first guru, or teacher, was Nanak, who lived from 1469 to 1539. Born into a Hindu family in modern Pakistan, Nanak as a young man sought out the teaching of Muslim and Hindu mystics and holy men. At the age of thirty he began to wander through India searching for disciples who would accept his message of love and reconciliation between Hindus and Muslims. He taught that external religious acts such as bathing in the sacred Ganges River or making a pilgrimage to Mecca are worthless before God unless inward sincerity and true morality accompany them. As a strict and uncompromising monotheist, he declared that love of God alone is sufficient to free any person of any caste from the law of Karma, bringing an end to the cycle of reincarnation and resulting in the absorption into the One.

The following poems come from the holy book of Sikhism, known as the *Adi-Granth*, or *Granth Sahid*. Compiled by Arjan (1563–1606), the fifth guru, it consists mostly of hymns and poetry composed by Nanak and other early gurus. It attained its final form in 1705–1706, when the tenth and last guru, Gobind Singh (1666-1708), added a number of hymns and declared that from then on the *Adi-Granth* itself, not any individual, was Sikhism's true guru. The following excerpts are taken from poems of Nanak.

## QUESTIONS FOR ANALYSIS

1. What Muslim elements can be found in Nanak's message? What Hindu elements? What Hindu and Muslim practices does he reject?
2. Which religion, Hinduism or Islam, seems to have had the stronger impact on Nanak's religious views?
3. Once Sikhism was established, Hindu and Muslim authorities persecuted it. Why would the Sikhs' religion constitute such a serious threat to both Muslim and Hindu societies?
4. What parallels can you discover between Nanak's message and Martin Luther's (Chapter 1, source 1)? What differences?

There is one God,
Eternal Truth is His Name;
Maker of all things,
Fearing nothing and at enmity with nothing,
Timeless is His Image;
Not begotten, being of His own Being;
By the grace of the Guru, made known to men.

. . .

It is not through thought that He is to be comprehended
Though we strive to grasp Him a hundred thousand times;
Nor by outer silence and long deep meditation
Can the inner silence be reached;
Nor is man's hunger for God appeasable
By piling up world-loads of wealth.
All the innumerable devices of worldly wisdom
Leave a man disappointed; not one avails.
How then shall we know the Truth?
How shall we rend the veils of untruth away?
Abide thou by His Will, and make thine own,
His will, O Nanak, that is written in thy heart.

. . .

He cannot be installed like an idol,
Nor can man shape His likeness.
He made Himself and maintains Himself
On His heights unstained forever;
Honored are they in His shrine
Who meditate upon Him.

. . .

Those who have inner belief in the Name,
Always achieve their own liberation,
Their kith and kin are also saved.
Guided by the light of the Guru
The disciple steers safe himself.
And many more he saves;
Those enriched with inner belief
Do not wander begging.
Such is the power of His stainless Name,
He who truly believes in it, knows it.

. . .

There is no counting men's prayers,
There is no counting their ways of adoration.
Thy lovers, O Lord, are numberless;
Numberless those who read aloud from the Vedas,[1]

---

[1]Basic Hindu texts that originally were sacred books of the Aryans, Sanskrit-speaking invaders from the steppes of western Asia who by 1500 B.C.E. ruled northwest India.

Numberless those Yogis[2] who are detached
from the world;

Numberless are Thy Saints contemplating,
Thy virtues and Thy wisdom;
Numberless are the benevolent, the lovers of
their kind.

Numberless Thy heroes and martyrs[3]
Facing the steel of their enemies;
Numberless those who in silence
Fix their deepest thoughts upon Thee;
. . .

Pilgrimages, penances, compassion and
almsgiving
Bring a little merit, the size of sesame seed.
But he who hears and believes and loves the
Name
Shall bathe and be made clean
In a place of pilgrimage within him.
. . .

When in time, in what age, in what day of the
month or week
In what season and in what month did'st Thou
create the world?
The Pundits[4] do not know or they would have
written it in the Puranas,[5]
The Qazis do not know, or they would have
recorded it in the Qur'an,
Nor do the Yogis know the moment of the day,
Nor the day of the month or the week, nor the
month nor the season.
Only God Who made the world knows when
He made it.
The Vedas proclaim Him,
So do the readers of the Puranas;
The learned speak of Him in many discourses;
Brahma[7] and Indra[8] speak of Him,
Shiva[9] speaks of Him, Siddhas[10] speak of Him,
The Buddhas[11] He has created, proclaim Him.
. . .

Maya, the mythical goddess;[12]
Sprang from the One, and her womb brought
forth
Three acceptable disciples of the One:
Brahma, Vishnu and Shiva.
Brahma, it is said bodies forth the world,
Vishnu it is who sustains it;
Shiva the destroyer, who absorbs,
He controls death and judgment.

God makes them to work as He wills,
He sees them ever, they see Him not;
That of all is the greatest wonder.
. . .

I have described the realm of *dharma*.
Now I shall describe the realm of Knowledge;

How many are the winds, the fires, the waters.
How many are the Krishnas[13] and Shivas,
How many are the Brahmas fashioning the
worlds,
Of many kinds and shapes and colors;
How many worlds, like our own there are,
Where action produces the consequences.

. . . How many adepts, Buddhas and Yogis are
there,
How many goddesses and how many images of
the goddesses;
How many gods and demons and how many
sages;

How many hidden jewels in how many oceans,
How many the sources of life;
How many the modes and diversities of
speech,

How many are the kings, the rulers and the
guides of men;
How many the devoted there are, who pursue
this divine knowledge.
His worshipers are numberless, saith Nanak.

---

[2]Persons with occult powers achieved through discipline
of the body.
[3]Muslim warriors.
[4]Brahmins learned in Hindu religion and law.
[5]A collection of popular Hindu books containing stories of
the gods.
[6]Muslim judges.
[7]The Hindu creator-god.
[8]The war-god of the Aryans and the embodiment of

strength, courage, and leadership; a prominent figure in
the Vedas.
[9]The god of destruction, death, and fertility.
[10]A class of demigods, beings more powerful than mortals
but not divine.
[11]Those who have been enlightened.
[12]A Hindu goddess who symbolizes material creation.
[13]The most popular of the god Vishnu's incarnations.

# Chapter 4

## Continuity and Change in East and Southeast Asia

Important changes took place in East and Southeast Asia during the sixteenth and seventeenth centuries, but in a political and cultural context that remained what it had been for more than a millennium. In terms of size, wealth, population, technology, and military might, China, as it had for centuries, overshadowed the smaller states and nomadic societies that surrounded it. With some justification the Chinese considered their state the "central kingdom" and viewed all other peoples as barbarians. Three neighboring states — Japan, Korea, and Vietnam — had borrowed extensively from the Chinese, but all three maintained their political independence and cultural distinctiveness. Southeast Asia, which includes both the Asian mainland east of India and south of China and also the thousands of islands that today comprise Indonesia and the Philippines, remained an area of small kingdoms, city-states, and stateless societies. The dominance of Islam and Buddhism in the region reflects the many centuries that India, not China, had been the main cultural influence.

Until the sixteenth century direct contacts between these East Asian societies and Europe had been exceptionally rare. True, trade between the two regions had existed for centuries, but it had been carried on by Arab, Indian, and central Asian intermediaries. It is also true that a small number of European missionaries, diplomats, and merchants had taken advantage of Eurasia's relative peace and order under Mongol rule to travel to China in the late thirteenth and early fourteenth centuries. But after the Mongol Empire broke apart around 1350, travel between China and Europe became virtually impossible, and direct contacts between east and west Eurasia ended.

Then, in the early 1500s, the Portuguese began to arrive in the coastal cities of East and Southeast Asia, seeking spices and converts to Christianity. The Spanish, Dutch, and English followed, and in time these Europeans would have an immense impact on the region. Hints of that impact were already evident in the first years of contact. The major port city of Malacca on the Malaysian Peninsula was conquered by the Portuguese in 1511, the Philippines were annexed by the Spaniards in the 1500s, and regions of northwest Java were taken over by the Dutch in the early seventeenth century; Roman Catholic missionaries became active in Japan, the Philippines, and eastern Indonesia; firearms became more available; and existing commercial networks were considerably altered with the arrival of aggressive Portuguese and Dutch traders.

Yet for most of the region the arrival of Europeans was a notable but not decisive event. In sixteenth- and seventeenth-century Japan, for example, the most significant development was the end of civil war and the rise of the Tokugawa shogunate in the early 1600s. Japan's new rulers did all they could to snuff out European influences. Missionaries were expelled, and Christianity was outlawed. Firearms were confiscated, and trade was reduced to the one Dutch ship per year permitted in the port of Nagasaki.

Similarly the Europeans' arrival had no bearing on China's politics. After taking power in 1368, the Ming restored native Chinese rule after a century of Mongol dominance and revived traditional practices such as the civil service examinations that the Mongols had abandoned. In the sixteenth century the quality and effectiveness of Ming rulers deteriorated, and by the early 1600s the Chinese experienced rising taxes, bureaucratic factionalism, neglect of public works, peasant rebellion, and military weakness — indications throughout Chinese history of a dynasty in decline. The last Ming emperor, Sizong, paid the price when a peasant rebellion ended his rule in 1644 and led to the founding of a new foreign dynasty under the Manchus.

The European impact was greatest in Southeast Asia. The decline of Malacca as the region's major commercial center is just one example of how the Portuguese and Dutch disrupted regional trade patterns. Even in Southeast Asia, however, only a small amount of territory came under European political control, and long-established cultural, political, and religious patterns persisted despite the Europeans' arrival.

# Confucianism in China and Japan

No philosopher has influenced the values and behavior of more human beings than the Chinese thinker Kong Fuzi (ca. 551–479 B.C.E.), known in the West by his Latinized name Confucius. Like many other thinkers of his day, Confucius was distressed by the political fragmentation and turbulence that plagued China during the Eastern Zhou Era (771–221 B.C.E.). A scholar intent on pursuing a career in public service, he turned to teaching only after his efforts to achieve a position as a ruler's trusted advisor had failed. He proved to be a gifted teacher, one who is reputed to have had more than three thousand students, some of whom collected his sayings in a book entitled *Lun-yu,* or *Analects.*

Confucius taught that China's troubles were rooted in the failure of its people and leaders to understand and act according to the rules of proper conduct. Proper conduct meant actions conforming to the standards of an idealized Chinese past, when all of China was structured along lines of behavior and authority paralleling those of a harmonious family. Confucius taught that just as fathers, wives, sons, and daughters have specific roles and obligations within families, individuals have roles and obligations in society that depend on age, gender, marital status, ancestry, and social standing. Subjects owed rulers obedience, and rulers were expected to be models of virtue and benevolence. Children owed parents love and reverence, and parents, especially fathers, were expected to be kind and just. Children learned from parents, and subjects from rulers. Confucius also taught that whatever one's status, one must live according to the principles of *jen,* which meant humaneness, benevolence, and love, and *li,* a term that encompasses the concepts of ceremony, propriety, and good manners. Because the wisdom and practices of ancient sages were central to his teaching, Confucius taught that his disciples could achieve virtue only by studying the literature, history, and rituals of the past. Education in traditional values and behavior was the path to sagehood, the quality of knowing what is proper and good and acting accordingly.

Although Confucius' philosophy competed with many other schools of thought in his own time, during the Han Dynasty (206 B.C.E.–220 C.E.) it became the official program of studies for anyone seeking an office in the imperial administration. Mastery of the Confucian Classics and their commentaries was the only path to success on the civil service examinations by which China chose its officials. Although the examination system was abolished by China's Mongol rulers during the Yuan Era (1264–1368), it was revived under the Ming (1368–1644) and continued in use until 1905. For almost two thousand years, China was administered by a literary elite devoted to Confucianism.

Confucianism's influence was not limited to China. Although it had to compete with Buddhism and other indigenous religions, Confucianism deeply affected the thought, politics, and everyday life of Korea, Vietnam, and Japan.

# "Doing Good" in Seventeenth-Century China

▼▼▼

## 28 ▼ *MERITORIOUS DEEDS AT NO COST*

During the sixteenth and seventeenth centuries, interpretations of Confucianism drew mainly on the work of scholars from the Song Era (960–1279 C.E.). Known as Neo-Confucianists, these scholars had brought new energy and rigor to the Confucian tradition after several centuries of stagnation and declining influence. The greatest Neo-Confucianist was Zhu Xi (1130–1200), who presided over a huge project of historical research and wrote detailed commentaries on most of the Confucian Classics. His commentaries came to be viewed as the orthodox version of Confucianism and the official interpretation for evaluating performance on the civil service examinations during the Ming and Qing eras.

Confucian scholarship in the 1500s and 1600s, however, was more than simply rehashing and refining old ideas and formulas. With generous support from the emperor and high officials, Ming scholars completed vast research projects on history, medicine, ethics, and literature. They explored new interpretations of Confucianism that sought to apply the Sage's wisdom to a China experiencing population growth, commercialization, urbanization, and ultimately dynastic decline and foreign conquest. Many endeavored to make Confucianism less elitist and more "popular."

Traditional Confucianism had taught that the qualities of erudition and virtue necessary for true sagehood were theoretically attainable by anyone, but that in reality they could rarely be achieved except by a small number of privileged males who had the wealth, leisure, and intelligence for years of study and self-cultivation. Women, artisans, peasants, and even merchants were capable of understanding and internalizing aspects of Confucian teaching by observing the words and deeds of their superiors, but serious scholarship, true morality, and sagehood were beyond them. At the beginning of the sixteenth century such ideas were challenged by Wang Yangming (1472–1529), a widely published scholar who taught that everyone, regardless of his or her station, was capable of practicing exemplary morality and achieving sagehood. An official as well as a scholar, Wang was also convinced that a healthy Chinese polity depended on effectively teaching sound moral principles to people of all classes.

Wang's ideas were well received in a China where urbanization, increased literacy, and growing wealth were creating a burgeoning demand for books, many of which brought Confucian ideas to the broad reading public. These included summaries of the Confucian Classics, editions of the Classics themselves, manuals to prepare candidates for the civil service examinations, and what were termed "morality books." Morality books, which first appeared in the Song and Yuan eras, discussed good and bad behavior not just for the learned elite but for all classes of people, irrespective of social status, economic position, gender, and formal education. People read these books avidly. With titles such as *A Record of the Practice of Good Deeds* and *Establishing One's Own Destiny,* morality books convinced people that good deeds would be rewarded by worldly success, robust health, many sons, and a long life.

Among the most popular morality books of the era was the anonymous *Meritorious Deeds at No Cost,* which appeared around the middle of the seventeenth century. Unlike other such books, which recommended costly good deeds such as paying for proper family rituals in connection with marriage, coming of age, funerals, and ancestral rites, *Meritorious Deeds at No Cost* discussed laudable acts that required little or no outlay of money. It lists actions considered good for "people in general," but mainly concentrates on good deeds appropriate to specific groups ranging from local gentry and scholars to soldiers and household servants. Its prescriptions provide insights into both basic Confucian values and also contemporary Chinese views of class, family, and gender.

*Meritorious Deeds at No Cost* begins with the "local gentry," a term that refers to individuals who have the rank and status of members of the official class, but who reside at home and may not have any specific political responsibilities. The author discusses the gentry's social responsibilities in the local community, but not their political role in the imperial bureaucracy. The next group, "scholars," refers to individuals at various stages of preparing for the civil service examinations. As educated individuals and potential officials, their status placed them below the gentry but above the common people. The recommended meritorious deeds for this group reveal that many "scholars" were also teachers.

## QUESTIONS FOR ANALYSIS

1. In what ways do the responsibilities of the various groups differ from one another? In what ways do they reflect certain underlying assumptions about what makes a good society?
2. According to this document, what should be the attitude of the upper classes (gentry and scholars) to those below them? Conversely, how should peasants, merchants, and artisans view their social superiors?
3. What views of women and sexuality are stated or implied in this treatise?
4. What views of money and moneymaking are stated or implied in this treatise?
5. According to this treatise, what specific kinds of behaviors and attitudes are components of filial piety?
6. Taking the document as a whole, what conclusions can be drawn about the ultimate purpose or highest good the author hopes to achieve through the various kinds of behaviors he describes?

## LOCAL GENTRY

Take the lead in charitable donations.
Rectify your own conduct and transform the common people.

Make a sincere effort to inform the authorities of what would be beneficial to the people of your locality. . . .
If people have suffered a grave injustice, expose and correct it.

Settle disputes among your neighbors fairly.

When villagers commit misdeeds, admonish them boldly and persuade them to desist.

Do not let yourself be blinded by emotion and personal prejudices.

Be tolerant of the mistakes of others.

Be willing to listen to that which is displeasing to your ears.

Do not make remarks about women's sexiness.

Do not harbor resentment when you are censured.

Protect virtuous people.

Hold up for public admiration women who are faithful to their husbands and children who are obedient to their parents.

Restrain those who are stubborn and unfilial.[1]

Prevent plotting and intrigue.

Endeavor to improve manners and customs. . . .

Prevent the younger members of your family from oppressing others by taking advantage of your position. . . .

Do not be arrogant, because of your own power and wealth, toward relatives who are poor or of low status. . . .

Do not ignore your own relatives and treat others as if they were your kin.

Influence other families to cherish good deeds. . . .

Do not disport yourself with lewd friends. . . .

Do not allow yourself to be overcome by personal feelings and therefore treat others unjustly. . . .

Restrain others from arranging lewd theater performances. . . .

Instruct your children, grandchildren, and nephews to be humane and compassionate toward all and to avoid anger and self-indulgence.

Do not deceive or oppress younger brothers or cousins.

Encourage others to read and study without minding the difficulties.

Urge others to esteem charity and disdain personal gain.

Do not underestimate the value of others [or underpay them]. . . .

Persuade others to settle lawsuits through conciliation.

Try to settle complaints and grievances among others. . . .

Curb the strong and protect the weak.

Show respect to the aged and compassion for the poor.

Do not keep too many concubines.

Do not keep catamites.[2] . . .

## SCHOLARS

Be loyal to the emperor and filial to your parents.

Honor your elder brothers and be faithful to your friends.

Establish yourself in life by cleaving to honor and fidelity.

Instruct the common people in the virtues of loyalty and filial piety.

Respect the writings of sages and worthies.

Be wholehearted in inspiring your students to study. . . .

Try to improve your speech and behavior.

Teach your students also to be mindful of their speech and behavior. . . .

Be patient in educating the younger members of poor families.

If you find yourself with smart boys, teach them sincerity; and with children of the rich and noble, teach them decorum and duty. . . .

Do not speak or write thoughtlessly of what concerns the women's quarters.

Do not expose the private affairs of others or harbor evil suspicions about them.

Do not write or post notices which defame other people.

---

[1]Being disobedient or disrespectful to one's parents.

[2]Boys kept by men for sexual purposes.

Do not write petitions or accusations to higher authorities. . . .

Do not encourage the spread of immoral and lewd novels [by writing, reprinting, expanding, etc.]. . . .

Do not attack or vilify commoners; do not oppress ignorant villagers. . . .

Do not ridicule other people's handwriting. . . .

Make others desist from unfiliality toward their parents or unkindness toward relatives and friends.

Educate the ignorant to show respect to their ancestors and live in harmony with their families. . . .

## PEASANTS

Do not miss the proper time for farm work. . . .

Do not obstruct or cut off paths. Fill up holes that might give trouble to passersby. . . .

Do not steal and sell your master's grain in connivance with his servants.

Do not damage crops in your neighbors' fields by leaving animals to roam at large, relying on your landlord's power and influence to protect you.

Do not encroach [on others' property] beyond the boundaries of your own fields and watercourses, thinking to ingratiate yourself with your landlord. . . .

In plowing, do not infringe on graves or make them hard to find. . . .

Do not damage the crops in neighboring fields out of envy because they are so flourishing.

Do not instigate your landlord to take revenge on a neighbor on the pretext that the neighbor's animals have damaged your crops.

Do not through negligence in your work do damage to the fields of others.

Do not become lazy and cease being conscientious because you think your landlord does not provide enough food and wine or fails to pay you enough.

Fill up holes in graves.

Take good care of others' carts and tools. . . .

Keep carts and cattle from trampling down others' crops.

## CRAFTSMEN

. . . Whenever you make something, try to make it strong and durable.

Do not be resentful toward your master if he fails to provide enough food and drink. . . .

When making things, do not leave them unfinished or rough. . . .

Do not reveal and spread abroad the secrets of your master's house.

Do not make crude imitations.

Finish your work without delay.

In your trade with others, do not practice deceit through forgery.

Do not mix damaged articles with good.

Do not break or damage finished goods.

Do not recklessly indulge in licentiousness.

Do not spoil the clothes of others.

Do not steal the materials of others.

Do not use the materials of others carelessly. . . .

## MERCHANTS

Do not deceive ignorant villagers when fixing the price of goods.

Do not raise the price of fuel and rice too high.

When the poor buy rice, do not give them short measure.

Sell only genuine articles.

Do not use short measure when selling and long measure when buying.

When sick people have urgent need of something, do not raise the price unreasonably.

Do not deceitfully serve unclean dishes or leftover food to customers who are unaware of the fact.

Do not dispossess or deprive others of their business by devious means.

Do not envy the prosperity of others' business and speak ill of them wherever you go.

Be fair in your dealings.

Treat the young and the aged on the same terms as the able-bodied.

When people come in the middle of the night with an urgent need to buy something, do not refuse them on the ground that it is too cold [for you to get up and serve them].

Pawnshops should lend money at low interest.

Give fair value when you exchange silver for copper coins. Especially when changing money for the poor, be generous to them.

When a debtor owes you a small sum but is short of money, have mercy and forget about the difference. Do not bring him to bankruptcy and hatred by refusing to come to terms.

When the poor want to buy such things as mosquito nets, clothing, and quilts, have pity on them and reduce the price. Do not refuse to come to terms.

## PEOPLE IN GENERAL

Do not show anger or worry in your parents' sight.

Accept meekly the reproaches and anger of your parents.

Persuade your parents to correct their mistakes and return to the right path.

Do not divulge your parents' faults to others.

Do not let your parents do heavy work.

Do not be disgusted with your parents' behavior when they are old and sick.

Do not yell at your parents or give them angry looks.

Love your brothers.

Keep close to your relatives.

Be attentive and obedient to the principles of Heaven and the laws of the ruler. . . .

If you are poor, do not entertain thoughts of harming the rich.

If you are rich, do not deceive and cheat the poor. . . .

Do not speak of others' humble ancestry.

Do not talk about the private [women's] quarters of others. [Commentary: When others bring up such things, if they are of the younger generation, reprimand them with straight talk, and if they are older or of the same generation as you, change the subject.] . . .

Respect women's chastity. . . .

Do not instigate quarrels. . . .

Do not stir up your mind with lewd and wanton thoughts.

Do not besmirch others' honor or chastity.

Do not intimidate others to satisfy your own ambition.

Do not assert your own superiority by bringing humiliation upon others. . . .

Do not dwell on others' faults while dilating [expounding at length] on your own virtues.

Try to promote friendly relations among neighbors and relatives. . . .

Do not get angry with household slaves when they give you cause for anger, but instead instruct them with kind words.

Propagate among others the law of moral retribution. . . .

Do not gossip about others' wrongdoing. . . .

Do not be avaricious. . . .

When you hear someone speaking about the failings of others, make him stop.

When you hear a man praising the goodness of others, help him to do so. . . .

When you see a man about to go whoring or gambling, try to dissuade him.

Do not speak deceitful words.

Do not say sharp or cruel things. . . .

Do not deceive cripples, fools, old men, the young, or the sick. . . .

Make peace between husbands and wives who are about to separate.

Do not forget the kindness of others; do not remember the wrongdoing of others. . . .

Show the way to those who have become lost.

Help the blind and disabled to pass over dangerous bridges and roads.

Advise others where a river is shallow or deep to cross.

Cut down thorns by the roadside to keep them from tearing people's clothes. . . .

Put stones in muddy places [to make them passable].

Lay wooden boards where the road is broken off.

At night, light a lamp for others.

Lend rainwear to others in case of rain.

Look after the household slaves lest they suffer from heat or cold, hunger or illness. . . .

Do not let your young children mistreat household slaves.

Do not listen to your wife or concubines if they should encourage you to neglect or abandon your parents. . . .

Do not humiliate or ridicule the aged, the young, or the crippled.

Do not trample down others' crops along the pathways. . . .

Do not say words which are harmful to morals and customs.

Do not stealthily peep at others' womenfolk when they are exposed by a fire in their home. . . .

Do not be impudent toward your superiors.

Do not instigate quarrels among relatives. . . .

Do not sell faithful dogs to dog butchers. . . .

Even if you see that the good sometimes suffer bad fortune and you yourself experience poverty, do not let it discourage you from doing good.

Even if you see bad men prosper, do not lose faith in ultimate recompense.

Never fail to give rice cakes or drugs first of all to your parents and only after that to your children and grandchildren. . . .

In all undertakings, think of others.

# Teaching the Young in Tokugawa Japan
▼▼▼

## 29 ▼ *Kaibara Ekiken,*
## *COMMON SENSE TEACHINGS*
## *FOR JAPANESE CHILDREN*
## *and GREATER LEARNING FOR WOMEN*

Although Chinese Neo-Confucianism had been brought to Japan by Zen Buddhist monks during the fourteenth and fifteenth centuries, it had little influence on Japan's aristocratic ruling class until the Tokugawa Era, when the early shoguns actively supported it. The shoguns were attracted to Confucianism because it emphasized the need for social hierarchy and obedience to the ruler and officials of a centralized state. Hayashi Razan (1583–1657), a leading Confucian scholar, was an advisor of Tokugawa Ieyasu, and the school founded by the Hayashi family at Edo in 1630 with shogunal financial support became the center of Confucian scholarship and education in Japan. Many provincial lords founded similar academies in their domains, and the education samurai received in these schools and from private tutors helped transform Japan's warrior aristocracy into a literate bureaucratic ruling class committed to the ethical values of Confucianism.

Among the Confucian scholars of the early Tokugawa period, few matched the literary output and popularity of Kaibara Ekiken (1630–1714). After studying in Kyoto and Edo, he served the Kuroda lords of the Fukuoka domain in southwestern Japan as physician, tutor, and scholar-in-residence. He wrote more than one hundred works on medicine, botany, philosophy, and education.

This selection draws on material from two of Ekiken's works. The first part is excerpted from his *Common Sense Teachings for Japanese Children,* a manual for tutors of children in aristocratic households. The second part is taken from *Greater Learning for Women,* a discussion of moral precepts for girls. It is thought that this treatise was written in collaboration with Token, Ekiken's wife.

## QUESTIONS FOR ANALYSIS

1. According to *Common Sense Teachings for Japanese Children,* what moral qualities should be inculcated in students?
2. What attitudes toward the lower classes are expressed in these two treatises?
3. How do the goals and purposes of education differ for Japanese boys and girls? How are they similar?
4. What do these treatises say about Japanese marriage customs and family life?
5. How do the attitudes toward women in Ekiken's treatise compare with views of women in sixteenth-century Europe (Chapter 1, sources 6–8) and Ottoman Turkey (Chapter 3, source 26)?
6. What is there in Ekiken's educational treatises that would have furthered the Tokugawa shoguns' ambition to provide Japan with stable and peaceful government?

## COMMON SENSE TEACHINGS FOR JAPANESE CHILDREN

In January when children reach the age of six, teach them numbers one through ten, and the names given to designate 100, 1,000, 10,000 and 100,000,000. Let them know the four directions, East, West, North and South. Assess their native intelligence and differentiate between quick and slow learners. Teach them Japanese pronunciation from the age of six or seven, and let them learn how to write. . . . From this time on, teach them to respect their elders, and let them know the distinctions between the upper and lower classes and between the young and old. Let them learn to use the correct expressions.

When the children reach the age of seven, do not let the boys and girls sit together, nor must you allow them to dine together. . . .

For the eighth year. This is the age when the ancients began studying the book *Little Learning.*[1] Beginning at this time, teach the youngsters etiquette befitting their age, and caution them not to commit an act of impoliteness. Among those which must be taught are: daily deportment, the manners set for appearing before one's senior and withdrawing from his presence, how to speak or respond to one's senior or guest, how to place a serving tray or replace it

---

[1]The *Little Learning* was written in 1187 by the Song scholar Liu Zucheng, a disciple of Zhu Xi. A book of instruction for young children, it contains rules of behavior and excerpts from the Classics and other works.

for one's senior, how to present a wine cup and pour rice wine and to serve side dishes to accompany it, and how to serve tea. Children must also learn how to behave while taking their meals.

Children must be taught by those who are close to them the virtues of filial piety and obedience. To serve the parents well is called filial piety, and to serve one's seniors well is called obedience. The one who lives close to the children and who is able to teach must instruct the children in the early years of their life that the first obligation of a human being is to revere the parents and serve them well. Then comes the next lesson which includes respect for one's seniors, listening to their commands and not holding them in contempt. One's seniors include elder brothers, elder sisters, uncles, aunts, and cousins who are older and worthy of respect. . . . As the children grow older, teach them to love their younger brothers and to be compassionate to the employees and servants. Teach them also the respect due the teachers and the behavior codes governing friends. The etiquette governing each movement toward important guests — such as standing, sitting, advancing forward, and retiring from their presence — and the language to be employed must be taught. Teach them how to pay respect to others according to the social positions held by them. Gradually the ways of filial piety and obedience, loyalty and trustworthiness, right deportment and decorum, and sense of shame must be inculcated in the children's minds and they must know how to implement them. Caution them not to desire the possessions of others, or to stoop below one's dignity in consuming excessive amounts of food and drink. . . .

Once reaching the age of eight, children must follow and never lead their elders when entering a gate, sitting, or eating and drinking. From this time on they must be taught how to become humble and yield to others. Do not permit the children to behave as they please. It is important to caution them against "doing their own things."

At the age of ten, let the children be placed under the guidance of a teacher, and tell them about the general meaning of the five constant virtues and let them understand the way of the five human relationships.[2] Let them read books by the Sage[3] and the wise men of old and cultivate the desire for learning. . . . When not engaged in reading, teach them the literary and military arts. . . .

Fifteen is the age when the ancients began the study of the *Great Learning*.[4] From this time on, concentrate on the learning of a sense of justice and duty. The students must also learn to cultivate their personalities and investigate the way of governing people. . . .

Those who are born in the high-ranking families have the heavy obligations of becoming leaders of the people, of having people entrusted to their care, and of governing them. Therefore, without fail, a teacher must be selected for them when they are still young. They must be taught how to read and be informed of the ways of old, of cultivating their personalities, and of the way of governing people. If they do not learn the way of governing people, they may injure the many people who are entrusted to their care by the Way of Heaven. That will be a serious disaster. . . .

## GREATER LEARNING FOR WOMEN

Seeing that it is a girl's destiny, on reaching womanhood, to go to a new home, and live in submission to her father-in-law, it is even more incumbent upon her than it is on a boy to receive with all reverence her parents' instructions. Should her parents, through their tenderness,

---

[2]The *five virtues* are human heartedness, righteousness, propriety, wisdom, and good faith. The *five relationships* are ruler–subject, father–son, husband–wife, older brother–younger brother, and friend–friend.

[3]In this context, the term *Sage* refers to Confucius.
[4]The *Great Learning*, a chapter taken from the *Record of Rituals*, was one of the four relatively short works that came to be known within the Confucian Classics as the Four Books.

allow her to grow up self-willed, she will infalli-bly show herself capricious in her husband's house, and thus alienate his affection; while, if her father-in-law be a man of correct principles, the girl will find the yoke of these principles intolerable. She will hate and decry her father-in-law, and the end of those domestic dissen-sions will be her dismissal from her husband's house and the covering of herself with ignominy. Her parents, forgetting the faulty education they gave her, may indeed lay all the blame on the father-in-law. But they will be in error; for the whole disaster should rightly be attributed to the faulty education the girl received from her parents.

▾ ▾ ▾

More precious in a woman is a virtuous heart than a face of beauty. The vicious woman's heart is ever excited; she glares wildly around her, she vents her anger on others, her words are harsh and her accent vulgar. When she speaks, it is to set herself above others, to upbraid others, to envy others, to be puffed up with individual pride, to jeer at others, to outdo others — all things at variance with the way in which a woman should walk. The only qualities that befit a woman are gentle obedience, chastity, mercy, and quietness.

▾ ▾ ▾

From her earliest youth a girl should observe the line of demarcation separating women from men. The customs of antiquity did not allow men and women to sit in the same apartment, to keep their wearing apparel in the same place, to bathe in the same place, or to transmit to each other any-thing directly from hand to hand. A woman go-ing out at night must in all cases carry a lighted lamp; and . . . she must observe a certain dis-tance in her relations even with her husband and with her brothers. In our days the women of lower classes, ignoring all rules of this nature, behave disorderly; they contaminate their reputations, bring down reproach upon the head of their parents and brothers, and spend their whole lives

in an unprofitable manner. Is not this truly lamentable?

▾ ▾ ▾

It is the chief duty of a girl living in the parental house to practice filial piety towards her father and mother. But after marriage her duty is to honor her father-in-law and mother-in-law, to honor them beyond her father and mother, to love and reverence them with all ardor, and to tend them with practice of every filial piety. . . . Even if your father-in-law and mother-in-law are inclined to hate and vilify you, do not be angry with them, and murmur not. If you carry piety towards them to its utmost limits, and minister to them in all sincerity, it cannot be but that they will end by becoming friendly to you.

▾ ▾ ▾

The great lifelong duty of a woman is obedience. . . . When the husband issues his instructions, the wife must never disobey them. In a doubtful case, she should inquire of her husband and obe-diently follow his commands. . . .

Should her husband be roused at any time to anger, she must obey him with fear and trem-bling, and not set herself up against him in anger and forwardness. A woman should look upon her husband as if he were Heaven itself, and never weary of thinking how she may yield to her husband and thus escape celestial castigation.

▾ ▾ ▾

Her treatment of her servant girls will require circumspection. Those low-born girls have had no proper education; they are stupid, obstinate, and vulgar in their speech. . . . Again, in her dealings with those lowly people, a woman will find many things to disapprove of. But if she be always reproving and scolding, and spend her time in hustle and anger, her household will be in a continual state of disturbance. When there is real wrongdoing, she should occasionally no-tice it, and point out the path of amendment, while lesser faults should be quietly endured without anger. . . .

# Chinese Merchants in a Confucian World
▼▼▼

## 30 ▼ *Wang Daokun,*
## *THE BIOGRAPHIES OF ZHU JIEFU*
## *AND GENTLEMAN WANG*

The Confucian tradition viewed merchants as a necessary evil and relegated them to the bottom of the social order. They were considered unproductive, lacking in skills and learning, and self-centered in their pursuit of wealth. Their travels kept them away from the ancestral hearth and prevented them from performing their duties to parents and ancestral spirits. Such views permeated the Chinese imperial bureaucracy, comprised of Confucianists who were mostly drawn from the landed gentry. Thus, Chinese commerce grew despite, not because of, the state, which closely regulated trade and often treated merchants capriciously and contemptuously. The merchants themselves were affected by their Confucian environment. Many, for example, based business decisions more on family considerations than the hard-headed pursuit of profit and, once successful, often bought land or even a scholar's degree and abandoned business to escape the onus of a merchant's low status.

Wang Daokun (1525–1593) combined a merchant's background with a Confucian education and a career in the imperial bureaucracy. His father and grandfather were salt merchants, but the gifted Wang passed the civil service examinations while in his twenties and entered government service. He served as governor of several provinces and filled important offices in the upper echelons of the Chinese army. In 1575 he abandoned his career to care for his aged parents. For the rest of his life he occupied himself by writing treatises on subjects that included card playing, drinking games, and sacrifices to ancestral spirits. He also wrote a series of biographies of Ming Era merchants, many of whom combined business success with dedication to Confucian principles. Wang's sketches provide many insights into Confucian ethics and the business climate of late Ming China.

## QUESTIONS FOR ANALYSIS

1. What, according to Wang Daokun, are the virtues of Zhu Jiefu and Gentleman Wang? To what extent do the two merchants represent different virtues?
2. What is the point of the story about Gentleman Wang and Magistrate Xu?
3. What does this source reveal about Chinese attitudes toward the elderly? Toward political authority? Toward wealth? Toward women?
4. What do these biographies reveal about the government's attitudes and policies in regard to merchants? What specific episodes illustrate these attitudes?
5. Do the author's sympathies lie with the merchants or the government officials in their dealings with one another?

## THE BIOGRAPHY OF ZHU JIEFU

Zhu Jiefu . . . started as a Confucian scholar. He was from Tunxi . . . and his father Hsing . . . was a salt merchant who lived away from home at Wulin. Hsing had taken Shaoji of Wulin as his concubine[1] but she was barren. Later, when he returned home for his father-in-law's birthday, his primary wife became pregnant and gave birth to Zhu Jiefu. In his early childhood, Zhu Jiefu lived in Wulin with his father and went to school there. Shaoji, relying on the father's favor, did not treat him as her son. Jiefu, however, served her respectfully and worked diligently in school. At the age of fourteen, he officially registered Wulin as his native place and was designated an official student of that place.[2] Shortly thereafter, his father died at Wulin. His concubine took the money and hid it with some of her mother's relatives and would not return to her husband's hometown. Jiefu wept day and night, saying, "However unworthy I may be, my late father was blameless." Finally the concubine arranged for the funeral and burial of her husband in his hometown. Thus, everything was done properly.

After the funeral, Jiefu was short of funds. Since for generations his family had been in commerce, he decided not to suffer just to preserve his scholar's cap. Therefore he handed in his resignation to the academic officials and devoted himself to the salt business. He thoroughly studied the laws on salt merchandising and was always able to talk about the strengths and weaknesses of the law. . . . Therefore, all the other salt merchants respected him as their leader.

During the Jiaqing period [1522–1567], salt affairs were handled by the Central Law Officer,[3] who increased the taxes suddenly, causing great inconvenience for the merchants. They gathered in Jiefu's house and asked him to serve as their negotiator. Jiefu entered the office and stated the advantages and disadvantages of the new law eloquently in thousands of words. Leaning against his couch, the Central Law Officer listened to Jiefu's argument and finally adopted his suggestion.

At that time, the merchants suffered greatly from two scoundrels who often took them to court in the hopes of getting bribes from them. During tense moments at trials, the merchants usually turned to Jiefu as their spokesman. Being lofty and righteous, he always disclosed the scoundrels' crimes and condemned them. The merchants thus esteemed Jiefu for his virtue and wanted to give him a hundred taels[4] of gold as a birthday present. But he protested: "Even if my acts have not been at the lofty level of a knight-errant, I did not do them for the sake of money." Thus, the merchants respected him even more and no longer talked about giving him money.

When there was a dispute among the merchants which the officials could not resolve, Jiefu could always mediate it immediately. Even when one group would go to his house and demand his compliance with their views, he would still be able to settle the dispute by indirect and gentle persuasion. Hence, people both far and near followed each other, coming to ask him to be their arbitrator. Yet, after settling a dispute, Jiefu would always step aside and never take credit himself.

The populace in Tunxi city where Jiefu lived was militant and litigious. When he returned home for his father's funeral, slanderous rumors were spread about him, but Jiefu humbled himself and never tried to get back at the instigators. Later, when he grew rich rapidly, people became even more critical. Jiefu merely behaved with even greater deference. When the ancestral shrine fell into disrepair, Jiefu on his own sent

---

[1]It was common for men to have concubines, in some cases several of them, in addition to their legal wives. No legal impediments prevented children of concubines from inheriting their father's property.

[2]This meant that Zhu Jiefu was being groomed to take the Chinese civil service examinations for entry into the imperial bureaucracy.

[3]An official of the imperial bureaucracy.

[4]A coin weighing approximately an ounce and a half.

workmen to repair it. When members of his lineage started talking about it, he had the workmen work during the day and consulted with his relatives in the evening. Finally the whole lineage got together and shared the task with him.

Once Jiefu bought a concubine in Wulin who bore a child after only a few months. His family was about to discard the child but Jiefu upbraided them, saying, "I love my children dearly. How could I cause someone else's child to die in the gutter?" He brought the child up and educated him until he was able to support himself. . . .

Jiefu finally discontinued his salt business and ordered his son to pursue a different career. By that time he was already planning to retire to his hometown. Then in 1568 a Central Law Officer who was appointed to inspect the salt business started to encourage secret informants. Soon Jiefu was arrested, an enemy having laid a trap for him. However, the official could not find any evidence against him. But then Ho, whose son Jiefu had once scolded, came forward to testify. Consequently, Jiefu was found guilty. When the litigation against him was completed, he was sentenced to be a frontier guard at Dinghai. The merchants said, in describing Jiefu's case: "Beating the drum, the official seized a lamb and claimed it to be a tiger; pretending to net a big fish, he actually aimed at the big bird."

When Jiefu received his sentence to enter the army, he controlled his feelings and immediately complied. His son, fearing his father would acquire a bad name, suggested that he send a petition to the Emperor. Jiefu merely sighed and said, "Your father must have offended Heaven. The truth is that the Central Law Officer is a representative of his Heavenly Majesty, not that your father is falsely charged."

Frontier General Liu had heard of Jiefu and therefore summoned him to work in his own encampment. At that time, a friend of the General's moved to Xintu upon his retirement. The General sent Jiefu to Xintu as his personal messen-

ger but within a short time Jiefu became seriously ill. He advised his son, Zhengmin: "Your father's name has been recorded in the official labor records. Now he is about to die as a prisoner. Never let your father's example stop you from behaving righteously. Remember this." Then, at the age of sixty-five, he died.

## THE BIOGRAPHY OF GENTLEMAN WANG

. . . Mr. Wang lives in Shanghai. Being open and confident he has attracted the respect of many capable and prosperous people who compete to attach themselves to him. At first, Mr. Wang's capital was no greater than the average person's. Later, as he grew more prosperous every day, the number of his associates also steadily increased. To accommodate his apprentices, Mr. Wang built buildings with doors on four sides. Whenever customers came, they could be taken care of from all four directions; thus, no one ever had to wait very long.

Mr. Wang set up the following guidelines for his associates: do not let anyone who lives in another county control the banking; when lending money, never harass law-abiding people unnecessarily or give them less than they need; charge low interest on loans; do not aim at high profit and do not ask for daily interest. These principles led customers to throng to him, even ones from neighboring towns and provinces. Within a short time, Mr. Wang accumulated great wealth; in fact, of all the rich people in that area he became the richest.

Mr. Wang liked to help people and to give assistance to the poor. If anyone among his kinsmen could not afford a funeral for his parents, Mr. Wang would always buy some land and build a tomb for him. As soon as he heard someone could not make ends meet, he would buy land to rent to him. Whenever he was out traveling and met some unburied spirit, he would bid his servants bury it and present some offerings.

During the Jiaqing period there was a serious drought, and the Prefect[5] proposed opening the granary. Considering the hardship this would cause the people, Mr. Wang sent a written report to the Prefect, as follows:

> This proposal will cause starving people to travel here from hundreds of li[6] away to wait for the distribution. Even if there are no delays on route, they may die before they get here. Yet if we make them stay home and wait for a pint of food, it will be like abandoning them to die in the gutters. I suggest that we exchange the grain for money and distribute it around the area. All the wealthy people ought to donate some money to help the poor. I myself will start with a donation of a hundred taels of gold.

The Prefect accepted his suggestion and everyone said that this was much more convenient. Then Mr. Wang also prepared some food to feed people in his own county and caused similar actions to be taken throughout the whole of Shanghai. Thus most people in this area survived. . . .

Whenever there was a dispute, Mr. Wang could always resolve it immediately, even if it was quite serious. When Magistrate Xu was in charge of Shanghai, he imprisoned someone named Zhu, who died in jail. The victim's father then presented a petition to the Emperor which worried the Magistrate. The officials, el-ders, and local leaders were willing to offer the father a thousand taels of gold on the Magistrate's behalf, but on discussing it, they decided only Mr. Wang could settle the matter, and indeed he persuaded the father to accept the terms. Then the Magistrate was transferred to another position. Upon learning this fact, the officials, elders, and local leaders all quickly dispersed. Mr. Wang sighed and said, "It isn't easy to collect a thousand taels of gold but I will not break the promise made to the Magistrate in trouble." He then paid the thousand taels of gold and the Magistrate was out of his difficulties. Even when Magistrate Xu was dismissed soon thereafter, Mr. Wang did not voice any concern, and after two years Xu returned the thousand taels of gold to him. . . .

When Mr. Wang is at home he is always in high spirits. He likes to make friends with the chivalrous youths. In his later years he has become particularly fond of chess, often staying up all night until he either wins or loses a game. The youths say that Mr. Wang is no ordinary person, that he must have received instruction from Heaven.

Now Mr. Wang is almost one hundred years old. He has at least thirty sons and grandsons living at home with him. It is said, "One who seeks perfection will attain it." This describes Mr. Wang perfectly.

---

[5]Also an official of the imperial bureaucracy.

[6]A Chinese measure of distance, approximately a third of a mile.

# Humanity and Nature in Chinese Painting

▼▼▼

## 31 ▼ *Zhang Hung, LANDSCAPE OF SHIXIE HILL; Sheng Maoye, SCHOLARS GAZING AT A WATERFALL*

Chinese painters over the centuries have produced portraits, religious works, pictures of animals and plants, and courtly scenes, but their greatest contribution to the world's art has been the landscape. Chinese painters began to develop their distinctive approach to landscape painting during the Tang Dynasty (618–907 C.E.) and brought it to fruition in the eleventh century during the era of the Song (960–1279). From then until the twentieth century, the painting of landscapes on silk or paper with ink and muted watercolor shading has inspired China's greatest painters and attracted countless collectors and connoisseurs. The Chinese devotion to landscape painting was closely tied to the philosophies of Daoism and Confucianism, both of which viewed the natural world as a metaphor for the moral and metaphysical order underlying the universe. Thus despite the many different schools and styles of landscape painting, all Chinese landscape painters sought to capture the inner quality, or vital spirit (*qi*), of nature rather than simply to reproduce what the eye perceives. By communicating this inner quality the artist enabled viewers to see how the ever-changing, infinitely variegated phenomena of the visible landscape — wind, rain, mountains, rivers, lakes, trees, storms, mist, and snow — reveal a higher reality that Confucianists called the "supreme ultimate" and Daoists called the "Way."

Ming Era landscape painting was characterized by many different schools and a profusion of individual styles. Some artists considered themselves amateur "scholar painters" while others were viewed as professionals. Some drew inspiration from the masters of the Song Era while others sought to recapture the stylistic qualities of painters during the Yuan Era (1264–1368). Individual artists depicted nature's vital spirit as tranquil, powerful, charming, wild, forbidding, lonely, or cold. Each artist had a distinctive style of brushwork and color.

Because of this diversity of styles, the two paintings included here cannot be considered typical Ming landscapes. But they do capture some of the general characteristics of landscape painting of the period. The first is Zhang Hung's *Landscape of Shixie Hill,* a painting in ink and light colors approximately five feet high and two feet wide. Although Zhang was one of the outstanding painters of the age, little is known about his life other than that he was born in 1577, lived most of his life in Suzhou, and probably died in 1652. The inscription on the upper-right corner of the painting reads, "In early summer of 1613, I traveled to Shixie with my revered older brother Chunyu and painted this for him." One must look closely to see the human beings in the painting. A group of travelers is gathering at the bridge at the bottom of the painting, perhaps planning to walk up the mountain. Farther up the stream one finds four gentleman-scholars gazing at a waterfall, while a Buddhist monk approaches them with tea. Their two servants stand idly by, looking away.

The second painting is *Scholars Gazing at a Waterfall* by Sheng Maoye. Painted on silk in 1630, it is slightly longer and approximately a foot wider than Zhang's painting. Sheng's works are dated from 1594 to 1640, but the dates of the artist's birth and death are unknown. The poetic inscription reads "Pines and rocks are proper to old age; / Wisteria vines do not count the years." As in Zhang's painting, learned scholars contemplate the rushing torrent while their servants look away.

*(See page 134 for Questions for Analysis.)*

*Zhang Hung,* Landscape of Shixie Hill

*Sheng Maoye,* Scholars Gazing at a Waterfall

## QUESTIONS FOR ANALYSIS

1. How would you characterize the "inner spirit" of nature each artist seeks to communicate? How are the two artists' visions similar and different?
2. How are the human beings in each picture interacting with nature?
3. What message does each painting communicate about humanity's relationship to the natural world? Consider both the actions of the human beings in each painting as well as the man-made structures in Zhang's painting.
4. Both paintings show learned scholars contemplating a waterfall, a scene depicted in literally hundreds of Chinese paintings. Why would the contemplation of a waterfall be particularly meaningful?
5. In each painting the scholars' servants are not paying any attention to the waterfall. What message does this communicate?

▼▼▼

# Political Decline and Recovery in China and Japan

Eighteenth-century China and Japan were models of well-governed, prosperous states with enlightened rulers and obedient subjects. This had seemed highly unlikely a century and a half earlier, when both societies faced severe political and social problems. Japan, in the midst of a devastating civil war, seemed on the brink of disintegrating into hundreds of small feuding states. China, meanwhile, was suffering from the incompetent rule of a declining Ming Dynasty.

The incessant civil strife of sixteenth-century Japan was rooted in long-standing tensions inherent in Japan's feudal society. In the 1300s power had begun to shift away from the shogun, a military commander who since the late twelfth century had ruled Japan through his armed retainers in the name of the emperor, to local military families who controlled districts and provinces. With a weakened central government, local wars and feuds became endemic among the *daimyo,* the emerging provincial lords, who enlisted both commoners and *samurai,* lesser members of the nobility, to fight in their armies. The warfare intensified between 1467 and 1568, a period sometimes called the *Warring States* era.

This ruinous feudal anarchy ended as a result of the efforts of three strong military leaders bent on unifying Japan. Oda Nobunaga (1534–1582) abolished the powerless Ashikaga shogunate and brought approximately half of Japan under his rule before a traitorous vassal assassinated him. His successor, Toyotomi Hideyoshi (1536–1598), continued the work of consolidation. It was completed by Tokugawa Ieyasu (1542–1616), who conquered his rivals and had himself declared shogun in 1603. Ieyasu and his successors stabilized Japan by imposing a sociopolitical order that lasted until 1867.

China's problems resulted more from the failure of individual rulers than the defects of a political system. The dedication and competence of Ming rulers suddenly and disastrously declined in the sixteenth century, especially during the interminable reign of the Wanli emperor (1573–1620). So great was the void created by the apathetic late Ming emperors that the efforts of several capable ministers could not save the dynasty. Factional strife, oppressive taxation, corruption, unchecked banditry, and bankruptcy led to rebellion, the dynasty's collapse, and foreign conquest. In 1644 a rebel leader, Li Zicheng (1605–1645), captured Beijing, and in despair the last Ming emperor hanged himself. Within months, however, Li was driven from the city by the Manchus, northern invaders from the region of the Amur River. In the following decades the Manchus extended their authority over all of China, established China's last dynasty, the Qing, and breathed new life into the imperial system.

## Symptoms of Ming Decline
▼▼▼

## 32 ▼ *Yang Lien, MEMORIAL TO EMPEROR MING XIZONG CONCERNING EUNUCH WEI ZHONGXIAN*

The challenges confronting China's late Ming rulers were in most respects no different from those of countless previous emperors and ministers. They had to keep expenditures in line with revenues; defend China's borders; maintain roads, dams, and bridges; make large and small decisions; and carry out the countless tasks that were part of the daily functioning of government. From the 1580s onward, however, emperors either ignored or were distracted from such tasks and failed to deal effectively with new problems such as Manchu pressure in the north, pirate raids, and mounting banditry. Rebellion finally overwhelmed the government and brought about the fall of the Ming in 1644.

The following selection, a memorial directed to the emperor by a high official, Yang Lien, highlights another problem of late Ming government, namely the growing influence of court eunuchs, castrated males whose theoretical purpose was to guard and administer the emperor's harem, but whose functions often extended to other areas of administration and government. Under Emperor Ming Xizong (r. 1620–1627), a young man mainly interested in carpentry, the eunuch Wei Zhongxian (1568–1627), who had served as a butler for the emperor's mother, rose to power in 1623 on the basis of his friendship with the young emperor's former wet nurse. Backed by a small eunuch army in the palace and spies throughout the empire, Wei purged his enemies, levied new taxes, and flouted rules and procedures. He was bitterly opposed by Confucian scholar-officials, especially elite members of the Donglin party, made up of scholar-officials and former office holders connected with the Donglin (Eastern Forest) Academy at Wusih on the lower Yangzi River.

Yang Lien, a member of the Donglin party, submitted the following memorial (memorandum) to the emperor in 1624 in which he described twenty-four crimes of Eunuch Wei. He was carrying out his duties as a member of the Board of Censors, a branch of the imperial administration that served as the "eyes and ears" of the emperor by investigating officials' conduct, hearing subjects' complaints, and reporting problems to the emperor. Emperor Ming Xizong ignored the letter, and in 1625 Yang was accused of treason, tortured, and executed on orders of Wei. Wei himself fell from power in 1627 when the new emperor, Ming Chongzhen (r. 1627–1644) exiled him to the Anhui province, where Wei hanged himself rather than face an offical inquiry into his conduct.

## QUESTIONS FOR ANALYSIS

1. According to Yang, what motivated him to write this memorandum to the emperor?
2. This excerpt contains only a few of Wei's twenty-four alleged "crimes." How many of them can you find in the excerpt?
3. What is it about Wei's actions that particularly violate the Confucian sensibilities of Yang?
4. What does the memorandum reveal about the basis of Wei's authority and political strength?
5. What does the memorandum tell us about the qualities of the Emperor Ming Xizong?

A treacherous eunuch has taken advantage of his position to act as emperor. He has seized control and disrupted the government, deceived the ruler and flouted the law. He recognizes no higher authority, turns his back on the favors the emperor has conferred on him, and interferes with the inherited institutions. I beg Your Majesty to order an investigation so that the dynasty can be saved.

When Emperor Hongwu[1] first established the laws and institutions, eunuchs were not allowed to interfere in any affairs outside the palace; even within it they did nothing more than clean up. Anyone who violated these rules was punished without chance of amnesty, so the eunuchs prudently were cautious and obedient. The succeeding emperors never changed these laws. . . .

How would anyone have expected that, with a wise ruler like Your Majesty on the throne, there would be a chief eunuch like Wei Zhongxian, a man totally uninhibited, who destroys court pre-

cedents, ignores the ruler to pursue his selfish ends, corrupts good people, ruins the emperor's reputation as a Yao or Shun,[2] and brews unimaginable disasters? The entire court has been intimidated. No one dares denounce him by name. My responsibility really is painful. But when I was supervising secretary of the office of scrutiny for war, the previous emperor personally ordered me to help Your Majesty become a ruler like Yao and Shun. I can still hear his words. If today out of fear I also do not speak out, I will be abandoning my determination to be loyal and my responsibility to serve the state. I would also be turning my back on your kindness in bringing me back to office after retirement and would not be able to face the former emperor in Heaven.

I shall list for Your Majesty Zhongxian's twenty-four most heinous crimes. Zhongxian was originally an ordinary, unreliable sort. He had himself castrated in middle age in order to enter the palace. He is illiterate. . . . Your Majesty was impressed by his minor acts of service and

---

[1] The first Ming emperor, who ruled from 1368 to 1398.
[2] Legendary emperors from China's prehistoric past, famous for their virtue and wisdom.

plucked him out of obscurity to confer honors on him. . . .

Our dynastic institutions require that re-scripts[3] be delegated to the grand secretaries. This not only allows for calm deliberation and protects from interference, but it assures that someone takes the responsibility seriously. Since Zhongxian usurped power, he issues the imperial edicts. If he accurately conveys your orders, it is bad enough. If he falsifies them, who can argue with him? Recently, men have been forming groups of three or five to push their ideas in the halls of government, making it as clamorous as a noisy market. Some even go directly into the inner quarters without formal permission. It is possible for a scrap of paper in the middle of the night to kill a person without Your Majesty or the grand secretaries knowing anything of it. The harm this causes is huge. The grand secretaries are so depressed that they ask to quit. Thus Wei Zhongxian destroys the political institutions that had lasted over two hundred years. . . .

One of your concubines, of virtuous and pure character, had gained your favor. Zhongxian was afraid she would expose his illegal behavior, so conspired with his cronies. They said she had a sudden illness to cover up his murdering her. Thus Your Majesty is not able to protect the concubines you favor. . . .

During the forty years that your father the former emperor was heir apparent, Wang An[4] was unique in worrying about all the dangers he faced, protecting him from harm, never giving in to intimidation or temptation. Didn't he deserve some of the credit for your father's getting to the throne? When he died and Your Majesty succeeded, Wang An protected you, so he cannot be called disloyal. Even if he had committed some offense, Your Majesty should have explained what he had done wrong publicly for all to see. Instead Zhongxian, because of his personal hatreds, forged an imperial order and had him killed in Nanhai park. His head and body were sepa-

rated, his flesh given to the dogs and pigs. This not only revealed his enmity toward Wang An, but his enmity toward all the former emperor's old servants, even his old dogs and horses. It showed him to be without the slightest fear. From that time on, which of the eunuchs was willing to be loyal or principled? I do not know how many thousands or hundreds of the rest of the eunuchs, important and unimportant alike, were slaughtered or driven away for no crime. . . .

Doesn't Your Majesty remember the time when Zhongxian, against all rules, rode his horse in the palace grounds? Those who are favored too much become arrogant; those who receive too many favors grow resentful. I heard that this spring when he rode a horse in front of Your Majesty, you shot and killed the horse, but forgave Zhongxian. Despite your generosity, Zhongxian did not beg to die for his offense, but rather acted more arrogantly in Your Majesty's presence and spoke resentfully of Your Majesty when away. He is on guard morning and night, missing nothing. His trusted followers keep guard all the time. In the past traitors and bandits have struggled to wreak havoc and take over. This is in fact what Your Majesty now faces. How can you release a tiger right by your elbow? Even if Zhongxian were cut into mincemeat, it would not atone for his sins. . . .

There is adequate evidence of his crimes. They are widely known and have been widely witnessed; they are not a matter of gossip. Zhongxian, guilty of these twenty-four great crimes, kills or replaces any eunuch he fears will expose his treachery. Thus those close at hand are terrified and keep silent. He expels or imprisons any of the officials he fears will expose his villainy, so the officials also all look the other way and keep silent. There are even ignorant spineless fellows eager to get rich and powerful who attach themselves to him or hang around his gate. They praise whatever he likes and criticize whatever he hates, doing whatever is needed.

---

[3]Official decrees and edicts.

[4]The eunuch Wang An was a supporter of the Donglin party and a bitter opponent of Wei Zhongxian. He was killed on Wei's orders in 1621.

Thus whatever he inside wants they do outside, whatever they outside say he responds to inside. Disaster or good luck can depend on slight movements. And if per chance the evil deeds of the inner court are revealed, there is still Lady Ke[5] to make excuses or cover up.

As a consequence, everyone in the palace recognizes the existence of Zhongxian but not of Your Majesty; everyone in the capital recognizes the existence of Zhongxian but not of Your Majesty. Even the major and minor officials and workers, by turning toward the sources of power, unconsciously show that they do not recognize the existence of Your Majesty, only of Zhongxian. Whenever they see that some matter needs urgent attention or an appointment needs to be made, they always say, "It must be discussed with the eunuch." When a matter cannot be handled or a person appointed, they just explain that the eunuch is not willing. All matters, large and small, in both the palace and the government offices, are decided by Zhongxian alone. . . .

In the tenth year of the first emperor of the dynasty [1377], there was a eunuch who had been in service a long time but carelessly mentioned a governmental matter. The emperor dismissed him that very day and told his officials, "Even though we attribute the fall of the Han and Tang[6] dynasties to the eunuchs, it was the rulers who made it possible by trusting and loving them. If in the past eunuchs had not commanded troops or participated in politics, they would not have been able to cause disorder no matter what they wanted. This eunuch has admittedly served me a long time, but I cannot overlook his mistake.

Getting rid of him decisively will serve as a warning to those to come." How brilliant! A eunuch who mentioned a governmental matter became a warning for the future. What about Zhongxian who deceives his ruler, recognizes no one above him, and piles up crimes? How can he be left unpunished?

I beg Your Majesty to take courage and thunder forth. Take Zhongxian to the ancestral temple in fetters. Assemble the military and civil officials of all ranks and have the judicial officials interrogate him. Check all the precedents from previous reigns on eunuchs having contacts with the outside, usurping imperial authority, breaking dynastic laws, disrupting court business, alienating the people, and violating the trust of the ruler. Sentence him in a way that will please the gods and satisfy public indignation. . . .

If all this is done and yet Heaven does not show its pleasure, the people do not rejoice, and there is not a new era of peace within the country and at its borders, then I ask that you behead me as an offering to Zhongxian. I am well aware that once my words become known, Zhongxian's clique will detest me, but I am not afraid. If I could get rid of the one person Zhongxian and save Your Majesty's reputation as a Yao and Shun, I would fulfill the command of the former emperor and could face the spirits of all ten of the former [Ming] emperors. My lifetime goal has been to serve loyally. I would not regret having to die as a way of paying back the extraordinary favors I have received during two reigns. I hope Your Majesty recognizes my passion and takes prompt action.

---

[5]Lady Ke, who had been the emperor's wet nurse, was instrumental in Wei's rise to power and reputedly his lover.

[6]The Han Dynasty ruled China from 206 B.C.E. to 220 C.E.; the Tang, from 618 to 906.

# The Tokugawa Formula for Japan
▼▼▼

## 33 ▼ *Tokugawa Hidetada,*
## *LAWS GOVERNING THE*
## *MILITARY HOUSEHOLDS*

In 1605, two years after defeating his enemies among the daimyo and becoming shogun, Tokugawa Ieyasu resigned the shogunate and conferred the office on his son, Hidetada, to ensure an orderly succession. Ieyasu, however, continued as *de facto* ruler until his death in 1616. In 1615 he issued under his son's name the following code for Japan's warrior aristocrats. Drawn up with the aid of Confucian scholars, it is a succinct statement of the Tokugawa formula for the social and political ills that had caused Japan's disintegration in the sixteenth century.

## *QUESTIONS FOR ANALYSIS*

1. What provisions of this edict are meant to ensure the shogun's control of the daimyo?
2. Even though the independence of the daimyo was limited by Tokugawa policies, the daimyo still retained certain political powers. How many can be identified in this document?
3. How does the code define the ideal samurai?
4. What sort of social order does the code envision?
5. Where in this document is it possible to detect the influence of Confucian principles?

1. The study of literature and the practice of the military arts, archery and horsemanship, must be cultivated diligently. . . .

From of old the rule has been to practice "the arts of peace on the left hand, and the arts of war on the right"; both must be mastered. Archery and horsemanship are indispensable to military men. Though arms are called instruments of evil, there are times when they must be resorted to. In peacetime we should not be oblivious to the danger of war. Should we not, then, prepare ourselves for it?

2. Drinking parties and wanton revelry should be avoided.

In the codes that have come down to us this kind of dissipation has been severely proscribed.

Sexual indulgence and habitual gambling lead to the downfall of a state.

3. Offenders against the law should not be harbored or hidden in any domain.

Law is the basis of social order. Reason may be violated in the name of the law, but law may not be violated in the name of reason. Those who break the law deserve heavy punishment.

4. Great lords [daimyo], the lesser lords, and officials should immediately expel from their domains any among their retainers or henchmen who have been charged with treason or murder.

Wild and wicked men may become weapons for overturning the state and destroying the people. How can they be allowed to go free?

5. Henceforth no outsider, none but the inhabitants of a particular domain, shall be permitted to reside in that domain.

Each domain has its own ways. If a man discloses the secrets of one's own country to another domain or if the secrets of the other domain are disclosed to one's own, that will sow the seeds of deceit. . . .

6. Whenever it is intended to make repairs on a castle of one of the feudal domains, the [shogunate] should be notified. The construction of any new castles is to be halted and stringently prohibited.

"Big castles are a danger to the state."[1] Walls and moats are the cause of great disorders.

7. Immediate report should be made of innovations which are being planned or of factional conspiracies being formed in neighboring domains.

Men all incline toward partisanship; few are wise and impartial. There are some who refuse to obey their masters, and others who feud with their neighbors.[2] Why, instead of abiding by the established order, do they wantonly embark upon new schemes?

8. Do not enter into marriage privately [i.e., without notifying the shogunate authorities].

Marriage follows the principle of harmony between yin and yang,[3] and must not be entered into lightly. In the *Book of Changes,*[4] . . . it says, "Marriage should not be contracted out of enmity (against another). Marriages intended to effect an alliance with enemies [of the state] will turn out badly." The Peach Blossom ode in *The Book of Poetry* also says that "When men and women are proper in their relationships and marriage is arranged at the correct time; then throughout the land there will be no loose women." To form an alliance by marriage is the root of treason.

9. Visits of the daimyo to the capital are to be in accordance with regulations.

The *Chronicles of Japan, continued*[5] contains a regulation that "Clansmen should not gather together whenever they please, but only when they have to conduct some public business; and also that the number of horsemen serving as an escort in the capital should be limited to twenty. . . ." Daimyo should not be accompanied by a large number of soldiers. Twenty horsemen shall be the maximum escort for daimyo with an income of from one million to two hundred thousand *koku* of rice.[6] For those with an income of one hundred thousand koku or less, the escort should be proportionate to their income. On official missions, however, they may be accompanied by an escort proportionate to their rank.

10. Restrictions on the type and quality of dress to be worn should not be transgressed.

Lord and vassal, superior and inferior, should observe what is proper to their station in life. [Then follows an injunction against the wearing of fine white damask or purple silk by retainers without authorization.]

---

[1]The quotation is a paraphrase from *The Tradition of Tso,* a commentary on *The Spring and Autumn Annals.*

[2]From the Seventeen Article Constitution of Prince Shotuku (573–621). While serving as regent for his aunt, Empress Suiko, the prince drew up seventeen principles of government designed to strengthen central authority and end disorder. He drew heavily on Confucian principles.

[3]*Yin* and *yang* are the two fundamental forces, tendencies, or elements in Chinese philosophy that since ancient times have been used to explain change in natural processes of all sorts. Yin suggests qualities that are female, weak, dark, cold, and connected with the moon; yang suggests qualities that are male, strong, warm, bright, and connected with the sun. Every being and substance contains both elements in varying proportions. As one of the elements increases within a being or substance, the other decreases but is never eliminated.

[4]*The Book of Changes,* a treatise on divination, and *The Book of Poetry,* a collection of songs, are among the oldest Confucian texts.

[5]*Nihongi, The Chronicles of Japan,* written in 720, is the oldest official history of Japan, covering the mythical age of the gods up to the time of the Empress Jito, who reigned from 686 to 697. This quotation comes from a sequel to *The Chronicles* called the *Shoku nihongi.*

[6]One *koku* equals about five bushels; a person's rank was determined by the amount of rice his lands produced.

11. Persons without rank shall not ride in palanquins.[7]

From of old there have been certain families entitled to ride in palanquins without special permission, and others who have received such permission. Recently, however, even the ordinary retainers and henchmen of some families have taken to riding about in palanquins, which is truly the worst sort of presumption. Henceforth permission shall be granted only to the lords of the various domains, their close relatives and ranking officials, medical men and astrologers, those over sixty years of age, and those ill or infirm. In the cases of ordinary household retainers or henchmen who willfully ride in palanquins, their masters shall be held accountable.

Exceptions to this law are the court families, Buddhist prelates, and the clergy in general.

12. The samurai of the various domains shall lead a frugal and simple life.

When the rich make a display of their wealth, the poor are humiliated and envious. Nothing engenders corruption so much as this, and therefore it must be strictly curbed.

13. The lords of the domains should select officials with a capacity for public administration.

Good government depends on getting the right men. Due attention should be given to their merits and faults; rewards and punishments must be properly meted out. If a domain has able men, it flourishes; if it lacks able men it is doomed to perish. This is the clear admonition of the wise men of old.

---

[7]Enclosed carriages, usually for one person, borne on the shoulders of carriers by means of poles.

---

▼▼▼

# Europeans in East and Southeast Asia

The Europeans' early impact on East and Southeast Asia varied from their conquest and domination of the Philippines to their rejection and expulsion from Japan. After several false starts the Spaniards subjugated the major Philippine islands between 1565 and 1571, established a regime modeled on New Spain in the Americas, and undertook the conversion of Filipinos to Catholicism. This was far different from the Europeans' experience in Japan, where their century-long presence as traders and missionaries ended in the 1630s when the shogun expelled all Europeans and decreed that only one Dutch ship a year would be permitted to trade with Japan at the tiny island of Deshima in Nagasaki Harbor. The shogun's seriousness was underscored by the experience of two Portuguese envoys who came to Japan in 1640 to petition for the reopening of trade and were promptly executed.

The rest of the region had experiences that fell somewhere between those of Japan and the Philippines. The Chinese treated the newly arrived Europeans like all other foreigners who sought trade and diplomatic relations with the Central Kingdom. Europeans would have to recognize China's superiority and realize that trade with China could take place only at the pleasure of the emperor and according to his rules. The Portuguese at first had trouble abiding by these rules, so the Chinese expelled them in 1522 and allowed them back only after restricting their commercial activity to the small peninsula of Macao, some seventy miles from Guongzhou. European trade with China continued but did not grow appreciably until the eighteenth century.

A small number of Chinese showed an interest in European culture and were attracted to Christianity. Jesuit fathers, learned in European mathematics and science, were welcomed to the emperor's court as long as they honored Confucius, wore Chinese garb, and assumed an attitude of subservience to the emperor. With their activities tolerated by the emperors, Catholic missionaries managed to convert several hundred thousand Chinese to Christianity by the late 1600s. In the eighteenth century, however, emperors and their officials took umbrage at the refusal of many non-Jesuit clergy to accommodate themselves to Chinese thought and practices. In the 1720s the suppression of Christianity began.

No area had more variety in its dealings with Europeans than Southeast Asia. In Burma, Cambodia, Vietnam, Thailand, and Laos, European impact was limited to small trading posts in no more than a dozen ports and an even smaller number of religious missions. In the so-called Spice Islands of modern Indonesia and in Malaysia, the Portuguese burst on the scene with their conquest of Malacca in 1511 and their establishment of fortified trading posts in other locations. Their thrust into the region soon stalled, however, and their dream of establishing a commercial monopoly was never realized. Their missionary efforts also foundered. Conversions were rare and, paradoxically, Portuguese aggressiveness might have even strengthened Islam, which came to be viewed as a symbol of resistance to the Europeans. The Netherlands, which became the dominant European power in the East Indies during the seventeenth century, established tighter control of the spice trade and displaced native rulers in Java and the Moluccas. But until the end of the 1600s, even the well-organized and single-minded Dutch were simply another new participant in the region's age-old patterns of commercial rivalry and politics.

# The Seclusion of Japan
▼▼▼

## 34 ▾ *Tokugawa Iemitsu,*
## *CLOSED COUNTRY EDICT OF 1635*

For close to a century Japan was the most spectacular European success story in Asia. Portuguese traders and missionaries began visiting Japan regularly in the 1540s, and the Spanish, Dutch, and English soon followed. The Japanese were fascinated by European goods such as eyeglasses and clocks and were quick to appreciate the military potential of European firearms and artillery. Some even adopted European dress. Daimyo on the island of Kyushu in southwestern Japan actively competed for European trade by tolerating the activities of Catholic missionaries and in a few cases converting to Christianity themselves. Oda Nobunaga, the military leader who unified approximately half of Japan in the 1570s and 1580s, encouraged the activities of Catholic missionaries in order to weaken his rivals, the powerful and wealthy Buddhist monasteries. Nobunaga's tolerance of missionary activity led to numerous conversions in the district of Kyoto, Japan's capital city. By the early seventeenth century approximately five hundred thousand Japanese had become Christians.

By then, however, anti-European sentiment was growing. Nobunaga's successor, Hideyoshi, became suspicious of Europeans after the Spaniards conquered the Philippines, and he began to question the loyalty of daimyo who had become Christians. In 1597 he ordered the crucifixion of nine Catholic missionaries and seventeen Japanese converts. The early Tokugawa shoguns, in their single-minded pursuit of stability and order, also feared the subversive potential of Christianity. They quickly moved to obliterate it, even at the expense of isolating Japan and severely limiting commercial contacts with China, Southeast Asia, and Europe.

Japan's isolation policy was fully implemented by Tokugawa Iemitsu, Ieyasu's grandson and shogun from 1623 to 1651. His edicts essentially closed Japan to all foreigners and prevented his subjects from leaving Japan. The following document, the most famous of Iemitsu's exclusion edicts, is directed to the two commissioners of Nagasaki, a port city in southern Japan and a center of Christianity.

## QUESTIONS FOR ANALYSIS

1. What steps are to be taken to suppress Christianity?
2. How are commercial dealings with foreigners to be handled before they are ended altogether?
3. In what ways did the edict affect the shogun's Japanese subjects?
4. Does trade or Christianity seem to have been the greater threat to Japan according to the edict?

1. Japanese ships are strictly forbidden to leave for foreign countries.

2. No Japanese is permitted to go abroad. If there is anyone who attempts to do so secretly, he must be executed. The ship so involved must be impounded and its owner arrested, and the matter must be reported to the higher authority.

3. If any Japanese returns from overseas after residing there, he must be put to death.

4. If there is any place where the teachings of the [Catholic] priests is practiced, the two of you must order a thorough investigation.

5. Any informer revealing the whereabouts of the followers of the priests must be rewarded accordingly. If anyone reveals the whereabouts of a high ranking priest, he must be given one hundred pieces of silver. For those of lower ranks, depending on the deed, the reward must be set accordingly.

6. If a foreign ship has an objection (to the measures adopted) and it becomes necessary to report the matter to Edo,[1] you may ask the Omura[2] domain to provide ships to guard the foreign ship. . . .

7. If there are any Southern Barbarians[3] who propagate the teachings of the priests, or otherwise commit crimes, they may be incarcerated in the prison. . . .

---

[1]Modern Tokyo, the seat of the Tokugawa government.
[2]The area around the city of Nagasaki.

[3]Westerners.

8. All incoming ships must be carefully searched for the followers of the priests.

9. No single trading city shall be permitted to purchase all the merchandise brought by foreign ships.

10. Samurai[4] are not permitted to purchase any goods originating from foreign ships directly from Chinese merchants in Nagasaki.

11. After a list of merchandise brought by foreign ships is sent to Edo, as before you may order that commercial dealings may take place without waiting for a reply from Edo.

12. After settling the price, all white yarns[5] brought by foreign ships shall be allocated to the five trading cities[6] and other quarters as stipulated.

13. After settling the price of white yarns, other merchandise [brought by foreign ships] may be traded freely between the [licensed] dealers. However, in view of the fact that Chinese ships are small and cannot bring large consignments, you may issue orders of sale at your discretion. Additionally, payment for goods purchased must be made within twenty days after the price is set.

14. The date of departure homeward of foreign ships shall not be later than the twentieth day of the ninth month. Any ships arriving in Japan later than usual shall depart within fifty days of their arrival. As to the departure of Chinese ships, you may use your discretion to order their departure after the departure of the Portuguese *galeota*.[7]

15. The goods brought by foreign ships which remained unsold may not be deposited or accepted for deposit.

16. The arrival in Nagasaki of representatives of the five trading cities shall not be later than the fifth day of the seventh month. Anyone arriving later than that date shall lose the quota assigned to his city.

17. Ships arriving in Hirado[8] must sell their raw silk at the price set in Nagasaki, and are not permitted to engage in business transactions until after the price is established in Nagasaki.

---

[4]Members of Japan's military aristocracy.
[5]Raw silk.
[6]The cities of Kyoto, Edo, Osaka, Sakai, and Nagasaki.

[7]A galleon, an ocean-going Portuguese ship.
[8]A small island in southwest Japan, not far from Nagasaki.

# Siamese-Dutch Tensions in the Seventeenth Century
▼▼▼

## 35 ▼ *LETTER TO THE DUTCH EAST INDIA COMPANY BOARD OF DIRECTORS*

The Dutch, having won their political independence from Spain at the close of the sixteenth century, immediately and aggressively entered the competition for profits in Asia. This meant the end of the commercial empire of Portugal, which lacked the wealth and organization to maintain its position against the Dutch East India Company, a joint stock company founded in 1602 and backed by the Dutch government, which had ample capital, military muscle, and a board of directors in Amsterdam (known as "the Seventeen") that controlled its operations. The fall of Malacca to the Dutch in 1641 ended the Portuguese empire in Southeast Asia except on the island of Timor, which the Portuguese held until the twentieth century. The Dutch also took political control of Java and the

Moluccas and defeated or weakened regional challengers such as the kingdom of Acheh.

As the following document shows, however, even with their wealth and organization, the Dutch still needed to cultivate good relations with the region's rulers to be successful. This letter was written by an agent of the Dutch East India Company stationed in Jakarta to the Seventeen in 1655. He expressed his concern about a diplomatic problem with the king of Siam (modern Thailand) and its implications for Dutch trade and prestige. Siam, with its capital to the north of Bangkok in Ayutthaya, was the strongest monarchy in Southeast Asia, with leaders who were skillful in playing off one European power against another. What prompted the letter was Siamese anger over the recent Dutch blockade of Tennasserim, a city in a Siamese vassal state on the Bay of Bengal, and the refusal of the Dutch to help the Siamese king suppress a rebellion in Singgora, another vassal state on the Bay of Siam.

## QUESTIONS FOR ANALYSIS

1. How would you characterize Siamese attitudes toward the Dutch?
2. How did the Dutch resident Westerwolt react when the Siamese court became antagonistic toward the Dutch? What does his behavior reveal about Dutch attitudes toward the Siamese?
3. According to the author and the views of Westerwolt he describes, how might the Dutch be weakened by their disfavor with the king?
4. How in the short run did the Dutch try to solve their problems with the unhappy Siamese king?
5. What does the document reveal about the competition the Dutch were facing from the English in Southeast Asia?

It appears that the merchant Hendrich Craijer Zalr had promised, so they[1] say, 20 ships, which was a very rash proceeding on his part, and thereupon they made the above-mentioned expedition, which they said, if our support did not appear, would be obliged to return unsuccessful and with shame and dishonor to the crown, as was actually the case. Moreover, it happened that a writing had come unexpectedly from the governor of Tennasserim that two Dutch ships had held the harbor there for 2 months, and had prevented the entrance and departure of foreign trad-

ers, which caused great annoyance in Siam, especially at Court, and embittered everyone against us. This gave the Companies[2] very favorable opportunity to blacken us and to make us odious to everyone, and to change the King's feeble opposition into open enmity, the more so since the news has from time to time been confirmed and assured, and no one there doubts it any longer.

Wherefore the resident Westerwolt,[3] who was convinced of the contrary, since he would certainly have been informed before any such action

---

[1] Refers to the Siamese royal court.
[2] The British East India Company; it is unclear why the plural is used.

[3] The resident agent of the Dutch East India Company at the Siamese royal court.

was taken, finally found himself obliged to ask that certain persons, on the King's behalf and on his own, should be deputed and sent overland to Tennasserim, in order to discover on the spot the truth of the case, which request was granted by the King, and on our behalf the junior merchant, Hugo van Crujlenburgh was sent.

Meanwhile the aforementioned resident Westerwolt had on various occasions made complaint of the bad and unreasonable treatment received, but got nothing by it but a summons to court, and before four Ojas or councilors was questioned on certain points to which he had to answer forthwith, and the answer was written down word for word, to be laid before the King, who sat by and waited, and every now and then asked whether one of the questions had yet been put. So that the resident was in very great embarrassment and did not know whether even his life was any longer safe. These questions were for the most part on the subject of the help asked for against Singgora, the Siamese professing to have gone to war with the Spanish on our account, and to have suffered much damage in the same, and that we now refused to assist his Majesty against the rebels with ships and men; whereas the beforementioned merchant, Hendrich Craijer, had definitely made him such promises. Therefore he [the king] had sent his forces to Ligor so as to cooperate with him [Craijer] on his arrival and keep his word: But instead we had sent our ships to Tennasserim and had taken possession of the place in order to keep foreigners away and to ruin their trade. In consequence of this inquiry Westerwolt was inclined to depart from Siam and so make an end of this business, as he had sometimes proposed to do, and as there were two of our ships lying ready at the bar . . . he thought he could initiate and carry his proposal into execution, but was warned that

no living soul would escape the power of the King since he could kill them all and trample them under foot and that his threats [of departing] were not at all to the purpose.

For all which reasons the aforesaid resident could not answer the questions put to him without embarrassment: And nothing followed thereon, except that four or five days later a prohibition was published that, for the future, neither Siamese nor Peguers[4] were to be allowed to serve the Dutch, thus putting great contempt upon the nation. From all which contemptuous proceedings the above-mentioned Westerwolt came to the conclusion that in case the long expected help could not be sent this year we should have trouble in Siam; also that this same year the Japanese cargoes were likely to be unimportant, even if he were allowed to ship and dispatch them. This gave us no small concern, for now, in addition to the war with Portugal, we had come to a rupture with the new government in England,[5] and it still continued impossible for us to spare any force in ships or men for Siam, and it was also inadvisable to continue to keep the King any longer in an uncertain hope, whereby our cause could only be made worse the longer it lasted, since it was quite uncertain whether we in the near future should have the power to help him. Besides it is not the Company's function nor does it agree with its maxims to interpose itself in the wars of foreign potentates over questions and quarrels which do not concern it in the least.

Nevertheless, it was decided and considered necessary to send thither at least one good flyboat[6] to take the cargo for Japan,[7] if it were allowed, or, in case of refusal, to sail to Taiwan, in order to return hither at its proper time with sugar. For which purpose the aforesaid *Crowned Charity* was again employed, departing on the

---

[4]A city in modern Myanmar (Burma), then a vassal state of Siam.

[5]Actually, the first Anglo–Dutch War, fought over English efforts to block Dutch ships from entering English ports, had ended in 1654, but the news seems not to have reached the author.

[6]A small sea-going vessel for carrying cargo.

[7]The Dutch were the only traders allowed in Japan after the Japanese seclusion acts of the 1630s. There was some question in the author's mind about how strictly they were being enforced.

21st May from this roadstead with a letter and a handsome present to the King, also one to the Oja Zebartiban above mentioned, in answer to his [letter] written to us from Ligor: In which we have made known clearly and definitely our inability to send assistance, and that it was impossible to say when it could be sent on account of the wars referred to above. That so his Majesty should therefore no longer wait for it and that we should be freed from the vexations which would otherwise probably be renewed every year. We have also sent on the 5th September the ship *Schiedam* in order that, all being well, it should return hither at once, laden with rice, sapan wood[8] and other necessaries, or if it can get no cargo, to sail to the Moluccas and bring us thence as much pepper as it can take in. . . .

---

[8]A Southeast Asian wood that yields a red dye.

# Part Two

▼▼▼

# *A World of Transformation and Tradition, from the Mid Seventeenth to Early Nineteenth Century*

Two themes — growing tension between innovation and tradition, and greater interaction among human societies — stand out in world history from the mid seventeenth to the early nineteenth century. Neither theme was new. Except for a few rare exceptions, groups of human beings throughout history had interacted with one another through conquest, trade, missionary activity, migration, travel, and the exchange of ideas and technology. In part for this very reason the need to balance the conflicting claims of tradition and innovation had also been a frequent challenge for past societies. But from the mid 1600s to the early 1800s interaction among the world's peoples was increasingly global rather than local or regional, and the forces of change were more profound and intense, more threatening to old ways, and less avoidable.

The conflict between change and tradition was most pronounced in Europe and its offshoots in the Americas. In the realm of ideas, intellectuals abandoned much of the heritage of medieval and Renaissance Europe and formulated views of society, morality, and human nature that were increasingly secular and scientific. In politics, revolutions on both sides of the Atlantic challenged royal authority, aristocratic privilege, and state-controlled churches, and sought a new political order based on popular sovereignty, constitutionalism, legal equality, and freedom. In economics, the Atlantic assumed ever-greater importance in world trade, while in Europe population growth, urbanization, commercial expansion, and greater productivity in agriculture and manufacturing further undermined the traditional feudal-agrarian order. As the century progressed, the mechanization of the English textile and iron industries heralded an even more profound transformation in human affairs, the Industrial Revolution.

The clash between innovation and tradition was not limited to Europe and the Americas, however. In Russia a deep division opened between those who supported the Westernizing efforts of Peter the Great (r. 1682–1725) and Catherine the Great (r. 1762–1796) and those who sought to preserve the essentials of traditional Russian culture and religion. In the Ottoman Empire advocates of military and political reform clashed with religious leaders and defenders of the status quo. In Japan, new intellectual currents, economic growth, and urbanization weakened the foundations of the Tokugawa regime, while in China Manchu rule brought inevitable changes and adjustments.

The subjugation of China by the Manchus, subsequent Chinese expansion into central Asia, and further Russian expansion into Siberia are all examples of growing interaction among the world's peoples through conquest. But the main cause of globalization was Europe's continuing commercial and political expansion. Through migration and internal growth the number of Europeans in the Americas swelled, and in their churches, universities, political institutions, social mores, racial attitudes, and much else, they transplanted European practices and perspectives to the Western Hemisphere. The growing importance of the Americas as a market for European manufactured goods and as a source for agricultural products and raw materials led to increased transatlantic trade, which in the eighteenth century included more than six million Africans who were sold into slavery in the Americas.

Europeans also intensified their involvement in Asia. During the 1600s, the Dutch drove Portuguese traders from Southeast Asia and established political control over the island of Java. By the late eighteenth century the British ruled the Indian state of Bengal, were flooding the Chinese market with opium, and were pressuring the Chinese government to open more ports to foreign trade. Europeans in the late 1700s also began to explore, exploit, and settle New Zealand, Australia, and other islands of the South Pacific, bringing the world's last isolated region into global patterns of political influence, cultural interchange, and commerce. More so than at any time in history, isolation among the world's peoples was melting away.

*Chapter 5*

▼▼▼

# Europe and the Americas in an Age of Science, Economic Growth, and Revolution

On October 24, 1648, the work of hundreds of diplomats and dozens of heads of state finally came to an end when signatures were affixed to the last agreements that collectively make up the Treaty of Westphalia, named after the northwest German territory where negotiations had taken place for the previous six years. With this, one of Europe's most devastating and demoralizing wars, the Thirty Years' War, finally ended. In no small measure because of this war's horrors and destructiveness, this was the last European war in which religious antagonism played a significant role. After a century of attempting to exterminate their religious enemies with armies, the executioner's axe, and instruments of the torture chamber, Europeans came to accept the permanence of Europe's Protestant-Catholic divisions.

Religion was not the only area in which tensions eased in the second half of the seventeenth century. In politics, Louis XIV of France (r. 1643–1715) and his much-imitated residence at Versailles symbolized the continentwide triumph of absolutist monarchs over rebellious nobles and independent-minded cities and provinces. In only a handful of states, including the Netherlands and England, were wealthy landowners and merchants able to strengthen representative assemblies and limit royal authority. In these states too, however, conflicts over fundamental constitutional issues were resolved.

An end of uncertainty also took place in the realm of ideas. The work of Isaac Newton (1642–1727) settled perplexing scientific issues that had emerged in the sixteenth century when Nicholas Copernicus and others revealed the flaws of ancient Greek science but sought in vain for a coherent, all-encompassing model to replace it. Newton's theory of universal gravitation provided such a model. It enabled scientists to understand a host of natural phenomena, including the Earth's tides, the acceleration of falling bodies, and lunar and planetary movement. The broad acceptance of Newton's theories along with advances in mathematics and other branches of science encouraged a belief in the powers of human reason and inspired the secularism of Europe's Age of Enlightenment.

Building on late-seventeenth-century foundations, Europe was more civil, more orderly, and more tranquil in the eighteenth century than it had been in hundreds of years. Wars were fought, but with military discipline tightened, religious tensions eased, and pitched battles rare, none matched the devastation of the Reformation era's religious wars. Steady economic growth, much of it fueled by trade with the Americas, modest inflation, and greater agricultural productivity increased per capita wealth in Europe's expanding population. Peasant revolts and urban violence declined, and old class antagonisms seemed to have abated.

The Atlantic community's outward tranquility was deceptive, however. One does not have to look far below the surface to see tensions that led to anticolonial revolts in the Americas and revolutions in France and other European states at century's end. A host of issues — commercial, political, and ideological — increasingly divided the governments of Spain and Great Britain from colonists across the Atlantic who now considered themselves more American than European. In Europe too discontent was growing. Peasants, who as always were taxed to their limit and beyond, now faced land shortages and higher rents as a result of rural population growth. Artisans felt pinched by decades of gradual inflation. Merchants, manufacturers, lawyers, and other members of the upper middle class prospered, but they resented the nobles' privileges and their rulers' ineptitude.

Their resentment, especially in France, was justified. While promoting themselves as defenders of liberty against royal tyranny, French nobles selfishly protected their privileges and tax exemptions even at the cost of bankrupting the state.

Faced with spiraling deficits, Louis XV (r. 1715–1774) pursued his pleasures, and Louis XVI (r. 1774–1792) embraced then abandoned one solution after another. The intellectual atmosphere of the Age of Enlightenment, which fostered a belief in reason and progress, heightened political expectations, as did recent events in North America, where between 1776 and 1783 the thirteen colonies threw off British rule and established a new government based on constitutionalism and popular sovereignty. The meeting of the moribund French representative assembly, the Estates-General, in May 1789 was the first step toward a revolution in France that reverberated throughout Europe and ultimately affected every corner of the globe.

In England another revolution, an economic revolution, was also underway by century's end. The adoption of new spinning and weaving devices driven by water power and steam was transforming the textile industry, while new methods of smelting and casting brought fundamental changes to the production of iron. As guilds and domestic industry gave way to factory production, output soared, urban populations swelled, and work was redefined. These economic changes, collectively known as the Industrial Revolution, even more than the political revolution in France, reshaped the human condition.

▼▼▼

# Science, Reason, and Progress

A series of remarkable scientific breakthroughs changed European thought during the seventeenth and eighteenth centuries. Science or, as it was known at the time, natural philosophy, was nothing new for Europeans. Medieval and Renaissance scholars had sought to understand the natural world, but their need to make science conform to Catholic theology and their conviction that virtually everything worth knowing in science had already been discovered by the ancients discouraged speculation and hampered new discoveries.

The first major break from ancient science was made by the Polish astronomer Nicholas Copernicus, who, in his *On the Revolutions of the Heavenly Spheres* (1543), theorized that the sun, not the Earth, was the center of the observable universe. By the time of Galileo Galilei (1564–1642), whose discussion of science and religion can be found in Chapter 1, most scientists accepted Copernican heliocentrism, even though it raised perplexing theoretical questions. Most of these questions were answered by Isaac Newton (1642–1727), whose *Mathematical Principles of Natural Philosophy* (1687) explained planetary and earthly motion through the universal law of gravitation. This law stated that every object, large or small, exerts a force on every other object directly proportional to the product of the two masses and inversely proportional to the square of the distance between them. Newton's discoveries provided a coherent alternative to the discredited Greek scientific model and fully revealed the power of a new scientific method based on observation, experiment, and mathematical analysis.

The Scientific Revolution was the major inspiration for the Enlightenment, the dominant intellectual movement of eighteenth-century Europe. Centered in France and led by intellectuals who called themselves *philosophes* (French for philosophers), the Enlightenment popularized and glorified science and proclaimed that human reason could be applied to social, political, and economic problems with results as spectacular as those achieved by Galileo and Newton in their study of nature. Freed from religious opinion and ancient authority, reason, so the philosophes claimed, could expose the weaknesses, errors, flaws, and injustices inherited from the past.

The philosophes were social and political critics, known for their condemnation of their era's legal codes, schools, churches, government policies, slave trade, wars, sexual mores, class privileges, and much else. The Enlightenment was not, however, purely negative. The philosophes rejected passive acceptance of the status quo, and proclaimed that human beings through reason could plot and achieve a better future. They disagreed about what that future would be like, but none doubted that improvement of the human condition was not just possible, but inevitable, if only reason were given freedom to inquire, question, plan, and inspire.

# The Promise of Science
▼▼▼

## 36 ▼ *Francis Bacon, NEW ORGANON*

Along with the Frenchman René Descartes (1596–1650), the English thinker Francis Bacon (1561–1626) was instrumental in formulating the strategies and methods of the new science. Both men rejected the medieval and Renaissance doctrine that scientific truth was attained by the careful study and analysis of authoritative texts from antiquity. Descartes, a superb mathematician and an advocate of the deductive method, stated in his *Discourse on Method* (1637) that humans could find scientific truth by carefully drawing conclusions from a few general, self-evident propositions. Bacon, a proponent of the inductive method, believed that experiment, observation, and the collection of data would reveal nature's laws. In his view, only after scientists had studied many individual phenomena could they generalize about the laws of nature. He also believed that by understanding nature humans would have the power to use and control it for the betterment of their condition.

Bacon's *New Organon* (1620), or "New Method of Inquiry," was meant to replace the "old organon," which refers to the "old method of inquiry" based on the system of logic devised by Aristotle. Written in Latin, and hence directed to a learned audience, *New Organon* consists of 130 aphorisms — concise statements of principles — that summarize Bacon's views on scientific knowledge and its potential.

## QUESTIONS FOR ANALYSIS

1. What does Bacon see as the major impediments to scientific progress?
2. According to Bacon, what are the roles of experiment, mathematics, and technology in scientific generalization?
3. What does Bacon mean when he says that a scientist must be like a bee rather than an ant or a spider?
4. What role in the future of humanity does Bacon see for science?
5. How do Bacon's concerns about potential roadblocks to scientific progress differ from those of Galileo (Chapter 1, source 10)?

1. Man, being the servant and interpreter of Nature, can do and understand so much and so much only as he has observed in fact or in thought of the course of nature: beyond this he neither knows anything nor can do anything.

2. Neither the naked hand nor the understanding left to itself can effect much. It is by instruments and helps that the work is done, which are as much wanted for the understanding as for the hand. And as the instruments of the hand either give motion or guide it, so the instruments of the mind supply either suggestions for the understanding or cautions.

3. Human knowledge and human power meet in one; for where the cause is not known the effect cannot be produced. Nature to be commanded must be obeyed; and that which in contemplation is as the cause is in operation as the rule. . . .

8. Even the works already known are due to chance and experiment rather than to sciences; for the sciences we now possess are merely systems for the peculiar arrangements and setting forth of things already invented; not methods of invention or directions for new works.

9. The cause and root of nearly all evils in the sciences is this — that while we falsely admire and extol the powers of the human mind we neglect to seek for its true helps. . . .

19. There are and can be only two ways of searching into and discovering truth. The one flies from the senses and particulars to the most general axioms, and from these principles, the truth of which it takes for settled and immovable, proceeds to judgment and to the discovery of middle axioms. And this way is now in fashion. The other derives axioms from the senses and particulars, rising by a gradual and unbroken ascent, so that it arrives at the most general axioms last of all. This is the true way, but as yet untried. . . .

22. Both ways set out from the senses and particulars, and rest in the highest generalities; but the difference between them is infinite. For the one just glances at experiment and particulars in passing, the other dwells duly and orderly among them. The one, again, begins at once by establishing certain abstract and useless generalities, the other rises by gradual steps to that which is prior and better known in the order of nature. . . .

31. It is idle to expect any great advancement in science from the superinducing[1] and engrafting of new things upon old. We must begin anew

---

[1]To introduce a concept over and above some already existing concept.

from the very foundations, unless we would revolve for ever in a circle with mean and contemptible progress. . . .

36. One method of delivery alone remains to us; which is simply this: we must lead men to the particulars themselves, and their series and order; while men on their side must force themselves for a while to lay their notions by and begin to familiarize themselves with facts. . . .

95. Those who have handled sciences have been either men of experiment or men of dogmas. The men of experiment are like the ant; they only collect and use: the reasoners resemble spiders, who make cobwebs out of their own substance. But the bee takes a middle course; it gathers its material from the flowers of the garden and of the field, but transforms and digests it by a power of its own. Not unlike this is the true business of philosophy; for it neither relies solely or chiefly on the powers of the mind, nor does it take the matter which it gathers from natural history and mechanical experiments and lay it up in the memory whole, as it finds it; but lays it up in the understanding altered and digested. Therefore from a closer and purer league between these two faculties, the experimental and the rational, (such as has never yet been made) much may be hoped. . . .

108. So much then for the removing of despair and the raising of hope through the dismissal or rectification of the errors of past time. We must now see what else there is to ground hope upon. And this consideration occurs at once — that if many useful discoveries have been made by accident or upon occasion, when men were not seeking for them but were busy about other things; no one can doubt but that when they apply themselves to seek and make this their business, and that too by method and in order and not by desultory impulses, they will discover far more.

109. Another argument of hope may be drawn from this, — that some of the inventions already known are such as before they were discovered it

could hardly have entered any man's head to think of; they would have been simply set aside as impossible. . . .

If, for instance, before the invention of ordnance,[2] a man had described the thing by its effects, and said that there was a new invention, by means of which the strongest towers and walls could be shaken and thrown down at a great distance; men would doubtless have begun to think over all the ways of multiplying the force of catapults and mechanical engines by weights and wheels and such machinery for ramming and projecting; but the notion of a fiery blast suddenly and violently expanding and exploding would hardly have entered into any man's imagination or fancy. . . .

In the same way, if before the discovery of silk, any one had said that there was a kind of thread discovered for the purposes of dress and furniture, which far surpassed the thread of linen or of wool in fineness and at the same time in strength, and also in beauty and softness; men would have begun immediately to think of some silky kind of vegetable, or of the finer hair of some animal, or of the feathers and down of birds; but of a web woven by a tiny worm, and that in such abundance, and renewing itself yearly, they would assuredly never have thought. Nay, if any one had said anything about a worm, he would no doubt have been laughed at as dreaming of a new kind of cobwebs.

So again, if before the discovery of the magnet, any one had said that a certain instrument had been invented by means of which the quarters and points of the heavens could be taken and distinguished with exactness; men would have been carried by their imagination to a variety of conjectures concerning the more exquisite construction of astronomical instruments; but that anything could be discovered agreeing so well in its movements with the heavenly bodies, and yet not a heavenly body itself, but simply a substance of metal or stone, would have been judged altogether incredible. . . .

---

[2]Cannon and artillery.

There is therefore much ground for hoping that there are still laid up in the womb of nature many secrets of excellent use, having no affinity or parallelism with any thing that is now known, but lying entirely out of the common track of our imagination, which have not yet been found out. They too no doubt will some time or other, in the course and revolution of many ages, come to light of themselves, just as the others did; only by the method of which we are now treating they can be speedily and suddenly and simultaneously presented and anticipated.

## Two Images of Seventeenth-Century Science
▼▼▼

### 37 ▼ *Sébastien Le Clerc,*
### *THE ROYAL ACADEMY AND ITS*
### *PROTECTORS and A DISSECTION*
### *AT THE JARDIN DES PLANTES*

The most significant institutional development in Europe's scientific revolution was the foundation of scientific societies, sanctioned and usually supported by royalty, and whose membership included most of the leading scientists of the day. The four most prestigious academies were the Academy of Experiments (f. 1657), located in Florence and supported by Prince Leopold de Medici; the Royal Society of London (f. 1660), licensed but not financially supported by Charles II; the French Royal Academy of Sciences (f. 1661), lavishly supported by Louis XIV; and the Berlin Academy of Sciences (f. 1700), created under the auspices of King Frederick I of Brandenburg-Prussia. Although these academies varied in size and differed in their organization and activities, they all encouraged scientific investigation, rewarded successful researchers, and disseminated their members' observations and discoveries through the publication of books and journals.

Many Europeans were introduced to the ideals and goals of the French Royal Academy of Sciences through the engravings of Sébastien Le Clerc (1637–1714), a gifted artist with a lifelong interest in mathematics and science. He made the engravings for many of the Academy's books and set a new standard for accurate scientific illustration. He also completed a series of engravings depicting the activities of the academicians. These engravings appeared in several of the Academy's publications, with individual copies made for the king, interested courtiers, and collectors. Two of them are reproduced here.

The first, *The Royal Academy and Its Protectors* (1671), centers on Louis XIV, with two high nobles, the Prince of Condé and the Duke of Orléans, to his right and Colbert, the French controller general of finance, to his left. They are surrounded by members of the Academy and their scientific instruments. Through the window is seen a formal garden and the Royal Observatory, which is under construction. The second engraving is titled *A Dissection at the Jardin des Plantes* (1671). At the center two academicians are dissecting a fox, with their observations being recorded by the individual seated to their right. In the foreground Charles Perrault, a member of the Academy, points to a printed book where this

*Sébastien Le Clerc,* The Royal Academy and Its Protectors

*Sébastien Le Clerc*, A Dissection at the Jardin des Plantes

information will be published, and behind the table stands Le Clerc himself, who is displaying a page of his scientific engravings. On the far left two figures are making observations with a magnifying glass and microscope, and on the right stand Colbert and another courtier.

Neither engraving is realistic. Louis XIV did not visit the Academy until 1681, ten years after *The Royal Academy and Its Protectors* was completed. And none of the Academy's rooms would have afforded a window view of the Royal Observatory. Furthermore, the room where dissections were carried out was notoriously rank, probably closer in appearance to a butcher shop than the genteel scene portrayed by Le Clerc. The artist's goal, however, was not to depict the day-to-day reality of the Academy's activities but to communicate an idealized vision of its methods and purposes.

---

### QUESTIONS FOR ANALYSIS

1. How many different pieces of scientific equipment can you identify in the engravings? What does the equipment and other paraphernalia reveal about the scientific interests and methodology of the academicians?
2. What is the significance of the picture toward which Colbert is pointing? What might be the significance of the map that lays on the floor?
3. What point is Le Clerc trying to make about the Academy in the following details from the engraving of the dissection room: the two figures at the window, the figure pointing to the book, and the artist pointing to the page of engravings.
4. Note the formal gardens that can be seen through the windows in both engravings. What attitude toward nature is implied in gardens such as these? How does this view of nature compare with the impression given in the Chinese paintings in source 31?

## An Affirmation of Human Progress
▼▼▼

## 38 ▼ *Marquis de Condorcet,*
## *SKETCH OF THE PROGRESS*
## *OF THE HUMAN MIND*

Throughout history most human beings have valued tradition and resisted change. Reform of governments, religious institutions, and social relationships was deemed possible, but it typically did not mean going forward to institute something new but going back to recapture features of a lost golden age. Serious thinkers who studied the past and contemplated the future concluded that the human condition had always been more or less the same, or that history ran in cycles, or that it was the story of gradual decline from a mythological state of perfection. Only in the West in the eighteenth and nineteenth centuries did intellectuals and much of the general populace come to believe that the past was a burden and that human beings could effect changes in their condition that were beneficial, not destructive. In a word, people began to believe in progress.

The West's belief in progress can be traced back to the eighteenth century when during the Age of Enlightenment many thinkers became convinced that well-intentioned human beings could employ reason to erase at least some of the cruelties, superstitions, and prejudices that diminished the human condition. By the end of the eighteenth century some went further and developed a theory of human progress that saw humanity ascending from ignorance and darkness to a utopian future. The most famous prophet of progress was the Marquis de Condorcet (1743–1794), a mathematician, philosopher, and educational reformer. He supported the French Revolution but, like many moderates, fell afoul of the radical Jacobins and was forced to go into hiding in July 1793. It was then he wrote his *Sketch of the Progress of the Human Mind,* which traces human progress in ten stages from the dawn of history to the French Revolution and into the future. Having completed his work in March 1794, he emerged from hiding, was arrested immediately, and was found dead the next morning of unknown causes.

The following excerpts come from "The Ninth Stage," in which he discusses developments from the mid seventeenth century to the beginning of the French Revolution, and "The Tenth Stage," in which he describes the future.

## QUESTIONS FOR ANALYSIS

1. What factors, according to Condorcet, have impeded progress in the past?
2. According to Condorcet, scientific achievement was the outstanding feature of humanity's "ninth stage." In what ways did science in this era change human thinking and affect human society?
3. Condorcet is not proud of the Europeans' record in dealing with the peoples of Asia, Africa, and the Americas. What groups does he blame for the Europeans' unenlightened behavior in these regions?
4. Why is Condorcet confident that Europeans will modify their behavior in Asia and Africa? What will be the result? Does Condorcet show any interest in preserving the customs and beliefs of the Asians and Africans?
5. What in Condorcet's view caused the oppression of women in the past? Why does he reject such oppression, and what positive results in his view will result from ending it?
6. What role will technology play in humanity's tenth stage? How are Condorcet's views on this issue similar to those expressed by Francis Bacon (source 36)?

## NINTH EPOCH

### *From Descartes to the Formation of the French Republic*

Until now we have demonstrated the progress of philosophy only in those men who have cultivated, deepened, and perfected it: it now remains to reveal what have been its effects on general opinion, and how reason, while ascending at last to a sure method of discovering and recognizing truth, learned how to preserve itself from the errors into which respect for authority and the imagination have often dragged it: at the same time it destroyed within the general mass of people the prejudices that have afflicted and corrupted the human race for so long a time.

Humanity was finally permitted to boldly proclaim the long ignored right to submit every opinion to reason, that is, to utilize the only instrument given to us for grasping and recognizing the truth. Each human learned with a sort of pride that nature had never destined him to believe the word of others. The superstitions of antiquity and the abasement of reason before the madness of supernatural religion disappeared from society just as they had disappeared from philosophy. . . .

If we were to limit ourselves to showing the benefits derived from the immediate applications of the sciences, or in their applications to man-made devices for the well-being of individuals and the prosperity of nations, we would be making known only a slim part of their benefits. The most important, perhaps, is having destroyed prejudices and re-established human intelligence, which until then had been forced to bend down to false instructions instilled in it by absurd beliefs passed on to the children of each generation by the terrors of superstition and the fear of tyranny. . . .

The advances of scientific knowledge are all the more deadly to these errors because they destroy them without appearing to attack them, while lavishing on those who stubbornly defend them the degrading taunt of ignorance. . . .

Finally this progress of scientific knowledge, which neither the passions nor self-interest is going to disturb, results in a belief that not birth, professional status, or social standing gives anyone the right to judge something he does not understand. This unstoppable progress cannot be observed without having enlightened men search unceasingly for ways to make the other branches of learning follow the same path. It offers them at every step a model to follow, according to which they will be able to judge their own efforts and recognize false paths on which they have embarked. It protects them from skepticism, credulity, blind caution, and even exaggerated submission to the knowledgeable and famous. . . .

## TENTH EPOCH

### *The Future Progress of the Human Mind*

Our hopes for the future of the human species may be reduced to three important points: the destruction of inequality among nations; the progress of equality within nations themselves; and finally, the real improvement of humanity. Should not all the nations of the world approach one day the state of civilization reached by the most enlightened peoples such as the French and the Anglo-Americans? Will not the slavery of nations subjected to kings, the barbarity of African tribes, and the ignorance of savages gradually disappear? Are there on the globe countries whose very nature has condemned them never to enjoy liberty and never exercise their reason? . . .

If we cast an eye at the existing state of the globe, we will see right away that in Europe the principles of the French constitution are already those of all enlightened men. We will see that they are too widely disseminated and too openly professed for the efforts of tyrants and priests to prevent them from penetrating into the hovels of their slaves, where they will soon rekindle those embers of good sense and that muffled indignation that the habit of suffering and terror have failed to totally extinguish in the minds of the oppressed. . . .

Can it be doubted that either wisdom or the senseless feuds of the European nations themselves, working with the slow but certain effects of progress in their colonies, will not soon produce the independence of the new world; and that then the European population, spreading rapidly across that immense land, must either civilize or make disappear the savage peoples that now inhabit these vast continents?

If one runs through the history of our undertakings and establishments in Africa and Asia, you will see our commercial monopolies, our treacheries, our bloodthirsty contempt for people of a different color and belief; the insolence of our usurpations; the extravagant missionary activities and intrigues of our priests which destroy their feelings of respect and benevolence that the superiority of our enlightenment and the advantages of our commerce had first obtained. But the moment is approaching, without any doubt, when ceasing to present ourselves to these peoples as tyrants or corrupters, we will become instruments of their improvement and their noble liberators. . . .

---

▷ Slavery will be abolished, free trade established on the world's oceans, and European political authority in Asia and Africa ended.

---

Then the Europeans, limiting themselves to free trade, too knowledgeable of their own rights to show contempt for the rights of others, will respect this independence that until now they have violated with such audacity. Then their settlements, instead of being filled with government favorites by virtue of their rank or privileges who hasten by pillaging and dishonesty to amass fortunes so they can return to Europe to buy honors and titles, will be populated by hard-working men, seeking in these happy climates the affluence that eluded them in their homeland. . . . These settlements of robbers will become colonies of citizens who will plant in

Africa and Asia the principles and the example of European liberty, enlightenment, and reason. In place of clergy who carry to these people nothing but the most shameful superstitions and who disgust them and menace them with a new form of domination, one will see men taking their place who are devoted to spreading among the nations useful truths about their happiness, and explaining to them both the concept of their own interest and of their rights. . . .

Thus the day will come when the sun will shine only on free men born knowing no other master but their reason; where tyrants and their slaves, priests and their ignorant, hypocritical writings will exist only in the history books and theaters; where we will only be occupied with mourning their victims and their dupes; when we will maintain an active vigilance by remembering their horrors; when we will learn to recognize and stifle by the force of reason the first seeds of superstition and tyranny, if ever they dare to appear! . . .

---

▷ Condorcet explains how education and scientific knowledge will be made available to all.

---

If we consider the human creations based on scientific theories, we shall see that their progress can have no limits; that the procedures in constructing them can be improved and simplified just like those of scientific procedures; that new tools, machines, and looms will add every day to the capabilities and skill of humans; they will improve and perfect the precision of their products while decreasing the amount of time and labor needed to produce them. Then the obstacles in the path of this progress will disappear, accidents will be foreseen and prevented, the unhealthful conditions that are due either to the work itself or the climate will be eliminated.

A smaller piece of land will be able to produce commodities of greater usefulness and value than before; greater benefits will be obtained with less waste; the production of the same industrial product will result in less destruction of raw materials and greater durability. We will be able to choose for each type of soil the production of goods that will satisfy the greatest number of wants and with the least amount of labor and expenditure. Thus without any sacrifice, the means of achieving conservation and limiting waste will follow the progress of the art of producing various goods, preparing them, and making them into finished products. Thus . . . each individual will work less but more productively and will be able to better satisfy his needs. . . .

Among the advances of the human mind we should reckon as most important for the general welfare is the complete destruction of those prejudices that have established an inequality of rights between the sexes, an inequality damaging even to the party it favors. One will look in vain for reasons to justify it on the basis of differences in physical make up, the strength of intellect, and moral sensibility. This inequality has no other root cause than the abuse of force, and it is to no purpose to try to excuse it through sophistical arguments. We will show how the abolition of practices condoned by this prejudice will increase the well-being of families and encourage domestic virtues, the prime foundation of all others; how it will favor the progress of education, and especially make it truly universal, partly because it will be extended to both sexes more equitably, and partly because it cannot be truly universal even for males without the co-operation of mothers in families. . . .

Would it not produce what until now has been a dream, namely national manners and customs, gentle and pure, not shaped by prideful displays of asceticism, hypocritical appearances, or modesty inspired by fear of shame or religious terrors, but by freely acquired habits inspired by nature and approved by reason?

The most enlightened people, having seized for themselves the right to control their life and treasure, will slowly come to perceive war as the deadliest plague and the most monstrous of crimes. . . . They will understand that they cannot become conquerors without losing their liberty; that perpetual alliances are the only way to

preserve independence; and that they should seek their security not power. . . .

We may conclude then that the perfectibility of humanity is indefinite. However, until now, we have imagined humanity with the same natural abilities and physical make-up as at the present. How great will our certitude be, and how limitless our hopes, if one were to believe that these natural abilities themselves, this physical make-up, are also capable of improvement? This is the last question we shall consider.

The organic perfectibility or degeneration of species of plants and animals may be regarded as one of the general laws of nature. This law is also applicable to the human species. No one can doubt that progress in preventive medicine, the use of healthier food and housing, a way of living that increases strength through exercise without destroying it through excess, and finally, the destruction of the two most persistent causes of deterioration, poverty and excessive wealth, will lengthen for human beings the average life span and assure more good health and a stronger constitution. Clearly, improvements in medical practices resulting from the progress of reason and the order of society, will cause transmittable and contagious diseases to disappear as well as diseases caused by climate, nourishment, and certain vocations. . . . Would it be absurd then to imagine . . . that we will arrive at a time when death will be nothing more than the result of extraordinary accidents or of the gradual destruction of vital forces, and that as a result, the interval between birth and the time of that destruction will no longer have a fixed term? . . .

Finally, can we not also extend the same hopes to the intellectual and moral faculties? . . . Is it not also probable that education, while perfecting these qualities, will also influence, modify, and improve that bodily nature itself? Analogy, analysis of the development of human faculties, and even certain facts seem to prove the reality of such conjectures, which extend even further the limits of our hopes. . . .

How much does this picture of the human species, freed of all chains, released from the empire of blind fate and the enemies of progress, and marching with a firm and sure pace on the path of truth, virtue, and honor, present the philosopher with a scene that consoles him for the errors, crimes, and injustices that still defile the earth and often victimize him? In contemplation of this scene he receives the reward for his efforts on behalf of the advance of reason and the defense of liberty. . . . Such contemplation is a place of refuge where the memories of his persecutors cannot follow him, where living with the thought of humans established in their natural rights and dignity, he forgets the way greed, fear, and envy have tormented and corrupted them. It is there he truly exists with his fellow humans in an Elysium[1] which his reason has created and which his love of humanity adorns with the purest pleasures.

---

[1]In Greek mythology, Elysium, also known as the Elysian Fields or the Isles of the Blessed, was the dwelling place after death of virtuous mortals or those given immortality by divine favor.

▼▼▼

# From Mercantilism to Laissez Faire

During the seventeenth and eighteenth centuries, European governments pursued a policy known as *mercantilism,* a system of economic regulation designed to strengthen the state and increase its gold and silver supply by encouraging industry, the growth of commerce, and self-sufficiency in agriculture and the production of raw materials. Although Europe's national and local governments had regulated economic activities since the Middle Ages, mercantilism was a new approach to regulation that reflected the growing competitiveness of the European state system and the authority of the absolutist state. Mercantilists viewed economic activity as a form of warfare in which each nation competed for economic advantages that would increase tax revenue, add to its hoard of gold and silver, maintain high employment, and sustain a favorable balance of trade, all at the expense of its rivals. On balance, its early impact was positive, with government encouragement of commerce and protection of industries contributing to Europe's economic expansion.

By the eighteenth century, however, mercantilism had many critics who argued that it inflated prices, stifled innovation, and smothered the entrepreneurial spirit. In addition, mercantilism was opposed by many intellectuals connected with the Enlightenment who prized individual liberty, deplored government intrusiveness, and were convinced that a nation's economy, like nature itself, worked best when its own "natural laws" operated without interference. The critics of mercantilism in France were known as *Physiocrats,* a term rooted in the Greek words meaning the "rule of nature."

The most famous critic of mercantilism was a Scot, Adam Smith, whose *Wealth of Nations* (1776) called for free trade and economic competition at every level. His disciples, the economic liberals of the nineteenth century, convinced governments to abandon a good part of old-style mercantilism, enabling thousands of investors and entrepreneurs to take advantage of the unparalleled opportunities provided by industrialization.

# The Advantages of Mercantilism
▼▼▼

## 39 ▼ Jean-Baptiste Colbert, *"MEMORANDUM ON ENGLISH ALLIANCES" and "MEMORANDUM TO THE KING ON FINANCES"*

Born to a family of merchants in Reims in 1619, Jean-Baptiste Colbert was the best known and most powerful minister of Louis XIV (r. 1643–1715). During the 1660s Colbert held several positions in the royal administration, the most important of which was controller general of finance. Colbert's goal was to strengthen the French economy to provide Louis the resources necessary to fight his wars. No statesman better represents the policies of seventeenth-century mercantilism; for the French, the words *mercantilisme* and *Colbertisme* are virtually synonymous.

## QUESTIONS FOR ANALYSIS

1. Why does Colbert feel that French commercial expansion can come only at the expense of France's competitors?
2. How much does the economic welfare of the French people figure in Colbert's plans and strategies?
3. Who among the French people will benefit from and who will be harmed by mercantilism? In what ways?
4. What types of industries is Colbert especially interested in supporting? What do they reveal about the overall purposes of mercantilism?
5. Drawing on Colbert's memoranda and the biographies of Ming merchants in Chapter 4 (source 30), what comparisons can you make between the attitudes toward merchants on the part of the seventeenth-century French government and the sixteenth-century Chinese government?

## MEMORANDUM ON ENGLISH ALLIANCES (1669)

The commerce of all Europe is carried on by ships of every size to the number of 20,000, and it is perfectly obvious that this number cannot be increased, because the number of people in all states remains the same and the consumption of goods also remains the same. . . .

It must be added that commerce causes a per-petual combat both in peacetime and during war among the nations of Europe as to who will win the most of it. . . . Each nation works incessantly to have its legitimate share of it and to gain an advantage over other nations. The Dutch currently are fighting this war with 15,000 to 16,000 ships, a government of merchants, all of whose principles and power are directed solely toward preservation and increase of their commerce, and more dedication, hard work, and thrift than any other nation.

The English fight with 3,000 to 4,000 vessels, less industriousness and attention, and more expenses. The French fight with 500 to 600 ships. The last two cannot improve their commerce except by increasing their number of vessels, and cannot increase this number except from the 20,000 that carry all the commerce, and consequently by cutting into the 15,000 or 16,000 of the Dutch.

## MEMORANDUM TO THE KING ON FINANCES (1670)

. . . The well-being and economic recovery of the people depend on apportioning what they pay into the public treasury with the amount of money that circulates in commerce. This ratio has always been 150 million livres[1] to 45 million livres. At present it is at 120 million to 70 million. As a result, it is in excess by a wide margin, and as would be expected, the people are falling into great misery.

It will be necessary to do one of two things to stop this evil: either lower tax impositions and expenditures, or increase the amount of money in public commerce. For the first, impositions have been lowered already. . . . For the second, it consists of three parts: increase money in public commerce by attracting it from other lands; by keeping it inside the kingdom and keeping it from leaving; by giving the people the means to make a profit.

In these points consist the greatness and the power of the state and the magnificence of the king, . . . and this magnificence is all the greater in that it weakens at the same time all the neighboring states, because, there being only a given quantity of money circulating in all of Europe, and this quantity is increased from time to time by what comes in from the West Indies, it is certain and clear if there is only 150,000,000 livres that circulate publicly in France, that one cannot succeed in increasing it by 20,000,000, 30,000,000 or even 50,000,000 without at the same time taking the same quantity from neighboring states; which is the cause of the double success of the past few years, the one increasing the power and greatness of your majesty, the other abasing that of his enemies and those who are jealous of him.

Thus in these three areas was concentrated all the work and attention to finances since the beginning of your majesty's administration; and since it is commerce alone and what depends on it that can produce such a great result, it was a task to introduce it into the realm because neither the general population nor individuals have applied themselves to it, and in a way it is even contrary to the genius of the nation. . . . For this, it was necessary to see what was done to attract money into the kingdom and to keep it there; . . .

The Dutch, English, and other nations take from the kingdom wine, brandy, vinegars, linen, paper, articles of clothing, and wheat when needed. . . . But they brought us woolen cloth and other goods made of wool and animal hair; sugar, tobacco, and indigo from the Americas; all the spices, drugs, [illegible word] in oils, silks, cotton cloths, leather goods, and an infinity of other goods from the East Indies; the same merchandise from the Levant.[2] . . . All the merchandise necessary for ship construction, such as wood, masts, iron from Sweden and Galicia,[3] copper, tar, cannons, hemp, rope, tin coated sheet iron, brass, navigation instruments, musket balls, iron anchors, and generally everything necessary for the construction of vessels for the fleet for the king and for his subjects.

Gunpowder, fuses, muskets, cannon shot, lead, pewter, clothes, serge[4] from London, silk and wool stockings from London, barracans, damask,

---

[1]The livre was the basic unit of French money.
[2]The eastern Mediterranean.
[3]A region of east central Europe then part of the Austrian Hapsburg Empire, today divided between Poland and Ukraine.

[4]Serge is a fabric, as are barracan, damask, camlet, dimities, and twills, all mentioned later in Colbert's memorandum.

camlet, and other fabrics from Flanders, lacework from Venice and Holland, trimming from Flanders, camlet from Brussels, carpets of Flanders; beef and mutton from Germany, hides and horses from every land, silk fabrics from Milan, Genoa, and Holland. . . .

By these means and an infinity of others that would be too long to enumerate, the Dutch, English, merchants of Hamburg, and others bring into the kingdom a quantity of merchandise much greater than they take away, withdraw the surplus in cash, which produced both their prosperity and the poverty of the kingdom, and as a result, unquestionably, added to their power and our weakness.

It is necessary next to examine the steps taken to change this fate. First, in 1662, your majesty sustained the right to 50 *sols*[5] for ton of freight carried on foreign vessels, which has had the impressive result that the number of French ships has increased every year, and in seven or eight years the Dutch have been almost excluded from port-to-port commerce. . . . Finally, after carefully considering the matter, your majesty ordered the tariff of 1664, in which the duties are regulated by a completely different principle, that is, all the merchandise and manufactured goods of the realm were notably favored, and the prices of foreign goods increased; . . . this change began to offer the opportunity to manufacture these same items in the kingdom; and to this end:

The fabric manufacture of Sedan was re-established, and the number of looms increased from 12 to 62. New establishments have been built at Abbeville, Dieppe, Fecamp, and Rouen, at which there are presently more than 200 looms; the factory for barracan was established at Ferte-sous-Jouarre with 120 looms; a factory for small Brussels damask at Meaux, composed of 80 looms; a carpet factory in the same city with 20 looms; for camlets at Amiens and Abbeville with 120 looms; dimities and twills

of Bruges and Brussels at Montmorin, St. Quentin, and Avranches, with 30 looms; for fine Dutch linens, at Bresle, Louviers, Laval, and other places, with 200 looms; serge of London at Gournay, Auxerre, Autun, and other places with 300 looms; English woolen stockings . . . in 32 towns and cities; that for tin in Nivernois; that for French lace in 52 towns and cities, in which more than 20,000 workers toil; the making of brass established in Champagne; brass wire in Burgundy; gold thread of Milan in Lyons; the manufacture of silks in the same city.

The search for saltpeter,[6] and at the same time the manufacture of gunpowder; that of match; the establishment of the manufacture of muskets and weapons of all sorts . . . ; the distribution of stud horses, which has produced and certainly will continue to produce the re-establishment of stud farms and will considerably decrease the import of foreign horses. . . .

And since your majesty wished to work hard for the restoration of his navy . . . it was absolutely necessary to try hard to find within the kingdom, or to establish everything needed for the great design.

To this end, the manufacture of tar was established at Médoc, Auvergne, Dauphiné and Provence; iron cannons in Burgundy, Nivernois, Saintonge, and Périgord; anchors in Dauphiné, Nivernois, Brittany, and Rochefort; sailcloth in Dauphiné; cloth for banners at Auvergne; pilots' instruments at Dieppe and la Rochelle; wood cutting for ships . . . ; wood for masts, which was unknown in the kingdom, has been found in Provence, Languedoc, Auvergne, Dauphiné, and in the Pyrenees. Iron, which was obtained from Sweden and Biscay, is now made within the kingdom. High quality hemp for rope, which came from Prussia and Piedmont, is now obtained from Burgundy, Maconnais, Bresse, and Dauphiné.

In a word, everything needed for the construction of vessels is at present established in the kingdom, so that your majesty can do without

---

[5]A *sol* was a French coin equal to one-twentieth of a livre. Colbert is referring to the royal tariff of 1662.

[6]Potassium nitrate, used in making gunpowder.

foreigners for the navy, and even in a short time can supply them with what they need and extract their money. . . .

In addition, to prevent the Dutch from profiting from American commerce, which they have gotten hold of and excluded the French, with annual profits of a million livres in gold, your majesty has established the West India Company and invested in it almost 4 million livres; he has also had the satisfaction of taking away from the Dutch that million livres per year that maintained more than 4,000 of their subjects who continually sailed among these islands on their 200 ships. . . . In addition, to prevent the same

Dutch from taking more than 10 million livres out of the kingdom through all the goods they bring from the East Indies and the Levant, your majesty formed companies for the same areas, in which he has invested more than 5 million livres. . . .

All these great undertakings, however, and an infinity of others that are in a sense innovations . . . are still in their infancy and can be carried to perfection only with work and stubborn application and can exist only with the resources of the state, since considerable expenditures are always necessary to support all of this great system. . . .

# Capitalism's Prophet
▼▼▼

## 40 ▾ *Adam Smith, THE WEALTH OF NATIONS*

Surprisingly few biographical details are known about Adam Smith, the economist famed for his devastating critique of mercantilism in *The Wealth of Nations.* Born in 1723 in a small Scottish fishing village and educated at Glasgow and Oxford, between 1751 and 1763 he held chairs in logic and moral philosophy at the University of Glasgow. The publication of his *Theory of Moral Sentiments* in 1759 ensured his literary and philosophical reputation. In 1763 he became the tutor of an English aristocrat's son and lived for three years in France, where he met many prominent French intellectuals. From 1767 to 1776 he lived in semi-retirement in Scotland and finished *The Wealth of Nations,* published in 1776. In 1778 he became commissioner of customs in Scotland and died in Edinburgh in 1790.

*The Wealth of Nations* went through five English editions and was published in several European translations in the eighteenth century. Its importance lies in its general approach to economics, which brought systematic analysis to wages, labor, trade, population, rents, and money supply, and in its unrelenting assault on mercantilism. The key to economic growth, Smith asserted, was not regulation but free competition among individuals and among nations.

---

### QUESTIONS FOR ANALYSIS

1. Smith denies that a nation's wealth consists of the amount of gold and silver it controls. What arguments does he present to defend his position, and what are their implications for trade policy?
2. Smith suggests a paradox that each individual by pursuing his or her own self-interest promotes the general welfare of society. What specific

examples of this paradox are provided? What implications does this paradox have for government policy?

3. What groups in society would you expect to be most enthusiastic about Smith's ideas? Why? What groups might be expected to oppose them?

4. The novelty of Smith's ideas can best be understood by comparing them with those of Colbert (source 39). How do the two men disagree about the following issues: (a) the benefits of government economic regulation, (b) economic competition among nations, and (c) the meaning of the balance of trade?

## SELF-INTEREST AND THE FREE MARKET

1. This division of labor,[1] from which so many advantages are derived, is not originally the effect of any human wisdom, which foresees and intends that general opulence to which it gives occasion. It is the necessary, though very slow and gradual consequence of a certain propensity in human nature which has in view no such extensive utility; the propensity to truck,[2] barter, and exchange one thing for another.

2. Whether this propensity be one of those original principles in human nature, of which no further account can be given; or whether, as seems more probable, it be the necessary consequence of the faculties of reason and speech, it belongs not to our present subject to enquire. It is common to all men, and to be found in no other race of animals, which seem to know neither this nor any other species of contracts. . . . Nobody ever saw a dog make a fair and deliberate exchange of one bone for another with another dog. Nobody ever saw one animal by its gestures and natural cries signify to another, this is mine, that yours; I am willing to give this for that. . . . In almost every other race of animals each individual, which it is grown up to maturity, is entirely independent, and in its natural

state has occasion for the assistance of no other living creature. But man has almost constant occasion for the help of his brethren, and it is in vain for him to expect it from their benevolence only. He will be more likely to prevail if he can interest their self-love in his favor, and show them that it is for their own advantage to do for him what he requires of them. Whoever offers to another a bargain of any kind, proposes to do this. Give me that which I want, and you shall have this which you want, is the meaning of every such offer; and it is in this manner that we obtain from one another the far greater part of those good offices which we stand in need of. It is not from the benevolence of the butcher, the brewer, or the baker, that we expect our dinner, but from their regard to their own interest. We address ourselves, not to their humanity but to their self-love, and never talk to them of our own necessities but of their advantages. Nobody but a beggar chooses to depend chiefly upon the benevolence of his fellow-citizens. . . .

## PRICES AND THE FREE MARKET

The quantity of every commodity brought to market naturally suits itself to the effectual demand. It is the interest of all those who employ their land, labor, or stock,[3] in bringing any com-

---

[1]This section of *The Wealth of Nations* follows a long discussion of the *division of labor*. As utilized by Smith, this term refers to economic specialization, both in terms of different professions and in terms of the separate tasks carried out by different individuals in the process of manufacturing or preparing commodities for the market.

[2]A synonym for barter.
[3]Money or capital invested or available for investment or trading.

modity to market, that the quantity never should exceed the effectual demand; and it is the interest of all other people that it never should fall short of that demand.

If at any time it exceeds the effectual demand, some of the component parts of its price must be paid below their natural rate. If it is rent,[4] the interest of the landlords will immediately prompt them to withdraw a part of their land; and if it is wages or profit, the interest of the laborers in the one case, and of their employers in the other, will prompt them to withdraw a part of their labor or stock from this employment. The quantity brought to market will soon be no more than sufficient to supply the effectual demand. All the different parts of its price will rise to their natural rate, and the whole price to its natural price.

If, on the contrary, the quantity brought to market should at any time fall short of the effectual demand, some of the component parts of its price must rise above their natural rate. If it is rent, the interest of all other landlords will naturally prompt them to prepare more land for the raising of this commodity; if it is wages or profit, the interest of all other laborers and dealers will soon prompt them to employ more labor and stock in preparing and bringing it to market. The quantity brought thither will soon be sufficient to supply the effectual demand. All the different parts of its price will soon sink to their natural rate, and the whole price to its natural price. . . .

The monopolists, by keeping the market constantly under-stocked, by never fully supplying the effectual demand, sell their commodities much above the natural price, and raise their emoluments,[5] whether they consist in wages or profit, greatly above their natural rate.

The price of monopoly is upon every occasion the highest which can be got. The natural price, or the price of free competition, on the contrary, is the lowest which can be taken, not upon every occasion, indeed, but for any considerable time together. The one is upon every occasion the highest which can be squeezed out of the buyers, or which, it is supposed, they will consent to give: The other is the lowest which the sellers can commonly afford to take, and at the same time continue their business.

The exclusive privileges of corporations, statutes of apprenticeship,[6] and all those laws which restrain, in particular employments, the competition to a smaller number than might otherwise go into them, have the same tendency, though in a less degree. They are a sort of enlarged monopolies, and may frequently, for ages together and in whole classes of employments, keep up the market price of particular commodities above the natural price, and maintain both the wages of the labor and the profits of the stock employed about them somewhat above their natural rate.

## MERCANTALIST FALLACIES

That wealth consists in money, or in gold and silver, is a popular notion which naturally arises from the double function of money, as the instrument of commerce, and as the measure of value. In consequence of its being the instrument of commerce, when we have money we can more readily obtain whatever else we have occasion for, than by means of any other commodity. The great affair [thing to do], we always find, is to get money. . . .

A rich country, in the same manner as a rich man, is supposed to be a country abounding in money; and to heap up gold and silver in any country is supposed to be the readiest way to enrich it. . . .

In consequence of these popular notions, all the different nations of Europe have studied, though to little purpose, every possible means

---

[4]In this sense, the cost of land in terms of the payments made by tenants to their landlord.

[5]The returns from employment, usually in the form of compensation.

[6]Laws that restricted the number of individuals who could receive training in trades through apprenticeship.

of accumulating gold and silver in their respective countries. Spain and Portugal, the proprietors of the principal mines which supply Europe with those metals, have either prohibited their exportation under the severest penalties, or subjected it to a considerable duty. The like prohibition seems anciently to have [been] made a part of the policy of most other European nations. When those countries became commercial, the merchants found this prohibition, upon many occasions, extremely inconvenient. . . .

They represented [stated forcefully], first, that the exportation of gold and silver in order to purchase foreign goods, did not always diminish the quantity of those metals in the kingdom. . . .

They represented, secondly, that this prohibition could not hinder the exportation of gold and silver, which, on account of the smallness of their bulk in proportion to their value, could easily be smuggled abroad. . . .

Those arguments . . . were solid so far as they asserted that the exportation of gold and silver in trade might frequently be advantageous to the country. They were solid too, in asserting that no prohibition could prevent their exportation, when private people found any advantage in exporting them. But they were sophistical in supposing, that either to preserve or to augment the quantity of those metals required more the attention of government, than to preserve or to augment the quantity of any other useful commodities, which the freedom of trade, without any such attention, never fails to supply in the proper quantity. . . .

A country that has no mines of its own must undoubtedly draw its gold and silver from foreign countries, in the same manner as one that has no vineyards of its own must draw its wines. It does not seem necessary, however, that the attention of government should be more turned towards the one than towards the other object. A country that has wherewithal to buy wine, will always get the wine which it has occasion for; and a country that has wherewithal to buy gold and silver, will never be in want of those metals.

They are to be bought for a certain price like all other commodities, and as they are the price of all other commodities, so all other commodities are the price of those metals. We trust with perfect security that the freedom of trade, without any attention of government, will always supply us with the wine which we have occasion for: and we may trust with equal security that it will always supply us with all the gold and silver which we can afford to purchase or to employ, either in circulating our commodities, or in other uses.

▼ ▼ ▼

By restraining, either by high duties, or by absolute prohibitions, the importation of such goods from foreign countries as can be produced at home, the monopoly of the home market is more or less secured to the domestic industry employed in producing them. . . . But whether it tends either to increase the general industry of the society, or to give it the most advantageous direction, is not, perhaps, altogether so evident. . . .

Every individual is continually exerting himself to find out the most advantageous employment for whatever capital he can command. It is his own advantage, indeed, and not that of the society, which he has in view. But the study of his own advantage, naturally, or rather necessarily, leads him to prefer that employment which is most advantageous to the society.

First, every individual endeavors to employ his capital as near home as he can, and consequently as much as he can in the support of domestic industry, provided always that he can thereby obtain the ordinary, or not a great deal less than the ordinary, profits of stock.

Secondly, every individual who employs his capital in the support of domestic industry, necessarily endeavors so to direct that industry, that its produce may be of the greatest possible value. . . .

As every individual, therefore, endeavors as much as he can both to employ his capital in the support of domestic industry, and so to direct that industry that its produce may be of the greatest value, every individual necessarily labors to render the annual revenue of the society as great as he can. He generally, indeed, neither intends to promote the public interest, nor knows how much he is promoting it. By preferring the support of domestic to that of foreign industry, he intends only his own security; and by directing that industry in such a manner as its produce may be of the greatest value, he intends only his own gain, and he is in this, as in many other cases, led by an invisible hand to promote an end which was no part of his intention. Nor is it always the worse for the society that it was no part of it. By pursuing his own interest he frequently promotes that of the society more effectually than when he really intends to promote it. . . .

What is the species of domestic industry which his capital can employ, and of which the produce is likely to be of the greatest value, every individual, it is evident, can, in his local situation, judge much better than any statesman or lawgiver can do for him. The statesman who should attempt to direct private people in what manner they ought to employ their capital, would not only load himself with a most unnecessary attention, but assume an authority which could safely be trusted, not only to no single person, but to no council or senate whatever, and which would nowhere be so dangerous as in the hands of a man who had folly and presumption enough to fancy himself fit to exercise it.

To give the monopoly of the home market to the produce of domestic industry, in any particular art or manufacture, is in some measure to direct private people in what manner they ought to employ their capital, and must, in almost all cases, be either a useless or a hurtful regulation. If the produce of domestic [industry] can be brought there as cheap as that of foreign industry, the regulation is evidently useless. If it cannot, it must generally be hurtful. It is the maxim of every prudent master of a family, never to attempt to make at home what it will cost him more to make than to buy. . . .

What is prudence in the conduct of every private family, can scarce be folly in that of a great kingdom. If a foreign country can supply us with a commodity cheaper than we ourselves can make it, better buy it of them with some part of the produce of our own industry, employed in a way in which we have some advantage. . . .

To expect, indeed, that the freedom of trade should ever be entirely restored in Great Britain, is as absurd as to expect that an Oceania or Utopia should ever be established in it. Not only the prejudices of the public, but what is much more unconquerable, the private interests of many individuals, irresistibly oppose it. . . .

The undertaker of a great manufacture, who, by the home markets being suddenly laid open to the competition of foreigners, should be obliged to abandon his trade, would no doubt suffer very considerably. That part of his capital which had usually been employed in purchasing materials and in paying his workmen might, without much difficulty perhaps, find another employment. But that part of it which was fixed in workhouses, and in the instruments of trade, could scarce be disposed of without considerable loss. The equitable regard, therefore, to his interest requires that changes of this kind should never be introduced suddenly, but slowly, gradually, and after a very long warning.

▼▼▼

# Russia and the West
# in the Eighteenth Century

After two centuries of Mongol rule ended in the late 1400s, Russia embarked on a period of remarkable expansion in which the tsars consolidated their control of European Russia, then extended their authority eastward across the Urals into Siberia. By the 1630s Russia stretched all the way to the Pacific and was the largest nation in the world.

Russia's western border, however, remained insecure. The Livonian War (1558–1582), launched against Poland and Sweden, resulted in territorial losses, and during the period of political breakdown known as the Time of Troubles (1604–1613), Poland and Sweden sent armies deep into Russian territory. In 1612 the Russians drove out the invaders, and for the next several decades the Thirty Years' War (1618–1648) diverted European rulers from Russian adventures. The Turks remained a threat, however, and in the late 1600s the Poles and the Swedes resumed their pressure.

Russia's vulnerability set the stage for an emotional debate among the Russians in the 1700s that continues even today. The issue was straightforward: Should the Russians abandon much or all of their past and strive to emulate the technologically superior, wealthier, and ostensibly more successful nations of Western Europe?

Tsar Peter the Great (r. 1682–1725) gave an unequivocally positive response to this question. He was determined to pull Russia out of its perceived backwardness by mandating the adoption of Western European institutions and mores. Many Russians found his goals and policies abhorrent. They treasured Russia's uniqueness and believed that in certain respects their country was superior to the nations of Western Europe. These lovers of Russia's Slavic traditions (later known as *Slavophiles*) argued that abandonment of Russia's past was too high a price to pay for Europeanization.

Variations of Russia's Westernizer-Slavophile debate later appeared among many peoples of Asia and Africa. As Europeans forced themselves into their lives, these people too had to ask themselves how willing they were, if at all, to abandon cultural and religious traditions for the lure of Western science, military power, and material gain. They, like the Russians, would find no easy answer to this question.

# Peter the Great's Blueprint for Russia
▼▼▼

## 41 ▼ Peter the Great, EDICTS AND DECREES

Peter the Great stands out as one of history's most significant figures during the past three hundred years. This remarkable man developed an interest in Western Europe when as a boy he spent hours smoking and drinking in the German quarter, the Moscow district where visiting Europeans resided. His fascination grew during two visits to Western Europe, where Dutch and British commerce and naval technology especially impressed him.

But the urgency of Peter's efforts to Europeanize Russia indicates that he was motivated more by his sense of Russia's vulnerability than a personal admiration of things European. In 1700 a decisive defeat by the Swedes at the Battle of Narva spurred him into action. With characteristic energy and single-mindedness he embarked on his campaign to transform Russia, issuing in the next twenty-five years no fewer than three thousand decrees on everything from the structure of government to male shaving habits. A few examples are included here.

### QUESTIONS FOR ANALYSIS

1. What do these decrees reveal about Peter the Great's motives for his reforms?
2. What can be learned from these decrees about Russian social relationships and the state of the Russian economy?
3. Why do you think Peter believed it was important that the Russians change their dress, shaving habits, and calendar for his ultimate goals to be achieved?
4. What evidence do these edicts provide about opposition or indifference to Peter's reforms on the part of his subjects?
5. What do these edicts reveal about Peter's views of the state and its relationship to his individual subjects?
6. What groups within Russia might have been most likely to oppose Peter's reforms? Why?

### LEARNING FROM EUROPE

*(Decree on the New Calendar {1699})*

It is known to His Majesty that not only many European Christian lands, but also Slavic nations which are in total accord with our Eastern Orthodox Church . . . agree to count their years from the eighth day after the birth of Christ, that is from the first day of January, and not from the creation of the world,[1] because of the many difficulties and discrepancies of this reckoning. It is now the year 1699 from the birth of Christ, and from the first of January will begin both the new year 1700 and a new century; and so His

---

[1]Before January 1, 1700, the Russian calendar started from the date of the creation of the world, which was reckoned at 5508 B.C.E. The year began on September 1.

Majesty has ordered, as a good and useful measure, that from now on time will be reckoned in government offices and dates be noted on documents and property deeds, starting from the first of January 1700. And to celebrate this good undertaking and the new century . . . in the sovereign city of Moscow . . . let the reputable citizens arrange decorations of pine, fir, and juniper trees and boughs along the busiest main streets and by the houses of eminent church and lay persons of rank. . . . Poorer persons should place at least one shrub or bough on their gates or on their house. . . . Also, on the first day of January, as a sign of rejoicing, wishes for the new year and century will be exchanged, and the following will be organized: when fireworks are lit and guns fired on the great Red Square, let the boyars,[2] the Lords of the Palace, of the Chamber, and the Council, and the eminent personages of Court, Army, and Merchant ranks, each in his own grounds, fire three times from small guns, if they have any, or from muskets and other small arms, and shoot some rockets into the air.

## (Decree on the Invitation of Foreigners {1702})

Since our accession to the throne all our efforts and intentions have tended to govern this realm in such a way that all of our subjects should, through our care for the general good, become more and more prosperous. For this end we have always tried to maintain internal order, to defend the state against invasion, and in every possible way to improve and to extend trade. With this purpose we have been compelled to make some necessary and salutary changes in the administration, in order that our subjects might more easily gain a knowledge of matters of which they were before ignorant, and become more skillful in their commercial relations. We have therefore given orders, made dispositions, and founded institutions indispensable for increasing our trade

with foreigners, and shall do the same in the future. Nevertheless we fear that matters are not in such a good condition as we desire, and that our subjects cannot in perfect quietness enjoy the fruits of our labors, and we have therefore considered still other means to protect our frontier from the invasion of the enemy, and to preserve the rights and privileges of our State, and the general peace of all Christians. . . .

To attain these worthy aims, we have endeavored to improve our military forces, which are the protection of our State, so that our troops may consist of well-drilled men, maintained in perfect order and discipline. In order to obtain greater improvement in this respect, and to encourage foreigners, who are able to assist us in this way, as well as artisans profitable to the State, to come in numbers to our country, we have issued this manifesto, and have ordered printed copies of it to be sent throughout Europe. . . . And as in our residence of Moscow, the free exercise of religion of all other sects, although not agreeing with our church, is already allowed, so shall this be hereby confirmed anew in such manner that we, by the power granted to us by the Almighty, shall exercise no compulsion over the consciences of men, and shall gladly allow every Christian to care for his own salvation at his own risk.

## (An Instruction to Russian Students Abroad Studying Navigation {1714})

1. Learn how to draw plans and charts and how to use the compass and other naval indicators.

2. Learn how to navigate a vessel in battle as well as in a simple maneuver, and learn how to use all appropriate tools and instruments; namely, sails, ropes, and oars, and the like matters, on row boats and other vessels.

3. Discover as much as possible how to put ships to sea during a naval battle. . . . Obtain from foreign naval officers written statements,

---

[2]Members of the hereditary nobility.

bearing their signatures and seals, of how adequately you are prepared for naval duties.

4. If, upon his return, anyone wishes to receive from the Tsar greater favors, he should learn, in addition to the above enumerated instructions, how to construct those vessels aboard which he would like to demonstrate his skills.

5. Upon his return to Moscow, every foreign-trained Russian should bring with him at his own expense, for which he will later be reimbursed, at least two experienced masters of naval science. They the returnees will be assigned soldiers, one soldier per returnee, to teach them what they have learned abroad. . . .

## CREATING A NEW RUSSIAN

### (Decree on Western Dress {1701})

Western dress shall be worn by all the boyars, members of our councils and of our court . . . gentry of Moscow, secretaries . . . provincial gentry, gosti,[3] government officials, streltsy,[4] members of the guilds purveying for our household, citizens of Moscow of all ranks, and residents of provincial cities . . . excepting the clergy and peasant tillers of the soil. The upper dress shall be of French or Saxon cut, and the lower dress . . . — waistcoat, trousers, boots, shoes, and hats — shall be of the German type. They shall also ride German saddles. Likewise the womenfolk of all ranks, including the priests', deacons', and church attendants' wives, the wives of the dragoons, the soldiers, and the streltsy, and their children, shall wear Western dresses, hats, jackets, and underwear — undervests and petticoats — and shoes. From now on no one of the above-mentioned is to wear Russian dress or Circassian[5] coats, sheepskin coats, or Russian peasant coats, trousers, boots, and shoes. It is also forbidden to ride Russian saddles, and the crafts-

men shall not manufacture them or sell them at the marketplaces.

### (Decree on Shaving {1705})

Henceforth, in accordance with this, His Majesty's decree, all court attendants . . . provincial service men, government officials of all ranks, military men, all the gosti, members of the wholesale merchants' guild, and members of the guilds purveying for our household must shave their beards and moustaches. But, if it happens that some of them do not wish to shave their beards and moustaches, let a yearly tax be collected from such persons; from court attendants . . . Special badges shall be issued to them from the Administrator of Land Affairs of Public Order . . . which they must wear. . . . As for the peasants, let a toll of two half-copecks[6] per beard be collected at the town gates each time they enter or leave a town; and do not let the peasants pass the town gates, into or out of town, without paying this toll.

## MILITARY AND ECONOMIC REFORMS

### (Decree on Promotion to Officer's Rank {1714})

Since there are many who promote to officer rank their relatives and friends — young men who do not know the fundamentals of soldiering, not having served in the lower ranks — and since even those who serve [in the ranks] do so for a few weeks or months only, as a formality; therefore . . . let a decree be promulgated that henceforth there shall be no promotion [to officer rank] of men of noble extraction or of any others who have not first served as privates in the Guards. This decree does not apply to soldiers of lowly

---

[3]Merchants who often served the tsar in some capacity.
[4]Members of the imperial guard stationed in Moscow.
[5]Circassia was a Russian territory between the Caspian and Black seas.

[6]One-twentieth a ruble, the basic unit of Russian money.

origin who, after long service in the ranks, have received their commissions through honest service or to those who are promoted on the basis of merit, now or in the future; it applies exclusively to those who have remained in the ranks for a short time, only as a formality, as described above.

### (Statute for the College of Manufactures[7] {1723})

His Imperial Majesty is diligently striving to establish and develop in the Russian Empire such manufacturing plants and factories as are found in other states, for the general welfare and prosperity of his subjects. He [therefore] most graciously charges the College of Manufactures to exert itself in devising the means to introduce, with the least expense, and to spread in the Russian Empire these and other ingenious arts, and especially those for which materials can be found within the empire. . . .

His Imperial Majesty gives permission to everyone, without distinction of rank or condition, to open factories wherever he may find suitable. This provision must be made public everywhere. . . .

Factory owners must be closely supervised, in order that they have at their plants good and experienced [foreign] master craftsmen, who are able to train Russians in such a way that these,

in turn, may themselves become masters, so that their produce may bring glory to the Russian manufactures. . . .

By the former decrees of His Majesty commercial people were forbidden to buy villages [i.e. to own serfs], the reason being that they were not engaged in any other activity beneficial for the state save commerce; but since it is now clear to all that many of them have started to found manufacturing establishments and build plants, both in companies and individually, which tend to increase the welfare of the state — and many of them have already started production; therefore permission is granted both to the gentry and to men of commerce to acquire villages for these factories without hindrance, [but] with the permission of the College of Manufactures. . . .

In order to stimulate voluntary immigration of various craftsmen from other countries into the Russian Empire, and to encourage them to establish factories and manufacturing plants freely and at their own expense, the College of Manufactures must send appropriate announcements to the Russian envoys accredited at foreign courts. The envoys should then, in an appropriate way, bring these announcements to the attention of men of various professions, urge them to come to settle in Russia, and help them to move.

---

[7]One of several administrative boards created by Peter in 1717. Based on Swedish precedent.

# A Russian Critic of Westernization
▼▼▼

## 42 ▼ *Mikhail Shcherbatov,* ON THE CORRUPTION OF MORALS IN RUSSIA

During the reign of Catherine the Great (1762–1796) Russian society continued to evolve along the lines laid down by Peter the Great. With the imperial court now in St. Petersburg, Peter's "window on the West," the German-born Catherine courted French intellectuals, encouraged the publication of Western European books, and proposed educational and political reforms inspired by Western models. Russian aristocrats spoke French, wore the latest European fashions, and congratulated themselves on Russia's growing prestige and their newly acquired sophistication and refinement. As the following selection reveals, however, some Russians had misgivings about Russia's transformation.

Prince Mikhail Shcherbatov (1733–1790) was born into a distinguished aristocratic family with a tradition of service to the state. Having developed a keen interest in Western European thought and literature through his knowledge of French, he moved as a young man from Moscow to St. Petersburg, where he contributed to literary journals and joined in the political discussions sparked by Catherine's policies and proposals. His major work was a seven-volume *History of Russia from Earliest Times,* still unfinished at the time of his death. During the 1780s he experienced growing disillusionment with the changes in Russia since the reign of Peter the Great. He stated his reservations in his *On the Corruption of Morals in Russia,* written in 1787 but not published until 1897.

## QUESTIONS FOR ANALYSIS

1. According to Shcherbatov what were the salient characteristics of Russia before the reforms of Peter the Great?
2. What changes instituted by Peter does Shcherbatov approve of? Why?
3. What reservations does Shcherbatov have concerning Peter's religious policies?
4. How would you describe Shcherbatov's vision of the ideal Russian society and government?
5. What specifically in Shcherbatov's view should Peter have done differently to prevent the moral decline of the Russian people?

I cannot but wonder at the short time in which morals in Russia have everywhere become corrupt. I can truly say that if, after entering later than other nations upon the path of enlightenment, nothing more remained for us than to follow prudently in the steps of nations previously enlightened, then indeed, in sociability and in various other things, it may be said that we have made wonderful progress and have taken gigantic steps to correct our outward appearance. But at the same time, with much greater speed, we have hastened to corrupt our morals, and have even come to this: that faith and God's Law have been extinguished in our hearts, Divine mysteries have fallen into disrepute and civil laws have become objects of scorn.

Children have no respect for parents, and are not ashamed to flout their will openly and to mock their old-fashioned behavior. Parents have no love for their offspring; . . . often they sacrifice them for profit, and many have become vendors of their daughters' honor for the sakes of ambition and luxury.[1] There is no genuine love between husbands and wives, who are often coolly indifferent to each other's adulteries; others, on some slight pretext, destroy the marriage concluded between them by the Church and are not merely unashamed but rather seem to take pride in this conduct. There is no family feeling, for the family name counts for nothing, and each lives for himself. There is no friendship, for everyone will sacrifice a friend for his own advan-

---

[1]A reference to the marriage of girls of noble birth into merchant families.

tage. There is no loyalty to the monarch, for the chief aim of almost everyone is to deceive his sovereign, in order to receive from him ranks and lucrative rewards. There is no patriotism, for almost all men serve for their own advantage rather than for that of the nation. . . .

## RUSSIA BEFORE PETER THE GREAT

Not only the subjects, but even our very monarchs led a very simple life. Their palaces were not large, as is attested by the old buildings that remain. Seven, eight, or at most, ten rooms, were sufficient for the monarch's accommodation.

These very palaces had no great embellishments, for the walls were bare, and the benches were covered with crimson cloth. . . .

For such a small number of rooms, not much lighting would be needed; but even here, they not only did not use, but considered it a sin to use wax candles,[2] and the rooms were lit by tallow candles, and even these were not set out in tens or hundreds; it was a large room indeed where four candles were set out on candlesticks.

Now let us consider the Czars' clothing. . . . Their ceremonial robes glittered all over with gold, jewels and diamonds. But their normal apparel, in which they looked for comfort rather than magnificence, was simple, and hence could not give rise to voluptuousness; . . . Generally speaking, there were no exquisite or perishable articles of finery, nor a large number of outfits, but when the Czar or Czarina had five, six, or, at most, ten outfits, then this was considered sufficient, and even these clothes were worn until they wore out, unless they were given to someone by the monarch out of special favor. The chief luxury in the Czar's ordinary clothing consisted of the precious furs, which they used for lining and on the edges of their garments; but these furs were not purchased or imported from foreign states, but were a tribute, collected from the Siberian peoples. . . . The boyars and other dignitaries, according to their means, led a similar life, striving, however, out of respect for the Czar's rank, never to approach even this simple magnificence. But what kept them from voluptuousness most of all was the fact that they had no conception of changing fashions, but, what grandfathers wore, grandsons also wore and used, without considering themselves old-fashioned.

## REIGN OF PETER THE GREAT

Peter the Great, in imitating foreign nations, not only strove to introduce to his realm a knowledge of sciences, arts and crafts, a proper military system, trade, and the most suitable forms of legislation; he also tried to introduce the kind of sociability, social intercourse and magnificence, which he first learnt from Lefort,[3] and which he later saw for himself.[4] Amid essential legislative measures, the organization of troops and artillery, he paid no less attention to modifying the old customs which seemed crude to him. He ordered beards to be shaved off, he abolished the old Russian garments, and instead of long robes he compelled the men to wear German coats,[5] and the women to wear bodices, skirts, gowns and long dresses, and instead of skull-caps, to adorn their heads with fontanges and cornettes.[6] He established various assemblies where the women, hitherto segregated from the company of men, were present with them at entertainments.

It was pleasant for the female sex, who had hitherto been almost slaves in their own homes, to enjoy all the pleasures of society, to adorn themselves with clothes and fineries, which en-

---

[2]Wax candles were to be used only in churches.
[3]Franz Lefort, a Genevan Swiss, was a mercenary in the Russian army who became Peter's close friend and advisor. He encouraged Peter's admiration of the West.
[4]A reference to Peter's protracted visit to Western Europe between March 1697 and September 1698.

[5]The phrase refers to any coat tailored in the Western European style.
[6]Forms of a tall headdress for fashionable women in France in the late seventeenth and early eighteenth centuries.

hanced the beauty of their faces and set off their fine figures. It also gave them no small pleasure to be able to see in advance with whom they were to be joined for life, and that the faces of their husbands and betrothed were no longer covered with prickly beards.

And on the other hand, it was pleasant for men who were young and not set in the old ways to mix freely with the female sex and to be able to see in advance and make the acquaintance of their brides-to-be; for previously they married, relying on their parents' choice. . . . And this in itself meant that women, previously unaware of their beauty, began to realize its power; they began to try to enhance it with suitable clothes, and used far more luxury in their adornments than their ancestors.

If the passion to be pleasing produced such an effect on women, it could not fail to have an effect on men too, who wished to be attractive to them; thus, the same striving after adornment gave rise to the same luxury. And now they ceased to be content with one or two long coats, but began to have many made, with galoon, embroidery and point-d'espagne.[7] . . .

The monarch himself kept to the old simplicity of morals in his dress . . . so he never wore anything costly. . . . However, for all his personal simplicity, he wanted his subjects to have a certain magnificence. I think that this great monarch, who did nothing without farsightedness, had it as his object to stimulate trade, industries and crafts through the magnificence and luxury of his subjects, being certain that in his lifetime excessive magnificence and voluptuousness would not enthrone themselves at the royal court.

---

▷ According to the author, despite Peter's reservations, the taste for luxury grew.

---

With this change in the way of life, first of the leading officials of state, and then, by imitation, of the other nobles, and as expenditure reached such a point that it began to exceed income, people began to attach themselves more and more to the monarch and the grandees, as sources of riches and rewards.

## PETER'S RELIGIOUS POLICIES

In Russia, the beard was regarded as being in the image of God, and it was considered a sin to shave it off, and through this, men fell into the heresy of the Anthropomorphites.[8] Miracles, needlessly performed, manifestations of icons,[9] rarely proven, were everywhere acclaimed, attracted superstitious idolatry, and provided incomes for dissolute priests.

Peter the Great strove to do away with all this. He issued decrees, ordering beards to be shaved off, and he placed a check on false miracles and manifestations and also on unseemly gatherings at shrines set up at crossways. . . .

But when did he do this? At a time when the nation was still unenlightened, and so, by taking superstition away from an unenlightened people, he removed its very faith in God's Law. This action of Peter the Great may be compared to that of an unskilled gardener, who, from a weak tree, cuts off the water-shoots which absorb its sap. If it had strong roots, then this pruning would cause it to bring forth fine, fruitful branches; but since it is weak and ailing, the cutting-off of these shoots . . . means that it fails; its wounds fail to heal over with sap, and hollows are formed which threaten to destroy the tree. Thus, the cutting-off of all superstitions did harm to the most basic articles of the faith; superstition decreased, but so did faith. The servile fear of Hell disappeared, but so did love of

---

[7]Galoon is a tightly woven braid of gold, silver, or silk thread; *point d'espagne* is French for a type of lace embroidery.
[8]Ascribing human characteristics to God.
[9]A religious image — usually of Christ, the Virgin Mary,

or one of the saints — painted on a small wooden panel used in the devotions of Orthodox Christians. Many icons were thought to have miracle-working qualities or to have been produced in heaven.

God and his Holy Law; and morals, which for lack of other enlightenment used to be improved by faith, having lost this support began to fall into dissolution.

And so, through the labors and solicitude of this monarch, Russia acquired fame in Europe and influence in affairs. Her troops were organized in a proper fashion, and her fleets covered the White Sea and the Baltic; with these forces she overcame her old enemies and former conquerors, the Poles and the Swedes, and acquired important provinces and sea-ports. Sciences, arts and crafts began to flourish there, trade began to enrich her, and the Russians were transformed — from bearded men to clean-shaven men, from long-robed men to short-coated men; they became more sociable, and polite spectacles[10] became known to them.

But at the same time, true attachment to the faith began to disappear, sacraments began to fall into disrepute, resoluteness diminished, yielding place to brazen, aspiring flattery; luxury and voluptuousness laid the foundation of their power, and hence avarice was also aroused, and, to the ruin of the laws and the detriment of the citizens, began to penetrate the law-courts.

___
[10]Plays performed in a theater.

▷  Only the reign of a truly virtuous monarch can save Russia.

Then exiled virtue, leaving the deserts will enthrone herself amid the cities and at the Court itself. Justice will not tilt her scales whether for bribery or for fear of violence; fear and corruption will be banished from the grandees; patriotism will ensconce itself in the hearts of the citizens. Men will boast, not of luxurious living and riches, but of impartiality, merit and disinterestedness. They will not reckon who is in or out of favor at Court, but with law and virtue as their object, will consider them as compass, able to lead them to both rank and fortune. The nobles will serve in various offices with a zeal proper to their calling; merchants will cease to aspire to be officers and noblemen; each will keep to his own class, and trade will flourish with the decrease in the import of foreign goods which give rise to voluptuousness, and with the export of Russian goods. Arts and crafts will increase so as to produce within Russia whatever is needed for the luxury and magnificence of a certain number of people.

▾▾▾

# Revolutions in England and France

**Revolutions involve more than changing leaders or replacing one ruling faction with another. Revolutions entail fundamental changes in the political order itself, often resulting in the transfer of power from one social group to another. Moreover, they affect more than politics. Revolutions reshape legal systems, schools, religious life, and economic practices and redefine relationships between rich and poor, males and females, old and young.**

**Because revolutions occur in societies already undergoing intellectual, economic, and social transformations, it is not surprising that revolutions first took place in Western Europe and the Americas, where economic and intellectual changes undermined the feudal-agrarian basis of society and traditional religious and political authorities. Nor is it surprising that in recent history revolutions have**

spread to other parts of the world, as new ideologies and economic and social changes have affected one society after another.

In the 1600s England experienced two revolutions: the Puritan Revolution (or English Revolution or English Civil War) in the 1640s and 1650s and the Glorious Revolution of 1688 and 1689. They limited royal authority, confirmed the fiscal and legislative powers of the Parliament, and guaranteed many basic rights for the English people, especially those with property. They also affirmed the constitutional principle that governments must not operate according to the whims of rulers but by established laws that apply to subjects and rulers alike.

The French Revolution had a greater impact than the English revolutions. A wider spectrum of society — peasants, urban workers, and women — participated, and it inspired more people around the globe. More important, the French Revolution went beyond liberalism and constitutionalism. It championed the principle of democracy — that every person, irrespective of social standing, should have a voice in government — and the principle of equality — that before the law all people should be treated identically. It also aroused the first nationalist movements in Europe and inspired disaffected groups throughout the world to seek political and social change through revolution. It ranks as one of the most significant events that have shaped the modern world.

# The Foundations of Parliamentary Supremacy in England
▼▼▼

## 43 ▼ *ENGLISH BILL OF RIGHTS*

The acceptance of the English Bill of Rights ended a clash between the Crown and Parliament that had convulsed English politics for almost a century. During the reigns of the first two Stuart kings, James I (r. 1603–1625) and his son Charles I (r. 1625–1649), the landowners, merchants, and lawyers who dominated the House of Commons fought the monarchy over religious, economic, diplomatic, and political issues that all centered on the fundamental question of Parliament's place in England's government.

A political impasse over new taxes led to civil war between Parliamentarians and Royalists in 1642. After a triumphant Parliament ordered the execution of Charles I in 1649, a faction of Puritans led by Oliver Cromwell seized power and for the next eleven years sought to impose its strict Protestant beliefs on the English people. The Puritans' grip on England loosened after the death of Cromwell in 1658 and was lost altogether when a newly elected Parliament restored the Stuarts in 1660.

Charles II (r. 1660–1685) and his brother James II (r. 1685–1688), however, also alienated their subjects through pro-French and pro-Catholic policies and disregard for Parliament. James II was a professed Catholic, and when a male heir was born in 1688, this raised the possibility of a long line of English Catholic kings. Most of his predominantly Protestant subjects found this unacceptable, and the result was the Glorious Revolution of 1688–1689. In a change that resembled a coup d'état more than a revolution, Parliament offered the Crown to James's Protestant daughter Mary and her husband William of Orange of Holland. After James mounted only token resistance and then fled the country, his son-in-law and daughter became King William III and Queen Mary II and signed the English Bill of Rights, passed by Parliament in 1689. By doing so they accepted parliamentary limitations on royal authority that became a permanent part of England's constitutional framework.

---

## QUESTIONS FOR ANALYSIS

1. What abuses of royal power seem to have most disturbed the authors of the English Bill of Rights?
2. Were the authors most concerned with political, economic, or religious issues?
3. What role does the Bill of Rights envision for the English Crown?
4. When the Bill of Rights speaks of "rights," to whose rights does it refer?
5. In what ways might the common people of England benefit from the Bill of Rights?

Whereas the late King James the Second, by the assistance of diverse evil counselors, judges and ministers employed by him, did endeavor to subvert and extirpate the Protestant religion and the laws and liberties of this kingdom;

By assuming and exercising a power of dispensing with and suspending of laws and the execution of laws without consent of Parliament;

By committing and prosecuting diverse worthy prelates for humbly petitioning to be excused from concurring to the said assumed power;

By issuing and causing to be executed a commission under the great seal for erecting a court called the Court of Commissioners for Ecclesiastical Causes;[1]

By levying money for and to the use of the Crown by pretense of prerogative for other time and in other manner than the same was granted by Parliament;

By raising and keeping a standing army within this kingdom in time of peace without consent of Parliament, and quartering soldiers contrary to law;

By causing several good subjects being Protestants to be disarmed at the same time when papists were both armed and employed contrary to law;

By violating the freedom of election of members to serve in Parliament; . . .

And whereas of late years partial corrupt and unqualified persons have been returned and served on juries in trials, and particularly diverse jurors in trials for high treason which were not freeholders;

And excessive bail hath been required of persons committed in criminal cases to elude the benefit of the laws made for the liberty of the subjects;

And excessive fines have been imposed;

And illegal and cruel punishments inflicted;

And several grants and promises made of fines and forfeitures before any conviction or judgment

---

[1]A special royal court established to try religious cases.

against the persons upon whom the same were to be levied;

All which are utterly and directly contrary to the known laws and statutes and freedom of this realm;

And whereas the said late King James the Second having abdicated the government and the throne being thereby vacant, his Highness the prince of Orange (whom it hath pleased Almighty God to make the glorious instrument of delivering this kingdom from popery and arbitrary power) did . . . cause letters to be written to the Lords Spiritual and Temporal being Protestants, and other letters to the several counties, cities, universities, boroughs and cinque ports,[2] for the choosing of such persons to represent them as were of right to be sent to Parliament, to meet and sit at Westminster upon the two and twentieth day of January in this year one thousand six hundred eighty and eight,[3] in order to make such an establishment as that their religion, laws and liberties might not again be in danger of being subverted, upon which letters elections having been accordingly made;

And thereupon the said Lords Spiritual and Temporal and Commons,[4] pursuant to their respective letters and elections, being now assembled in a full and free representative of this nation, taking into their most serious consideration the best means for attaining the ends aforesaid, do in the first place (as their ancestors in like case have usually done) for the vindicating and asserting their ancient rights and liberties declare;

That the pretended power of suspending of laws or the execution of laws by regal authority without consent of Parliament is illegal;

That the pretended power of dispensing with laws or the execution of laws by regal authority,

as it hath been assumed and exercised of late, is illegal;

That the commission for erecting the late Court of Commissioners for Ecclesiastical Causes, and all other commissions and courts of like nature, are illegal and pernicious;

That levying money for or to the use of the Crown by pretense of prerogative, without grant of Parliament, for longer time, or in other manner than the same is or shall be granted, is illegal;

That it is the right of the Subjects to petition the king, and all commitments and prosecutions for such petitioning are illegal;

That the raising or keeping a standing army within the kingdom in time of peace, unless it be with consent of Parliament, is against law;

That the subjects which are Protestants may have arms for their defense suitable to their conditions and as allowed by law;

That election of members of Parliament ought to be free;

That the freedom of speech and debates or proceedings in Parliament ought not to be impeached or questioned in any court or place out of Parliament;

That excessive bail ought not to be required, nor excessive fines imposed nor cruel and unusual punishments inflicted;

That jurors ought to be duly impaneled and returned, and jurors which pass upon men in trials for high treason ought to be freeholders;[5]

That all grants and promises of fines and forfeitures of particular persons before conviction are illegal and void;

And that for redress of all grievances, and for the amending, strengthening and preserving of the laws, Parliaments ought to be held frequently.

And they do claim, demand and insist upon all and singular the premises as their undoubted

---

[2]Five maritime towns in southeast England that during the Middle Ages gained the right to send representatives to Parliament in return for aiding the naval defense of the realm.

[3]Until the eighteenth century the English new year began on March 25, not January 1; by modern reckoning the year should be 1689.

[4]The Lords Spiritual were the prelates of the Anglican Church who sat in the House of Lords; the Lords Temporal were titled peers who sat in the House of Lords; Commons refers to the House of Commons, to which nontitled Englishmen were elected.

[5]Property holders.

rights and liberties, and that no declarations, judgments, doings or proceedings to the prejudice of the people in any of the said premises ought in any wise [manner] to be drawn hereafter into consequence or example; to which demand of their rights they are particularly encouraged by the declaration of his Highness the prince of Orange as being the only means for obtaining a full redress and remedy therein. Having therefore an entire confidence that his said Highness the prince of Orange will perfect the deliverance so far advanced by him, and will still preserve them from the violation of their rights which they have here asserted, and from all other attempts upon their religion, rights and liberties, the said Lords Spiritual and Temporal and Commons assembled at Westminster do resolve that William and Mary, prince and princess of Orange, be and be declared king and queen of England, France[6] and Ireland and the dominions thereunto belonging.

---

[6]An anachronistic reference to the time in the Middle Ages when English kings ruled parts of France as fiefdoms and, for a time, claimed the French throne.

## A Program for Revolutionary Change in France

▼▼▼

### 44 ▼ *CAHIER OF THE THIRD ESTATE OF THE CITY OF PARIS*

The French Revolution began because of a problem that has plagued rulers since the beginning of organized government — King Louis XVI and his ministers could not balance their budget. In 1788, having exhausted every other solution, the king agreed to convene a meeting of the Estates General, France's representative assembly, which had last met in 1614. He hoped it would solve the government's fiscal plight by approving new taxes. The nobility, having fended off every effort to curtail its tax exemptions and privileges, saw the convening of the Estates General as an opportunity to increase its power at the expense of the monarchy. For both king and nobility the calling of the Estates General had unexpected results: The nobility lost its privileges, and the king lost most of his power and, in 1793, having been judged a traitor to the Revolution, his head.

Neither Louis nor the nobles had comprehended the French people's disgust with royal absolutism and aristocratic privilege. Nor had they sensed the degree to which the Enlightenment and the English and American revolutions had committed the people to fundamental change. Having convened in May 1789, within months the Estates General transformed itself into a National Assembly, dismantled the laws and institutions of the Old Regime, and set about creating a new political order based on constitutionalism, equality, and natural rights.

Even before the Estates General met, the French populace was in a high pitch of political excitement as a result of the procedures adopted for choosing delegates. The delegates representing the three orders of French society — the First Estate, or clergy, the Second Estate, or nobility, and the Third Estate, everyone else from peasants to wealthy city-dwellers — were to be chosen in a complicated process that began with village and neighborhood assemblies and ended at the level of *baillages,* larger districts based on divisions in the French judicial system. At each electoral assembly, of which there were forty thousand, those attending were encouraged to draw up a *cahier de doléances,* a memorandum of grievances, in which all kinds of ideas on local and national affairs could be expressed. These would be passed on to editorial committees at the baillage level, whose members would sift through them and integrate them into final cahiers to send on to Versailles, where the Estates General would meet.

We have chosen to include excerpts from the cahier of the Third Estate of the city of Paris. A document largely created by lawyers and businessmen, it presents a fair sampling of the grievances and expectations of urban, upper-middle-class Frenchmen who, with the help of peasants, artisans, shopkeepers, and women, provided the impetus for the unfolding revolution.

## QUESTIONS FOR ANALYSIS

1. How does the proposed declaration of rights in this cahier compare to the political rights outlined in the English Bill of Rights (source 43)?
2. What view of monarchy is expressed in the cahier? How does it compare with the views of monarchy expressed in the English Bill of Rights (source 43)?
3. What views are expressed in the cahier about the position of the nobility and clergy in French society?
4. It has been said that the French Revolution was about legal privilege, not monarchy. Do the thoughts expressed in this cahier bear this out?
5. What solutions does the cahier offer for the French government's fiscal crisis?
6. In what ways does this document represent the interests of the urban middle class? To what extent does it show concern for other groups in French society?
7. What kind of government does the cahier envision for France?
8. In its discussion of government, does the cahier ignore or gloss over any issues that later might prove controversial once the revolution began?

## DECLARATION OF RIGHTS

In every political society all men are equal in rights.

All power emanates from the nation, and can be utilized only for its wellbeing.

The general will makes the law; public might ensures its execution.

The nation alone can grant the means to support the government; it has the right to determine the amount, to limit its duration, to amend it, to determine its use, to demand an accounting of it; and to insist on the accounting's publication.

Laws exist only to guarantee each individual's ownership of his property and the security of his person. All property is inviolable.

No citizen may be arrested or punished except by legal trial.

Every citizen has the right to be admitted to all employments, professions, and offices.

The natural, civil, and religious liberty of each man, his personal security, and his absolute independence of every authority except that of the law, bar all enquiry into his opinions, speech, writings, and actions, so long as they do not disturb public order, and do not infringe on the rights of others.

In keeping with the declaration of rights of the nation, our delegates shall demand the end of: personal servitude; compulsory militia service; the violation of the public faith in regard to letters entrusted to the mail; and all exclusive privileges except to inventors, to whom they will be granted for a limited time only.

As a result of these principles, liberty of the press is to be granted on the condition that authors sign their writings; that the publisher be known, and that both will be held responsible for the consequences of their publications.

The declaration of these natural, civil and political rights shall become the national charter and the basis of the French government.

## CONSTITUTION

In the French monarchy, legislative power belongs to the nation conjointly with the king; executive power belongs to the king alone.

No tax can be established except by the nation.

The Estates General shall meet at three-year intervals.

Any person convicted of having done anything tending to prevent the meeting of the Estates General shall be declared a traitor to the nation, guilty of high treason, and punished as such. . . .

The order and form of the convening of the Estates General and of the national representation shall be fixed by law.

Our delegates shall approve of the demand of the colony of Saint Domingue[1] to be admitted to the Estates General; they shall demand that representatives of other colonies shall also be admitted, as they are our brothers, and should share in all the advantages of the French constitution.

The monarch's person is sacred and inviolable. The succession to the throne is hereditary in the reigning family, in the male line, by order of primogeniture, to the exclusion of women and their descendants, male or female, and can only fall on a prince born French, within lawful marriage. . . .

At the beginning of each new reign the king shall swear an oath to the nation, and the nation to the king; the form of which shall be determined by the Estates General.

No citizen may be arrested, nor his home violated, by virtue of *lettres de cachet*,[2] or any other order emanating from the executive power, . . . all persons who have solicited, countersigned, and executed them being subject to special prosecution and corporal punishment. . . .

The whole kingdom will be divided into provincial assemblies, made up of people who live in the province, elected freely by all the orders. . . .

Public administration, in all matters having to do with the allocation and collection of taxes, agriculture, commerce, manufacturing, communications, public works projects, construction, and public morals shall be entrusted to the provincial assemblies.

Cities, towns, and villages shall likewise have elected municipal authorities which, like the assemblies, shall administer local affairs.

Judicial authority shall be exercised in France in the name of the king by tribunals composed of members completely independent of any act by the executive power.

Nobles will be able to participate in commerce and other useful professions without losing their status.[3] The Estates General shall establish a civic

---

[1]Saint Domingue was a French colony on the western third of the island of Hispaniola, acquired by treaty from Spain in 1697. At the time of the revolution, its population of 520,000 consisted of 450,000 slaves and 30,000 mulattos. The remaining 40,000 were whites of French extraction.
[2]Literally "sealed letters;" a form of warrant issued under the king's signature for arbitrary arrest and imprisonment in prerevolutionary France.

[3]According to French law, members of the nobility lost their noble status if they participated in business activities involving commerce, manufacturing, and banking, all considered "middle class" professions. Nobles were expected to derive their income from landholding, investments, or government service.

and honorary award, personal and not hereditary, which will be conferred by the king without discrimination on citizens of any order who merit it by the loftiness of their patriotic virtue and by the importance of their public service.

The charter of the constitution shall be engraved on a public monument raised for this purpose. A reading of it shall be made to the king at the ascension to his throne, and then shall be followed by his oath. . . . All agents of the executive power, civil and military, all judicial magistrates, all municipal officers shall swear an oath to uphold the charter. Every year on the anniversary of its approval, the charter shall be read and posted in the churches, courts, schools, and at the headquarters of each regiment and on naval vessels. The day will be a day of solemn celebration in every country under French dominion.

## FINANCES

The Estates General shall void every special tax, on persons or on property, such as the *taille,* the *franc-fief,* head tax, military service, the *corvée,*[4] the billeting of troops, and others, and replace them as needed by general taxes, payable by all citizens of every order.

The Estates General in the outright replacement of taxes, shall consider principally direct taxes, which will bear equally on all citizens and all provinces and which will be simplest and less expensive to collect.

## AGRICULTURE

The deputies will be especially charged to demand the total abolition of *capitaineries;*[5] they are in such contradiction to every principle of morality that they cannot be tolerated, even under the pretext of getting rid of some of their worst abuses.

It is the natural right of any proprietor of land to be able to destroy on his land destructive game and other animals.[6] In regard to hunting rights and the means of employing them, whether for their suppression or preservation, we look to the Estates General to suppress their abuses in a timely manner.

## LEGISLATION

The object of the laws is to protect liberty and property. Their perfection is to be humane and just, clear and general, to be in keeping with the national character and morality, to protect people of every order and every class equally, and to punish without distinction of persons whoever violates the law.

## TREATMENT OF CRIMINALS

No citizen can be arrested or obliged to appear before any judge without an order coming from a competent judge. Every accused person, even before his first interrogation, shall have the right to call a lawyer.

A law will be passed to suppress the use of all torture before a criminal is executed and all practices that add prolonged and cruel suffering to the execution.

The death penalty should be limited to the smallest number of cases as possible, and reserved for truly atrocious crimes.

Those guilty of the same crime, no matter what order of society they are from, should undergo the same punishment.

---

[4]*Taille:* a tax on land paid mainly by peasants; *franc-fief:* a fee paid by a nonnoble on the acquisition of land; *corvée:* unpaid labor demanded mainly from peasants by their landlords.
[5]Hunting monopolies granted mainly to members of the high nobility.

[6]Laws prevented peasants from destroying crop-damaging birds and rabbits; their purpose was to protect the supply of animals hunted by the nobility.

Prisons should have the purpose not of punishing prisoners but of securing their persons. Underground dungeons should be suppressed. Efforts should be made to make the interior of other prisons healthier, and to establish rules for the moral conduct of the prisoners.

The Estates General should consider the plight of black slaves and men of color, in the colonies as well as in France.

## RELIGION

[Religion's] ministers, as citizens of the state, are subject to the law; as property owners, they must bear a share of all public expenditure.

The Christian religion ordains civil toleration; every citizen must enjoy private liberty of conscience, but the requirements of law and order require only one dominant religion. . . .

# Women's Issues on the Eve of the French Revolution
▼▼▼

## 45 ▼ PETITION OF PARISIAN WOMEN OF THE THIRD ESTATE TO LOUIS XVI

Aside from its undisputed importance in political and legal history, the French Revolution has a special place in the history of feminism. To a degree without precedent, French women, especially in the early 1790s, ceased being passive observers of political developments and became active participants in the revolutionary process. Their most dramatic act took place on October 5, 1789, when approximately seven thousand Parisian women marched to Versailles, where they invaded the royal apartments and demanded that the king address issues of unemployment, inflation, and shortages of bread. In response to their demands and threats (some demonstrators threatened to "rip out the queen's heart and fricassee her liver") the royal family and the National Assembly moved to Paris, where, in this city's politically charged atmosphere, the Revolution unfolded. Women's involvement was not limited to this one notable act. Women helped storm the Paris Bastille in July 1789, wrote revolutionary manifestos, organized women's political clubs, engaged in political debates, wrote letters to newspapers, and rioted both for and against the Revolution.

Many female revolutionaries saw the upheaval in France as more than an opportunity to eradicate absolutism and aristrocratic privilege. They demanded that the Revolution's leaders consider issues that pertained uniquely to women — marriage and divorce, education, inheritance laws, vocational opportunities, and female political rights. A few of the women's political clubs demanded women's rights to bear arms and fight in the revolutionary armies. Female activism declined after 1793 when Jacobin leaders in the National Convention outlawed women's political clubs and denied women the right to speak in political assemblies. The regime instituted after the fall of the Jacobins in 1794, known as the Directory, revoked much earlier legislation that had favored women's rights. In 1804 the Napoleonic Code once more legalized the dominance of husbands over wives and curtailed married women's control of their wages, property, and inheritance. Despite these setbacks, the women revolutionaries raised issues that would not go away. The ground had been prepared for the feminist movements that flourished in Europe and the Americas during the nineteenth and twentieth centuries.

The following petition was written in January 1789 by a group of Parisian women of the Third Estate. Although unable to vote in the election of delegates to the Estates General and excluded from the process of drawing up the *cahiers de doléances,* these women, no less than their male counterparts, had hopes for revolutionary change.

## QUESTIONS FOR ANALYSIS

1. The authors of the petition chose to address their concerns to the king rather than the Estates General. Why?
2. What attitudes toward men are stated or implied in the petition?
3. According to the petition, what laws and social customs of France determine women's vocational and matrimonial prospects?
4. What specific steps do the authors hope the king will take on their behalf?
5. If these steps are taken, what kind of future do these women envision for themselves in France?
6. How does the tone and political rhetoric of the women's petition resemble and differ from that of the cahier of the Paris Third Estate, a document written by men (see source 45)?
7. What guesses can be made about the status and educational background of the women who wrote this petition?

Sire,

At a time when the various orders of the state are busy with their interests, when everyone is trying to assert his titles and his rights, when some people are worrying about recalling centuries of servitude and anarchy, when others are making every effort to shake off the last links which still bind them to the imperious remains of the feudal system, women — continual objects of the admiration and scorn of men — women, wouldn't it be possible for them also to make their voices heard amidst this general agitation?

Excluded from the national assemblies by laws too well consolidated for them to hope to break, they do not ask, Sire, for your permission to send their deputies to the Estates General; they know too well how great a role interest would play in an election and how easy it would be for the representatives to impede the freedom of the votes.

We prefer, Sire, to place our cause at your feet; not wishing to obtain anything except from your heart, we address our complaints and confide our miseries to it.

The women of the Third Estate are almost all born without fortune; their education is very neglected or very defective: it consists in their being sent to schools at the house of a teacher who himself does not know the first word of the language he is teaching. They continue going there until they are able to read the service of the Mass in French and Vespers[1] in Latin. Hav-

---

[1] A Catholic religious service in the late afternoon or evening, consisting of hymns, scriptural readings, and prayers.

ing fulfilled the first duties of religion, they are taught to work; having reached the age of fifteen or sixteen, they can make five or six *sous*[2] a day. If nature has refused them beauty, they get married without dowry[3] to unfortunate artisans, lead aimless, difficult lives stuck away in the provinces, and give birth to children they are incapable of raising. If, on the contrary, they are born pretty, without culture, without principles, without any idea of morals, they become the prey of the first seducer, commit a first sin, come to Paris to bury their shame, end by losing it altogether, and die victims of licentious ways.

Today, when the difficulty of subsisting forces thousands of them to put themselves up for auction, when men find it easier to buy them for a spell than to win them over forever, those whom a happy penchant inclines to virtue, who are consumed by the desire to learn, who feel themselves led by a natural taste, who have overcome the deficiencies of their education and know a little of everything without having learned anything, those, to conclude, whom a haughty soul, a noble heart, a pride of sentiment cause to be called *prudish*, are forced to throw themselves into cloisters where only a modest dowry is required, or forced to hire themselves out when they do not have enough courage, enough heroism, to share the generous devotion of the daughters of Vincent de Paul.[4]

Also, several, solely because they are born girls, are disdained by their parents, who refuse to set them up, preferring to concentrate their fortune on the head of a son whom they designate to carry on their name in the capital; for it is good that Your Majesty understands that we also have names to keep up. Or, if old age finds them spinsters, they spend it in tears and see themselves the object of the scorn of their nearest relatives.

To prevent so many ills, Sire, we ask that men not be allowed, under any pretext, to exercise trades that are the prerogative of women — such as seamstress, embroiderer, *marchande de mode*,[5] etc., etc.; if we are left at least with the needle and the spindle, we promise never to handle the compass or the square.

We ask, Sire, that your benevolence provide us with the means of putting to use the talents with which nature will have furnished us, notwithstanding the impediments which are forever being placed on our education.

May you assign us positions, which we alone will be able to fill, which we will occupy only after having passed a strict examination, after trustworthy inquiries concerning the purity of our morals.

We ask to be enlightened, to have work, not in order to usurp men's authority, but in order to be better esteemed by them, so that we might have the means of living out of the way of misfortune and so that poverty does not force the weakest among us, who are blinded by luxury and swept along by example, to join the crown of unfortunate beings who overpopulate the streets and whose debauched audacity is a disgrace to our sex and to the men who keep them company.

We would want this class of women to wear a mark of identification. Today, when they go so far as to adopt the modesty of our dress, when they mingle everywhere in all kinds of clothing, we often find ourselves taken for them; some men are mistaken and make us blush because of their scorn. It would be necessary that under pain of having to work in the public workshops for the benefit of the poor (it is known that work is the greatest punishment that can be inflicted on them), they never be able to remove this mark.

---

[2]Figuratively, a tiny amount of money; a few cents.
[3]Money or goods that a woman brings to her husband at the time of marriage. In prerevolutionary France the money would be controlled by the husband but returned to the woman if she became a widow. Without a dowry a young woman's chances of marrying were severely diminished.

[4]The Daughters of Charity, a religious order founded in 1633 by the French religious leader St. Vincent de Paul (1581–1660), was noted for its work among the poor and orphans.
[5]One who makes or sells women's hats.

. . . [*sic*] However, it occurs to us that the empire of fashion would be destroyed and one would run the risk of seeing many too many women dressed in the same color.

We implore you, Sire, to set up free schools where we could learn our language on the basis of principles [and] religion and ethics. May one and the other be offered to us in all their grandeur, entirely stripped of the petty applications which attenuate their majesty; may our hearts be formed there; may we be taught above all to practice the virtues of our sex: gentleness, modesty, patience, charity; as for the arts that please, women learn them without teachers. Sciences? . . . They serve only to inspire us with a stupid pride, lead us to pedantry, go against the desires of nature, make of us mixed beings who are rarely faithful wives and still more rarely good mothers of families.

We ask to come out of the state of ignorance, to be able to give our children a sound and reasonable education so as to make of them subjects worthy of serving you. We will teach them to cherish the beautiful name of Frenchmen; we will transmit to them the love we have for Your Majesty, for we are willing to leave valor and genius to men, but we will challenge them over the dangerous and precious gift of sensitivity; we defy them to love you better than we; they run to Versailles,[6] most of them for their interests, and when we, Sire, see you there, with difficulty and with pounding hearts, and are able to gaze for an instant upon your August Person, tears flow from our eyes. The idea of Majesty, of Sovereign, vanishes, as we see in you only a tender Father, for whom we would sacrifice our lives a thousand times.

---

[6]The French royal residence, the construction of which was begun during the reign of Louis XIV in the 1680s.

▼▼▼

# Anticolonialism and Revolution in the Americas

Despite the many contrasts between the British colonies of eastern North America and the Portuguese-Spanish colonies of Mexico and Central and South America, all of them won independence from European rule between the 1770s and the 1830s. Although the independence movements in North and Latin America unfolded differently, throughout the Americas the rebels had similar grievances and ideals. Grievances included mercantilist restrictions on trade, high taxes, and a lack of self-government; the ideals were provided by English constitutionalism, the Enlightenment, and, in the case of Latin America, the revolutions in North America and France.

The governments that emerged after the revolutions differed markedly. In the northern thirteen colonies, opponents of British rule coalesced in a unified movement under the Continental Congress and George Washington, and after independence this unity was ultimately preserved in the U.S. Constitution. In South America, where struggles for independence were waged on a regional basis under generals such as Simón Bolívar, Bernardo O'Higgins, and José de San Martín, the departure of Spain and Portugal resulted in more than a dozen independent states. In North America, federal and state governments drew on the principles of English constitutionalism to guarantee basic freedoms and extend political rights to a majority of adult white males. In Latin America, with its traditions of Spanish/Portuguese absolutism and aristocracy, wealthy landowners controlled the new states and excluded the peasant masses from politics.

Social and economic relationships also differed markedly in the postcolonial era. Although the new U.S. government preserved slavery and continued to restrict women's legal and political rights, property holding was widespread. A fluid class structure and economic expansion ensured that not just the political elite but the common people too would benefit from independence. In Latin America, however, continuation of the colonial class structure meant that the economic and social chasm between the mass of propertyless Indian peasants and the narrow elite of white property owners remained. Even more so than in North America, the independence movement in Latin America transformed political relationships but was not a true revolution.

# "Simple Facts, Plain Arguments, and Common Sense"

## 46 ▼ Thomas Paine, *COMMON SENSE*

After more than a decade of growing tension over taxes, British imperial policy, the power of colonial legislatures, and a host of other emotionally charged issues, in April 1775 the American Revolution began with the clash between British regulars and American militiamen at the Battle of Lexington and Concord. In May the Green Mountain Boys under Ethan Allen took Fort Ticonderoga on Lake Champlain, and in June the British defeated colonial troops in the Battle of Bunker Hill outside of Boston but at the cost of more than a thousand casualties.

Despite these events, in the summer and fall of 1775 most Americans still hoped reconciliation with Great Britain was possible. They were convinced that evil ministers, not the king, were responsible for British policy and that views of conciliatory British politicians such as Edmund Burke would prevail. Then in January 1776 there appeared in Philadelphia a thirty-five page pamphlet entitled *Common Sense* written by Thomas Paine (1737–1809), a bankrupt one-time corset-maker, sailor, tobacconist, and minor customs official, who had immigrated to Pennsylvania from England only fourteen months earlier to escape debtor's prison. Despite his background, Paine produced what was far and away the most brilliant political pamphlet written during the American Revolution, and perhaps ever in the English language.

Within three months *Common Sense* sold more than one hundred thousand copies, one for every four or five adult males in the colonies. It "burst from the press," wrote Benjamin Rush, the Pennsylvania physician and signer of the Declaration of Independence, "with an effect which has rarely been produced in any age or country." Written with passion and vivid imagery, Paine's pamphlet brought into focus American reservations about England and the European world and expressed American aspirations for creating a newer, freer, more open society as an independent nation. It accelerated the move toward the events of July 2, 1776, when the delegates to the Second Continental Congress created the United States of America, and of July 4, when they signed the Declaration of Independence.

During the Revolutionary War Paine fought in Washington's army and composed pamphlets to bolster American spirits. In the late 1780s he returned to England but in 1792 was forced to flee to France after his public support of the French Revolution led to his indictment for sedition. Chosen as a delegate to the French National Convention (although he knew no French), Paine was later imprisoned for ten months during the Reign of Terror, and on release resided with James Monroe, the American ambassador to France. While in France he attacked Christianity in his pamphlet *The Age of Reason,* the notoriety of which was such that on his return to the United States in 1802 he was vilified as an atheist. Impoverished and disgraced, he died unheralded in New York City in 1809.

## QUESTIONS FOR ANALYSIS

1. What are Paine's views of the origins and defects of monarchy as a form of government and hereditary succession as a principle of government?
2. What are his views of King George III?
3. What characteristics does Paine ascribe to Great Britain in general and the British government in particular? How might his background explain his negative views?
4. How does Paine counter the arguments of Americans who still sought reconciliation with Great Britain?
5. Despite Paine's rejection of the British government, do his ideas in *Common Sense* owe a debt to the principles of the English Bill of Rights?
6. What is there about the pamphlet's language, tone, and arguments that might explain its enormous popularity?

## REMARKS ON THE ENGLISH CONSTITUTION

I draw my idea of the form of government from a principle in nature which no art can overturn, viz. that the more simple anything is, the less liable it is to be disordered, and the easier repaired when disordered; and with this maxim in view, I offer a few remarks on the so much boasted constitution of England. That it was noble for the dark and slavish times in which it was erected, is granted. When the world was overrun with tyranny, the least remove therefrom was a glorious rescue. But that it is imperfect, subject to convulsions, and incapable of producing what it seems to promise, is easily demonstrated.

Absolute governments (though the disgrace of human nature) have this advantage with them, they are simple; if the people suffer, they know the head from which their suffering springs; know likewise the remedy; and are not bewildered by a variety of causes and cures. But the constitution of England is so exceedingly complex that the nation may suffer for years together without being able to discover in which part the fault lies; some will say in one and some in another, and every political physician will advise a different medicine.

An inquiry into the *constitutional errors* in the English form of government is at this time highly necessary; for as we are never in a proper condition of doing justice to others while we continue under the influence of some leading partiality, so neither are we capable of doing it to ourselves while we remain fettered by any obstinate prejudice. And as a man who is attached to a prostitute is unfitted to choose or judge of a wife, so any prepossession in favor of a rotten constitution of government will disable us from discerning a good one.

## OF MONARCHY AND HEREDITARY SUCCESSION

Government by kings was first introduced into the world by the heathens, from whom the children of Israel copied the custom. It was the most prosperous invention the Devil ever set on foot for the promotion of idolatry. The heathens paid divine honors to their deceased kings, and the Christian world has improved on the plan by doing the same to their living ones.[1] How impious is the title of sacred Majesty applied to a worm, who in the midst of his splendor is crumbling into dust! . . .

To the evil of monarchy we have added that of hereditary succession; and as the first is a degradation and lessening of ourselves, so the second, claimed as a matter of rights, is an insult and imposition on posterity. For all men being originally equals, no *one* by *birth* could have a right to set up his own family in perpetual preference to all others forever, and though himself might deserve *some* decent degree of honors of his contemporaries, yet his descendants might be far too unworthy to inherit them. . . .

Secondly, as no man at first could possess any other public honors than were bestowed upon him, so the givers of those honors could have no power to give away the right of posterity, and though they might say "we choose you for our head," they could not without manifest injustice to their children say "that your children and your children's children shall reign over our's forever." Because such an unwise, unjust, unnatural compact might perhaps, in the next succession put them under the government of a rogue or a fool. . . .

This is supposing the present race of kings in the world to have had an honorable origin; whereas it is more than probable that, could we take off the dark covering of antiquity and trace them to their first rise, we should find the first of them nothing better than the principal ruffian of some restless gang. . . . England, since the conquest, hath known some few good monarchs, but groaned beneath a much larger number of bad ones; yet no man in his senses can say that their claim under William the Conqueror is a very honorable one. A French bastard, landing with an armed banditti and establishing himself king of England against the consent of the natives, is in plain terms a very paltry rascally original. It certainly hath no divinity in it. . . .

The most plausible plea which hath ever been offered in favor of hereditary succession is that it preserves a nation from civil wars; and were this true, it would be weighty; whereas, it is the most barefaced falsity ever imposed upon mankind. The whole history of England disowns the fact. Thirty kings and two minors have reigned in that distracted kingdom since the conquest, in which time there have been (including the Revolution) no less than eight civil wars and nineteen rebellions. Wherefore instead of making for peace, it makes against it, and destroys the very foundation it seems to stand upon. . . .

In short, monarchy and succession have laid (not this or that kingdom only) but the world in blood and ashes. 'Tis a form of government which the word of god bears testimony against, and blood will attend it.

---

[1]The reference is to the theory of divine right monarchy, which asserted that kings were God's specially chosen lieutenants to rule his subjects, and were even in some limited sense divine figures themselves.

## THOUGHTS ON THE PRESENT STATE OF AMERICAN AFFAIRS

In the following pages I offer nothing more than simple facts, plain arguments, and common sense; and have no other preliminaries to settle with the reader, than that he will divest himself of prejudice and prepossession, and suffer his reason and his feelings to determine for themselves; that he will put on, or rather that he will not put off, the true character of a man, and generously enlarge his views beyond the present day.

Volumes have been written on the subject of the struggle between England and America. Men of all ranks have embarked in the controversy, from different motives, and with various designs; but all have been ineffectual, and the period of debate is closed. Arms as the last resource decide the contest; the appeal was the choice of the king, and the continent has accepted the challenge. . . .

The sun never shined on a cause of greater worth. 'Tis not the affair of a city, a county, a province, or a kingdom; but of a continent — of at least one-eighth part of the habitable globe. 'Tis not the concern of a day, a year, or an age; posterity are virtually involved in the contest, and will be more or less affected even to the end of time by the proceedings now. Now is the seedtime of continental union, faith, and honor. The least fracture now will be like a name engraved with the point of a pin on the tender rind of a young oak; the wound would enlarge with the tree, and posterity read it in full grown characters. . . .

I have heard it asserted by some, that as America has flourished under her former connection with Great Britain, the same connection is necessary towards her future happiness. . . . Nothing can be more fallacious than this kind of argument. We may as well assert that because a child has thrived upon milk, that it is never to have meat, or that the first twenty years of our lives is to become a precedent for the next twenty. But even this is admitting more than is true; for

I answer roundly that America would have flourished as much, and probably much more, had no European power taken any notice of her. The commerce by which she hath enriched herself are the necessaries of life, and will always have a market while eating is the custom of Europe.

But she has protected us, say some. That she hath engrossed[2] us is true, and defended the continent at our expense as well as her own is admitted; and she would have defended Turkey from the same motive, viz., for the sake of trade and dominion. . . .

We have boasted the protection of Great Britain without considering that her motive was *interest,* not *attachment;* and that she did not protect us from *our enemies* on *our account,* but from her enemies on her own account, from those who had no quarrel with us on any *other account,* and who will always be our enemies on the *same account.* . . .

As I have always considered the independency of this continent an event which sooner or later must arrive, so from the late rapid progress of the continent to maturity, the event cannot be far off. Wherefore, on the breaking out of hostilities, it was not worth the while to have disputed a matter which time would have finally redressed, unless we meant to be in earnest; otherwise it is like wasting an estate on a suit at law, to regulate the trespasses of a tenant whose lease is just expiring. No man was a warmer wisher for a reconciliation than myself, before the fatal nineteenth of April, 1775, but the moment the event of that day was made known, I rejected the hardened, sullen-tempered Pharaoh of England forever; and disdain the wretch, that with the pretended title of FATHER OF HIS PEOPLE can unfeelingly hear of their slaughter, and composedly sleep with their blood upon his soul.

But admitting that matters were now made up, what would be the event? I answer, the ruin of the continent. And that for several reasons.

*First.* The powers of governing still remaining in the hands of the king, he will have a negative[3] over the whole legislation of this continent. And as he hath shown himself such an inveterate en-

---

[2]To occupy with troops.

[3]A veto.

emy to liberty, and discovered such a thirst for arbitrary power, is he, or is he not, a proper person to say to these colonies, *You shall make no laws but what I please!* . . .

*Secondly.* That as even the best terms which we can expect to obtain can amount to no more than a temporary expedient, or a kind of government by guardianship, which can last no longer than till the colonies come of age, so the general face and state of things in the interim will be unsettled and unpromising. Emigrants of property will not choose to come to a country whose form of government hangs but by a thread, and who is every day tottering on the brink of commotion and disturbance; and numbers of the present inhabitants would lay hold of the interval to dispose of their effects, and quit the continent. . . .

If there is any true cause of fear respecting independence, it is because no plan is yet laid down. Men do not see their way out. Wherefore, as an opening into that business I offer the following hints; at the same time modestly affirming that I have no other opinion of them myself than that they may be the means of giving rise to something better. . . .

Let the assemblies be annual, with a president only. The representation more equal, their business wholly domestic, and subject to the authority of a continental congress.

Let each colony be divided into six, eight, or ten, convenient districts, each district to send a proper number of delegates to congress, so that each colony send at least thirty. The whole number in congress will be at least 390. Each congress to sit and to choose a president by the following method. When the delegates are met, let a colony be taken from the whole thirteen colonies by lot, after which let the congress choose (by ballot) a president from out of the delegates of that province. In the next congress, let a colony be taken by lot from twelve only, omitting that colony from which the president was taken in the former congress, and so proceeding on till the whole thirteen shall have had their proper rotation. And in order that nothing may pass into a law but what is satisfactorily just, not less than three fifths of the congress to be called a majority. He that will promote discord, under a government so equally formed as this, would have joined Lucifer in his revolt. . . .

But where, say some, is the king of America? I'll tell you, friend, he reigns above, and doth not make havoc of mankind like the Royal Brute of Great Britain. Yet that we may not appear to be defective even in earthly honors, let a day be solemnly set apart for proclaiming the charter; let it be brought forth placed on the divine law, the Word of God; let a crown be placed thereon, by which the world may know, that so far as we approve of monarchy, that in America THE LAW IS KING. For as in absolute governments the king is law, so in free countries the law *ought* to BE king, and there ought to be no other. But lest any ill use should afterwards arise, let the crown at the conclusion of the ceremony be demolished, and scattered among the people whose right it is. . . .

Ye that tell us of harmony and reconciliation, can ye restore to us the time that is past? Can ye give to prostitution its former innocence? Neither can ye reconcile Britain and America. The last cord now is broken, the people of England are presenting addresses against us. There are injuries which nature cannot forgive; she would cease to be nature if she did. As well can the lover forgive the ravisher of his mistress, as the continent forgive the murders of Britain. . . .

O ye that love mankind! Ye that dare oppose not only the tyranny but the tyrant, stand forth! Every spot of the old world is overrun with oppression. Freedom hath been hunted round the globe. Asia and Africa have long expelled her. Europe regards her like a stranger, and England hath given her warning to depart. O receive the fugitive, and prepare in time an asylum for mankind.

# Bolívar's Dreams for Latin America
▼▼▼

## 47 ▼ Simón Bolívar, THE JAMAICA LETTER

Simón Bolívar, proclaimed "Liberator" by his own people and the most renowned leader of the Latin American independence movement, was born to a wealthy Venezuelan landowning family in 1783. Orphaned at an early age, he was educated by a private tutor who inspired in his pupil an enthusiasm for the principles of the Enlightenment and republicanism. After spending three years in Europe, Bolívar returned to New Spain in 1803, where the death of his new bride plunged him into grief and caused his return to France and Italy. In 1805 in Rome he took a vow to dedicate his life to the liberation of his native land. On his return he became a leading member of the republican-minded group in Caracas that in 1808 began to agitate for independence and in 1810 deposed the colonial governor. Until his death in 1830, Bolívar dedicated himself to the Latin American independence movement as a publicist, diplomat, theoretician, and statesman. His greatest contribution was as the general who led the armies that defeated the Spaniards and liberated the northern regions of South America.

The so-called Jamaica Letter was written in 1815 during a self-imposed exile in Jamaica. It was addressed to "an English gentleman," probably the island's governor, the Duke of Manchester. The Venezuelan Republic had collapsed in May as a result of a viciously fought Spanish counteroffensive, divisions among the revolutionaries, and opposition from many Indians, blacks, and mulattos, who viewed the Creole landowners, not the Spaniards, as their oppressors. The letter was written in response to a request from the Englishman for Bolívar's insights into the background and prospects of the liberation movement.

---

## QUESTIONS FOR ANALYSIS

1. Why does Bolívar believe that Spain's efforts to hold on to its American territories are doomed?
2. What Spanish policies, according to Bolívar, have made Spanish rule odious to him and other revolutionaries?
3. In Bolívar's view, what complicates the task of predicting Spanish America's political future?
4. Does Bolívar's letter reveal concern for the economic and social condition of South America's nonwhite population? What are some of the implications of Bolívar's attitudes?
5. Based on your reading of Bolívar, what guesses can you make about the reasons why the new nations of South America found it difficult to achieve stable republican governments?

With what a feeling of gratitude I read that passage in your letter in which you say to me: "I hope that the success which then followed Spanish arms may now turn in favor of their adversaries, the badly oppressed people of South America." I take this hope as a prediction, if it is justice that determines man's contests. Success will crown our efforts, because the destiny of America has been irrevocably decided; the tie that bound her to Spain has been severed. Only a concept maintained that tie and kept the parts of that immense monarchy together. That which formerly bound them now divides them. The hatred that the Peninsula[1] inspired in us is greater than the ocean between us. It would be easier to have the two continents meet than to reconcile the spirits of the two countries. The habit of obedience; a community of interest, of understanding, of religion; mutual goodwill; a tender regard for the birthplace and good name of our forefathers; in short, all that gave rise to our hopes, came to us from Spain. As a result there was born a principle of affinity that seemed eternal, notwithstanding the misbehavior of our rulers which weakened that sympathy, or, rather, that bond enforced by the domination of their rule. At present the contrary attitude persists: we are threatened with the fear of death, dishonor, and every harm; there is nothing we have not suffered at the hands of that unnatural step-mother — Spain. The veil has been torn asunder. We have already seen the light, and it is not our desire to be thrust back into darkness. . . . For this reason America fights desperately, and seldom has desperation failed to achieve victory. . . .

It is . . . difficult to foresee the future fate of the New World, to set down its political principles, or to prophesy what manner of government it will adopt. . . . We inhabit a world apart, separated by broad seas. We are young in the ways of almost all the arts and sciences, although, in a certain manner, we are old in the ways of civilized society. . . . But we scarcely retain a vestige of what once was; we are, moreover, neither Indian nor European, but a species midway between the legitimate proprietors of this country and the Spanish usurpers. In short, though Americans by birth we derive our rights from Europe, and we have to assert these rights against the rights of the natives, and at the same time we must defend ourselves against the invaders. This places us in a most extraordinary and involved situation. . . .

The role of the inhabitants of the American hemisphere has for centuries been purely passive. Politically they were non-existent. We are still in a position lower than slavery, and therefore it is more difficult for us to rise to the enjoyment of freedom. . . . States are slaves because of either the nature or the misuse of their constitutions; a people is therefore enslaved when the government, by its nature or its vices, infringes on and usurps the rights of the citizen or subject. Applying these principles, we find that America was denied not only its freedom but even an active and effective tyranny. Under absolutism there are no recognized limits to the exercise of governmental powers. The will of the great sultan, khan, bey, and other despotic rulers is the supreme law, carried out more or less arbitrarily by the lesser pashas, khans, and satraps of Turkey and Persia, who have an organized system of oppression in which inferiors participate according to the authority vested in them. To them is entrusted the administration of civil, military, political, religious, and tax matters. But, after all is said and done, the rulers of Isfahan are Persians; the viziers of the Grand Turk are Turks; and the sultans of Tartary are Tartars. . . .

How different is our situation! We have been harassed by a conduct which has not only deprived us of our rights but has kept us in a sort of permanent infancy with regard to public affairs. If we could at least have managed our domestic affairs and our internal administration,

---

[1]Refers to the Iberian Peninsula, consisting of Spain and Portugal.

we could have acquainted ourselves with the processes and mechanics of public affairs. . . .

Americans today, and perhaps to a greater extent than ever before, who live within the Spanish system occupy a position in society no better than that of serfs destined for labor, or at best they have no more status than that of mere consumers. Yet even this status is surrounded with galling restrictions, such as being forbidden to grow European crops, or to store products which are royal monopolies, or to establish factories of a type the Peninsula itself does not possess. To this add the exclusive trading privileges, even in articles of prime necessity, and the barriers between American provinces, designed to prevent all exchange of trade, traffic, and understanding. In short, do you wish to know what our future held? — simply the cultivation of the fields of indigo, grain, coffee, sugar cane, cacao, and cotton; cattle raising on the broad plains; hunting wild game in the jungles; digging in the earth to mine its gold — but even these limitations could never satisfy the greed of Spain.

So negative was our existence that I can find nothing comparable in any other civilized society, examine as I may the entire history of time and the politics of all nations. Is it not an outrage and a violation of human rights to expect a land so splendidly endowed, so vast, rich, and populous, to remain merely passive?

As I have just explained, we were cut off and, as it were, removed from the world in relation to the science of government and administration of the state. We were never viceroys or governors, save in the rarest of instances; seldom archbishops and bishops; diplomats never; as military men, only subordinates; as nobles, without royal privileges. In brief, we were neither magistrates nor financiers and seldom merchants — all in flagrant contradiction to our institutions. . . .

It is harder, Montesquieu[2] has written, to release a nation from servitude than to enslave a free nation. This truth is proven by the annals of all times, which reveal that most free nations have been put under the yoke, but very few enslaved nations have recovered their liberty. Despite the convictions of history, South Americans have made efforts to obtain liberal, even perfect, institutions, doubtless out of that instinct to aspire to the greatest possible happiness, which, common to all men, is bound to follow in civil societies founded on the principles of justice, liberty, and equality. But are we capable of maintaining in proper balance the difficult charge of a republic? Is it conceivable that a newly emancipated people can soar to the heights of liberty, and, unlike Icarus, neither have its wings melt nor fall into an abyss? Such a marvel is inconceivable and without precedent. There is no reasonable probability to bolster our hopes.

More than anyone, I desire to see America fashioned into the greatest nation in the world, greatest not so much by virtue of her area and wealth as by her freedom and glory. Although I seek perfection for the government of my country, I cannot persuade myself that the New World can, at the moment, be organized as a great republic. Since it is impossible, I dare not desire it; yet much less do I desire to have all America a monarchy because this plan is not only impracticable but also impossible. Wrongs now existing could not be righted, and our emancipation would be fruitless. The American states need the care of paternal governments to heal the sores and wounds of despotism and war. . . .

From the foregoing, we can draw these conclusions: The American provinces are fighting for their freedom, and they will ultimately succeed. Some provinces as a matter of course will form federal and some central republics; the larger areas will inevitably establish monarchies, some of which will fare so badly that they will disintegrate in either present or future revolu-

---

[2]Montesquieu (1689–1755) was a French philosopher, historian, and jurist best known for his *Spirit of the Laws* (1755) and his theory that the powers of government — executive, legislative, and judicial — must be separated to ensure individual freedom.

tions. To consolidate a great monarchy will be no easy task, but it will be utterly impossible to consolidate a great republic.

It is a grandiose idea to think of consolidating the New World into a single nation, united by pacts into a single bond. It is reasoned that, as these parts have a common origin, language, customs, and religion, they ought to have a single government to permit the newly formed states to unite in a confederation. But this is not possible. . . .

When success is not assured, when the state is weak, and when results are distantly seen, all men hesitate; opinion is divided, passions rage, and the enemy fans these passions in order to win an easy victory because of them. As soon as we are strong and under the guidance of a liberal nation which will lend us her protection, we will achieve accord in cultivating the virtues and talents that lead to glory. Then will we march majestically toward that great prosperity for which South America is destined. . . .

# Chapter 6

# Africa, Southwest Asia, and India in the Seventeenth and Eighteenth Centuries

Around 1600, Southwest Asia and India, dominated by three large and powerful states, the Ottoman, Safavid, and Mughal empires, would seem to have had little in common with Africa, with its hundreds of kingdoms, confederations, chieftainships, and city-states and extensive regions with no formal states whatsoever. South and Southwest Asia, moreover, had but two major religions, Hinduism and Islam, while Africa had many religious faiths, including Christianity in Ethiopia, Islam in the Sudan, the Mediterranean north, and the east coast, and numerous varieties of animism throughout the continent. In comparison to Africa, India and Southwest Asia were more densely populated and more urbanized, and had more commercial and cultural contacts with Europe and East Asia.

Despite these many differences, during the seventeenth and eighteenth centuries Africa and South and Southwest Asia had a number of broad similarities. Both areas, for example, experienced increasing political instability and witnessed the decline, and in some cases disappearance, of once formidable states. Political deterioration was most striking in Asia, where the Persian Safavid Empire collapsed and disappeared in the 1730s, and the Mughal Empire was reduced to impotence and irrelevancy by the mid 1700s. The Ottoman Empire survived, but with shrunken borders, a demoralized populace, and an army that was a pale shadow of the force that had gone from victory to victory in the fifteenth and sixteenth centuries.

Africa too had its examples of political disintegration. The Songhai Empire in the western Sudan fell apart after a major defeat by invading Moroccans in 1591. The Kingdom of Monomotapa in southeast Africa had a similar fate after 1685 when it was overrun by a former client state, the Changamire Kingdom. Other African states slowly declined. These included Ethiopia, the Christian kingdom in east Africa; Benin, one of the great West African forest kingdoms; and Kanem-Bornu, in the central Sudan. Political weakness in Africa was not universal, with new states such as Dahomey, the Asante Confederation, and Oyo becoming formidable and many peoples throughout the continent preserving traditional chieftainships and clan relationships. Overall, however, African political life became less stable and more subject to conflict in the 1600s and 1700s.

Africa, India, and Southwest Asia also shared the experience of becoming more fully integrated into the global economy. Although some groups and individuals benefited from this development, its overall impact in both regions was negative. In India and Southwest Asia, increased trade with Europe brought new and cheaper goods but also widespread inflation and economic ruin for many thousands of artisans. Political corruption, oppressive taxes, rebellion, and warfare further damaged these regions' economies. In Africa, trade boomed on the west coast, but it came at great cost. Its most important commodities were human beings, whose capture, sale, and enslavement in the Americas destabilized African politics and degraded millions of human beings.

In all these regions European pressure increased in the 1600s and 1700s. In 1652, a small group of Dutch farmers arrived at the southern tip of Africa and established the first permanent European settlement on the continent. During the eighteenth century the descendants of these settlers pushed inland, and their appetite for land and slaves led to a series of wars with the Bantu who lived in the interior. A century later in India officials of the British East India Company took advantage of the Mughal Empire's disintegration and established its political authority in Bengal in northeast India and in regions of India's east coast. From this base the British extended their control of the whole subcontinent in the nineteenth century. Meanwhile on Africa's west coast Europeans were orchestrating a dramatic increase in the transatlantic slave trade in response to demands for slaves from sugar growers in Brazil and the West Indies. Over six million Africans were transported to the Americas as slaves in the 1700s. On Africa's east coast, where slaving had been insignificant, Dutch,

Portuguese, Arab, and especially French merchants by the end of the eighteenth century were selling many thousands of Africans per year to customers in Arabia, India, and French-controlled islands in the Indian Ocean. This spectacular growth of the slave trade underlined Africa's vulnerability in an age of growing global interaction.

▼▼▼

# Africa's Curse: The Slave Trade

Slavery has been practiced throughout history, in every corner of the globe and as part of every conceivable social-economic system. Slavery has existed in small farming villages in China and in great imperial cities such as ancient Rome; it has been practiced by pastoral nomads, plantation owners, rulers of empires, and modern totalitarian dictators. Slavery was mentioned in ancient Sumerian law codes during the fourth millennium B.C.E., and is still the lot of millions of human beings today despite its official condemnation by most of the world's governments.

In recent history slavery most affected the people of Africa, who became a source of unpaid labor in many parts of the world, especially the Americas. The Atlantic slave trade began in the fifteenth century under the Portuguese, who at first made small shipments of Africans to Portugal to serve as domestics and then larger shipments to the Canary Islands, the Madeiras, and São Tomé to work on sugar plantations. By 1500, approximately five hundred slaves were exported each year. That number did not grow appreciably until the mid 1500s, when the plantation system was established in Brazil and subsequently spread to Spanish America, the West Indies, and British North America. By the eighteenth century, when Great Britain became the leading purveyor of slaves, the transatlantic slave trade peaked, with more than six million slaves transported to the Americas.

Almost every aspect of modern African slavery is the subject of debate among historians. Did the enslavement of Africans result from racism, or were Africans enslaved because they were available and convenient to the market across the Atlantic? Did the loss of millions of individuals to slavery over five hundred years have serious or minimal demographic consequences for Africa? Was the political instability of various African states linked to the slave trade or other factors? Did reliance on selling slaves to Europeans impede Africa's economic development? Did European governments abolish the slave trade because of humanitarianism and religious convictions or hard-headed economic calculation?

One thing is certain. For the millions of Africans who were captured, shackled, wrenched from their families, branded, sold, packed into the holds of ships, sold once more, and put to work in American mines and fields, enslavement meant pain, debasement, and horror. For them, slavery was an unmitigated and terrible curse.

# The Path to Enslavement in America
▼▼▼

## 48 ▼ *Olaudah Equiano,*
## *THE INTERESTING NARRATIVE*
## *OF THE LIFE OF OLAUDAH EQUIANO*
## *WRITTEN BY HIMSELF*

Olaudah Equiano (1745?–1797) was born in Iboland, an area east of the Niger delta that today is part of southern Nigeria. Captured and sold into slavery when he was about eleven, during his teens he served several masters, including Michael Henry Pascal, a lieutenant in the British navy, and Robert King, a Quaker merchant from Philadelphia. Equiano accompanied Pascal on several naval campaigns during the Seven Years' War and, after having been sold to King, made a dozen voyages between London and the West Indies. He learned English, enabling him to pursue a career as a shipping clerk and navigator in England after King granted his freedom in the late 1760s. In the 1770s he joined the English abolitionist movement, speaking out against slavery in lecture tours that took him to dozens of cities in England, Scotland, and Ireland.

English abolitionists supported the publication of his autobiography, which went through eight editions after it appeared in 1789. Although written to turn the English public against the slave trade, Equiano's account of his experiences seems generally accurate and balanced. He describes the cruelties of the white slave traders as well as the acts of kindness of his white masters and English friends. He shows pride in his African ancestry but denounces the Africans who bought and sold slaves. In the following excerpt, Equiano describes his harsh introduction to slavery.

## QUESTIONS FOR ANALYSIS

1. On the basis of Equiano's account, describe the role of Africans in the slave trade.
2. What does Equiano's account reveal about the effect of slavery and the slave trade on African society?
3. What were the characteristics of slavery that Equiano encountered?
4. Once aboard the slave ship, what in the slaves' experiences contributed to their despair and demoralization, according to Equiano?
5. What factors might have contributed to the brutal treatment of the slaves by the ship's crew?

## TAKEN CAPTIVE

Generally when the grown people in the neighborhood were gone far in the fields to labor, the children assembled together in some of the neighbors' premises to play, and commonly some of us used to get up a tree to look out for any assailant or kidnapper that might come upon us, for they sometimes took those opportunities of our parents' absence to attack and carry off as many as they could seize. . . . One day, when all our people were gone out to their work as usual and only I and my dear sister were left to mind the house, two men and a woman got over our walls, and in a moment seized us both, and without giving us time to cry out or make resistance they stopped our mouths and ran off with us into the nearest wood. . . .

For a long time we had kept to the woods, but at last we came into a road which I believed I knew. I had now some hopes of being delivered, for we had advanced but a little way before I discovered some people at a distance, on which I began to cry out for their assistance: but my cries had no other effect than to make them tie me faster and stop my mouth, and then they put me into a large sack. They also stopped my sister's mouth and tied her hands, and in this manner we proceeded till we were out of the sight of these people. When we went to rest the following night they offered us some victuals, but we refused it, and the only comfort we had was in being in one another's arms all that night and bathing each other with our tears. But alas! we were soon deprived of even the small comfort of weeping together. The next day proved a day of greater sorrow than I had yet experienced, for my sister and I were then separated while we lay clasped in each other's arms. It was in vain that we besought them not to part us; she was torn from me and immediately carried away, while I was left in a state of distraction not to be described. I cried and grieved continually, and for several days I did not eat anything but what they forced into my mouth. At length, after many days' traveling, during which I had often changed

masters, I got into the hands of a chieftain in a very pleasant country. This man had two wives and some children, and they all used me extremely well and did all they could to comfort me, particularly the first wife, who was something like my mother. . . . This first master of mine, as I may call him, was a smith, and my principal employment was working his bellows, which were the same kind as I had seen in my vicinity. . . . I believe it was gold he worked, for it was of a lovely bright yellow color and was worn by the women on their wrists and ankles. I was there I suppose about a month, and they at last used to trust me some little distance from the house. This liberty I used in embracing every opportunity to inquire the way to my own home: and I also sometimes, for the same purpose, went with the maidens in the cool of the evenings to bring pitchers of water from the springs for the use of the house.

---

▷ Equiano escapes but, terrified of being alone in the forest at night, returns to his household.

---

Soon after this my master's only daughter and child by his first wife sickened and died, which affected him so much that for some time he was almost frantic, and really would have killed himself had he not been watched and prevented. However, in a small time afterwards he recovered and I was again sold. I was now carried to the left of the sun's rising, through many different countries and a number of large woods. The people I was sold to used to carry me very often when I was tired either on their shoulders or on their backs. I saw many convenient well-built sheds along the roads at proper distances, to accommodate the merchants and travelers who lay in those buildings along with their wives, who often accompany them; and they always go well armed.

---

▷ Equiano encounters his sister, but they are again quickly separated.

---

I was now more miserable, if possible, than before. The small relief which her presence gave me from pain was gone, and the wretchedness of my situation was redoubled by my anxiety after her fate and my apprehensions lest her sufferings should be greater than mine, when I could not be with her to alleviate them. Yes, thou dear partner of all my childish sports! thou sharer of my joys and sorrow! happy should I have ever esteemed myself to encounter every misery for you, and to procure your freedom by the sacrifice of my own. . . .

I did not long remain after my sister [departed]. I was again sold and carried through a number of places till, after traveling a considerable time, I came to a town called Tinmah in the most beautiful country I had yet seen in Africa. . . . I was sold here . . . by a merchant who lived and brought me there. I had been about two or three days at his house when a wealthy widow, a neighbor of his, came there one evening, and brought with her an only son, a young gentleman about my own age and size. Here they saw me; and, having taken a fancy to me, I was bought of the merchant, and went home with them. . . . The next day I was washed and perfumed, and when meal-time came I was led into the presence of my mistress, and ate and drank before her with her son. This filled me with astonishment; and I could scarce help expressing my surprise that the young gentleman should suffer me, who was bound, to eat with him who was free; and not only so, but that he would not at any time either eat or drink till I had taken first, because I was the eldest, which was agreeable to our custom. Indeed everything here, and all their treatment of me, made me forget that I was a slave. . . . There were likewise slaves daily to attend us, while my young master and I with other boys sported with our darts and bows and arrows, as I had been used to do at home. In this resemblance to my former happy state I passed about two months; and I now began to think I was to be adopted into the family, and was beginning to be reconciled to my situation, and to forget by degrees my misfortunes, when all at once the delusion vanished; for without the least previous knowledge, one morning early, while my dear master and companion was still asleep, I was wakened out of my reverie to fresh sorrow, and hurried away. . . .

At last I came to the banks of a large river, which was covered with canoes in which the people appeared to live with their household utensils and provisions of all kinds. I was beyond measure astonished at this, as I had never before seen any water larger than a pond or a rivulet: and my surprise was mingled with no small fear when I was put into one of these canoes and we began to paddle and move along the river. We continued going on thus till night, and when we came to land and made fires on the banks, each family by themselves, some dragged their canoes on shore, others stayed and cooked in theirs and laid in them all night. . . . Thus I continued to travel, sometimes by land, sometimes by water, through different countries and various nations, till at the end of six or seven months after I had been kidnapped I arrived at the sea coast.

## THE SLAVE SHIP

The first object which saluted my eyes when I arrived on the coast was the sea, and a slave ship which was then riding at anchor and waiting for its cargo. These filled me with astonishment, which was soon converted into terror when I was carried on board. I was immediately handled and tossed up to see if I were sound by some of the crew, and I was now persuaded that I had gotten into a world of bad spirits and that they were going to kill me. Their complexions too differing so much from ours, their long hair and the language they spoke (which was very different from any I had ever heard) united to confirm me in this belief. Indeed such were the horrors of my views and fears at the moment that, if ten thousand worlds had been my own, I would have freely parted with them all to have exchanged my condition with that of the meanest slave in my own country. When I looked round the ship too and saw a large furnace or copper boiling and a multitude of black people of every description chained together, every one of their countenances expressing dejection and sorrow, I no longer doubted of my fate; and quite overpowered with horror and anguish, I fell motionless on the deck and fainted. When I recovered a little I found some black people about me, who I believed were some of those who had brought me on board and had been receiving their pay; they talked to me in order to cheer me, but all in vain. . . .

I was soon put down under the decks, and there I received such a salutation in my nostrils as I had never experienced in my life: so that with the loathsomeness of the stench and crying together, I became so sick and low that I was not able to eat, nor had I the least desire to taste anything. I now wished for the last friend, death, to relieve me; but soon, to my grief, two of the white men offered me eatables, and on my refusing to eat, one of them held me fast by the hands and laid me across I think the windlass, and tied my feet while the other flogged me severely. I had never experienced anything of this kind before, and although, not being used to the water, I naturally feared that element the first time I saw it, yet nevertheless could I have got over the nettings I would have jumped over the side, but I could not; and besides, the crew used to watch us very closely who were not chained down to the decks, lest we should leap into the water: and I have seen some of these poor African prisoners most severely cut for attempting to do so, and hourly whipped for not eating. This indeed was often the case with myself. In a little time after, amongst the poor chained men I found some of my own nation, which in a small degree gave ease to my mind. I inquired of these what was to be done with us; they gave me to understand we were to be carried to these white people's country to work for them. I then was a little revived, and thought if it were no worse than working, my situation was not so desperate: but still I feared I should be put to death, the white people

looked and acted, as I thought, in so savage a manner; for I had never seen among my people such instances of brutal cruelty, and this not only shown towards us blacks but also to some of the whites themselves. One white man in particular I saw, when we were permitted to be on deck, flogged so unmercifully with a large rope near the foremast that he died in consequence of it; and they tossed him over the side as they would have done a brute. This made me fear these people the more, and I expected nothing less than to be treated in the same manner. . . .

At last, when the ship we were in had got in all her cargo, they made ready with many fearful noises, and we were all put under deck so that we could not see how they managed the vessel. But this disappointment was the last of my sorrow. The stench of the hold while we were on the coast was so intolerably loathsome that it was dangerous to remain there for any time, and some of us had been permitted to stay on the deck for the fresh air; but now that the whole ship's cargo were confined together it became absolutely pestilential. The closeness of the place and the heat of the climate, added to the number in the ship, which was so crowded that each had scarcely room to turn himself, almost suffocated us. This produced copious perspirations, so that the air soon became unfit for respiration from a variety of loathsome smells, and brought on a sickness among the slaves, of which many died, thus falling victims to the improvident avarice, as I may call it, of their purchasers. This wretched situation was again aggravated by the galling of the chains, now become insupportable, and the filth of the necessary tubs, into which the children often fell and were almost suffocated. The shrieks of the women and the groans of the dying rendered the whole a scene of horror almost inconceivable. Happily perhaps for myself I was soon reduced so low here that it was thought necessary to keep me almost always on deck, and from my extreme youth I was not put in fetters. . . .

One day, when we had a smooth sea and moderate wind, two of my wearied countrymen who were chained together (I was near them at the time), preferring death to such a life of misery, somehow made through the nettings and jumped into the sea: immediately another quite dejected fellow, who on account of his illness was suffered to be out of irons, also followed their example; and I believe many more would very soon have done the same if they had not been prevented by the ship's crew, who were instantly alarmed. Those of us that were the most active were in a moment put down under the deck, and there was such a noise and confusion amongst the people of the ship as I never heard before, to stop her and get the boat out to go after the slaves. However two of the wretches were drowned, but they got the other and afterwards flogged him unmercifully for thus attempting to prefer death to slavery. In this manner we continued to undergo more hardships than I can now relate, hardships which are inseparable from this accursed trade. Many a time we were near suffocation from the want of fresh air, which we were often without for whole days together. This and the stench of the necessary tubs carried off many. . . .

At last we came in sight of the island of Barbados, at which the whites on board gave a great shout and made many signs of joy to us. We did not know what to think of this, but as the vessel drew nearer we plainly saw the harbor and other ships of different kinds and sizes, and we soon anchored amongst them off Bridgetown. Many merchants and planters now came on board, though it was in the evening. They put us in separate parcels and examined us attentively. They also made us jump, and pointed to the land, signifying we were to go there. . . .

We were not many days in the merchant's custody before we were sold after their usual manner, which is this: On a signal given, (as the beat of a drum) the buyers rush at once into the yard where the slaves are confined, and make choice of that parcel they like best. The noise and clamor with which this is attended and the eagerness visible in the countenances of the buyers serve not a little to increase the apprehensions of the terrified Africans, who may well be supposed to consider them as the ministers of that destruction to which they think themselves devoted. In this manner, without scruple, are relations and friends separated, most of them never to see each other again. I remember in the vessel in which I was brought over, in the men's apartment there were several brothers who, in the sale, were sold in different lots; and it was very moving on this occasion to see and hear their cries at parting. O, ye nominal Christians! might not an African ask you, learned you this from your God who says unto you, Do unto all men as you would men should do unto you?

# The Economics of the Slave Trade
▼▼▼

## 49 ▼ James Barbot,
## *A VOYAGE TO THE NEW CALABAR RIVER*

For millions of Africans like Olaudah Equiano, the transatlantic slave trade was a nightmare. For many others it was a source of economic gain. One thinks immediately of wealth generated for European and American merchants, ship captains, plantation owners, and investors who profited from the slave trade and the exploitation of slave labor. As the following selection shows, however, there were also many others, not only in Europe but also in Africa and even Asia, who benefited economically.

James, or Jacques, Barbot, was a merchant from La Rochelle, France, who with his brother Jean moved to London in the late seventeenth century to escape religious persecution after Louis XIV revoked toleration for French Protestants in 1685. Both before and after leaving France the two brothers made several trading voyages to Africa, where they purchased slaves, and then to the Americas, where they sold their human cargo. In this selection Barbot describes his experiences on a voyage in 1699 to the Guinea Coast, a region of intense European commercial activity on Africa's west central coast. He and his ship, the *Albion,* visited a number of coastal towns, including Axim, Fida, Mina, Anamabou, New Calabar, Anischan, and Dony. Their main business took place in Bonny, a small island city-state on the Niger delta with a population of approximately 3,000. After negotiating with the king of Bonny, dubbed by Barbot as "King William," they set sail from Africa with over 600 slaves. This particular venture was a failure. After encountering bad weather en route, Barbot had fewer than 300 sick and emaciated slaves to sell when his ship reached the West Indies.

## QUESTIONS FOR ANALYSIS

1. What individuals and groups directly or indirectly profited from the slave trade? Do not limit yourself to Europeans.
2. What can you infer from Barbot's account about the effect of the slave trade on interior Africa?
3. How would you characterize trade on the Guinea Coast? Was it haphazard bargaining? A well-developed system with a specific currency? Something else?
4. What do the prices of the other commodities purchased by the Europeans say about the relative value of one slave?
5. What does the source reveal about the views of Europeans and slavery on the part of the Africans Barbot encountered?
6. What differences do you see between African attitudes toward the slave trade revealed in Barbot's account and those of King Afonso of Kongo some two hundred years earlier (Chapter 2, source 13)? How do you account for those differences?

April 8. Anchored before the Prussian fort, Great Fredericksburg.[1]

The Prussian general received us at his fort very civilly, but told us he had no need for any of our goods; the trade being everywhere on that coast at a standstill, as well by reason of the vast number of interlopers[2] and other trading ships; as for the wars among the natives . . . the armies had actually been in the field for eight months, which stopped all the routes for merchants to come down to the forts to trade; that it was expected there would be a battle soon between

---

[1]A fort built at Axim in 1684 by the Africa Company, a trading company founded in 1682 in which the rulers of Brandenburg-Prussia and several smaller German states were the principal investors. The company failed, and its assets were sold to the Dutch West India Company in the early 1700s.

[2]Traders who encroached on the trading rights of others.

them; that the Hollanders, a people very jealous of their commerce at the coast, were very committed to have the war carried on among the blacks, to distract as long as possible the trade of other Europeans, and to that effect were always ready to assist upon all occasions the blacks, their allies, that they might beat their enemies, so the commerce would fall into their hands.

On the tenth of April, a small Portuguese ship anchored by us; the master a black said he had been but three weeks from São Tomé,[3] and that about three months before he saw there four tall French ships coming from the coast of Guinea, loaded with slaves, mostly at Fida: . . . Those ships had been obliged to give near fifty crowns[4] apiece, at Fida; slaves being then pretty thin at that place, and in great demand.

The Portuguese master begged our protection to convoy him safely to Cape Corso, on his way to Fida, fearing the Hollanders at Mina, who, whenever they can, force all Portuguese ships to pay them a very high toll for the permission of trading at the coast.

We have abundance of our men sick, and several already dead, the weather being intolerably scorching hot, and we can hardly get any provisions for them, but a few goats very dear: we had from the Portuguese, one goat, one hog, and seven chickens, for five akies[5] in gold.

Here we perceived that above a hundred pounds worth of horse-beans we had bought at London, for subsisting our slaves in the voyage were quite rotten and spoiled, for want of being well stowed and looked after ever since.

On the twenty-first of April, we set sail, and anchored at Anamabou; where we purchased with much trouble, and at a very dear rate, a quantity of Indian wheat; . . . we paid three akies for every chest of corn, which is excessively expensive;

but having lost all our large stock of horse-beans, were forced to get corn at all rates.

The tenth of May, we sent the boat to Anischan for fuel; and bought a loading of wood chunks at three akies for each hundred, very expensive wood. . . .

The twenty-sixth, as we worked our small anchor aboard, both cable and buoy-rope breaking, we were forced to sail, leaving the anchor behind, which was hitched among the rocks at the bottom; and having purchased sixty-five slaves along the Gold Coast,[6] besides gold and elephants' teeth,[7] saluted the three European forts, each with nine guns; and steered east southeast, for four or five leagues, then south-east by east for twenty-eight leagues, towards New Calabar, to buy more slaves. . . .

June 23. Our man reported that the ship we could see within the river was English, commanded by one Edwards, who had got his complement of slaves, being five hundred, in three weeks time; and was ready to sail for the West-Indies: and that he would spare us an anchor of about eleven hundred weight, which rejoiced us much.

He reported further, that as soon as the blacks could see our ship off at sea, they immediately went up the river to buy slaves, besides a hundred and fifty that were actually at Bonny when he left it; and that king William had assured him, he engaged to furnish five hundred slaves for our loading, all lusty and young. Upon which, we consulted aboard with the officers, and unanimously agreed to carry up the ship, if possible, for the greater expedition.

On the twenty-fifth of June in the morning . . . we went ashore also to compliment the king, and make him overtures of trade, but he gave us to understand he expected one bar of iron[8] for

---

[3]A small island off the Guinea Coast controlled by Portugal.
[4]A former English coin worth five shillings.
[5]*Akie* or *accy* was a unit of money used in some parts of the African coast; apparently derived from the English word "account."

[6]Europeans referred to various parts of the Guinea Coast as the Gold Coast, Ivory Coast, Grain Coast, and Slave Coast.
[7]Elephant tusks.
[8]A bar of iron meant just that, but was also the basis for computing the value of other goods and types of currency.

each slave, more than Edwards had paid for his; and also objected much against our basins, tankards, yellow beads, and some other merchandise, as of little or no demand there at that time. The twenty-sixth, we had a conference with the king and principal natives of the country about trade, which lasted from three o-clock till night, without any result, they insisting to have thirteen bars of iron for a male, and ten for a female slave; objecting that they were now scarce, because of the many ships that had exported vast quantities of late. The king treated us at supper, and we took leave of him. . . .

The thirtieth, being ashore, had a new conference, which produced nothing; and then Pepprell, the king's brother, made a speech as from the king, reporting, "He was sorry we would not accept his proposals; that it was not his fault, he having a great esteem and regard for the Whites, who had much enriched him by trade. That what he so earnestly insisted on thirteen bars for a male, and ten for female slaves, came from the country people holding up the price of slaves at their inland markets, seeing so many large ships resort to Bonny for them; but to moderate matters, and encourage trading with us, he would be contented with thirteen bars for males, and nine bars and two brass rings for females, etc." Upon which we offered thirteen bars for men, and nine for women, and proportionably for boys and girls, according to their ages; after this we parted, without concluding anything further.

On the first of July, the king sent for us to come ashore; we stayed there till four in the afternoon, and concluded the trade on the terms offered them the day before; the king promising to come the next day aboard to confirm it, and be paid his duties. . . .

July 2. At two o-clock we fetched the king from shore, attended by all his caboceiros[9] and

officers, in three large canoes; and entering the ship, was saluted with seven guns. . . .

We had again a long discourse with the king and Pepprell his brother, concerning the rates of our goods and his customs. This Pepprell being a sharp blade, and a mighty talking black, perpetually making sly objections against something or other, and teasing us for this or that, . . . as well as for drinks, etc. it were to be wished, that such a one as he were out of the way, to facilitate trade.

We filled them with drams of brandy and bowls of punch till night, at such a rate that they all, being about fourteen with the king, had such loud clamorous discourses among themselves, as were hardly to be endured.

Thus, with much patience, all our affairs were adjusted after the fashion of a people who are not very scrupulous when it comes to finding excuses for not keeping literally to a verbal contract; for they have not the art of reading and writing, and therefore we are forced to stand to their agreement, which often is no longer than they think fit to hold it themselves. The king ordered the public crier to proclaim permission to trade with us; with the noise of his trumpets, being elephants' teeth made much after the same fashion as is used at the Gold Coast, we paying sixteen brass rings to the fellow for his fee. The blacks objected much against our wrought pewter, and tankards, green beads, and other goods, which they would not accept.

We gave the usual presents to the king and his officers; that is,

To the king a hat, a firelock, and nine bunches of beads, instead of a coat.

To captain Forty, the king's general, captain Pepprell, captain Boileau, alderman Bougsby, my lord Willyby, duke of Monmouth, drunken Henry,[10] and some others, two firelocks, eight hats, nine narrow Guinea stuffs.[11]

---

[9]A Portuguese term in this context meaning "middlemen" or "associates."
[10]Whimsical nicknames made up by Barbot for the members of the king's entourage.

[11]Inexpensive wool cloths.

We adjusted with them the reduction of our merchandise into bars of iron, as the standard coin.

One bunch of beads, one bar. Four strings of rings, ten rings in each, one bar. Four copper bars, one bar. One piece of narrow Guinea stuff, one bar. One broad piece of felt, one bar. One piece Nicanees,[12] three bars. . . . And so on, for every other sort of goods.

The price of provisions and wood was also regulated.

Sixty king's yams, one bar; one hundred and sixty slaves' yams,[13] one bar; for fifty thousand yams to be delivered to us. A large cask of water, two rings. For the length of wood, seven bars, which is expensive; but they were to deliver it ready cut into our boat. For a goat, one bar. A cow, ten or eight bars, according to its bigness. A hog, two bars. A calf, eight bars. A jar of palm-oil one bar and a quarter.

We paid also the king's duties in goods; five hundred slaves, to be purchased at two copper rings a head.

The fifth of August, the king sent aboard thirty slaves, men and women; of which we picked nineteen, and returned the rest.

The sixth, the king came aboard with four slaves, which, with the nineteen others of the day before, made twenty-three, for which we paid him two hundred and forty seven bars, three of the women having each a child. . . .

Thus from day to day, from this time to the twenty-ninth of August following, either by means of our armed sloop making several voyages to New Calabar town, and to Dony, to purchase slaves and provisions; or by the contract made with the king and his people of Bonny, and nearby trading places; we had by degrees aboard six hundred and forty-eight slaves, of all sexes and ages, including the sixty-five we purchased at the Gold Coast, all very fresh and sound, very few exceeding forty years of age; besides provisions of yams, goats, hogs, fowls, wood and water, and some cows and calves. As for fish, this river did not afford us any great quantity, which was a great loss to us, being forced to supply the ship's crew with fresh meat from land, at a great expense, it being here pretty expensive, and most of our salt meat being spent, and have but for three months more of sea biscuit left in the bread-room. Several of our sailors are tormented with colic, and some few dead.

---

[12] A type of Indian cotton textile.

[13] The value of the yams depended on size and quality.

# Rules for Slaves and Masters
▼▼▼

## 50 ▼ *THE BLACK CODE*

Having experienced capture in Africa, purchase by Europeans on Africa's coast, and the transatlantic crossing, what kind of life did newly enslaved Africans face on reaching the Americas? Some answers to this question can be gleaned by analyzing the various legal codes pertaining to slavery that existed in all the American colonies. These codes were issued by European governments and occasionally refined by colonial officials or legislatures to address local conditions. They covered a wide range of issues, including work conditions, manumission, punishments, slave families, sexual relations between slaves and freemen, standards for the care for slaves, and much else. Although many of their provisions were difficult to enforce and hence often ignored, slave codes provide valuable insights into the values of slave-owning societies, the concerns of slave owners, and the realities of slavery itself.

The French *Code Noir,* or Black Code, issued by King Louis XIV in 1685, technically remained in force until 1848. Its rules and regulations were meant to apply to French holdings in the West Indies, the most important of which were Martinique, Guadeloupe, and from the 1670s onward the western parts of Hispaniola, or Saint Domingue. In these colonies, as elsewhere in the Caribbean, until the mid seventeenth century relatively few European colonists had grown tobacco on modest-sized farms with labor supplied mainly by indentured servants. However, in response to competition from Virginia tobacco and the ever-increasing demand for sweets in Europe, beginning in the 1650s the economy of the West Indies shifted decisively to sugar cane, which was grown and processed on large plantations by an ever-greater number of African slaves. By the mid eighteenth century African slaves comprised 90 percent of the population on islands where sugar was grown.

As West Indian planters became dependent on massive amounts of slave labor, the French government in Versailles turned its attention to producing a suitable legal code for the regulation of slavery. Under the direction of Jean-Baptiste Colbert, the French controller general of finance (see Chapter 5, source 39), the government collected testimony and suggestions from lawyers, colonial officials, and planters, and then issued the Black Code in 1685. This was two years after Colbert's death and the same year in which the French withdrew religious toleration for French Protestants by revoking the Edict of Nantes.

## QUESTIONS FOR ANALYSIS

1. What part does religion play in the various regulations in the Black Code? What in the code indicates that religious issues had such a prominent place?
2. On the basis of the various provisions of the code, what conclusions can be drawn about the lives and experiences of slaves in the French colonies?
3. What does the code reveal about fears and worries of the slave masters?
4. What does the code reveal about the legal and economic relationship between slaves and masters?
5. What underlying racial attitudes are revealed in the provisions of the code, especially those pertaining to sexual relations between slaves and freemen?
6. What provisions of the code do you think would be most difficult to enforce? Why?

Louis, by God's grace King of France and Navarre,[1] greetings to all people now and in the future: Whereas we are obligated to care for all the people the Divine Providence has placed under our authority, we have been pleased to have had reviewed in our presence the memoranda which have been sent us by our officials in the American islands: we have been informed of the need they have for our authority and justice to maintain the discipline of the Catholic Church,

---

[1]The northern part of the province of Navarre, which straddles the western Pyrenees, was united with France in the late sixteenth century when Henry of Navarre ascended the French throne as King Henry IV (r. 1589–1610).

Apostolic and Roman, and to make rules for them concerning the state and quality of the slaves in those said islands; we desire to be able and to make it known to them that even though they live infinitely far from our normal residence, we are always with them, not only by the wide range of our power, but also by the promptness of our attention to care for them in their needs.

For these reasons, on the advice of our Council, with our certain knowledge, full power, and royal authority, we have proclaimed, legislated, and ordered what follows. . . .

2. All slaves in our islands shall be baptized and instructed in the Catholic religion, Apostolic and Roman. We instruct the colonists buying newly arrived slaves that they should inform the Governor and intendant[2] of it within one week at the latest, on pain of a summary fine, and they shall give the necessary orders to have them instructed and baptized in due course. . . .

4. No overseer shall be put in charge of Negroes who does not profess the Catholic religion, on pain of the confiscation of the said Negroes from the masters who have appointed them and the summary punishment of the overseers who shall have accepted such an appointment.

6. We order all our subjects, whatever their status, to observe Sundays and Holy Days which are kept by our subjects of the Catholic faith, Apostolic and Roman. We forbid them to work, and we order them not to make their slaves work on these days from midnight to midnight on field work, the production of sugar, and any and all other types of work, on pain of a fine and punishment of the masters, and the confiscation by our officials of however much sugar was produced by those slaves. . . .

9. Freemen who shall have had one or more children by cohabitation with slaves, also masters who shall have allowed it, shall each be sub-

ject to a fine of 200 pounds of sugar, and should they be the masters of the slaves by whom they have had the said children, in addition they shall be deprived of the slave and the children and she and they shall be transferred to the hospital, without the possibility of emancipation. . . .

11. Priests are strictly forbidden to conduct slave marriages if they do not appear to be with the consent of their masters. Masters are also forbidden to use any sanction on their slaves to make them marry against their wish.

12. Children born of slave marriages shall be slaves and shall belong to the masters of the female slaves and not those of her husband if the husband and wife have different masters.

13. We wish that if a slave husband has married a free woman, the children, whether male or female, shall be the status of their mother and shall be free like her . . . ; and also if the father is free and the mother a slave, the infants likewise shall be slaves.

14. Slave masters should have baptized slaves buried in hallowed ground in a cemetery set apart for that specific purpose; those who die unbaptized should be interred at night in whatever field can be found near to the place where they have died.

15. Slaves are forbidden to carry any arms or large clubs on pain of whipping and confiscation of the arms by those who have caught them; the only exception are those who have been sent by their master to go hunting and who carry with them a signed letter of permission from their master.

16. Slaves belonging to different masters are also forbidden to gather together by day or by night under the pretext of marriages or other occasions, either on their masters' estates or otherwise, and even less in the open road or distant spots, on pain of corporal punishment which cannot be less than whipping and branding, and in repeated cases or other aggra-

---

[2]An *intendant* was a royal official with responsibilities for tax collection, enforcement of laws, and communicating with the royal administration.

vating circumstances can be punished by death. . . .

17. Masters who are convicted of having permitted or tolerated such gatherings of slaves will be sentenced to make reparations to their neighbors for any damage as a result of these said gatherings and to pay a fine of ten *écus*[3] for the first offense and twice that much in case of a repeat offense.

22. Masters shall be obliged to provide each week to their slaves of eighteen years or older for food 2 1/2 measures of cassava[4] flour, or three cassavas weighing 2 1/2 pounds each at least, or some equivalent provisions, with 2 pounds of salt beef or three pounds of fish, or something of equal value; and to children weaning until ten years old half the above sustenance.

23. It is prohibited to give slaves brandy or fermented cane juice to take the place of rations mentioned in the previous article.

24. It is prohibited to decrease the provisions for slaves by permitting them instead to work on their own account on certain days of the week.

25. It is required that each master supply to each and every slave two cloth outfits or four ells[5] of cloth, according to the preference of the said master.

26. Slaves who are not fed, clothed, and maintained by their masters, as we have here ordained, may report the fact to our Procurator General[6] and put their complaints in his hands, in each case, or if the information comes from others, the masters shall be summoned at their request but without cost; which will be the same process as we would wish pursued for crimes and barbarous and inhumane treatment by masters against their slaves.

27. Slaves made infirm by old age, sickness or other causes, whether the disease is curable or not, must be nourished and taken care of by their masters; and in the instance where a slave has been abandoned, the slave shall be sent to a hospital to which the master will be obligated to pay six *sols*[7] a day for the slave's upkeep and nourishment.

28. We declare that slaves may own nothing which does not belong to their masters; and everything which they receive for their work, or through the gift of other people, or otherwise, whatever their claims might be, shall be regarded fully the property of their masters, even the children of slaves. . . .

33. Any slave who has struck his master, his mistress or their children to cause bruising or bleeding, or on the face, shall be punished by death.

34. Violence or assaults committed by slaves against any free person, shall be severely punished even with death. . . .

36. Slaves stealing sheep, goats, pigs, poultry, sugar cane, millet, manioc[8] or other vegetables grown by slaves, should be punished according to the type of goods stolen; at their discretion, judges may order the slaves to be beaten with a rod or branded.

37. Masters will be obligated in case of robbery or other damage caused by their slaves to make reparations for the damage on their behalf, or if they prefer, to give away the slave to the party that is owed damages. . . .

38. Runaway slaves who have been missing for a month from the day their master has reported it to the Justice, shall have their ears cut and shall be branded on the shoulder; if they run away for another month, also from the day of the report, they shall have their tongue slit, and be branded on the other shoulder, and the third time, they shall be put to death.

42. Masters are only permitted to have their slaves bound in chains and beaten with rods or whips when they believe their slaves merit it; we prohibit the use of torture and mutilation on the pain of confiscation of the slave and further judicial proceedings against these masters.

---

[3]An *écu*, or crown, was a silver coin worth three *livres*.
[4]Any of several plants grown in the tropics for their starchy roots.
[5]A unit of measurement, slightly more than a meter.

[6]A judicial official appointed by the crown.
[7]A silver coin worth one-sixtieth of an *écu*.
[8]Another word for cassava.

43. We instruct our officials to take criminal proceedings against masters or overseers who killed a slave belonging to them or under their command, and shall punish the murderer according to the brutality of the circumstances. . . .

47. It is not permitted to seize[9] or sell separately a husband and wife and their children when they are all under the authority of the same master; we declare null and void all previous sales that have led to separation. . . .

59. We grant to those who have been emancipated the same rights, privileges, and immunities enjoyed by people born free; wishing that the benefits of acquired liberty may produce in them, as much for their persons as for their goods, the same effects that the good fortune of natural liberty offers to our other subjects.

---

[9]Seize for payment of a debt or some other financial obligation.

▼▼▼

# Political Change in the Islamic World

Empires are forged through military conquest, and most disintegrate in the wake of military defeat. So it was for the Muslim empires of Southwest Asia, Africa, and India from the late sixteenth century onward. The Songhai Empire of Africa, which had dominated the western Sudan since the late fifteenth century, fell apart and was replaced by a number of small regional states after a musket-bearing Moroccan army defeated its forces at the Battle of Tondibi outside of Gao in 1591. The Safavid Empire came to an abrupt end in 1722 when Afghan warriors took the capital city of Isfahan, and the Safavids fled to the hills, leaving the empire open to Ottoman invasion, decades of anarchy, and ultimately the establishment of the weak Qajar Dynasty in the 1790s. The Mughal Empire in India broke apart when the warlord Nadir Shah, having seized power from the Afghans after the fall of the Safavids, in 1739 invaded India and sacked Delhi, the Mughal capital. The Ottoman Empire outlasted the other Islamic empires, but in the end it too disappeared after military defeat, in this case in World War I.

In each one of these empires decay had set in long before the military defeats that led to their final demise. Like countless previous empires, all of them faced deteriorating financial situations once their expansion ended. Large armies were still needed to defend borders and maintain authority over newly conquered racial, ethnic, and religious groups, many of whom resented their new rulers and resisted integration into the new state. Rulers themselves added to the financial strain by spending large sums on court life, the arts, and ambitious building programs. During the time of imperial expansion such costs were met by confiscating the wealth of newly conquered peoples and adding them to the tax roles. After expansion ended, expenses could be met only by raising taxes, running deficits, and selling offices and titles. Such expedients impeded economic growth, encouraged government corruption and inefficiency, and simply put off the day of final fiscal reckoning.

All of these empires were plagued by succession struggles and deteriorating leadership. In the Ottoman and Safavid empires the practice of raising the rulers' sons as indulged prisoners in the palace to prevent rebellions resulted in a long series of uninformed, inexperienced, and often debauched sultans and shahs. In the Ottoman Empire decisive rulers and fierce warriors such as Selim the Grim (r. 1512–1520) and Suleiman the Magnificent (r. 1520–1566) gave way to incompetents such as Selim the Sot (r. 1566–1574) and Ibrahim the Crazy (r. 1640–1648). In Persia, the distinguished reign of Shah Abbas I (1587–1629) was followed by the murderous rule of Shah Safi, Abbas's grandson, who took power after Abbas had ordered the murder of one of his sons and the blinding of two others. In Songhai, of the eight sixteenth-century rulers who followed the empire's founders, Sunni Ali (r. 1469–1492) and Askia Muhammad (r. 1493–1528), all but three were murdered in office or deposed. Not a one dealt effectively with succession-related conflicts, internal rivalries, or outside threats. Leadership also was a problem in Mughal India. Aurangzeb's (r. 1658–1707) persecution of his Hindu subjects and his costly military campaigns in the south set the stage for the religious conflicts and rebellions that undermined Mughal authority in the eighteenth century.

Although the causes of political decline in these empires were broadly similar, the consequences were quite different. After the breakup of the Songhai Empire, the western Sudan was ruled by a number of small regional states, some of which were conquered and merged around 1800 into a larger state, the Sokoto Caliphate, by the religious and political reformer Usman dan Fodio. Persia survived the civil wars of the immediate post-Safavid Era, but then languished for another century and a half under the Zand and Qajar dynasties. The Ottoman Empire continued, but the efforts of reforming sultans and ministers failed to halt territorial losses or prevent growing Western interference in its political and economic affairs. The fall of the Mughal Empire had the most significant result. It paved the way for the British takeover of the Indian subcontinent, the beginning of a new wave of European imperialism that by the late nineteenth century brought Africa and much of Asia under Western control.

# Ottoman Decline: An Insider's View

▼▼▼

## 51 ▼ *Mehmed Pasha,*
## *THE BOOK OF COUNSEL*
## *FOR VIZIERS AND GOVERNORS*

Along with battlefield defeats, fiscal crises, internal turmoil, and palace intrigues, another sign of Ottoman decline in the seventeenth and eighteenth centuries was the appearance of treatises with plans for reviving the empire's fortunes. Among the most candid and insightful works of this type was *The Book of Counsel for Viziers and Governors,* written in the early eighteenth century by an Ottoman treasury official, Mehmed Pasha. Although little is known about Mehmed Pasha's early life, it is likely that he was born into the family of a petty merchant in Istanbul in the 1650s. While in his teens, he became an apprentice for an official in the Ottoman treasury department, a branch of the government in which he worked for the rest of his career. His long service was rewarded in 1702, when he was named chief *defterdar,* or treasurer of the empire. Over the next fifteen years Mehmed Pasha lost and regained the office no less than seven times as one faction or another became ascendant in the sultan's administration. In 1717 he was executed on order of the sultan when his enemies blamed him for the loss of a fortress in the Balkans.

It is unknown when exactly Mehmed Pasha wrote *The Book of Counsel for Viziers and Governors,* but internal evidence suggests it was around 1703 or 1704. It is a book written by a man who had firsthand knowledge of the failings of the Ottoman state and was deeply disturbed by what he knew.

## QUESTIONS FOR ANALYSIS

1. Mehmed Pasha cites several examples of how the sultan's subjects suffer as a result of government policies and practices. What examples does he cite and what are their causes?
2. What, according to the author, are the reasons for the government's financial problems? What solutions does he propose?
3. How does Mehmed Pasha's description of the Ottoman military and government differ from the observations made by Ogier Ghiselin de Busbecq in the sixteenth century (Chapter 3, source 21)?
4. What do Mehmed Pasha's comments reveal about the economic situation in the Ottoman Empire around 1700?
5. Little was done to implement the changes suggested by Mehmed Pasha and other Ottoman reformers. What do you think made it so difficult to achieve meaningful reforms?

## THE RESULTS OF BRIBERY

It is essential to guard against giving office through bribery to the unfit and to tyrannical oppressors. For giving office to such as these because of bribes means giving permission to plunder the property of the subjects. An equivalent for the bribe which is given must be had. In addition to what is given as a bribe, he must make a profit for himself and his followers. Bribery is the beginning and root of all illegality and tyranny, the source and fountain of every sort of disturbance and sedition, the greatest of

calamities. . . . There is no more powerful engine of injustice and cruelty, for bribery destroys both faith and state. . . .

If it becomes necessary to give a position because of bribes, in this way its holder has permission from the government for every sort of oppression. Stretching out the hand of violence and tyranny against the poor subjects along his route of travel[1] and spreading fear among the poor, he destroys the wretched peasants and ruins the cultivated lands. As the fields and villages become empty of husbandmen, day by day weakness comes to land and property, which remain

---

[1]Officials traveling on government business were entitled to horses, food, and lodging from the people of the districts they visited.

destitute of profits, revenues, harvest, and benefit. In addition to the fact that it causes a decline in the productivity of the subjects and in the revenues of the Treasury, through neglect of the employment of tilling and lack of the work of agriculture, there is the greatest probability . . . that will cause scarcity, dearth, mishaps and calamities.

## FINANCIAL ISSUES

The business of the Treasury is among the most important and essential affairs of the Exalted Government. The man who is chief treasurer needs to know and understand . . . the Treasury employees who for their own advantage are the cause of ruin and destruction to the government service in obtaining tax farms.[2] He must know how they behave in getting money from the Treasury through "invalid receipts"[3] and in other cases, and he must understand what are their tricks and wiles. . . . Every one of them is waiting and watching in the corner of opportunity, taking care . . . to cause certain matters outside the regular procedure to appear correct. . . . In case the chief treasurer is not informed about such persons, they cause the wasting of the public wealth through various frauds, and of disordering affairs. . . .

Reliance must not be placed in the calumnies and lies of certain spitefully jealous persons regarding the chief treasurers. For most people, and especially some of the government officers, are always making proposals detrimental to the condition of the Treasury and to the property of the repository of money. . . . They want a man who gives out the public money freely. They say, "This treasurer is unjust," and set themselves to putting forward all sorts of improprieties of his. But let him not be quickly removed, without making very careful investigation and enquiry and search by dependable persons about his habits, and without having complete knowledge in this matter. . . . In short it is absolutely essential that freedom be given to those who are chief treasurers.

Those who are chief treasurers should be extremely circumspect in behavior, upright and devout, devoid of avarice and spite. . . . They . . . should strive to increase the income of the Treasury and to diminish expenditures.

But the reduction of expenditures cannot come about through the care and industry of the chief treasurer alone. These must be supplemented by the Sovereign and personal help of his imperial majesty the sultan, who is the refuge of the universe, and by the good management of his excellency the grand vizier.[4] . . .

Certain tax concessions, instead of being farmed out, should be committed to the charge of trustworthy and upright persons on government account.[5]

Let the janissary corps[6] not be increased. Let them be well disciplined, few but elite, and all present in time of need. In this connection also it is fitting to be extremely careful and to be attentive in keeping their rolls in proper order and in having the soldiers actually present. The late Lutfi Pasha, who was formerly grand vizier, has written: "Fifteen thousand soldiers are a great many soldiers. It is a heroic deed to pay the wages year by year of fifteen thousand men with no decrease." But under the present conditions the soldiers and pensioned veterans . . . who get pay and rations have exceeded all limits.

In order that the income and expenditure of the Treasury may be known and the totals in-

---

[2]Tax farms were purchased by private individuals who in return for paying the government a lump sum had the right to collect taxes owed the government.

[3]Forged documents showing that a person had paid taxes he owed.

[4]A *vizier* was a government minister. The *grand vizier* was chief minister.

[5]In other words, tax farming should be abandoned and taxes collected directly by government officials. The author does not develop this point further.

[6]Infantry fighters in the Ottoman army, originally recruited from the sultan's Christian subjects who were converted to Islam and given over to military training. Their effectiveness and discipline had severely declined by the eighteenth century.

spected, the rolls of the bureaus must be investigated and the numbers known. There are on a war footing 53,200 janissary footmen, consisting of janissaries of the imperial court and pensioned veterans, including those who are in the fortresses protecting the ever-victorious frontier. There are 17,133 cavalrymen of the sipahis, silihdars,[7] and four other regiments of cavalry. The armorers of the imperial court and artillerymen and artillery drivers and bostanjis[8] of the bodyguard ... and the aghas[9] of the imperial stirrup and müteferriqas[10] and sergeants and gatemen and those who belong to the imperial stables and the flourishing kitchens and to the dockyard and to the *peikan*[11] and to other units, making up 17,716 persons, the total of all these amounts to 96,727 persons.

The expense for meat and value of the winter allowance[12] together with the yearly pay of the janissaries of the lofty court and armorers and artillerymen and artillery drivers in the fortresses on the ever-victorious frontier exceeds a total of ten thousand purses of aspers.[13] And in addition to these, the local troops in the fortresses on the ever-victorious frontier number seventy thousand persons and certain veterans pensioned from the income of the custom house and tax farms, together with those who have the duty of saying prayers amount to twenty-three thousand five hundred. Their yearly pay amounts to five thousand nine hundred and ten purses. Those who are on the government galleys total six thousand persons and their yearly pay eight hundred purses. Accordingly, the total of those who receive pay and have duties is 196,227 and their yearly pay amounts to 16,710 purses.[14]

In addition to these salaries there are incomes of the illustrious princes and princesses and the grand vizier and the yearly allowance of the Tatar princes[15] and of the commanders of the sea and the expenditures of the imperial kitchens and stables, of the flourishing dockyards, of the prefect of the capital, of the chief butcher, of the agha of Istanbul, of the chief biscuit maker, of the cannon factory, some expenditures of müteferriqas, and in addition to these, chance expenditures which do not come to mind. ... For this reason the income does not cover the expenditure, and of necessity the farmed taxes, and other taxes such as the capitation tax,[16] have each fallen a year or two in arrears.

## THE STATE OF THE MILITARY

The troops on the frontiers are actually too numerous on their rolls and in the summaries given, although it is certain that in their appointed places each battalion is deficient, some being perhaps half lacking and others even more, nevertheless they let the salaries be sent from here for all. As for the extra money which they get, they have agreed to divide it among themselves. Care and thought and trustworthiness and uprightness in the officers is needed for the separation and distinguishing of those who are present and those who are absent. ...

Everyone knows that there are very many people outside the corps who pretend they are janissaries. Especially in recent times, because of the long continuance of campaigns which have taken place against the Magyars[17] and in various other regions according to the necessity of the moment, outsiders have joined and mixed themselves among this janissary corps more than among all the others. Becoming mingled with all sorts of people, the janissaries have broken

---

[7]*Sipahis* and *silihdars* were cavalry troops supported by land grants from the sultan.

[8]Infantry troops who maintained the palace grounds in Istanbul.

[9]Generals.

[10]Mounted bodyguards who accompanied diplomats on missions.

[11]An elite bodyguard numbering thirty to forty men who wore distinctive gilded helmets.

[12]Payments over and above the troops' regular salary.

[13]A *purse* was a unit of money made up of approximately 420 *piasters;* one piaster equaled 120 *aspers*.

[14]A sum that exceeded the estimated annual income of the government.

[15]Chieftains on the border of the empire who were allies of the Ottomans.

[16]A tax on individuals; a head tax.

[17]The term *Magyar,* meaning Hungarian, was used to refer to any of the Ottomans' Christian enemies in southeastern Europe.

down their fixed regulations. In the towns and villages situated on the coasts of Anatolia and in many regions of Rumelia[18] likewise, many of the subject population, in order to free their necks from the obligations which are incumbent upon them, have changed their dress.[19] Because of their pretensions of being janissaries and because of aid from the commanders of the latter,[20] the civilians cannot be separated from the janissaries. There is no distinction between this sort of men and the faithful guardians of the frontier, veterans who have undergone fatigue and hard usage on campaigns, who have perhaps been several times wounded and injured, who have suffered cuts and bruises for the welfare of faith and state, who have pillowed their heads on stones and lain down to sleep upon the ground. . . .

At the present time special care is necessary in the repairing of castles. If they be built solidly they will not become dilapidated, and frequent repairs will not be needed. But the execution of repairs must not be committed to any chance person, for the appropriation from the Treasury may be embezzled and wasted. It must be committed to a man who abstains from profiteering and avarice.

When either the glorious commander-in-chief or the generals go on campaign their true purpose should be the animating of religion and the execution of the words of the Prophet. . . . Let them not be unjust or oppressive to any one, but just and equitable, and let them seek to win affection and praises. While not oppressing or tyrannizing over the military corps, let them safeguard proper discipline.

For when soldiers are charged with a campaign, they join in bands and agree together to consider one of themselves as chief. Practicing brigandage, they are not satisfied with free fodder for their horses and food for their own bellies from the villages they meet. They covet the horse-cloth and rags of the peasants, and if they can get their hands on the granaries they become joyful, filling their sacks with barley and oats for provisions and fodder. While they behave in this way, . . . the sighs and groans of mankind attain the heavens and it is certain that they will be accursed. . . .

## ECONOMIC REGULATIONS

It is essential at all times for every ruler to keep track of the small things relating to the general condition of the people. He must set the proper market prices. Everything must be sold at the price it is worth. For in case the sultan and the viziers say: "The fixing of market prices, though part of the public business, is insignificant," and are not diligent about it, the city judge alone cannot carry it out. . . . Under such circumstances everyone buys and sells as he pleases. Through senseless avarice the venom of vipers is added to lawful goods. The most contemptible of the people, useless both for the services of the sultan and for warfare, become possessors of all the wealth . . . while the great men of the people who deserve respect, becoming poor and powerless, pursue the road of bankruptcy. Then, when it comes about that both horsemen and footmen who go on campaign must sell all their property,[21] it is troublesome and difficult to determine all at once how to restrain those men who have them by the throat and how to change their demeanor and diminish their arrogance (may God forbid it!). . . . The fruiterers and merchants put a double price on provisions and supplies and reap a harvest of profits. They rob the people. It is apparent that neglect in this matter redounds to the harm of believers in time of trouble and to the benefit of fruiterers and merchants.[22]

---

[18]An area north of Greece, including the regions of Albania, Macedonia, and Thrace.

[19]The people have purchased and wear the uniforms of the janissaries and claim to be members of the corps to avoid taxes.

[20]The commanders have accepted bribes to enter their names on the corps' roles.

[21]Many soldiers paid for their own military equipment and provisions before a campaign. They hoped to recoup their expenses through plunder.

[22]Many merchants were Christian Armenians or Jews.

# Fatal Flaws of the Mughal Empire
▼▼▼

## 52 ▼ *François Bernier, LETTER TO JEAN-BAPTISTE COLBERT ON THE MUGHAL EMPIRE*

In 1658 Aurangzeb, the son of Shah Jahan and grandson of Jahangir, became India's new emperor as a result of a three-year succession struggle that resulted in the execution of two of his brothers, the death in battle of another, and the imprisonment of his father, Shah Jahan, for the last year of his life. Aurangzeb, who ruled until 1707, is often blamed for the rapid demise of the Mughal Empire that followed his death. True, his abandonment of his predecessors' tolerant policy toward Hinduism proved disastrous. His decisions to raise Hindus' taxes and level their temples led to resentment and rebellion, not the conversions to Islam he had anticipated. It is also true that his long military campaigns in the south left an empty treasury and an exhausted and demoralized army. As the following source reveals, however, the Mughal Empire that Aurangzeb inherited was deeply flawed. His policies accelerated the empire's disintegration, but they were not its underlying cause.

The author of the following letter, François Bernier (ca. 1620–1688), was born in the French city of Angers and originally hoped to pursue a career as a Catholic churchman. While a student at the University of Paris, however, he abandoned theology, joined a circle of intellectuals led by the materialist philosopher Pierre Gassendi, and in the late 1640s traveled through much of north central Europe in the service of a French diplomat. He then obtained his medical degree from the University of Montpellier and immediately departed for Asia and Africa, where he visited Syria, Egypt, and finally India in the hope of establishing some sort of career as a physician.

Bernier's travels had surprising results. In 1658 he became the personal physician of no less a figure than the new Mughal emperor, Aurangzeb. He left his post in 1669, returning to France to write books on Asia and edit Gassendi's philosophical works. In 1670 he took time to communicate his thoughts about India in a letter to Colbert, France's controller general of finance. Bernier was an acute political observer. Beneath the wealth and splendor of the Mughal Empire he detected inherent weaknesses that within only a few decades brought about the empire's ruin.

---

## QUESTIONS FOR ANALYSIS

1. What is Bernier's overall assessment of the Mughal government? What are its major weaknesses?
2. What seems to impress Bernier most about India? As a European what does he most deplore in Indian society?
3. In what ways does he see a relationship between India's political situation and its economy?

4. According to Bernier what problems resulted from the fact that Aurangzeb was a Muslim?
5. Compare Bernier's critique of Mughal government and society with the observations of Mehmed Pasha concerning the problems of the Ottoman Empire (source 51). To what extent are the problems of the governments similar and different?

I think I have shown that the precious metals must abound in Hindustan,[1] although the country be destitute of mines; and that the Great Mughal, lord and master of the greater part, must necessarily be in the receipt of an immense revenue, and possess incalculable wealth.

But there are many circumstances to be considered, as forming a counterpoise to these riches.

First. — Of the vast tracts of country constituting the empire of Hindustan, many are little more than sand, or barren mountains, badly cultivated, and thinly peopled; and even a considerable portion of the good land remains untilled from want of laborers; many of whom perish in consequence of the bad treatment they experience from the Governors. These poor people, when incapable of discharging the demands of their rapacious lords, are not only often deprived of the means of subsistence, but are bereft of their children, who are carried away as slaves. Thus it happens that many of the peasantry, driven to despair by so execrable a tyranny, abandon the country, and seek a more tolerable mode of existence, either in the towns, or camps; as bearers of burdens, carriers of water, or servants to horsemen. Sometimes they fly to the territories of a Raja,[2] because there they find less oppression, and are allowed a greater degree of comfort.

Second. — The empire of the Great Mughal comprehends several nations, over which he is not absolute master. Most of them still retain their own peculiar chiefs or sovereigns, who obey the Mughal or pay him tribute only by compulsion. In many instances this tribute is of trifling amount; in others none is paid. . . .

The petty sovereignties bordering the Persian frontiers, for example, seldom pay tribute either to the Mughal or to the King of Persia. . . . Nor can the former be said to receive anything considerable from the Baluchi, Afghans,[3] and other mountaineers, who indeed seem to feel nearly independent of him. . . .

The Pathans[4] are ungovernable. . . . They hold the Indians, both Hindus and Mughals, in the utmost contempt; and, recollecting the consideration in which they were formerly held in India, they mortally hate the Mughals, by whom their fathers were dispossessed of great principalities, and driven to the mountains far from Dehli and Agra. . . .

The King of Bijapur,[5] so far from paying tribute to the Mughal, is engaged in perpetual war with him, and contrives to defend his dominions. . . . His Kingdom is at a great distance from Agra and Dehli, the Mughal's usual places of residence; the capital city, called also Bijapur, is strong, and not easily accessible to an invad-

---

[1]*Hindustan* is the Persian word for India. It is usually used in reference to the whole of India north of the Deccan, the region of southern India below the Narmada and Kistna rivers.

[2]A Hindu prince; in this context one who paid tribute to the Mughal emperor but who maintained his political independence.

[3]Peoples who lived in provinces loosely linked to the Mughal Empire in regions of modern-day Pakistan and Afghanistan.

[4]The Pathans were a people originally from the region of modern southeastern Afghanistan and northwest Pakistan. Rulers of the Lodi Dynasty, the last dynasty that held the Delhi sultanate, they were Parthans; they were defeated by the founder of the Mughal Empire, Babur, in 1526.

[5]Bijapur and Golconda (mentioned in the next paragraph) were both Muslim states in south central India.

ing army, because of the bad water and scarcity of forage in the surrounding country; and several Rajas for the sake of mutual security join him, when attacked, with their forces. . . .

There is again the wealthy and powerful King of Golconda, who secretly supplies the King of Bijapur with money, and constantly keeps an army on the frontiers, with the double object of defending his own territories and aiding Bijapur in the event of that country being closely pressed.

Similarly, among those not paying tribute may be numbered more than a hundred Rajas, or Hindu sovereigns of considerable strength, dispersed over the whole empire, some near and some at a distance from Agra and Dehli. Fifteen or sixteen of these Rajas are rich and formidable, and if [they] . . . chose to enter into an offensive league, they would prove dangerous opponents to the Mughal. . . .

Third. — It is material to remark that the Great Mughal is a Muslim, of the sect of the Sunnis, who, believing with the Turks that Osman was the true successor of Muhammad, are distinguished by the name of Osmanlys.[6] The majority of his courtiers, however, being Persians, are of the party known by the appellation of Shiites,[7] believers in the real succession of Ali. Moreover, the Great Mughal is a foreigner in Hindustan, a descendant of Tamerlane,[8] . . . who, about the year 1401, overran and conquered the Indies. Consequently he finds himself in a hostile country, or nearly so; a country containing hundreds of Hindus to one Mughal, or even to one Muslim. To maintain himself in such a country, in the midst of domestic and powerful enemies, and to be always prepared against any hostile movement on the side of Persia or Uzbek, he is under the necessity of keeping up numerous armies, even in the time of peace. . . .

It is also important to remark the absolute necessity which exists of paying the whole of this army every two months . . . for the King's pay is their only means of sustenance. In France, when the exigencies of the times prevent the government from immediately discharging an arrear of debt, an officer, or even a private soldier, may contrive to live for some time by means of his own private income; but in the Indies, any unusual delay in the payment of the troops is sure to be attended with fatal consequences; after selling whatever trifling articles they may possess, the soldiers disband and die of hunger. Toward the close of the late civil war, I discovered a growing disposition in the troopers to sell their horses, which they would, no doubt, soon have done if the war had been prolonged. And no wonder; for consider, My Lord, that it is difficult to find in the Mughal's army, a soldier who is not married, who has not wife, children, servants, and slaves, all depending upon him for support. I have known many persons lost in amazement while contemplating the number of persons, amounting to millions, who depend for support solely on the King's pay. Is it possible, they have asked, that any revenue can suffice for such incredible expenditure? seeming to forget the riches of the Great Mughal, and the peculiar manner in which Hindustan is governed.

But I have not enumerated all the expenses incurred by the Great Mughal. He keeps in Delhi and Agra from two to three thousand fine horses, always at hand in case of emergency; eight or nine hundred elephants, and a large number of baggage horses, mules, and porters, intended to carry the numerous and capacious tents, with their fittings, his wives and women, furniture, kitchen apparatus, water, and all the other articles necessary for the camp, which the Mughal has always about him, as in his capital, things which are not considered necessary in our kingdoms in Europe.

Add to this, if you will, the enormous expenses of the harem, where the consumption of fine

---

[6]The Ottomans believed that Osman I (r. 1299–1326) and his descendants were caliphs, successors of Muhammad and heads of the Islamic community.

[7]Shi'ite Muslims believed that the true caliphs were de-

scendants of Muhammad's son-in-law, Ali. See Chapter 3, source 24.

[8]Tamerlane, or Timur the Lame (1336–1405), was a great Turkic conqueror.

cloths of gold, and brocades, silks, embroideries, pearls, musk, amber and sweet essences, is greater than can be conceived.

Thus, although the Great Mughal be in receipt of an immense revenue, his expenditure being much in the same proportion, he cannot possess the vast surplus of wealth that most people seem to imagine. I admit that his income exceeds probably the joint revenues of the Grand Seignior[9] and of the King of Persia; but if I were to call him a wealthy monarch, it would be in the sense that a treasurer is to be considered wealthy who pays with one hand the large sums which he receives with the other. . . .

Toward the conclusion of the last war, Aurangzeb was perplexed how to pay and supply his armies, notwithstanding that the war had continued but five years, that the pay of the troops was less than usual, that, with the exception of Bengal . . . , a profound tranquillity reigned in every part of Hindustan, and that he had so lately appropriated to himself a large portion of the treasures of his father Shah Jahan. . . .

Before I conclude, I wish to explain how it happens that, although this Empire of the Mughal is such an abyss for gold and silver;[10] as I said before, these precious metals are not in greater plenty here than elsewhere; on the contrary, the inhabitants have less the appearance of a moneyed people than those of many other parts of the globe.

In the first place, a large quantity is melted, re-melted, and wasted, in fabricating women's bracelets, both for the hands and feet, chains, ear-rings, nose and finger rings, and a still larger quantity is consumed in manufacturing embroideries; alachas, or striped silken stuffs; touras, or fringes of gold lace, worn on turbans; gold and silver cloths, scarfs, turbans, and brocades. The quantity of these articles made in India is incredible.

In the second place, the King, as proprietor of the land, makes over a certain quantity to military men, as an equivalent for their pay; and this grant is called jah-ghir . . . the word jagir signifying the spot from which to draw, or the place of salary. Similar grants are made to governors, in lieu of their salary, and also for the support of their troops, on condition that they pay a certain sum annually to the King out of any surplus revenue that the land may yield. The lands not so granted are retained by the King as the peculiar domains of his house, and are seldom, if ever, given in the way of jagir; and upon these domains he keeps contractors, who are also bound to pay him an annual rent.

The persons thus put in possession of the land, whether as governors or contractors, have an authority almost absolute over the peasantry, and nearly as much over the artisans and merchants of the towns and villages within their district; and nothing can be imagined more cruel and oppressive than the manner in which it is exercised. There is no one before whom the injured peasant, artisan, or tradesman can pour out his just complaints; no great lords, parliaments, or judges of local courts, exist, as in France, to restrain the wickedness of those merciless oppressors, and the judges are not invested with sufficient power to redress the wrongs of these unhappy people. This sad abuse of the royal authority may not be felt in the same degree near capital cities such as Delhi and Agra, or in the vicinity of large towns and seaports, because in those places acts of gross injustice cannot easily be concealed from the court.

This debasing state of slavery obstructs the progress of trade and influences the manners and mode of life of every individual. There can be little encouragement to engage in commercial pursuits, when the success with which they may be attended, instead of adding to the enjoyments

---

[9]The king of France, in this case Louis XIV.
[10]Bernier had already discussed the reasons why as a result of the balance of trade India received and kept large amounts of gold and silver.

of life, provokes the cupidity of a neighboring tyrant possessing both power and inclination to deprive any man of the fruits of his industry. When wealth is acquired, as must sometimes be the case, the possessor, so far from living with increased comfort and assuming an air of independence, studies the means by which he may appear indigent: his dress, lodging, and furniture, continue to be mean, and he is careful, above all things, never to indulge in the pleasures of the table. In the meantime, his gold and silver remain buried at a great depth in the ground. . . .

The misery of this ill-fated country is increased by the practice which prevails too much at all times, but especially on the breaking out of an important war, of selling the different government offices for immense sums in hard cash. Hence it naturally becomes the principal object of the individual thus appointed Governor, to obtain repayment of the purchase-money, which he borrowed as he could at a ruinous rate of interest. Indeed whether the government of a province has or has not been bought, the Governor,

as well as the treasurer and the farmer of the revenue must find the means of making valuable presents, every year, to a vizier, a Eunuch, a lady of the harem, and to any other person whose influence at court he considers indispensable. The Governor must also enforce the payment of the regular tribute to the King; and although he was originally a wretched slave, involved in debt, and without the smallest patrimony, he yet becomes a great and opulent lord.

Thus do ruin and desolation overspread the land. The provincial governors, as before observed, are so many petty tyrants, possessing a boundless authority; and as there is no one to whom the oppressed subject may appeal, he cannot hope for redress, let his injuries be ever so grievous or ever so frequently repeated.

It is true that the Great Mughal sends agents to the various provinces; that is, persons whose business it is to communicate every event that takes place; but there is generally a disgraceful collusion between these officers and the governor, so that their presence seldom restrains the tyranny exercised over the unhappy people.

---

[11]A financier who in return for making a lump-sum payment to the government received the right to collect taxes in a given district.

---

▼▼▼

# The Continuing Vitality of Islam

The resurgence of Islam in the late twentieth century, characterized by political militancy, intensification of personal devotion, and a drive to create societies based on Islamic law and teaching, has roots deep in Islamic history. Time and again Islam has been revitalized and renewed by movements inspired by visionaries and reformers who have exhorted believers to purify doctrine and ritual and to rededicate their lives to God. Many of these reformers spoke of the need for *Jihad*, Arabic for exertion or struggle. In formal religious terms this meant the struggle of Muslims to overcome unbelief and sin. It could also mean holy war against unbelievers.

The eighteenth century was such a period of Islamic revitalization despite the demoralizing political and military failures of the major Muslim empires. While the Ottomans were losing battles to European armies and the Safavid and Mughal empires were disintegrating, Islam continued to make converts in Southeast Asia and Africa and spread into areas such as eastern Bengal through migration. In addition, movements of reform and renewal took root in many parts of the Islamic world, including the religion's historic center in Arabia and its outermost fringes in Southeast Asia and West Africa.

Given the dissimilar environments in which these movements took place, it is not surprising that their doctrines and impact varied greatly. Most were led by legal or Qur'anic scholars or by Muslims with ties to *sufism,* the mystical dimension of Islam that emphasizes personal experience and closeness to God through devotion. Many reformers traveled widely and drew inspiration from ideas they encountered in religious centers such as Baghdad, Cairo, Mecca, and Medina. Some called for a purification of Muslim practices and a return to Islam's fundamentals as revealed in the Qur'an and the teachings and deeds of Muhammad. Many were convinced that Islam had been tainted by accommodating itself to local religious customs and beliefs. Some urged Muslims to seek social justice, while others preached a message of puritanical rigor and personal regeneration. A few called on their followers to take up the sword against unbelievers and heretics.

Eighteenth-century Islamic reform movements were not anti-Western in any meaningful sense. They did, however, affect interaction between the West and the Islamic world in the nineteenth and twentieth centuries. To many earlier Islamic intellectuals and religious leaders, certain Western and Islamic views were not necessarily incompatible, and Muslim thinkers had integrated aspects of Western thought, especially ancient Greek science, into Islamic learning. The message of many eighteenth-century reformers, however, was that Islam was sufficient unto itself. It should be more exclusivist, more centered on its own writings and traditions, and more suspicious of outside ideas and practices. Such views were one of many factors that shaped the tone of interactions between the Muslim and Western worlds in the modern era.

## A Call to Recapture Islam's Purity

▼▼▼

### 53 ▼ *'Abdullah Wahhab,* *THE HISTORY AND DOCTRINES* *OF THE WAHHABIS*

Muhammad ibn-Abd al-Wahhab (1703–1792) was a native of Nejd, a region in the east central part of the Arabian Peninsula, who as a student and teacher visited Mecca, Medina, Basra, Damascus, and Baghdad. In the course of his studies he embraced the ideas of Ahmad ibn Hanbal, the ninth-century jurist and founder of the *Hanbali* school of Sunni Muslim law, which asserted that the sole source of Islamic law was the Qur'an and *hadith,* the Prophet Muhammad's sayings and practices as recorded by those who knew him. Returning home, Wahhab began to denounce the Arabs' religious failings. These included magical rituals, faith in holy men, worship of saints and their tombs, and veneration of supposedly sacred wells and trees. Rejecting Sufi mysticism and rationalist attempts to understand God's nature and purposes, he sought to recapture the pure faith revealed to the Prophet and set forth in Hanbali doctrines. Wahhab urged his listeners to focus on Islam's central doctrine that only God was worthy of worship. Calling themselves *Muwahhidin,* or "unitarians," to emphasize their exclusive devotion to Allah, Wahhab's followers gained military backing when an Arabian chieftain, Muhammad ibn-Sa'ud, accepted their message and dedicated himself to spreading it by force.

In 1803, eleven years after Abd al-Wahhab's death, his followers captured the holy city of Mecca, the immediate aftermath of which is described in the following selection. The excerpt is taken from a pamphlet written by the founder's grandson, 'Abdullah Wahhab, who participated in the conquest of Mecca and was executed when an army sent by the Ottoman sultan took the city in 1818. The pamphlet was written to answer critics and clarify the true beliefs of the Muwahhidin.

---

## QUESTIONS FOR ANALYSIS

1. In the Wahhabi view what are the most serious threats to the purity of Islam?
2. How did the Wahhabis attempt to change Mecca after they captured it? What do their acts reveal about their beliefs and purposes?
3. The Wahhabis have been characterized as puritanical and intolerant. Is such a view justified on the basis of this document?
4. The Wahabbis strongly opposed Shi'ism and the use of logic as a means of discovering religious truth. Why? (See the introduction to source 24 for a discussion of Shi'ism.)
5. How do the Wahabbis perceive their role in the history of Islam?

In the name of God, the compassionate and merciful! Praise be to God, the Lord of the Universe, and blessing and peace be upon our prophet Muhammad, the faithful, and on his people and his companions, and those who lived after them, and their successors of the next generation! Now I was engaged in the holy war, carried on by those who truly believe in the Unity of God, when God, praised be He, graciously permitted us to enter Mecca, the holy, the exalted, at midday, on the 6th day of the week on the 8th of the month Muharram, 1218, Hijrí.[1] Before this, Sa'ud, our leader in the holy war, whom the Lord protect, had summoned the nobles, the divines, and the common people of Mecca; for indeed the leaders of the pilgrims and the rulers of Mecca had resolved on battle, and had risen up against us in the holy place, to exclude us from the house of God. But when the army of the true believers advanced, the Lord filled their hearts with terror, and they fled hither and thither. Then our commander gave protection to everyone within the holy place, while we, with shaven heads and hair cut short,[2] entered with safety, crying "Labbayka,"[3] without fear of any created being, and only of the Lord God. Now, though we were

---

[1] April 1803 on the Islamic calendar.
[2] A custom during the pilgrimage to Mecca.

[3] The loud cry uttered by Muslims as they begin their pilgrimage activities in Mecca.

more numerous, better armed and disciplined than the people of Mecca, yet we did not cut down their trees, neither did we hunt,[4] nor shed any blood except the blood of victims, and of those four-footed beasts which the Lord has made lawful by his commands.

When our pilgrimage was over, we gathered the people together on the forenoon of the first day of the week, and our leader, whom the Lord saves, explained to the divines what we required of the people, . . . namely, a pure belief in the Unity of God Almighty. He pointed out to them that there was no dispute between us and them except on two points, and that one of these was a sincere belief in the unity of God, and a knowledge of the different kinds of prayer of which *du'a*[5] was one. He added that to show the significance of *shirk,*[6] the prophet (may he be blessed!) had put people to death on account of it; that he had continued to call upon them to believe in the Unity of God for some time after he became inspired, and that he had abandoned shirk before the Lord had declared to him the remaining four pillars[7] of Islam. The second point related to actions lawful and unlawful as prohibited. . . .

Then they jointly and severally admitted that our belief was best, and promised the Emir to be guided by the Qur'an and the Sunnah. . . . They then acknowledged our belief, and there was not one among them who doubted or hesitated to believe that that for which we condemned men to death, was the truth pure and unsullied. And they swore a binding oath, although we had not asked them, that their hearts had been opened and their doubts removed, and that they were

convinced whoever said, "Oh prophet of God!" or "Oh Ibn 'Abbes!" or "Oh 'Abdul Qadir!"[8] or called on any other created being, thus entreating him to turn away evil or grant what is good, (where the power belongs to God alone) such as recovery from sickness, or victory over enemies, or protection from temptation, etc.; he is a *Mushrik,*[9] guilty of the most heinous form of shirk, his blood shall be shed and property confiscated. Nor is it any excuse that he believes the effective first cause in the movements of the universe is God, and only supplicates those mortals . . . to intercede for him or bring him nearer the presence of God, so that he may obtain what he requires from Him through them or through their intercession. Again, the tombs which had been erected over the remains of the pious, had become in these times as it were idols where the people went to pray for what they required; they humbled themselves before them, and called upon those lying in them, in their distress, just as did those who were in darkness before the coming of Muhammad.

When this was over, we razed all the large tombs in the city which the people generally worshipped and believed in, and by which they hoped to obtain benefits or ward off evil, so that there did not remain an idol to be adored in that pure city, for which God be praised. Then the taxes and customs we abolished, all the different kinds of instruments for using tobacco we destroyed, and tobacco itself we proclaimed forbidden.[10] Next we burned the dwellings of those selling *hashish,* and living in open wickedness, and issued a proclamation, directing the people to constantly exercise themselves in prayer. They

---

[4]Not cutting down a defeated enemy's trees or hunting the enemy's animals was considered an act of mercy by the victor.

[5]A personal prayer uttered by a Muslim.

[6]*Shirk* is the opposite of surrender to God and the acceptance and recognition of His reality. It may mean atheism, paganism, or polytheism. It is the fundamental error at the root of all sin and transgression.

[7]The first pillar of Islam is the creed, which affirms "There is no god but God, and Muhammad is the messenger of God." The four other pillars are daily prayer; almsgiving;

fasting during the month of Ramadan; and pilgrimage, at least once in every Muslim's life if possible, to Mecca, the city of Muhammad's birth and revelation.

[8]Calling out in prayer the name of Muhammad or these early caliphs in the Abbassid line detracted from the majesty of God.

[9]A person guilty of shirk.

[10]The Wahhabis saw no Qur'anic basis for the use of tobacco; its use is still rare in modern Saudi Arabia, where Wahhabi Islam is predominant.

were not to pray in separate groups according to the different Imams;[11] but all were directed to arrange themselves at each time of prayer behind any Imam who is a follower of any of the four Imams (may the Lord be pleased with them!). For in this way the Lord would be worshiped by as it were one voice, the faithful of all sects would become friendly disposed towards each other, and all dissensions would cease. . . .

We believe that good and evil proceed from God, the exalted; that nothing happens in His kingdom, but what He commands; that created beings do not possess free will, and are not accountable for their own acts; but on the contrary they obtain rank and spiritual reward, merely as an act of grace, and suffer punishment justly, for God is not bound to do anything for His slaves. We believe that the faithful will see Him in the end, but we do not know under what form, as it was beyond our comprehension. And in the same way we follow Imam Ahmad Ibn Hanbal in matters of detail; but we do not reject anyone who follows any of the four Imams, as do the Shi'ites, the Zaidiyyahs, and the Imamiyyahs,[12] &c. Nor do we admit them in any way to act openly according to their vicious creeds; on the contrary, we compelled them to follow one of the four Imams. We do not claim to exercise our reason in all matters of religion, and of our faith, save that we follow our judgment where a point is clearly demonstrated to us in either the Qur'an or the Sunnah. . . . We do not command the destruction of any writings except such as tend to cast people into infidelity to injure their faith, such as those on Logic, which have been prohibited by all Divines. But we are not very exacting with regard to books or documents of this nature, if they appear to assist our opponents, we destroy them. . . . We do not consider it proper

to make Arabs prisoners of war, nor have we done so, neither do we fight with other nations. Finally, we do not consider it lawful to kill women or children. . . .

We believe that our prophet Muhammad is more exalted by God than any other created being; that he is alive, lives in his grave a life quicker [more animated] than that declared by revelation unto martyrs, and that he can hear the salutations of those who salute him. We consider pilgrimage is supported by legal custom, but it should not be undertaken except to a mosque, and for the purpose of praying in it. Therefore, whoever performs pilgrimage for this purpose, is not wrong, and doubtless those who spend the precious moments of their existence in invoking the Prophet, shall, according to Hadith,[13] obtain happiness in this world and the next, and he will dispel their sorrows. We do not deny miraculous powers to the saints, but on the contrary allow them. They are under the guidance of the Lord, so long as they continue to follow the way pointed out in the laws and obey the prescribed rules. But whether alive or dead, they must not be made the object of any form of worship. . . .

We prohibit those forms of Bid'ah[14] that affect religion or pious works. Thus drinking coffee, reciting poetry, praising kings, do not affect religion or pious works and are not prohibited. . . .

All games are lawful. Our prophet allowed play in his mosque. So it is lawful to chide and punish persons in various ways; to train them in the use of different weapons; or to use anything which tends to encourage warriors in battle, such as a war-drum. But it must not be accompanied with musical instruments. These are forbidden, and indeed the difference between them and a war drum is clear. . . .

---

[11]The author uses the term *imam* to refer to the founders of the four major schools of Sunni Muslim jurisprudence: Abu Hanifah (d. 767), founder of the Hanafite school; Malik ibn Anas (d. 795), founder of the Malikite school; al-Shafi (d. 820), founder of the Shafiite school; and Ahmad ibn Hanbal (d. 855), founder of the Hanbali school. The Wahhabis were Hanbalis, but did not reject the authority of the other schools.

[12]Zaidiyyahs and Imamiyyahs were Shi'ite sects.

[13]The tradition, or written record, of the thought and deeds of Muhammad as recorded by his companions.

[14]Erroneous or improper customs that grew after the third generation of Muslims died out.

Whoever is desirous of knowing our belief, let him come to us at al Dir'iyya,[15] and he will see what will gladden his heart, and his eyes will be pleased in reading the compilations on the different kinds of knowledge. . . . He will see God praised in a pleasing manner; the assistance He gives in establishing the true faith; the kindness, which He exerts among the weak and feeble,

between inhabitants and travelers. . . . He is our Agent, our Master, our Deliverer. May peace and the blessing of God be upon our prince Muhammad and on his family and his companions!

'Abdullah, son of Muhammad, son of 'Abdul-Wahhab, wrote this in Muharram, 1218. [April 1803]

---

[15]The Wahhabi capital, some fifteen miles northeast of Riyadh.

## *Jihad* in the Western Sudan
▼▼▼

### 54 ▼ *Usman dan Fodio,*
### *SELECTIONS FROM HIS WRITINGS*

Although merchants and teachers from North Africa and Arabia had introduced Islam to Africa's western and central Sudan as early as the tenth century, by 1800 Islam was not truly dominant in the region. It was still a religion of the cities, where resident Muslim merchants had established Islamic communities, built mosques, introduced Arabic, and made converts. Many converts, however, continued non-Muslim religious rites and festivals, and in rural areas peasants and herders remained animists. Rulers became Muslims in name, but often less for religious reasons than to ingratiate themselves with the merchant community and to attract Islamic scholars to their service as advisors, interpreters, and scribes. Most rulers tolerated their subjects' pagan practices, and many participated in such practices themselves.

This all changed as a result of a series of *jihads,* or holy wars, that swept across the Sudan in the eighteenth and especially the nineteenth centuries. Dedicated Muslims took up arms against non-Muslim or nominal Muslim rulers, and, after seizing power, suppressed traditional African religion and imposed a pure and strict form of Islam on their new subjects. In a matter of decades, these movements redrew the political and religious maps of the Sudan.

The first major jihad of the era, known as the Sokoto Jihad, took place in Hausaland in the early nineteenth century under the leadership of Usman dan Fodio (1754–1817). Hausaland, an area that straddles the Niger River and today makes up the northern part of Nigeria, had been settled by Hausa speakers in the tenth century but also had a substantial population of Fulani, pastoralists who had begun to migrate into the area in the 1500s. The region was divided into approximately a dozen principalities, all of which had emerged after the Songhai Empire's collapse around 1600.

Usman dan Fodio, a member of a Fulani clan with a tradition of Islamic scholarship and teaching, was a member of the *Qadiriyya,* a Sufi brotherhood that dates back to the twelfth century. Beginning in the 1770s, he began to travel and preach throughout rural Hausaland, denouncing corrupt Islamic practices and the tyrannical and venal rulers who tolerated them. His calls for religious and political renewal gained him many followers among the Fulani, who considered themselves oppressed by their rulers, and some Hausa farmers, who were feeling the effects of drought and land shortages. In 1804 when the Sultan of Gobir denounced Usman and prepared to attack the reformer's followers, Usman called on his supporters to take up arms and begin a jihad against Hausaland's rulers. By the late 1810s, Usman controlled Hausaland and established the Kingdom of Sokoto. After his retirement from public life Usman's son and brother extended the campaign to the south and east. The era of Sudanese jihads had begun in earnest.

Usman wrote close to one hundred books on politics, religion, marriage customs, and education. Brief excerpts from four of them are included here. Together they provide a sampling of his thoughts on religion, government, and society.

---

## QUESTIONS FOR ANALYSIS

1. What policies and values of the Hausa sultans does Usman criticize? Why?
2. How do the religious failings of the Hausa princes prevent them from being just and equitable rulers?
3. What groups in Hausa society would have been most likely to respond positively to Usman's criticisms of the sultans?
4. What is Usman's message concerning the treatment of Muslim women? Is it a message of equality with men?

## THE FAULTS OF THE HAUSA RULERS[1]

And one of the ways of their government is the building of their sovereignty upon three things: the people's persons, their honor, and their possessions; and whomsoever they wish to kill or exile or violate his honor or devour his wealth they do so in pursuit of their lusts, without any right in the *Shari'a*.[2] One of the ways of their government is their imposing on the people monies not laid down by the *Shari'a*. One of the ways of their government is their intentionally eating whatever food they wish, whether it is religiously permitted or forbidden, and wearing

whatever clothes they wish, whether religiously permitted or forbidden, and drinking what beverages they wish, whether religiously permitted or forbidden, and riding whatever riding beasts they wish, whether religiously permitted or forbidden, and taking what women they wish without marriage contract, and living in decorated palaces, whether religiously permitted or forbidden, and spreading soft carpets as they wish, whether religiously permitted or forbidden.

. . . One of the ways of their government is to place many women in their houses, until the number of women of some of them amounts to one thousand or more. One of the ways of their government is that a man puts the affairs of his

---

[1]An excerpt from *Kitab al-farq,* "The Book of Difference between the Government of Muslims and Unbelievers," probably written around 1806.

[2]*Shari'a,* or literally "path" in Arabic, is the word for Islamic law.

women into the hands of the oldest one, and every one of the others is like a slave-woman under her. One of the ways of their government is to delay in the paying of a debt, and this is injustice. One of the ways of their government is what the superintendent of the market takes from all the parties to a sale, and the meat which he takes on each market day from the butchers, . . . and one of the ways of their government is the cotton and other things which they take in the course of the markets. . . . One of the ways of their governments is the taking of people's beasts of burden without their permission to carry the sultan's food to him. Whoever follows his beast to the place where they unload it, they return it to him but he who does not follow, his beast is lost.

. . . One of the ways of their government which is also well known is that whoever dies in their country, they take his property, and they call it "inheritance," and they know that it is without doubt injustice.[3] One of the ways of their government is to impose tax on merchants, and other travellers. One of the ways of their government, which is also well known, is that one may not pass by their farms, nor cross them without suffering bad treatment from their slaves. One of the ways of their government, which is also well known, is that if the people's animals go among their animals, they do not come out again unless they give a proportion of them, and if the sultan's animals stray, and are found spoiling the cultivated land and other things, they are not driven off. . . .

One of the ways of their government, which is also well known, is that if you have an adversary in law and he precedes you to them, and gives them some money, then your word will not be accepted by them, even though they know for a certainty of your truthfulness, unless you give them more than your adversary gave. One of the ways of their government is to shut the door in the face of the needy. . . . Therefore do not follow their way in their government, and do not imitate them. . . .

## ROYAL RELIGION[4]

It is well known that in our time Islam in these countries mentioned above is widespread among people other than the sultans. As for the sultans, they are undoubtedly unbelievers, even though they may profess the religion of Islam, because they practice polytheistic rituals and turn people away from the path of God and raise the flag of worldly kingdom above the banner of Islam. All this is unbelief according to the consensus of opinion.[5]

The government of a country is the government of its king without question. If the king is a Muslim, his land is Muslim; if he is an Unbeliever, his land is a land of Unbelievers. In these circumstances it is obligatory for anyone to leave it for another country.[6] There is no dispute that the sultans of these countries venerate certain places, certain trees, and certain rocks and offer sacrifice to them. This constitutes unbelief according to the consensus of opinion.

I say this on the basis of the common practice known about them, but I do not deny the existence of some Muslims here and there among them. Those however are rare and there is no place for what is rare in legal decisions.

## THE TREATMENT OF WOMEN AND SLAVES[7]

Most of our educated men leave their wives, their daughters, and the slaves morally abandoned, like beasts, without teaching them what God prescribes should be taught them, and without instructing them in the articles of the Law which

---

[3]A grievance of foreign Muslim merchants who might die while residing in a Hausa city.

[4]From *Tanbih al-ikhwan 'ala ahwal ard al-Sudan,* "Concerning the Government of Our Country and Neighboring Countries in the Sudan," written around 1811.

[5]Consensus of the Muslim community, usually interpreted to mean the opinions of leading legal scholars, was a recognized source of Muslim law.

[6]Usman did just this when he led his followers out of the sultanate of Gobir after its ruler had turned against him.

[7]From *Nur al-albab,* "Light of the Intellects."

concern them. Thus, they leave them ignorant of the rules regarding ablutions,[8] prayer, fasting, business dealings, and other duties which they have to fulfil, and which God commands that they should be taught.

Men treat these beings like household implements which become broken after long use and which are then thrown out on the dung-heap. This is an abominable crime! Alas! How can they thus shut up their wives, their daughters, and their slaves in the darkness of ignorance, while daily they impart knowledge to their students? In truth, they act out of egoism, and if they devote themselves to their pupils, that is nothing but hypocrisy and vain ostentation on their part.

Their conduct is blameworthy, for to instruct one's wives, daughters, and captives is a positive duty, while to impart knowledge to students is only a work over and above what is expected, and there is no doubt but that the one takes precedence over the other.

Muslim women — Do not listen to the speech of those who are misguided and who sow the seed of error in the heart of another; they deceive you when they stress obedience to your husbands without telling you of obedience to God and to his Messenger,[9] (May God show him bounty and grant him salvation), and when they say that the woman finds her happiness in obedience to her husband.

They seek only their own satisfaction, and that is why they impose upon you tasks which the Law of God and that of his Prophet have never especially assigned to you. Such are — the preparation of food-stuffs, the washing of clothes, and other duties which they like to impose upon you, while they neglect to teach you what God and the Prophet have prescribed for you.

Yes, the woman owes submission to her husband, publicly as well as in intimacy, even if he is one of the humble people of the world, and to disobey him is a crime, at least so long as he does not command what God condemns; in that case she must refuse, since it is wrong of a human creature to disobey the Creator.

## THE CALL TO HOLY WAR[10]

That to make war upon the heathen king who does not say "There is no God but Allah" on account of the custom of his town, and who makes no profession of Islam, is obligatory by assent,[11] and that to take the government from him is obligatory by assent.

And that to make war upon the king who is an apostate, and who has abandoned the religion of Islam for the religion of heathendom is obligatory by assent, and that to take the government from him is obligatory by assent; And that to make war against the king who is an apostate — who has not abandoned the religion of Islam as far as the profession of it is concerned, but who mingles the observances of Islam with the observances of heathendom, like the kings of Hausaland for the most part — is also obligatory by assent, and that to take the government from him is obligatory by assent.

And to make war upon backsliding Muslims who do not own allegiance to any of the Emirs of the Faithful,[12] is obligatory by assent, if they be summoned to give allegiance and they refuse, until they enter into allegiance; . . .

And that residence in enemy territory is unlawful by assent; . . .

And to enslave the freeborn among the Muslims is unlawful by assent, whether they reside in the territory of Islam, or in enemy territory;

And to make war upon the oppressors is obligatory by assent, and that wrongfully to devour their property is unlawful by assent, for "Use is made of their armor against them, and afterwards it is returned to them"; and their enslavement is unlawful by assent; . . .

---

[8]Washing one's body as part of a religious rite.
[9]Muhammad.
[10]From *Wathiqat ahl al-Sudan wa man sha' Allah min al-ikhwan*, "Dispatch to the Folk of the Sudan and to Whom

so Allah Wills among the Brethren," probably written in 1804 or 1805.
[11]"By assent" refers to the consensus of the Muslim community.
[12]"Emirs of the faithful" were Usman's lieutenants.

# Chapter 7

### ▼▼▼

# Change and Continuity in East Asia and Oceania

For the Ottoman, Safavid, and Mughal empires the seventeenth and eighteenth centuries were times of turmoil and decline after an era of strength and expansion. In East and Southeast Asia, this pattern was reversed. Japan endured civil war throughout the sixteenth century, a period that also saw the arrival of Europeans with their firearms and Catholic religious beliefs. China entered into a period of dynastic decline at the end of the sixteenth century when the quality and effectiveness of Ming emperors deteriorated. Factionalism paralyzed the central administration, and peasant violence escalated in the face of rising taxes and official corruption. Then in 1644 military weakness and internal decay led to invasion by the Manchus, who seized power and established China's last imperial dynasty, the Qing. Southeast Asia, which produced the spices so coveted by Europeans, also experienced turmoil in the sixteenth century. The Spaniards conquered the Philippines, while the Portuguese took over Malacca on Malaysia's west coast and bullied their way into the region's trade networks.

During the seventeenth century, however, conflict and tensions abated. In Japan recovery began in 1603 when the Tokugawa clan took power and ended the century-long civil war, while in China it began in 1644 when Manchu invaders replaced the Ming and began to reinvigorate the government. Although China and Japan did not lack problems in the seventeenth and eighteenth centuries, in comparison to what had gone before and what would follow, these were years of orderly government and social harmony.

These also were years in which European influence in the region grew but slightly, if at all. China's Manchu rulers continued to limit European merchants' activities to Macao and Guangzhou, and beginning in the early 1700s they curtailed European missionary activity. The Manchus also checked Russian expansion in the Amur Valley. In 1689 they negotiated the Treaty of Nerchinsk, by which the Russians abandoned their trading posts in Manchuria in return for modest commercial privileges in Beijing. In Japan the Tokugawa shoguns expelled all foreigners, outlawed Christianity, and limited trade with Europeans to one Dutch ship a year. In the East Indies the Dutch, after forcing out the Portuguese and establishing a political base in Java, were content after the mid 1600s to protect rather than expand their gains. Spain's involvement in the region never extended beyond the Philippines.

By the end of the 1700s, however, signs of change were evident. In Japan economic expansion, urbanization, and political tranquility created new tensions by enriching merchants while undermining the function and financial base of the military aristocracy. In China rapid population growth caused hardship among the peasant masses by driving up the cost of land; moreover, around 1800 budgetary shortfalls, higher taxes, abuses of the civil service examination system, and neglect of roads, bridges, and dikes were signs of impending dynastic decline.

In addition, European pressures in the region once more were growing. In the 1780s, the English began to settle Australia and New Zealand. French missionaries increased their activities in Vietnam. In 1800 the Dutch government stripped the Dutch East India Company of its administrative responsibilities in Southeast Asia and tightened its grip on the region's agriculture and trade. From their base in India British merchants opened a new chapter in the history of trade with China after finding a product that millions of Chinese deeply craved. The product, grown and processed in India, packed into 133-pound chests, shipped to Guangzhou, sold for silver to Chinese merchants, and sold again to millions of addicts, was opium. For East and Southeast Asians and for the peoples of the South Pacific islands, a new era of upheaval was about to begin.

▼▼▼

# China's Revival under the Qing

After the last Ming emperor hanged himself in April 1644 and the bandit-emperor Li Zicheng fled Beijing in June, Manchu invaders placed the child emperor Shunzhi on the throne, and China's last dynasty, the Qing, began its rule. During the next thirty-five years, Manchu armies fought from Burma to Taiwan, hunting down and executing Ming supporters, crushing their armies, and suppressing rebellion. By 1680 the Manchus controlled China and could fully attend to the challenge of ruling their 150 million new subjects.

The Manchus made it clear from the start that they were the rulers and the Chinese their subjects. They ordered courtiers and government officials to abandon the loose-fitting robes of the Ming for the high-collared tight jackets favored by the Manchus. They also required all males to shave their foreheads and braid their hair in the back in a Manchu style despised by the Chinese.

In most other ways, however, the Manchus maintained Chinese institutions and adapted to Chinese culture. They embraced the Chinese principle of centralized monarchy, learned the Chinese language, and supported Confucian scholarship. They reinstated the civil service examinations, which had been abandoned during the last decades of Ming rule. Although Manchus were disproportionately represented in the bureaucracy, Chinese were allocated half of all important offices, and gradually Chinese scholar-officials began to support and serve the new foreign dynasty.

From 1661 through 1799, China had but three emperors: Kangxi (r. 1661–1722), Yongzhen (r. 1722–1736), and Qianlong (r. 1736–1796), who resigned as emperor in 1796 to avoid exceeding the long reign of his grandfather Kangxi but who actually ruled until 1799. By any standard, the years of their rule were among the most impressive in all of Chinese history. China reached its greatest size as a result of military campaigns in central Asia. Agriculture flourished, trade expanded, and China's population grew from an estimated 150 million at the end of the seventeenth century to over 300 million a century later. China's cultural vitality was no less remarkable. The era's literary output included China's greatest novel, *The Dream of the Red Chamber* by Cao Xueqin, and painting and scholarship flourished under Qing patronage. Kangxi sponsored a dictionary of the Chinese language and an encyclopedia that reached 5,000 volumes. Qianlong supported the work of scholars and copyists who compiled an anthology of 3,450 historical, literary, and philosophical texts which with commentaries totaled 36,000 volumes.

Toward the end of Qianlong's reign, however, the first signs of decline began to appear. Rural poverty worsened, military effectiveness declined, and factionalism and favoritism at the imperial court resurfaced. Nonetheless, it was neither farfetched nor fanciful when France's leading eighteenth-century writer, Voltaire, described Qing China as a model of moral and ethical government and praised Qianlong as the ideal philosopher-king.

# Emperor Kangxi Views His World
▼▼▼

## 55 ▼ Kangxi, SELF-PORTRAIT

In 1661 a seven-year-old boy became the second emperor of the Qing Dynasty after the unexpected death of his father, Shunzhi. His name was Kangxi, and during his long reign, which lasted until 1722, he brought order to a China racked by decades of Ming misrule, internal chaos, and invasion. He crushed the last vestiges of Ming resistance, fortified China's borders, revitalized the civil service examination system, won the support of China's scholar-officials, managed to ease tensions between ethnic Chinese and their Manchu conquerors, and brought new vigor and direction to government. A generous supporter of writers, artists, poets, scholars, and craftsmen, Kangxi himself was also a scholar and writer of distinction. He studied Confucianism, Latin, music, mathematics, and science and left behind a rich store of poems, essays, aphorisms, letters, edicts, and sayings.

In 1974, the historian Jonathan Spence drew on these writings and statements to compile a self-portrait of the emperor. In the following excerpts the emperor expresses his views on justice, government administration, and Europeans, with whom China's relations took a decisive turn for the worse during his reign.

Since the late sixteenth century, members of the Society of Jesus, a Catholic religious order, had provided an intellectual and cultural link between China and the West. Prized by emperors for their knowledge of astronomy and mathematics and their skills as cartographers, artists, and architects, these Jesuit fathers had been welcomed at the imperial court in Beijing, where they wore Chinese garb, learned Chinese, and paid homage to the emperor. They also managed to convert some two hundred court officials, who in keeping with a policy initiated by the founder of the Jesuit mission in China, Matteo Ricci (1552–1610), were permitted to practice Chinese rites such as ceremonies in honor of deceased ancestors and public homage to Confucius. Kangxi had an avid interest in Western learning, and in 1692 he granted toleration to Christianity and permission to the Jesuits to preach outside Beijing. By the early eighteenth century as many as three hundred thousand Chinese may have been Roman Catholics.

In the early 1700s, however, the Catholic missionary effort experienced a fatal schism. Members of the Franciscan and Dominican religious orders, fresh from their successful missionary efforts in the Philippines and relative newcomers to the field of Chinese missions, attacked the Jesuit position on Confucian rites and successfully won over Pope Clement XI to their point of view. In 1706 a papal envoy to China, Charles de Tournon, announced the pope's decision that traditional Confucian ceremonies were religious, not civil rites, and henceforth would be prohibited for Chinese Catholics. An angry Kangxi responded with a ban on Christian preaching, and the Qing assault on Christianity was underway. Under Kangxi's successor, the Jesuits lost their position at Beijing, and the main source of contact between the imperial court and the intellectual world of the West disappeared.

## QUESTIONS FOR ANALYSIS

1. What does Kangxi's treatment of delinquent and dishonest government officials reveal about his philosophy of government?
2. How do Confucian values affect Kangxi's decisions about whether to be lenient to men accused of killing their wives?
3. What are Kangxi's views of the civil service examination system? What ideas did he have about improving the system?
4. What role do eunuchs play in Kangxi's administration? How does this compare with the situation during the late Ming Era (Chapter 4, source 32)?
5. According to Kangxi, what are the strengths and limitations of Western science and mathematics?
6. According to Kangxi, what specific issues were involved in the dispute over Chinese rites?
7. What other characteristics and actions of the missionaries led to Kangxi's decision to ban further Christian preaching?

## AN EMPEROR'S RESPONSIBILITIES

Giving life to people and killing people — those are the powers that the emperor has. He knows that administrative errors in government bureaus can be rectified, but that a criminal who has been executed cannot be brought back to life any more than a chopped string can be joined together again. He knows, too, that sometimes people have to be persuaded into morality by the example of an execution. . . .

Hu Jianzheng was a subdirector of the Court of Sacrificial Worship whose family terrorized their native area in Jiangsu, seizing people's lands and wives and daughters, and murdering people after falsely accusing them of being thieves. . . . I ordered . . . that he be executed with his family and in his native place, so that all the local gentry might learn how I regarded such behavior. Corporal Yambu was sentenced to death for gross corruption in the shipyards. I not only agreed to the penalty but sent guards officer Uge to supervise the beheading, and ordered that all

shipyard personnel from generals down to private soldiers kneel down in full armor and listen to my warning that execution would be their fate as well unless they ended their evil ways. . . .

The final penalty of lingering death[1] must be given in cases of treason, as the Legal Code requires. . . . When Ilaguksan Khutuktu, who had had his spies in the lamas' residences so that they would welcome Galdan's[2] army into China, and had plotted with Galdan and encouraged him in his rebellion, was finally caught, I had him brought to Beijing and cut to death in the Yellow Temple, in the presence of all the Manchu and Mongol princes, and the senior officials, both civil and military. . . .

Of all the things that I find distasteful, none is more so than giving a final verdict on the death sentences that are sent to me for ratification. . . .

Each year we went through the lists, sparing sixteen out of sixty-three at one session, eighteen out of fifty-seven at another, thirty-three out of eighty-three at another. For example, it was clear to me that the three cases of husbands

---

[1] A slow, painful, and humiliating punishment in which a person died from the administration of numerous cuts on the body.

[2] A lama was a Buddhist priest, or monk, in Tibet, Mongolia, and western China. Galdan was a leader of a Western Mongol tribe who in the late seventeenth century conquered much of Chinese Turkestan and Outer Mongolia; when he threatened Beijing, Kangxi raised an army and crushed him in 1696.

killing wives that came up . . . were all quite different. The husband who hit his wife with an ax because she nagged at him for drinking, and then murdered her after another domestic quarrel . . . how could any extenuating circumstances be found? But Baoer, who killed his wife for swearing at his parents; and Meng, whose wife failed to serve him properly and used foul language so that he killed her — they could have their sentences reduced. . . .

## EUNUCHS AND BUREAUCRATS

You have to define and reward people in accordance with their status in life. If too much grace is shown to inferiors they become lazy and uppity and will be sure to stir up trouble — and if you neglect them they will abuse you behind your back. That was why I insisted on such strictness when the eunuch Jian Wenzai beat a commoner to death, saying strangulation was not enough. For eunuchs are basically Yin[3] in nature. They are quite different from ordinary people; when weak with age they babble like babies. In my court I never let them get involved with government — even the few eunuchs-of-the-presence with whom I might chatter or exchange family jokes were never allowed to discuss politics. I only have about four hundred, as opposed to the immense numbers there were in the Ming, and I keep them working at menial jobs; I ignore their frowns and smiles and make sure that they stay poor. Whereas in the later Ming Dynasty, besides being so extravagant and reckless, they obtained the power to write endorsements on the emperors' memorials, for the emperors were unable to read the one- or two-thousand-character memorials that flowed in; and the eunuchs in turn passed the memorials on to *their* subordinates to handle.

▾ ▾ ▾

There are too many men who claim to be pure scholars and yet are stupid and arrogant; we'd be better off with less talk of moral principle and more practice of it. Even in those who have been the best officials in my reign there are obvious failings. . . . Peng Peng was always honest and courageous — when robbers were in his district he simply put on his armor, rode out, and routed them — but when angry he was wild and vulgar in his speech, and showed real disrespect. Zhao Shenjiao was completely honest, traveled with only thirteen servants and no personal secretaries at all, but was too fond of litigation and was constantly getting the common people involved in complex cases. . . . And Zhang Pengke, whom I praised so often and kept in the highest offices, could write a memorial so stupid that I ordered it printed up and posted in major cities so that everyone could read it — for he claimed that the drop in the river's level was due to a miracle performed by the spirit of the waters, when the real reason was that no rain had fallen for six months in the upper reaches of the Yellow River. . . .

This is one of the worst habits of the great officials, that if they are not recommending their teachers or their friends for high office then they recommend their relations. This evil practice used to be restricted to the Chinese: they've always formed cliques and then used their recommendations to advance the other members of the clique. Now the practice has spread to the Chinese Bannermen[4] like Yu Chenglong, and even the Manchus, who used to be so loyal, recommend men from their own Banners, knowing them to have a foul reputation, and will refuse to help the Chinese. . . .

In 1694 I noted that we were losing talent because of the ways the exams were being

---

[3]In East Asian thought, Yin and Yang were the two complementary principles or forces that make up all aspects and phenomena of life. Yin is conceived of as Earth, female, dark, passive, and absorbing.

[4]The banner system was a method of military organization under the Qing in which fighting men were grouped in divisions identified by different colored banners. Bannermen were given grants of land and small stipends for their service. Chinese (as opposed to Manchu) bannermen were originally drawn from the ranks of Chinese soldiers and officers who had surrendered to the Manchus and joined their cause early in their struggle against Ming supporters.

conducted: even in the military exams most of the successful candidates were from Zhejiang and Jiangnan, while there was only one from Henan and one from Shanxi.[5] The successful ones had often done no more than memorize old examination answer books, whereas the best *should* be selected on the basis of riding and archery. Yet it is always the strong men from the western provinces who are eager to serve in the army, while not only are troops from Zhejiang and Jiangnan among the weakest, they also pass on their posts to their relatives who are also weak.

Even among the examiners there are those who are corrupt, those who do not understand basic works, those who ask detailed questions about practical matters of which they know nothing, those who insist entirely on memorization of the *Classics*[6] and refuse to prescribe essays, those who put candidates from their own geographical area at the top of the list, or those who make false claims about their abilities to select the impoverished and deserving. . . . Other candidates hire people to sit [take] the exams for them, or else pretend to be from a province that has a more liberal quota than their own. It's usually easy enough to check the latter, since I've learnt to recognize the accents from thirteen provinces, and if you watch the person and study his voice you can tell where he is really from. As to the other problems, one can overcome some of them by holding the exams under rigorous armed supervision and then reading the exam papers oneself.

## DEALING WITH EUROPEANS

The rare can become common, as with the lions and other animals that foreign ambassadors like to give us and my children are now accustomed to; . . .

Western skills are a case in point: in the late Ming Dynasty, when the Westerners first brought the gnomon,[7] the Chinese thought it a rare treasure until they understood its use. And when the Emperor Shunzhi got a small chiming clock in 1653, he kept it always near him; but now we have learned to balance the springs and to adjust the chimes and finally to make the whole clock, so that my children can have ten chiming clocks each to play with, if they want them. Similarly, we learned in a short time to make glassware that is superior to that made in the West, and our lacquer would be better than theirs, too, were it not that their wet sea climate gives a better sheen than the dry and dusty Chinese climate ever could. . . .

I realized, too, that Western mathematics has its uses. . . . I ordered the Jesuits Thomas, Gerbillon, and Bouvet to study Manchu also, and to compose treatises in that language on Western arithmetic and the geometry of Euclid.[8] In the early 1690's I often worked several hours a day with them. With Verbiest I had examined each stage of the forging of cannons, and made him build a water fountain that operated in conjunction with an organ, and erect a windmill in the court; with the new group — who were later joined by Brocard and Jartoux, and worked in the Yangxin Palace under the general direction of my Eldest Son Yinti — I worked on clocks and mechanics. Pereira taught me to play the tune, *"P'u-yen-chou"* on the harpsichord and the structure of the eight-note scale, Pedrini taught my sons musical theory, and Gherardini painted portraits at the Court. I also learned to calculate the weight and volume of spheres, cubes, and cones, and to measure distances and the angle of river banks. On inspection tours later I used these Western methods to show my officials how to make more accurate calculations when planning their river works. . . . I showed them how to

---

[5]Zhejiang and Jiangnan were southeast coastal regions of China; Henan and Shanxi were north-central provinces.
[6]A clearly specified set of books from Chinese antiquity, thought to embody Confucian wisdom.

[7]A sundial.
[8]The ancient Greek mathematician who lived around 300 B.C.E., and whose work laid the foundation for the study of geometry.

calculate circumferences and assess the area of a plot of land, even if its borders were as jagged as dogs' teeth, drawing diagrams for them on the ground with an arrow; and calculated the flow of river water through a lock gate by multiplying the volume that flowed in a few seconds to get a figure for the whole day. . . .

But I was careful not to refer to these Westerners as "Great Officials." . . . For even though some of the Western methods are different from our own, and may even be an improvement, there is little about them that is new. The principles of mathematics all derive from the *Book of Changes,*[9] and the Western methods are Chinese in origin: this algebra — "A-erh-chu-pa-erh" — springs from an Eastern word.[10] And though it was indeed the Westerners who showed us something our ancient calendar experts did not know — namely how to calculate the angle of the northern pole — this but shows the truth what Zhu Xi[11] arrived at through his investigation of things: the earth is like the yolk within an egg.

▼ ▼ ▼

On the question of the Chinese Rites that might be practiced by the Western missionaries, de Tournon[12] would not speak, though I sent messages to him repeatedly. I had agreed with the formulation the Beijing fathers had drawn up in 1700: that Confucius was honored by the Chinese as a master, but his name was not invoked in prayer for the purpose of gaining happiness, rank, or wealth; that worship of ancestors was an expression of love and filial remembrance, not intended to bring protection to the worshiper; and that there was no idea when an ancestral

tablet was erected, that the soul of the ancestor dwelt in that tablet. And when sacrifices were offered to Heaven it was not the blue existent sky that was addressed, but the lord and creator of all things. If the ruler Shang-ti was sometimes called Heaven, *T'ien,* that had no more significance than giving honorific names to the emperor.

If de Tournon didn't reply, the Catholic Bishop Maigrot[13] did, . . . telling me that Heaven is a material thing and should not be worshiped, and that one should invoke only the name "Lord of Heaven" to show the proper reverence. Maigrot wasn't merely ignorant of Chinese literature, he couldn't even recognize the simplest Chinese characters; yet he chose to discuss the falsity of the Chinese moral system. . . .

Even little animals mourn their dead mothers for many days; these Westerners who want to treat their dead with indifference are not even equal to animals. How could they be compared with Chinese? We venerate Confucius because of his doctrines of respect for virtue, his system of education, his inculcation of love for superiors and ancestors. Westerners venerate their own saints because of their actions. They paint pictures of men with wings and say, "These represent heavenly spirits, swift as if they had wings, though in reality there are no men with wings." I do not find it appropriate to dispute this doctrine, yet with superficial knowledge Maigrot discussed Chinese sanctity. . . .

Every country must have some spirits that it reveres. This is true for our dynasty, as for Mongols or Mohammedans, Miao or Lolo,[14] or other foreigners. Just as everyone fears some-

---

[9]One of the Classics, the *Book of Changes* was a work of divination that relied on the analysis of trigrams and hexagrams.
[10]*Algebra* is derived from the Arabic word *Al-jabr.* Kangxi is correct when he asserts that China had a long tradition of achievement in algebra, geometry, and trigonometry dating back at least as far as the Han Dynasty (206 B.C.E.– 220 C.E.).
[11]Zhu Xi (1130–1200 C.E.) was a famous commentator on Confucius and was China's leading philosopher after the classical age.
[12]Charles de Tournon (1668–1710) was a special papal envoy sent to India and China to oversee Catholic missions.

His demand that Chinese Christians abandon traditional rites was deeply offensive to Kangxi. The emperor ordered him to prison, where he died in 1710.
[13]Charles Maigrot (1652–1730) was the apostolic vicar to China. His opposition to the Jesuit position on rites led to his expulsion from China in 1707.
[14]The Miao (also known as the Hmong) and Lolo were indigenous people of southwest China and upland Southeast Asia.

thing, some snakes but not toads, some toads but not snakes; and as all countries have different pronunciations and different alphabets. But in this Catholic religion, the Society of Peter[15] quarrels with the Jesuits, . . . and among the Jesuits the Portuguese want only their own nationals in their church while the French want only French in theirs. This violates the principles of religion. Such dissension cannot be inspired by the Lord of Heaven but by the Devil, who, I have heard the Westerners say, leads men to do evil since he can't do otherwise.

▾ ▾ ▾

Since I discovered on the Southern Tour of 1703 that there were missionaries wandering at will over China, I had grown cautious and determined to control them more tightly: to bunch them in the larger cities and in groups that included men from several different countries, to catalogue their names and residences, and to permit no new establishments without my express permission. . . . I made all missionaries who wanted to stay on in China sign a certificate, stating that they would remain here for life and follow Ricci on the Rites. Forty or fifty who refused were exiled to Guangzhou; de Tournon was sent to Macao,[16] his secretary, Appiani, we kept in prison in Beijing.

Despite these sterner restrictions, the Westerners continued to cause me anxiety. Our ships were being sold overseas; reports came of iron-wood for keel blocks being shipped out of Guangdong; Luzon and Batavia[17] became havens for Chinese outlaws; and the Dutch were strong in the Southern Seas. I ordered a general inquiry among residents of Beijing who had once lived on the coast, and called a conference of the coastal governors-general. "I fear that some time in the future China is going to get into difficulties with these various Western countries," I said. "That is my prediction."

[15]There is no such religious order as the "Society of Peter." Kangxi is probably referring to supporters of the papal position on rites; according to Catholics the authority of the pope can be traced back to the apostle Peter.
[16]Macao was the trading settlement some one hundred miles from Guangzhou where by imperial order Western merchants were permitted to do business.
[17]Luzon was the major island of the Spanish-ruled Philippines; Batavia was the Dutch name for the island of Java in the East Indies.

## China Rejects Increased Western Trade
▾▾▾

### 56 ▾ *Emperor Qianlong,* *LETTER TO KING GEORGE III*

Chinese restrictions on Western commerce in the eighteenth century increasingly frustrated and angered the British, who were strenuously seeking to expand their trade in East Asia. Agents of the East India Company could trade only outside the city walls of Guangzhou with government-appointed merchants and had to depart as soon as their business was completed. They were subject to Chinese laws and required to avoid activities that disturbed the Chinese such as entering Guangzhou city limits, learning Chinese, being accompanied by their wives, and much else. When the East India Company sent a representative, James Flint, to Beijing in 1759 to negotiate changes in the Guangzhou system, the unfortunate envoy was imprisoned for three years because he had learned Chinese, sailed to unapproved ports, and improperly addressed the emperor.

In 1792 the East India Company tried another approach by enlisting the British government in its cause. In 1792 Lord George Macartney, a diplomat with previous service in Russia, the West Indies, and India, sailed to China on a British warship loaded with magnificent gifts for Emperor Qianlong (r. 1736–1796). He also delivered a letter to the emperor from King George III, requesting an easing of trade regulations, the publication of tariff lists, and permission to trade in cities other than Guangzhou. The request elicited the following response from the emperor.

---

## QUESTIONS FOR ANALYSIS

1. What view of China's place in the world is revealed in Qianlong's letter?
2. What are the emperor's stated reasons for rejecting any expansion of British trade?
3. What unstated reasons may have affected the emperor's decision?
4. The British government made no immediate effort to change Qianlong's mind. But if it had made such an attempt, how might it have responded to Qianlong's arguments?

You, O King, from afar have yearned after the blessings of our civilization, and in your eagerness to come into touch with our converting influence have sent an Embassy across the sea bearing a memorial.[1] I have already taken note of your respectful spirit of submission, have treated your mission with extreme favor and loaded it with gifts, besides issuing a mandate to you, O King, and honoring you with the bestowal of valuable presents. Thus has my indulgence been manifested.

Yesterday your Ambassador petitioned my Ministers to memorialize me regarding your trade with China, but his proposal is not consistent with our dynastic usage and cannot be entertained. Hitherto, all European nations, including your own country's barbarian merchants, have carried on their trade with our Celestial Empire at Guangzhou. Such has been the procedure for many years, although our Celestial Empire possesses all things in prolific abundance and lacks no product within its own borders. There was therefore no need to import the manufactures of outside barbarians in exchange for our

own produce. But as the tea, silk, and porcelain which the Celestial Empire produces are absolute necessities to European nations and to yourselves, we have permitted, as a signal mark of favor, that *hongs*[2] should be established at Guangzhou, so that your wants might be supplied and your country thus participate in our beneficence. But your Ambassador has now put forward new requests which completely fail to recognize the Throne's principle to "treat strangers from afar with indulgence," and to exercise a pacifying control over barbarian tribes the world over. Moreover, our dynasty, ruling over the myriad races of the globe, extends the same benevolence towards all. Your England is not the only nation trading at Guangzhou. If other nations, following your bad example, wrongfully importune my ear with further impossible requests, how will it be possible for me to treat them with easy indulgence? Nevertheless, I do not forget the lonely remoteness of your island, cut off from the world by intervening wastes of sea, nor do I overlook your excusable ignorance of the usages of our Celestial Empire. I have con-

---

[1]Memorandum.
[2]Approximately ten Chinese merchant guilds that alone were licensed to trade with Westerners.

sequently commanded my Ministers to enlighten your Ambassador on the subject, and have ordered the departure of the mission. But I have doubts that after your Envoy's return he may fail to acquaint you with my view in detail or that he may be lacking in lucidity, so that I shall now proceed . . . to issue my mandate on each question separately. In this way you will, I trust, comprehend my meaning. . . .

Your request for a small island near Zhoushan,[3] where your merchants may reside and goods be warehoused, arises from your desire to develop trade. As there are neither *hongs* nor interpreters in or near Zhoushan, where none of your ships has ever called, such an island would be utterly useless for your purposes. Every inch of the territory of our Empire is marked on the map and the strictest vigilance is exercised over it all: even tiny islets and far-lying sand-banks are clearly defined as part of the provinces to which they belong. Consider, moreover, that England is not the only barbarian land which wishes to establish . . . trade with our Empire: supposing that other nations were all to imitate your evil example and beseech me to present them each and all with a site for trading purposes, how could I possibly comply? This also is a flagrant infringement of the usage of my Empire and cannot possibly be entertained.

The next request, for a small site in the vicinity of Guangzhou city, where your barbarian merchants may lodge or, alternatively, that there be no longer any restrictions over their movements at Macao,[4] has arisen from the following causes. Hitherto, the barbarian merchants of Europe have had a definite locality assigned to them at Macao for residence and trade, and have been forbidden to encroach an inch beyond the limits assigned to that locality. . . . If these restrictions were withdrawn, friction would inevitably occur between the Chinese and your barbarian subjects, and the results would militate against the benevolent regard that I feel towards you. From every point of view, therefore, it is best that the regulations now in force should continue unchanged. . . .

Regarding your nation's worship of the Lord of Heaven, it is the same religion as that of other European nations. Ever since the beginning of history, sage Emperors and wise rulers have bestowed on China a moral system and inculcated a code, which from time immemorial has been religiously observed by the myriads of my subjects.[5] There has been no hankering after heterodox doctrines. Even the European officials[6] in my capital are forbidden to hold intercourse with Chinese subjects; they are restricted within the limits of their appointed residences, and may not go about propagating their religion. The distinction between Chinese and barbarian is most strict, and your Ambassador's request that barbarians shall be given full liberty to disseminate their religion is utterly unreasonable.

It may be, O King, that the above proposals have been wantonly made by your Ambassador on his own responsibility, or peradventure you yourself are ignorant of our dynastic regulations and had no intention of transgressing them when you expressed these wild ideas and hopes. . . . If, after the receipt of this explicit decree, you lightly give ear to the representations of your subordinates and allow your barbarian merchants to proceed to Zhejiang and Tianjin,[7] with the object of landing and trading there, the ordinances of my Celestial Empire are strict in the extreme, and the local officials, both civil and military, are bound reverently to obey the law of the land. Should your vessels touch the shore, your merchants will assuredly never be permitted to land or to reside there, but will be subject to instant expulsion. In that event your barbarian merchants will have had a long journey for nothing. Do not say that you were not warned in due time! Tremblingly obey and show no negligence! A special mandate!

---

[3]A group of islands in the East China Sea at the entrance to Hangzhou Bay.
[4]Island colony west of Hong Kong where Europeans were allowed to carry on their trade.

[5]A reference to Confucianism.
[6]Missionaries.
[7]Two Chinese port cities.

▼▼▼

# Social and Economic Change in Tokugawa Japan

Tokugawa Ieyasu and his early successors implemented a four-part plan to strengthen their authority and stabilize Japan. They tightened control of powerful *daimyo* families, who maintained authority in their domains but whose ability to launch rebellions was crippled; they virtually severed contacts between Japan and the outside world; they officially sanctioned and supported Confucianism, with its conservativism and respect for authority; and they sought to freeze class divisions with military aristocrats at the top and farmers, artisans, and merchants below them. These policies were remarkably successful. Their subjects, who yearned for order as much as their rulers, experienced internal peace and stable government well into the nineteenth century.

Paradoxically, the demise of the Tokugawa regime in 1867 resulted in part from its success. Decades of peace fostered economic expansion accompanied by population growth, urbanization, and social mobility. Japan's population grew from approximately 18 million in 1600 to 30 million by the 1750s, and Edo (modern Tokyo) grew from a small village into a city with over a million inhabitants. These changes increased demand for all types of goods, especially rice, and certain groups such as richer peasants and merchants benefited. Most peasants, however, could not take advantage of the commercialization of agriculture, and by the mid eighteenth century, many were hard hit by land shortages and rising rents. In addition, Japan's military aristocrats, the daimyo and samurai, failed to benefit from the economic boom. Lavish personal spending and, in the case of the daimyo, the need to maintain residences in both Edo and their own domain, caused many to fall into debt.

While economic change was undermining the social basis of the Tokugawa regime, intellectual ferment was eroding its ideological underpinnings. As the memory of the sixteenth-century civil wars faded, the conservativism of Confucianism lost some of its appeal, and foreign ideas seemed less dangerous. In the eighteenth century two intellectual developments challenged state-sponsored Confucianism. Proponents of *National Learning,* or *Kokugaku,* rejected foreign influence, especially Confucianism, and dedicated themselves to the study and glorification of Japan's ancient literature and religious beliefs. Others developed an intense interest in European ideas, especially in medicine but also in botany, cartography, and gunnery. These endeavors were known as *Dutch Studies* because the only information about Europe came from the Dutch, who continued to trade on a limited basis with Japan even after the seclusion policy was adopted. By the late eighteenth century those who were dissatisfied with the Tokugawa regime did not lack models for a different future, something that solidly Confucian China did not have.

# A Japanese Merchant Views His World
▼▼▼

## 57 ▼ *Mitsui Takafusa,*
## *SOME OBSERVATIONS ON MERCHANTS*

Among the hundreds of family businesses begun in the early Tokugawa period, none can match the long-term economic success and political clout of the multi-faceted business enterprise founded by the Mitsui family. With interests at first in *sake* brewing, pawn brokerage, and money changing, the family opened a dry goods store in Edo in 1673 and continued to diversify into banking, shipping, rice marketing, and mining. By 1800 it employed one thousand workers in its Edo shops alone, and a century later it was Japan's largest business conglomerate and a powerful force in creating the new industrialized Japan.

None of this could have been foreseen by Mitsui Takahira (1653–1737), the second head of the family business. He had seen too many new businesses flourish at the start only to fail because of high living and poor business sense on the part of second- and third-generation owners. In the hope that the Mitsui firm would avoid such a fate, in 1722 he drew up the Mitsui Family Code, a set of precepts of personal and business behavior for members of the family. He also compiled a set of sketches of approximately fifty business families from Osaka, Edo, and Kyoto, whose businesses had failed. The purpose of these sketches was to illustrate the points he had made in the code. Sometime in the late 1720s Mitsui Takahira's son, Takafusa, collated and edited his father's sketches and added an introduction and conclusion. Posterity has credited the son with the authorship of *Some Observations on Merchants,* even though it mainly contains his father's recollections and ideas. It is an invaluable source of information about the business world of early Tokugawa Japan and the values and experiences of the merchants who were part of it.

---

## QUESTIONS FOR ANALYSIS

1. What is the message of the source concerning the ideal qualities of a successful merchant?
2. What is likely to lead to business failure?
3. What does the source reveal about the level of commercialization in the Japanese economy?
4. What perspectives does the source offer concerning the merchant's place in Japanese society, in particular the relationship of merchants to the daimyo and samurai?
5. What differences and similarities do you see between the ideal merchant described by the Mitsui and the ideal merchant of Ming China described by Wang Daokun (Chapter 4, source 30)?

## QUALITIES OF A SUCCESSFUL MERCHANT

There was a man of Edo rather ill-favored by nature. He had, nevertheless, a considerable fortune. Once when he met with other persons of the same status, they all asked: "What should we do to make money like yourself? Please pass on the formula." Thereupon he replied, "If only you are fond of money, you can do it any time." The people answered that there was no one who was not fond of money. "In that case," the man inquired, "if each of you now had as much money as he wanted, what would you do? I would like to have your reflections on the subject." They each gave their views, that if they had so much money they would put so much aside and with the rest restore their unsightly houses or pay off their debts and so on. "Since this is how you all feel," the man said, "you cannot have money. You actually are planning to spend it before you even have it. I do not worry about the state of my house. Nor do I have clothes made. The only thing I am keen on is money." How truly right these golden words are. This little story should be weighed thoroughly.

▾ ▾ ▾

When a deficiency appears in their financial positions, they should own up immediately to their poverty and declare their inability to pay. This should be the time to make plans to stay in business, but what they do is to think first of their reputations and borrow as much as they can to cover up their financial position. When at their wit's end, they are exposed and thus wind up like this [bankrupt]. . . . This is the meaning of the maxim that a bud may be nipped with the hand but if left will later have to be chopped with an axe.

▾ ▾ ▾

Whatever business you get your start in, you must always continue to recognize the value of that business and put your heart and soul into it. Most people, however, when they have made a fortune, with large holdings of gold and silver, forget where it came from and think that the way to make a living is to engage in financing, which does not require many assistants. They leave their former business clerks and think they can live at ease through financing, but it is scarcely possible to make a living as easily as that. There are many examples in this world of people eventually going bankrupt by risking not only their own capital but even borrowed money. After all, though it may be a slower process, if you pay for all your personal expenses out of the profits of the trade in which you originally prospered, regard the money which you have as your stock in trade and work single-mindedly at your own business, it is only natural that as a divine reward your house will continue. . . .

## MERCHANTS' MISSTEPS

This business of lending to daimyo is like gambling. Instead of being cut in the first place while they are small, losses become a kind of bait. Using the argument that if further loans are made the original ones will be reactivated, the officials and financial agents of daimyo who raise loans decoy the lenders with specious talk. This is like setting fried bean curd for mice, as the saying has it, and finally they are caught in the trap. They thus incur heavier losses than before. Such being the case, one should give up making loans of this sort. However, no gambler places a bet expecting from the beginning that he will lose. . . . If in lending to daimyo the dealings go according to contract, certainly there is no better business. It does not require a large staff. With one account book and one pair of scales, the thing is settled. This is really genuinely making money while you sleep. As the classical saying goes, however, "for every profit there is a loss." Such a fine business as this is liable to turn out very badly in the end. Consider well that you should never rely on lending to daimyo.

▾ ▾ ▾

Samurai employ stratagems with victory as their sole aim. To do so is their military duty. Merchants may think that they can make profits to a reasonable extent and write off their losses. Samurai, however, are the highest of the four social classes, and their officials, who combine cleverness with cunning, see through your tricks and turn the tables on you. As soon as they have what they want out of the other party, they seize control and default. The bamboo spears of merchants, you might say, are pitted against the true swords of samurai, and you are no match for your adversary. As lending to daimyo is such an unreasonable business from the start, who would invest his precious money in it? . . . In books on military strategy, it is said that only he who knows the enemy as well as his own side can be called a great general. Any merchant who tries to trick samurai does not know his enemy.

▼ ▼ ▼

Many in times both past and present have ruined their families through becoming involved in speculative ventures. In Edo, by so-called gold extraction,[1] or the smelting of gold from copper, people obtained some gold from bar copper and showed it to amateurs, whom they tricked into putting a lot of money into the idea. Eventually those "gold extractors" absconded with the money they had raised. They say that a little gold generally can be extracted by processing copper. If the cost of charcoal and laborers is taken into account, however, it hardly provides a living. I am told that in Holland they do smelt gold from copper. In Japan, though how to do this is known, it does not pay for the above reason, and so the copper is handed over as it is.

As regards gold mines, they say that small amounts of gold and silver exist everywhere but that the mining of them is not a commercial

proposition because, as with the extraction of gold from copper, the yield is too small. Despite this, just because someone shows them something supposed to be ore from a mine and talks glibly, there are many people about who, being somewhat rash by nature, are ready to risk everything and, finally being talked into it, and by losing what little they had.

## THE MERCHANT'S PLACE IN SOCIETY

The Jūemon I and Jūemon II[2] possessed many fine household articles which they had bought. One of these was the "Misoya Katatsuki" tea container, which was bought from Kameya someone or other for a thousand gold pieces. They say the purchase money was loaded on a cart and dragged around in broad daylight to make the payment and take delivery.

Jūemon II built a Zen temple at Narutaki, on the western side of Kyoto. He deposited with the temple an image of Hitomaro[3] and built for it a hall called Hitomaro Hall. The interior of this he lined with gold brocade. It is commonly known as the Gold Brocade Hall of Narutaki. Through his interest in Japanese poetry, he, though a merchant, mixed with distinguished Court nobles, forgot the real nature of his status and finally lost his large fortune. He was one who did not know his proper station.

▼ ▼ ▼

Again, a merchant called Ishikawa Rokubei, of Edo, who started off in the brokerage business, had a wife who was extraordinarily extravagant and went to the limit in finery. Retribution finally caught up with them. Along the route of the valiant, when this Rokubei's wife and her servants were all decked out, the valiant prince,

---

[1] The process of extracting gold or silver from copper ore by smelting it with the addition of lead was introduced to Japan by Europeans in the late sixteenth century.

[2] "Jūemon I" is Itoya Jūemon, a Kyoto-based rice trader. "Jūemon II" and "Jūemon III" were his son and grandson, respectively.

[3] Kakinomoto Hitomaro was a famous poet of the late seventh and the early eighth centuries venerated as the God of Poetry.

thinking that she was the wife of a daimyo or of some family of high rank, graciously had his aides make inquiries and was told that she was the wife of that fellow [the merchant]. After he had returned to the palace, Rokubei and his wife were summoned to the office of the town magistrate. It was considered that their extravagance beyond their station and particularly their lack of respect for their superiors were outrageous. Their family property was forfeited, and, by the Shogun's mercy, they got off with banishment from Edo.

As they say, a curse always falls on the house where the hen does the crowing. If a wife is extravagant in defiance of her husband and runs the household just as she likes, it is the same as for a hen to crow the time. This must be the meaning of the golden words which say that such a house invariably perishes. . . .

## THE MERCHANT'S CALLING

. . . When great men are extravagant, they lose their territories, but lesser folk lose their liveli-hood. Even if one cannot add further profits to the money which one's forebear, acquiring merit through difficulties, accumulated by sweating away at money-making day and night, one at least should reflect on the debt of gratitude ow-ing to one's forebear and take good care to keep his fortune intact. What can we say of one who does neither of these things and finally ruins his family through extravagance! Losses through miscalculation in trading, as well as losses in fi-nancial operations, may be due to insufficient concentration of one's proper calling. This is your livelihood, however, and as such cannot be shirked. Understand thoroughly that these things are only matters of prudence. . . . It is the law of nature that birds and beasts and in fact all things which dwell between heaven and earth — and above all, human beings — should seek their sustenance by working at their callings. This being so, such behavior on the part of people far from being in their dotage displays ignorance of the will of heaven.

## The Social Ills of Tokugawa Japan
▼▼▼

## 58 ▼ *Honda Toshiaki,*
## *A SECRET PLAN OF GOVERNMENT*

Honda Toshiaki, born in northern Japan in 1721, was a perceptive critic of late Tokugawa society and a prophet of Japan's future. After studying and teaching mathematics, astronomy, and fencing in Edo, he devoted most of his life to ob-serving and analyzing the state of contemporary Japan. In his travels he was par-ticularly interested in observing conditions among the poor and learning the reasons for their misery. He concluded that as a small island nation, Japan needed to expand its commerce and colonize, rather than concentrate on agriculture, as a large continental country like China could do. In his view Japan's seclusion policy should be abandoned and efforts made to teach the Japanese modern navi-gation and weaponry. Honda publicized his ideas to students and correspondents, but his influence on Japan's political leaders came only after his death. His only government service was as advisor to the lord of Kaga, a minor daimyo. In 1821 he died in Edo.

Honda's *A Secret Plan for Government,* written in 1798, is his most important work. In it he elaborates an economic and political plan for Japan based on what he called the "four imperative needs" — to learn the effective use of gunpowder, to develop metallurgy, to increase trade, and to colonize both nearby islands and distant lands. The following excerpt comes at the end of a long discourse on Japanese history in which Honda analyzes the roots of Japan's problems.

## QUESTIONS FOR ANALYSIS

1. What is Honda's view of the daimyo? How does it compare to Mitsui's views of the daimyo?
2. How do merchants contribute to Japan's problems, according to Honda?
3. How does Honda justify his assertion that fifteen-sixteenths of all Japanese rice production goes to the merchants? Are his arguments plausible?
4. Why is Europe rather than China the better model for Japan's revival, according to Honda?
5. What Confucian influence is evident in Honda's *Plan?* In what ways does Honda reject Confucianism?

Not until Tokugawa Ieyasu used his power to control the strong and give succor to the weak did the warfare that had lasted for three hundred years without a halt suddenly abate. Arrows were left in their quivers and spears in their racks. If now, in a time of peace, the country were ruled in accordance with the four imperative needs, the prices of all commodities would be stabilized, and the discontent of the people would thus be cut off at the root. This is the true method of establishing a permanent foundation for the nation, so that the people will become honest in their hearts and cultivate orderly ways even if they are not governed. It must have been because he realized how difficult it would be to preserve the empire for all ages to come if the people were not honest in their hearts that Ieyasu, in his testament, exhorted shoguns who would succeed him to abstain from any irregularities in government, and to rule on a basis of benevolence and honesty. It was his counsel that the shoguns should serve as models to the people, and by their

honesty train the people in the ways of humanity and justice. He taught that the shogun should not compel obedience merely by the use of force, but by his acts of benevolence should keep the nation at peace. . . .

He taught the daimyo that the duties of a governor consisted in the careful attempt to guide the people of their domains in such a way as both to bring about the prosperity of the land and to encourage the literary and military arts.

However, in recent days there has been the spectacle of lords confiscating the allocated property of their retainers on the pretext of paying back debts to the merchants. The debts do not then decrease, but usually seem rather to grow larger. One daimyo with an income of 60,000 *koku*[1] so increased his borrowings that he could not make good his debts, and there was a public suit. The court judgment in the case was said to have been over 1,180,000 *ryo*.[2] Even if repayment had been attempted on the basis of his income of 60,000 koku, the debt would not have

---

[1] A *koku* is approximately five bushels of rice and was used to measure daimyo income.

[2] A measurement of the weight of gold.

been completely settled for fifty or sixty years, so long a time that it is difficult to imagine the day would actually come.

All the daimyo are not in this position, but there is not one who has not borrowed from the merchants. Is this not a sad state of affairs? The merchant, watching this spectacle, must feel like a fisherman who sees a fish swim into his net. Officials of the daimyo harass the farmers for money, which they claim they need to repay the daimyo's debts, but the debts do not diminish. Instead, the daimyo go on contracting new ones year after year. The officials are blamed for this situation, and are dismissed as incompetent. New officials then harass and afflict the farmers in much the same way as the old ones, and so it goes on. However talented the officials may be, they become disgusted and abandon the effort. Some pretend sickness and remain in their homes; others are indiscreet and die young.

No matter how hard the daimyo and their officials rack their brains, they do not seem to be able to reduce the debts. The lords are "sunk in a pool of debts," as it is popularly said, a pool from which their children and grandchildren will be unable to escape. Everything will be as the merchants wish it. The daimyo turn over their domains to the merchants, receiving in return an allowance with which to pay their public and private expenses. Such daimyo give no thought at all to Heaven, to fulfilling their duties as samurai, or to the proper way of looking after the farmers.

Many fields have turned into wasteland since the famine of 1783, when thousands of farmers starved to death. Wherever one goes . . . , one hears people say, "There used to be a village here. . . . The land over there was once part of such-and-such a county, but now there is no village and no revenue comes from the land." . . . When so many farmers starved, reducing still further their already insufficient numbers, the amount of uncultivated land greatly increased. If the wicked practice of infanticide, now so prevalent, is not stopped, the farming population will dwindle until it tends to die out alto-

gether. Generous protective and relief measures must be put into effect immediately if this evil practice is to be stamped out.

A wise ruler could end this practice in short order and create an atmosphere favorable to the prosperity of the nation by establishing a system based on generosity and compassion. When a woman of one of the lower classes becomes pregnant, a government agent should be sent to investigate the situation. The mother of the child should then be given two sacks of rice each year from the month the child is born until he is ten years old. The practice of infanticide would soon stop. Thus by spending a mere twenty sacks of rice over a period of ten years, the country would at the same time gain a good farmer and atone for the misery caused in the past. . . .

The Confucian scholars of ancient and modern times have talked a great deal about benevolence and compassion, but they possess neither in their hearts. Officials and authorities talk about benevolent government, but they have no understanding of what that means. Whose fault is it that the farmers are dying of starvation and that good fields are turning into wasteland? The fault lies entirely with the ruler. . . .

---

▷  There follows an enthusiastic but often inaccurate account of Europe's accomplishments.

---

Because astronomy, calendar making, and mathematics are considered the ruler's business, the European kings are well versed in celestial and terrestrial principles, and instruct the common people in them. Thus even among the lower classes one finds men who show great ability in their particular fields. The Europeans as a result have been able to establish industries with which the rest of the world is unfamiliar. It is for this reason that all the treasures of the world are said to be attracted to Europe. There is nowhere the Europeans' ships do not go in order to obtain the different products and treasures of the world. They trade their own rare products, superior implements, and unusual inventions for the precious metals and valuable goods of others, which they bring back to enrich their own countries. Their prosperity makes them strong, and it is because of their strength that they are never invaded or pillaged, whereas for their part they have invaded countless non-European countries. . . .

There is no place in the world to compare with Europe. It may be wondered in what way this supremacy was achieved. In the first place, the European nations have behind them a history of five to six thousand years. In this period they have delved deep into the beauties of the arts, have divined the foundations of government, and have established a system based on a thorough examination of the factors that naturally make a nation prosperous. Because of their proficiency in mathematics, they have excelled also in astronomy, calendar making, and surveying. They have elaborated laws of navigation such that there is nothing simpler for them than to sail the oceans of the world. . . .

In spite of this example, however, the Japanese do not look elsewhere than to China for good or beautiful things, so tainted are the customs and temperament of Japan by Chinese teachings. Japanese are therefore unaware of such things as the four imperative needs, since they do not figure in the teachings of the Chinese sages.

China is a mountainous country that extends as far as Europe and Africa. It is bounded by the ocean to the south, but water communication within the country is not feasible. Since it is impossible to feed the huge population of cities when transport can be effected only by human or animal strength, there are no big cities in China away from the coast. China is therefore a much less favored country than Japan, which is surrounded by water, and this factor shows in the deficiencies and faults of Chinese state policies. China does not merit being used as a model. Since Japan is a maritime nation, shipping and

trade should be the chief concerns of the ruler. Ships should be sent to all countries to obtain products needed for national consumption and to bring precious metals to Japan. A maritime nation is equipped with the means to increase her national strength.

By contrast, a nation that attempts to get along on its own resources will grow steadily weaker. . . . To put the matter more bluntly, the policies followed by the various ruling families until now have determined that the lower classes must lead a hand-to-mouth existence. The best part of the harvests of the farmers who live on the domains of the empire is wrenched away from them. The lords spend all they take within the same year, and if they then do not have enough, they oppress the farmers all the more cruelly in an effort to obtain additional funds. This goes on year after year. . . .

It is a great shame that such conditions prevail, but it is said that "even the thoughts of an ant may reach up to Heaven." Though their conditions differ, the highest and the lowest alike are human beings, and the rulers ought to think about those who are less fortunate than themselves. Soon all the gold and silver currency will pass into the hands of the merchants, and only merchants will be deserving of the epithets "rich" and "mighty." Their power will thus grow until they stand first among the four classes. When I investigated the incomes of present-day merchants, I discovered that fifteen-sixteenths of the total income of Japan goes to the merchants, with only one-sixteenth left for the samurai. As proof of this statement, I cite the following case. When there are good rice harvests at Yonezawa in Dewa or in Semboku-gun in Akita[3] the price is five or six *mon* for one *sho.*[4] The rice is sold to merchants who ship it to Edo, where the price is about 100 mon, regardless of the original cost. At this rate, if one bought 10,000 ryos worth of rice in Dewa, sent it to Edo, and sold it there, one's capital would be increased to 160,000 ryo. If the

---

[3]Dewa and Akita are provinces in northern Honshu.

[4]A *mon* was a copper coin; a *sho* was about 3.2 pints.

160,000 ryo in turn were used as capital, the return in Edo would be 2,560,000 ryo. With only two exchanges of trade it is possible to make enormous profits.

It may be claimed that of this sum part must go for shipping expenses and pack-horse charges, but the fact remains that one gets back sixteen times what one has paid for the rice. It is thus apparent that fifteen-sixteenths of the nation's income goes to the merchants. In terms of the production of an individual farmer, out of thirty days a month he works twenty-eight for the merchants and two for the samurai; or, out of 360 days in a year, he works 337 1/2 for the merchants and 22 1/2 for the samurai. Clearly, then, unless the samurai store grain it is impossible for them to offer any relief to the farmers in years of famine. This may be why they can do no more than look on when the farmers are dying of starva-

tion. And all this because the right system has not been established. It is a most lamentable state of affairs that the farmers have to shoulder the weight of this error and die of starvation as inevitably as "water collecting in a hollow."

By means of the plans outlined in the account of the four imperative needs . . . the present corrupt and jejune society could be restored to its former prosperity and strength. The ancient glories of the warrior-nation of Japan would be revived. Colonization projects would gradually be commenced and would meet with great success. A capital city would be built . . . for northern Japan. The central capital would be at Edo, and the southern one at Osaka. The capital of the entire nation would alternate among these three locations. Then, under enlightened government, Japan could certainly be made the richest and strongest country in the world.

▼▼▼

# The Opening of Oceania

Slowly, in a process that began as long as forty thousand or even sixty thousand years ago when people from Asia reached Australia and ended only in 900 C.E. when the Maori settled New Zealand, human beings populated the thousands of islands that stretch across the South Pacific from Asia to the Americas. The details of this process are dimly understood, but one thing is certain: Once established, these island societies existed in isolation from the rest of the world until the 1700s. The single exception is the Chamorro people of Guam and the Marianas, islands that were conquered and occupied by the Spaniards in the late 1600s to serve as refreshment stations for their galleons sailing between Mexico and the Philippines. Elsewhere, even in Australia, which is not far from the East Indies or even the Southeast Asian mainland, native Australians had no documented contact with outsiders from approximately 8000 B.C.E. until the arrival of the Dutch explorer Abel Janszoon Tasman in 1642. Tasman and his backers, the Dutch East India Company, concluded that the island had few economic prospects, and the next outsiders to visit Australia were Englishmen under the command of Captain James Cook, who claimed the subcontinent for Great Britain in 1770.

Cook's Pacific voyages, which between 1770 and 1779 took him to Tahiti, New Zealand, Hawaii, and dozens of other Pacific islands, initiated a new era of European and U.S. colonization in Oceania. Although glossed over in many histories, it is nonetheless an interesting and significant story. Because the Western move into the Pacific was rapid and on a comparatively small scale, it provides sharp insights into the complex phenomenon of Western expansion. One extreme is represented by the seal hunters who were among the first Westerners attracted to New Zealand, Australia, and Tasmania. Their slaughter of seals was so furious that the seal population was all but exterminated within a generation. Their treatment of the Maori and Aborigines was not much different. They kidnapped and sexually abused the women, enslaved the men, and subjected both to brutal punishment or death for minor acts of theft or disobedience. When the seals were gone, most of the hunters moved on.

On the other extreme were the missionaries, many of whom came from Protestant lands such as England, where a strong missionary spirit took hold later than in Catholic Spain, Portugal, and France. These missionaries were sincere idealists who endured great hardship to carry Christianity and what they perceived as the benefits of civilization to the "less fortunate" pagans of the Pacific islands. Yet the germs they carried in their bodies and the ideas they carried in their minds were lethal to the peoples they encountered, no matter how noble their intentions. The missionaries from the West did a measure of good but, like the sealers, also a measure of harm.

# Early Reports from New Zealand
▼▼▼

## 59 ▼ Committee of the Church of England Missionary Society, *MEMORANDUM TO THE EARL OF BATHURST, SECRETARY OF STATE OF THE COLONIES*

The islands that make up modern New Zealand were uninhabited by humans until the Maori, a Polynesian people, arrived during the ninth century C.E. They numbered approximately 250,000 when the Dutch explorer Abel Janszoon Tasman visited in 1642. More than a century later, after the Englishman James Cook charted the islands in 1769, whalers and sealers from Australia, Europe, and the United States were drawn to New Zealand's shores, and permanent settlers soon followed. Clashes between the Maori and the settlers, many of whom were former convicts from the English penal colony of Australia, soon began.

Missionary efforts in New Zealand sponsored by the Church of England began in 1814 under the direction of Reverend Samuel Marsden (1764–1838), the son of a blacksmith. As a young man Marsden abandoned his studies at Cambridge University to minister to convicts who had been shipped to Australia. When he shifted his activities to New Zealand, Marsden and his assistants had three goals: to protect the Maori from abuse, to teach them agricultural and craft skills, and to convert them to Christianity.

As the following letter written in 1817 shows, Marsden and the other ministers faced formidable obstacles. Massacres of the Maori and other abuses prompted

British government intervention but also more resistance from the Maori. Conversions came slowly, and a series of bloody wars was fought against the Maori before they acquiesced to English rule. The Maori survived their encounter with the Europeans. Today they number approximately three hundred thousand and comprise 10 percent of New Zealand's population. Some of them are Christians.

## QUESTIONS FOR ANALYSIS

1. How do the authors view the intellectual and moral capacities of the Maori?
2. What solutions do the authors suggest to end the abuses they describe?
3. How does the document depict Maori attitudes toward the Europeans?
4. On the basis of the examples cited, what were the causes of the conflicts between the Maori and Europeans?

The memorial[1] of the Committee of the Church of England Missionary Society for Africa and the East humbly sheweth, —

That the Church Missionary Society has been engaged for eight years in endeavoring to propagate the knowledge of the Christian religion among the idolatrous nations of Africa and the East, and thereby to promote their civilization, as well as their spiritual and eternal welfare.

That in the prosecution of these designs the Society has directed its attention to the inhabitants of the islands of the South Seas, and especially to those of New Zealand, whose active and intelligent character appeared to offer a favorable field for their exertions. In the course of the year 1814, having obtained a grant of land from one of the chiefs of the country, the Society established a settlement in the Bay of Islands in New Zealand, at which three missionary settlers, with their families, have been since resident.

That the efforts of these settlers, as far as it has been possible hitherto to extend them, have been attended with most encouraging success. They have found the natives in the vicinity of a frank and affectionate character, desirous to cultivate their friendship, and to receive instruction, and

the Society entertain a confident hope that by the establishment of schools and by other means of instruction they shall in due time be enabled, under the Divine blessing, to diffuse the knowledge of Christianity throughout this populous and benighted land, and to rescue a noble race of men from the horrible superstitions and savage customs by which they are now degraded. The Society feels warranted also to hope that its exertions will tend in other ways to meliorate the condition of the islanders. Their settlers have already introduced among them the cultivation of wheat and other grain, and a foundation may perhaps be thus laid for the agricultural improvement of this fertile and productive country, which may hereafter render it not an unimportant object of commercial attention.

That the hopes which your memorialists thus entertain have been greatly checked by the intelligence continually received by them of the atrocities committed by the European traders in the South Seas, by which not only the most grievous injuries are inflicted on the natives, but their minds are exasperated to acts of barbarous revenge, all tendency to a milder and more civilized character is repressed, confidence in the character and designs of the European settlers is

---

[1]A statement of facts addressed to a government, often accompanied by a petition or request.

weakened, and the lives of themselves and their families are seriously endangered. . . .

In the year 1810 the ship *Boyd* sailed from Port Jackson to Whangarooa in New Zealand with some natives on board, one of them the son of the head chief of the place. These persons were very ill used during the voyage. The young chief, who had fallen sick and was unable to work as a sailor, was severely flogged, treated with great indignity, and sent on shore, lacerated with stripes. When the treatment which he had received became known to his friends and people it roused them to fury; they seized the ship, and put the captain and all the crew to death. Soon after this Tippahee, a chief belonging to the Bay of Islands, and who was well known and respected at Port Jackson, was accused of having been concerned in the massacre. In consequence of this report, the whalers, who were on the coast, manned and armed seven boats, landed on the island of Tippahee, and shot every man, woman, and child that came in their way. Tippahee was severely wounded. It has since been ascertained that this chief so far from being guilty of the crime imputed to him, he exerted himself to save the lives of the crew. His people must have been known to be guiltless, for their territory was forty miles distant from Whangarooa; yet thus have the unoffending inhabitants of a whole island been exterminated by a lawless act of private vengeance.

A year or two before this the captain of an English ship which was sailing by one of the islands fired, without any provocation, five or six large guns, loaded with grape shot, among a multitude of natives, men, women, and children, who were assembled on the beach to look at the vessel, and killed and wounded several of them. When remonstrated with for this act of wanton barbarity he only said it was necessary to strike terror into the minds of these natives, and convince them of what power we possessed.

In 1812 the schooner *Parramatta* put into the Bay of Islands, in distress, for provisions and water. She was supplied by the natives with potatoes, pork, and fish to the extent of their wants, and when they required payment they were thrown overboard, fired at, and wounded. The schooner immediately weighed anchor, but was soon after driven on shore in a storm, and the islanders revenged themselves by putting the crew to death.

In the same year the brig *Daphne* was off the Island of Riematerra when eighteen natives came off in three canoes with fruit; they were invited on board, behaved in the most friendly and respectful manner, and delivered their cargoes of supplies, for which they received a trifling remuneration. The captain then ordered the crew to turn them out of the ship; this was done in the most barbarous manner; they were beaten with ropes to force them over the sides of the ship into the sea; they swam to their canoes, which were swamped, and fourteen of them were drowned within sight of the brig. . . .

That your memorialists will not dwell on the various instances in which potato grounds (the chief culture of these islands) have been destroyed, and the produce stolen; in which the property of the natives has been forcibly taken or fraudulently obtained, under presence of purchase, and no equivalent given; in which their chiefs have been imprisoned and ill treated in order to extort a ransom; and all these misdeeds too often accompanied by circumstances of wanton cruelty.

That in a recent case proceedings have been instituted at Port Jackson[2] against the captain of a trading vessel for acts of oppression and cruelty against the chiefs and other natives of one of the Marquesas Islands,[3] in which after a full investigation a conviction took place on the whole of the charges; but the party convicted has escaped with impunity, on account of the

---

[2]Sydney's original name.
[3]An island group just south of the equator and to the east of Hawaii.

inadequacy of the powers vested in the Magistrates to punish the offence.

That your memorialists are informed that there is no competent jurisdiction in New South Wales for the cognizance and punishment of such offences as have been enumerated, nor any adequate means for their prevention; and that no remedy at present exists but sending persons charged with the perpetration of such enormities to be tried at the Admiralty Sessions in England.[4] . . .

That even the establishment of a tribunal with adequate power of punishment in New South Wales would not in all cases be effectual to remedy the evil, since it frequently happens that the vessels whose captains and crews have committed these atrocities do not return thither, and that some further measure seems therefore req-

uisite for the protection of the islanders, and the prevention of the crimes by which the moral character of Great Britain is degraded by the conduct of her subjects trading in those seas.

That, in consequence of the want at present of any sufficient provision by colonial tribunals or otherwise for the prevention or the punishment of crimes committed in the islands of the South Seas, your memorialists submit that not only the lives of the missionaries and settlers in those islands are exposed to the most imminent hazard, but that all endeavors to extend the blessings of Christianity and civilization among the natives must thereby be in a great measure frustrated, and the reasonable hope of advantage which might be derived therefrom even to our own country is destroyed.

---

[4]An English court that handled cases involving ships on the seas.

# The Plight of the Tasmanians

▼▼▼

## 60 ▼ *George A. Robinson,* *REPORT TO THE LIEUTENANT* *GOVERNOR-GENERAL OF TASMANIA*

The island of Tasmania, off the southeastern coast of Australia and about the size of West Virginia, was first inhabited by humans twenty thousand years ago when a land bridge connected it to the Australian mainland. When the seas rose ten thousand years later, the bridge disappeared, and the Tasmanian Aborigines were isolated until the arrival of Europeans in the seventeenth century. Hunters and gatherers who were organized into approximately ten tribes, the Tasmanian Aborigines numbered three to four thousand around 1800.

In the early nineteenth century Australian, English, and American sealers established themselves on the northern shore, and English officials began sending convicts to three new penal colonies. Conflicts with the Aborigines erupted immediately over such issues as kangaroo hunting and soon intensified when farmers and sheepherders took over much of the island in the 1820s. By 1830 Tasmania supported nearly twenty-five thousand settlers, more than five hundred thousand sheep, but only two thousand Aborigines, whose numbers had been halved by disruption and disease.

In the 1830s English administrators attempted to solve the "Aborigine problem" by forcing them to live in one area where they could be protected, educated, taught Christianity, and kept out of the way. Many Aborigines were killed resisting captivity, so that only several hundred were shipped to the aboriginal settlement established on Flinders Island, off Tasmania's north shore. There they came under the direction of George A. Robinson, a carpenter who had come to Tasmania in 1824 and had directed the roundup of Aborigines in the early 1830s. A deeply religious man, who viewed the Aborigines as his "brothers in Christ," he honestly believed they would benefit from living on Flinders Island. He wrote the following letter to the lieutenant governor of Tasmania in 1837, three years after the founding of the colony.

None of the letter's optimistic predictions came true. Infection, alcoholism, and poor diet further diminished the Aborigine population, and the colony on Flinders Island was disbanded in the early 1840s. Many whites now believed the Aborigines were beyond redemption. The survivors of Flinders Island were sent to the village of Oyster Cove, where the last full-blooded male Aborigine died in 1868, and the last female, Truganini, died in 1871. Her skeleton was displayed as a scientific curiosity in a Hobart museum until 1947 when public opposition forced the Royal Society of Tasmania to put it in storage. In 1976, after appeals from Tasmanians of mixed Aborigine-European descent, her remains were cremated and scattered on the beach where she had played as a girl.

## QUESTIONS FOR ANALYSIS

1. What encouraging signs does Robinson see in the first years of the Flinders Island colony's existence?
2. What are Robinson's views of the skills and mental capacities of the Aborigines?
3. In Robinson's view, what are the concrete signs that the Aborigines are becoming "civilized"?
4. According to Robinson, what general lessons of colonial policy can be learned from the experience at Flinders Island?
5. Despite the rosy picture Robinson painted of Flinders Island, the colony soon failed. From reading Robinson's letter, what can you surmise about the reasons?

Sir,

I have the honor to submit, for the information of his Excellency the Lieutenant-governor, the subjoined particulars relative to this experimental and interesting institution, since the transmission of my previous report; and I have much satisfaction in stating that this settlement continues as heretofore in a very quiet and tranquil state, and that the same order and regularity is maintained as mentioned on former occasions. . . .

I have much satisfaction in stating that the wants of the aborigines are amply and abundantly supplied, and that the provisions furnished by the Government are of the best description; and though, notwithstanding, the fatality to which I have heretofore alluded is of painful character, still it must be conceded that the same is quite providential, and might have occurred in their own native districts; . . . and hence, amid the calamity that has happened, it is a pleasing reflection to know that everything has been done which ingenuity could devise or humanity suggest to alleviate their condition, and of which the aborigines themselves have marked their appreciation, and oft repeated their acknowledgements for . . . the kind intention of the Government towards them.

The advantages to the aborigines by their removal have been manifold, and many of them of the highest order. In their native forests they were without the knowledge of a God, hence but little removed from the brute themselves. Their mode of life was extremely precarious, and to the juveniles distressing in the extreme; and though in their insidious and deadly attacks on the white inhabitants they invariably eluded pursuit, yet they themselves were not without dangers and alarms, and might reasonably be said to exist by excitement alone. . . . Anterior to their arrival . . . they were in a deplorable state of mental degradation. Such is not now the case: they not only possess the knowledge of a Deity, but are acquainted with the principles of Christianity.

From the time I first took charge of the settlement, now near two years since, religious knowledge has been daily imparted to them, and religious principles inculcated. In this laudable object the whole of the officers and my family have untiredly assisted, a duty in which they have evinced the greatest aptitude and delight; and I myself can testify with what avidity and eagerness they have attended to and sought after religious knowledge. . . .

## DOMESTIC ECONOMY

Their time is wholly employed in useful labor, harmless amusements, in their attendance at school, and religious exercises, and not, as heretofore, wandering about the settlement with listless and careless indifference to what was going on; but on the contrary, evinced by their general conduct, their prompt attention to instruction, and their persevering industry, that they have an interest in the affairs of the settlement, and

which it has ever been my aim on all occasions to bring them to participate. They are no longer idle spectators, but actors and ready agents to assist, as far as strength and ability will permit, in every useful undertaking.

I have already alluded to their proficiency in useful arts, viz. knitting and fancy network, and though from the paucity of their numbers the manufacture cannot be done to any great extent, still in whatever light we view it, whether as a branch of useful industry, or as an amusement, one thing is certain, that it displays a precocity of intellect of no ordinary kind, and proves that those whom civilized men despised as beings without mind, are, like all God's creatures, perfect in every form, and which only requires the adoption of proper means, when the latent intellect of the degraded savage will be made manifest, and be developed.

There are many and numerous incidents that might be cited to mark their improvement in domestic economy: suffice to say, they are not now, as formerly, content to sit upon the ground, but require seats, both as an article of convenience and a preservation from soiling their clothes. Those among them who have knives and forks habitually use them, and which the residue are anxious to possess; they now also confine themselves more closely to their domiciles, and not interchanging or crouching under bushes or lolling about in idleness.

The aborigines are becoming cleanly in their persons; they now perform the necessary ablutions daily, and the greater part of them have shorn beards; they are not now satisfied as heretofore with one garment, *i.e.,* a frock coat, but require trousers also, and their raiment is in general kept in clean and proper order.

The females are equally as anxious to possess clothes of a European fashion. Several pieces of print[1] bought on their account, and sold at the market, were purchased with avidity and manufactured into gowns; they likewise wear under garments, which they keep in clean and good

---

[1]Printed cotton fabric.

order. They now evince great desire for domestic comforts, and which, though amply supplied, can only be attained by industry and good conduct. Their primitive habits are now all but forgotten: the use of ochre[2] and grease, with which they used formerly to bedaub themselves, is now entirely abolished. Their nocturnal orgies . . . , which hurt the repose of the settlement and impaired the health of the natives, as adverted to in my previous reports, never occur.

## ABORIGINAL POLICE

The police of this establishment consists of four special constables, and their two chiefs, to whom the conservation of the aborigines is confided. The constables are chosen from each of the two remnant tribes in full assembly, convened for the occasion.

The constables act under the orders of their chiefs; the latter determine all points of disputes, and on several occasions have displayed tact and judgment highly creditable, and in every instance have administered impartial justice. When this police was first established, it was done as an experiment, and solely with a view to assimilate the natives as much as it was possible to the customs and usages of Europeans. . . .

## CHRISTIAN INSTRUCTION

The work of Christian instruction and civilization, which has taken place under the auspices of the local government at this settlement, has succeeded beyond the most sanguine expectation,

and has determined a question hitherto deemed impracticable.

If, as is made evident, so much has been effected for a people said to possess so little intellectual capacity, a people reputed to be but one remove from the brute creation, and of whom it was said they were but a link between the human and brute species; if so much has been done for such a people, how much more might be performed with those of a different character; and I do trust that the time is not far distant when the experiment will be tried among the numerous tribes inhabiting New Holland; for from the appalling accounts received, and from what I myself have witnessed, as well as from information heretofore communicated, there appears a prompt necessity that some efficient protection be extended to those ill-used and persecuted people. Humanity, religion, and justice require that every effort should be made on their behalf.

The primeval occupants of Van Diemen's Land[3] are not deserving of the obloquy which has been heaped upon them. The hostile feeling evinced by them towards the whites, and their attacks upon the lonely settlement of the colony, are only considered as just retaliation for the wrongs due to them and to their progenitors. They are now well disposed and bear no ill-will or animosity to the white inhabitants. . . .

The effects that have been produced on the minds of these people will forever put to silence the cavils of the most sceptical and prejudicially minded; and if (as I understand) in the sister colony the attempts hitherto brought into operation for the amelioration of the aborigines have failed, it can only be attributed to a defect in the system, and not to the people themselves.

---

[2]An earthy clay containing iron ore and usually reddish in color.
[3]After finding Tasmania in 1642, the Dutch explorer Tasman named it Van Diemen's Land in honor of the governor-general of the Dutch East India Company in Jakarta.

# Part Three

▼▼▼

## *The World in the Age of Western Dominance: 1800–1914*

The direction of world history during the nineteenth century is perhaps best symbolized by the experience of Africa. In 1800, except for the far southern regions settled by the Dutch and the areas on each coast where slaves were traded, Africa was largely untouched by Europeans. A century later, except for Ethiopia and Liberia, the whole continent had succumbed to the control of the European powers, who accomplished their takeover with scant regard for the interests and wishes of the Africans. In 1884 and 1885 rules for dividing Africa were established, with the rule makers all Europeans. Meeting at the Congress of Berlin, diplomats agreed that each power had to give the others proper notice if it intended to annex African lands and, on doing so, could not simply ink in its name on a map. It had to have real troops or administrators on the scene. Only three decades later, during World War I, thousands of Africans were dispatched to battlefronts in Africa, Europe, and the Middle East, where many gave their lives for their new colonial masters.

The Europeans' land-grab in Africa was striking in terms of its suddenness, rapidity, and magnitude, but it was not unique. During the nineteenth century Burma, India, Vietnam, Cambodia, Laos, Malaya, Indonesia, and many South Pacific islands also came under direct European or U.S. control. Other states such as Cuba, Nicaragua, Haiti, the Dominican Republic, the Ottoman Empire, Egypt, and China, although independent, were forced to accept varying degrees of Western control of their finances and foreign policy. Australia and New Zealand became European settler colonies. Canada, South Africa, the Philippines, and most of the West Indies remained parts of pre-nineteenth-century empires, although Canada in 1867 and South Africa in 1910 were granted extensive powers of self-government and the Philippines in 1898 changed masters from Spain to the United States. Mexico and most nations of Central and South America retained full political sovereignty but saw many of their economic assets — banks, railroads, industries, and even their farms — taken over by Western investors and corporations. Only Japan, by adopting the technology, military organization, and industrial economy of the West, avoided subservience to the West and became an imperialist power itself.

Never had world economic and political relationships been as one-sided as they were when World War I began in 1914. A handful of nations led by Great Britain, France, and the newly emerging powers, Germany and the United States, were masters of Africa and large parts of Asia and exerted political influence throughout the world. These same nations controlled much of the world's economy and channeled a disproportionate amount of the world's wealth and resources to their own societies.

This expansion of the West resulted in part from the inner dynamics of capitalism, with its drive for new markets, resources, and investment opportunities. It also resulted from nationalist rivalries among the Western powers themselves, most of whose leaders and citizens were convinced that prestige and prosperity depended on empire building and overseas investment. It also resulted from the huge disparity between the military and economic strength of Europe and the United States and that of the rest of the world. During the nineteenth century once powerful states, such as the Ottoman Empire and China, faced formidable internal problems or, like Mughal India, collapsed completely. Europe and the United States, however, continued to industrialize, develop new technologies, and build the most powerful armies and navies in history. Thus the Western nations faced no effective resistance when they sought to extend their economic grasp and political authority throughout the world.

The people of Asia and Africa now faced questions and, to the degree it was within their power to do so, made choices similar to those confronting the Russians during and after the reign of Peter the Great. Do we want to Westernize? If so, how thoroughly? At what human cost? How? How quickly? No one people answered these questions identically, and the choices they made led to a wide range of experiences. But ignoring the West was no longer an option.

# Chapter 8

▼▼▼

# The West in the Age of Industrialization and Imperialism

As far-reaching as the transformation of Western civilization since the Renaissance had been, no one around 1800 could have predicted the even greater changes about to occur in the nineteenth century. When Napoleon met defeat at Waterloo in 1815, Europe's population was 200 million, with as many as 25 million people of European descent living in the rest of the world. By 1914, when World War I began, these numbers had increased to 450 million and 150 million, respectively. In 1815 a large majority of Europeans and Americans lived in rural villages and worked the land; by 1914, in highly industrialized nations such as Great Britain, a majority of the population lived in cities and had abandoned farming. In 1815, despite two decades of democratic revolution, most governments were still aristocratic and monarchical; in 1914 representative government and universal manhood suffrage were the norm in most of Europe, the United States, and the British dominions of Canada, Australia, and New Zealand. In 1815 most governments limited their activities to defense, the preservation of law and order, and some economic regulation; in 1914 governments in industrialized states subsidized education, sponsored scientific research, oversaw public health, monitored industry, provided social welfare care, maintained huge military establishments, and, as a result, had grown enormously.

Europe's global role also changed dramatically. In 1815 it appeared that European political authority around the world was declining. Great Britain no longer ruled its thirteen American colonies, Portugal and Spain were losing their colonies in Mexico and Central and South America, and France had lost Haiti and sold 800,000 square miles of North American territory to the United States through the Louisiana Purchase. Decisions of several European states to outlaw the slave trade seemed to be a step toward a diminished European role in Africa, and there was little to suggest that Western nations had the ability or inclination to extend their power in the Middle East or East Asia. Only the continuing expansion of Great Britain in India hinted at what the nineteenth century would bring — the Western nations' takeover of Africa and Southeast Asia, their intrusion into the politics of China and the Middle East, and their dominance of the world's economy.

Many factors contributed to the West's transformation and expansion in the nineteenth century. But the single most important cause was the *Industrial Revolution* — that series of wide-ranging economic changes involving the application of new technologies and energy sources to industrial production, communication, and transportation. The Industrial Revolution began in England in the late eighteenth century when power-driven machines began to produce textiles in unprecedented quantities. By 1914 industrialization had taken root in Europe, Japan, and the United States and was spreading to Canada, Russia, and parts of Latin America. As much as the discovery of agriculture many centuries earlier, industrialization profoundly altered the human condition.

▼▼▼

# Middle Class and Working Class in Early Industrial Europe

The English were the first and, for many decades, the only people in the world to experience the material benefits and social costs of industrialization. Favored by an abundant labor supply, strong domestic and foreign markets, rich coal deposits, plentiful capital, a sound banking system, good transportation, a favorable business climate, and government stability, England began to industrialize in the eighteenth century. By the 1760s new mechanical devices for spinning and weaving were beginning to transform the textile industry, and by the early 1800s, coal-burning steam engines were being applied not just to textile manufacture but also to iron-smelting, brewing, milling, and a host of other industrial processes. In 1830, the first steam-driven locomotive made the trip between Liverpool and Manchester, and within only two decades railroads were moving people and goods throughout England.

During the nineteenth century industrialization spread from England to continental Europe, the United States, and Japan, and in the process changed considerably. During the final decades of the nineteenth century small family-owned businesses gave way to large corporations, monopolies, and cartels; finance capital became more important; new energy sources such as petroleum and electricity were introduced; and, most importantly, new scientific discoveries, especially in chemistry, transformed thousands of industrial processes.

The Industrial Revolution was a revolution in every sense of the term. It affected politics, work, people's standards of living, marriage, child-rearing, leisure, and, most fundamentally, the structure of society itself. In preindustrial Europe landowning aristocrats dominated society and politics, and peasants were the largest socioeconomic group. Preindustrial cities consisted of a middle class, or bourgeoisie, made up of merchants and professionals at the top and artisans and small shopkeepers below them. These cities also contained numerous servants and unskilled workers who earned wages as porters and laborers.

Industrial Europe looked quite different. Cities grew enormously, especially industrial centers like Birmingham, England, which grew from 73,000 to 250,000 between 1801 and 1850, and Liverpool, which grew from 77,000 to 400,000 in the same half-century. Europe in 1800 had twenty-one cities with populations over 100,000. By 1900 the number of such cities had reached one hundred twenty. Within these cities there had emerged a new class of factory workers, the "proletariat," who took their place in the working class alongside skilled tradesmen, servants, and day laborers. Industrialization and urbanization also increased the numbers, diversity, and wealth of the middle class. To the ranks of merchants, lawyers, doctors, and shopkeepers, there now were added industrialists, managers, government officials, white-collar workers, and skilled professionals in such fields as engineering, architecture, accounting, chemistry, and higher education.

This new and expanding middle class dominated the nineteenth century. Its members controlled Europe's liberal, parliamentary governments, set the standards of taste in literature, music, and art, and drove forward and reaped the benefits from Europe's ongoing industrialization. In their view they were responsible for the material and moral progress of the age. In the view of others, however, the rise of the middle class had a different meaning. To Karl Marx, the German socialist, the bourgeoisie were selfish materialists, exploiters and oppressors of the workers, and responsible for the poverty and squalor of the industrial age. Marx and his followers looked forward to the coming revolution in which workers would rise up and destroy the bourgeoisie, end class exploitation, and initiate a new era of cooperation, harmony, and equality.

# English Workers in the Early Industrial Revolution

▼▼▼

## 61 ▼ TESTIMONY BEFORE PARLIAMENTARY COMMITTEES ON WORKING CONDITIONS IN ENGLAND

A key to England's early industrial growth was the large pool of workers willing to accept low wages for long hours of labor in factories and mines. Many of these workers were displaced farmers or farm workers, forced from rural areas because of land shortages caused by population growth and the consolidation of small farms into large estates by wealthy landowners. Rural families moved to cities or coal-mining towns, where they provided the workforce for the emerging industrial society. Few avoided poverty, crowded housing, and poor health.

Eventually, the British government abandoned its commitment to free enterprise, and Parliament passed laws to protect factory workers and miners, especially children, from exploitation. When considering legislation, parliamentary committees held hearings to gather testimony from workers, employers, physicians, clergy, and local officials. Their statements present a vivid picture of working-class conditions in the first half of the nineteenth century.

Section 1 includes testimony from the records of the Sadler Committee, chaired by Michael Thomas Sadler in 1831 and charged with investigating child labor in cotton and linen factories; section 2 includes testimony taken by a parliamentary commission appointed in 1833 to investigate working conditions in other textile industries; section 3 presents evidence taken in 1842 by the committee chaired by Lord Ashley to investigate conditions in coal mines.

---

## QUESTIONS FOR ANALYSIS

1. What differences were there between working conditions in the mines and in the cotton factories?
2. As revealed by the questions they asked, what did the committee members consider the worst abuses of working conditions in the factories and mines?
3. What does the testimony of Hannah Richardson and George Armitage reveal about (a) the economic circumstances of working-class families and (b) attitudes of working-class families toward their children?
4. Consider the testimony of the workers themselves. Do the workers express anger? Do they demand changes? What might explain their attitudes?
5. For what reasons do William Harter and Thomas Wilson oppose factory laws? In what ways do their views reflect the economic philosophy of Adam Smith in the *Wealth of Nations* (source 40)?

▷  1. Testimony before the Sadler Committee, 1831

## ELIZABETH BENTLEY

What age are you? — Twenty-three. . . .

What time did you begin to work at a factory? — When I was six years old. . . .

What kind of mill is it? — Flax-mill. . . .

What was your business in that mill? — I was a little doffer.[1]

What were your hours of labor in that mill? — From 5 in the morning till 9 at night, when they were thronged.[2]

For how long a time together have you worked that excessive length of time? — For about half a year.

What were your usual hours of labor when you were not so thronged? — From 6 in the morning till 7 at night.

What time was allowed for your meals? — Forty minutes at noon.

Had you any time to get your breakfast or drinking? — No, we got it as we could.

And when your work was bad, you had hardly any time to eat it at all? — No; we were obliged to leave it or take it home, and when we did not take it, the overlooker took it, and gave it to his pigs.

Do you consider doffing a laborious employment? — Yes.

Explain what it is you had to do. — When the frames are full, they have to stop the frames, and take the flyers off, and take the full bobbins off, and carry them to the roller; and then put empty ones on, and set the frames on again.

Does that keep you constantly on your feet? — Yes, there are so many frames and they run so quick.

Your labor is very excessive? — Yes; you have not time for any thing.

Suppose you flagged a little, or were too late, what would they do? — Strap us.

Are they in the habit of strapping those who are last in doffing? — Yes.

Constantly? — Yes.

Girls as well as boys? — Yes.

Have you ever been strapped? — Yes.

Severely? — Yes.

Could you eat your food well in that factory? — No, indeed, I had not much to eat, and the little I had I could not eat it, my appetite was so poor, and being covered with dust; and it was no use to take it home, I could not eat it, and the overlooker took it, and gave it to the pigs. . . .

Did you live far from the mill? — Yes, two miles.

Had you a clock? — No, we had not.

Supposing you had not been in time enough in the morning at the mills, what would have been the consequence? — We should have been quartered.

What do you mean by that? — If we were a quarter of an hour too late, they would take off half an hour; we only got a penny an hour, and they would take a halfpenny more. . . .

Were you generally there in time? — Yes, my mother has been up at 4 o'clock in the morning, and at 2 o'clock in the morning; the colliers used to go to their work about 3 or 4 o'clock, and when she heard them stirring she has got up out of her warm bed, and gone out and asked them the time, and I have sometimes been at Hunslet Car at 2 o'clock in the morning, when it was streaming down with rain, and we have had to stay till the mill was opened. . . .

▷  2. Commission for Inquiry into the Employment of Children in Factories, Second Report, 1833

## JOHN WRIGHT[3]

Are silk-mills clean in general? — They are; they are swept every day, and whitewashed once a year.

---

[1]A worker, usually a young child, whose job was to clean the machines used in textile manufacturing.

[2]Busy.

[3]A silk factory worker in his mid thirties.

What is the temperature of silk-mills? — I don't know exactly the temperature, but it is very agreeable.

Is any artificial heat required? — In the winter it is heated by steam.

To what degree? — I cannot speak positively; but it is not for the work, only to keep the hands warm and comfortable.

Why, then, are those employed in them said to be in such a wretched condition? — In the first place, the great number of hands congregated together, in some rooms forty, in some fifty, in some sixty, and I have known some as many as 100, which must be injurious to both health and growing. In the second place, the privy is in the factory, which frequently emits an unwholesome smell; and it would be worth while to notice in the future erection of mills, that there be betwixt the privy door and the factory wall a kind of a lobby of cage-work. 3dly, The tediousness and the everlasting sameness in the first process preys much on the spirits, and makes the hands spiritless. 4thly, the extravagant number of hours a child is compelled to labor and confinement, which for one week is seventy-six hours, which makes 3,952 hours for one year, we deduct 208 hours for meals within the factory which makes the net labor for one year 3,744; but the labor and confinement together of a child between ten years of age and twenty is 39,520 hours, enough to fritter away the best constitution. 5thly, About six months in the year we are obliged to use either gas, candles, or lamps, for the longest portion of that time, nearly six hours a day, being obliged to work amid the smoke and soot of the same; and also a large portion of oil and grease is used in the mills.

What are the effects of the present system of labor? — From my earliest recollections, I have found the effects to be awfully detrimental to the well-being of the operative; I have observed frequently children carried to factories, unable to walk, and that entirely owing to excessive labor and confinement. The degradation of the

workpeople baffles all description: frequently have two of my sisters been obliged to be assisted to the factory and home again, until by-and-by they could go no longer, being totally crippled in their legs. . . .

## WILLIAM HARTER[4]

What effect would it have on your manufacture to reduce the hours of labor to ten? — It would instantly much reduce the value of my mill and machinery, and consequently far prejudice my manufacture.

How so? — They are calculated to produce a certain quantity of work in a given time. Every machine is valuable in proportion to the quantity of work which it will turn off in a given time. It is impossible that the machinery could produce as much work in ten hours as in twelve. If the tending of the machines were a laborious occupation, the difference in the quantity of work might not always be in exact proportion to the difference of working time; but in my mill, and silk-mills in general, the work requires the least imaginable labor; therefore it is perfectly impossible that the machines could produce as much work in ten hours as in twelve. The produce would vary in about the same ratio as the working time.

What may be said about the sum invested in your mill and machinery? — It is not yet near complete, and the investment is a little short of 20,000 pounds.

Then to what extent do you consider your property would be prejudiced by a bill limiting the working hours to ten? — All other circumstances remaining the same, it is obvious that any property in the mill and machinery would be prejudiced to the extent of one-sixth its value, or upwards of 3,000 pounds.

How would the reduction in the hours of labor affect the cost of your manufactures? — The cost of our manufactures consists in the price of the raw material and of the expense of putting

---

[4]The owner of a silk mill in Manchester.

that said material into goods. Now the mere interest of the investment in buildings and machinery, and the expense of keeping the same in repair, forms a large item in the cost of manufacturing. Of course it follows, that the *gross* charge under this head would be the same upon a production of 10,000 pounds and 12,000 pounds, and this portion of the cost of manufacturing would consequently be increased by about 16%.

Do you mean to say, that to produce the same quantity of work which your present mill and machinery is capable of, it requires an additional outlay of upwards of 3,000 pounds? — I say distinctly, that to produce the same quantity of work under a ten-hours bill will require an additional outlay of 3,000 or 4,000 pounds; therefore a ten-hours bill would impose upon me the necessity of this additional outlay in such perishable property as buildings and machinery, or I must be content to relinquish one-sixth portion of my business.

---

▷　3. *Testimony before the Ashley Committee on the Conditions in Mines, 1842*

---

## EDWARD POTTER

I am a coal viewer, and the manager of the South Hetton colliery. We have about 400 bound people (contract laborers), and in addition our bank people (foremen), men and boys about 700. In the pits 427 men and boys; of these, 290 men. . . .

Of the children in the pits we have none under eight, and only three so young. We are constantly beset by parents coming making application to take children under the age, and they are very anxious and very dissatisfied if we do not take the children; and there have been cases in times of brisk trade, when the parents have threatened to leave the colliery, and go elsewhere if we did not comply. At every successive binding, which takes place yearly, constant attempts are made to get the boys engaged to work

to which they are not competent from their years. In point of fact, we would rather not have boys until nine years of age complete. If younger than that, they are apt to fall asleep and get hurt: some get killed. It is no interest to the company to take any boys under nine. . . .

## HANNAH RICHARDSON

I've one child that works in the pit; he's going on ten. He is down from 6 to 8. . . . He's not much tired with the work, it's only the confinement that tires him. He likes it pretty well, for he'd rather be in the pit than go to school. There is not much difference in his health since he went into the pit. He was at school before, and can read pretty well, but can't write. He is used pretty well; I never hear him complain. I've another son in the pit, 17 years old. . . . He went into the pit at eight years old. It's not hurt his health nor his appetite, for he's a good size. It would hurt us if children were prevented from working till 11 or 12 years old, because we've not jobs enough to live now as it is. . . .

## MR. GEORGE ARMITAGE

I am now a teacher at Hoyland school; I was a collier at Silkstone until I was 22 years old and worked in the pit above 10 years. . . . I hardly know how to reprobate the practice sufficiently of girls working in pits; nothing can be worse. I have no doubt that debauchery is carried on, for which there is every opportunity; for the girls go constantly, when hurrying, to the men, who work often alone in the bank-faces apart from every one. I think it scarcely possible for girls to remain modest who are in pits, regularly mixing with such company and hearing such language as they do — it is next to impossible. I dare venture to say that many of the wives who come from pits know nothing of sewing or any household duty, such as women ought to know — they lose all disposition to learn such things; they are rendered unfit for learning them also by being overworked and not being trained to the habit of it. I have worked in pits for above 10 years, where girls were constantly employed, and I can safely say it is an abominable system; indecent language is quite common. I think, if girls were trained properly, as girls ought to be, that there would be no more difficulty in finding suitable employment for them than in other places. Many a collier spends in drink what he has shut up a young child the whole week to earn in a dark cold corner as a trapper. The education of the children is universally bad. They are generally ignorant of common facts in Christian history and principles, and, indeed, in almost everything else. Little can be learned merely on Sundays, and they are too tired as well as indisposed to go to night schools. . . .

## THE REV. ROBERT WILLAN, CURATE OF ST. MARY'S, BARNSLEY

I have been resident here as chief minister for 22 years. I think the morals of the working classes here are in an appalling state. . . . The ill manners and conduct of the weavers are daily presented to view in the streets, but the colliers work under ground and are less seen, and we have less means of knowing. . . . The master-sin among the youths is that of gambling; the boys may be seen playing at pitch-and-toss on the Sabbath and on week-days; they are seen doing this in all directions. The next besetting sin is promiscuous sexual intercourse; this may be much induced by the manner in which they sleep — men, women, and children often sleeping in one bed-room. I have known a family of father and mother and 12 children, some of them up-grown, sleeping on a kind of sacking and straw bed, reaching from one side of the room to the other, along the floor; they were an English family. Sexual intercourse begins very young. This and gambling pave the way; then drinking ensues, and this is the vortex which draws in every other sin.

## THOMAS WILSON, ESQ., OWNER OF THREE COLLIERIES

I object on general principles to government interference in the conduct of any trade, and I am satisfied that in the mines it would be productive of the greatest injury and injustice. The art of mining is not so perfectly understood as to admit of the way in which a colliery shall be conducted being dictated by any person, however experienced, with such certainty as would warrant an interference with the management of private business. I should also most decidedly object to placing collieries under the present provisions of the Factory Act[5] with respect to the education of children employed therein. First, because, if it is contended that coal-owners, as employers of children, are bound to attend to their education, this obligation extends equally to all other employers, and therefore it is unjust to single out one class only; secondly, because, if the legislature asserts a right to interfere to secure education, it is bound to make that interference general; and thirdly, because the mining population is in this neighborhood so intermixed with other classes, and is in such small bodies in any one place, that it would be impossible to provide separate schools for them.

---

[5]The Factory Act of 1833, which regulated employment of children and women, applied to textile factories.

# Middle-Class Success and How to Achieve It
▼▼▼

## 62 ▼ Samuel Smiles,
## SELF-HELP and THRIFT

No writer expressed the hopes, fears, expectations, and values of nineteenth-century Europe's middle class more faithfully and successfully than the Scottish biographer, essayist, and businessman, Samuel Smiles (1812–1904). Born into the family of a papermaker and shopkeeper, Smiles received a medical degree, worked as a journalist in Leeds, and held several managerial posts in the railroad industry. He wrote biographies, histories, and travel narratives, but achieved worldwide fame through his inspirational books on morality and personal behavior. After it had been rejected by six publishers, his book *Self-Help* (1859) became a bestseller that in the nineteenth century went through dozens of editions and was translated into seventeen languages, including Arabic, Chinese, and Japanese. With an upbeat message that hard work, discipline, and high moral standards guaranteed success, *Self-Help* was followed by *Character* (1871), *Thrift* (1875), and *Duty* (1880). With his life spanning the century that saw the triumph of the middle-class values he championed, he died in 1904 at the age of ninety-three.

In the following excerpt, the first two sections, "Self-Help and Individualism" and "Habits of Successful Men," are from *Self-Help,* and the third section, "Faults of the Poor," is from *Thrift*.

---

## QUESTIONS FOR ANALYSIS

1. Why does Smiles consider government incapable of solving the social and economic problems confronting early industrial England? In his view what should be government's proper role and function?
2. What definition would Smiles offer for the word "individualism"?
3. How would you define the "middle-class ethic" discussed by Smiles? What are its components?
4. According to Smiles, who is responsible for the widespread poverty in England? In his view, what can be done about it?
5. If given a chance to testify before one of the parliamentary committees about the effects of industrialization on the working class, what might Smiles have said?
6. How do Smiles's views resemble and differ from those of Adam Smith in *The Wealth of Nations?* (See source 40.)

## SELF-HELP AND INDIVIDUALISM

"Heaven helps those who help themselves" is a well-tried maxim, embodying in a small compass the results of vast human experience. The spirit of self-help is the root of all genuine growth in the individual; and, exhibited in the lives of many, it constitutes the true source of national vigor and strength. . . . Whatever is done *for* men or classes, to a certain extent takes away the stimulus and necessity of doing for themselves; and where men are subjected to over-guidance and over-government, the inevitable tendency is to render them comparatively helpless.

Even the best institutions can give a man no active help. Perhaps the most they can do is, to leave him free to develop himself and improve his individual condition. But in all times men have been prone to believe that their happiness and well-being were to be secured by means of institutions rather than by their own conduct. Hence the value of legislation as an agent in human advancement has usually been much overestimated. . . . Moreover, it is every day becoming more clearly understood, that the function of Government is negative and restrictive, rather than positive and active; being resolvable principally into protection — protection of life, liberty, and property. Laws, wisely administered, will secure men in the enjoyment of the fruits of their labor, whether of mind or body, at a comparatively small personal sacrifice; but no laws, however stringent, can make the idle industrious, the thriftless provident, or the drunken sober. Such reforms can only be effected by means of individual action, economy, and self-denial; by better habits, rather than by greater rights. . . .

National progress is the sum of individual industry, energy, and uprightness, as national decay is of individual idleness, selfishness, and vice. What we are accustomed to decry as great social evils, will for the most part be found to be but the outgrowth of man's own perverted life; and though we may endeavor to cut them down and extirpate them by means of Law, they will only spring up again with fresh luxuriance in some other form unless the conditions of personal life

and character are radically improved. If this view be correct, then it follows that the highest patriotism and philanthropy consist, not so much in altering laws and modifying institutions as in helping and stimulating men to elevate and improve themselves by their own free and independent individual action.

## HABITS OF SUCCESSFUL MEN

Practical industry, wisely and vigorously applied, always produces its due effects. It carries a man onward, brings out his individual character, and stimulates the action of others. All may not rise equally, yet each, on the whole, very much according to his deserts. . . .

On the whole, it is not good that human nature should have the road of life made too easy. Better to be under the necessity of working hard and faring meanly, than to have every thing done ready to our hand and a pillow of down to repose upon. Indeed, to start in life with comparatively small means seems so necessary as a stimulus to work, that it may almost be set down as one of the conditions essential to success in life. Hence, an eminent judge, when asked what contributed most to success at the bar, replied, "Some succeed by great talent, some by high connections, some by miracle, but the majority by commencing without a shilling."

The necessity of labor may, indeed, be regarded as the main root and spring of all that we call progress in individuals, and civilization in nations; and it is doubtful that any heavier curse could be imposed on a man than the gratification of all his wishes without effort on his part, leaving nothing for his hopes, desires, or struggles. . . .

Attention, application, accuracy, method, punctuality, and dispatch are the principal qualities required for the efficient conduct of business of any sort. . . . They are little things, it is true; but human life is made up of comparative trifles. It is the repetition of little acts which constitutes not only the sum of human character, but which determines the character of nations. And where men or nations have broken down, it will almost invariably be found that neglect of little things was the rock on which they split. Every human being has duties to be performed, and, therefore, has need of cultivating the capacity for doing them; whether the sphere of action be the management of a household, the conduct of a trade or profession, or the government of a nation. . . .

Men of business are accustomed to quote the maxim that Time is money; but it is more; the proper improvement of it is self-culture, self-improvement, and growth of character. An hour wasted daily on trifles or in indolence, would, if devoted to self-improvements, make an ignorant man wise in a few years, and, employed in good works, would make his life fruitful, and death a harvest of worthy deeds. Fifteen minutes a day devoted to self-improvement, will be felt at the end of the year.

## FAULTS OF THE POOR

England is one of the richest countries in the world. Our merchants are enterprizing, our manufacturers are industrious, our labourers are hard-working. There is an accumulation of wealth in the country to which past times can offer no parallel. The Bank[1] is gorged with gold. There never was more food in the empire; there never was more money. There is no end to our manufacturing productions, for the steam-engine never tires. And yet, notwithstanding all this wealth, there is an enormous mass of poverty. Close alongside the Wealth of Nations, there gloomily stalks the Misery of Nations, — luxurious ease resting upon a dark background of wretchedness.

Parliamentary reports have again and again revealed to us the miseries endured by certain portions of our working population. They have described the people employed in factories, workshops, mines, and brickfields, as well as in the pursuits of country life. We have tried to grapple with the evils of their condition by legislation, but it seems to mock us. Those who sink into poverty are fed, but they remain paupers. Those who feed them, feel no compassion; and those who are fed, return no gratitude. . . . Thus the Haves and the Have-nots, the opulent and the indigent, stand at the two extremes of the social scale, and a wide gulf is fixed between them. . . .

With respect to the poorer classes, — what has become of them in the midst of our so-called civilization? An immense proportion of them remain entirely uncivilized. . . .

They work, eat, drink, and sleep: that constitutes their life. They think nothing of providing for tomorrow, or for next week, or for next year. They abandon themselves to their sensual appetites; and make no provision whatever for the future. The thought of adversity, or of coming sorrow, or of the helplessness that comes with years and sickness, never crosses their minds. In these respects, they resemble the savage tribes, who know no better, and do no worse. Like the North American Indians, they debase themselves by the vices which accompany civilization, but make no use whatever of its benefits and advantages. . . .

No one can reproach the English workman with want of industry. He works harder and more skilfully than the workman of any other country; and he might be more comfortable and independent in his circumstances, were he as prudent as he is laborious. . . . In prosperous times they are not accustomed to make provision for adverse times; and when a period of social pressure occurs, they are rarely found more than a few weeks ahead of positive want.

Hence, the skilled workman, unless trained in good habits, may exhibit no higher a life than that of the mere animal; and the earning of increased wages will only furnish him with increased means for indulging in the gratification of his grosser appetites. . . .

This habitual improvidence — though of course there are many admirable exceptions —

---

[1]The Bank of England, England's central bank.

is the real cause of the social degradation of the artisan. This too is the prolific source of social misery. But the misery is entirely the result of human ignorance and self-indulgence. For though the Creator has ordained poverty, the poor are not necessarily, nor as a matter of fact, the miserable. Misery is the result of moral causes, — most commonly of individual vice and improvidence. . . .

Complaining that the laws are bad, and that the taxes are heavy, will not mend matters. Aristocratic government, and the tyranny of masters, are nothing like so injurious as the tyranny of vicious appetites. Men are easily led away by the parade of their miseries, which are for the most part voluntary and self-imposed, — the results of idleness, thriftlessness, intemperance, and misconduct. To blame others for what we suffer, is always more agreeable to our self-pride, than to blame ourselves. But it is perfectly clear that people who live from day to day without plan, without rule, without forethought — who spend all their earnings, without saving anything for the future — are preparing beforehand for inevitable distress. To provide only for the present, is the sure means of sacrificing the future. What

hope can there be for a people whose only maxim seems to be, "Let us eat and drink, for tomorrow we die"?

All this may seem very hopeless; yet it is not entirely so. The large earnings of the working classes is an important point to start with. The gradual diffusion of education will help them to use, and not abuse, their means of comfortable living. The more extended knowledge of the uses of economy, frugality, and thrift, will help them to spend their lives more soberly, virtuously, and religiously. . . . Social improvement is always very slow. . . . It requires the lapse of generations before its effect can be so much as discerned; for a generation is but as a day in the history of civilization. . . . From the days in which our British progenitors rushed to battle in their war-paint, — or those more recent times when the whole of the labouring people were villeins and serfs, bought and sold with the soil which they tilled, — to the times in which we now live, — how wide the difference, how gratifying the contrast. Surely it ought not to be so difficult to put an end to the Satanic influences of thriftlessness, drunkenness, and improvidence!

# The Marxist Critique of Industrial Capitalism
▼▼▼

## 63 ▼ Karl Marx and Friedrich Engels, *THE COMMUNIST MANIFESTO*

As factories, steam engines, and railroads transformed Europe's economy in the first half of the nineteenth century, industrialization brought fundamental changes to European society, transformed politics, and sparked animated discussion and debate among intellectuals. Journalists, politicians, academics, factory owners, social reformers, and clergy examined workers' grievances, explored the moral dimensions of capitalism, and debated what industrialization meant for Europe's future. Out of this ferment of ideas a potent new ideology, socialism, emerged.

Although Karl Marx (1818–1883) is by far the most important figure in the history of socialism, he was not the movement's founder. Europe's first socialists were visionaries and idealists such as Count Henri de Saint-Simon (1760–1825), Charles Fourier (1772–1837), and Etienne Cabet (1788–1856), whose dreams of reordering European society on the basis of equality, cooperation, and justice lacked philosophical rigor and political savvy. Marx, the son of a German lawyer and a graduate of the University of Berlin, where he studied philosophy, shared these thinkers' moral outrage over the poverty and cutthroat competition fostered by the early Industrial Revolution. But he found their ideas too unrealistic — too "utopian" — and set for himself the task of utilizing history, economics, and science to provide the intellectual foundations of *scientific socialism,* capable of describing the mechanisms by which socialism would ultimately replace capitalism.

Among Marx's many writings, none rivals the importance of *The Communist Manifesto,* which he published in 1848 with his coauthor Friedrich Engels (1820–1895). Marx met Engels, an ardent critic of capitalism despite the fortune he built from managing a textile mill in Manchester, England, in Paris in 1844 after Marx had been exiled from Germany because of his radical editorials in a Cologne newspaper. In 1847, they both joined the Communist League, a revolutionary society dominated by German political exiles in France and England. They wrote the *Manifesto* to publicize the League's program. After 1848, the two men remained friends, with Engels giving the impoverished Marx enough money to continue his writing and political activities while living in London. Both men continued to write on behalf of socialism, but Marx's works, especially his masterpiece, *Das Kapital (Capitalism),* assumed the far greater role in shaping modern socialist thought. Furthermore, Marx's views of history, human behavior, and social conflict have influenced not just politics but also philosophy, religion, literature, and all the social sciences.

## QUESTIONS FOR ANALYSIS

1. How do Marx and Engels define class, and what do they mean by the "class struggle"?
2. According to Marx and Engels, how is the class struggle in nineteenth-century Europe unique?
3. In their view, what characterizes the bourgeoisie?
4. Marx and Engels believe that bourgeois society is doomed and that the bourgeoisie will be the cause of their own destruction. Why?
5. The authors dismiss the importance of ideas as a force in human affairs. On what grounds? Ultimately, what is the cause of historical change in their view?
6. What do you believe explains the popularity and influence of *The Communist Manifesto* among the working class and those who sympathized with their plight?
7. How does *The Communist Manifesto*'s vision of the past and future resemble that of Condorcet's *Sketch of the Progress of the Human Mind* (source 38)?
8. How would Marx and Engels have responded to the point of view represented by Samuel Smiles in *Self-Help* and *Thrift* (source 62)?

# I. THE BOURGEOISIE AND PROLETARIAT

The history of all hitherto existing society is the history of class struggles.

Freeman and slave, patrician and plebeian, lord and serf, guild-master and journeyman, in a word, oppressor and oppressed, stood in constant opposition to one another, carried on an uninterrupted, now hidden, now open fight, a fight that each time ended, either in a revolutionary reconstitution of society at large, or in the common ruin of the contending classes. . . .

The modern bourgeois society that has sprouted from the ruins of feudal society has not done away with class antagonisms. It has but established new classes, new conditions of oppression, new forms of struggle in place of the old ones.

Our epoch, the epoch of the bourgeoisie, possesses, however, this distinctive feature: It has simplified the class antagonisms. Society as a whole is more and more splitting up into two great hostile camps, into two great classes directly facing each other — bourgeoisie and proletariat.

From the serfs of the Middle Ages sprang the chartered burghers of the earliest towns. From these burgesses the first elements of the bourgeoisie were developed.

The discovery of America, the rounding of the Cape, opened up fresh ground for the rising bourgeoisie. The East-Indian and Chinese markets, the colonization of America, trade with the colonies, the increase in the means of exchange and in commodities generally, gave to commerce, to navigation, to industry, an impulse never before known, and thereby, to the revolutionary element in the tottering feudal society, a rapid development.

The feudal system of industry, in which industrial production was monopolized by closed guilds, now no longer sufficed for the growing wants of the new markets. The manufacturing system took its place. The guild-masters were pushed aside by the manufacturing middle class; division of labor between the different corporate guilds vanished in the face of division of labor in each single workshop.

Meantime the markets kept ever growing, the demand ever rising. Even manufacture no longer sufficed. Thereupon, steam and machinery revolutionized industrial production. The place of manufacture was taken by the giant, modern industry, the place of the industrial middle class by industrial millionaires, the leaders of whole industrial armies, the modern bourgeois. . . .

We see, therefore, how the modern bourgeoisie is itself the product of a long course of development, of a series of revolutions in the modes of production and of exchange. . . .

The bourgeoisie, historically, has played a most revolutionary part.

The bourgeoisie, wherever it has got the upper hand, has put an end to all feudal, patriarchal, idyllic relations. It has pitilessly torn asunder the motley feudal ties that bound man to his "natural superiors," and has left no other nexus between man and man than naked self-interest, than callous "cash payment." . . . It has resolved personal worth into exchange value, and in place of the numberless indefeasible chartered freedoms, has set up that single, unconscionable freedom — Free Trade. In one word, for exploitation, veiled by religious and political illusions, it has substituted naked, shameless, direct, brutal exploitation. . . .

We see then: the means of production and of exchange, on whose foundation the bourgeoisie built itself up, were generated in feudal society. At a certain stage in the development of these means of production and of exchange, the conditions under which feudal society produced and exchanged, the feudal organization of agriculture and manufacturing industry, in one word, the feudal relations of property became no longer compatible with the already developed productive forces; they became so many fetters. They had to be burst asunder; they were burst asunder.

Into their place stepped free competition, accompanied by a social and political constitution adapted to it, and by the economic and political sway of the bourgeois class.

A similar movement is going on before our own eyes. Modern bourgeois society with its relations of production, of exchange and of property, a society that has conjured up such gigantic means of production and of exchange, is like the sorcerer who is no longer able to control the powers of the nether world whom he has called up by his spells. For many a decade past the history of industry and commerce is but the history of the revolt of modern productive forces against modern conditions of production, against the property relations that are the conditions for the existence of the bourgeoisie and of its rule. It is enough to mention the commercial crises that by their periodical return put the existence of the entire bourgeois society on its trial, each time more threateningly. In these crises a great part not only of the existing products, but also of the previously created productive forces, are periodically destroyed. In these crises there breaks out an epidemic that, in all earlier epochs, would have seemed an absurdity — the epidemic of overproduction.

And how does the bourgeoisie get over these crises? On the one hand, by enforced destruction of a mass of productive forces; on the other, by the conquest of new markets, and by the more thorough exploitation of the old ones. That is to say, by paving the way for more extensive and more destructive crises, and by diminishing the means whereby crises are prevented.

The weapons with which the bourgeoisie felled feudalism to the ground are now turned against the bourgeoisie itself.

But not only has the bourgeoisie forged the weapons that bring death to itself; it has also called into existence the men who are to wield those weapons — the modern working class — the proletarians. . . .

Modern industry has converted the little workshop of the patriarchal master into the great factory of the industrial capitalist. Masses of laborers, crowded into the factory, are organized like soldiers. As privates of the industrial army they are placed under the command of a perfect hierarchy of officers and sergeants. Not only are they slaves of the bourgeois class, and of the bourgeois state; they are daily and hourly enslaved by the machine, by the overseer, and, above all, by the individual bourgeois manufacturer himself. The more openly this despotism proclaims gain to be its end and aim, the more petty, the more hateful and the more embittering it is. . . .

The lower strata of the middle class — the small tradespeople, shopkeepers, and retired tradesmen generally, the handicraftsmen and peasants — all these sink gradually into the proletariat, partly because their diminutive capital does not suffice for the scale on which modern industry is carried on, and is swamped in the competition with the large capitalists, partly because their specialized skill is rendered worthless by new methods of production. Thus the proletariat is recruited from all classes of the population.

But with the development of industry the proletariat not only increases in number; it becomes concentrated in greater masses, its strength grows, and it feels that strength more. The various interests and conditions of life within the ranks of the proletariat are more and more equalized, in proportion as machinery obliterates all distinctions of labor, and nearly everywhere reduces wages to the same low level. The growing competition among the bourgeois, and the resulting commercial crises, make the wages of the workers ever more fluctuating. The unceasing improvement of machinery, ever more rapidly developing, makes their livelihood more and more precarious; the collisions between individual workmen and individual bourgeois take more and more the character of collisions between two classes. Thereupon the workers begin to form combinations (trade unions) against the bourgeois; they club together in order to keep up the rate of wages; they found permanent associations in order to make provision beforehand for these occasional revolts. Here and there the contest breaks out into riots.

Now and then the workers are victorious, but only for a time. The real fruit of their battle lies, not in the immediate result, but in the ever expanding union of the workers. This union is helped on by the improved means of communication that are created by modern industry, and that place the workers of different localities in contact with one another. It was just this contact that was needed to centralize the numerous local struggles, all of the same character, into one national struggle between classes. . . .

This organization of the proletarians into a class, and consequently into a political party, is continually being upset again by the competition between the workers themselves. But it ever rises up again, stronger, firmer, mightier. . . .

Further, as we have already seen, entire sections of the ruling classes are, by the advance of industry, precipitated into the proletariat, or are at least threatened in their conditions of existence. These also supply the proletariat with fresh elements of enlightenment and progress.

Finally, in times when the class struggle nears the decisive hour, the process of dissolution going on within the ruling class, in fact within the whole range of old society, assumes such a violent, glaring character, that a small section of the ruling class cuts itself adrift, and joins the revolutionary class, the class that holds the future in its hands. Just as, therefore, at an earlier period, a section of the nobility went over to the bourgeoisie, so now a portion of the bourgeoisie goes over to the proletariat, and in particular, a portion of the bourgeois ideologists, who have raised themselves to the level of comprehending theoretically the historical movement as a whole.

## II. PROLETARIANS AND COMMUNISTS

The distinguishing feature of communism is not the abolition of property generally, but the abolition of bourgeois property. But modern bourgeois private property is the final and most complete expression of the system of producing and appropriating products that is based on class antagonisms, on the exploitation of the many by the few.

In this sense, the theory of the Communists may be summed up in the single sentence: Abolition of private property. . . .

You are horrified at our intending to do away with private property. But in your existing society, private property is already done away with for nine-tenths of its population; its existence for the few is solely due to its nonexistence in the hands of those nine-tenths. You reproach us, therefore, with intending to do away with a form of property, the necessary condition for whose existence is the nonexistence of any property for the immense majority of society.

In one word, you reproach us with intending to do away with your property. Precisely so; that is just what we intend. . . .

The Communists are further reproached with desiring to abolish countries and nationality.

The working men have no country. We cannot take from them what they have not got. . . .

National differences and antagonism between peoples are daily more and more vanishing, owing to the development of the bourgeoisie, to freedom of commerce, to the world market, to uniformity in the mode of production and in the conditions of life corresponding thereto.

The supremacy of the proletariat will cause them to vanish still faster. United action of the leading civilized countries at least, is one of the first conditions for the emancipation of the proletariat.

In proportion as the exploitation of one individual by another is put an end to, the exploitation of one nation by another will also be put an end to. In proportion as the antagonism between classes within the nation vanishes, the hostility of one nation to another will come to an end.

The charges against communism made from a religious, a philosophical and, generally, from an ideological standpoint, are not deserving of serious examination.

Does it require deep intuition to comprehend that man's ideas, views, and conceptions, in one word, man's consciousness, change with every change in the conditions of his material existence, in his social relations and in his social life?

What else does the history of ideas prove, than that intellectual production changes its character in proportion as material production is changed? The ruling ideas of each age have ever been the ideas of its ruling class. . . .

## IV. POSITION OF THE COMMUNISTS IN RELATION TO THE VARIOUS EXISTING OPPOSITION PARTIES

The Communists turn their attention chiefly to Germany, because that country is on the eve of a bourgeois revolution that is bound to be carried out under more advanced conditions of European civilization and with a much more developed proletariat than that of England was in the seventeenth, and of France in the eighteenth century, and because the bourgeois revolution in Germany will be but the prelude to an immediately following proletarian revolution.

In short, the Communists everywhere support every revolutionary movement against the existing social and political order of things.

In all these movements they bring to the front, as the leading question in each, the property question, no matter what its degree of development at the time. . . .

The Communists disdain to conceal their views and aims. They openly declare that their ends can be attained only by the forcible overthrow of all existing social conditions. Let the ruling classes tremble at a communist revolution. The proletarians have nothing to lose but their chains. They have a world to win.

Working men of all countries, unite!

▼▼▼

# Middle-Class Women in Emerging Industrial Society

Women's political and legal rights became a subject of public debate and controversy in the 1790s during the early stages of the French Revolution. Feminist leaders such as Olympe de Gouges demanded political rights for women and an end to laws and customs that served as the foundation for Europe's patriarchal society. These early French feminists made few long-term gains. In 1793 Jacobin leaders of the Revolution flatly rejected women's demands for political rights. A decade later, early revolutionary laws that had given women control of their property, legal equality with their husbands, and inheritance rights were annulled when a more conservative law code, the *Code Napoléon,* was adopted. Despite the Revolution's rhetoric about the Rights of Man, it was clear that to most politicians, even those sympathetic with the ideals of the Revolution, *Man* in this context did not mean humanity in general, but just men.

Most women, especially those of the middle class, also lost ground economically in the early 1800s with the spread of industrialization. In the early phases of industrialization, single and married working-class women had jobs in factories and mines, and middle-class women often assisted their husbands in newly established factories or stores. Once businesses were well established and family incomes increased, however, most middle-class women lost their formal work roles, and middle-class daughters were discouraged from working before marriage.

By the 1820s and 1830s, middle-class women were consigned to a domestic role centered on child care, housekeeping, supervising servants, and providing husbands with a tranquil haven where they could escape the pressures of business and politics. Young girls from the working class held paying jobs before marriage, but, if finances permitted, once married they too were expected to abandon their jobs outside the home.

To justify the notion that men and women had their "separate spheres," male and female writers developed a gender ideology that depicted men as rational, aggressive, decisive, and practical, and women as loving, nurturing, morally pure, emotional, and lacking in sexual appetite. Men should be given a rigorous academic education to prepare them for business and politics, while women should be taught etiquette, housekeeping skills, and the genteel arts of singing and piano playing to prepare them for child care, homemaking, and charitable work. An example of this point of view is provided by source 64, excerpted from Sarah Stickney Ellis's *The Wives of England,* published in 1843.

Such stereotypes continued to influence thinking about men and women well into the twentieth century, but by the mid 1800s, European and American women, many with ties to the temperance and antislavery movements, renewed the call for women's rights. A landmark in the history of nineteenth-century feminism (a word coined in France in the 1830s) was the women's rights convention held in the upstate New York town of Seneca Falls in 1848, which adopted a series of resolutions proclaiming the equality of men and women and demanding for women the vote, divorce and property rights, and equal employment and educational opportunities. Such issues also were the focus of feminists in England beginning in the 1850s and in France and Germany later in the century.

Some gains were made in the 1800s, especially in the areas of women's education and legal status. In addition, professions such as nursing and teaching provided new opportunities for many middle-class women, and a few women established careers in medicine and law. But little progress was made in the area of women's political rights before World War I. By then only Australia, New Zealand, Finland, Norway, and a dozen states in the western United States had granted women full voting privileges. Elsewhere they were permitted to vote only in municipal elections or, more frequently, not at all.

The efforts of nineteenth-century feminists were not in vain, however. After World War I, women received the right to vote in most democratic states, and those who carried on the struggle for women's rights in the twentieth century continued to draw inspiration from their ideals and actions.

# Women's "Separate Sphere"
▼▼▼

## 64 ▼ *Sarah Stickney Ellis, THE WIVES OF ENGLAND*

Little is known about the childhood and education of the widely read novelist, poet, and moralist Sarah Stickney Ellis. Born into a Quaker family in Holderness, England, in 1799, at some point she renounced Quakerism and became a Congregationalist before becoming the second wife of William Ellis (1794–1872) in 1837. By then her husband, who had served as a missionary in Madagascar, the South Pacific, and Hawaii, had taken a position at the home office of the London Missionary Society. In addition to her writing, Ellis was active in the temperance movement and founded a school for girls in London. The author of five novels and a book of poetry, Ellis turned her attention to the "woman question" in 1838 with the publication of her advice book *The Women of England.* Well received on both sides of the Atlantic, it was followed in the next five years by the *The Daughters of England, The Mothers of England,* and *The Wives of England,* which is excerpted here. She died in 1872, one week after the death of her husband.

## QUESTIONS FOR ANALYSIS

1. According to Ellis, what are the differences between men and women?
2. What implications do these differences have for women's political activity?
3. In Ellis's view, why would equality between men and women be a mistake?
4. According to Ellis, what does marriage mean for a wife? What does it mean for a husband?
5. What implications do Ellis's views have for female education?

## DIFFERENT NATURES

As it is the natural characteristic of woman's love in its most refined, as well as its most practical development, to be perpetually doing something for the good or the happiness of the object of her affection, it is but reasonable that man's personal comfort should be studiously attended to; and in this, the complacence and satisfaction which most men evince on finding themselves placed at table before a favourite dish, situated beside a clean hearth, or accommodated with an empty sofa, is of itself a sufficient reward for any sacrifice such indulgence may have cost. In proofs of affection like these, there is something tangible which speaks home to the senses — something which man can understand without an effort; and he will sit down to eat, or compose himself to rest, with more hearty good-will towards the wife who has been thoughtful about these things, than if she had been all day busily employed in writing a treatise on morals for his especial benefit. . . .

Those who argue for the perfect equality — the oneness of women in their intellectual na-

ture with men, appear to know little of that higher philosophy, by which both, from the very distinctness of their characters, have been made subservient to the purposes of wisdom and of goodness; and after having observed . . . the operation of mind on mind, the powerful and instinctive sympathies which rule our very being, and the associated influence of different natures, all working together, yet too separate and distinct to create confusion; . . . I own it does appear an ignorant and vulgar contest, to strive to establish the equality of that, which would lose not only its utility, but its perfection, by being assimilated with a different nature. . . .

## SEPARATE SPHERES

It may be said to be a necessary part of man's nature, and conducive to his support in the position he has to maintain, that he should, in a greater degree than woman, be sufficient unto himself. The nature of his occupations, and the character of his peculiar duties, require this. The contending interests of the community at large, the strife of public affairs, and the competition of business, with the paramount importance of establishing himself as the master of a family, and the head of a household, all require a degree of concentrated effort in favour of self, and a powerful repulsion against others, which woman, happily for her, is seldom or never called upon to maintain. . . .

The love of woman appears to have been created solely to minister; that of man, to be ministered unto. It is true, his avocations lead him daily to some labour, or some effort for the maintenance of his family; and he often conscientiously believes that this labour is for his wife. But the probability is, that he would be just as attentive to his business, and as eager about making money, had he no wife at all — witness the number of single men who provide with as great care, and as plentifully, according to their wants, for the maintenance of a house without either wife or child.

It is unquestionably the inalienable right of all men, whether ill or well, rich or poor, wise or foolish, to be treated with deference, and made much of in their own houses. It is true that in the last mentioned case, this duty may be attended with some difficulty in the performance; but as no man becomes a fool, or loses his senses by marriage, the woman who has selected such a companion must abide by the consequences; and even he, whatever may be his degree of folly, is entitled to respect from her, because she has voluntarily placed herself in such a position that she must necessarily be his inferior. . . .

## WOMEN AND POLITICS

That mode of conversation which I have been accustomed to describe as *talking on a large scale,* is, except on very important occasions, most inimical to the natural softness and attractiveness of woman. . . . The excellence of woman as regards her conversation, consists rather of quick, and delicate, and sometimes playful turns of thought, with a lively and subtle apprehension of the bearings, tendencies, and associations of

ideas; so that the whole machinery of conversation . . . may be made, by her good management, to turn off from one subject, and play upon another, as if the direction of some magic influence, which will ever be preserved from detection by the tact of an unobtrusive and sensitive nature.

It is in this manner, and this alone, that women should evince their interest in those great political questions which arise out of the state of the times in which they live. Not that they may be able to attach themselves to a party, still less that they may *make speeches* either in public or in private; but that they may think and converse like rational beings on subjects which occupy the attention of the majority of mankind; . . . If, for instance, a wife would converse with her husband about a candidate for the representation of the place in which they live, she may, if she choose, discuss the merits of the colour which his party wears, and wish it were some other, as being more becoming; she may tell with delight how he bowed especially to her; and she may wish from her heart that the number of votes may be in his favour, because he kissed her child, and called it the prettiest he had ever seen. It is this kind of prattle which may properly be described as *small talk,* and which it is to be feared denotes a littleness of soul. Yet this style of talk may be, and sometimes is, applied by women to all sorts of subjects, not excepting politics, philosophy, and even religion. . . .

## TRIALS OF MARRIED LIFE

Amongst the trials peculiar to married life, we will first speak of those of temper; and . . . in order to judge more candidly on this subject, let us single out a few instances of the most familiar kind on both sides; and if the merit of unconsciousness, and absence of design, does not preponderate on the side of man, I shall be much mistaken in my calculations.

It is a well known fact, that men in general appear to consider themselves justly entitled to the privilege of being out of humour about their food. Thus the whole pleasure of a social meal is sometimes destroyed by some trifling error in the culinary department, or the non-appearance of some expected indulgence. But here again, our forbearance is called into existence, by remembering the probability there is, that such men have had silly mothers, who made the pleasures of their childhood to consist chiefly of such as belong to the palate: and here too, if the wife cannot remedy this evil, and in all probability it will be beyond her power to do so, she may, by her judicious efforts to promote the welfare of the rising generation, impart to the youthful minds committed to her care, or subject to her influence, a juster estimate of what belongs to the true enjoyment of intellectual and immortal beings.

With all occasions of domestic derangement, such as washing-days, and other renovations of comfort and order, some men of irritable temperament wage open and determined war. But, may we not ask, in connection with this subject, whether their prejudices against these household movements have not been remotely or immediately excited, by the extreme and unnecessary confusion and disturbance with which they are too frequently accompanied? . . . And if properly managed, so as to interfere as little as possible with his personal comfort, and conducted with general cheerfulness and good humour, such a man might easily be brought to consider them as necessary to the good of his household, as the refreshing shower is to the summer soil.

A causeless and habitual neglect of punctuality on the part of the master of a house, is certainly a grievance very difficult to bear; because as he is the principal person in the household, and the first to be considered, the whole machinery of domestic management must necessarily be dependent upon his movements; and more especially, since it so happens, that persons who are the most accustomed to keep others waiting, have the least patience to wait for others. . . .

Now, as the time of women, if properly employed, is too precious to be wasted, something surely may be done, not by endeavouring to control the movements of such a man so as to make him true to his own appointment, but by convincing him, that common honesty requires him simply to state the actual time at which he does intend to be ready. . . .

But we have not yet sufficiently examined that one consideration, which ever remains to be weighed in the balance against the trials of patience arising out of the conduct of men. And here we must first ask — Have you yourself no personal peculiarities exactly opposed to your husband's notions of what is agreeable? — such as habits of disorder, dressing in bad taste, or any other of those minor deviations from delicacy or good breeding which he might not have had an opportunity of observing before marriage? . . .

But if such peculiarities as these are of sufficient importance to cast a shadow over the sunny spots of life, what must we say of some others occasionally observable in the character and conduct of women, to which it is scarcely possible that much charity should be extended? And here I would ask, if you have never treasured up against your husband some standing cause of complaint, to be thrown at him when an opportunity is offered by the presence of a friend, or a stranger, for discharging this weapon from the household quiver with perfect safety to yourself? . . .

Have you never made the most of household troubles, spread forth the appurtenances of a wash, allowed the affairs of the kitchen to extend themselves to the parlour, complained unnecessarily of servants and work-people, and appeared altogether in your own person more harassed, exhausted, and forlorn, after your husband's return home, than you did before, on purpose that he might be compelled, not only to pity you, but to bear a portion of your domestic discomfort himself?

When a concatenation of cross occurrences, hinderances, or mistakes, have rendered every moment one of perplexity and haste; have you never, when involved with your husband in such circumstances, added fuel to the fire by your own petulance, or by your still more provoking exclamations of triumph, that you "thought it would come to that?" . . .

Now, it is impossible for any woman of right feelings to hide from her conscience, that if she chooses to marry, she places herself under a moral obligation to make her husband's home as pleasant to him as she can. Instead, therefore, of behaving as if it was the great business of married life to complain, it is her peculiar duty as a wife, and one for which, by her natural constitution, she is especially fitted, to make all her domestic concerns appear before her husband to the very best advantage. She has time for her troubles and turmoils, . . . when her husband is absent, or when she is engaged exclusively in her own department; and if she would make his home what it ought to be to him — "an ever-sunny place," she will studiously shield him, as with the wings of love, from the possibility of feeling that his domestic annoyances give weight and poignancy to those more trying perplexities, which most men, engaged either in business, or in public affairs, find more than sufficient for their peace of mind.

# American Women Demand Equality
▼▼▼

## 65 ▼ *Ohio Women's Convention of 1850, RESOLUTIONS*

In 1850, two years after the first U.S. women's rights convention was held in Seneca Falls, New York, a group of Ohio women met in Salem, in eastern Ohio, to draw up resolutions on the status of women for submission to a forthcoming convention that was to consider amendments to the state constitution. The Salem meeting has a special place in the history of feminist movements because, although men attended, they were not allowed to speak, vote, or make proposals. At the close of the meeting the men in attendance organized their own association, and as their first act, voted to endorse the resolutions the women had drawn up without their help. The resolutions were received less favorably at the constitutional convention, where the delegates, all men, ignored them.

*QUESTIONS FOR ANALYSIS*

1. What specific demands do the resolutions make in the areas of education, the family, politics, and employment?
2. For the authors of the resolutions, *dependency* is a key concept in their views of women's place in society. What do they mean by this term, and what social and political practices contribute to it?
3. What specific demands do the resolutions make in the areas of political rights, employment, education, and the family?
4. The authors admit that not all women share their views. How do they view women who are content to accept their "idle lives" and "sterile submission"? How do they explain these women's indifference to women's plight?
5. In what ways do these resolutions resemble the concerns of the middle-class Parisian women who petitioned Louis XVI in 1789 (source 45)? How do they differ, and why?

Whereas, all men are created equal and endowed with certain God-given rights, and all just government is derived from the consent of the governed; and whereas, the doctrine that "man shall pursue his own substantial happiness" is acknowledged by the highest authority to be the great precept of Nature; and whereas, this doctrine is not local, but universal, being dictated by God himself; therefore,

Resolved, That the prohibition of Woman from participating in the enactment of the laws by which she is governed is a direct violation of this precept of Nature, as she is thereby prevented from occupying that position which duty points out, and from pursuing her own substantial happiness by acting up to her conscientious convictions; and that all statutes and constitutional provisions which sanction this prohibition are null and void.

Resolved, That all rights are *human* rights, and pertain to human beings, without distinction of sex; therefore justice demands that all laws shall be made, not for man, or for woman, but for mankind, and that the same legal protection be afforded to the one sex as to the other.

Resolved, That the servile submission and quiet indifference of the Women of this country in relation to the unequal and oppressive laws by which they are governed, are the fruit either of ignorance or degradation, both resulting legitimately from the action of those laws.

Resolved, That the evils arising from the present social, civil, and religious condition of women proclaim to them in language not to be misunderstood, that not only their *own* welfare, but the highest good of the race demands of them, as an imperative duty, that they should secure to themselves the elective franchise.

Resolved, That in those laws which confer on man the power to control the property and person of woman, and to remove from her at will the children of her affection, we recognize only the modified code of the slave plantation; and that thus we are brought more nearly in sympathy with the suffering slave, who is despoiled of all his rights.

Resolved, That we, as human beings, are entitled to claim and exercise all the rights that belong by nature to any members of the human family.

Resolved, That all distinctions between men and women in regard to social, literary, pecuniary, religious or political customs and institutions, based on a distinction of sex, are contrary to the laws of Nature, are unjust, and destructive to the purity, elevation and progress in knowledge and goodness of the great human family, and ought to be at once and forever abolished.

Resolved, That the practice of holding women amenable to a different standard of propriety and morality from that to which men are held amenable, is unjust and unnatural, and highly detrimental to domestic and social virtue and happiness.

Resolved, That the political history of Woman demonstrates that tyranny, the most degrading, cruel and arbitrary, can be exercised and produced the same in effect under a mild and republican form of government as by an hereditary despotism.

Resolved, That while we deprecate thus earnestly the political oppression of Woman, we see in her social condition, the regard in which she is held as a moral and intellectual being, the fundamental cause of that oppression.

Resolved, That amongst the principal causes of such social condition we regard the public sentiment which withholds from her all, or almost all, lucrative employment, and enlarged spheres of labor.

Resolved, That in the difficulties thus cast in the way of her self-support, and in her consequent *dependence* upon man, we see the greatest influence at work in imparting to her that tone of character which makes her to be regarded as the "weaker vessel." . . .

Resolved, That we regard those women who content themselves with an idle, aimless life, as involved in the guilt as well as the suffering of their own oppression; and that we hold those who go forth into the world, in the face of the frowns and the sneers of the public, to fill larger spheres of labor, as the truest preachers of the cause of Woman's Rights.

Whereas, one class of society dooms woman to a life of drudgery, another to one of dependence and frivolity; and whereas, the education she generally receives is calculated to cultivate vanity and dependence, therefore,

Resolved, That the education of woman should be in accordance with responsibility in life, that she may acquire the self-reliance and true dignity so essential to the proper fulfillment of the important duties devolving on her.

Resolved, That as woman is not permitted to hold office, nor have any voice in the government, she should not be compelled to pay taxes out of her scanty wages to support men who get eight dollars a-day for *taking* the right to *themselves* to enact laws *for* her.

Resolved, That we, the Women of Ohio, will hereafter meet annually in Convention to consult upon and adopt measures for the removal of various disabilities — political, social, religious, legal and pecuniary — to which women as a class are subjected, and from which results so much misery, degradation, and crime.

▼▼▼

# Nationalism and Imperialism in the Late Nineteenth Century

Nationalism, simply defined, is dedication to and identification with the interests, purposes, and well-being of one's nation-state, a political entity consisting ideally of individuals with shared values and a common language, history, and vision. As such, nationalism takes precedence over competing loyalties to religion, locality, and even family. No other political force in modern history has matched its ability to stir deep emotions, inspire heroism and self-sacrifice, and justify war and oppression.

Nationalism emerged during the first years of the French Revolution when the French people transformed themselves from "subjects" to "citizens" by abolishing class privilege and establishing a regime based on equality and popular sovereignty. When war broke out in 1792 between republican France and anti-revolutionary Austria and Prussia, previously apathetic Frenchmen eagerly volunteered to fight, and defense of the Revolution became a national crusade. The French people's devotion saved the Revolution in the 1790s and in the early 1800s contributed to the stunning victories under Napoleon Bonaparte that gave France control of most of Europe by 1810. French conquests in turn aroused nationalism among Germans, Italians, Poles, and Russians, who fought to throw off French rule and establish self-government. Although successful in defeating France on the battlefield, nationalists had their hopes dashed in 1815 at the Congress of Vienna, when diplomats rejected their claims. They gave Norway to Sweden, Belgium to the Netherlands, and much of Italy to Austria; divided Poland among Russia, Prussia, and Austria; and kept Germany fragmented. But nationalism could not be snuffed out by redrawing maps and striking diplomatic compromises. Strengthened by romanticism, Darwinist notions of competition and struggle, economic rivalries, and popular journalism, nationalism continued to intensify in the nineteenth century, not just in areas of foreign rule and political fragmentation, but also in established states such as Great Britain and France. It contributed to some of the nineteenth century's most important political developments: the revolutions of 1830 and 1848, the unification of Italy in 1870 and of Germany in 1871, runaway militarism among the Great Powers, the emergence of new states in the Balkans, and what concerns us in this section, late-nineteenth-century imperialism.

Unlike nationalism, a new historical phenomenon, European imperialism has a history dating back to the medieval crusades and the conquests of the Americas in the sixteenth and seventeenth centuries. Western expansionism continued in the late eighteenth and early nineteenth centuries, despite the loss of their American colonies by France, Great Britain, Portugal, and Spain. The British extended their authority in India, the French subdued Algeria between 1830 and 1847, and the Western powers led by England forced China to open its ports to European trade after the Opium War (1839–1842). Then in the closing decades of the 1800s — the "Era of Imperialism" — the long history of Western expansion culminated in an unprecedented and astounding land grab. Between 1870 and 1914 Great Britain added 4.25 million square miles of territory and 66 million people to its empire; France, 3.5 million square miles of territory and 26 million people; Germany, 1 million square miles and 13 million people; and Belgium, 900,000 square miles and 13 million people. Italy, the United States, and the Netherlands also made imperialist conquests.

These enormous acquisitions were made possible by a number of key technological developments. The replacement of sailing vessels by metal-hulled steamships reduced two-month ocean voyages to two weeks; undersea telegraph lines enabled governments and businessmen to communicate in seconds, not weeks or months; medical advances and new drugs protected Europeans from diseases that flourished in warm, humid climates; rapid-fire rifles and machine guns gave Western troops an insurmountable advantage over any Africans or Asians who resisted the invaders of their lands.

Technological capability alone, however, cannot explain the expansionist fever that swept through the West in the late 1800s. Anticipated economic gains, missionary fervor, racism, and a faith in the West's civilizing mission all contributed. But the most important cause was nationalism. Politicians, journalists, and millions of people from every walk of life were convinced that foreign conquests brought respect, prestige, a sense of national accomplishment, and pride. To have colonies was a sure sign of great power status.

## Racism, Militarism, and the New Nationalism
▼▼▼

## 66 ▼ *Heinrich von Treitschke,*
## *Extracts from HISTORY OF GERMANY*
## *IN THE NINETEENTH CENTURY and*
## *HISTORICAL AND POLITICAL WRITINGS*

As nationalism grew in nineteenth-century Europe, it also changed. In the first half of the century, when nationalists saw conservative monarchical governments as the main obstacle to national self-determination, nationalism was linked to republicanism and liberalism. During the middle of the century, especially in Germany and Italy, nationalism was championed by pragmatic and moderate leaders, who believed that hard-headed politics, not romantic gestures and lofty republican ideals, would bring about their people's unification or independence from foreign rule. By century's end nationalism was increasingly associated with racism and identified with conservative if not reactionary groups that used it to justify large military outlays, promote imperialism and aggressive foreign policies, and lure the masses away from socialism and democracy.

The German historian Heinrich von Treitschke (1834–1896) represents this later link between nationalism and militarism, racism, and authoritarianism. The son of a Prussian general, Treitschke taught history at several universities, including the prestigious University of Berlin, where he concluded his career. He also was a member of the German representative assembly, the Reichstag, from 1871 to 1884. His best-known work is his seven-volume *History of Germany in the Nineteenth Century.* In this and his numerous other writings, lectures, and speeches, Treitschke acclaimed militarism, authoritarianism, and war as the path to German greatness. His views struck a responsive chord among many Germans who feared socialism and democracy and yearned for the day when Germany would be recognized as the world's most powerful nation.

---

### QUESTIONS FOR ANALYSIS

1. What, according to Treitschke, is the relationship between the state and the individual?
2. Why, according to Treitschke, is monarchy superior to democracy?
3. What qualities of Germans set them apart from other peoples, especially the English and the Jews, according to Treitschke?
4. Early nineteenth-century nationalists believed that all nations had a contribution to make to human progress. What is Treitschke's view?
5. What, according to Treitschke, is the value of war for a nation?

## ON THE GERMAN CHARACTER

Depth of thought, idealism, cosmopolitan views; a transcendent philosophy which boldly oversteps (or freely looks over) the separating barriers of finite existence, familiarity with every human thought and feeling, the desire to traverse the world-wide realm of ideas in common with the foremost intellects of all nations and all times. All that has at all times been held to be characteristic of the Germans and has always been praised as the essence of German character and breeding.

The simple loyalty of the Germans contrasts remarkably with the lack of chivalry in the English character This seems to be due to the fact that in England physical culture is sought, not in the exercise of noble arms, but in sports like boxing, swimming, and rowing, sports which undoubtedly have their value, but which obviously tend to encourage a brutal and purely athletic point of view, and the single and superficial ambition of getting a first prize.[1]

## ON THE STATE

The state is a moral community, which is called upon to educate the human race by positive achievement. Its ultimate object is that a nation should develop in it, a nation distinguished by a real national character. To achieve this state is the highest moral duty for nation and individual alike. All private quarrels must be forgotten when the state is in danger.

At the moment when the state cries out that its very life is at stake, social selfishness must cease and party hatred be hushed. The individual must forget his egoism, and feel that he is a member of the whole body.

The most important possession of a state, its be-all and end-all, is power. He who is not man enough to look this truth in the face should not meddle in politics. The state is not physical power as an end in itself, it is power to protect and promote the higher interests. Power must justify itself by being applied for the greatest good of mankind. It is the highest moral duty of the state to increase its power.

The true greatness of the state is that it links the past with the present and future, consequently, the individual has no right to regard the state as a means for attaining his own ambitions in life. Every extension of the activities of the state is beneficial and wise if it arouses, promotes, and purifies the independence of free and reasoning men; it is evil when it kills and stunts the independence of free men. It is men who make history.

The state does not stand for the whole life of the nation. Its function is essentially protective and administrative. The state does not swallow up everything; it can only influence by external compulsion. It represents the nation from the point of view of power. For in the state it is not only the great primitive forces of human nature that come into play; the state is the basis of all national life. Briefly, it may be affirmed that a state which is not capable of forming and maintaining an external organization of its civilizing activities deserves to perish.

Only the truly great and powerful states ought to exist. Small states are unable to protect their subjects against external enemies; moreover, they are incapable of producing genuine patriotism or national pride and are sometimes incapable of *Kultur*[2] in great dimensions. Weimar produced a Goethe and a Schiller;[3] still these poets would have been greater had they been citizens of a German national state.

---

[1]Treitschke is correct in drawing a distinction between English and German sports. In the nineteenth century the English prized competitive athletic contests, while the Germans favored group calisthenics and exercises.
[2]German for *culture* or *civilization*.

[3]Johann Wolfgang von Goethe (1749–1832) and Johann von Schiller (1759–1805) were German poets and dramatists who lived before Germany became a unified state. They both spent a good part of their adult lives in the city of Weimar, the capital of the Duchy of Saxe-Weimar.

## ON MONARCHY

The will of the state is, in a monarchy, the expression of the will of one man who wears the crown by virtue of the historic right of a certain family; with him the final authority rests. Nothing in a monarchy can be done contrary to the will of the monarch. In a democracy, plurality, the will of the people, expresses the will of the state. A monarchy excels any other form of government, including the democratic, in achieving unity and power in a nation. It is for this reason that monarchy seems so natural, and that it makes such an appeal to the popular understanding. We Germans had an experience of this in the first years of our new empire.[4] How wonderfully the idea of a united Fatherland was embodied for us in the person of the venerable Emperor! How much it meant to us that we could feel once more: "That man is Germany; there is no doubting it!"

## ON WAR

The idea of perpetual peace is an illusion supported only by those of weak character. It has always been the weary, spiritless, and exhausted ages which have played with the dream of perpetual peace. A thousand touching portraits testify to the sacred power of the love which a righteous war awakes in noble nations. It is altogether impossible that peace be maintained in a world bristling with arms, and even God will see to it that war always recurs as a drastic medicine for the human race. Among great states the greatest political sin and the most contemptible is feebleness. . . .

War is elevating because the individual disappears before the great conception of the state.

The devotion of the members of a community to each other is nowhere so splendidly conspicuous as in war.

Modern wars are not waged for the sake of goods and resources. What is at stake is the sublime moral good of national honor, which has something in the nature of unconditional sanctity, and compels the individual to sacrifice himself for it.

## ON THE ENGLISH

The hypocritical Englishman, with the Bible in one hand and a pipe of opium[5] in the other, possesses no redeeming qualities. The nation was an ancient robber-knight, in full armor, lance in hand, on every one of the world's trade routes.

The English possess a commercial spirit, a love of money which has killed every sentiment of honor and every distinction of right and wrong. English cowardice and sensuality are hidden behind unctuous, theological fine talk which is to us free-thinking German heretics among all the sins of English nature the most repugnant. In England all notions of honor and class prejudices vanish before the power of money, whereas the German nobility has remained poor but chivalrous. That last indispensable bulwark against the brutalization of society — the duel — has gone out of fashion in England and soon disappeared, to be supplanted by the riding whip.[6] This was a triumph of vulgarity. The newspapers, in their accounts of aristocratic weddings, record in exact detail how much each wedding guest has contributed in the form of presents or in cash; even the youth of the nation have turned their sports into a business, and contend for valuable prizes, whereas the German students wrought havoc on their countenances for the sake of a real or imaginary honor.[7]

---

[4]When Germany became a unified state in 1871, the king of Prussia, William I, became emperor of Germany.

[5]Treitschke is making a point about what he considers the hypocrisy of the British, professed Christians who nonetheless sell opium to the Chinese. See Lin Zexu's Letter to Queen Victoria in Chapter 10 (source 80).

[6]Aristocratic males frequently settled disputes concerning their honor by dueling. To Treitschke, abandoning the duel

for less manly pursuits such as hunting and horseback riding was a sign of decadence.

[7]Treitschke is again using examples from sports to underscore the differences between the Germans and English. By the end of the nineteenth century English sports such as rugby and football (American soccer) were organized into professional leagues; the Germans were still willing to be scarred in duels to defend their honor.

## ON JEWS

The Jews at one time played a necessary role in German history, because of their ability in the management of money. But now that the Aryans[8] have become accustomed to the idiosyncrasies of finance, the Jews are no longer necessary.

The international Jew, hidden in the mask of different nationalities, is a disintegrating influence; he can be of no further use to the world. It is necessary to speak openly about the Jews, undisturbed by the fact that the Jewish press befouls what is purely historical truth.

---

[8]Today, the term *Aryan,* or Indo-Iranian, refers to a branch of the Indo-European family of languages, which also includes Baltic, Slavic, Armenian, Greek, Celtic, Latin, and Germanic. Indo-Iranian includes Bengali, Persian, Punjabi, and Hindi. In Treitschke's day *Aryan* was used not only to refer to the prehistoric language from which all these languages derived but also to the racial group that spoke the language and migrated from its base in central Asia to Europe and India in the distant past. In the racial mythology that grew in connectlon with the term and later was embraced by Hitler and the Nazis, the Aryans provided Europe's original racial stock.

## A Defense of French Imperialism

▼▼▼

## 67 ▼ *Jules Ferry,* SPEECH BEFORE THE FRENCH NATIONAL ASSEMBLY

Jules Ferry (1832–1893) was a French politician and ardent imperialist who twice served as premier of France. During his premierships (1880–1881, 1883–1885) France annexed Tunisia and parts of Indochina and began exploring parts of Africa. In debates in the French National Assembly he frequently defended his policies against socialist and conservative critics who opposed French imperialism. The following selection from his speech on July 28, 1883, summarizes his reasons for supporting French expansionism; it also sheds light on his opponents' views.

---

## QUESTIONS FOR ANALYSIS

1. According to Ferry, what recent developments in world trade have made France's need for colonies more urgent?
2. What ideological arguments against imperialism are proposed by Ferry's critics? How does Ferry counter them?
3. Aside from providing markets for French goods, what other economic advantages do colonies offer, according to Ferry?
4. How does Ferry's appeal for colonies reflect nineteenth-century nationalism?
5. Given the opportunity to have heard Ferry's speech, how might Condorcet have reacted to it (source 38)?

M. JULES FERRY    Gentlemen, it embarrasses me to make such a prolonged demand upon the gracious attention of the Chamber, but I believe that the duty I am fulfilling upon this platform is not a useless one: It is as strenuous for me as for you, but I believe that there is some benefit in summarizing and condensing, in the form of arguments, the principles, the motives, and the various interests by which a policy of colonial expansion may be justified; it goes without saying that I will try to remain reasonable, moderate, and never lose sight of the major continental interests which are the primary concern of this country. What I wish to say, to support this proposition, is that in fact, just as in word, the policy of colonial expansion is a political and economic system; I wish to say that one can relate this system to three orders of ideas: economic ideas, ideas of civilization in its highest sense, and ideas of politics and patriotism.

In the area of economics, I will allow myself to place before you, with the support of some figures, the considerations which justify a policy of colonial expansion from the point of view of that need, felt more and more strongly by the industrial populations of Europe and particularly those of our own rich and hard working country: the need for export markets. Is this some kind of chimera? Is this a view of the future or is it not rather a pressing need, and, we could say, the cry of our industrial population? I will formulate only in a general way what each of you, in the different parts of France, is in a position to confirm. Yes, what is lacking for our great industry, drawn irrevocably on to the path of exportation by the (free trade) treaties of 1860,[1] what it lacks more and more is export markets. Why? Because next door to us Germany is surrounded by barriers, because beyond the ocean,

the United States of America has become protectionist, protectionist in the most extreme sense, because not only have these great markets, I will not say closed but shrunk, and thus become more difficult of access for our industrial products, but also these great states are beginning to pour products not seen heretofore into our own markets. . . . It is not necessary to pursue this demonstration any further. . . .

. . . Gentlemen, there is a second point, a second order of ideas to which I have to give equal attention, but as quickly as possible, believe me; it is the humanitarian and civilizing side of the question. On this point the honorable M. Camille Pelletan[2] has jeered in his own refined and clever manner; he jeers, he condemns, and he says "What is this civilization which you impose with cannon-balls? What is it but another form of barbarism? Don't these populations, these inferior races, have the same rights as you? Aren't they masters of their own houses? Have they called upon you? You come to them against their will, you offer them violence, but not civilization." There, gentlemen, is the thesis; I do not hesitate to say that this is not politics, nor is it history: it is political metaphysics. ("Ah, Ah" *on far left.*)[3]

. . . Gentlemen, I must speak from a higher and more truthful plane. It must be stated openly that, in effect, superior races have rights over inferior races. (*Movement on many benches on the far left.*)

M. JULES MAIGNE    Oh! You dare to say this in the country which has proclaimed the rights of man!

M. DE GUILLOUTET    This is a justification of slavery and the slave trade!

M. JULES FERRY    If M. Maigne is right, if the declaration of the rights of man was written for

[1]Refers to a treaty between Great Britain and France that lowered tariffs between the two nations.
[2]Pelletan (1846–1915) was a radical republican politician noted for his strong patriotism.
[3]Going back to a tradition begun in the legislative assemblies of the French Revolution, democrats and republicans sat on the left, moderates in the center, and conservatives and monarchists on the right. By the 1880s the "left" also included socialists.

the blacks of equatorial Africa, then by what right do you impose regular commerce upon them? They have not called upon you.

M. RAOUL DUVAL   We do not want to impose anything upon them. It is you who wish to do so!

M. JULES MAIGNE   To propose and to impose are two different things!

M. GEORGES PERIN[4]   In any case, you cannot bring about commerce by force.

M. JULES FERRY   I repeat that superior races have a right, because they have a duty. They have the duty to civilize inferior races. . . . *(Approbation from the left. New interruptions from the extreme left and from the right.)* . . .

That is what I have to answer M. Pelletan in regard to the second point upon which he touched.

He then touched upon a third, more delicate, more serious point, and upon which I ask your permission to express myself quite frankly. It is the political side of the question. The honorable M. Pelletan, who is a distinguished writer, always comes up with remarkably precise formulations. I will borrow from him the one which he applied the other day to this aspect of colonial policy.

"It is a system," he says, "which consists of seeking out compensations in the Orient with a circumspect and peaceful seclusion which is actually imposed upon us in Europe."

I would like to explain myself in regard to this. I do not like this word "compensation," and, in effect, not here but elsewhere it has often been used in a treacherous way. If what is being said or insinuated is that a republican minister could possibly believe that there are in any part of the world compensations for the disasters which we have experienced,[5] an injury is being inflicted . . . and an injury undeserved by that government. *(Applause at the center and left.)* I will ward off this injury with all the force of my patrio-

tism! *(New applause and bravos from the same benches.)*

Gentlemen, there are certain considerations which merit the attention of all patriots. The conditions of naval warfare have been profoundly altered. ("Very true! Very true!")

At this time, as you know, a warship cannot carry more than fourteen days' worth of coal, no matter how perfectly it is organized, and a ship which is out of coal is a derelict on the surface of the sea, abandoned to the first person who comes along. Thence the necessity of having on the oceans provision stations, shelters, ports for defense and revictualling. *(Applause at the center and left. Various interruptions.)* And it is for this that we needed Tunisia, for this that we needed Saigon and the Mekong Delta, for this that we need Madagascar, that we are at Diégo-Suarez and Vohemar[6] and will never leave them! *(Applause from a great number of benches.)* Gentlemen, in Europe as it is today, in this competition of so many rivals which we see growing around us, some by perfecting their military or maritime forces, others by the prodigious development of an ever growing population; in a Europe, or rather in a universe of this sort, a policy of peaceful seclusion or abstention is simply the highway to decadence! Nations are great in our times only by means of the activities which they develop; it is not simply "by the peaceful shining forth of institutions" *(Interruptions on the extreme left and right)* that they are great at this hour. . . .

As for me, I am astounded to find the monarchist parties becoming indignant over the fact that the Republic of France is following a policy which does not confine itself to that ideal of modesty, of reserve, and, if you will allow me the expression, of bread and butter *(Interruptions and laughter on the left)* which the representatives of fallen monarchies wish to impose upon France. *(Applause at the center.)* . . .

---

[4]Maigne, Guilloutet, Duval, and Perin were all members of the assembly.

[5]Refers to France's defeat by Prussia and the German states in the Franco-Prussian War of 1870 to 1871.

[6]Madagascar port cities.

(The Republican Party) has shown that it is quite aware that one cannot impose upon France a political ideal conforming to that of nations like independent Belgium and the Swiss Republic; that something else is needed for France: that she cannot be merely a free country, that she must also be a great country, exercising all of her rightful influence over the destiny of Europe, that she ought to propagate this influence throughout the world and carry everywhere that she can her language, her customs, her flag, her arms, and her genius. *(Applause at center and left.)*

# Images of Imperialism in Great Britain
▼▼▼

## 68 ▼ ADVERTISEMENTS AND ILLUSTRATIONS FROM BRITISH BOOKS AND PERIODICALS

Although late-nineteenth-century imperialism had its critics, there is no doubt that in the major imperialist states it had broad support, not just from investors, missionary groups, and civil servants who had direct interests in Africa and Asia but also from the general populace. People avidly read accounts of military victories in distant lands, followed the exploits of explorers and missionaries, and celebrated each time another piece of Africa or Asia came under their nation's control. Imperialism had this appeal for several reasons. For many it confirmed their faith in progress and their belief in the superiority of white, Christian Europeans over the rest of the world's peoples. For ardent nationalists it was an endeavor that tested and demonstrated the nation's strength and vigor. For those who found their lives in industrial society drab and tedious, it provided vicarious adventure, excitement, and a sense of the exotic.

Late-nineteenth-century popular culture provides ample evidence of the public's enthusiasm for imperialism. Especially in Great Britain, the premier imperialist power, novels, poetry, plays, children's books, advertisements, music hall entertainment, and publications of missionary societies were filled with positive imperialist images, themes, and motifs. Youth organizations such as the Boy Scouts (f. 1908) and the Girl Guides (f. 1910) sought to inculcate the values of service to Britain's imperial cause. This constant exposure of the public to material connected with the British Empire reinforced imperialism's appeal and strengthened support for the government's expansionist policies.

The selections in this section provide several examples of how British popular culture propagated imperial values. The first group of illustrations (page 299) appeared in *An ABC for Baby Patriots* by Mrs. Earnest Ames. Designed to be read to young children, it was published in 1898 in London and went through several printings.

The second illustration (page 300) is taken from *The Kipling Reader,* a collection of stories written for young adults by Rudyard Kipling (1865–1936); it was published in 1908 and illustrated by J. Macfarlane. Kipling, one of the most popular British writers of the era, is best remembered for his glorification of the British Empire and the heroism of the British soldier in India and Burma. This particular illustration depicts Scott, a character in the story "William the Conqueror." Set in India during a famine, the story centers on the romance between Scott and

*(text continued on p. 300)*

From *An ABC for Baby Patriots*

E.

E is our Empire
Where the sun never sets;
The larger we make it
The bigger it gets.

I.

I is for India,
Our land in the East
Where everyone goes
To shoot tigers and feast.

W.

W is the Word
Of an Englishman true;
When given, it means
What he says, he will do.

*From* The Kipling Reader

a young woman nicknamed "William" while they toil to save Indians from star-vation. Scott has saved hundreds of babies by feeding them milk from a herd of goats he has managed to maintain. In this illustration he approaches William, who sees "a young man, beautiful as Paris, a god in a halo of gold dust, walking slowly at the head of his flocks, while at his knee ran small naked Cupids."

The third illustration (page 301) is the masthead of a weekly newspaper pub-lished in 1866 by the London Missionary Society, one of a dozen major British missionary groups that supported their government's imperialist policies.

The last illustration (page 301) is an advertisement for Lipton Teas, which ap-peared in 1897 in the popular weekly the *Illustrated London News.* The Lipton Company was founded in Glasgow, Scotland, by the son of a poor Irish shop-keeper, Thomas Lipton (1850–1931). He opened a small food shop in Glasgow in 1871 and by 1890 owned three hundred food stores throughout Great Britain. In 1890 the multimillionaire decided to cash in on the British taste for tea. Growing tea on plantations he owned in India and Ceylon and marketing it in inexpensive small packets that guaranteed freshness, the Lipton Company soon became syn-onymous with tea drinking throughout Europe and the United States. Advertise-ments for its tea appeared regularly in the *Illustrated London News* during the 1890s and early 1900s.

*Masthead from* The Missionary News, *a weekly newspaper published by the London Missionary Society*

*Advertisement for Lipton Teas, which appeared in the* Illustrated London News, *a weekly publication*

*QUESTIONS FOR ANALYSIS*

1. What views of Africans and Asians are being communicated in each of the illustrations?
2. What message is being communicated about the benefits colonial subjects are accruing from their status?
3. What images are being communicated about the British in their role as imperialists?
4. What concrete examples of nationalism can you see in the various illustrations?
5. How many of the justifications for imperialism presented in Jules Ferry's speech (source 67) can you find represented in the illustrations?
6. Using evidence in the illustrations alone, what conclusions can you draw about the reasons for imperialism's popularity within the general British population?

▼▼▼

# Europeans on the Move: Nineteenth-Century Migrations

Migration — over land and water, by craftsmen and conquerors, hunters and herdsmen, farmers and traders — has been a part of human history from its beginning. But in the nineteenth century more people were on the move over longer distances than ever before. Indians migrated to Southeast Asia, the West Indies, Africa, and South America; Chinese moved to Malaya, Singapore, and the Americas; Japanese moved to Canada, the United States, and South America. And most dramatically of all, millions of Europeans migrated to Argentina, Australia, New Zealand, Africa, Canada, and especially the United States.

Although a small number of nineteenth-century migrants left their homes to escape political or religious oppression, the overwhelming majority did so to improve their economic condition, or, to be more precise, to escape economic disaster. Throughout Eurasia decades of population growth had created widespread economic hardship. China's population increased from 142 million in the mid eighteenth century to 432 million around 1850, and to more than 450 million in 1900. India's population increased from 150 million in 1850 to 250 million in 1881, while the population of Europe grew from 187 million in 1800, to 266 million at midcentury, and 435 million by 1914. This demographic surge was especially damaging to peasants, who faced land shortages and rising rents. In Europe problems were compounded by the mechanization of agriculture, which limited the need for rural labor, and by the mechanization of the textile industry, which took away the employment of thousands of home-based spinners and weavers.

For millions of land-hungry Europeans, the open spaces and cheap land of Australia, New Zealand, and the Americas beckoned, as did the demand for labor in heavy industry, construction, mining, commerce, food processing, manufacturing, and services. These Europeans could now think seriously of long-distance migration because railroads and steamships made travel cheaper, more reliable, and quicker than in the age of stagecoach and sail. The average sailing time from Europe to the Americas in the 1860s was forty-four days, but by then steamers were already making the trip in fourteen days, and by 1900 the trip was reduced to ten days or a week. At the same time competition among steamship companies and booking agents and subsidies from labor-starved employers drove down the price of ocean travel. As a result, by the end of the century it made economic sense for a large number of Italians, known as "swallows," to travel to Argentina every year to harvest the wheat crop, then return home once the work was done.

From the early nineteenth century to 1914, approximately seventy million migrants left Europe, of whom slightly better than 70 percent went to North America, slightly more than 20 percent went to South America, and the remainder, primarily English, went to South Africa, Australia, and New Zealand. It was the greatest migration in human history. It caused profound changes and created innumerable tensions, both in the lands the migrants left and in those that received them.

## The Lures and Pitfalls of Migration
▼▼▼

## 69 ▼ *Gottfried Menzel,*
## *THE UNITED STATES OF NORTH AMERICA,*
## *WITH SPECIAL REFERENCE TO*
## *GERMAN EMIGRATION*

The era of mass migration from Europe to the United States dates from the 1840s and 1850s, when 4.2 million immigrants landed from Europe. Just short of three quarters of these immigrants arrived between 1845 and 1855, the decade that witnessed the largest immigration in proportion to the total population (around 20 million) in U.S. history. The bulk of these immigrants came from Ireland and Germany, and a small percentage came from Great Britain, Norway, Sweden, the Netherlands, and Switzerland. Unlike the Irish immigrants, who were overwhelmingly Roman Catholic peasants who left Ireland because of eviction from their lands or the famine following the potato blight from 1845 to the early 1850s, the German immigrants included Lutherans, Catholics, and Jews, who by occupation were a mix of farmers, artisans, professionals, and tradespeople. They left Germany because of population pressures, land shortages, and guild restrictions, and in a few instances because of the failure of the liberal/nationalist German revolution of 1848. Growing from 400,000 German immigrants in the 1840s to a peak of more than 1.5 million in the 1890s, immigration from Germany then rapidly declined when German industrialization created a large demand for labor at home.

During the first decade of large-scale German migration, dozens of guides and "advice books" were published for would-be German immigrants to the United

States. Most had a strong bias in favor of migration, and tended to depict the United States positively and unrealistically. A more balanced point of view characterized the guide book written by the German botanist Gottfreid Menzel (1798–1889), who had visited the United States in the early 1840s. His book, *The United States of North America,* appeared in 1853.

---

## QUESTIONS FOR ANALYSIS

1. What can be inferred from Menzel's guidebook about the motives for German emigration? Make sure to consider his list of "noteworthy advantages" offered by the United States.
2. Why, according to Menzel, do many German immigrants have inaccurate notions about their prospects in the United States?
3. What can be inferred about the target audience of Menzel's book?
4. What are the main obstacles to a German immigrant's success in the United States, according to Menzel?
5. According to Menzel, what kind of reception can the German immigrant expect from Americans?
6. What is Menzel's overall conclusion about the German migrant and the United States? In his view, was emigration a worthwhile gamble?

In Germany as in most of the European states many people are dissatisfied with the state organization and institutions. They feel themselves hampered by the government, complain of lack of freedom, of too much government, and the like, and direct their gaze to the free states of the great North American Republic, as the land of desired freedom. . . .

Germans who voluntarily exchanged their homes in Germany for new homes in North America to obtain greater freedom, especially those who have emigrated since the year 1848,[1] always say in their accounts from America that they are entirely satisfied with American freedom, and sincerely pity all those who are not yet sharers in it. But through the newspapers of the day other opinions are heard. There are many things with which they are really dissatisfied. . . .

Much greater is the number of those who leave their fatherland on account of the poverty of its material resources and in order to better their condition in America. For many people industrial conditions in Germany are such that you cannot blame them for emigrating when they learn that in North America there are far greater productive natural resources and that work has a greater value than in Germany.

He who in Germany has to suffer from want and misery, or must expect these in the near future, finds that hope of better fortune overcomes his attachment to the Fatherland. He easily separates himself from his old home and wanders to a distant land believing that he will find life more favorable there.

That it is easier to make a living in America cannot be denied; but it is a matter of regret that those who could better their condition in this way frequently lack the means. Many people who take this risk find only their misfortune or ruin. The numbers of those who return to Germany

---

[1] In 1848 a wave of liberal, nationalist revolutions swept through the German states, but the revolutions were suppressed, and Germany remained politically divided and authoritarian. It is estimated that ten to fifteen thousand Germans migrated to the United States for political reasons as a result of these failed revolutions.

from America prove that many are not successful there. When an emigrant ship is prepared to sail from the harbor of New York for Hamburg or Bremen, there are usually twenty or more people leaving the land of their disappointed hopes for the old home country after one or two years' bitter experiences. They have left, out of their fortunes, with scarcely the necessary money for the return passage. Still others would follow them if they had the means for the trip or if they were not ashamed to return.

Therefore everyone who is thinking of emigrating to America should take care to determine whether or not he is fit for America. He should carefully weigh what he leaves here against what he may find there, lest he should be guilty of too great haste or light-mindedness and make a mistake that he may regret only too soon and bitterly. . . .

A great many books about emigration to America have been written, and every year new ones appear. . . . A book written against emigration, or one advising emigration only for the few, would have little charm and would find few purchasers. But as soon as a book appears which describes the land to which the emigrant would go as a land of paradise, then it is sold and read diligently, and thousands are moved in this way to become emigrants. . . . Through this one-sided presentation of American conditions many are lured to emigrate. It is obvious that the countless speculators who every year gain many millions from emigrants will make a great effort to bring to the attention of the people many books through which the desire for emigration is awakened and increased. They are themselves completely indifferent to the fate of the emigrants, and if emigration turns out to be for their ruin they do not care. . . .

But the descriptions and the letters of the emigrants to their relatives and friends and acquaintances — are they not then true and reliable? This I deny. First, because no one who has emigrated will confess that he was disappointed, that he had not found there that on which he had counted with certainty and which he had so joyfully anticipated. He is very right in thinking that few in the old home will have sympathetic pity for him, and many only malicious joy and bitter ridicule. . . .

Secondly, the immigrants wish, for many reasons, to have many of their relatives and countrymen follow them and settle near them. On the one hand, because of the neighborly society and support, the need of which many of them have bitterly experienced. On the other hand, one desires everywhere new arrivals of immigrants because they will buy land, and stock, and so on from those already settled, by which ready money, of which there is always need, comes into this part of the country and the value of the land and its produce increases. . . .

## WHAT DOES NORTH AMERICA OFFER THAT IS GOOD?

This great country offers its inhabitants noteworthy advantages which may be summarized as follows:

— Although the citizens of the United States are not, as is popularly supposed, free from taxes, yet the taxes on land and cattle which the farmer has to pay are not high, and artisans pay no taxes on their business.

— The citizens are, during a certain age, under obligation to serve in the militia, but except in the case of war this is rarely asked of them except perhaps for suppression of a riot. For regular military service volunteers are always available, since they are well paid. The quartering of soldiers in time of peace is not allowed.

— Complete freedom in the trades and professions, hunting and fishing is allowed to everyone. . . .

— There is no difference in rank. The terms "upper class" and "lower class" have no significance. The public official has no advantage not shared by the farmer, the merchant, or the teamster.

— North America, as a country with fertile land still partly unoccupied, a country thinly populated with flourishing trade and general freedom of trade, offers far greater and more abundant means of livelihood than Germany.

— Labor there has a high, and cost of living a lower, value; therefore on the whole the people are far less oppressed by want and need and the tormenting anxiety for one's daily bread.

Against the advantages just enumerated . . . the following disadvantages will not please those who are eager to emigrate.

— The German in America is a complete stranger. Everything is strange, the country, the climate, laws, and customs. One ought to realize what it means to be an alien in a far distant land. More than this, the German in America is despised as alien, and he must often hear the nickname "Dutchman,"[2] at least until he learns to speak English fluently. It is horrible what the German immigrants must endure from the Americans, Irish, and English. I was more than once a witness to the way German immigrants were forced by the American captain or pilot with terrible brutality, kicking, etc., to carry wood from the shore to the boat, although they had paid their full fare and had not been engaged for those duties. Only in the places where the Germans are in the majority does the newly arrived immigrant find, after all the hardships of the journey, an endurable existence. The Americans are accustomed to alter their behavior to him only after he has become Americanized. The rabble who also emigrated from Germany in former times have brought the German name into discredit.

— The educational institutions are, in America, defective and expensive or they are completely lacking. Therefore parents can give their children the necessary education only through great sacrifices or, in case they are poor, the children must be allowed to run wild. . . .

— The majority of the Germans emigrating to America wish to seek their fortunes in agriculture. But the purchase of land has its dangers and difficulties. The price of the land is, in proportion to its productivity, not so low as is generally believed. . . . Where labor is so dear and where agricultural products are so cheap, there no one can exist except the man who is able and willing to do all his own work and does not need to employ outside labor. . . .

I have been approached since my return from North America by a large number of persons for information concerning conditions there and for advice concerning their projected plan of emigration. Either because of their personal qualifications or circumstances, hardly one-fourth of these people could be advised with confidence to undertake this important step. I found most of them unsuitable for emigration for the following more or less serious reasons:

*A weak constitution or shattered health.* — The emigrant to America needs a strong and healthy body.

*Advanced age.* — The man who is already over forty years of age, unless he has some sons who can help him with their labor, cannot count upon success and prosperity in America.

*Childlessness with somewhat advanced age.* — What will a married couple do when their capacity to labor disappears with the years? They could not earn enough when young to support them in later years. If they have a substantial property to bring over from Germany, then emigration would be a very unwise step for them, since for the man without employment living is much higher in America than in Europe, especially if one needs servants or cannot do without the comforts and luxuries of life.

*Lack of experience in the field of labor on the part of those who expect to establish their fortunes there through hard labor.* — . . . Many harbor the delusion that they are already accustomed to the labor required there, or that they will easily learn it if they have worked a little here in this country. But he who has not from his youth up been performing continuously the most severe labor, so much the more will he lack, in America, where work is harder, the necessary strength and ability. He will

---

[2]The term "Dutchman" was derived from the German word for German, *deutsch,* pronounced "doitch."

certainly not be a competent and contented working man. . . . Those who spent their youth in schools, offices, or in other sedentary work, play in America a very sad and pitiable rôle.

*A slow easy-going habit of living a life of ease and comfort.* — One may find in the great cities of North America all the comforts and conveniences which European cities offer, but in America they are only for the few — for the rich — and to this class German emigrants do not usually belong. Not many persons in America can command even the comforts of the ordinary citizen of Europe. Many people seek compensation in whiskey for their many privations and hardships and this is the way to certain ruin.

*Destitution.* — If the passage for a single emigrant costs only 50 thaler, at least as much again must be counted for the land journey here and in America. Unfortunately this amount is beyond the reach of those who would have the best chance of improving their condition in America. The artisan, even though he cannot carry on his business there independently but must work in great workshops and factories must often make yet a further land journey in order to find the most suitable place, and he needs, especially if he has a family, a not inconsiderable amount of money. . . . If the means of traveling are not available, he falls into difficulties and distress, is obliged to sell the effects he brought with him for a trifling sum, or considers himself fortunate if he finds a job anywhere at the lowest wage — a wage that will barely keep him and his family from hunger.

## "The Gates Should No Longer Be Left Unguarded"

▼▼▼

## 70 ▼ Henry Cabot Lodge, *SPEECH TO THE UNITED STATES SENATE, MARCH 16, 1896*

In the decades following the Civil War, immigration to the United States reached new heights, with more than twenty million new arrivals between 1870 and 1910. Although these millions included an appreciable number of Japanese and Chinese, close to 98 percent of them came from Europe. Unlike previous European migrants who had mostly come from England, Germany, and Ireland, the migrants of the late nineteenth century were mainly from Italy, the Austro-Hungarian Empire, Russia, and Poland (then divided among Russia, Germany, and Austria-Hungary). Most were Roman Catholics or, in the case of many of the emigrants from Poland and Russia, Jews.

Anti-immigrant sentiment, or nativism, which had flared up in the 1840s and 1850s in response to the influx of Germans and Irish, once again became a powerful force in American life. Workers and small businessmen worried about competition from the new immigrants, many Protestants deplored the growing numbers of Catholics and Jews, and Americans in general wondered if the republic could survive if the country was overrun by people unfamiliar with democracy and constitutionalism. Anti-immigrant prejudice was given a "scientific" basis by contemporary theories of race, which ranked the world's races in a hierarchy with northern European whites (except the Irish) at the top. Although authors disagreed about where specifically other peoples should be ranked, most agreed that among Europeans, Italians, Slavs, and Jews were near the bottom but at least were superior to Asians and Africans.

Anti-immigrant groups had some legislative success. In 1870 Congress passed the Naturalization Act, which barred Chinese from citizenship. This was followed in 1882 by the Chinese Exclusion Act, which barred Chinese immigration altogether. Then in the 1890s the Immigration Restriction League (IRL), founded in 1894, pushed for legislation to require new immigrants to pass a literacy test, which, IRL members hoped, most would fail. A leader in the fight for immigration restriction was the distinguished Bostonian Henry Cabot Lodge, who served in the House of Representatives from 1887 to 1893 and the Senate from 1893 until his death in 1924. He presented the following remarks to the Senate in support of anti-immigration legislation under consideration in 1896. The bill failed to pass, and millions of immigrants continued to pour into the United States until Congress passed a series of restrictive laws in the 1920s.

## QUESTIONS FOR ANALYSIS

1. What according to Lodge distinguishes "desirable" and "undesirable" immigrants?
2. What fears does Lodge have about the future of the United States unless immigration is limited?
3. What are Lodge's views of race, and how do they affect his attitude toward immigration? According to Lodge what are the qualities of the various "races" he discusses?
4. The bill Lodge supported was defeated in the Senate. What arguments against immigration restriction do you think were made by the bill's opponents?

## RESTRICTING IMMIGRATION

This bill is intended to amend the existing law so as to restrict still further immigration to the United States. Paupers, diseased persons, convicts, and contract laborers are now excluded. By this bill it is proposed to make a new class of excluded immigrants and add to those which have just been named the totally ignorant. . . .

Three methods of obtaining this further restriction have been widely discussed of late years and in various forms have been brought to the attention of Congress. The first was the imposition of a capitation tax on all immigrants. . . .

The second scheme was to restrict immigration by requiring consular certification of immigrants.[1] . . .

The third method was to exclude all immigrants who could neither read nor write, and this is the plan which was adopted by the committee. . . . In their report the committee have shown by statistics, which have been collected and tabulated with great care, the emigrants who would be affected by this illiteracy test. . . . It is found, in the first place, that the illiteracy test will bear most heavily upon the Italians, Russians, Poles, Hungarians, Greeks, and Asiatics, and very lightly, or not at all, upon English-speaking

[1]U.S. consuls in overseas cities would make judgments about immigration eligibility.

emigrants or Germans, Scandinavians, and French. In other words, the races most affected by the illiteracy test are those whose emigration to this country has begun within the last twenty years and swelled rapidly to enormous proportions, races with which the English-speaking people have never hitherto assimilated, and who are most alien to the great body of the people of the United States.

On the other hand, immigrants from the United Kingdom and of those races which are most closely related to the English-speaking people, and who with the English-speaking people themselves founded the American colonies and built up the United States, are affected but little by the proposed test. These races would not be prevented by this law from coming to this country in practically undiminished numbers. These kindred races also are those who alone go to the Western and Southern states, where immigrants are desired, and take up our unoccupied lands. The races which would suffer most seriously by exclusion under the proposed bill furnish the immigrants who do not go to the West or South, where immigration is needed, but who remain on the Atlantic seaboard, where immigration is not needed and where their presence is most injurious and undesirable. . . .

## IMMIGRATION AND
## THE ECONOMY

There is no one thing which does so much to bring about a reduction of wages and to injure the American wage earner as the unlimited introduction of cheap foreign labor through unrestricted immigration. Statistics show that the change in the race character of our immigration has been accompanied by a corresponding decline in its quality. The number of skilled mechanics and of persons trained to some occupation or pursuit has fallen off, while the number of those without occupation or training, that is, who are totally unskilled, has risen in our recent immigration to enormous proportions. This low,

unskilled labor is the most deadly enemy of the American wage earner, and does more than anything else toward lowering his wages and forcing down his standard of living. . . .

There is no danger, at present at all events, to our workingmen from the coming of skilled mechanics or of trained and educated men with a settled occupation or pursuit, for immigrants of this class will never seek to lower the American standard of life and wages. On the contrary, they desire the same standard for themselves. But there is an appalling danger to the American wage earner from the flood of low, unskilled, ignorant, foreign labor which has poured into the country for some years past, and which not only takes lower wages but accepts a standard of life and living so low that the American workingman can not compete with it.

## IMMIGRATION AND CITIZENSHIP

The English-speaking race . . . has been made slowly during the centuries. Nothing has happened thus far to radically change it here. In the United States, after allowing for the variations produced by new climatic influences and changed conditions of life and of political institutions, it is still in the great essentials fundamentally the same race. The additions in this country until the present time have been from kindred people or from those with whom we have been long allied and who speak the same language. By those who look at this question superficially we hear it often said that the English-speaking people, especially in America, are a mixture of races. Analysis shows that the actual mixture of blood in the English-speaking race is very small, and that while the English-speaking people are derived through different channels, no doubt, there is among them nonetheless an overwhelming preponderance of the same race stock, that of the great Germanic tribes who reached from Norway to the Alps. They have been welded together by more than a thousand years of wars, conquests, migrations, and struggles, both at home and abroad, and in so doing they have attained a fixity and definiteness of national character unknown to any other people. . . .

When we speak of a race, then, we do not mean its expressions in art or in language, or its achievements in knowledge. We mean the moral and intellectual characters, which in their association make the soul of a race and which represent the product of all its past, the inheritance of all its ancestors, and the motives of all its conduct. The men of each race possess an indestructible stock of ideas, traditions, sentiments, modes of thought, an unconscious inheritance from their ancestors, upon which argument has no effect. What make a race are their mental and, above all, their moral characteristics, the slow growth and accumulation of centuries of toil and conflict. These are the qualities which determine their social efficiency as a people, which make one race rise and another fall, which we draw out of a dim past through many generations of ancestors, about which we cannot argue, but in which we blindly believe, and which guide us in our short-lived generation as they have guided the race itself across the centuries. . . .

Those qualities are moral far more than intellectual, and it is on the moral qualities of the English-speaking race that our history, our victories, and all our future rest. There is only one way in which you can lower those qualities or weaken those characteristics and that is by breeding them out. If a lower race mixes with a higher in sufficient numbers, history teaches us that the lower race will prevail. The lower race will absorb the higher, not the higher the lower, when the two strains approach equality in numbers. . . . The lowering of a great race means not only its own decline but that of human civilization. . . .

Mr. President, more precious even than forms of government are the mental and moral qualities which make what we call our race. While those stand unimpaired, all is safe. When those decline, all is imperiled. They are exposed to but a single danger and that is by changing the quality of our race and citizenship through the wholesale infusion of races whose traditions and inheritances, whose thoughts and whose beliefs are wholly alien to ours and with whom we have never assimilated or even been associated in the past. The danger has begun. . . .

The time has certainly come, if not to stop at least to check, to sift, and to restrict those immigrants. In careless strength, with generous hand, we have kept our gates wide open to all the world. If we do not close them, we should at least place sentinels beside them to challenge those who would pass through. The gates which admit men to the United States and to citizenship in the great republic should no longer be left unguarded.

# Chapter 9

## Western Pressures, Nationalism, and Reform in Africa, Southwest Asia, and India in the 1800s

Africa, Southwest Asia, and India all shared a common experience in the nineteenth century: All three were engulfed in a tidal wave of change set off by the political, economic, and cultural onslaught of Europe. Until the 1800s, contact with Europeans for the peoples and rulers of these regions mainly had meant dealing with merchants, who did their business on the coast and traded with the indulgence of local rulers who often benefited from their activities. Only in the case of the Ottoman Empire were relations with Europeans marked by warfare. And only in the case of India in the closing decades of the eighteenth century were Europeans, in this instance the British, able to establish extensive political authority. Until the nineteenth century, Europe's impact on the intellectual, cultural, and religious life of Africa, India, and Southwest Asia was negligible.

By the early twentieth century the politics of all three regions had been transformed as a result of European penetration. In the 1800s the British extended their Indian empire until it virtually encompassed the whole Indian subcontinent. Previously independent Africa also became a victim of European imperialism. The main difference was that India had but one colonial master; Africa had half a dozen. Persia experienced growing British and Russian interference in its affairs, culminating in the Anglo-Russian Agreement of 1907, which divided the country into a Russian-dominated north, a British-dominated south, and a nominally independent center.

The Ottoman Empire survived, but lost thousands of square miles of territory. In North Africa, which was still part of the Ottoman Empire despite the near independence of its rulers, Algeria and Tunisia became French colonies, and Egypt became a British protectorate. In southeastern Europe, Greece, Serbia, Romania, Bulgaria, Montenegro, and Albania all gained their independence from Ottoman rule, often with the aid of European powers. In addition, Europeans seriously compromised the sovereignty of the Ottoman state itself. Foreign businessmen, who controlled the empire's banks, railroads, and mines, regulated Ottoman tariff policy and were exempt from many of the empire's laws and taxes. Beginning in 1881 Europeans supervised the collection and disbursement of state revenues through the Ottoman Public Debt Administration, an agency established mainly to guarantee payment of the government's huge debts to European creditors.

In all three regions European penetration threatened ruling elites and traditional political institutions, making some irrelevant, destroying others, and inspiring reform in a few. It also undermined these regions' traditional economies. Europeans built railroads and telegraph lines, undertook huge engineering projects such as the Suez Canal, created new demands for raw materials and agricultural goods, and aggressively marketed their own manufactured products. European penetration also introduced unsettling new ideas and values through intensified missionary activity, the introduction of the printing press, and the promotion of Western science and education. In a matter of decades, the peoples of Africa, Southwest Asia, and India were wrenched from their past and forced to face an uncertain future.

# The European Assault on Africa

Paradoxically, the century that saw the near total submission of Africa to European rule began with an effort by Europeans to outlaw their main business in Africa, the slave trade. Responding to both humanitarian and economic arguments, several states, including Denmark, France, the United States, and, most importantly, Great Britain, banned slave trading around 1800. Unexpectedly, this led to more, not less, European involvement in Africa. Palm oil, ivory, cocoa, coffee, rubber, and other goods soon replaced slaves as items of trade, and by the 1850s this "legitimate" trade was more profitable for the British than the old slave trade. Then in the closing decades of the nineteenth century, African-European relations underwent a radical transformation, and the whole continent except Liberia and Ethiopia succumbed to European rule.

The takeover took just two decades. It began in earnest in 1878, when King Leopold II of Belgium (r. 1865–1909) and his business associates gained control of lands in the Congo River basin through the efforts of their representative, Welsh explorer Henry M. Stanley (1841–1904). In 1880 Italian-born explorer Pierre Savorgnan de Brazza (1852–1905) signed the first of hundreds of treaties with African chieftains that laid the basis for what became the sprawling colony of French Equatorial Africa. In 1881 France established a protectorate over Tunisia, and in 1882 Great Britain occupied Egypt. In 1884 and 1885 thirteen European nations and the United States attended the Congress of Berlin, which established guidelines for the European conquest of Africa. By 1914, when World War I began, Africa had become a vast European colony.

Africans did not passively acquiesce to the European onslaught. Many Africans fought back, but Europe's artillery, high-explosive shells, and machine guns doomed their efforts. In 1898 the Battle of Omdurman in modern Sudan resulted in some eleven thousand casualties for the Sudanese and forty for the British and their Egyptian troops.

# "With the View of Bettering . . . Our Country"
▼▼▼

## 71 ▼ Royal Niger Company, STANDARD TREATY

During the partition of Africa, African chieftains signed hundreds of treaties that effectively gave European states or trading companies control of African lands and resources. The following document is an example of such a treaty.

This "standard treaty" was utilized in the late 1880s by representatives of the Royal Niger Company, founded in 1879 as the United African Company by the merchant adventurer George Goldie Taubman. Competing with the French for trade on the Niger River outside the control of the African states on the Niger delta, the company was commissioned by Queen Victoria in 1886 as the Royal Niger Company and given a trade monopoly and the right to exercise political authority in the region. The numerous treaties it signed with the chieftains of the region served as the basis for the Niger Districts Protectorate, which in turn became the British colony of Nigeria. After receiving the royal charter, the company's representatives had to move quickly to head off the French, so they drew up a standard treaty for use throughout the region. One needed only to fill in the blanks.

## QUESTIONS FOR ANALYSIS

1. By accepting this treaty, what were the chieftains giving up?
2. What benefits were the Africans to receive by signing the treaty?
3. What does use of the standard treaty signify about English attitudes toward and knowledge of the Africans?
4. What does the treaty indicate about the motives of the British in Africa?

We, the undersigned Chiefs of _____, with the view to the bettering of the condition of our country and people, do this day cede to the Royal Niger Company, for ever, the whole of our territory extending from _____.

We also give to the said Royal Niger Company full power to settle all native disputes arising from any cause whatever, and we pledge ourselves not to enter into any war with other tribes without the sanction of the said Royal Niger Company.

We understand that the said Royal Niger Company have full power to mine, farm, and build in any portion of our country.

We bind ourselves not to have any intercourse with any strangers or foreigners except through the said Royal Niger Company.

In consideration of the foregoing, the said Royal Niger Company (Chartered and Limited) bind themselves not to interfere with any of the native laws or customs of the country, consistently with the maintenance of order and good government.

The said Royal Niger Company agree to pay native owners of land a reasonable amount for any portion they may require.

The said Royal Niger Company bind themselves to protect the said Chiefs from the attacks of any neighboring aggressive tribes.

The said Royal Niger Company also agree to pay the said Chiefs _____ measures native value.

We, the undersigned witnesses, do hereby solemnly declare that the _____ Chiefs whose names are placed opposite their respective crosses have in our presence affixed their crosses of their own free will and consent, and that the said _____ has in our presence affixed his signature.

Done in triplicate at _____, this _____ day of _____, 188_____.

*Declaration by interpreter*  I, _____, of _____, do hereby solemnly declare that I am well acquainted with the language of the country, and that on the _____ day of _____, 188_____, I truly and faithfully explained the above Agreement to all the Chiefs present, and that they understood its meaning.

# The Fate of the Ndebele

▼▼▼

## 72 ▼ *Ndansi Kumalo, HIS STORY*

If one seeks proof of the remarkable changes in Africa during the nineteenth and twentieth centuries, consider the fate of the *Ndebele* (pronounced en-duh-bee'-lee) and the life of one of their sons, Ndansi Kumalo. In the early nineteenth century the Ndebele were pastoralists living in southeastern Africa, a region of political turmoil and economic hardship as a result of overpopulation and drought. In the 1820s they fled from the warriors of the Zulu chieftain Shaka, who in just a few years created a large and formidable Zulu state in southeastern Africa. The Ndebele moved to a region north of the Vaal River but ten years later were forced off their land by Boer *trekkers,* Dutch pioneers from the south who sought grazing land for their cattle. The Ndebele moved north of the Limpopo River to a region that is part of modern Zimbabwe. Despite their years of flight, they were able to subdue other groups in the region and establish a sizable kingdom with a population of one hundred thousand.

But the Ndebele could not escape danger. This time it came from the British, who, under the famous imperialist, Cecil Rhodes, were anxious to exploit the region's mineral wealth. In 1888 the Ndebele chieftain, Lobengula, signed an agreement with Rhodes that gave the South Africa Company mining rights in exchange for one thousand rifles and a monthly stipend of one hundred pounds. Friction grew when European settlers began establishing farmsteads around 1890, and war broke out in 1893. The Ndebele were defeated, and they were defeated again when they rose up against the British in 1897. The Ndebele then made one last journey to a vast but arid reservation their new masters provided.

One of the Ndebele who made this journey was Ndansi Kumalo. Born in the late 1870s, he was raised as a warrior to protect Ndebele land and raid neighbors for wives and cattle. He fought against the British in the 1890s and took up farming after the Ndebele's defeat. In 1932 he caught the attention of a British filmmaker who was in Southern Rhodesia to make *Rhodes of Africa,* on the life of Cecil Rhodes. He was recruited to play the part of Lobengula, the Ndebele chieftain. To complete the film he traveled to England, where he took in the sights of London and made his first plane flight. While there, he also related his life story to the English Africanist, Margery Perham, whose transcription of it serves as the basis for the following excerpt. *Rhodes of Africa* was a modest success, and after it opened, Ndansi Kumalo returned to Africa, where he rejoined his large family. In the following excerpt he describes events of the 1890s.

---

## QUESTIONS FOR ANALYSIS

1. Who was to blame for the outbreak of hostilities between the Ndebele and the British in 1893?
2. How did conditions following the war lead to the 1897 rebellion?
3. The condition of the Ndebele rapidly deteriorated after the suppression of the rebellion. Why?

4. Aside from raising revenue, what might the British have hoped to achieve by imposing, then raising, taxes on the Ndebele?

5. What economic changes did the Ndebele experience as a result of their subjection to the Europeans?

6. Do you agree with Ndansi Kumalo that the arrival of Europeans was a mixed blessing? Why?

We were terribly upset and very angry at the coming of the white men, for Lobengula . . . was under her . . . [The Queen's] protection and it was quite unjustified that white men should come with force into our country.[1] . . . Lobengula had no war in his heart: he had always protected the white men and been good to them. If he had meant war, would he have sent our regiments far away to the north at this moment? As far as I know the trouble began in this way. Gandani, a chief who was sent out, reported that some of the Mashona[2] had taken the king's cattle; some regiments were detailed to follow and recover them. They followed the Mashona to Ziminto's people. Gandani had strict instructions not to molest the white people established in certain parts and to confine himself to the people who had taken the cattle. The commander was given a letter which he had to produce to the Europeans and tell them what the object of the party was. But the members of the party were restless and went without reporting to the white people and killed a lot of Mashonas. The pioneers were very angry and said, "You have trespassed into our part." They went with the letter, but only after they had killed some people, and the white men said, "You have done wrong, you should have brought the letter first and then we should have given you permission to follow the cattle." The commander received orders from the white people to get out, and up to a certain point which he could not possibly reach in the time allowed. A force followed them up and they defended themselves. When the pioneers turned out there was a fight at Shangani and at Bembezi. . . .

The next news was that the white people had entered Bulawayo; the King's kraal[3] had been burnt down and the King had fled. Of the cattle very few were recovered; most fell into the hands of the white people. Only a very small portion were found and brought to Shangani where the King was, and we went there to give him any assistance we could. . . . Three of our leaders mounted their horses and followed up the King and he wanted to know where his cattle were; they said they had fallen into the hands of the whites, only a few were left. He said, "Go back and bring them along." But they did not go back again; the white forces had occupied Bulawayo and they went into the Matoppos. Then the white people came to where we were living and sent word round that all chiefs and warriors should go into Bulawayo and discuss peace, for the King had gone and they wanted to make peace. . . . The white people said, "Now that your King has deserted you, we occupy your country. Do you submit to us?" What could we do? "If you are sincere, come back and bring in all your arms, guns, and spears." We did so. . . .

So we surrendered to the white people and were told to go back to our homes and live our usual lives and attend to our crops. But the white men sent native police who did abominable things; they were cruel and assaulted a lot of our people and helped themselves to our cattle and goats. These policemen were not our own people; any-

---

[1] In the agreement Lobengula signed with Rhodes in 1888 the British government (Her Majesty's government) guaranteed there would be no English settlers on Ndebele land and no decrease of Lobengula's authority. Lobengula's con-

cessions angered many of his warriors, who began to press for war against the Europeans.
[2] Pastoralists subject to the Ndebele.
[3] The stockade where the king lived.

body was made a policeman. We were treated like slaves. They came and were overbearing and we were ordered to carry their clothes and bundles. They interfered with our wives and our daughters and molested them. In fact, the treatment we received was intolerable. We thought it best to fight and die rather than bear it. How the rebellion started I do not know; there was no organization, it was like a fire that suddenly flames up. We had been flogged by native police and then they rubbed salt water in the wounds. There was much bitterness because so many of our cattle were branded and taken away from us; we had no property, nothing we could call our own. We said, "It is no good living under such conditions; death would be better — let us fight." Our King gone, we had submitted to the white people and they ill-treated us until we became desperate and tried to make an end of it all. We knew that we had very little chance because their weapons were so much superior to ours. But we meant to fight to the last, feeling that even if we could not beat them we might at least kill a few of them and so have some sort of revenge.

I fought in the rebellion. We used to look out for valleys where the white men were likely to approach. We took cover behind rocks and trees and tried to ambush them. We were forced by the nature of our weapons not to expose ourselves. I had a gun, a breech-loader. They — the white men — fought us with big guns and Maxims[4] and rifles.

I remember a fight in the Matoppos when we charged the white men. There were some hundreds of us; the white men also were as many. We charged them at close quarters: we thought we had a good chance to kill them but the Maxims were too much for us. We drove them off at the first charge, but they returned and formed up again. We made a second charge, but they were too strong for us. I cannot say how many white people were killed, but we think it was

quite a lot. . . . Many of our people were killed in this fight: I saw four of my cousins shot. One was shot in the jaw and the whole of his face was blown away — like this — and he died. One was hit between the eyes; another here, in the shoulder; another had part of his ear shot off. We made many charges but each time we were beaten off, until at last the white men packed up and retreated. But for the Maxims, it would have been different. . . .

So peace was made. Many of our people had been killed, and now we began to die of starvation; and then came the rinderpest[5] and the cattle that were still left to us perished. We could not help thinking that all these dreadful things were brought by the white people. We struggled, and the Government helped us with grain; and by degrees we managed to get crops and pulled through. Our cattle were practically wiped out, but a few were left and from them we slowly bred up our herds again. We were offered work in the mines and farms to earn money and so were able to buy back some cattle. At first, of course, we were not used to going out to work, but advice was given that the chief should advise the young people to go out to work, and gradually they went. At first we received a good price for our cattle and sheep and goats. Then the tax came. It was 10s.[6] a year. Soon the Government said, "That is too little, you must contribute more; you must pay £1." We did so. Then those who took more than one wife were taxed; 10s. for each additional wife. The tax is heavy, but that is not all. We are also taxed for our dogs; 5s. for a dog. Then we were told we were living on private land; the owners wanted rent in addition to the Government tax; some 10s. some £1, some £2 a year. . . .

Would I like to have the old days back? Well, the white men have brought some good things. For a start, they brought us European implements — plows; we can buy European clothes, which are an advance. The Government has arranged

---

[4]Invented by the American-born engineer Hiram S. Maxim, the Maxim gun was an early machine gun.

[5]An acute infectious disease of cattle.
[6]s. = shilling, one-twentieth of a pound.

for education and through that, when our children grow up, they may rise in status. We want them to be educated and civilized and make better citizens. Even in our own time there were troubles, there was much fighting and many innocent people were killed. It is infinitely better to have peace instead of war, and our treatment generally by the officials is better than it was at first. But, under the white people, we still have our troubles. Economic conditions are telling on us very severely. We are on land where the rainfall is scanty, and things will not grow well. In our own time we could pick our own country, but now all the best land has been taken by the white people. We get hardly any price for our cattle; we find it hard to meet our money obligations. If we have crops to spare we get very little for them; we find it difficult to make ends meet and wages are very low. When I view the position, I see that our rainfall has diminished, we have suffered drought and have poor crops and we do not see any hope of improvement, but all the same our taxes do not diminish. We see no prosperous days ahead of us. There is one thing we think an injustice. When we have plenty of grain the prices are very low, but the moment we are short of grain and we have to buy from Europeans at once the price is high. If when we have hard times and find it difficult to meet our obligations some of these burdens were taken off us it would gladden our hearts. As it is, if we do raise anything, it is never our own: all, or most of it, goes back in taxation. We can never save any money. If we could, we could help ourselves: we could build ourselves better houses; we could buy modern means of traveling about, a cart, or donkeys or mules.

As to my own life, I have had twelve wives altogether, five died and seven are alive. I have twenty-six children alive, five have died. Of my sons five are married and are all at work farming; three young children go to school. I hope the younger children will all go to school. I think it is a good thing to go to school.

There are five schools in our district. Quite a number of people are Christians, but I am too old to change my ways. In our religion we believe that when anybody dies the spirit remains and we often make offerings to the spirits to keep them good-tempered. But now the making of offerings is dying out rapidly, for every member of the family should be present, but the children are Christians and refuse to come, so the spirit-worship is dying out. A good many of our children go to the mines in the Union, for the wages are better there. Unfortunately a large number do not come back at all. And some send money to their people — others do not. Some men have even deserted their families, their wives, and children. If they cannot go by train they walk long distances.

# Imperialist Economics and Rebellion in German East Africa

▼▼▼

## 73 ▼ *RECORDS OF THE MAJI-MAJI REBELLION*

The Germans were latecomers to imperialism, but after they gained control of territories in Africa and Oceania, they were quick to adopt the view that colonies existed to serve the economic interests of the colonial master. This was clearly the philosophy that underlay their policies in German East Africa, a large and politically diverse region on Africa's east coast, surrounded by Kenya to the north, the Belgian Congo to the west, and Northern Rhodesia and Mozambique to the south. At first administered in the 1880s by the German East Africa Company, the colony came under direct control of the German government in 1890. German economic policy lacked direction in the 1880s and 1890s as the Germans (who numbered only 880 permanent settlers in 1914) struggled to overcome resistance to their rule and tried several strategies to force Africans to grow crops the Germans needed for their home industries, especially cotton.

In 1902 the Germans implemented a new plan to increase cotton cultivation in the coastal and southern sections of the colony. It required each village in the region to provide a quota of laborers to work growing cotton a certain number of days a year on government estates, settler plantations, or village fields. To encourage Africans to accept these low-paying jobs, the Germans instituted a head tax payable in cash only. African opposition to the German plan led to rebellion in 1905. Encouraged by religious leaders who supplied the rebels with *maji*, a magic water that supposedly made warriors impervious to bullets, the rebellion spread throughout the colony's central and southern regions. The Germans fought back with Maxim guns, mass executions, and the burning of villages. The rebellion ended in 1907, at a cost of seventy-five thousand African deaths, many by famine.

The following testimony concerning the Maji-Maji Rebellion and its background was gathered and published in a book by two Tanzanian historians, G. C. K. Gwassa and John Iffle, in 1967. Most of the information deals with the experiences of the Matumbi, highlanders who lived in the southeastern part of the colony.

## QUESTIONS FOR ANALYSIS

1. What do these records and testimonies reveal about Germany's administration of its colony?
2. Why did the Africans object so strongly to German agricultural policy?
3. What other aspects of German rule did the Africans find objectionable?
4. What does the source reveal about German views of Africans and their African colonies?
5. What information does the source provide about the role of women in the African village?

## [RECOLLECTION OF AMBROSE NGOMBALE MWIRU CONCERNING THE ARRIVAL OF A GERMAN AGENT IN 1897]

Then when that European arrived he asked, "Why did you not answer the call by drum to pay tax?" And they said, "We do not owe you anything. We have no debt to you. If you as a stranger want to stay in this country, then you will have to ask us. Then we will ask of you an offering to propitiate the gods. You will offer something and we will propitiate the gods on your behalf; we will give you land and you will get a place to stay in. But it is not for us as hosts to give you the offering. That is quite impossible."

## [RECOLLECTIONS OF NDUNDULE MANGAYA]

The cultivation of cotton was done by turns. Every village was allotted days on which to cultivate at Samanga Ndumbo[1] and at the Jumbe's[2] plantation. One person came from each homestead, unless there were very many people. Thus you might be told to work for five or ten days at Samanga. So a person would go. Then after half the number of days another man came from home to relieve him. If the new man did not feel pity for him, the same person would stay on until he finished. It was also like this at the Jumbe's. If you returned from Samanga then your turn at the Jumbe's remained, or if you began at the Jumbe's you waited for the turn at Samanga after you had finished. No woman went unless her husband ran away; then they would say she had hidden him. Then the woman would go. When in a village a former clan head was seized to go to cultivate he would offer his slave in his stead. Then after arriving there you all suffered very greatly. Your back and your buttocks were whipped, and there was no rising up once you stooped to dig. The good thing about the Germans was that all people were the same before the whip. If a jumbe or akida[3] made a mistake he received the whip as well. Thus there were people whose job was to clear the land of trees and undergrowth; others tilled the land; others would smooth the field and plant; another group would do the weeding and yet another the picking; and lastly others carried the bales of cotton to the coast . . . for shipping. Thus we did not know where it was taken. Then if that European gave out some bakshishi[4] to the akida or jumbe they kept it. We did not get anything. In addition, people suffered much from the cotton, which took three months to ripen and was picked in the fourth. Now digging and planting were in the months of Ntandatu and Nchimbi, and this was the time of very many wild pigs in this country.[5] If you left the chasing of the pigs to the women she could not manage well at night. In addition, the pigs are very stubborn at that

period and will not move even if you go within very close range. Only very few women can assist their husbands at night and these are the ones with very strong hearts. There were just as many birds, and if you did not have children it was necessary to help your wife drive away the birds, while at the same time you cleared a piece of land for the second maize crop, because your wife would not have time. And during this very period they still wanted you to leave your home and go to Samanga or to work on the jumbe's plantation. This was why people became furious and angry. The work was astonishingly hard and full of grave suffering, but its wages were the whip on one's back and buttocks. And yet he [the German] still wanted us to pay him the tax. Were we not human beings? And Wamatumbi . . . since the days of old, did not want to be troubled or ruled by any person. They were really fierce, ah! Given such grave suffering they thought it better for a man to die rather than live in such torment.

Thus they hated the rule which was too cruel. It was not because of agriculture, not at all. If it had been good agriculture which had meaning and profit, who would have given himself up to die? Earlier they had made troubles as well, but when he began to cause us to cultivate cotton for him and to dig roads and so on, then people said, "This has now become an absolute ruler. Destroy him."

## [RECOLLECTION OF NDULI NJIMBWI CONCERNING WORK ON A PLANTATION OWNED BY A GERMAN SETTLER NAMED STEINHAGEN]

During the cultivation there was much suffering. We, the labor conscripts, stayed in the front

---

[1] A coastal town.
[2] A chief or headman given low-level administrative responsibilities by the Germans.
[3] An official appointed by the Germans with functions simi-

lar to those of jumbes; akidas, however, were recruited from coastal towns and were usually Muslims.
[4] A bribe or, in this case, a payment.
[5] A threat to cultivated crops.

line cultivating. Then behind us was an overseer whose work it was to whip us. Behind the overseer there was a jumbe, and every jumbe stood behind his fifty men. Behind the line of jumbes stood Bwana Kinoo[6] himself. . . . [T]he overseer had a whip, and he was extremely cruel. His work was to whip the conscripts if they rose up or tried to rest, or if they left a trail of their footprints behind them.[7] Ah, brothers, God is great — that we have lived like this is God's Providence! And on the other side Bwana Kinoo had a bamboo stick. If the men of a certain jumbe left their footprints behind them, that jumbe would be boxed on the ears and Kinoo would beat him with the bamboo stick using both hands, while at the same time the overseer lashed out at us laborers.

## [EXCERPTS FROM AN INTERVIEW WITH A GERMAN OFFICIAL VON GEIBLER CONCERNING THE COMMUNAL PLOTS]

Village plots were set up in each akida's and headman's area early in 1902 (September–October). Bushland was mainly chosen. The people were consulted in choosing the post. Each headman made a plot for his area in the neighborhood of his headquarters. The principle was that every 30–50 men were to cultivate $2^{1}/_{2}$ acres. . . . Where possible, the advice of the natives was obtained as to the crop to be grown. So far as possible, one crop was to be grown on each plot, according to the type of soil. Some 2,000 acres were cleared and cultivated. The size varied from $2^{1}/_{2}$ to 35 acres; the average was about $12^{1}/_{2}$ acres.

In 1903–04 it was ordered that each village plot should be extended by at least a quarter. The total area in that year came to 3,215 acres. Maize, millet, simsim,[8] groundnuts, rice, and

coconut palms were grown during 1902–03. Cotton was added in 1903–04.

No extension took place in 1904–05, but the cultivation of other crops was abandoned in favor of cotton.

What was the labor situation and the supervision?

. . . According to returns by the headmen, the number of able-bodied men amounted to:

| | |
|---|---|
| 1902–03 | c. 25,000 men |
| 1903–04 | c. 26,000 men |
| 1904–05 | c. 25,000 men |

During the last year, women and children had to be brought in to help, since the men frequently refused to work.

In Herr von Geibler's opinion, two days' work a week, as proposed by the District Office order, was insufficient from the start; 50–100 per cent more had to be worked from the first. When cotton became a main crop, continuous work was sometimes necessary. . . .

The akidas were relied upon to report on the condition of the plots, and they were also responsible for punishing those whom the headmen reported as refractory workers. There was no European control of this — who among the natives worked, and for how many days — although agricultural students (some of them children) were sent out, each with a note-book, to judge the condition of the plots and the work performed, and to report to the District Officer. Only once a year did a European visit the plots, to measure them out and select the land. No lists of workers were kept anywhere; the profits were distributed only according to the total numbers. Work on most of the plots was *flatly* refused during 1904–05. The headmen complained that they no longer had the people in hand. The offi-

---

[6]The Matumbi's name for Steinhagen.
[7]Such a trail would mean that the person had walked away from his assigned work.

[8]Sesame.

cials of the Commune believed at the time that they could detect a state of ferment.

Were refractory workers punished, and by whom?

Last year (1904–05), following reports from the akidas and from Sergeant Holzhausen, who was sent to inspect the headmen, numerous headmen were punished by the District Office with imprisonment in chains or solitary confinement for totally neglecting their village plots as a result of the natives' refusal to work. The last, in June, was headman Kibasila, who got one month in chains.

What were the financial returns?

*1902–03:* . . .   Total receipts: Shs.[9] 25,530. . . .
Gives an average
   per headman:  Shs. 47.75
   per worker:    35 cents.

─────────

[9]An abbreviation for shilling, a unit of money.

*1903–04:* . . .   Very bad harvest as a result of drought. . . . Total receipts: Shs. 17,528 from 178 plots totaling 3,170 acres. 178 headmen and 26,186 workers were engaged in production. Mode of distribution:
   $1/2$ to workers
   $1/4$ to commune
   $1/4$ to headmen

. . . The last payment to the headmen and people took place early in October 1903, following the distribution plan of 1902–03.
   No subsequent distribution took place.

▼▼▼

# Southwest Asia under Siege

Each decade of the nineteenth century confirmed what had been apparent for at least a century, namely that years of misgovernment, economic stagnation, and military neglect had enfeebled the once-powerful and culturally sophisticated Persian and Ottoman empires. The Ottoman Empire lost its territories in north Africa and southeastern Europe, and escaped embarrassing and potentially fatal military defeats by Russia and its one-time province, Egypt, only because Great Britain and France dreaded the consequences of its disintegration and intervened on its behalf. Under the Qajar Dynasty, Persia lost territory on each side of the Caspian Sea to Russia and lands around the Persian Gulf to Great Britain. At times Russian and British consular officials in Teheran, not the shah and his officials, appeared to be in charge of Persian affairs.

What economic development occurred in the region mainly benefited European investors. Ottoman, Persian, and Egyptian governments all welcomed European investors and borrowed heavily from European financiers, who then "rescued" them from their unpayable debts in return for monopolies, control of governmental expenditures, and a guaranteed cut of tax revenues. When in 1876 the Egyptian government failed to make required payments on its massive loans, two officials, one British and one French, took over its finances and became the real rulers of Egypt. They hired well-paid Europeans to administer the country, and made debt liquidation the fiscal priority of the state. In 1882, following anti-European demonstrations and an attempted military revolt led by Colonel Ahmad Urabi, the British bombarded Alexandria, occupied Cairo, and established a protectorate over Egypt, making it for all intents and purposes a British colony until 1936.

Intellectuals, military men, and religious leaders throughout the region debated the causes and significance of these developments, and government officials, especially within the Ottoman state, took action by implementing reforms. Such reformers loosely fit into one of two categories. Moderates, or as they are sometimes called, "conservative modernizers," sought to reorganize the army, end corruption, improve tax collection, and reform the judiciary while preserving the authority of the sultan, shah, or khedive. Reformers in this camp cautiously approved greater intellectual and cultural contacts with the West and accepted the need for European investment. By the 1870s, other more progressive reformers, such as the Young Ottomans, went beyond proposals for military and administrative reform; they sought greater acceptance of Western science and secularism and demanded parliaments, written constitutions, elections, and guarantees of individual freedoms.

Reformers in both camps faced formidable obstacles. Powerful families and well-placed officials who benefited from the status quo naturally opposed them. So too did many religious leaders, who feared that all reforms at some level were European-inspired and thus would inevitably weaken Islam and encourage secularization. True reform, they believed, would come not from modern weapons and new law codes, but from rededication to Islamic spirituality and morality. Islamic religious leaders thus generally approved the autocratic and reactionary reign of the Ottoman Sultan Abbul Hamid II (1876–1909) and undercut the parliamentary regime established by the Persian Revolution of 1906 by demanding a legal system based on Islamic law rather than Western legal codes.

The reformers' biggest obstacle was lack of money. The costs of modern armies, schools, roads, telegraph lines, bridges, and steamships outstripped revenues, forcing governments to rely on European loans and investments and to accept European control of taxes and expenditures. In other words, the reformers' policies fostered greater economic dependency on the West, one of the things they most wished to avoid.

In the end, reformers and revolutionaries in the Middle East were unable to halt Western intervention or stave off political disaster. Egypt remained a British protectorate. In 1907 Persia was divided into a Russian north and British south, with only the central portion under the control of the Qajars, who were overthrown by a military coup in 1925. The Ottoman Empire lost all but a tiny sliver of its European territories as a result of the Balkan Wars of 1912 and 1913 and lost its Arab provinces during World War I. It disappeared altogether when the sultan's government was overthrown by Turkish nationalists in 1920 and replaced by the modern state of Turkey.

# Ottoman Reforms in the Tanzimat Era
▼▼▼
## 74 ▼ *Sultan Abdul Mejid, IMPERIAL RESCRIPT*

Serious efforts to reverse the Ottoman Empire's political and military decline can be traced back to the reign of Selim III (r. 1789–1807), who sought to revitalize the Ottoman army by importing foreign officers, updating weapons, and tightening discipline. These modest reforms were bitterly opposed by many Islamic religious leaders and by the janissaries, once the elite of the Ottoman army, but now mainly concerned with protecting their privileges. As a result, Selim was deposed in 1807 and then murdered. Mahmud II (r. 1808–1839) achieved more permanent military and administrative reforms, largely because of his destruction of the reactionary janissary corps in 1826 and his success in weakening some of the authority of conservative Islamic judges. Despite his efforts, his armies were badly defeated when he sent them into battle against the forces of the Egyptian pasha Muhammad Ali in 1832 and 1839. Yet another era of reform began during the reign of Abdul Mejid (r. 1839–1861). Inspired by the sultan's foreign minister and later grand vizier, Mustafa Reshid, it came to be known as the era of *Tanzimat,* which literally means restructuring. This movement, which maintained its momentum until early in the reign of Abdul Hamid II (r. 1876–1909), sought to save the empire by administrative reform, expansion of education, and the adoption of Western legal concepts and practices.

Two of the most important documents in the Tanzimat Era were proclamations issued by Sultan Abdul Mejid (r. 1839–1861). The first, known as the Noble Rescript, was issued shortly after he became sultan in 1839. In it he committed himself to ending government corruption, confirming the rights of non-Muslims, and protecting all subjects from arbitrary arrest. Seventeen years later, in 1856, he made a second, broader statement, known as the Imperial Rescript. This represented the high point of efforts to reform the Ottoman Empire while maintaining its authoritarian government and traditional mix of Muslim, Christian, and Jewish subjects.

---

## QUESTIONS FOR ANALYSIS

1. What benefits were the emperor's non-Muslim subjects to receive as a result of this proclamation?
2. What efforts were to be made to improve the empire's system of justice?
3. What do the decrees dealing with the economy suggest about the state of the empire's economic situation?
4. To what extent does this document extend meaningful political rights to the emperor's subjects?
5. In what respects does this document reflect Western liberal ideals of individual freedom and religious toleration?

Let it be done as herein set forth. . . . It being now my desire to renew and enlarge still more the new Institutions ordained with the view of establishing a state of things conformable with the dignity of my Empire and — . . . by the kind and friendly assistance of the Great Powers, my noble Allies,[1] . . . The guarantees promised on our part by the Hatti-Humaïoun of Gülhané,[2] and in conformity with the Tanzimat, . . . are today confirmed and consolidated, and efficacious measures shall be taken in order that they may have their full and entire effect.

All the privileges and spiritual immunities granted by my ancestors from time immemorial, and at subsequent dates, to all Christian communities or other non-Muslim persuasions established in my empire, under my protection, shall be confirmed and maintained.

Every Christian or other non-Muslim community shall be bound within a fixed period, and with the concurrence of a commission composed . . . of members of its own body, to proceed with my high approbation and under the inspection of my Sublime Porte,[3] to examine into its actual immunities and privileges, and to discuss and submit to my Sublime Porte the reforms required by the progress of civilization and of the age. The powers conceded to the Christian Patriarchs and Bishops[4] by the Sultan Mehmed II[5] and his successors, shall be made to harmonize with the new position which my generous and beneficient intentions ensure to these communities. . . . The principles of nominating the Patriarchs for life, after the revision of the rules of election now in force, shall be exactly carried out. . . . The ecclesiastical dues, of whatever sort of nature they be, shall be abolished and replaced by fixed revenues of the Patriarchs and heads of communities. . . . In the towns, small boroughs, and villages, where the whole population is of the same religion, no

obstacle shall be offered to the repair, according to their original plan, of buildings set apart for religious worship, for schools, for hospitals, and for cemeteries. . . .

Every distinction or designation tending to make any class whatever of the subjects of my Empire inferior to another class, on account of their religion, language, or race, shall be forever effaced from Administrative Protocol. The laws shall be put in force against the use of any injurious or offensive term, either among private individuals or on the part of the authorities. . . .

As all forms of religion are and shall be freely professed in my dominions, no subject of my Empire shall be hindered in the exercise of the religion that he professes. . . . No one shall be compelled to change their religion . . . and . . . all the subjects of my Empire, without distinction of nationality, shall be admissible to public employments. . . . All the subjects of my Empire, without distinction, shall be received into the civil and military schools of the government. . . . Moreover, every community is authorized to establish public schools of science, art, and industry. . . .

All commercial, correctional, and criminal suits between Muslims and Christian or other non-Muslim subjects, or between Christian or other non-Muslims of different sects, shall be referred to Mixed Tribunals. The proceedings of these Tribunals shall be public; the parties shall be confronted, and shall produce their witnesses, whose testimony shall be received, without distinction, upon an oath taken according to the religious law of each sect. . . .

Penal, correctional, and commercial laws, and rules of procedure for the Mixed Tribunals, shall be drawn up as soon as possible, and formed into a code. . . . Proceedings shall be taken, for the reform of the penitentiary system. . . .

---

[1]During the Crimean War (1853–1856) Turkey was allied with Great Britain and France against Russia. France and Great Britain at the time were encouraging Turkish military reform to offset the power of Russia in the region.
[2]This refers to the Noble Rescript of 1839.
[3]"Sublime Porte" refers to the building that housed the grand vizier and other high officials of the Ottoman state.

It is a translation of the Turkish words *Bab-i-Ali,* or "high gate." The term is used to refer to Ottoman leadership in much the same way that the "White House" refers to the American presidency.
[4]The reference is to ruling officials of the Greek and Armenian churches in the Ottoman Empire.
[5]Ottoman ruler from 1451 to 1481.

The organization of the police . . . shall be revised in such a manner as to give to all the peaceable subjects of my Empire the strongest guarantees for the safety both of their persons and property. . . . Christian subjects, and those of other non-Muslim sects, . . . shall, as well as Muslims, be subject to the obligations of the Law of Recruitment. The principle of obtaining substitutes, or of purchasing exemption, shall be admitted.

Proceedings shall be taken for a reform in the constitution of the Provincial and Communal Councils, in order to ensure fairness in the choice of the deputies of the Muslim, Christian, and other communities, and freedom of voting in the Councils. . . .

As the laws regulating the purchase, sale, and disposal of real property are common to all the subjects of my Empire, it shall be lawful for foreigners to possess landed property in my dominions. . . .

The taxes are to be levied under the same denomination from all the subjects of my Empire, without distinction of class or of religion. The most prompt and energetic means for remedying the abuses in collecting the taxes, and especially the tithes, shall be considered. The system

of direct collection shall gradually, and as soon as possible, be substituted for the plan of farming,[6] in all the branches of the revenues of the state.

A special law having been already passed, which declares that the budget of the revenue and the expenditure of the state shall be drawn up and made known every year, the said law shall be most scrupulously observed. . . .

The heads of each community and a delegate, designated by my Sublime Porte, shall be summoned to take part in the deliberations of the Supreme Council of Justice on all occasions which might interest the generality of the subjects of my Empire. . . .

Steps shall be taken for the formation of banks and other similar institutions, so as to effect a reform in the monetary and financial system, as well as to create funds to be employed in augmenting the sources of the material wealth of my empire.

Everything that can impede commerce or agriculture shall be abolished. To accomplish these objects means shall be sought to profit by science, the art, and the funds of Europe, and thus gradually to execute them.

---

[6]Tax farming, in which the government contracted with private financiers, who collected taxes for a profit.

# Persian Opposition to the Tobacco Concession
▼▼▼

## 75 ▼ Sayyid Jamal ad-Din, *LETTER TO HASAN SHIRAZI*

European imperialism did not always involve gunboats, invading armies, and control by colonial administrators. It frequently was more economic than political. Both the Ottoman Empire and Persia remained independent states in the 1800s, but their finances and economies were increasingly controlled and manipulated by European bondholders, bankers, businessmen, and speculators. Their experience is as much a part of the West's imperialist expansion as that of India, Africa, and Southeast Asia.

For Persia, economic imperialism was epitomized by the numerous concessions granted to foreign businessmen by the shah's government. These agreements gave Europeans exclusive control over a sector of the nation's economy, usually in return for a one-time payment and an annual percentage of profits. Viewed as a painless way to attract foreign capital, solve budget problems, and generate bribes, such arrangements were irresistible to Persia's shahs and their ministers. Hundreds of concessions were granted for activities ranging from railroad construction to the founding and administration of a national lottery. By far the most ambitious such agreement was the concession granted in 1872 to Baron Julius de Reuter, a British subject. De Reuter gained control of much of Persia's economy — factories, minerals, irrigation works, agricultural improvements, new forms of transportation, and virtually any other enterprise that had to do with Persia's economic modernization — for a period of seventy years. The Russians and many of the shah's subjects were outraged, and largely because of their opposition, government officials found reasons to withdraw the concession, even though they kept the payments (legal and illegal) de Reuter had made.

Despite the outcry over the de Reuter concession in 1872, the number of concessions granted by Shah Nasir al-Din and his ministers mounted in the 1870s and 1880s. Many Persians experienced deep frustration over their inability to dissuade their autocratic and concession-loving ruler from selling off the nation's wealth and economic future to foreigners. This changed, however, in 1891, when for the first and only time in history a government abandoned an unpopular policy after the adult population "kicked the habit" and gave up tobacco smoking.

In 1891 Persians learned of a new concession granted to the British Imperial Tobacco Corporation for the purchase, processing, and sale of tobacco, for which it paid the shah fifteen thousand pounds and promised him 25 percent of annual profits. The English expected profits of approximately five hundred thousand pounds per year, but the Persians expected to pay inflated prices for a product they grew, used heavily, and previously had marketed themselves. Persia erupted with demonstrations, angry sermons, calls for boycotts, destruction of tobacco warehouses, and denunciations of the shah. Then in December Persia's most prominent Shi'ite religious leader, Hasan Shirazi, ordered Persians to give up tobacco smoking until the concession was lifted. A nation of heavy smokers obeyed, and within only a few days the concession was canceled.

A key figure in the campaign against the tobacco concession was the Islamic intellectual Sayyid Jamal ad-Din "al Afghani," who since 1889 had resided in Teheran. Born in 1838 or 1839 in Persia and raised as a Shi'ite, he was educated in Persia, learned of the West while visiting British India and Europe, and traveled and taught throughout the Middle East. In his many writings and speeches Jamal ad-Din blended Islamic traditionalism and a pragmatic and selective acceptance of Western science, technology, and values. He taught that only a religious and intellectual revival that transcended state boundaries and sectarian differences could save Islam from subservience to the West.

From the time he moved to Teheran, Jamal ad-Din was a vocal critic of the shah. Fearing arrest, he sought sanctuary at a holy shrine, but the shah's soldiers forcefully removed him in January 1891 and deported him to Ottoman territory. From exile, in April 1891 he wrote the following letter to Hasan Shirazi. It is unclear how much influence Jamal ad-Din's letter had, but as Jamal ad-Din had hoped, Shirazi did abandon his apolitical stance by denouncing the shah and then issuing the antismoking decree that ended the concession.

The shah stayed in power and the foreigners remained, but for the first time in their modern history, all Persians, rural and urban, religious and secular, had united for a political end. Such unity of purpose reappeared in the Persian Revolution of 1906, which, for a time, established a parliamentary government for Persia.

---

## QUESTIONS FOR ANALYSIS

1. What strategies does Jamal ad-Din use to convince Hasan Shirazi that he should speak out against the shah? What does he claim would be the consequences of inaction?
2. According to Jamal ad-Din, what are the personal faults of the shah? Are his criticisms based more on religious or nonreligious considerations?
3. What has been the result of the shah's fiscal and economic policies, according to the author?
4. What view of the West is expressed in the letter?
5. What seems to be Jamal ad-Din's vision of Persia's future?
6. What differences do you see between the ideas and spirit of Jamal ad-Din's letter and those of the rescript of Sultan Abdul Mejid (source 74)?
7. What does the letter reveal about the prospects and progress of reform in Persia, as compared to the Ottoman Empire?

---

Religious leader of the people, Ray of the Imams[1] Light, Pillar of the edifice of Religion, Tongue attuned to the exposition of the Unhidden Law, Your Reverence . . . Hasan Shirazi — may God protect by your means the fold of Islam, and avert the plots of the vile unbelievers! —

God has set you apart for this supreme vice regency, . . . and has chosen you out of the true communion, and has committed to your hands the reins to guide the people obediently to the most luminous Law, and thus to protect their rights, and to guard their hearts from errors and doubts. He has entrusted to you out of all mankind (so that you have become the heir of the Prophet) the care of those weighty interests by which the people shall prosper in this world and

attain happiness in the hereafter. He has assigned to you the throne of authority, and has bestowed on you such supremacy over his people as empowers you to save and defend their country and testify for them to the ways of those who have gone before. . . .

O most mighty Religious Guide! Verily the Shah's purpose wavers, his character is impure, his perceptions are failing and his heart is corrupt. He is incapable of governing the land, or managing the affairs of his people, and has entrusted the reins of government in all things great and small to the hands of a wicked freethinker,[2] a tyrant and usurper, who reviles the Prophets openly, and heeds not God's Law, who counts for nothing the religious authorities, curses the doc-

---

[1]According to Shi'ite doctrine, *imams* were descendants of Muhammad's son-in-law, Ali, with special powers to interpret the Qur'an. Most Shi'ites believe that the Twelfth Imam

mysteriously disappeared in the ninth century but would ❧ return as the savior *(mahdi)* of humanity.
[2]Amin al-Sultan, the shah's grand vizier.

tors of the Law, rejects the pious, condemns honorable Sayyids[3] and treats preachers as one would treat the vilest of mankind. Moreover since his return from Europe he has taken the bit between his teeth, drinks wine openly,[4] associates with unbelievers and displays enmity toward the virtuous. Such is his private conduct; but in addition to this he has sold to the foes of our Faith the greater part of the Persian lands and the profits derived from them, for example, the mines, the roads leading to them, the roads connecting them with the frontiers of the country, the inns about to be built by the side of these extensive means of travel which will spread out through all parts of the kingdom, and the gardens and fields surrounding them. Also the river Karun[5] and the guesthouses which will arise on its banks up to its very source, and the gardens and meadows which adjoin it, and the highway from Ahwaz to Teheran, with the buildings, inns, gardens, and fields surrounding it. Also tobacco, with the chief centers of its cultivation, the lands on which it is grown, and the warehouses, carriers, and sellers, wherever these are found. He has similarly disposed of the grapes used for making wine, and the shops, factories, and winepresses pertaining to this trade throughout the whole of Persia; and so likewise soap, candles, and sugar, and the factories connected with their manufacture. Lastly there is the Bank:[6] what must you understand about the Bank? It means the complete handing over of the reins of government to the enemy of Islam, the enslaving of the people to that enemy, the surrendering of them and of all dominion and authority into the hands of the foreign foe.

After this the ignorant traitor, desiring to pacify the people by his futile arguments, pretended that these agreements were temporary, and these compacts were only for a limited period which would not exceed a hundred years!

God! what an argument, the weakness of which amazed even the traitors! . . .

In short this criminal has offered the provinces of Persia to auction among the Powers,[7] and is selling the realms of Islam and the abodes of Muhammad and his household (on whom be greeting and salutation) to foreigners. But by reason of the vileness of his nature and meanness of his understanding he sells them for a paltry sum and at a wretched price. (Yea, thus it is when meanness and avarice are mingled with treason and folly!)

And you, O Proof, if you will not arise to help this people, and will not unite them in purpose, and pluck them forth, by the power of the Holy Law from the hands of this sinner, verily the realms of Islam will soon be under the control of foreigners, who will rule . . . as they please and do what they will. If this opportunity is lost . . . and this thing happens while you are alive, verily you will not leave behind . . . a fair record in the register of time and on the pages of history. And you know that the *ulama*[8] of Persia and the Persian people . . . with one accord (their spirits being troubled and their hearts distressed) await a word from you with which they shall behold their happiness and by which their deliverance shall be effected. How then can it seem that one on whom God has bestowed such power as this to be so reluctant to use it or to leave it suspended?

I further assure Your Eminence, speaking as one who knows and seeks, that the Ottoman Government will rejoice in your undertaking of this effort and will aid you in it, for it is well aware that the intervention of Europeans in the Persian domains and their ascendancy there will assuredly prove injurious to its own dominions. Moreover all the ministers and lords of Persia will rejoice in a word in this sense uttered by you, seeing that all of them naturally detest these

---

[3]Descendants of Muhammad.
[4]A forbidden act according to the Qur'an.
[5]In 1888 an Englishman had been granted a concession to open steamship traffic on the Karun River.
[6]The Imperial Bank of Persia had been granted a sixty-year

concession to issue bank notes and carry on other banking activities.
[7]The Great Powers of Europe.
[8]Those learned in religion; the Muslim clergy.

innovations and are constitutionally opposed to these agreements, which your actions will give them the opportunity to annul, that perhaps they may restrain this evil of covetousness which has been sanctioned and approved. . . . All is from you, by you and in you, and you are responsible for all before God and men. . . .

As for my own story and what that ungrateful tyrant did to me . . . the wretch [the shah] commanded me to be dragged, when I was in sanctuary in the shrine of Shah 'Abdu'l-'Azim and grievously ill, through the snow to the capital with such circumstances of disrespect, humiliation and disgrace as cannot be imagined for wickedness (and all this after I had been plundered and despoiled). Verily we belong to God and verily unto Him do we return!

Thereafter his miserable lackeys placed me, despite my illness, on a pack-saddle, loading me with chains, and this in the winter season, amid the snow-drifts and bitter, icy blasts, and a company of horsemen conveyed me to Khaniqin,[9] guarded by an escort. And he had previously written to the . . . Turkish governor, requesting him to remove me to Basra, knowing well that, if he left me alone, I should come to you, . . . and inform you of his doings and of the state of the people, and explain to you what had befallen the lands of Islam through the evil deeds of this

infidel, and would invoke your help, O Proof, for the True Faith, and convince you to come to the assistance of the Muslims. For he knew for a certainty that, should I succeed in meeting you, it would not be possible for him to continue in his office, involving as it does the ruin of the country, the destruction of the people, and the encouragement of unbelief. . . . Moreover his conduct was made more blameworthy and mean in that, in order to avert a general revolt and quiet the popular agitation, he accused the party whom zeal for religion and patriotism had impelled to defend the sanctuary of Islam and the rights of the people of belonging to the Babi sect.[10] . . . What is this weakness? What this cowardice? How is it possible that a low-born vagabond and contemptible fool should be able to sell the Muslims and their lands for a vile price and a paltry sum, scorn the *ulama*, treat with disrespect the descendants of the Prophet, and slander in such fashion Sayyids of the House of 'Ali? Is there no hand able to pluck up this evil root and so to appease the wrathful indignation of the Muslims, and avenge the descendants of the Chief of God's Apostles (upon whom and whose household be blessings and salutation)? . . .

Peace be upon thee, and the Mercy of God, and His Blessings.

---

[9]A Turkish frontier post on the road from Persia to Baghdad.
[10]*Babism* was a religious movement inspired by Sayyid Ali Muhammad (d. 1852), who claimed to be the *Bab,* or Gate, between the realm of flesh and the realm of spirit and the

means by which the Twelfth Imam communicated to the faithful. Accused of plotting against the shah, the Bab was executed in 1850.

## A Turkish Nationalist Statement

▼▼▼

## 76 ▾ PROCLAMATION OF THE YOUNG TURKS

During the 1870s a group of reformers known as the Young Ottomans began to seek changes that went beyond the Tanzimat reforms. They believed that only a constitutional regime could save their country from continued deterioration. Led by Grand Vizier Ahmed Midhat Pasha (1822–1884), a career administrator, a committee of ministers produced the Constitution of 1876, which the new sultan, Abdul Hamid II (r. 1876–1909), accepted with seeming enthusiasm. He revealed his true beliefs in 1877, however, when in response to a rebellion in Bosnia and Herzegovina he abolished the first elected parliament and established an autocratic regime stubbornly dedicated to maintaining the status quo.

Opposition to Abdul Hamid was centered in a secret revolutionary society founded in 1889, officially named the Committee of Union and Progress but commonly known as the Young Turks. Fierce nationalists, they called for the resignation of Abdul Hamid and the restoration of the Constitution of 1876. Many members were imprisoned or went into exile, and those who remained in Turkey lived in dread of the secret police. The Young Turks' opportunity came in 1908, when, after an army mutiny, they came into the open and demanded the restoration of the Constitution of 1876. The sultan acquiesced, and a parliamentary regime was reestablished. Shortly after the constitution was reinstated, the Young Turks outlined their plans for a new Turkey in the proclamation that follows.

*QUESTIONS FOR ANALYSIS*

1. How would the proposals in the proclamation affect the empire's various ethnic groups?
2. To what extent does this document express the nationalism of the Young Turks?
3. What view of the relationship between the Turkish state and Islam is expressed in the proclamation?
4. To what extent does this document reflect a commitment to the Western principles of liberalism and democracy?
5. How does this document differ from the Imperial Rescript (source 74) of 1856 on the issue of the status of religious minorities within the empire?

All the general rights accorded by the Constitution of 1293 (1876) and confirmed by the Imperial decree communicated to the Sublime Porte[1] the 4th of *redjeb* 1326[2] (1908), as well as the parts of those rights which are not in opposition to the foresaid Constitution, will be respected and preserved intact, as long as they are not abolished by the Parliament.

1. The basis for the Constitution will be respect for the predominance of the national will. One of the consequences of this principle will be to require without delay the responsibility of the minister before the Chamber, and, consequently, to consider the minister as having resigned when he does not have a majority of the votes of the Chamber.

2. Provided that the number of senators does not exceed one third the number of deputies, the Senate will be named (which is not provided for in article 62 of the Constitution) as follows: one third by the Sultan and two thirds by the nation, and the term of senators will be of limited duration;

3. It will be demanded that all Ottoman subjects having completed their twentieth year, regardless of whether they possess property or fortune, shall have the right to vote. Those who have lost their civil rights will naturally be deprived of this right.

[1]See note 3 of source 74.

[2]July 24 on the Western calendar.

4. It will be demanded that the right freely to constitute political groups be inserted in a precise fashion in the constitutional charter, in order that article 1 of the Constitution of 1293 (1876) be respected. . . .

7. The Turkish tongue will remain the official state language. Official correspondence and discussion will take place in Turkish. . . .

9. Every citizen will enjoy complete liberty and equality, regardless of nationality or religion, and be submitted to the same obligations. All Ottomans, being equal before the law as regards rights and duties relative to the State, are eligible for government posts, according to their individual capacity and their education. Non-Muslims will be equally liable to the military law.

10. The free exercise of the religious privileges which have been accorded to different nationalities will remain intact.

11. The reorganization and distribution of the State forces, on land as well as on sea, will be undertaken in accordance with the political and geographical situation of the country, taking into account the integrity of the other European powers. . . .

14. Provided that the property rights of landholders are not infringed upon (for such rights must be respected and must remain intact, according to the law), it will be proposed that peasants be permitted to acquire land, and they will be accorded means to borrow money at a moderate rate. . . .

16. Education will be free. Every Ottoman citizen, within the limits of the prescriptions of the Constitution, may operate a private school in accordance with the special laws.

17. All schools will operate under the surveillance of the state. In order to obtain for Ottoman citizens an education of a homogeneous and uniform character, the official schools will be open, their instruction will be free, and all nationalities will be admitted. Instruction in Turkish will be obligatory in public schools. In official schools, public instruction will be free.

Secondary and higher education will be given in the public and official schools indicated above; it will use the Turkish tongue. . . . Schools of commerce, agriculture and industry will be opened with the goal of developing the resources of the country. . . .

Steps shall also be taken for the formation of Roads and Canals to increase the facilities of communication and increase the sources of the wealth of the country. Everything that can impede commerce or agriculture shall be abolished.

# The Beginnings of Arab Nationalism
▼▼▼

## 77 ▼ *ANNOUNCEMENT TO THE ARABS, SONS OF QATHAN*

Of all the ethnic groups in the Ottoman Empire, the Arabs were the sultan's least troublesome subjects during the nineteenth century. Attached to the Ottoman state through deeply ingrained habits of loyalty and the perception of the sultan/caliph as protector of the Islamic community, or *umma,* the Arabs, unlike the Balkan Christians, Kurds, and Armenians, experienced no surge of nationalism and made no demands for independence or greater autonomy within the empire. This changed in the years directly preceding the outbreak of World War I, when Arab nationalism suddenly intensified. It gained strength during the Arab revolt against the Ottomans in World War I and has continued to be a significant part of the region's politics to the present day.

Although Arab nationalism became a political force only on the eve of World War I, its roots can be traced back to the nineteenth century, when publications of Arabic language printing houses and the establishment of schools and universities in major Arab cities under the auspices of French Jesuit and American Presbyterian missionaries sparked renewed interest in Arab history and literature. These same missionary schools also introduced Arab students to Western science and Western ideas of constitutionalism and liberalism. Continued Ottoman misrule and military losses in the Balkans also encouraged the growth of Arab consciousness. The Ottoman Empire, some suggested, was no longer capable of defending the interests of Islam, and a few went further to suggest that the Islamic community would continue to decline until its founders and natural leaders, the Arabs, regained control.

Arab discontent intensified after the Young Turk Revolution of 1908. Although many Arabs had supported the Young Turks' political agenda before the revolution, especially their demand to revive the Constitution of 1876, they turned against the new regime after it replaced Arab officials with Turks, stripped many old Arab families of their local authority, mandated the use of Turkish throughout the empire, and encouraged the further secularization of education and the law. Arab political organizations formed in Cairo, Beirut, Damascus, Baghdad, and Aleppo, with some, like the Decentralization Party, advocating greater Arab autonomy with the empire, and others, like *al-Fatat,* demanding Arab independence.

Independence clearly was the goal of the author or authors of the following "announcement" to the Arabs, which appeared in Cairo in the summer of 1914. It may have been written by a supporter of Major Aziz Ali-al-Misri, a decorated Arab officer in the Ottoman Army and founder of the Covenant, an organization of Arab officers dedicated to Arab independence. Arrested and condemned to death by Ottoman officials in early 1914, he was released later in the year and allowed to go to Cairo as a result of foreign pressure and public outcry among the Arabs.

## QUESTIONS FOR ANALYSIS

1. The author's nationalism is directed against both the Turks and the West. What, specifically, are his views of each?
2. Does he have a deeper aversion for the Turks or for the Western nations? Why?
3. In the view of the author, what lessons can the Arabs learn from the Armenians?
4. How does the author define "Arab"?
5. What role does religion play in connection with the author's nationalism? How committed is he to Islam?
6. What are the author's ultimate goals for the Arab people? How does he believe these goals can be attained?

O Sons of Qahtan! O Descendants of Adnan![1] Are you asleep? And how long will you remain asleep? How can you remain deep in your slumber when the voices of the nations around you have defeated everyone? Do you not hear the commotion all around you? Do you not know that you live in a period when he who sleeps dies, and he who dies is gone forever? When will you open your eyes and see the glitter of the bayonets which are directed at you, and the lightning of the swords which are drawn over your heads? When will you realize the truth? When will you know that your country has been sold to the foreigner? See how your natural resources have been alienated from you and have come into the possession of England, France, and Germany. Have you no right to these resources? You have become humiliated slaves in the hands of the usurping tyrant; the foreigner unjustly dispossesses you of the fruit of your work and labor and leaves you to suffer the pangs of hunger. How long will it be before you understand that you have become a plaything in the hand of him who has no religion but to kill the Arabs and forcibly to seize their possessions? The Country is yours, and they say that rule belongs to the people, but those who exercise rule over you in the name of the Constitution[2] do not consider you part of the people, for they inflict on you all kinds of suffering, tyranny, and persecution. How, then, can they concede to you any political rights? In their eyes you are but a flock of sheep whose wool is to be clipped, whose milk is to be drunk, and whose meat is to be eaten. . . .

The Armenians, small as their numbers are when compared to yours, have won their administrative autonomy in spite of the opposition of the Turkish state, and they will presently become independent.[3] Their people will then become self-governing, free and advanced, free and active in the social organization of humanity, in contrast to you, who will remain ever enslaved to the descendants of Genghis and Hulagu[4] who brought to an end your advanced Arab government in Baghdad, the Abode of Peace; and to the descendants of Tamerlane[5] who built a tower composed of the heads of eighty thousand Arabs in Aleppo. Till when will you go on acquiescing in this utter humiliation, when your honor is made free of, your wives raped, your children orphaned, your habitations destroyed, so that the Byzantine capital should be defended, your money taken to be spent in the palaces of Constantinople, full as they are with intoxicating drink, musical instruments, and all kinds of wealth and luxury, and your young men driven to fight your Arab brethren. . . . Has your Arab blood become congealed in your veins, and has it changed into dirty water? You have become, by God, a byword among the nations, a laugh-

---

[1]Qahtan, or Kahtan, was supposedly the ancient ancestor of all south Arabs; Adnan was the ancestor of north Arabs.
[2]The Constitution of 1876, restored for a time by the Young Turks.
[3]These claims are exaggerated. Slightly more than one million Armenians were Ottoman subjects, with most of them living in the eastern provinces of Anatolia. An upsurge in Armenian nationalism at the end of the nineteenth century led to a proliferation of Armenian political groups, anti-government terrorism, and public demonstrations against Turkish rule. Abdul Hamid's government responded by ordering, or at least condoning, massacres of perhaps as many as one hundred thousand Armenians by Ottoman troops and mobs between 1894 and 1897. Another massacre of approximately twenty thousand Armenians took place in the village of Adana in 1909. Such atrocities outraged world opinion, and European governments pressured the Ottomans to implement reforms on behalf of the Armenians. A plan worked out in 1914 established two large provinces with heavy Armenian populations in eastern

Anatolia and placed them under the administrative authority of Europeans, who would be named by the Ottoman government and approved by the European powers. With the outbreak of World War I, however, the plan was dropped. During the war government-ordered evacuations of Armenians from their homelands and attacks on Armenian communities resulted in more than a million Armenian deaths.
[4]Chinggis Khan (1167–1227) was the ruler who after uniting the Mongols, conquered northern China, central Asia and Persia; his grandson Hulagu, or Hülegü, led the Mongol armies that sacked Baghdad in 1258, killing an estimated two hundred thousand inhabitants and bringing an end to the Abbasid Dynasty.
[5]Tamerlane (ca. 1336–1405) was a conqueror of Turko-Mongol ancestry. His armies carved a short-lived empire that stretched from Asia Minor to India. His most notorious custom was to pile his victims' skulls in huge pyramids after a city had been sacked.

ingstock of the world, a subject of mockery and derision among the peoples. You have almost become proverbial in your humility, weakness, and acquiescence in great loss.

Compare how well the Turks treat the Armenians and how they seek to humor them, with the harsh treatment which they reserve for you Arabs. See how the Turkish government adopts the stance of obedience before them, how it humbly begs them to accept more than their due share of parliamentary representation. As for you, O how we grieve for you! The government directs against you those armies which had been defeated on the Russian front and in the Balkans,[6] in order to kill you, destroy your liberty, destroy your noble Arab race, and finally to finish you off, as though it can have no power but over you. . . .

What is the reason of all this? Is it not because you have sunk into passivity and accepted the yoke of the Turks? Till when will you remain acquiescent in these oppressions, witnessing all the while the annihilation of your people? . . .

O sons of Qahtan! Do you not know that man is meant to live here on earth a goodly life, in honor and prosperity, a life full of spiritual values, and that he founds states which safeguard these things, the most precious gift of God to the sons of Adam, to which they hold very fast? What, then, is the value of life, when honor is stained, possessions robbed, and souls destroyed? What is the meaning of a life spent in humiliation and subjection, without honor, without possessions, without enjoyment of liberty and independence? . . .

Arise, O ye Arabs! Unsheathe the sword from the scabbard, ye sons of Qahtan! Do not allow an oppressive tyrant who has only disdain for you to remain in your country; cleanse your country from those who show their enmity to you, to your race and to your language. . . .

O ye Arabs! Warn the people of the Yemen, of Asir, of Nejd, and of Iraq[7] against the intrigues of your enemies. Be united, in the Syrian and Iraqi provinces, with the members of your race and fatherland. Let the Muslims, the Christians, and the Jews be as one in working for the interest of the nation and of the country. You all dwell in one land, you speak one language, so be also one nation and one land. Do not become divided against yourselves according to the designs and purposes of the troublemakers who feign Islam, while Islam is really innocent of their misdeeds. . . .

Unite then and help one another, and do not say, O ye Muslims: This is a Christian, and this is a Jew, for you are all God's dependents, and religion is for God alone. God has commanded us, in his precious Arabic Book and at the hand of his Arab Adnanian Prophet, to follow justice and equality, to deal faithfully with him who does not fight us, even though his religion is different, and to fight him who uses us tyrannously. Who, then, have tyrannized over the Arabs? Have the Christian Arabs or any others sent armed expeditions to the Yemen, to Nejd, or to Iraq? Is it not the band of Constantinople who fight you and seek to exterminate some of the Arabs by means of sword and fire, and others by means of quarrels and dissensions, following the maxim "divide and rule"? . . .

Every tyrannical government is an enemy and a foe to Islam; how more so, then, if the government destroys Islam, considers it lawful to shed the blood of the people of the Prophet of Islam, and seeks to kill the language of Islam in the name of Islamic government and the Islamic caliphate? . . . Therefore, he who supports these unionists[8] because he considers them Muslims is in clear error, for none of them have done a good deed for Islam. . . . Fanatic in its cause, they fight

---

[6]The Ottoman government had been fighting and losing wars in the Balkans since the 1820s; their most recent defeat had come in the Balkan War of 1912–1913. The last major war with Russia had been fought in 1877 and 1878 with disastrous results for the Ottomans.

[7]Yemen, Asir, and Nejd are all regions of the Arabian Pen-

insula; Iraq was a province centered on the Tigris/Euphrates rivers. The Ottoman government had sent troops to all these regions to quell disturbances or control local Arab rulers.

[8]Refers to the Committee of Union and Progress, the political party of the Young Turks.

the Qur'an and the tradition of the Arabic Prophet. Is this the Islam which it is incumbent on them to respect? It is not notorious that they seek to kill the Arabic language? Did they not write books to show that it must be abandoned, and that prayers and the call to prayers should be made in Turkish? And if Arabic dies, how can the Qur'an and the traditions live? And if the Book and the traditions cease to be known, what remains of Islam?

And O ye Christian and Jewish Arabs, combine with your brethren the Muslim Arabs, and do not follow in the footsteps of him who says to you, whether he be one of you or not: The Arab Muslims are sunk in religious fanaticism, therefore we prefer the irreligious Turks. This is non-sensical speech which proceeds from an ignorant man who knows neither his own nor his people's interest. . . . Our ancestors were not fanatical in this sense, for Jews and Christians used to study in the mosques of Baghdad and the Andalus like brethren. Let them, both sides, aim at tolerance and at the removal of these ugly fanaticisms. For you must know that those who do not speak your tongue are more harmful to you than the ignorant fanatics among the Arabs, since you can reach understanding with the Arabs who are your brethren in patriotism and race, while it is difficult for you to reach agreement with these contemptible creatures who are at the same time your enemies and the enemies of the Muslim Arabs. See how, when you are friendly to them, they maltreat you, look down on you, and withhold your rights. Combine with your fellow countrymen and your kin, and know that ugly fanaticism will inevitably disappear. A day will come when fanaticism will disappear from our country, leaving no trace, and that day shall be when our affairs will be in our own hands, and when our affairs, our learning, and the verdicts of our courts will be conducted in our own language. If we are united, such a day is not far off.

Know, all ye Arabs, that a *fada'i* society has been formed which will kill all those who fight the Arabs and oppose the reform of Arab lands. The reform of which we speak is not on the principle of decentralization coupled with allegiance to the minions of Constantinople, but on the principle of complete independence and the formation of a decentralized Arab state which will revive our ancient glories and rule the country on autonomous lines, according to the needs of each province.

▼▼▼

# India under British Domination

As Great Britain took control of India during the nineteenth century, administrators, policymakers, and the British public all agreed that this new colony should serve the economic interests of the mother country. It would be a source of raw materials, an area for investment, and a market for British manufactured goods. Other issues, however, sparked lively debate. Most of the British assumed that at some point in the future they would leave India, and their colony would become a self-governing, independent state. They had no timetable for leaving, however, and they disagreed about how to prepare their subjects for that day of independence. They would bring some Indians into the colonial administration, but how many and at what levels? They would provide India with schools and colleges, but would they offer Western or traditional Indian learning? They would attempt to "civilize" the Indians, but in doing so, how much traditional Indian culture were they willing to obliterate?

The debate among the British was complicated by sharp disagreements among Indians about their relationship to their colonial masters. Many Indians at first believed that British rule was a blessing and would enable them to attain the benefits of Western science, constitutional government, and economic development. Such views persisted into the twentieth century, but by the late 1800s only a minority embraced them. Many Indians came to resent the British assumption that Western ways were superior to centuries-old Indian beliefs and practices. They were also offended by Britain's one-sided economic policies, which drained India's resources, stifled development, and damaged traditional industries. Finally, they were angered by Great Britain's reluctance to consider seriously Indian self-rule.

As the following documents reveal, an evaluation of the benefits and harm of British rule in India is no simple matter. Historians continue to debate the issue down to the present day.

## A Plea for Western Schools
▼▼▼

## 78 ▼ *Rammohun Roy,*
### *LETTER TO LORD AMHERST*

Rammohun Roy, the father of modern India, was born into a devout high-caste Hindu family in 1772. He showed an early genius for languages and a keen interest in religions. By the age of twenty he had learned Arabic, Persian, Greek, and Sanskrit (the ancient language of India) and had spent five years wandering through India seeking religious enlightenment. He then learned English and entered the service of the British East India Company, ultimately attaining the highest administrative rank possible for an Indian. In 1814, at the age of forty-two, he retired to Calcutta, where he established several newspapers, founded a number of schools, and campaigned to abolish the practice of widow burning, or *sati*. He also established the Society of God, dedicated to combining Christian ethical teaching with certain Hindu beliefs. He spent his final years in England, where he died in 1833.

Roy wrote the following letter in 1823 to the British governor-general of India, Lord Amherst (1773–1857), to oppose a British plan to sponsor a school in Calcutta to teach Sanskrit and Hindu literature. Roy believed that Indians should study English and receive a Western education.

In 1835 the debate over Indian education was settled when a committee appointed by the British government decided that Indian schools should offer an English-style education. In the words of the committee's chair, Thomas B. Macaulay (1800–1859), the goal was to produce young men who were "Indian in blood and color, but English in taste, in opinions, in morals, and in intellect."

## QUESTIONS FOR ANALYSIS

1. How would you characterize Roy's attitude toward the British? Does he seem comfortable offering the British advice? Explain your answer.
2. What does he especially admire in Western civilization?
3. What does he consider to be the weaknesses of an education based on traditional Indian learning?
4. According to Roy, what implications would a Hindu-based educational system have for India's political future?

To His Excellency the Right Honorable Lord Amherst, Governor-General in Council

My Lord,

Humbly reluctant as the natives of India are to obtrude upon the notice of government the sentiments they entertain on any public measure, there are circumstances when silence would be carrying this respectful feeling to culpable excess. The present rulers of India, coming from a distance of many thousand miles to govern a people whose language, literature, manners, customs, and ideas, are almost entirely new and strange to them, cannot easily become so intimately acquainted with their real circumstances as the natives of the country are themselves. We should therefore be guilty of a gross dereliction of duty to ourselves and afford our rulers just grounds of complaint at our apathy did we omit, on occasions of importance like the present, to supply them with such accurate information as might enable them to devise and adopt measures calculated to be beneficial to the country, and thus second by our local knowledge and experience their declared benevolent intentions for its improvement.

The establishment of a new Sanskrit School in Calcutta evinces the laudable desire of government to improve the natives of India by education — a blessing for which they must ever be grateful, and every well-wisher of the human race must be desirous that the efforts made to pro-

mote it should be guided by the most enlightened principles, so that the stream of intelligence may flow in the most useful channels.

When this seminary of learning was proposed, we understood that the government in England had ordered a considerable sum of money to be annually devoted to the instruction of its Indian subjects. We were filled with sanguine hopes that this sum would be laid out in employing European gentlemen of talent and education to instruct the natives of India in mathematics, natural philosophy, chemistry, anatomy, and other useful sciences, which the natives of Europe have carried to a degree of perfection that has raised them above the inhabitants of other parts of the world.

While we looked forward with pleasing hope to the dawn of knowledge thus promised to the rising generation, our hearts were filled with mingled feelings of delight and gratitude, we already offered up thanks to Providence for inspiring the most generous and enlightened nations of the West with the glorious ambition of planting in Asia the arts and sciences of modern Europe.

We find that the government are establishing a Sanskrit school under Hindu pandits[1] to impart such knowledge as is already current in India. This seminary (similar in character to those which existed in Europe before the time of Lord Bacon)[2] can only be expected to load the minds of youth with grammatical niceties and meta-

---

[1] Wise and learned men of Hindu India.
[2] The reference is to the English philosopher and prophet of science, Francis Bacon (1561–1626). Excerpts from his *New Organon* are included in source 36.

physical distinctions of little or no practical use to the possessors or to society. The pupils will there acquire what was known two thousand years ago with the addition of vain and empty subtleties since then produced by speculative men such as is already commonly taught in all parts of India.

The Sanskrit language, so difficult that almost a lifetime is necessary for its acquisition, is well known to have been for ages a lamentable check to the diffusion of knowledge, and the learning concealed under this almost impervious veil is far from sufficient to reward the labor of acquiring it. But if it were thought necessary to perpetuate this language for the sake of the portion of valuable information it contains, this might be much more easily accomplished by other means than the establishment of a new Sanskrit College; for there have been always and are now numerous professors of Sanskrit in the different parts of the country engaged in teaching this language, as well as the other branches of literature which are to be the object of the new seminary. Therefore their more diligent cultivation, if desirable, would be effectually promoted, by holding out premiums and granting certain allowances to their most eminent professors, who have already undertaken on their own account to teach them, and would by such rewards be stimulated to still greater exertion. . . .

Neither can much improvement arise from such speculations as the following which are the themes suggested by the Vedanta.[3] In what manner is the soul absorbed in the Deity? What relation does it bear to the Divine Essence? Nor will youths be fitted to be better members of

society by the Vedantic doctrines which teach them to believe that all visible things have no real existence, that as father, brother, etc., have no real entity, they consequently deserve no real affection, and therefore the sooner we escape from them and leave the world the better. . . .

If it had been intended to keep the British nation in ignorance of real knowledge, the Baconian philosophy would not have been allowed to displace the system of the schoolmen which was the best calculated to perpetuate ignorance. In the same manner the Sanskrit system of education would be the best calculated to keep this country in darkness, if such had been the policy of the British legislature. But as the improvement of the native population is the object of the government, it will consequently promote a more liberal and enlightened system of instruction, embracing mathematics, natural philosophy, chemistry, anatomy, with other useful sciences, which may be accomplished with the sums proposed by employing a few gentlemen of talent and learning educated in Europe and providing a college furnished with necessary books, instruments, and other apparatus.

In presenting this subject to your Lordship, I conceive myself discharging a solemn duty which I owe to my countrymen, and also to that enlightened sovereign and legislature which have extended their benevolent care to this distant land, actuated by a desire to improve the inhabitants, and therefore humbly trust you will excuse the liberty I have taken in thus expressing my sentiments to your Lordship.

I have the honor, etc.,

Rammohun Roy

---

[3]A major school of Hindu philosophy based on the study and analysis of three ancient texts, the *Upanishads,* the *Vedanta-sutras,* and the *Bhagavad Gita.* The various schools of Vedanta have different views concerning the nature of Brahman, the relationship of the individual to Brahman, and the nature and means of liberation from the cycle of reincarnation.

# Indian Railroads and the People's Welfare
▼▼▼

## 79 ▼ *G. V. Joshi,*
## *"THE ECONOMIC RESULTS OF FREE TRADE AND RAILWAY EXTENSION"*

An enduring monument to British imperialism in India is the Indian railway system, which at the time of independence in 1947 had more track mileage than that of any European state and less than only the United States, Canada, and the Soviet Union. The first railway track was laid in India in 1850, and by 1915 India had better than forty thousand miles of track and approximately one hundred million railroad passengers per year. Indian railway building was supported by several powerful groups: British cotton manufacturers, for whom railways were a cheap and efficient way to get cotton to the coast for shipment to England; British industrialists, who supplied India with most of its rails, locomotives, moving stock, and equipment; colonial officials, who saw railroads as a way to move troops quickly to trouble spots and an essential part of the Indian postal system; and millions of Indians, who, rather to the surprise of the British, took to rail travel with great alacrity.

But was India's new railway system a good investment? Did it contribute to India's overall economic development? Did it justify its enormous costs? Among those who answered "no" to these questions, few were as eloquent or persistent in their criticisms of British economic policy as G. V. Joshi (1851–1911), a schoolteacher and schoolmaster by profession, but also one of India's leading economic writers of the nineteenth century. His essay on public works and free trade in India was published in 1884.

---

## QUESTIONS FOR ANALYSIS

1. What benefits for the Indian people does Joshi see in the program of railroad construction?
2. What is Joshi's overall assessment of the priorities and goals of the Indian colonial government?
3. According to Joshi, what were Lord Dalhousie's motives for building India's railway system?
4. Why is Joshi so deeply opposed to the doctrine of free trade?
5. What long-term effects has India's railway system had on India's economic situation according to Joshi?
6. If Joshi had been given an opportunity to draw up a blueprint for India's economic development what would it have looked like?

## ECONOMIC REALITIES

In this country, which is economically in such a primitive and backward condition, a too exclusive policy of pushing on Railways at American speed, beyond the resources of Indian finance, will, unless accompanied by other economic measures of far greater importance, only end in national impoverishment. We are not opposed to the growth of Railways *per se*. They are good in their own way as providing cheap transit, and promoting national solidarity, and facilitating trade-movements, but when their extension is made the ultimate goal of State action on its economic side, their tendency to prevent, in a country like India, a healthy material advance on *normal lines* must be duly taken into account; for, unless they are accompanied by other and more important measures conducive to a better organisation of national industries, they do not add to the intensive strength of the country, which alone furnishes a firm foundation to its expansive greatness. . . .

Every consideration, therefore, of prudence and justice alike dictate that the action of Government,[1] in such circumstances, shall be thoroughly national in its aims, purposes, and principles of execution. It might employ foreign talent for the prosecution of such works; it might borrow foreign capital for the purpose. But it is on no grounds justified in bringing the foreigner with his talent and capital into the country, and suffering him to appropriate permanently the national field of improvement, to the exclusion of the native element, and forming the nucleus of a domineering foreign aristocracy in the land with purposes and interests adverse to those of the nation — a result which cannot but be regarded as at once a serious political danger, and a great economic evil. . . .

## THE EFFECTS OF FREE TRADE

The Public Works policy of the Government of India was first formulated by Lord Dalhousie,[2] under whose administration the proposal of a separate Department for the promotion of Public Works undertaken on Government account, or with Government guarantee,[3] was carried out. . . . It was Lord Dalhousie's dream to strengthen the domination not only of English rule, but of English trade and commerce in India, and the permanent interests of this country were subordinated to this all-engrossing ambition. The contemporaneous rise of the school of Free Trade[4] in England, and the great reputation which its apostles enjoyed, furnished the metaphysical ground-work for this essentially selfish and grasping policy. The value of India to the British nation was measured by the quantity of raw material which the resources of Indian agriculture enabled it to export for the feeding and maintenance of the Lancashire manufactures.[5] India was to devote all its energies to raise the raw exports; and canals, Railroads and improved communications were to be pushed on at any cost to facilitate the export of raw articles and the import of English manufactures. India's own industrial needs were of comparatively no consequence. . . . A splendid opportunity for fruitful

---

[1]The "Government," or the "Government of India," consisted of a British governor-general, his six-man Executive Council, and a Legislative Council consisting of the Executive Council and six to twelve additional members. All these various Councils were dominated by the British.

[2]The Marquis of Dalhousie had been head of the Railway Department of the English Board of Trade before serving as governor-general of India between 1848 and 1856. He was a strong advocate of India's economic modernization and sponsored a host of public works projects, including railroads, canals, roads, and irrigation systems. He created the Department of Public Works to oversee the many new undertakings.

[3]The "guarantee" was a policy by which railroad companies were guaranteed a 5 percent profit on their investment and were reimbursed by the government if profits fell below that percentage.

[4]Advocates of free trade espoused the teachings of Adam Smith in the *Wealth of Nations* (1776) (see source 40). They called for the abolition of all tariffs on imports and exports. In England such doctrines were popular among industrialists who believed the lowering or end of tariffs would ensure markets for British manufactured goods and keep down the price of imported foodstuffs.

[5]The region of England where cotton manufacturing was concentrated.

State activity was thus thrown away, and abused by aggravating the naturally unfavourable conditions presented by the free contact of the two countries. So far as this result was inevitably due to natural conditions, we have no fault to find with Government. But surely it was not a legitimate exercise of the State's parental functions to help with Indian resources the one country which needed no such help, at the cost of paralyzing its great unfortunate dependency, whose salvation from its depression of ages depends upon its industrial growth in all directions. . . .

The extent of the mischief that has been worked already is admitted by the more keensighted of English statesmen, and is witnessed to by the ghastly spectacle so recently witnessed of a condition of things when six millions of people died during a single year of scanty rainfall, . . . and one-third of the population lives from hand to mouth on a single meal a day. And yet Government professes itself to be powerless to raise its little finger to stop the drain,[6] or divert it into less exhaustive channels. It cannot undertake to subsidize native industrial growth, or stimulate local manufactures without exposing itself to the fire of Free-Trade fanatics, and the opposition of the vested foreign interests which it has created. . . . The abolition of these duties [on imports to India] has worked mischief in that it has exposed to the unrestricted competition of the world the rude and undeveloped industries of the country. These duties were not, as in England, levied upon raw products, but upon finished articles such as cotton, silk and woollen manufactured goods, and wrought metal. These imported articles were all of them machine-made, and necessarily displaced the hand-made products of native skill. This displacement was to a certain extent inevitable, but Government, as the protector of national Indian interests, should not have gone out of its way to

stimulate this process of the violent disintegration of important industries in this country. . . . People point out with pride to the fact that, in the course of fifty years, the imports have risen from six to sixty crores of Rupees.[7] To enable our readers to understand the true character of these figures, we append below a table showing the growth in the import of manufactured goods during the last 25 years.

| Articles | 1859–60 | 1870–71 | 1881–82 |
|---|---|---|---|
| | £ | £ | £ |
| Woollen goods | 358,557 | 582,330 | 1,276,263 |
| Cotton goods | 11,698,928 | 19,044,869 | 24,000,237 |
| Metal | 454,457 | 850,319 | 2,772,178 |
| Sugar | 220,270 | 555,801 | 1,243,758 |
| Umbrellas | 136,670 | Not available | 209,572 |

These figures show what displacement has occurred in the consumption of the chief manufactured goods of home production. It cannot be maintained for one moment that India did not clothe itself in cotton or other fabrics in times past. As a matter of fact, India did not only clothe itself, but even so late as the first quarter of this century, it exported its fine muslins[8] to Europe in large quantities, and even to this day the raw material of cotton and wool is exported in larger quantities than the imported goods. . . .

## NATIVE VERSUS FOREIGN MANAGEMENT

A little judicious protection to local manufactures, and a little encouragement in the way of technical education, would have easily enabled India to displace its rude hand-made goods by improved machine-made articles.

When such protection was for a time enforced upon an unwilling Government by its financial necessities, Indian capital organised itself, and

---

[6]A term used by critics of British colonialism to describe the loss of Indian wealth to Britain through taxes and trade.
[7]The rupee was the basic coin in the Indian currency system; one crore equaled ten million rupees.

[8]A term for a number of types of plain, finely woven cotton textiles.

put forth its energies in the manufacture of cotton and other goods. In 1882 there were 62 cotton Mills and many times the number of cotton presses and gins, 3 silk manufactures, 14 tanneries, 14 iron and brass foundries, 12 sugar refineries, 4 soap companies, 4 paper mills, 68 collieries, and a large number of jute companies in Bengal. . . . Even where native capitalists have embarked their capital in such enterprises, they are not able to command native skill of management, but find it necessary to import foreign talent and skill. With a partial exception in Bombay, these new industries are all managed throughout by European skill, thus giving the foreigners a monopoly of the advantages reaped, over and above their natural monopoly as shippers, and carriers and insurers. Even in those departments of money dealings where the native has a natural claim to succeed, European enterprise has driven out native talent. We refer here to the banking enterprise of the country. As many as 323 banking companies have been established in this country since 1861, and 140 of these establishments are in active operation to this day. All these are managed by Europeans, though their dealings are for the most part with native customers, and their funds are derived to a large extent from native depositors.

## RAILWAYS AND TECHNICAL TRAINING

Notwithstanding this financially burdensome and economically ruinous policy of the Government . . . the people of India would have had good reason to welcome this diversion of public funds by the State, if the vast expenditure incurred for railway construction had the effect of training the nation by suitable arrangements for their technical education, and liberal association in the management, to take up in course of time in their own hands the new sphere of industrial activity represented by railway enterprise. . . . The people of India needed above all things a technical training in mechanical arts and manufacturing processes, and pecuniary aid in the shape of State subsidies in starting new enterprises. Above all, they had to be protected from the predominance of a foreign plutocracy, with vested interests opposed to those of the Native producer. None of these considerations have attracted the attention of Government as they deserved. The system of public education, . . . is mainly intended to qualify native youths for inferior service in the State departments. The scientific branches of the service are all but sealed to the natives by reason of their education not fitting them to take their natural place in mechanical and engineering enterprises. The subventions were paid to the foreigner, and in consequence of these State guarantees, a powerful foreign aristocracy of stock-holders has been created with interests adverse to the nation. . . . The result is that, after 25 years of continuous State direction, the natives of the country are as unfitted to take up this work of railway construction or management, as ever they were when Lord Dalhousie first sanctioned the proposal of covering India with a net-work of railway lines. The railway establishments in all the higher grades are a close preserve for the foreigner and even the lower duties of collecting or clipping tickets are entrusted to other hands than those of the natives of the country. A few native guards and drivers and fitters are all that the companies can show in the way of training natives for higher work, and the position and status of these people are anything but comfortable. . . . Everything for the people, and nothing by the people, this was the maxim of the great Napoleon, and in no country in the world has it been more vigorously carried out than in India, where the foreigner does everything for the people, who look upon all that is done with rustic amazement.

# Chapter 10

▾▾▾

# East Asia Confronts the West

During the nineteenth century the ancient rhythms of life in East and Southeast Asia were irrevocably altered by upheavals that felled governments, intensified social conflict, introduced new ideas and technologies, and transformed long-standing diplomatic relationships. These changes were caused in part by social and political forces generated from within these societies themselves, but in greater measure they resulted from new pressures and incursions from the West. Until the nineteenth century, Western involvement in East and Southeast Asia had been limited to commerce and a modicum of generally ineffectual missionary activity. Only the Dutch in Java and the Spaniards in the Philippines exercised direct political authority, and only the Filipinos had been converted to Christianity. Elsewhere in the region rulers and their subjects remained politically independent and culturally indifferent to the West.

Much of this changed during the nineteenth century. Like Africa, most states in Southeast Asia became European colonies. By the time World War I began in 1914, Burma, Laos, Cambodia, Vietnam, Singapore, the states of Malaysia, and much of the East Indies had joined the Philippines and Java as part of Western empires. Thailand remained independent, but lost territory to France and Great Britain.

China faced severe internal problems and experienced relentless economic and military pressure from the European powers, the United States, and Japan. Imperial China had survived domestic turbulence and foreign threats before, but this time its problems were fatal. More than two thousand years of imperial rule ended as a result of the revolution of 1911, when the Qing Dynasty fell and no dynasty replaced it. China now faced an uncharted future — without the authority of an emperor, the rule of scholar-officials, and the guidance of official Confucian ideology.

Japan also experienced the demise of a once-successful government system and the abandonment of many traditions, but otherwise its history differs sharply from China's. After an intense debate over Japan's future in the mid nineteenth century, a group of patriotic aristocrats led a revolt that abolished the Tokugawa shogunate, restored the emperor, and set the stage for Japan's rapid modernization. By the 1890s Japan had avoided becoming a victim of imperialism and instead was becoming an imperialist power itself.

▼▼▼

# The Disintegration of Imperial China

Only a half century after Emperor Qianlong sent King George III of England his condescending rejection of the British appeal for trade concessions (see source 56), Emperor Daoguang (r. 1821–1850) saw no choice in 1842 but to sign the Treaty of Nanjing, which opened five Chinese ports to British trade, ceded Hong Kong to the British, and required the Chinese to pay the London government $21 million, free all British prisoners, lower tariffs, and avoid insulting foreigners. These were the results of the Chinese defeat in the Opium War, the climax of early Chinese efforts to halt the British sale of opium in China.

The Treaty of Nanjing was only a foretaste of the galling indignities the Chinese experienced during the rest of the nineteenth century. The government was forced to open dozens of coastal cities to foreign trade, lost control of Korea, granted foreigners the right to collect customs duties, lost legal authority over resident foreigners, and promised to protect the lives and property of Christian missionaries. When the Chinese fought back, they suffered defeat and further humiliation.

Even without the foreign onslaught, nineteenth-century China faced enormous problems, many of them resulting from its spiraling population. By the mid nineteenth century China's population reached 450 million, more than three times the level of 1500. The inevitable results were land shortages, famine, and deepening poverty among the peasantry. Heavy taxes, inflation, and greedy local officials compounded the peasants' woes. Meanwhile, the government neglected public works and the military, and as bureaucratic efficiency declined, landowners, secret societies, and military strongmen took over local affairs by default. Some officials proposed reforms, but the government either rejected them or executed them poorly. Rebellion, lawlessness, and foreign exploitation continued to plague the Qing regime until the Revolution of 1911 caused it, and China's ancient imperial tradition, to pass into history.

# The Curse of Opium
▼▼▼

## 80 ▼ *Lin Zexu, LETTER TO QUEEN VICTORIA*

Although the opium poppy was grown in China and opium derivatives had been used by the Chinese in medicine for centuries, smoking opium as a narcotic dates from the seventeenth century, shortly after tobacco smoking was introduced by Spaniards and Portuguese. By the early 1800s millions of Chinese at every socio-economic level were addicted to opium, and almost two million pounds of opium were being sold in China every year. Most of it was imported by British merchants, who in India had access to one of the world's major poppy-growing areas.

Chinese officials viewed opium addiction with increasing alarm, but until 1838 efforts to restrict the opium trade were half-hearted and ineffectual. In that year, Emperor Daoguang decided to ban the importation of opium altogether and sent one of his officials, Lin Zexu (1785–1850), to Guangzhou to implement his decree. Lin had served in the Hanlin Academy, China's leading center for Confucian studies in Beijing, and had held various provincial posts, including terms in Hubei and Hunan, where he had tried to suppress opium smoking. On arrival in Guangzhou he launched a campaign of moral persuasion and force to discourage opium smoking among Chinese and end the sale of opium by Chinese and foreign merchants. Insight into his thinking is provided by a letter he wrote to Great Britain's Queen Victoria in 1839, imploring her to halt her subjects' sale of opium.

Nothing came of his letter (which was never delivered to the queen), and the refusal of British merchants in Guangzhou to cooperate drove him to more drastic steps. He arrested the leading English opium trader and blockaded the foreign community until its merchants agreed to hand over twenty thousand chests of opium. On receiving the opium, he then had it mixed with water, salt, and lime and flushed into the sea. In response, the British government dispatched a fleet and mobilized Indian troops to protect British interests in China. While the flotilla of almost fifty vessels was on its way to China in late 1839, fighting between the Chinese and the English had already started around Guangzhou; the Opium War was under way.

---

## QUESTIONS FOR ANALYSIS

1. According to Lin, what is the role of the Chinese emperor, and how does it affect his dealings with Queen Victoria?
2. What differences does Lin see in the motives of Chinese and Europeans in regard to trade?
3. What moral arguments does Lin use to persuade Victoria to order the end of opium trading? What other arguments does he use?
4. What seems to be Lin's understanding of the powers of Victoria as queen of England?
5. How does Lin's view of the outside world differ from that of Emperor Qianlong (source 56)?

His Majesty the Emperor comforts and cherishes foreigners as well as Chinese: he loves all the people in the world without discrimination. Whenever profit is found, he wishes to share it with all men; whenever harm appears, he likewise will eliminate it on behalf of all of mankind. His heart is in fact the heart of the whole universe.

Generally speaking, the succeeding rulers of your honorable country have been respectful and obedient. Time and again they have sent petitions to China, saying: "We are grateful to His Majesty the Emperor for the impartial and favorable treatment he has granted to the citizens of my country who have come to China to trade," etc. I am pleased to learn that you, as the ruler of your honorable country, are thoroughly familiar with the principle of righteousness and are grateful for the favor that His Majesty the Emperor has bestowed upon your subjects. Because of this fact, the Celestial Empire, following its traditional policy of treating foreigners with kindness, has been doubly considerate towards the people from England. You have traded in China for almost 200 years, and as a result, your country has become wealthy and prosperous.

As this trade has lasted for a long time, there are bound to be unscrupulous as well as honest traders. Among the unscrupulous are those who bring opium to China to harm the Chinese; they succeed so well that this poison has spread far and wide in all the provinces. You, I hope, will certainly agree that people who pursue material gains to the great detriment of the welfare of others can be neither tolerated by Heaven nor endured by men. . . .

Your country is more than 60,000 *li*[1] from China. The purpose of your ships in coming to China is to realize a large profit. Since this profit is realized in China and is in fact taken away from the Chinese people, how can foreigners return injury for the benefit they have received by sending this poison to harm their benefactors? They may not intend to harm others on purpose, but the fact remains that they are so obsessed with material gain that they have no concern whatever for the harm they can cause to others. Have they no conscience? I have heard that you strictly prohibit opium in your own country, indicating unmistakably that you know how harmful opium is.[2] You do not wish opium to harm your own country, but you choose to bring that harm to other countries such as China. Why?

The products that originate from China are all useful items. They are good for food and other purposes and are easy to sell. Has China produced one item that is harmful to foreign countries? For instance, tea and rhubarb[3] are so important to foreigners' livelihood that they have to consume them every day. Were China to concern herself only with her own advantage without showing any regard for other people's welfare, how could foreigners continue to live? Foreign products like woolen cloth and beiges[4] rely on Chinese raw materials such as silk for their manufacturing. Had China sought only her own advantage, where would the foreigners' profit come from? The products that foreign countries need and have to import from China are too numerous to enumerate: from food products such as molasses, ginger, and cassia[5] to useful necessities such as silk and porcelain. The imported goods from foreign countries, on the other hand, are merely playthings which can be easily dispensed with without causing any ill effect. Since we do not need these things really, what harm would come if we should decide to stop foreign trade altogether? The reason why we unhesitantly allow foreigners to ship out such Chinese products as tea and silk is that we feel that wherever there is an advantage, it should be shared by all the people in the world. . . .

---

[1]A Chinese measurement of distance, approximately one-third of a mile.

[2]Actually, the use of opium was not prohibited in England when Lin wrote his letter.

[3]Rhubarb roots were used in medicines.

[4]A soft wool fabric unbleached and undyed, thus having a tan color.

[5]A spice similar to cinnamon.

I have heard that you are a kind, compassionate monarch. I am sure that you will not do to others what you yourself do not desire. I have also heard that you have instructed every British ship that sails for Guangzhou not to bring any prohibited goods to China. It seems that your policy is as enlightened as it is proper. The fact that British ships have continued to bring opium to China results perhaps from the impossibility of making a thorough inspection of all of them owing to their large numbers. I am sending you this letter to reiterate the seriousness with which we enforce the law of the Celestial Empire and to make sure that merchants from your honorable country will not attempt to violate it again.

I have heard that the areas under your direct jurisdiction such as London, Scotland, and Ireland do not produce opium; it is produced instead in your Indian possessions such as Bengal, Madras, Bombay, Patna, and Malwa. In these possessions the English people not only plant opium poppies that stretch from one mountain to another but also open factories to manufacture this terrible drug. As months accumulate and years pass by, the poison they have produced increases in its wicked intensity, and its repugnant odor reaches as high as the sky. Heaven is furious with anger, and all the gods are moaning with pain! It is hereby suggested that you destroy and plow under all of these opium plants and grow food crops instead, while issuing an order to punish severely anyone who dares to plant opium poppies again. If you adopt this policy of love so as to produce good and exterminate evil, Heaven will protect you, and gods will bring you good fortune. Moreover, you will enjoy a long life and be rewarded with a multitude of children and grandchildren! In short, by taking this one measure, you can bring great happiness to others as well as yourself. Why do you not do it?

The right of foreigners to reside in China is a special favor granted by the Celestial Empire, and the profits they have made are those realized in China. As time passes by, some of them stay in China for a longer period than they do in their own country. For every government, past or present, one of its primary functions is to educate all the people living within its jurisdiction, foreigners as well as its own citizens, about the law and to punish them if they choose to violate it. Since a foreigner who goes to England to trade has to obey the English law, how can an Englishman not obey the Chinese law when he is physically within China? The present law calls for the imposition of the death sentence on any Chinese who has peddled or smoked opium. Since a Chinese could not peddle or smoke opium if foreigners had not brought it to China, it is clear that the true culprits of a Chinese's death as a result of an opium conviction are the opium traders from foreign countries. Being the cause of other people's death, why should they themselves be spared from capital punishment? A murderer of one person is subject to the death sentence; just imagine how many people opium has killed! This is the rationale behind the new law which says that any foreigner who brings opium to China will be sentenced to death by hanging or beheading. Our purpose is to eliminate this poison once and for all and to the benefit of all mankind.

Our Celestial Empire towers over all other countries in virtue and possesses a power great and awesome enough to carry out its wishes. But we will not prosecute a person without warning him in advance; that is why we have made our law explicit and clear. If the merchants of your honorable country wish to enjoy trade with us on a permanent basis, they must fearfully observe our law by cutting off, once and for all, the supply of opium. Under no circumstance should they test our intention to enforce the law by deliberately violating it. You, as the ruler of your honorable country, should do your part to uncover the hidden and unmask the wicked. It is hoped that you will continue to enjoy your country and become more and more respectful and obeisant. How wonderful it is that we can all enjoy the blessing of peace!

# The Plight of the Emperor's Subjects
▼▼▼

## 81 ▼ Zeng Guofan, *MEMORANDUM TO EMPEROR XIANFENG*

Zeng Guofan (1811–1872) was one of nineteenth-century China's truly impressive statesmen. Born into a farm family in the province of Hunan, Zeng received a Confucian education and passed the highest civil service examination at age twenty-eight. During his career as a government official, his greatest achievement was the organization and leadership of a potent military force, the Xiang Army, which was instrumental in suppressing the Taiping Rebellion, a massive peasant revolt that raged through China between 1850 and 1864. Knowing well the problems of the regime and the unrest among the people, Zeng drew up the following memorandum on February 7, 1852, for Emperor Xianfeng (r. 1851–1861). It provides a clear and balanced assessment of China's problems at midcentury.

---

### QUESTIONS FOR ANALYSIS

1. According to Zeng, what is the key to keeping China peaceful and secure?
2. Which aspects of the government's tax policies does Zeng deplore?
3. How, according to Zeng, does the behavior of local officials, soldiers, and magistrates affect the lives of the Chinese people?
4. Zeng states at the end of his memorandum that he will draft a plan to address the shortcomings of the tax system. What do you guess he will propose?
5. How does Zeng propose to remedy the problem of corruption? Does his solution have a reasonable chance of success? Why or why not?

The danger to a nation is not so much the paucity of material wealth as the lack of coherence among its people. In the course of our history rarely was a time so prosperous as the Sui Dynasty during Wendi's reign.[1] Yet the country was soon plunged into chaos, and the Sui regime eventually came to an end. Why? Because the people had lost faith in their government despite the country's material wealth. Conversely, seldom was the nation so poor as she was during the reign of Han Chaodi.[2] Yet the country was peaceful and her people secure. Why? Because the people had faith and confidence in their own government. For a period of fifteen years, from the first to the sixteenth year of Kangxi[3] during the present dynasty, the Yellow River broke its dikes every year with the exception of one, and flood damage was extremely heavy over a large

---

[1]Wendi, the founder of the Sui Dynasty, reigned from 589 to 604 C.E.

[2]Han Chaodi reigned from 86 to 74 B.C.E.
[3]1662–1677.

region. . . . As if this were not enough, the Three Viceroys' Rebellion erupted[4] and ravaged nine provinces; it took the government seven years to suppress it. By then the treasury was almost empty, emptier than it is today. Yet the dynasty remained secure and the country undisturbed. Why? Because the Saintly Progenitor[5] loved the people more than he did himself, and the people, in response, continued to pledge to him their unswerving allegiance and rallied for his support. Though Your Majesty undeniably loves your subjects to the same extent as the Saintly Progenitor loved his, local officials, being indifferent to the plight of their charges, have failed in conveying your compassionate sentiments to the people and bringing to your attention their grievances. Because of this lack of communication, your humble servant wishes to take this opportunity to describe in some detail the ills from which our people suffer most.

The first ill concerns the high price of silver which affects adversely the peasants' ability to fulfill their tax obligations. The tax load in Suzhou, Songjiang, Zhangzhou, and Jinjiang[6] is the heaviest in the nation, and the people in these districts also suffer most. The yield for each *mou*[7] of land is anywhere from 15 to 20 pecks[8] of polished rice, and the landowner, after dividing it with his tenant on a fifty-fifty basis, receives approximately 8 pecks as his rent. Though his regular tax is only 2 pecks per *mou,* he has to pay another 2 pecks as rice tribute and 2 pecks more for miscellaneous requisitions, totaling 6 pecks altogether. Thus, for each *mou* of land he owns, his net income is only 2 pecks of polished rice per year. If all these taxes could be paid in rice, the situation would not be so serious. But most of them have to be paid in silver. . . . Since a farmer reaps only rice, he has to sell his harvest for standard coins[9] in order to obtain the neces-

sary cash; since the price of standard coins is high in terms of rice, he has understandable grievances. Moreover, in order to pay his taxes, he has to convert his standard coins into silver. . . . Formerly, selling 3 pecks of rice would bring enough silver to pay taxes for one *mou* of land; now, selling 6 pecks will not be enough to achieve the same purpose. While the return to the government remains the same, the burden to the people has been doubled. Besides, there are additional taxes on houses and family cemeteries, all of which have been doubled in terms of rice because they, like most of other taxes, have also to be paid in silver.

Under the circumstances it is not surprising that a large number of taxpayers have become delinquent, despite local governments' effort to enforce payment. Often special officials are assigned to help tax collections, and day and night soldiers are sent out to harass taxpayers. Sometimes corporal punishments are imposed upon tax delinquents; some of them are so badly beaten to exact the last penny that blood and flesh fly in all directions. Cruel though it is, this practice does not necessarily reflect the evil nature of local officials who, more often than not, do not believe that they have a better choice. If they fail to collect 70 percent of the amount due, not only will they be impeached and punished as a matter of routine, they may also have to pay the balance with their own money, that sometimes amounts to thousands of taels,[10] and ruin their families in the process. In short, they are forced to do what they loathe. . . .

Under the circumstances it is not surprising that the people are complaining and angry, and often the resistance to tax payment bursts forth and mushrooms into full-fledged riot. . . .

The second ill of our nation is the great number of bandits which threaten the security of our law-abiding citizens. . . . Lately your humble

---

[4]Also known as the Revolt of the Three Feudatories, 1673–1681.

[5]Emperor Kangxi, who ruled from 1662 to 1722 (see source 55).

[6]All are located in the south-central region of China.

[7]One-sixth of an acre.

[8]One peck equals one-quarter of a bushel.

[9]Coins made of copper.

[10]Chinese silver coins, each weighing approximately 1 1/4 ounces.

servant has heard that the bandits have become bolder and more numerous, robbed and raped in broad daylight, and kidnapped people for ransom. Whenever an act of banditry is reported to the government, the local official announces in advance his intention to send troops against the bandits and advertises it in public proclamations, so as to make sure that the bandits know the soldiers are coming. Upon arriving at the village where the banditry took place, the official-in-charge expects to learn from the village chiefs, who are afraid of the bandits, that the offenders have already fled. Without anything worthwhile to do, he orders the burning of some of the houses in the village before his departure, so as to impress the villagers with the power of his office. Meanwhile his soldiers use a variety of excuses to exact payment from the bandits' victim, who by then is only too regretful that he reported the banditry to the government in the first place. While the soldiers are busy taking away from his house whatever they can carry, the bandits are still at large, hiding somewhere in the village. Sometimes the official announces that the responsible bandit has in fact been killed and that the case is therefore closed; then he proceeds to show off the bandit's body, after killing some prisoner in his jail who has nothing to do with this particular crime. Not only does the bandits' victim fail to get his grievances redressed and his stolen properties restored; he may also lose everything he has and go bankrupt. After all this, he will probably swallow his tears in silence and make no more complaint, since by then he is no longer financially able to make any appeals.

Suppose he does appeal and that the government responds by mobilizing a large force in its attempt to arrest the bandits. Since these soldiers have always been in collusion with the bandits, they will release the offenders soon after their capture, in return for a handsome bribe, and the offenders will quickly disappear without leaving a trace. Sometimes the soldiers use the reported presence of bandits as an excuse to blackmail the villagers; if the latter refuse to pay

the bribes they demand, they will accuse them as the bandits' accomplices, burn their houses, and bring them to the city in chains. . . .

The third ill which your humble servant wishes to stress is the great number of cases in which innocent men are condemned and the inability on the part of the people to have a wrong redressed. Since his appointment at the Ministry of Justice, your humble servant has reviewed several hundred cases of appeal. . . . In most cases, . . . it was the plaintiffs who received punishment in the end, on the ground that they had made false accusations, while the defendants went through the whole litigation unscathed and free. Generally speaking, the officials-in-charge invoke the following rules in the law as legitimate ground to impose heavy penalties upon the plaintiffs. First, the plaintiff has failed to present the truth in his petition, and for such failure he is to receive one hundred blows by a striking rod. Second, the case he presents is not serious enough for him to bypass the local courts and to go straight to the nation's capital, and for such offense he is to be punished by banishment to the frontier as a soldier. Third, he intimidates the government under the pretense of offering constructive suggestions, and for such offense he is to be punished by banishment to a nearby area as a soldier. Fourth, he harbors personal grudges against the official under whose jurisdiction he lives and falsely accuses him of wrongdoing before the latter's superior. For this offense he is to be punished by banishment to the malarious regions as a soldier. . . .

Who can believe that when an ordinary citizen is a plaintiff and a government official a defendant, the defendant is always right and the plaintiff always wrong? The answer to both questions would have to be a clear "No one" if we had conscientious, enlightened officials sitting on the bench as judges. . . .

These three ills are the most serious the nation faces today, and the search for their cure is our most urgent task. Insofar as the second and the third ills — the widespread banditry and the condemnation of innocent men — are concerned,

Your Majesty is hereby requested to issue a strict order to all the governors-general and governors to think carefully about them and to devise ways for their cure. As for the first ill or the increasingly higher price of silver, we should find remedies in terms of stabilizing the existing price. Your humble servant is at present drafting a proposal aimed at the attainment of this goal, which, when completed, will be presented to Your Majesty for reference purposes.

## A Revolutionary Formula for China's Revival
▼▼▼

### 82 ▼ *Sun Yat-sen,*
### *THE THREE PEOPLE'S PRINCIPLES AND*
### *THE FUTURE OF THE CHINESE PEOPLE*

By 1900 the prognosis for China's Manchu regime had deteriorated from poor to critical. It had survived massive peasant revolts, military defeats at the hands of the British, French, and Japanese, and a series of one-sided treaties that made a mockery of China's self-image as the world's greatest power. But the Manchu government was doing little more than surviving. In 1898 a desperate attempt to revamp government, encourage education, promote agriculture and commerce, and strengthen the armed forces resulted in a flurry of decrees from Emperor Guangxu during the period known as the One Hundred Days' Reforms. The emperor's efforts, however, were scuttled by court reactionaries led by the Empress Dowager Cixi. Cixi then lent her support to the antiforeign secret societies known as the Boxers, who in 1899 and 1900 converged on Beijing intent on killing or driving away the foreigners. The Boxer Rebellion was suppressed by a multinational force, and China was forced to accept another humiliating treaty — one that included an indemnity of $333,990,000. Support for the government virtually disappeared, and many intellectuals, students, generals, secret society members, and Chinese living abroad began plotting the downfall of the Qing.

The leading revolutionary was Sun Yat-sen (1866–1925), a man far different from previous Chinese reformers. Born to a poor rural family near Guangzhou, Sun was educated in Hawaiian and Chinese missionary schools and developed a world view more Western than Confucian. Galled by his nation's military impotence and Qing ineptitude, in 1894 he founded the secret Revive China Society, which in 1895 laid plans for a military uprising to overthrow the government. The plot was uncovered, and Sun was forced into exile. After sixteen years of traveling, planning, writing, and organizing, his hopes were realized when the revolution that ended the Qing Era broke out in 1911.

On his return to China from the United States (he read about the revolution in a Denver newspaper while en route to Kansas City), he was elected provisional president of the United Provinces of China on December 30, 1911. Sun's moment of glory was short-lived. Without an armed force or an organized political party to back him up, Sun resigned as president in 1912 in favor of the military strong man Yuan Shikai, who one year later sent Sun into exile as part of his plan to establish a dictatorship. Sun returned to Guangzhou in 1917 and attempted to establish a parliamentary government, but by then China had descended into the chaos of warlord rule. When Sun died in 1925 the prospects of national unity and orderly government for China still seemed dim.

In the following selection Sun presents an early formulation of his "three people's principles," which served as the ideology of the United League, an organization he founded in 1905 in Tokyo that combined secret societies from China, overseas Chinese groups, and Chinese students in Japan. When the United League joined with several other groups to form the Guomindang, or Nationalist, party in 1912, Sun's three principles provided the platform for the new party. Sun presented the following analysis of his three principles in a speech to the United League in Tokyo in 1906 to help celebrate the first anniversary of the League's publication, *Min Pao (The People's Journal )*.

## QUESTIONS FOR ANALYSIS

1. What is meant by Sun's principle of nationalism? Against whom are his nationalist sentiments directed? How is his principle of nationalism linked to the principle of democracy?
2. What does he mean by the principle of democracy, and why does he feel it is so important to the future of China?
3. What, according to Sun, have been the good and bad effects of "the advances of civilization"? Why have the benefits of these advances been so poorly distributed?
4. Briefly describe Sun's "land valuation procedure" and its relation to the principle of livelihood. What are its strengths and weaknesses?
5. What is Sun's attitude toward the West? How and in what ways will the future government and society of China be superior to those of the West?
6. To what extent are Sun's ideas inspired by Western ideologies and to what extent do they draw on traditional Chinese thought and practice?

A person always recognizes his parents and never confuses them with strangers. Nationalism is analogous to this. It has to do with human nature and applies to everyone. Today, more than 260 years have passed since the Manchus entered China proper, yet even as children we Han[1] would certainly not mistake them for fellow Han. This is the root of nationalism. On the other hand, we should recognize that nationalism does not mean discriminating against people of different nationality. It simply means not allowing such people to seize our political power, for only when we Han are in control politically do we have a nation. . . .

Let us pause to consider for a moment: Where is the nation? Where is the political power? Actually, we are already a people without a nation! The population of the globe is only one billion, several hundred million; we Han, being 400 million, comprise one-fourth of that population. Our nation is the most populous, most ancient, and most civilized in the world, yet today we are

[1]*Han* in the Chinese language means the Chinese people. Essentially it applies to those who speak the Chinese language and share a common Chinese culture and history.

a lost nation. Isn't that enormously bizarre? The African nation of the Transvaal has a population of only 200,000, yet when Britain tried to destroy it, the fighting lasted three years.[2] The Philippines have a population of only several million, but when America tried to subdue it, hostilities persisted for several years.[3] Is it possible that the Han will gladly be a lost nation?

We Han are now swiftly being caught up in a tidal wave of nationalist revolution, yet the Manchus continue to discriminate against the Han. They boast that their forefathers conquered the Han because of their superior unity and military strength and that they intend to retain these qualities so as to dominate the Han forever. . . . Certainly, once we Han unite, our power will be thousands of times greater than theirs, and the success of the nationalist revolution will be assured.

As for the Principle of Democracy, it is the foundation of the political revolution. In the future, to be sure, the vicious politics of today will be swept away after the nationalist revolution triumphs, but it will also be necessary to eradicate the roots of such politics. For several thousand years China has been a monarchical autocracy, a type of political system intolerable to those living in freedom and equality. A nationalist revolution is not itself sufficient to get rid of such a system. Think for a moment: When the founder of the Ming dynasty expelled the Mongols and restored Chinese rule, the nationalist revolution triumphed, but his political system was only too similar to those of the Han, Tang, and Song dynasties.[4] Consequently, after another three hundred years, foreigners again began to invade China. This is the result of the inadequacy of the political system, so that a po-

litical revolution is an absolute necessity. . . . The aim of the political revolution is to create a constitutional, democratic political system. In the context of the current political situation in China, a revolution would be necessary even if the monarch were a Han. . . .

▾ ▾ ▾

Now, let me begin by discussing the origins of the Principle of the People's Livelihood, a principle that began to flourish only in the latter part of the nineteenth century. Before that it did not flourish because civilization was not as highly developed. . . . As civilization advanced, people relied less on physical labor and more on natural forces, since electricity and steam could accomplish things a thousand times faster than human physical strength. For example, in antiquity a single man tilling the land could harvest at best enough grain to feed a few people, notwithstanding his toil and trouble. Now, however, as a result of the development of scientific agriculture, one man can grow more than enough to feed a thousand people because he can use machinery instead of his limbs, with a consequent increase in efficiency. . . .

Once we adopt this method, the more civilization advances, the greater the wealth of the nation, and then we can be sure our financial problems will not become difficult to handle. After the excessive taxes of the present have been abolished, the price of consumer goods will gradually fall and the people will become increasingly prosperous. We will forever abolish the vicious taxation policies that have prevailed for several thousand years. Even Europe, America, and Japan, although rich and powerful, impose taxes and rents that are too heavy on their people.

---

[2]The reference is to the South African War, also known as the Boer War (1899–1902), fought between Great Britain and Transvaal and the Orange Free State, the two Afrikaner, or Boer, states in South Africa. It resulted from cultural friction and political conflict between the British settlers and administrators in the region and the Dutch settlers of the two states.

[3]Between 1899 and 1901 Filipinos under the leadership of Emilio Aguinaldo fought against their new colonial master, the United States, after the United States took over the Philippines from Spain at the conclusion of the Spanish-American War.

[4]The Han (206 B.C.E.–220 C.E.), Tang (618–907 C.E.), and Song (960–1279 C.E.) were dynastic periods in Chinese history.

After China's social revolution is accomplished, private individuals will never again have to pay taxes. The collection of land revenues alone will make China the richest nation on earth. . . .

▼ ▼ ▼

Obviously, . . . it is necessary to give considerable attention to what the constitution of the Republic of China should be. . . . The British constitution embodies the so-called separation of powers into executive, legislative, and judicial, all mutually independent. . . . The Frenchman Montesquieu[5] later embraced the British system and melded it with his own ideals to create his own school of thought. The American constitution was based on Montesquieu's theories but went further in clearly demarcating the separation of powers. . . . As to the future constitution of the Republic of China, I propose that we introduce a new principle, that of the "five separate powers."

Under this system, there will be two other powers in addition to the three powers just discussed. One is the examination power. . . . American officials are either elected or appointed. Formerly there were no civil service examinations, which led to serious shortcomings with respect to both elected and appointed officials. With respect to elections, those endowed with eloquence ingratiated themselves with the public and won elections, while those who had learning and ideals but lacked eloquence were ignored. Consequently, members of America's House of Representatives have often been foolish and ignorant people who have made its history quite ridiculous. As for appointees, they all come and go with the president. The Democratic and Republican parties have consistently taken turns holding power, and whenever a president is replaced, cabinet members and other officials, comprising no fewer than 60,000–70,000 people, including the postmaster general, are also re-

placed. As a result, the corruption and laxity of American politics are unparalleled among the nations of the world. . . . Therefore, the future constitution of the Republic of China must provide for an independent branch expressly responsible for civil service examinations. Furthermore, all officials, however high their rank, must undergo examinations in order to determine their qualifications. . . . This procedure will eliminate such evils as blind obedience, electoral abuses, and favoritism. . . .

▼ ▼ ▼

Everyone in Europe and America should be living in a state of plenty and happiness undreamed of in antiquity. If we look around, however, we see that conditions in those countries are precisely the opposite. Statistically, Britain's wealth has increased more than several thousandfold over the previous generation, yet poverty of the people has also increased several thousandfold over the previous generation. Moreover, the rich are extremely few, and the poor extremely numerous. This is because the power of human labor is no match for the power of capital. In antiquity, agriculture and industry depended completely on human labor; but now, with the development of natural forces that human labor cannot match, agriculture and industry have fallen completely into the hands of capitalists. . . . Unable to compete, the poor have naturally been reduced to destitution. . . .

Indeed, this constitutes a lesson for China. . . . Civilization yields both good and bad fruits, and we should embrace the good and reject the bad. In the countries of Europe and America, the rich monopolize the good fruits of civilization, while the poor suffer from its evil fruits. . . .

Why have Europe and America failed to solve their social problems? Because they have not solved their land problem. Generally speaking, wherever civilization is advanced, the price of

[5]Montesquieu (1689–1755) was a French political philosopher whose *Spirit of the Laws* (1748) described the separation of powers as a means to protect individual liberty.

land increases with each passing day. . . . In China capitalists have not yet emerged, so that for several thousand years there has been no increase in land prices. . . . After the revolution, however, conditions in China will be different. For example, land prices in Hong Kong and Shanghai are currently as much as several hundred times higher than those in the interior. This increment is the result of the advance of civilization and the development of communications. It is inevitable that, as the entire nation advances, land prices everywhere will rise accordingly. . . . This is evidence of the clearest sort, from which we can see that in the future the rich will get richer every day, and the poor, poorer. In another ten years, social problems will become even more pressing. . . . Consequently, we must come up with a solution now. . . .

With respect to a solution, although the socialists have different opinions, the procedure I most favor is land valuation. For example, if a landlord has land worth 1,000 dollars, its price can be set at 1,000 or even 2,000 dollars. Perhaps in the future, after communications have been developed, the value of his land will rise to 10,000 dollars; the owner should receive 2,000, which entails a profit and no loss, and the 8,000

increment will go to the state. Such an arrangement will greatly benefit both the state and the people's livelihood. Naturally, it will also eliminate the shortcomings that have permitted a few rich people to monopolize wealth. This is the simplest, most convenient, and most feasible method. . . .

The other power is the supervisory power, responsible for monitoring matters involving impeachment. For reasons that should be evident to all, such a branch is indispensable to any nation. The future constitution of the Republic of China must provide for an independent branch. Since ancient times, China had a supervisory organization, the Censorate,[6] to monitor the traditional social order. Inasmuch as it was merely a servant of the monarchy, however, it was ineffectual. . . .

With this added to the four powers already discussed, there will be five separate powers. That constitution will form the basis of the sound government of a nation that belongs to its own race, to its own citizens, and to its own society. This will be the greatest good fortune for our 400 million Han people. I presume that you gentlemen are willing to undertake and complete this task. It is my greatest hope.

---

[6]The Censorate, or Board of Censors, was a unique feature of Ming and Qing government. Members of the board reviewed the conduct of officials, both in the provinces and in Beijing, and reported to the emperor when they discovered dereliction of duty. They were considered the "eyes and ears" of the emperors.

---

▼▼▼

# The Emergence of Modern Japan

In the late nineteenth century the Japanese accomplished what no other people had or has been able to do. Within only three decades and without recourse to foreign loans or investments, Japan changed from a secluded, preindustrial society vulnerable to foreign exploitation into a powerful, industrialized nation that shocked the world by winning wars against China in 1895 and Russia in 1905. What made this transformation even more remarkable was that it was accompanied by little social upheaval and that, despite its magnitude, the Japanese retained many of their hallowed ideals and beliefs.

Japan's transformation began in 1867 when a faction of aristocrats led a rebellion that abolished the Tokugawa shogunate and then orchestrated the move of the previously secluded and ceremonial emperor from Kyoto to Edo to assume titular authority over a government that they controlled. This is known as the Meiji Restoration, based on the Japanese word for "brilliant rule," *meiji,* chosen by Emperor Mutsuhito as his reign name.

The Meiji Restoration came after almost a century in which the foundations of Tokugawa society had been weakened by population growth, urbanization, intellectual ferment, social change, and the erosion of Confucian values. Peasant revolts, urban riots, and bolder and more frequent denunciations of the shogun by restive aristocrats all were signs of a troubled regime.

Then in July 1853 an event that many Japanese had feared for decades finally took place. Into Edo Bay steamed four naval vessels, flying U.S. colors and under the command of the forceful and flamboyant Commodore Matthew Perry. Perry demanded that the Japanese agree to open their ports to U.S. merchants, and Japan acquiesced. Within a decade, Japan also granted trading privileges to the Netherlands, Russia, Great Britain, and France.

Patriotic Japanese now bitterly turned against a government lacking the will, strength, and broad-based support to protect them from such indignities. Opponents of the shogun raised the cry, "Honor the Emperor, Expel the Barbarians!" They were convinced that only the semidivine emperor could inspire the national effort needed to overcome the foreigners. On January 3, 1868 (by the Japanese calendar, the ninth day of the twelfth month of 1867), forces led by the Satsuma and Chosu clans seized the shogun's palace and declared the restoration of the emperor. Mutsuhito accepted the invitation of the rebels to head the government, and after his supporters crushed the shogun's resistance, more than 250 years of Tokugawa rule ended. Japan now entered the Meiji Era, a period of transformation unparalleled in recent history.

## Eastern Ethics and Western Science
▼▼▼

### 83 ▼ *Sakuma Shozan,* *REFLECTIONS ON MY ERRORS*

After Commodore Perry left Tokyo in the summer of 1853, promising to return within a year to receive answers to his demands, government officials, daimyo, samurai, intellectuals, merchants, and courtiers entered into an intense debate about the crisis at hand and their nation's future. Although the immediate reaction was to reject all things Western and "Expel the Barbarians," many soon realized that threats were no match for superior ships and firepower. Thus, as the debate went on, increasing numbers of Japanese were willing to consider the ideas of Sakuma Shozan, whose philosophy is summarized by the motto he made famous: "Eastern ethics and Western science."

Born into a samurai family in 1811, Sakuma had a Confucian education before entering the service of one of Japan's leading aristocrats, Sanada Yukitsura. When the shogun put Sanada in charge of Japan's coastal fortifications in 1841, Sakuma was pushed into the world of artillery, naval strategy, and shipbuilding. He learned Dutch, read all he could of Western science, and became an advocate of adopting

Western weaponry. In the 1840s such views were unpopular within the shogun's government, and as a result both Sakuma and his lord were dismissed from the shogun's service. Sakuma experienced more problems in 1854, when at his urging a student of his attempted to stow away on one of Perry's ships as it left Japan. According to the Seclusion Laws (see source 34), this was a capital offense, but through his aristocratic connections, Sakuma and his student received a jail sentence of only several months.

Sakuma wrote his deceptively titled *Reflections on My Errors* on his release from prison. Far from being an apology for his "errors," it was a vigorous self-defense made up of fifty-two brief commentaries on various issues. Although he claimed that the work was to be "locked up in a box" and shown only to his descendants, it was widely circulated among Japan's military and political leaders.

After completing *Reflections,* Sakuma continued to advocate the opening of Japan and cooperation between shogun and emperor. His ideas angered those who sought to abolish the shogunate completely and they arranged his assassination in 1864.

---

## QUESTIONS FOR ANALYSIS

1. What is the meaning of the parable about the "man who is grieved by the illness of his lord or his father"?
2. What does Sakuma mean by Eastern ethics? Does he see any difficulty reconciling them with Western science? In what way?
3. What does Sakuma see as the major weaknesses of Japan's military leaders and Confucian scholars? How can their deficiencies be rectified?
4. What does Sakuma see as the main reason for studying mathematics and science?
5. Aside from his admiration of Western science, how would you characterize Sakuma's attitude toward the West?
6. What similarities and differences do you see between Sakuma's ideas and those of Honda Toshiaki (source 58)?

In the summer of Kaei 7, the fourth month [May, 1854], I, because of an incident, went down into prison. During my seven months of imprisonment, I pondered over my errors, and, as a result, there were things that I should have liked to say concerning them. However, brush and ink-stone were forbidden in the prison, and I was therefore unable to keep a manuscript. Over that long period, then, I forgot much. Now that I have come out, I shall record what I remember, deposit the record in a cloth box, and bequeath it to my descendants. As for publicizing what I have to say, I dare do no such thing. . . .

2. Take, for example, a man who is grieved by the illness of his lord or his father, and who is seeking medicine to cure it. If he is fortunate enough to secure the medicine, and is certain that it will be efficacious, then, certainly, without questioning either its cost or the quality of its name, he will beg his lord or father to take it. Should the latter refuse on the grounds that he

dislikes the name, does the younger man make various schemes to give the medicine secretly, or does he simply sit by and wait for his master to die? There is no question about it: the feeling of genuine sincerity and heartfelt grief on the part of the subject or son makes it absolutely impossible for him to sit idly and watch his master's anguish; consequently, even if he knows that he will later have to face his master's anger, he cannot but give the medicine secretly. . . .

20. The gentleman has five pleasures, but wealth and rank are not among them. That his house understands decorum and righteousness and remains free from family rifts — this is one pleasure. That exercising care in giving to and taking from others, he provides for himself honestly, free, internally, from shame before his wife and children, and externally, from disgrace before the public — this is the second pleasure. That he expounds and glorifies the learning of the sages, knows in his heart the great Way, and in all situations contents himself with his duty, in adversity as well as in prosperity — this is the third pleasure. That he is born after the opening of the vistas of science by the Westerners, and can therefore understand principles not known to the sages and wise men of old — this is the fourth pleasure. That he employs the ethics of the East and the scientific technique of the West, neglecting neither the spiritual nor material aspects of life, combining subjective and objective, and thus bringing benefit to the people and serving the nation — this is the fifth pleasure. . . .

28. The principal requisite of national defense is that it prevents the foreign barbarians from holding us in contempt. The existing coastal defense installations all lack method; the pieces of artillery that have been set up are improperly made; and the officials who negotiate with the foreigners are mediocrities who have no understanding of warfare. The situation being such,

even though we wish to avoid incurring the scorn of the barbarians, how, in fact, can we do so? . . .

30. Of the men who now hold posts as commanders of the army, those who are not dukes or princes or men of noble rank, are members of wealthy families. As such, they find their daily pleasure in drinking wine, singing, and dancing; and they are ignorant of military strategy and discipline. Should a national emergency arise, there is no one who could command the respect of the warriors and halt the enemy's attack. This is the great sorrow of our times. For this reason, I have wished to follow in substance the Western principles of armament, and, by banding together loyal, valorous, strong men of old, established families not in the military class — men of whom one would be equal to ten ordinary men — to form a voluntary group which would be made to have as its sole aim that of guarding the nation and protecting the people. Anyone wishing to join the society would be tested and his merits examined; and, if he did not shirk hardship, he would then be permitted to join. Men of talent in military strategy, planning, and administration would be advanced to positions of leadership, and then, if the day should come when the country must be defended, this group could be gathered together and organized into an army to await official commands. It is to be hoped that they would drive the enemy away and perform greater service than those who now form the military class. . . .

35. Mathematics is the basis for all learning. In the Western world after this science was discovered military tactics advanced greatly, far outstripping that of former times. This development accords with the statement that "one advanced from basic studies to higher learning." In the *Art of War*[1] of Sunzi, the statement about "estimation, determination of quantity, calculation, judgment, and victory" has reference to

---

[1]A classic work on military strategy written during the early fourth century B.C.E.

mathematics. However, since Sunzi's time nei-ther we nor the Chinese have ceased to read, study, and memorize his teachings, and our art of war remains exactly as it was then. It conse-quently cannot be compared with that of the West. There is no reason for this other than that we have not devoted ourselves to basic studies. At the present time, if we wish really to com-plete our military preparations, we must develop this branch of study. . . .

40. What do the so-called scholars of today actually do? Do they clearly and tacitly under-stand the way in which the gods and sages es-tablished this nation, or the way in which Yao, Shun, and the divine emperors of the three dy-nasties governed?[2] Do they, after having learned the rites and music, punishment and administra-tion, the classics and governmental system, go on to discuss and learn the elements of the art of war, of military discipline, of the principles of machinery? Do they make exhaustive studies of conditions in foreign countries? Of effective de-fense methods? Of strategy in setting up strong-holds, defense barriers, and reinforcements? Of the knowledge of computation, gravitation, ge-ometry, and mathematics? If they do, I have not heard of it! Therefore I ask what the so-called scholars of today actually do. . . .

47. In order to master the barbarians there is nothing so effective as to ascertain in the begin-ning conditions among them. To do this, there is no better first step than to be familiar with barbarian tongues. Thus, learning a barbarian language is not only a step toward knowing the barbarians, but also the groundwork for master-ing them. . . .

49. Last summer the American barbarians ar-rived in the Bay of Uraga[3] with four warships, bearing their president's message. Their deport-ment and manner of expression were exceedingly arrogant, and the resulting insult to our national dignity was not small. Those who heard could but gnash their teeth. A certain person on guard in Uraga suffered this insult in silence, and, hav-ing been ultimately unable to do anything about it, after the barbarians had retired, he drew his knife and slashed to bits a portrait of their leader, which they had left as a gift. Thus he gave vent to his rage. In former times Zao Wei of Song,[4] having been demoted, was serving as an official in Shensi, and when he heard of the character of Chao Yuanhao, he had a person skillful in draw-ing paint Chao's image. Zao looked at this por-trait and knew from its manly appearance that Chao would doubtless make trouble on the bor-der in the future. Therefore Zao wished to take steps toward preparing the border in advance, and toward collecting together and examining men of ability. Afterwards, everything turned out as he had predicted. Thus, by looking at the por-trait of his enemy, he could see his enemy's abili-ties and thereby aid himself with his own preparations. It can only be regretted that the Japanese guard did not think of this. Instead of using the portrait, he tore it up. In both cases there was a barbarian; in both cases there was a portrait. But one man, lacking the portrait, sought to obtain it, while the other, having it, destroyed it. Their depth of knowledge and far-sightedness in planning were vastly different.

---

[2]According to the most widespread version of earliest Chi-nese history, China was governed by three early rulers *(huang),* followed by five emperors and then three dynas-ties, the Xia, Shang, and Zhou. Yao and Shun, the last two of the "five emperors," were revered for their wisdom and virtue.
[3]A small bay at the mouth of Tokyo Bay.
[4]The Chinese Song Dynasty ruled from 960 to 1279 C.E.

# Patriotic Duty and Business Success
▼▼▼

## 84 ▾ *Iwasaki Yataro,* *LETTER TO MITSUBISHI EMPLOYEES*

A priority for the Meiji reformers was to establish a strong industrial economy, both to support the army and navy and to protect the country from foreign exploitation. After a rocky start in the 1870s, Japanese industrialization proceeded rapidly, and by 1900 the nation had become a major economic power through a combination of government subsidies and individual entrepreneurship.

The greatest success story in Japan's economic transformation was Iwasaki Yataro (1835–1885), the founder of one of the nation's most powerful business conglomerates, Mitsubishi. Born into a poor farming family, Iwasaki gained a rudimentary education and held several low-level business jobs before he found employment as an administrator in the domain of the aristocratic Tosa family in the mid 1860s. He was given the task of managing and reducing the domain's huge debt, the result of massive purchases of firearms and artillery. His policies, which included paying some debtors with counterfeit money, quickly eliminated the domain's deficit. In 1871, when the domain abandoned its direct ownership of business enterprises, it gave Iwasaki eleven steamships and all the assets connected with its enterprises in silk, coal mining, tea, and lumber. In return, Iwasaki was expected to pay off some new Tosa debts and provide employment for former samurai. With this to build on, he systematically wiped out foreign and domestic competition and, through a series of shrewd (and frequently cutthroat) business moves, turned Mitsubishi into Japan's second largest conglomerate, with interests in shipbuilding, mining, banking, insurance, and manufacturing.

Iwasaki wrote the following letter to his employees in 1876 during Mitsubishi's battle with the British Peninsula and Oriental Steam Navigation Company over control of Japanese coastal trade. He had just cut fares in half but had also reduced wages by a third.

---

## QUESTIONS FOR ANALYSIS

1. Why does Iwasaki believe that the Japanese must prevent foreigners from becoming involved in the coastal trade?
2. According to Iwasaki, what is at stake in the competition for control of Japan's coastal trade?
3. What advantages and disadvantages does Iwasaki's company have in its rivalry with the Peninsula and Oriental Steamship Company?
4. How does Iwasaki attempt to inspire greater dedication and effort from his workers?
5. To what extent is Iwasaki's letter similar in spirit to Sakuma Shozan's *Reflections on My Errors* (source 83)?

Many people have expressed differing opinions concerning the principles and advantages of engaging foreigners or Japanese in the task of coastal trade. Granted, we may permit a dissenting opinion which suggests that in principle both foreigners and Japanese must be permitted to engage in coastal trade, but once we look into the question of advantages, we know that coastal trade is too important a matter to be given over to the control of foreigners. If we allow the right of coastal navigation to fall into the hands of foreigners in peacetime it means loss of business opportunities and employment for our own people, and in wartime it means yielding the vital right of information to foreigners. In fact, this is not too different from abandoning the rights of our country as an independent nation.

Looking back into the past, in Japan at the time when we abandoned the policy of seclusion and entered into an era of friendly intercourse and commerce with foreign nations, we should have been prepared for this very task. However, due to the fact that our people lack knowledge and wealth, we have yet to assemble a fleet sufficient to engage in coastal navigation. Furthermore, we have neither the necessary skills for navigation nor a plan for developing maritime transportation industry. This condition is the cause of attracting foreign shipping companies to occupy our major maritime transport lines. Yet our people show not a sense of surprise at it. Some people say that our treaties with foreign powers contain an express provision allowing foreign ships to proceed from Harbor A to Harbor B, and others claim that such a provision must not be regarded as granting foreign ships the right to coastal navigation inasmuch as it is intended not to impose unduly heavy taxes on them. While I am not qualified to discuss it, the issue remains an important one.

I now propose to do my utmost, and along with my 35 million compatriots, perform my duty as a citizen of this country. That is to recover the right of coastal trade in our hands, and not to delegate that task to foreigners. Unless we propose to do so, it is useless for our government to revise the unequal treaties[1] or to change our entrenched customs. We need people who can respond, otherwise all the endeavors of the government will come to naught. This is the reason why the government protects our company, and I know that our responsibilities are even greater than the full weight of Mt. Fuji[2] thrust upon our shoulders. There have been many who wish to hinder our progress in fulfilling our obligations. However, we have been able to eliminate one of our worst enemies, the Pacific Mail Company of the United States, from contention by application of appropriate means.[3] Now, another rival has emerged. It is the Peninsula & Oriental Steam Navigation Company of Great Britain which is setting up a new line between Yokohama and Shanghai, and is attempting to claim its right over the ports of Nagasaki, Kobe, and Yokohama. The P & O Company comes to compete for the right of coastal navigation with us. How can we decline the challenge? Heretofore, our company has received protection from the government, support from the nation, and hard work from its employees through which it has done its duty. However, our company is young and not every phase of its operation is well conducted. In contrast, the P & O Company is backed by its massive capital, its large fleet of ships, and by its experiences of operations in Oriental countries. In competing against this giant, what methods can we employ?

I have thought about this problem very carefully and have come to one conclusion. There is no other alternative but to eliminate unnecessary positions and unnecessary expenditures. This is a time-worn solution and no new wisdom is involved. Even though it is a familiar saying, it is much easier said than done, and this indeed

---

[1] The various commercial treaties the shogunate signed after Admiral Perry's mission.
[2] The highest mountain in Japan, near Tokyo.
[3] The American firm abandoned its effort to crack the Japanese market when it found it could not compete with Mitsubishi's price slashing, made possible largely by hefty government subsidies.

has been the root cause of difficulties in the past and present times. Therefore, starting immediately I propose that we engage in this task. By eliminating unnecessary personnel from the payroll, eliminating unnecessary expenditures, and engaging in hard and arduous work, we shall be able to solidify the foundation of our company. If there is a will there is a way. Through our own effort, we shall be able to repay the government for its protection and answer our nation for its confidence shown in us. Let us work together in discharging our responsibilities and not be ashamed of ourselves. Whether we succeed or fail, whether we can gain profit or sustain loss, we cannot anticipate at this time. Hopefully, all of you will join me in a singleness of heart to attain this cherished goal, forebearing and undaunted by setbacks to restore to our own hands the right to our own coastal trade. If we succeed it will not only be an accomplishment for our company alone but also a glorious event for our Japanese Empire, which shall let its light shine to all four corners of earth. We can succeed or fail, and it depends on your effort or lack of effort. Do your utmost in this endeavor!

# Images of the West in Late Tokugawa and Meiji Japan
▼▼▼

## 85 ▼ *PRINTS AND DRAWINGS, 1853–1887*

In the decades after the first Europeans arrived in Japan in 1542, their ideas, dress, weapons, and religion proved attractive to many Japanese. As many as five hundred thousand Japanese converted to Catholicism, military leaders put European firearms to use in the Japanese civil wars, and in the 1580s and 1590s there was even a groundswell of interest in European fashion and cuisine. After the suppression of Christianity and the implementation of the seclusion policy by the Tokugawa in the seventeenth century, however, knowledge of the West soon came to be limited to the few merchants who traded with the Dutch in Nagasaki and a handful of intellectuals who maintained interest in European thought, or Dutch studies. For most Japanese, memory of the South Sea Barbarians disappeared.

The arrival of Commodore Perry in 1853 and the opening of Japan to foreign trade in 1854 changed this dramatically. Inspired by a mixture of fear, awe, and curiosity, the Japanese developed a deep interest in the West, and a flood of printed material about Europe and the United States appeared in the 1850s and 1860s. Then after the Meiji Restoration of 1868, imitation of the West became a patriotic duty. Employing Western science, technology, military organization, and government practices would make Japan strong and prosperous; adopting Western fashion, etiquette, grooming habits, architecture, and culture would make the Japanese respected and admired. What can only be described as a craze for things Western took hold of Japan in the early Meiji period. In the late 1880s, however, a reaction against overzealous Westernization set in. Since then, the Japanese have managed to strike a successful balance between borrowing from the West what was necessary for their modernization while preserving the essentials of their traditional culture.

The six following illustrations, covering the period from the 1850s to the late 1880s, provide insights into changing Japanese views of the West. They also serve as reminders that these changes in attitudes underlay the political, military, and economic transformation that made Japan a world power.

The first two illustrations (page 365) are tile prints that appeared shortly after the arrival of Commodore Perry in 1853. Forerunners of modern newspapers, tile prints could be produced quickly and cheaply after newsworthy events and sold for a few cents. Since the printmakers feared government censorship, their prints, like those included here, often appeared without the name of the artist or publisher. The first print depicts one of Perry's "black ships," so called because of the dark smoke that belched from their smokestacks. The Japanese text provides information on the ship's dimensions and the length of its voyage to Japan. The second print depicts Commander Henry Adams, Perry's second-in-command.

The next two illustrations both appeared when the drive to emulate Europeans was fully underway. The first illustration (page 366) is part of a series of woodblock prints published in the 1880s entitled *Self-Made Men Worthy of Emulation.* The individual depicted here is Fukuchi Gen'ichiro (1841–1909), a journalist who served as editor-in-chief of Tokyo's first daily newspaper. He is shown as a war correspondent covering the Satsuma Rebellion of 1877, an antigovernment rebellion by disgruntled samurai against the new Meiji order that was suppressed by the imperial army. The accompanying text (with an erroneous birthdate) reads:

> Fukuchi Gen'ichiro was born in Nagasaki in 1844. An exceptionally bright child, he could recognize characters at the age of five and had begun to read and write at about the age of seven. He resolved to enter the service of the shogunate and, upon coming of age, entered the government, in the service of which he traveled three times to Europe. He then entered into a successful business career. In 1874 he became president of the Reporters' Association. He personally covered the Satsuma Rebellion in the south. Received by the emperor, he respectfully reported his observations to the throne. His style seemed almost supernatural in its logic, force, and lucidity. He is one of the truly great men of Meiji.

The next illustration (page 367, top) appeared in a popular book, written by Kanagaki Robun and published in serial form in the 1870s. Entitled *Hiking through the West,* it relates the adventures of two Japanese travelers during a trip to London and back. The illustration depicts, from right to left, an "unenlightened man," dressed in the garb of a samurai, a "half-enlightened man," and an "enlightened man."

Even in the years when the Japanese enthusiasm for things Western reached its height, there were those who opposed Japan's headlong rush to Westernize. Government censorship caused most of these critics to keep their opinions to themselves, but a few managed to get their ideas into print. Cartoonists Honda Kinkichiro and Kobayashi Kyochika were two such individuals. Honda's cartoons, usually accompanied by English captions and a Japanese text, appeared in the 1870s and 1880s in the weekly humor magazine, *Marumara Chimbun.* His cartoon "Monkey Show Dressing Room" (page 367, bottom) was published in 1879, shortly after Dr. Edward S. Morse introduced Darwin's theory of evolution in a series of lectures at the newly founded Department of Zoology at Tokyo University. The text reads, "Mr. Morse explains that all human beings were

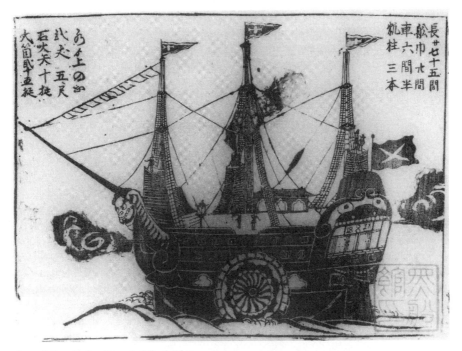

*One of Commodore Perry's Black Ships*

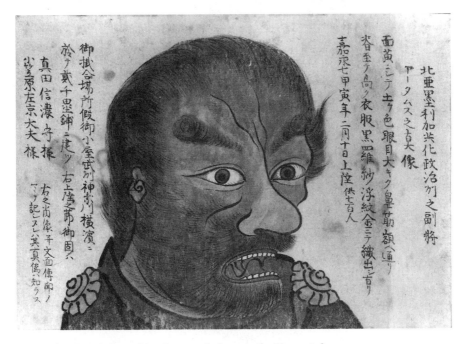

*Commodore Perry's Second-in-Command, Commander Henry Adams*

*Kobayashi Kyochika, Fukuchi Gen'ichiro*

*Kanagaki Robun, Hiking through the West*

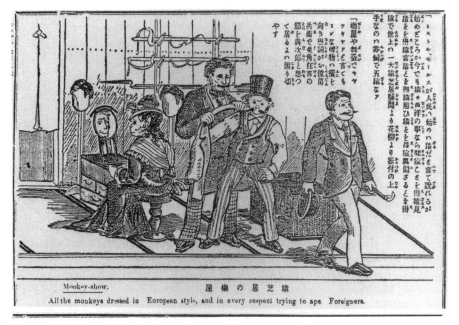

*Honda Kinkichiro, "Monkey Show Dressing Room"*

*Kobayashi Kiyochika, "Hands Dance, Feet Stomp, Call Out Hurrah!"*

monkeys in the beginning. In the beginning — but even now aren't we still monkeys? When it comes to Western things we think the red beards [a Japanese nickname for Westerners] are the most skillful at everything." Kobayashi, who contributed cartoons to *Marumara Chimbun* in the 1880s, published his cartoon (above) in the *Tokyo Daily News* in 1891. It depicts the New Year's Dance held in the Rokumeikan, a pavilion built by the government in 1883 to serve as a venue for fancy-dress balls and other entertainments involving Westerners and Japan's elite. Above the dance floor, dominated by ill-matched Western and Japanese couples, is a sign that reads, "Hands Dance, Feet Stomp, Call Out Hurrah!"

## QUESTIONS FOR ANALYSIS

1. What impression of the West is conveyed by the prints of Perry's ship and his second-in-command, Commander Adams? What specific details help convey this impression?
2. In the top illustration on page 367, what are the most significant differences between the three figures? How does the artist convey a sense of the "enlightened man's" superiority?
3. What is there in the drawing of Fukuchi Gen'ichiro and in the accompanying text that makes him "a man worthy of emulation"?

4. Why do you think the artist chose to depict Fukuchi while he was covering the Satsuma Rebellion?
5. What messages are Honda and Kobayashi attempting to convey about Japan's campaign to westernize?
6. Compare and contrast the depiction of Westerners in "Hands Dance . . ." with the earlier depiction of Commander Adams.

▼▼▼

# Southeast Asia in the Era of Imperialism

The Western takeover of Southeast Asia in the nineteenth century was more gradual than the European seizure of Africa but was motivated by the same mixture of nationalism, anticipated economic benefits, missionary zeal, and perceived strategic imperatives. The British move into Burma, which took place in three stages following wars fought in the 1820s, 1850s, and 1880s, was to prevent Burmese interference in India and head off French influence in the region. In contrast, the British takeover of the Malay Peninsula was mainly inspired by economic motives. The British annexed Singapore in 1819 after they discovered that Malacca, conquered from the Dutch in 1795, had lost much of its commercial prominence. They then extended their authority over the remainder of the peninsula to protect their interest in the region's tin mines and rubber plantations.

The French subjugation of Vietnam, which began in 1862 with the takeover of Saigon and the southern provinces, was ostensibly for religious reasons. The French intervened to protect Vietnamese Christians and European Catholic missionaries from persecution by the Vietnamese government. They subsequently took over northern Vietnam, Laos, and Cambodia, and lumped these territories into their colony of Indochina.

The Dutch expanded their political control in the East Indies in the late nineteenth century to head off European competitors and to exploit the islands' tin, oil, rubber, and agricultural products. Finally, the United States became an imperialist power in the region when it took over the Philippines from Spain after the Spanish American War of 1898 and crushed Filipino resistance between 1899 and 1901.

Although Western colonialism in most of Southeast Asia was relatively brief, lasting on average only a century or less, it was still significant. In politics it brought administrative cohesion to diverse island groupings such as the East Indies, and throughout the region it weakened or destroyed the authority of traditional leaders. It also altered the region's economy by stimulating enterprises such as tin mining and rubber production, introducing new crops such as the oil palm, improving communications, and promoting the building of new harbors and rail systems. In part because of this economic development, the region's population soared from approximately 26 million in 1830 to 123 million in the 1940s. Western colonialism also expanded education and introduced the ideologies of nationalism, liberalism, and democracy. Inevitably, these developments inspired anticolonial movements and, after World War II, the emergence of independent states throughout the region.

# Reform from Above in Thailand
▼▼▼

## 86 ▼ King Chulalongkorn, *EDICTS AND PROCLAMATIONS*

Unlike the rulers of Burma, who underestimated the British threat, and the rulers of Vietnam, who provoked the French by persecuting Christians, the kings of Thailand pursued a policy of compromise with the West and a program of European-inspired reform. As a result, Thailand survived Europe's imperialist drive into Southeast Asia with territorial losses but its independence intact.

Thailand had been largely immune from Western interference since the seventeenth century, but in the 1820s the British began to petition for trading privileges, and missionaries, many of them American Protestants, increased their activities. The missionaries made few converts among Thailand's devout Buddhists, but they introduced Western medicine, science, and the country's first printing press. They also influenced King Mongkut (r. 1851–1868), the ruler who formulated Thailand's strategy to deal with the West. Before becoming king, Mongkut spent twenty-seven years in a Buddhist monastery, where in addition to his religious studies he learned Western languages and developed an interest in Western science and mathematics. As king, he sought to modernize Thailand's army and economy and to accommodate Western powers by opening Thailand to trade.

Mongkut's policies were continued under his son Chulalongkorn (one of the eighty children Mongkut fathered after abandoning monastic celibacy at age forty-seven), who reigned from 1868 to 1910. Chulalongkorn's experiences included trips to India, Java, and Malaya and toward the end of his reign two visits to Europe. He delicately balanced his diplomatic relations with Great Britain, colonial master of Burma and Malaya, and France, which dominated Indochina. He also worked to introduce railroad, postal, and telegraph systems, founded schools, and abolished slavery.

The following excerpts from Chulalongkorn's speeches and writings provide insights into his motives and style as a reformer. The first selection is from a speech to his advisors in 1864 on the subject of slavery, a centuries-old institution in Thailand. Large numbers of Thais sold themselves into slavery to cancel debts or escape poverty, and all their children became slaves. The state put a value on slaves at various ages, and slaves could gain their freedom if they paid their master their worth. Few could do this, so most slaves were slaves for life. Chulalongkorn gradually liberalized Thailand's slavery laws and in 1895 abolished slavery altogether.

The other two sections deal with education, the expansion of which was crucial to Chulalongkorn's plans to modernize his country. He advocated the teaching of Western languages, mathematics, and science while preserving Thailand's cultural and literary heritage.

## QUESTIONS FOR ANALYSIS

1. What seem to be the motives for Chulalongkorn's interest in mitigating the conditions of slavery?
2. Why does he believe that immediately ending slavery would be a mistake?
3. What were Chulalongkorn's convictions about education, and how were they linked to his strategy for ending slavery?
4. What kind of person should Thailand's educational system seek to produce, according to Chulalongkorn?
5. In Chulalongkorn's view, what are the major deficiencies of missionary schools?
6. How does Chulalongkorn's approach to reform differ from that of Russia's Peter the Great (source 41)?

I wish to see whatever is beneficial to the people accomplished gradually according to circumstances and unjust, though well-established, customs abolished. But, as it is impossible to change everything overnight, steady pruning is necessary to lighten the burden. If this practice is adopted, things will proceed smoothly and satisfactorily as time goes by. As far as slavery is concerned, children born to slaves in their creditors' houses are considered by present legislation to be slaves. For this purpose, male slaves born in such circumstances from the age of 26 to 40 are worth each, according to present legislation, 14 *tamlungs,*[1] while female ones are worth each 12 *tamlungs.* In the case of male slaves of more than 40 and female ones of more than 30, value declines gradually with advancing age until at 100 male slaves are worth 1 *tamlung* while female ones 3 *baht.*

I feel that children born to slaves in their creditor's houses, who are slaves as from the time of delivery and are worth something even beyond 100, have not been treated kindly. Children thus born have nothing to do with their parents' wrongdoing. The parents have not only sold themselves into slavery but also dragged their innocent children into lifetime slavery and suffering on their behalf. But to emancipate them

straight away now would put them into the danger of being neglected and being left to die by themselves, since unkind creditors, seeing no use in letting mothers look after their children, will put these mothers to work. It is therefore felt that, if these children are of no use to their parents' creditors, they will meet with no kindness. If the burden borne at present is so reduced as to allow them to become free, it seems advisable. Slaves' children aged from 8 upwards can be depended upon to work, and thus their full worth should be calculated as from this age. With advancing years their worth should be reduced until at 21 they are emancipated just in time for ordination as priests and for embarking on their careers. Similarly, female slaves are emancipated just in time to get married and have children. . . . Thus at 21 they are emancipated, and, in view of the fact that they have served their masters up to 20, enough advantage has been derived by their masters. . . .

▷ Chulalongkorn expresses his hope that all slavery might be abolished.

However, I do not think that my proposal can be carried to its logical conclusions, since pres-

[1]A unit of Thai currency; one tamlung equaled four baht.

sure exists in the direction of making people want to become slaves despite our desire to see the contrary. Slaves do not have to pay high State dues and do not have to engage in any regular occupation, since they are maintained by their masters. They work when work comes to them; otherwise they are unoccupied. When there is nothing to do and they happen to come by a bit of money, they gamble, since there is no risk of losing their means of subsistence. To eradicate slavery it is necessary to go to its root causes; but whatever can be done in the circumstances should proceed step by step. . . . If my proposal really succeeds, I can think of one other thing which can effectively liberate slaves' children from slavery. Slaves' children are compelled to serve their masters from an early age and know nothing other than what pleases their masters. Instead of getting vocational training, they spend their free time in gambling from early childhood so that this habit becomes ingrained, thereby preventing them from seeing any value in having a career. If they really have to quit slavery, they do not possess sufficient knowledge to improve their status and are compelled to return to slavery. It is because of this that there should be an institution for education similar to the old almshouse where, by royal command, education was given to children. There have been a good many men educated in this manner, and many available clerks at the time came from such institution. . . . At the present time, there are not enough clerks [literate people] to go round. Literate people are in great demand among the noblemen and will not readily remain slaves. This is why I feel that education can really free slaves. . . . Once they can read and write, various subjects including those derived from translated European texts can be taught. At 17 or 18 they should be able to apply their knowledge to various branches of the civil service as petty officials or clerks, or secure employment outside the civil service. There is little likelihood, then, of their going to the dogs, unless they are inherently bad. But school education is an increasingly expensive undertaking, and should begin in a small way with possibilities of gradual expansion. This will not only reduce the number of slaves but will also bring prosperity to the country, paving the way for a more drastic reform in the future. . . .

## ROYAL PROCLAMATION ON EDUCATION

. . . Chulalongkorn, Lord of Siam, considers that, though the long-established practice in education in Siam has been to use the monastery as the seat of learning and the home as the center of vocational training in the family, in modern times the increasing tempo of international communications by means of steamers at sea and railways on land and the increasing international contacts caused by the necessity of nations to exchange commodities, have dictated a reorientation of academic and technical training in a correct and useful manner and also a proper adjustment of outmoded disciplines and arts.

At a time when international contacts were difficult, international disparities in academic and technical advance could persist; but, now that such contacts have been rendered so close, international differences in levels of academic and technical achievements are bound to disappear. . . .

The Government has for some time maintained schools; but the original purpose of training people for the needs of the civil service has misled some into thinking that learning is meant exclusively for those destined for the civil service and that it is no part of the masses' duty to seek knowledge. . . .

In actual fact, education leads to intelligence and proper behavior and skill in earning one's living. No matter what a person's career is, whether it be in teaching, medicine, trade or mechanics, prior learning is essential for success in life. . . .

Having taken all this into consideration, His Majesty has graciously commanded his people in the following terms:

From now on it shall be the duty of parents and guardians to teach their children and afford them such opportunity for education as their status and financial means allow. The Government will, for its part, lay down the framework of national education as a guideline to be announced later by officials of the Ministry of Education. The purpose of such education and training shall be to inculcate the following qualities: inquisitiveness for knowledge to whet intelligence and capability, good and righteous behavior, concern for family welfare, generosity to relatives, unity and harmony with spouses, faithfulness to friends, economy, kindness to others, regard for the public good, compliance with laws, willingness to serve the country with courage, loyalty to the throne in times of need, and gratefulness and loyalty to the throne at all times.

When all these elements of responsibility have become so deeply rooted in one's nature as to be manifested in all outward behavior, then training and education may be said to have succeeded, and any one who has successfully undergone the process may be said to be an eminently worthy citizen of Siam.

## LETTER TO THE THAI MINISTER OF EDUCATION, 1910

Dear Praya Paisal,

I have one more thing to tell you. At the celebration of my birthday the Kulstree School[2] for royal ladies sent me 6 copies of the Wadhana Widhaya magazine, which is a monthly and which you may have seen yourself. . . .

My reaction as I went through the magazine was initially that these missionaries had a working knowledge of Siamese and that our girl students had a working knowledge of English. On reflection, however, it was seen that the knowledge of contributors was confined to narrow limits, since there were many errors in respect, for instance, to geography and history about which nothing was known. What was known concerned only religion taught by teachers, and it is a pity that students should be thus confined. . . .

My conclusion from this was that, though the teaching of missionaries could bring about knowledge and intelligence in some matters, it could hardly foster patriotism, since the basic approach was already destructive of this. . . . In one place mention was made of liberty, which the Siamese were unlikely to understand when it was also made of riots in India. This is something we are not accustomed to and must be a novelty. . . . I think it should be our principle to think out the approach to education that will promote the welfare of that part of the globe in which we live rather that which missionaries set up. What they preach will be different from the principles of learning in particular countries. Do they all preach this in all places and do they succeed elsewhere? I do not think they do. They can only deceive softhearted and ignorant women into following them. Even then these people are in the minority and in an embarrassing position. They feel abashed to pay respect to Buddhist monks in the presence of Europeans, and are equally shameful to let the Siamese know their European faith. There are many such Siamese, and it is not in the nature of our good citizens to be so. Remember this. Religion is not important, and any religion is out of date in the context of the present day, unless we establish up-to-date religions. But, as we cannot establish religions, we should plan to keep up with the times and forget about an up-to-date religion. It is a waste of time to argue about something which is 2,000 years old.

---

[2]A school sponsored by the Anglican Church, England's state church, for educating princesses and daughters of the high nobility.

# The Fall of Vietnam
▼▼▼

## 87 ▼ *Phan Thanh Gian,*
### *LETTER TO EMPEROR TU DUC and*
### *LAST MESSAGE TO HIS ADMINISTRATORS*

Phan Thanh Gian (1796–1867) poignantly represents the submission of traditional Confucian Vietnam to French imperialism. The Nguyen (nuh-win´) Dynasty, having unified the country and moved its capital from Hanoi to Hué in 1802, attempted to govern strictly on the principles of Confucianism, which, in contrast to the Hindu-Buddhist or Muslim influence throughout the rest of the region, had largely shaped Vietnam's scholarship, politics, and values. The Nguyen emperors' efforts to turn Vietnam into a model Confucian society led directly to the persecution of Vietnamese Christians, who, as a result of efforts by French, Spanish, and Portuguese missionaries, numbered three hundred thousand by the nineteenth century. When Vietnamese Catholics were implicated in a rebellion in 1833, the emperor ordered the imprisonment and execution of converts and European missionaries. This step caused the French, who sixty years earlier had helped the Nguyen Dynasty gain power, to send troops to Vietnam in 1858, ostensibly to protect Christianity but also to advance French imperialism. Although the Vietnamese staunchly resisted, Emperor Tu Duc accepted a settlement in 1862 by which he ceded to the French three southern provinces around Saigon.

Four years later, an anti-French rebellion broke out in three provinces west of Saigon, then under the governorship of Phan Thanh Gian, one of Vietnam's leading statesmen and the head of a delegation sent to Paris in 1863 to negotiate with the French government. When he failed to suppress the revolts, the French sent in troops and demanded control of the provinces. Phan Thanh Gian acquiesced and then committed suicide, but not before he wrote the following two letters, one to Emperor Tu Duc and the other to administrators in his district.

## QUESTIONS FOR ANALYSIS

1. What is the basis of Phan Thanh Gian's hope that the emperor can save Vietnam from further humiliation at the hands of the French?
2. What is Phan Thanh Gian's view of the French?
3. What evidence of Phan Thanh Gian's Confucian training do you see in the letter?
4. Why did Phan Thanh Gian decide to acquiesce to the French?

## LETTER TO EMPEROR TU DUC

8, July 1867

I, Phan Thanh Gian, make the following report, in expressing frankly, with my head bowed, my humble sentiments, and in soliciting, with my head raised, your discerning scrutiny.

During the period of difficulties and misfortunes that we are presently undergoing, rebellion is rising around the capital, the pernicious influence[1] is expanding on our frontiers. The territorial question is rapidly leading to a situation that it is impossible to end.

My duty compels me to die. I would not dare to live thoughtlessly, leaving a heritage of shame to my Sovereign and my Father. Happily, I have confidence in my Emperor, who has extensive knowledge of ancient times and the present and who has studied profoundly the causes of peace and of dissension: . . . In respectfully observing the warnings of Heaven and in having pity on the misery of man . . . in changing the string of the guitar, in modifying the track of the governmental chariot, it is still possible for you to act in accordance with your authority and means.

At the last moment of life, the throat constricted, I do not know what to say, but, in wiping my tears and in raising my eyes toward you affectionately, I can only ardently hope that this wish will be realized. With respect, I make this report, Tu Duc, twentieth year, sixth moon, seventh day, Phan Thanh Gian.

## LAST MESSAGE
## TO HIS ADMINISTRATORS

Mandarins and people,

It is written: He who lives in accordance with the will of Heaven lives in virtue; he who does not live according to the will of Heaven lives in evil. To work according to the will of Heaven is to listen to natural reason. . . . Man is an intelligent animal created by Heaven. Every animal lives according to his nature, as water flows to low ground, as fire goes out on dry ground. . . . Men, to whom Heaven has given reason, must apply themselves to live in obedience to this reason which Heaven has given them.

The empire of our king is ancient. Our gratitude toward our kings is complete and always ardent; we cannot forget them. Now, the French are come, with their powerful weapons of war to cause dissension among us. We are weak against them; our commanders and our soldiers have been vanquished. Each battle adds to our misery. . . . The French have immense warships, filled with soldiers and armed with huge cannons. No one can resist them. They go where they want, the strongest ramparts fall before them.

I have raised my spirit toward Heaven and I have listened to the voice of reason. And I have said: "It would be as senseless for you to wish to defeat your enemies by force of arms as for a young fawn to attack a tiger. You attract uselessly great misfortunes upon the people whom Heaven has confided to you. I have thus written to all the mandarins and to all the war commanders to break their lances and surrender the forts without fighting.

But, if I have followed the Will of Heaven by averting great evils from the head of the people, I am a traitor to our king in delivering without resistance the provinces which belong to him. . . . I deserve death. Mandarins and people, you can live under the command of the French, who are only terrible during the battle, but their flag must never fly above a fortress where Phan Thanh Gian still lives."

---

[1]The French.

# Part Four

▼▼▼

## *Global Society and Its Challenges in the Twentieth Century*

It is impossible to predict how future historians will interpret the twentieth century, a century marked by spectacular human achievements and abysmal human failures. Their views of the past will be shaped by values and concerns unique to their age, and what seems of great consequence to us may be insignificant to them. It would be surprising, however, if their histories did not emphasize the dramatic shifts in world relationships that took place around the middle of the century. The world of the early 1900s was a Eurocentric world. Europeans were the best-educated and wealthiest people on Earth, and a few European states — Great Britain, Germany, and France, along with the Netherlands, Portugal, Belgium, Italy, and a European offshoot, the United States — were the colonial masters of Africa and much of Asia. When one spoke of Great Powers, they were all European states. Despite its new industrial might, the United States was still not a major player on the world scene. After the Second World War, Europe's primacy ended. The Europeans' colonial empires disintegrated, their paramount role in international relations shifted to the Soviet Union and the United States, and their economic importance declined in the face of global competition.

Future historians undoubtedly will also highlight the increasing global interrelatedness that developed during the twentieth century. Growing interaction among the world's regions and peoples had been an outstanding feature of history ever since the fifteenth and sixteenth centuries when Europeans first sailed to Africa, the Americas, and Asia and opened a new era in commerce, migration, and biological exchange. But during the twentieth century, breakthroughs in communications and transportation virtually obliterated the limitations of time and space, and the exchange of goods and ideas among the world's peoples reached undreamed-of levels. It became the age of *world* wars, *multinational* corporations, *global* communication networks, the *World Wide Web,* and thousands of *international* organizations.

Historians assuredly will also note other developments: the ongoing rush of scientific, medical, and technological discoveries; the spectacular expansion of the world's population (from approximately 1.7 billion in 1900 to more than 6 billion in 2000); the decline of the world's rural population and the growth of cities, best represented by megacities such as Tokyo, Mexico City, São Paulo, and Bombay; and the emergence at least superficially of a shared global culture, symbolized by the ubiquity of fast-food restaurants, blue jeans, popular music, and CNN.

What else historians will say about the twentieth century is open to conjecture. They undoubtedly will take note of the century's inhumanities and cruelties: its appalling war casualties, its use of torture, and its genocides, not just against Jews in World War II but also against Armenians in World War I, Cambodians in the 1970s, and Bosnians, Kosovars, and Tutsi in the 1990s. Will such developments be described as aberrations or the beginning of a new trend toward brutality and callousness in human relationships? Historians surely will discuss the emergence of over one hundred new independent states in Africa and Asia after the demise of colonialism. Will the story they tell be a celebration of economic and political achievement or a tale of failure and disillusionment? They will note that the twentieth century was marked by signs of both growing religious fervor and indifference; environmental disasters and growing environmental consciousness; and the globalization of culture and the continued appeal of nationalism and ethnic identification.

In looking toward the future, optimists affirm their faith in progress, holding fast to the dream that reasonable human beings are capable of shaping a future of peace, harmony, and a just sharing of the world's wealth. Pessimists ponder population projections, inevitable oil shortages, worsening pollution, and perhaps a nuclear winter, and warn of the coming of a new "dark age." However things develop, the twentieth century launched humankind on new paths that will determine its future for years to come.

# Chapter 11

▼▼▼

# The Industrialized World in Crisis

In 1922 the French intellectual Paul Valéry spoke these words in a speech to a university audience in Switzerland:

> The storm has died away, and still we are restless, uneasy, as if the storm is about to break. Almost all the affairs of men remain in terrible uncertainty. We think of what has disappeared, we are almost destroyed by what has been destroyed; we do not know what will be born, and we fear the future, not without reason. We hope vaguely, we dread precisely; . . . we confess that the charm of life is behind us, abundance is behind us, but doubt and disorder are in us and with us. There is no thinking man, however shrewd or learned he may be, who can hope to overcome this anxiety, to escape this darkness, to measure the probable duration of this period when the vital relations of humanity are disturbed profoundly.[1]

How stark a contrast between Valéry's despondency and the previous generation's limitless optimism! Before World War I the wealth, power, and scientific achievements of the West reached unimagined heights, and most Americans and Europeans were self-satisfied and proud to the point of arrogance. They took for granted their moral and intellectual superiority and were confident their world dominance would last indefinitely. The people of Japan, a new and successful entrant into the ranks of industrialized nations, had a different perspective on the future, but like the people of the West they looked forward to that future with high expectations. Only a few years later assurance gave way to doubt, hope to despair, and optimism to dread.

The turning point, especially for Europe, was World War I — the four-year exercise in death that resulted in thirty million casualties, billions of squandered dollars, and a disturbing

---

[1]Paul Valéry, *Variety* (New York: Harcourt-Brace, 1927), p. 252.

realization that human inventiveness could have dark and devastating consequences. The war and the treaties that followed set the stage for three decades of turmoil that included worldwide depression, totalitarianism, diplomatic failure, contempt for human rights, and finally, a second world war with a legacy of fifty to sixty million dead, the attempted annihilation of Europe's Jews, and the dropping of the first atomic bombs.

Intellectuals who shared Paul Valéry's anxiety and gloom prophesied the fall of Western civilization and drew analogies between the decline of the West in the twentieth century and the fatal problems of fifth-century Rome. Developments after World War II discredited much of their bleak pessimism. The industrialized nations, even devastated Germany and Japan, recovered from the decades of war and depression and have retained many of their distinctive characteristics. What changed was their role in the world. Empires disappeared, and formerly colonial peoples reestablished their political independence. The traumatic events that unfolded between 1914 and 1945 were largely responsible for these changes.

▼▼▼

# The Trauma of World War I

Why did Europeans find World War I so demoralizing, so unsettling, so devoid of any aspect or result that might have justified its appalling costs and casualties? War, after all, was nothing new for the people of Europe. Dynastic wars, religious wars, commercial wars, colonial wars, civil wars, wars to preserve or destroy the balance of power, wars of every conceivable variety fill the pages of European history books. Some of these wars convulsed the whole continent, and some can even be considered world wars. The Seven Years' War (1756–1763) was fought in Europe, the Americas, and India. The wars of the French Revolution and Napoleonic Era spilled over from Europe into Egypt and had reverberations in the Americas, South Africa, and Southeast Asia. Yet, as the sources in this section seek to show, none of these experiences prepared Europeans for the war they fought between 1914 and 1918.

The sheer number of battlefield casualties goes far to explain the war's devastating impact. The thirty-two nations that participated in the war mobilized approximately sixty-five million men, of whom just under ten million were killed and slightly more than twenty million were wounded. To present these statistics in another way, this means that for approximately fifteen hundred consecutive days during the war, on average six thousand men were killed. Losses were high on both the eastern and western fronts, but those in the West were more troubling.

Here, after the Germans almost took Paris in the early weeks of fighting, the war became a stalemate until the armistice on November 11, 1918. Along a four-hundred-mile front stretching from the English Channel through Belgium and France to the Swiss border, defense — a combination of trenches, barbed wire, land mines, poison gas, and machine guns — proved superior to offense — massive artillery barrages followed by charges of troops sent over the top across no man's land to overrun enemy lines. Such tactics produced unbearably long casualty lists but minuscule gains of territory.

Such losses would have been easier to endure if the war had led to a secure and lasting peace. But the hardships and antagonisms of the postwar years rendered such sacrifice meaningless. After the war, winners and losers alike faced inflation, high unemployment, and, after a few years of prosperity in the 1920s, the affliction of the Great Depression. Embittered by their defeat and harsh treatment by the victorious allies in the Versailles Treaty, the Germans abandoned their democratic Weimar Republic for Hitler's Nazi dictatorship in 1933. Japan and Italy, though on the winning side, were disappointed with their territorial gains, and in both nations this resentment played into the hands of ultranationalist politicians. The Arabs, who had fought against Germany's ally, the Turks, in the hope of achieving nationhood, were embittered when Great Britain and France denied their independence. The United States, disillusioned with war and great power wrangling, withdrew into diplomatic isolation, leaving Great Britain and France to enforce the postwar treaties and face the fearsome problems caused by the reordering of Europe and Russia's Bolshevik Revolution. Britain and France expanded their colonial empires in Africa and the Middle East, but this was scant compensation for their casualties, expenditures, and postwar problems of inflation, indebtedness, and loss of economic leadership. Even for them, victory in World War I was empty.

# The Romance of War
▼▼▼

## 88 ▼ POPULAR ART AND POSTER ART FROM GERMANY, ENGLAND, AUSTRALIA, AND FRANCE

When the soldiers marched off to war in the summer of 1914, crowds cheered, young men rushed to enlist, and politicians promised that "the boys would be home by Christmas." Without having experienced a general war since the defeat of Napoleon in 1815 and with little thought to the millions of casualties in the American Civil War, Europeans saw the war as a glorious adventure — an opportunity to fight for the flag or kaiser or queen, to wear splendid uniforms, and to win glory in battles that would be decided by élan, spirit, and bravery. The war they fought was nothing like the war they imagined, and the disparity between expectations and reality was one of the many reasons why the four-year struggle was fraught with such disillusionment and bitterness.

The four illustrations shown here portray the positive attitudes toward the war that all belligerents shared at the outset and that governments sought to perpetuate as the war dragged on. The first (page 383, left), entitled *The Departure,* shows a German troop train departing for the battlefront in late summer 1914. It originally appeared in the German periodical *Simplicissimus* in August 1914 and was the work of B. Hennerberg, an artist originally from Sweden and a regular contributor to the magazine. That *Simplicissimus* would publish such an illustration is a monument to the nationalist emotions the war generated. Noted before the war for its irreverent satire and criticism of German militarism, *Simplicissimus,* as a result of a decision by its editors, abandoned its antiestablishment stance and lent its full support to the war effort.

The second illustration (page 383, right) is one of a series of cards that the Mitchell Tobacco Company included in its packs of Golden Dawn Cigarettes in the early stages of the war. It shows a sergeant offering smokes to the soldiers under his command before battle. Tobacco advertising with military themes reached a saturation point in England during the war years.

An Australian recruitment poster issued in 1915 serves as the third illustration (page 384, left). Although Australia, like Canada, had assumed authority over its own internal affairs by the time the war started, its foreign policy was still controlled by Great Britain. Hence when Great Britain went to war, so did Australia. The Australian parliament refused to approve conscription, however, so the government had to work hard to encourage volunteers. This particular poster appeared in 1915, at a time when Australian troops were heavily involved in the Gallipoli campaign, the allied effort to knock the Ottoman Empire out of the war. Directing its message to the many young men who were members of sports clubs, it promised them the opportunity to enlist in a battalion made up entirely of fellow sportsmen. Such battalions had already been formed in England.

The fourth illustration (page 384, right), a poster from France, was designed to encourage the purchase of war bonds, which were sold by all major belligerents to finance the war. It appeared in 1916 in the midst of the Battle of Verdun, which lasted from February to November and resulted in more than five hundred thousand French casualties but hardly any change in the battle lines. The French soldier shouts, "On les aura!" ("We'll get them!"), words ascribed to General Henri Philippe Pétain, who was in charge of the Verdun defense until he was promoted and given command of all French armies in the field in the summer of 1916.

## QUESTIONS FOR ANALYSIS

1. What message about the war does each of the four illustrations seek to communicate?
2. In what specific ways does each example romanticize war and the life of a soldier?
3. What impression of combat do the English tobacco card and the French war bond poster communicate?
4. What does Hennerberg's painting suggest about women's anticipated role in the war?

*Advertisement card from Golden Dawn Cigarettes*

B. Hennerberg, *The Departure*

*French poster encouraging purchase of war bonds*

*Australian recruitment poster*

# The Reality of War in Verse

▼▼▼

## 89 ▼ Wilfred Owen, "DULCE ET DECORUM EST" and "DISABLED"

So great was the carnage of World War I that no historian has captured its horror as vividly as poets and writers of fiction. Every major belligerent had writers who evoked the desolation and inhumanity of trench warfare. Among the most powerful was the British poet Wilfred Owen (1893–1918), who enlisted in the British army in 1915 at the age of twenty-two, was wounded in 1917, hospitalized, released, sent back to the trenches, and killed on November 4, 1918, one week before the armistice.

Owen's poem "Dulce et Decorum Est," written in 1915, takes its title from a line by the ancient Roman poet Horace, "It is sweet and fitting to die for one's country." The subject of the poem is a poison gas attack. The Germans launched the first large-scale gas attack in April 1915 when they released chloride gas from cylinders so that it was carried by the wind toward French and Canadian troops in the vicinity of Ypres. Subsequently both sides used poison gas, with phosgene and mustard gas being delivered by artillery shells by 1918. "Disabled," also written in 1915, describes the situation of a badly mutilated Scottish soldier who enlisted before he was eighteen years old and now sits in a wheelchair in an institution where he survives but barely.

---

### QUESTIONS FOR ANALYSIS

1. How in "Dulce et Decorum Est" does Owen describe the mental and physical conditions of the foot soldiers?
2. What imagery does he apply to the body of the gas victim?
3. Why does Owen find the plight of the young Scottish soldier so compelling?
4. In what specific ways do Owen's poems attempt to dispel the illusions about war represented in the art in source 88?

### DULCE ET DECORUM EST

Bent double, like old beggars under sacks,
Knock-kneed, coughing like hags, we cursed
  through sludge,
Till on the haunting flares we turned our backs
And towards our distant rest began the trudge.
Men marched asleep. Many had lost their boots
But limped on, blood-shod. All went lame; all
  blind;
Drunk with fatigue; deaf even to the hoots
Of tired, outstripped Five-Nines[1] that dropped
  behind.

Gas! GAS! Quick, boys! — An ecstasy of
  fumbling,

---

[1]Slang for artillery shells used by the Germans.

Fitting the clumsy helmets just in time;
But someone still was yelling out and stum-
      bling,
And flound'ring like a man in fire or lime . . .
Dim, through the misty panes and thick green
      light,
As under a green sea, I saw him drowning.
In all my dreams, before my helpless sight,
He plunges at me, guttering, choking,
      drowning.

If in some smothering dreams you too could
      pace
Behind the wagon that we flung him in,
And watch the white eyes writhing in his face,
His hanging face, like a devil's sick of sin;
If you could hear, at every jolt, the blood
Come gargling from the froth-corrupted lungs,
Obscene as cancer, bitter as the cud
Of vile, incurable sores on innocent tongues,
My friend, you would not tell with such high
      zest,
To children ardent for some desperate glory.
The old Lie: Dulce et decorum est
Pro patria mori.

## DISABLED

He sat in a wheeled chair, waiting for dark,
And shivered in his ghastly suit of grey,
Legless, sewn short at elbow. Through the park
Voices of boys rang saddening like a hymn,
Voices of play and pleasure after day,
Till gathering sleep had mothered them from
      him.

About this time Town used to swing so gay
When glow-lamps budded in the light blue
      trees,
And girls glanced lovelier as the air grew
      dim, —
In the old times, before he threw away his
      knees.
Now he will never feel again how slim
Girls' waists are, or how warm their subtle
      hands.

All of them touch him like some queer disease.

There was an artist silly for his face,
For it was younger than his youth, last year.
Now, he is old; his back will never brace;
He's lost his colour very far from here,
Poured it down shell-holes till the veins ran
      dry,
And half his lifetime lapsed in the hot race
And leap of purple spurted from his thigh.

One time he liked a bloodsmear down his leg,
After the matches, carried shoulder-high.
It was after football, when he'd drunk a peg,
He thought he'd better join. — He wonders
      why.
Someone had said he'd look a god in kilts.
That's why; and maybe, too, to please his Meg,
Aye, that was it, to please the giddy jilts[2]
He asked to join. He didn't have to beg;
Smiling they wrote his lie; aged nineteen
      years.
Germans he scarcely thought of; all their guilt
And Austria's, did not move him. And no fears
Of Fear came yet. He thought of jewelled hilts
For daggers in plaid socks; of smart salutes;
And care of arms; and leave, and pay arrears;
*Esprit de corps;* and hints for young recruits.
And soon, he was drafted out with drums and
      cheers.

Some cheered him home, but not as crowds
      cheer Goal.
Only a solemn man who brought him fruits
*Thanked* him; and then inquired about his
      soul.

Now, he will spend a few sick years in Insti-
      tutes,
And do what things the rules consider wise,
And take whatever pity they may dole.
Tonight he noticed how the women's eyes
Passed from him to the strong men that were
      whole.
How cold and late it is! Why don't they come
And put him to bed? Why don't they come?

---

[2]Scottish slang for young girls.

# The Reality of War in Art

▼▼▼

## 90 ▼ *C. R. W. Nevinson, THE HARVEST OF BATTLE, and Otto Dix, SHOCK TROOP ADVANCING UNDER GAS ATTACK*

Many European artists fought in World War I or were sent to the front to serve as official painters. What they could draw and paint was carefully monitored by their governments. In England, for example, it was illegal to display a painting that portrayed a dead English soldier. Thus most of the paintings that expressed disillusionment with the war appeared only after hostilities ended. Such was the case with the two works shown here.

The first painting, *The Harvest of Battle,* was completed by C. R. W. Nevinson in 1919. Born in 1889, Nevinson was an art student in France when the war started. He served on the front line in the Red Cross and the Royal Army Medical Corps before rheumatic fever forced him out of active service in 1916. He returned to the war zone as an official painter in late 1917 and early 1918. On his return to England he produced a large number of war-related paintings and drawings, but only after the armistice could he express in them his deep emotions about the war's costs. *The Harvest of Battle* was painted in 1919. Nevinson found that the public had little interest in his war-related paintings in the 1920s, and he devoted the rest of his career to townscapes and flower pictures. While serving as a war artist in World War II he suffered a stroke and died in 1946.

Otto Dix (1891–1969), who created the etching *Shock Troop Advancing under Gas Attack,* is one of Germany's most important twentieth-century artists. Dix was on active duty throughout World War I, serving as a machine gunner, artilleryman, and aerial observer on both the eastern and western fronts. Deeply disillusioned with postwar society and its failure to appreciate the sacrifices of its veterans, Dix became an ardent pacifist, whose powerful antiwar drawings and paintings contributed to his condemnation and arrest under the Nazis. Only in the desperate closing days of World War II was he drafted into the army.

*Shock Troop Advancing under Gas Attack* was one of a series of fifty etchings Dix produced in 1923 and 1924 collectively entitled *War.* It depicts a group of attacking troops wearing gas masks.

---

## QUESTIONS FOR ANALYSIS

1. What statements about war is each artist attempting to make in his work?
2. What specific details help the artists put their messages across?
3. Why do you suppose Nevinson chose the title *The Harvest of Battle* for his work?

*C. R. W. Nevinson, The Harvest of Battle*

*Otto Dix, Shock Troop Advancing under Gas Attack*

▼▼▼

# The Russian Revolution and the Foundation of the Soviet State

Among the results of World War I, the downfall of Russia's tsarist regime and its replacement by a Marxist-inspired Bolshevik dictatorship is one of the most important. Tsar Nicholas II, facing defeat on the battlefield, defections within the army, and rioting in Petrograd, abdicated in March 1917. The tsarist autocracy was replaced by a liberal provisional government that sought to govern Russia until a constituent assembly could meet and devise a new constitution. Seven months later, the Bolsheviks wrested power from the provisional government, and after four years of civil war, established the world's first communist state.

Nicholas II's Russia was full of discontent. Its millions of peasants were no longer serfs, but they still lived in abysmal poverty. Some moved to Moscow or St. Petersburg to work in Russia's new factories, but without political power or unions, most exchanged the squalor of the rural village for the squalor of the urban slum. Meanwhile many intellectuals, mostly from the ranks of Russia's small middle class, became deeply alienated from the tsar's regime and espoused political causes ranging from anarchism to constitutional monarchy. With the fervor of religious zealots, they argued, organized, hatched plots, planned revolution, assassinated government officials (including Tsar Alexander II in 1881), published pamphlets by the thousands, and tried, not always successfully, to stay a step ahead of the secret police.

Nicholas II raised his subjects' hopes in 1905, when after rioting broke out in St. Petersburg (renamed *Petrograd* after World War I began), he promised a parliament and constitutional reforms. Russians soon realized, however, that their tsar had no intention of abandoning control of such crucial areas as finance, defense, and ministerial appointments. Meanwhile, workers and peasants cursed their government, and revolutionaries continued to plot. World War I provided the final push to a regime teetering on the brink of collapse.

After the Bolsheviks seized power in 1917 and survived the civil war that ended in 1921, their leaders faced the challenge of establishing the world's first Marxist state. After a decade of experiment and controversy, in the 1930s Soviet leaders created a framework of government that lasted until the breakup of the Soviet Union in the late 1980s. Under Communist direction the Soviet Union became a major industrial power and a highly centralized, one-party dictatorship that tolerated no dissent. Freedom and individual initiative played no role in this new society, based, so their leaders claimed, on the principles of Karl Marx.

# The Basic Tenets of Leninism
▼▼▼

## 91 ▼ *Lenin, "WHAT IS TO BE DONE?"*

The founder of the Soviet Union was Vladimir Ilyich Ulyanov (1870–1924), better known by his adopted revolutionary name, Lenin. The son of a government official, Lenin dedicated himself to revolution after the government executed his brother for plotting the assassination of Tsar Alexander III. After joining the Marxist-inspired Social-Democratic Party, founded in 1898, in 1903 he became the leader of the "majority men," or Bolsheviks, who, in opposition to the "minority men," or Mensheviks, demanded highly centralized party leadership, noncooperation with bourgeois liberals, and single-minded devotion to revolution.

Lenin described his ideas about revolutionary tactics in 1902 in a pamphlet entitled "What Is to Be Done?" It was directed against ideological enemies Lenin called "Economists," Marxists who believed that because Russia had just begun to industrialize, it was not ready for true socialism. Social-Democrats, they believed, should seek short-term economic gains for workers rather than revolution. Published in Germany, smuggled into Russia, and read by thousands of Social-Democrats, "What Is to Be Done?" established Lenin as a major party theoretician and a man to be reckoned with in the Social-Democratic Party. It marked the beginning of that distinctive variant of Marxism known as Leninism.

---

## QUESTIONS FOR ANALYSIS

1. According to Lenin, how does the "critical Marxism" of men such as Bernstein endanger the socialist movement?
2. In Lenin's view how are the goals and purposes of trade unionism similar to and different from those of the Social-Democratic Party?
3. Why, according to Lenin, have the workers been unable to develop true revolutionary consciousness? What does he believe must be done to change this?
4. What advantages does Lenin see in restricting the party to a small corps of dedicated revolutionaries?
5. What kinds of activities will these professional revolutionaries carry on to further the cause of revolution?
6. Compare and contrast the views of Lenin and Marx (see source 63) on the following topics: revolution, the working class, the role of the party.

## [SOCIALIST DIVISIONS]

In fact, it is no secret for anyone that two trends have taken form in present-day international Social-Democracy. . . . The essence of the "new" trend, which adopts a "critical" attitude towards "obsolete dogmatic" Marxism, has been clearly enough *presented* by Bernstein and *demonstrated* by Millerand.[1]

Social-Democracy must change from a party

---

[1]Eduard Bernstein (1850–1932) was a German socialist identified with revisionism, the idea that socialists should seek their goals not by revolution but through the democratic process. Alexandre Millerand (1859–1943) was the first French socialist to take a cabinet seat in a nonsocialist government.

of social revolution into a democratic party of social reforms. Bernstein has surrounded this political demand with a whole battery of well-attuned "new" arguments and reasonings. Denied was the possibility of putting socialism on a scientific basis and of demonstrating its necessity and inevitability from the point of view of the materialist conception of history. Denied was the fact of growing impoverishment, the process of proletarization, and the intensification of capitalist contradictions; the very concept, *"ultimate aim,"* was declared to be unsound, and the idea of the dictatorship of the proletariat was completely rejected. Denied was the antithesis in principle between liberalism and socialism. Denied was *the theory of the class struggle,* on the alleged grounds that it could not be applied to a strictly democratic society governed according to the will of the majority, etc. . . .

## [THE WORKERS AND REVOLUTION]

We have said that *there could not have been* Social-Democratic consciousness among the workers. It would have to be brought to them from without. The history of all countries shows that the working class, exclusively by its own effort, is able to develop only trade-union consciousness, i.e., the conviction that it is necessary to combine in unions, fight the employers, and strive to compel the government to pass necessary labor legislation, etc. . . .

The overwhelming majority of Russian Social-Democrats have of late been almost entirely absorbed by this work of organising the exposure of factory conditions. . . . — so much so, indeed, that they have lost sight of the fact that this, *taken by itself,* is in essence still not Social-Democratic work, but merely trade union work. As a matter of fact, the exposures merely dealt with the relations between the workers *in a given trade* and their employers, and all they achieved was that the sellers of labor-power learned to sell their "commodity" on better terms and to fight the

purchasers over a purely commercial deal. These exposures could have served . . . as a beginning and a component part of Social-Democratic activity; but they could also have led . . . to a "purely trade union" struggle and to a non-Social-Democratic working-class movement. Social-Democracy leads the struggle of the working class, not only for better terms for the sale of labor-power, but for the abolition of the social system that compels the propertyless to sell themselves to the rich. Social-Democracy represents the working class, not in its relation to a given group of employers alone, but in its relation to all classes of modern society and to the state as an organised political force. . . . We must take up actively the political education of the working class and the development of its political consciousness. . . .

Why do the Russian workers still manifest little revolutionary activity in response to the brutal treatment of the people by the police, the persecution of religious sects, the flogging of peasants, the outrageous censorship, the torture of soldiers, the persecution of the most innocent cultural undertakings, etc.? Is it because the "economic struggle" does not "stimulate" them to this, because such activity does not "promise palpable results," because it produces little that is "positive"? . . . We must blame ourselves, our lagging behind the mass movement, for still being unable to organize sufficiently wide, striking, and rapid exposures of all the shameful outrages. When we do that (and we must and can do it), the most backward worker will understand, *or will feel,* that the students and religious sects, the peasants and the authors are being abused and outraged by those same dark forces that are oppressing and crushing him at every step of his life. Feeling that, he himself will be filled with an irresistible desire to react, and he will know how to heckle the censors one day, on another day to demonstrate outside the house of a governor who has brutally suppressed a peasant uprising, on still another day to teach a lesson to the gendarmes in surplices who are doing the work of the Holy Inquisition,[2] etc. As yet we have done very little, almost nothing, *to bring* before the working masses prompt exposures on all possible issues. Many of us as yet do not recognize this as our *bounden duty* but trail spontaneously in the wake of the "drab everyday struggle," in the narrow confines of factory life. . . .

## [THE PARTY AND ITS PURPOSES]

If we begin with the solid foundation of a strong organisation of revolutionaries, we can ensure the stability of the movement as a whole and carry out the aims both of Social-Democracy and of trade unions proper. If, however, we begin with a broad workers' organisation, which is supposedly most "accessible" to the masses (but which is actually most accessible to the gendarmes and makes revolutionaries most accessible to the police), we shall achieve neither the one aim nor the other; we shall not eliminate our rule-of-thumb[3] methods, and, because we remain scattered and our forces are constantly broken up by the policy, we shall only make trade unions of the Zubatov and Ozerov[4] type the more accessible to the masses. . . .

"A dozen wise men can be more easily wiped out than a hundred fools." This wonderful truth (for which the hundred fools will always applaud you) appears obvious only because in the very midst of the argument you have skipped from one question to another. You[5] began by talking and continued to talk of the unearthing of a "committee," of the unearthing of an "organization," and now you skip to the question of unearthing the movement's "roots" in their "depths." The fact is, of course, that our move-

ment cannot be unearthed, for the very reason that it has countless thousands of roots deep down among the masses; but that is not the point at issue. . . . But since you raise the question of *organizations* being unearthed and persist in your opinion, I assert that it is far more difficult to unearth a dozen wise men than a hundred fools. This position I will defend, no matter how much you instigate the masses against me for my "anti-democratic" views, etc. As I have stated repeatedly, by "wise men," in connection with organization, I mean *professional revolutionaries,* irrespective of whether they have developed from among students or working men. I assert: (1) that no revolutionary movement can endure without a stable organization of leaders maintaining continuity; (2) that the broader the popular mass drawn spontaneously into the struggle, which forms the basis of the movement and participates in it, the more urgent the need for such an organization, and the more solid this organization must be (for it is much easier for all sorts of demagogues to side-track the more backward sections of the masses); (3) that such an organization must consist chiefly of people professionally engaged in revolutionary activity; (4) that in an autocratic state, the more we *confine* the membership of such an organization to people who are professionally engaged in revolutionary activity and who have been professionally trained in the art of combating the political police, the more difficult will it be to unearth the organization; and (5) the *greater* will be the number of people from the working class and from the other social classes who will be able to join the movement and perform active work in it.

I shall deal only with the last two points. The question as to whether it is easier to wipe out "a

---

[2]Refers to clergy of the Russian Orthodox Church; *gendarmes* means police; a surplice is part of the vestments worn by members of the clergy.

[3]A way of getting things done that is based on experience or practice rather than scientific knowledge.

[4]S. V. Zubatov (1864–1917), a colonel in the Moscow state police, was an ardent foe of revolutionary movements best

known for his efforts to establish "depoliticized" trade unions under the control of the police; he shot himself when the tsarist government fell during the Russian Revolution. I. K. Ozerov was a professor at the University of Moscow who supported Zubatov's "police socialism."

[5]"You" in this context refers to skeptical readers, not a specific individual.

dozen wise men" or "a hundred fools" reduces itself to the question, above considered, whether it is possible to have a mass *organization* when the maintenance of strict secrecy is essential. We can never give a mass organization that degree of secrecy without which there can be no question of persistent and continuous struggle against the government. To concentrate all secret functions in the hands of as small a number of professional revolutionaries as possible does not mean that the latter will "do the thinking for all" and that the rank and file will not take an active part in the *movement.* . . . Centralization of the secret functions of the *organization* by no means implies centralization of all the functions of the *movement.* . . . The active and widespread participation of the masses will not suffer; on the contrary, it will benefit by the fact that a "dozen" experienced revolutionaries, trained professionally no less than the police, will centralize all the secret aspects of the work — the drawing up of leaflets, the working out of approximate plans; and the appointing of bodies of leaders for each urban district, for each factory district, and for each educational institution. . . . Centralization of the most secret functions in an organization of revolutionaries will not diminish, but rather increase the extent and enhance the quality of the activity of a large number of other organizations, that are intended for a broad public and are therefore as loose and as non-secret as possible, such as workers' trade unions; workers' self-education circles and circles for reading illegal literature; and socialist, as well as democratic, circles among *all* other sections of the population; etc., etc. We must have such circles, trade unions, and organizations everywhere in *as large a number as possible* and with the widest variety of functions; but it would be absurd and harmful *to confound* them with the organization of *revolutionaries,* to efface the border-line between them, to make still more hazy the all too faint recognition of the fact that in order to "serve" the mass movement we must have people who will devote themselves exclusively to Social-Democratic activities, and that such people must *train* themselves patiently and steadfastly to be professional revolutionaries.

Yes, this recognition is incredibly dim. Our worst sin with regard to organization consists in the fact that *by our primitiveness we have lowered the prestige of revolutionaries in Russia.* A person who is flabby and shaky on questions of theory, who has a narrow outlook, who pleads the spontaneity of the masses as an excuse for his own sluggishness, who resembles a trade-union secretary more than a spokesman of the people, who is unable to conceive of a broad and bold plan that would command the respect even of opponents, and who is inexperienced and clumsy in his own professional art — the art of combating the political police — such a man is not a revolutionary, but a wretched amateur!

Let no active worker take offense at these frank remarks, for as far as insufficient training is concerned, I apply them first and foremost to myself. I used to work in a study circle[6] that set itself very broad, all-embracing tasks; and all of us, members of that circle, suffered painfully and acutely from the realization that we were acting as amateurs at a moment in history when we might have been able to say, varying a well-known statement: "Give us an organization of revolutionaries, and we will overturn Russia!" The more I recall the burning sense of shame I then experienced, the bitterer become my feelings towards those pseudo-Social-Democrats whose preachings "bring disgrace on the calling of a revolutionary," who fail to understand that our task is not to champion the degrading of the revolutionary to the level of an amateur, but *to raise* the amateurs to the level of revolutionaries.

---

[6]Workers, intellectuals, or students who met regularly to discuss and plan strategies to overcome Russia's social and political problems.

# The Soviet Model of Economic Planning
▼▼▼

## 92 ▼ *Joseph Stalin,* *THE RESULTS OF THE FIRST FIVE-YEAR PLAN*

Joseph Stalin (1879–1953), the son of a shoemaker from the Russian province of Georgia, was a candidate for the priesthood before he abandoned Christianity for Marxism and became a follower of Lenin in 1903. In 1917 he was named Bolshevik party secretary, an office he retained after the revolution. Following Lenin's death in 1924, Stalin fought a successful battle for party control with Leon Trotsky (1879–1940), the leader of the Red Army during the civil war and Lenin's heir apparent. Shortly after taking power in 1928 Stalin launched a bold restructuring of the Soviet economy.

In 1928 the New Economic Policy (NEP), which Lenin adopted in 1921, still guided Soviet economic life. Through the NEP, Lenin had sought to restore agriculture and industry after seven years of war, revolution, and civil strife. Although the state maintained control of banks, foreign trade, and heavy industry, peasants could sell their goods on the open market, and small businessmen could hire labor, operate small factories, and keep their profits. The NEP saved the Soviet Union from economic collapse, but its sanction of private profit and economic competition troubled Marxist purists, and it did little to foster rapid industrialization. Thus in 1928 Stalin abandoned the NEP and replaced it with the first Five-Year Plan, which established a centralized planned economy in which Moscow bureaucrats regulated agriculture, manufacturing, finance, and transportation. In agriculture, the plan abolished individual peasant holdings and combined them into large collectives and state farms. This meant the obliteration of the class of prosperous and successful peasant farmers known as *kulaks*. In manufacturing, the plan emphasized heavy industry and the production of goods such as tractors, trucks, and machinery. Second and third Five-Year Plans were launched in 1933 and 1938.

In the following report, delivered to the Central Committee of the Communist Party of the Soviet Union in January 1933, Stalin outlines the goals and achievements of the first Five-Year Plan.

---

## QUESTIONS FOR ANALYSIS

1. What were the overriding reasons, according to Stalin, for adopting the Five-Year Plan? Does socialist theory or the defense of the Soviet Union seem more important to him?
2. Why, in the industrial area, was it necessary to concentrate on heavy industry?
3. According to Stalin, why was the collectivization of agriculture such a key component of the Five-Year Plan?

4. What were the main obstacles to the success of the Five-Year Plan, according to Stalin?
5. In Stalin's view, how have the people of the Soviet Union benefited from the Five-Year Plan? What sacrifices have they been asked to make?
6. How, according to Stalin, does the success of the Five-Year Plan prove that communism is superior to capitalism?

The fundamental task of the Five-Year Plan was to convert the U.S.S.R. from an agrarian and weak country, dependent upon the caprices of the capitalist countries, into an industrial and powerful country, fully self-reliant and independent of the caprices of world capitalism.

The fundamental task of the Five-Year Plan was, in converting the U.S.S.R. into an industrial country, fully to eliminate the capitalist elements, to widen the front of socialist forms of economy, and to create the economic base for the abolition of classes in the U.S.S.R., for the construction of socialist society.

The fundamental task of the Five-Year Plan was to create such an industry in our country as would be able to re-equip and reorganize, not only the whole of industry, but also transport and agriculture — on the basis of socialism.

The fundamental task of the Five-Year Plan was to transfer small and scattered agriculture to the lines of large-scale collective farming, so as to ensure the economic base for socialism in the rural districts and thus to eliminate the possibility of the restoration of capitalism in the U.S.S.R.

Finally, the task of the Five-Year Plan was to create in the country all the necessary technical and economic prerequisites for increasing to the utmost the defensive capacity of the country, to enable it to organize determined resistance to any and every attempt at military intervention from outside. . . . But the execution of such a grand plan cannot be started haphazardly, just anywhere. In order to carry out such a plan it is necessary first of all to find its main link; for only after this main link has been found and grasped can all the other links of the plan be raised. . . .

The main link in the Five-Year Plan was heavy industry, with machine building at its core. For only heavy industry is capable of reconstructing industry as a whole, as well as the transport system and agriculture, and of putting them on their feet. . . . Hence, the restoration of heavy industry had to be made on the basis of the fulfillment of the Five-Year Plan. . . .

But the restoration and development of heavy industry, particularly in such a backward and poor country as our country was at the beginning of the Five-Year Plan period, is an extremely difficult task; for, as is well known, heavy industry calls for enormous financial expenditures and the availability of a certain minimum of experienced technical forces, without which, speaking generally, the restoration of heavy industry is impossible. Did the party know this, and did it take this into consideration? Yes, it did. . . . The party declared frankly that this would call for serious sacrifices, and that we must openly and consciously make these sacrifices if we wanted to achieve our goal. . . .

The facts have proved that without this boldness and this confidence in the forces of the working class the party could not have achieved the victory of which we are now so justly proud.

▾ ▾ ▾

What are the results of the Five-Year Plan in four years in the sphere of *industry?* . . .

We did not have an iron and steel industry, the foundation for the industrialization of the country. Now we have this industry.

We did not have a tractor industry. Now we have one.

We did not have an automobile industry. Now we have one.

We did not have a machine-tool industry. Now we have one.

We did not have a big and up-to-date chemical industry. Now we have one.

We did not have a real and big industry for the production of modern agricultural machinery. Now we have one.

We did not have an aircraft industry. Now we have one.

In output of electric power we were last on the list. Now we rank among the first.

In the output of oil products and coal we were last on the list. Now we rank among the first. . . .

And as a result of all this the capitalist elements have been completely and irrevocably eliminated from industry, and socialist industry has become the sole form of industry in the U.S.S.R.

And as a result of all this our country has been converted from an agrarian into an industrial country; for the proportion of industrial output, as compared with agricultural output, has risen from 48 per cent of the total in the beginning of the Five-Year Plan period (1928) to 70 per cent at the end of the fourth year of the Five-Year Plan period (1932). . . .

Finally, as a result of all this the Soviet Union has been converted from a weak country, unprepared for defense, into a country mighty in defense, a country prepared for every contingency, a country capable of producing on a mass scale all modern weapons of defense and of equipping its army with them in the event of an attack from without. . . .

We are told: This is all very well; but it would have been far better to have abandoned the policy of industrialization, . . . and to have produced more cotton, cloth, shoes, clothing, and other articles of general use. The output of articles of general use has been smaller than is required, and this created certain difficulties.

But, then, we must know and take into account where such a policy of relegating the task of industrialization to the background would have led us. Of course, out of the 1,500,000,000 rubles in foreign currency that we spent on purchasing equipment for our heavy industries, we could have set apart a half for the purpose of importing raw cotton, hides, wool, rubber, etc. Then we would now have more cotton cloth, shoes and clothing. But we would not have a tractor industry or an automobile industry; we would not have anything like a big iron and steel industry; we would not have metal for the manufacture of machinery — and we would be unarmed, while we are surrounded by capitalist countries which are armed with modern technique. . . . Our position would be more or less analogous to the present position of China, which has no heavy industry and no war industry of her own and which is pecked at by everybody who cares to do so. . . .

▼ ▼ ▼

The Five-Year Plan in the sphere of agriculture was a Five-Year Plan of collectivization. What did the party proceed from in carrying out collectivization?

The party proceeded from the fact that in order to consolidate the dictatorship of the proletariat and to build up socialist society it was necessary, in addition to industrialization, to pass from small, individual peasant farming to large-scale collective agriculture equipped with tractors and modern agricultural machinery, as the only firm basis for the Soviet power in the rural districts.

The party proceeded from the fact that without collectivization it would be impossible to lead our country onto the highroad of building the economic foundations of socialism, impossible to free the vast masses of the laboring peasantry from poverty and ignorance. . . .

The party has succeeded, in a matter of three years, in organizing more than 200,000 collective farms and about 5,000 state farms specializing mainly in grain growing and livestock raising, and at the same time it has succeeded, in the course of four years, in enlarging the crop area by 21,000,000 hectares.[1]

The party has succeeded in getting more than 60 per cent of the peasant farms, which account for more than 70 per cent of the land cultivated by peasants, to unite into collective farms, which means that we have *fulfilled* the Five-Year Plan *threefold*.

The party has succeeded in creating the possibility of obtaining, not 500,000,000 to 600,000,000 poods[2] of marketable grain, which was the amount purchased in the period when individual peasant farming predominated, but 1,200,000,000 to 1,400,000,000 poods of grain annually.

The party has succeeded in routing the kulaks as a class, although they have not yet been dealt the final blow; the laboring peasants have been emancipated from kulak bondage and exploitation, and a firm economic basis for the Soviet government, the basis of collective farming, has been established in the countryside.

The party has succeeded in converting the U.S.S.R. from a land of small peasant farming into a land where agriculture is run on the largest scale in the world. . . .

Do not all these facts testify to the superiority of the Soviet system of agriculture over the capitalist system? Do not these facts go to show that the collective farms are a more virile form of farming than individual capitalist farms? . . .

In putting into effect the Five-Year Plan for agriculture, the party pursued a policy of collectivization at an accelerated tempo. Was the party right in pursuing the policy of an accelerated tempo of collectivization? Yes, it was absolutely right, even though certain excesses were committed in the process.[3] In pursuing the policy of eliminating the kulaks as a class, and in destroying the kulak nests, the party could not stop half way. It was necessary to carry this work to completion. . . .

▾ ▾ ▾

What are the results of these successes as regards the improvement of the material conditions of the workers and peasants? . . .

In our country, in the U.S.S.R., the workers have long forgotten unemployment. Some three years ago we had about one and a half million unemployed. It is already two years now since unemployment has been completely abolished. And in these two years the workers have already forgotten about the unemployment, about its burden and its horrors. Look at the capitalist countries: what horrors are taking place there as a result of unemployment! There are now no less than thirty to forty million unemployed in those countries. . . .

Every day they try to get work, seek work, are prepared to accept almost any conditions of work but they are not given work, because they are "superfluous." And this is taking place at a time when vast quantities of goods and products are wasted to satisfy the caprices of the darlings of fate, the scions of capitalists and landlords. The unemployed are refused food because they have no money to pay for the food; they are refused shelter because they have no money to pay rent. How and where do they live? They live on the miserable crumbs from the rich man's table; by raking refuse cans, where they find decayed scraps of food; they live in the slums of big cities, and more often in hovels outside of the towns, hastily put up by the unemployed out of packing cases and the bark of trees. . . .

One of the principal achievements of the Five-Year Plan in four years is that we have abolished unemployment and have relieved the workers of the U.S.S.R. of its horrors.

The same thing must be said in regard to the peasants. They, too, have forgotten about the differentiation of the peasants into kulaks and poor peasants, about the exploitation of

---

[1]In the metric system a *hectare* is slightly less than 2.5 acres.
[2]A *pood* is a Russian measure of weight equal to about thirty-six pounds.

[3]Stalin is understating the case more than a little. In fact, several million kulaks were executed or deported to Siberia because of their opposition to collectivization.

the poor peasants by the kulaks, about the ruin which, every year, caused hundreds of thousands and millions of poor peasants to go begging. . . .

[The Five-Year Plan] has undermined and smashed the kulaks as a class, thus liberating the poor peasants and a good half of the middle peasants from bondage to the kulaks. . . . It has thus eliminated the possibility of the differentiation of the peasantry into exploiters — kulaks — and exploited — poor peasants. It has raised the poor peasants and the lower stratum of the middle peasants to a position of security in the collective farms, and has thereby put a stop to the process of ruination and impoverishment of the peasantry. . . .

Now there are no more cases of hundreds of thousands and millions of peasants being ruined and forced to hang around the gates of factories and mills. That is what used to happen; but that was long ago. Now the peasant is in a position of security; he is a member of a collective farm which has at its disposal tractors, agricultural machinery, a seed fund, a reserve fund, etc., etc.

Such are the main results of the realization of the Five-Year Plan in industry and agriculture; in the improvement of the conditions of life of the working people and the development of the exchange of goods; in the consolidation of the Soviet power and the development of the class struggle against the remnants and survival of the dying classes.

▼▼▼

# Ultranationalism in Germany and Japan

Nationalism, the most important single cause of World War I, became even more potent in the 1920s and 1930s, leading to a second world war many times more costly and horrifying than the struggle of 1914 to 1918. In Italy and Germany extreme nationalism was the driving force behind right-wing, antidemocratic movements personified by Benito Mussolini, whose Fascists seized power in Italy in 1922, and Adolf Hitler, whose Nazis took over Germany in 1933. In Japan ultranationalists never subverted the limited democracy established by the 1890 constitution, but in the 1930s their views inspired millions and became dogma within the Japanese military.

These three nations in which nationalism ran wild were similar in several respects. All three in a sense were recent creations: Italy gained national unity between 1859 and 1870; Germany achieved the same in 1871; and a new Japan was created after the Meiji Restoration of 1868. All three had weak parliamentary governments and lacked democratic experience. All three resented their treatment after World War I: The Germans were humiliated by the Versailles Treaty, and the Italians and Japanese were insulted by the refusal of Great Britain and France to recognize all their territorial claims. Finally, all three faced severe postwar economic problems — problems that extreme nationalists claimed could be eliminated by expansion and conquest.

Ultranationalism in each state also had the same tragic result: It led all three nations into catastrophic wars. After conquering Manchuria in 1931, invading China in 1937, attacking the United States at Pearl Harbor in 1941, and expanding into Southeast Asia, Japan conceded defeat only when atomic bombs devastated Hiroshima and Nagasaki in August 1945. Germany launched World War II in Europe with its attack on Poland in September 1939, but after conquering much of Western Europe and invading the Soviet Union in 1941, its armies were steadily pushed back until the leaders of a devastated land surrendered in May 1945. Italy entered World War II on the side of Germany in 1940, but its armies performed poorly, and only massive German support prevented its rapid collapse. Anti-Fascists captured Mussolini and shot him without trial on April 28, 1945, just a few days before Adolf Hitler committed suicide in his bunker under the rubble of what had been Berlin.

# Hitler's Dreams
▼▼▼

## 93 ▼ *Adolf Hitler, MEIN KAMPF*

Born the son of an Austrian customs official and his German wife in 1889, Adolf Hitler moved to Vienna at the age of nineteen to seek a career as an artist or architect. His efforts failed, however, and he lived at the bottom of Viennese society, drifting from one low-paying job to another. In 1912 he moved to Munich, where his life fell into the same purposeless pattern. Enlistment in the German army in World War I rescued Hitler, giving him comradeship and a sense of direction he had lacked. After the war a shattered Hitler returned to Munich, where in 1919 he joined the small German Workers' Party, which in 1920 changed its name to the National Socialist German Workers' Party, or Nazis.

After becoming leader of the National Socialists, Hitler staged an abortive coup d'état against the government of the German state of Bavaria in 1923. For this he was sentenced to a five-year prison term (serving only nine months), during which he wrote the first volume of his major work, *Mein Kampf (My Struggle)*. To a remarkable degree this work, completed in 1925, provided the ideas that inspired his millions of followers and guided the National Socialists until their destruction in 1945.

---

## QUESTIONS FOR ANALYSIS

1. What broad purpose does Hitler see in human existence?
2. What, in Hitler's view, are the basic dissimilarities between Aryans and Jews?
3. What is Hitler's view of political leadership?
4. What role do parliaments play in a "folkish" state, according to Hitler?
5. How does Hitler plan to reorient German foreign policy? What goals does he set for Germany, and how are they to be achieved?
6. Based on what Hitler says in these excerpts, what can you guess about his objections to the ideologies of democracy, liberalism, and socialism?
7. How do Hitler's views of race compare to those of van Treitschke (source 66) and Henry Cabot Lodge (source 70)?

## NATION AND RACE

There are some truths that are so plain and obvious that for this very reason the everyday world does not see them or at least does not apprehend them. . . .

So humans invariably wander about the garden of nature, convinced that they know and understand everything, yet with few exceptions are blind to one of the fundamental principles Nature uses in her work: the intrinsic segregation of the species of every living thing on the earth. . . . Each beast mates with only one of its own species: the titmouse with titmouse, finch with finch, stork with stork, field mouse with field mouse, house mouse with house mouse, wolf with wolf. . . . This is only natural.

Any cross-breeding between two not completely equal beings will result in a product that is in between the level of the two parents. That means that the offspring will be superior to the parent who is at a biologically lower level of being but inferior to the parent at a higher level. This means the offspring will be overcome in the struggle for existence against those at the higher level. Such matings go against the will of Nature for the higher breeding of life.

A precondition for this lies not in the blending of beings of a higher and lower order, but rather the absolute victory of the stronger. The stronger must dominate and must not blend with the weaker orders and sacrifice their powers. Only born weaklings can find this cruel, but after all, they are only weaker and more narrow-minded types of men; unless this law dominated, then any conceivable higher evolution of living organisms would be unthinkable. . . .

Nature looks on this calmly and approvingly. The struggle for daily bread allows all those who are weak, sick, and indecisive to be defeated, while the struggle of the males for females gives to the strongest alone the right or at least the possibility to reproduce. Always this struggle is a means of advancing the health and power of resistance of the species, and thus a means to its higher evolution.

As little as nature approves the mating of higher and lower individuals, she approves even less the blending of higher races with lower ones; for indeed otherwise her previous work toward higher development perhaps over hundreds of thousands of years might be rendered useless with one blow. If this were not the case, progressive development would stop and even deterioration might set in. . . .

All the great civilizations of the past died out because contamination of their blood caused them to become decadent. . . . In other words, in order to protect a certain culture, the type of human who created the culture must be preserved. But such preservation is tied to the inalterable law of the necessity and the right of victory of the best and the strongest.

Whoever would live must fight. Whoever will not fight in this world of endless competition does not deserve to live. Whoever ignores or despises these laws of race kills the good fortune that he believes he can attain. He interferes with the victory path of the best race and with it, the precondition for all human progress. . . .

It is an idle undertaking to argue about which race or races were the original standard-bearers of human culture and were therefore the true founders of everything we conceive by the word humanity. It is much simpler to deal with the question as it pertains to the present, and here the answer is simple and clear. What we see before us today as human culture, all the yields of art, science, and technology, are almost exclusively the creative product of the Aryans.[1] In-

---

[1]*Aryan,* strictly speaking, is a linguistic term referring to a branch of the Indo-European family of languages known as Indo-Iranian. It is also used to refer to a people who around 2000 B.C.E. began to migrate from their homeland in the steppes of western Asia to Iran, India, Mesopotamia, Asia Minor, and Europe. Their related family of languages, based on an even older language known as *Proto-Indo-European,* is believed to be the ancestor of all Indo-European languages, including Greek, Latin, Celtic, Persian, Sanskrit, and Balto-Slavonic, as well as their derivatives. In the nineteenth century, Aryan was used to refer to the *racial group* that spoke these languages. According to Hitler and the Nazis, the Aryans provided Europe's original racial stock and stood in contrast to other peoples such as the Jews, who spoke *Semitic* languages.

deed this fact alone leads to the not unfounded conclusion that the Aryan alone is the founder of the higher type of humanity, and further that he represents the prototype of what we understand by the word: MAN. He is the Prometheus[2] from whose brow the bright spark of genius has forever burst forth, time and again rekindling the fire, which as knowledge has illuminated the night full of silent mysteries, and has permitted humans to ascend the path of mastery over the other beings of the earth. Eliminate him — and deep darkness will again descend on the earth after a few thousand years; human civilization will die out and the earth will become a desert.

If we were to divide mankind into three categories — the founders of culture, the bearers of culture, and the destroyers of culture, only the Aryans can be considered to be in the first category. From them are built the foundations and walls of all human creations, and only the outward form and colors of these are to be attributed to varying characteristics of the other individual peoples. He provides the mightiest building stones and designs for all human progress. . . .

The Jew provides the greatest contrast to the Aryan. With no other people of the world has the instinct for self-preservation been so developed as by the so-called chosen race.[3] The best proof of this statement rests in the fact that this race still exists. Where can another people be found in the past 2,000 years that has undergone so few changes in its inner qualities, character, etc. as the Jews? What people has undergone upheavals as great as this one — and nonetheless has emerged unchanged from the greatest catastrophes of humanity? What an infinitely tenacious will to live and to preserve one's kind is revealed in this fact. . . .

Since the Jew . . . never had a civilization of his own, others have always provided the foundations of his intellectual labors. His intellect has always developed by the use of those cultural achievements he has found ready at hand around him. Never has it happened the other way around.

For though their drive for self-preservation is not smaller, but larger than that of other people, and though their mental capabilities may easily give the impression that their intellectual powers are equal to those of other races, the Jews lack the most basic characteristic of a truly cultured people, namely an idealistic spirit.

It is a remarkable fact that the herd instinct brings people together for mutual protection only so long as there is a common danger that makes mutual assistance necessary or unavoidable. The same pack of wolves that an instant ago combined to overcome their prey will soon after satisfying their hunger again become individual beasts. . . . It goes the same way with the Jews. His sense of self sacrifice is only apparent. It lasts only so long as it is strictly necessary. As soon as the common enemy departs, however, as soon as the danger is gone and the booty secured, the superficial harmony among the Jews ends, and original conditions return. Jews act together only when a common danger threatens them or a common prey attracts them. When these two things are lacking, then their characteristic of the crassest egoism returns as a force, and out of this once unified people emerges in a flash a swarm of rats fighting bloodily against one another.

If the Jews existed in the world by themselves, they would wallow in their filth and disasters; they would try to get the best of the other in a hate-filled struggle, and even exterminate one another, that is, if their absolute lack of a sense

---

[2]In Greek mythology Prometheus was the titan (titans were offspring of Uranus, Heaven, and Gaea, Earth) who stole fire from the gods and gave it to humans, along with all other arts and civilization. He was also variously regarded as the creator of man (from clay), the first mortal man (along with his brother Epimetheus), and humanity's preserver when Zeus threatened to kill all human beings.

[3]A reference to the Jewish conviction that God had chosen the Jews to enter into a special relationship or covenant in which God promised to be the God of the Hebrews and favor them in return for true worship and obedience.

of self sacrifice, which is expressed in their venality, did not turn this drama into comedy also. . . .

That is why the Jewish state — which should be the living organism for the maintenance and improvement of the race — has absolutely no borders. For the territorial definition of a state always demands a certain idealism of spirit on the part of the race which forms the state and especially an acceptance of the idea of work. . . . If this attitude is lacking then the prerequisite for civilization is lacking.

---

▷    Hitler describes the process by which Jews in concert with communists have come close to subverting and controlling the peoples and nations in Europe.

---

Here he stops at nothing, and his vileness becomes so monstrous that no one should be surprised if among our people the hateful figure of the Jew is taken as the personification of the devil and the symbol of evil. . . .

How close they see their approaching victory can be seen in the frightful way that their dealings with members of other races develop.

The black-haired Jewish youth, with satanic joy on his face, lurks in wait for hours for the innocent girls he plans to defile with his blood, and steal the young girl from her people. With every means at hand he seeks to undermine the racial foundations of the people they would subjugate. . . . For a people which is racially pure and is conscious of its blood, will never be able to be subjugated by the Jews. The Jew in this world will forever only be the masters of bastardized people. . . .

Around those nations which have offered sturdy resistance to their internal attacks, they surround them with a web of enemies; thanks to their international influence, they incite them

to war, and when necessary, will plant the flag of revolution, even on the battlefield.

In economics he shakes the foundations of the state long enough so that unprofitable business enterprises are shut down and come under his financial control. In politics he denies the state its means of self-preservation, destroys its means of self-maintenance and defense, annihilates faith in state leadership, insults its history and traditions, and drags everything that is truly great into the gutter.

Culturally, he pollutes art, literature and theater, makes a mockery of natural sensibilities, destroys every concept of beauty and nobility, the worthy and the good, and instead drags other men down to the sphere of its own lowly type of existence.

Religion is made an object of mockery, morality and ethics are described as old-fashioned, until finally the last props of a people for maintaining their existence in this world are destroyed.

## PERSONALITY AND THE IDEAL OF THE FOLKISH[4] STATE

*The folkish world view differs from the Marxist world view fundamentally in that it not only recognizes the value of race, but also that of the individual, and makes these the pillars of its very structure.* These are the sustaining factors in its view of the world.

The folkish state must care for the well-being of its citizens by recognizing in everything the worth of the person, and by doing so direct it to the highest level of its productive capability, thus guaranteeing for each the highest level of participation.

Accordingly, the folkish state must free the entire leadership, especially those in political leadership, from the parliamentary principle of majority rule by the multitude, so that the right of personality is guaranteed without any limita-

---

[4]The word Hitler uses, *völkisch,* is an adjective derived from *Volk,* meaning "people" or "nation," which Hitler defined in a racial sense; thus a "folkish" state is one that expresses the characteristics of and furthers the interests of a particular race, in this case, the Aryans.

tion. From this is derived the following realization. *The best state constitution and form is that which with unquestioned certainty raises the best minds from the national community to positions of leading authority and influence. . . .*

There are no majority decisions, rather only responsible individuals, and the word "advice" will once again have its original meaning. Each man will have advisers at his side, *but the decision will be made by one man.*

The principle that made the Prussian army in its time the most splendid instrument of the German people will have to become someday the foundation for the construction of our completed state: *authority of every leader downward and responsibility upward. . . .*

This principle of binding absolute responsibility with absolute authority will gradually bring forth an elite group of leaders which today in an era of irresponsible parliamentarianism is hardly thinkable.

## THE DIRECTION AND POLITICS OF EASTERN EUROPE

*The foreign policy of the folkish state has as its purpose to guarantee the existence on this planet of the race that it gathers within its borders. With this in mind it must create a natural and healthy ratio between the number and growth of the population and the extent and quality of the land and soil. The balance must be such that it accords with the vital needs of the people.* What I call a *healthy* ratio is one in which the support of the people is assured by its own land and soil. Any other condition, even if it lasts centuries or a thousand years, is nevertheless an unhealthy one and will lead sooner or later to damage, if not the total destruction of the affected people. *Only a sufficiently large space on the earth can assure the independent existence of a people. . . .*

*If the National Socialist Movement really is to be consecrated in history as fulfilling a great mission for the people, it must, spurred by knowledge and filled with pain over its true situation on this earth, boldly* *and with a clear sense of direction, take up the battle against the aimlessness and incompetence of our foreign policy. It must, without consideration of "traditions" or preconceived notions, find the courage to gather our people and their forces and advance them on the path from their present restricted living space to new land and soil. This will free the people from the dangers of disappearing from the earth altogether or becoming a slave people in the service of another.*

*The National Socialist movement must seek to eliminate the disproportion between our people's population and our territory — viewing this as a source of food as well as a basis for national power — and between our historical past and our present hopeless impotence.* While doing so it must remain conscious of the fact that we as protectors of the highest humanity on earth are bound also by the highest duty that will be fulfilled only if we inspire the German people with the racial ideal, so that they will occupy themselves not just with the breeding of good dogs, horses, and cats but also show concern about the purity of *their own* blood.

Against everything else we National Socialists must hold unflinchingly to our goal of foreign policy, namely, *to secure for the German people the land on this earth to which they are entitled. . . .*

*State boundaries are made by man and can be changed by man.*

The fact that a nation has acquired a large amount of land is no mandate that this should be recognized forever. This only goes to prove the strength of the conqueror and the weakness of the conquered. And only in force lies the right of possession. If today the German people are imprisoned within an impossible territorial area and for that reason are face to face with a miserable future, this is not the commandment of fate, any more than a revolt against such a situation would be a violation of the laws of fate; . . . the soil on which we now live was not bestowed upon our ancestors by Heaven; rather, they had to conquer it by risking their lives. So with us, in the future we will win soil and with it the means of existence of the people not through some sort of folkish grace but only through the power of the triumphant sword.

But we National Socialists must go further: *The right to land and soil will become an obligation if without further territorial expansion a great people is threatened with its destruction.* And that is particularly true when the people in question is not some little nigger people, but the German mother of life, which has given cultural shape to the modern world. *Germany will either become a world power or will no longer exist.* To achieve world power an expansion in size is needed, which will give the state meaning in today's world and will give life to its citizens. . . .

*And so we National Socialists consciously draw a line below the direction of our foreign policy before the war. We take up where we broke off six hundred years ago. We put a stop to the eternal pull of the Germans toward the south and western Europe and turn our gaze to the lands of the east. We put an end to the colonial and commercial policy of the prewar period and shift to the land-oriented policy of the future.*

When today we speak of new territory and soil in Europe, we think primarily of *Russia* and her subservient border states.

# The Destiny of Japan
▼▼▼

## 94 ▼ *"THE WAY OF SUBJECTS"*

In 1941, only a few months before the bombing of Pearl Harbor, the Japanese Ministry of Education issued "The Way of Subjects," a pamphlet that became required reading for high school and university students. It reflects the basic principles of Japanese ultranationalism, a growing force in the 1920s and 1930s.

Racial and cultural pride had characterized the Japanese for centuries and was a major reason for their wholehearted support of modernization during the Meiji period. In the 1920s and 1930s nationalism intensified and, as in Germany and Italy, became identified with antidemocratic and antisocialist movements. It grew in response to several developments, including resentment of the West for its treatment of Japan after World War I, fears of a reunified China under Chiang Kai-shek and the Nationalists, concerns about economic fluctuations and social tensions caused by the Great Depression, opposition to "dangerous" ideologies such as socialism and communism, and anxieties about Western influence on Japanese culture and politics.

The ultranationalists denounced democracy, socialism, and the influence of big business on Japanese life. They praised Japanese virtues of harmony and duty, idealized the past, demanded absolute obedience to the emperor, and called for the revival of warrior values. They also clamored for Japanese imperialist expansion, claiming that this alone could save Japan from overpopulation and economic isolation.

With strong support in the rural population and army, ultranationalism peaked between 1931 and 1936, when its disciples assassinated business leaders and politicians, including a prime minister, and plotted to overthrow the government. The most serious coup attempt took place in February 1936 when officers and troops of the Fifteenth Division attacked and held downtown Tokyo for three days before authorities suppressed their rebellion. The government survived, but to satisfy the extremists it cracked down on leftist politicians and acceded to many of the army's demands. The balance of Japanese politics had shifted to right-wing militarists, setting the stage for the invasion of China in 1937 and the bombing of Pearl Harbor in 1941.

## QUESTIONS FOR ANALYSIS

1. What is the stated purpose of "The Way of Subjects"?
2. According to the authors, what are the distinguishing characteristics of Western nations, and how is the West threatening Japan?
3. According to the authors, how do the Japanese differ from other people? What do they see as Japan's special mission?
4. What, according to the authors, is the role of individual Japanese in fulfilling the nation's mission?
5. To what extent do the authors' views of Japan's future resemble Hitler's dreams for Germany (source 93)?

## PREAMBLE

The way of the subjects of the Emperor issues from the polity of the Emperor, and is to guard and maintain the Imperial Throne coexistent with the Heavens and the Earth. This is not an abstract principle, but a way of daily practices based on history. The life and activities of the nation are all attuned to the task of strengthening the foundation of the Empire.

Looking to the past, this country has been widely seeking knowledge in the world since the Meiji Restoration, thereby fostering and maintaining the prosperity of the state. With the influx of European and American culture into this country, however, individualism, liberalism, utilitarianism, and materialism began to assert themselves, so that the traditional character of the country was much impaired and the virtuous habits and customs bequeathed by our ancestors were affected unfavorably.

With the outbreak of the Manchurian Affair[1] and further occurrence of the China Affair,[2] the national spirit started to be elevated gradually, but there is still much to be desired in point of the people's understanding the fundamental principle of polity as a whole and their consciousness as subjects of the Emperor. . . .

If this situation is left unremedied, it will be difficult to eradicate the evils of European and American thought that are deeply penetrating various strata of Japan's national life, and to achieve the unprecedentedly great tasks by establishing a structure of national solidarity of guarding and maintaining the prosperity of the Imperial Throne. Herein lies an urgent need to discard the self-centered and utilitarian ideas and to elevate and practice the way of the Emperor's subjects based on state service as the primary requisite.

## PART I

The thoughts that have formed the foundation of Western civilization since the early period of the modern age are individualism, liberalism, materialism, and so on. These thoughts regard the strong preying on the weak as reasonable, unstintedly promote the pursuit of luxury and pleasure, encourage materialism, and stimulate competition for acquiring colonies and securing trade, thereby leading the world to a veritable hell of fighting and bloodshed. . . . The self-destruction in the shape of the World War finally followed. It was only natural that cries were raised

---

[1]The Japanese invasion of Manchuria in 1931.

[2]The invasion of China in 1937.

even among men of those countries after the war that Western civilization was crumbling. A vigorous movement was started by Britain, France, and the United States to maintain the status quo by any means. Simultaneously, a movement aiming at social revolution through class conflict on the basis of thoroughgoing materialism like Communism also vigorously developed. On the other hand, Nazism and Fascism arose with great force. The basic principles of the totalitarianism in Germany and Italy are to remove the evils of individualism and liberalism.

That these principles show great similarity to Eastern culture and spirit is a noteworthy fact that suggests the future of Western civilization and the creation of a new culture. Thus, the orientation of world history has made the collapse of the old world order a certainty. Japan has hereby initiated the construction of a new world order based on moral principles.

The Manchurian Affair was a violent outburst of Japanese national life long suppressed. Taking advantage of this, Japan in the glare of all the Powers made a step toward the creation of a world based on moral principles and the construction of a new order. This was a manifestation of the spirit, profound and lofty, embodied in the founding of Empire, and an unavoidable action for its national life and world mission.

Japan's position was raised suddenly to the world's forefront as a result of the Russo-Japanese War of 1904–05. . . . The general tendency of world domination by Europe and America has begun to show signs of a change since then. Japan's victory attracted the attention of the entire world, and this caused a reawakening of Asiatic countries, which had been forced to lie prostrate under British and American influence, with the result that an independence movement was started.

Hopes to be free of the shackles and bondage of Europe and America were ablaze among the nations of India, Turkey, Arabia, Thailand, Vietnam, and others. This also inspired a new national movement in China. Amid this stormy atmosphere of Asia's reawakening, Japan has come to be keenly conscious of the fact that the stabilization of East Asia is her mission, and that the emancipation of East Asian nations rests solely on her efforts. . . .

## PART III

Viewed from the standpoint of world history, the China Affair is a step toward the construction of a world of moral principles by Japan. The building up of a new order for securing lasting world peace will be attained by the completion of the China Affair as a steppingstone. In this regard the China Affair would not and should not end with the mere downfall of the Chiang Kai-shek regime.[3] Until the evils of European and American influences in East Asia that have led China astray are eliminated, until Japan's cooperation with New China as one of the links in the chain of the Greater East Asian Coprosperity Sphere[4] yields satisfactory results, and East Asia and the rest of the world are united as one on the basis of moral principles, Japan's indefatigable efforts are sorely needed. . . .

Japan has a political mission to help various regions in the Greater East Asian Coprosperity Sphere, which are reduced to a state of quasi-colony by Europe and America, and rescue them from their control. Economically, this country will have to eradicate the evils of their exploitation and then set up an economic structure for coexistence and coprosperity. Culturally, Japan must strive to fashion East Asian nations to abandon their following of European and American culture and to develop Eastern culture for the purpose of contributing to the creation of a just world. The East has been left to destruction for the past several hundred years. Its rehabilitation

---

[3]Chiang Kai-shek (1887–1975), successor to Sun Yat-sen as head of the Nationalist Party, was the recognized leader of wartime China, even though the communists under Mao Zedong controlled large parts of the country.

[4]The Japanese term for their Asian empire.

is not an easy task. It is natural that unusual difficulties attend the establishment of a new order and the creation of a new culture. Overcoming these difficulties will do much to help in establishing a world dominated by morality, in which all nations can co-operate and all people can secure their proper positions. . . .

It is urgent for Japan to achieve the establishment of a structure of national unanimity in politics, economy, culture, education, and all other realms of national life. Defense is absolutely necessary for national existence. A nation without defense is one that belongs to a dream world. Whether defense is perfected or not is the scale that measures the nation's existence or ruin. . . .

With the change of war from a simple military matter to a complicated total affair, the distinction between wartime and peacetime has been clouded. When the world was singing peace, a furious economic and cultural war was staged behind the scenes, among nations. Unless a country is organized even in time of peace, so that the total struggle of the state and the people is constantly concentrated on the objective of the country, and the highest capacity is displayed, the country is predestined to be defeated before taking to arms. . . .

## PART IV

The cardinal objective of strengthening the total war organism is solely to help the Imperial Throne, and this can be attained by all the people fulfilling their duty as subjects through their respective positions in society. The Soviet Union has world domination through Communism as its objective, and for this that country follows the policy of using force through class dictatorship.

Standing on the national principle of blood and soil, Germany aims at destroying the world domination of the Anglo-Saxon race and the prevailing condition of pressure brought to bear upon Germany. . . . And for this she has succeeded in achieving thoroughgoing popular con-

fidence in, and obedience to, the dictatorship of the Nazis, and is adopting totalitarianism. Italy's ideals are the restoration of the great Roman Empire, and her policy for realizing them is not different from that of Germany. . . .

The ideals of Japan are to manifest to the entire world the spirit of her Empire-founding. . . . There is virtually no country in the world other than Japan having such a superb and lofty mission bearing world significance. So it can be said that the construction of a new structure and an armed state is all so that Japan may revive her proper national standing and return to her original status of supporting the Throne by the myriad subjects, thereby perfecting the workings of national strength and leaving no stone unturned in displaying her total power to the fullest extent.

## PART V

The Imperial Family is the fountain source of the Japanese nation, and national and private lives issue from this. In the past, foreign nationals came to this country only to enjoy the benevolent rule of the Imperial Family, and became Japanese subjects spiritually and by blood. The Imperial virtues are so great and boundless that all are assimilated into one. Here is the reason for the present glorious state, in which the Emperor and his subjects are harmonized into one great unit. . . .

The way of the subjects is to be loyal to the Emperor in disregard of self, thereby supporting the Imperial Throne coextensive with the Heavens and with the Earth. . . .

The great duty of the Japanese people to guard and maintain the Imperial Throne has lasted to the present . . . and will last forever and ever. To serve the Emperor is its key point. Our lives will become sincere and true when they are offered to the Emperor and the state. Our own private life is fulfillment of the way of the subjects; in other words, it is not private, but public, insofar as it is held by the subjects supporting the Throne.

"As far as the clouds float and as far as the mountains and valleys expand," the land is Imperial territory and the people living there are subjects of the Emperor. It is not correct to observe, therefore, that private life has nothing to do with the state and is quite free. Every action has not only a private side, but has more or less connection with the state. All must be unified under the Emperor. Herein lies the significance of national life in Japan.

▼▼▼

# The Legacy of World War II

In the two decades after World War I weapons became more destructive, nationalism more impassioned, and leaders' ambitions more fantastic. As a result, the war that began in Asia in 1937 and in Europe in 1939 — World War II — became the most devastating and destructive war in history. Modern communication and transportation systems enabled generals to plan and execute massive campaigns such as the German invasion of the Soviet Union in 1941 and the Allies' Normandy invasion in 1944. The airplane, only a curiosity in World War I, became an instrument of destruction in World War II, making possible the German assault on English cities in 1940, the Japanese attack on Pearl Harbor in 1941, the around-the-clock bombing of Germany by Britain and the United States from 1943 to 1945, and the American fire-bombing of Tokyo in 1945.

Only the closing months of the war, however, fully revealed the destructive possibilities of modern technology and large bureaucratic states. As Allied armies liberated Europe in the winter and spring of 1945, they found in the Third Reich's concentration and extermination camps the horrifying results of the Nazi assault on political enemies, religious dissidents, prisoners of war, gypsies, Slavs, and especially Jews. Then on August 6 the United States dropped an atomic bomb on Hiroshima, Japan. It killed nearly eighty thousand people, seriously injured twice that number, and obliterated three-fifths of the city. On August 9 the United States dropped a second atomic bomb on Nagasaki, intending to destroy the Mitsubishi shipyards. It missed its target but destroyed half the city and killed seventy-five thousand people.

A half century later the names Hiroshima and Nagasaki still evoke nightmares in a world where the number of nuclear powers grows, thousands of nuclear warheads exist, and many nations have the capacity to manufacture nuclear weapons many times more powerful than those dropped on Japan. Similarly, the Holocaust, the Nazi attempt to exterminate the Jews, continues to haunt the imagination. Racism and ethnic hatreds are universally condemned, but they flourish in many parts of the world. Anti-Semitism has resurfaced in Central and Eastern Europe, the Serbs have bombed and starved Bosnian and Kosovar towns and cities in the name of ethnic cleansing, Tutsi and Hutus have slaughtered one another in central Africa, and racial tensions plague the United States and dozens of other societies.

Was the Holocaust an aberration resulting from the unique prejudices of the Germans and the perverse views of a handful of their leaders? Or was something

much more basic in human nature involved? These are just two of the many
disturbing questions raised by the Nazi campaign to exterminate the Jews.

# "Führer, You Order. We Obey"
▼▼▼
## 95 ▼ *Rudolf Höss, MEMOIRS*

On gaining power, the Nazis began to implement the anti-Jewish policies Hitler
had promised in *Mein Kampf* and thousands of Nazi books, pamphlets, and
speeches. Jewish shops were plundered while police looked the other way, Jewish physicians were excluded from hospitals, Jewish judges lost their posts, Jewish students were denied admission to universities, and Jewish veterans were
stripped of their benefits. In 1935 the Nazis promulgated the Nuremberg Laws,
which deprived Jews of citizenship and outlawed marriage between Jews and
non-Jews. In November 1938 the regime organized nationwide violence against
Jewish synagogues and shops in what came to be known as *Kristallnacht,* or "night
of the broken glass."

After the war began, conquests in Eastern Europe gave the Nazis new opportunities to deal with the "Jewish problem." In early 1941 they began to deport Jews
from Germany and conquered territories to Poland and Czechoslovakia, where
Jews were employed as slave laborers or placed in concentration camps. In June
1941 special units known as *Einsatzgruppe* ("special action forces") were organized to exterminate Jews in territories conquered by German armies on the eastern front. In eighteen months, they gunned down over one million Jews and
threw them into open pits. Then in January 1942 at the Wannsee Conference
outside Berlin, the Nazis approved the Final Solution to the so-called Jewish problem. Their goal became the extermination of European Jewry, and to reach it they
constructed special camps where their murderous work could be done efficiently
and quickly.

When World War II ended, the Nazis had not achieved their goal of annihilat-
ing Europe's eleven million Jews. They did, however, slaughter close to six million, thus earning themselves a permanent place in the long history of man's
inhumanity to man.

The following excerpt comes from the memoirs of Rudolf Höss, the commandant of the Auschwitz concentration camp in Poland between 1940 and 1943.
Born in 1900, Höss abandoned plans to become a priest after serving in World
War I and became involved in a number of right-wing political movements, including the Nazi Party, which he joined in the early 1920s. After serving a jail
sentence for participating in the murder of a teacher suspected of "treason," Höss
became a farmer and then in 1934, on the urging of Heinrich Himmler, a member of the Nazi SS, or *Schutztaffel* (Guard Detachment). The SS under Himmler
grew from a small security force to guard Hitler and other high-ranking Nazis
into a powerful Nazi organization involved in police work, state security, intelligence gathering, administration of conquered territories, and management of the
concentration camps. After postings at the Dachau and Sachsenhausen camps,

Höss was appointed commandant of Auschwitz, which began as a camp for Polish political prisoners but became a huge, sprawling complex where over a million Jews were gassed or shot and tens of thousands of prisoners served as slave laborers in nearby factories. In 1943 Höss became overseer of all the Third Reich's concentration camps, but he returned to Auschwitz in 1944 to oversee the murder of four hundred thousand Hungarian Jews. After his capture in 1946, he was tried and convicted for crimes against humanity. He was hanged on April 16, 1947, within sight of the villa where he and his family had lived while he served as commandant at Auschwitz.

While awaiting trial, Höss was encouraged to compose his memoirs to sharpen his recollection of the events he experienced. In the following passage he discusses his views of the Jews and his reaction to the mass killings he planned and witnessed.

## QUESTIONS FOR ANALYSIS

1. What does Höss claim to have been his attitude toward the Jews?
2. How do his statements about the Jews accord with his assertion that he was a fanatic National Socialist?
3. Does Höss make any distinction between the Russians and Jews that he had exterminated?
4. What was Höss's attitude toward the Final Solution? How does Höss characterize his role in the mass extermination of the Jews?
5. How did his involvement in the Holocaust affect him personally? How, according to Höss, did it affect other German participants?
6. What would you describe as the key components of Höss's personality? To what extent was his personality shaped by the Nazi philosophy to which he was dedicated?
7. What insight does this excerpt provide about the issue of how much the German people knew of and participated in the Holocaust?

Since I was a fanatic National Socialist, I was firmly convinced that our idea would take hold in all countries, modified by the various local customs, and would gradually become dominant. This would then break the dominance of international Jewry. Anti-Semitism was nothing new throughout the whole world. It always made its strongest appearance when the Jews had pushed themselves into positions of power and when their evil actions became known to the general public. . . . I believed that because our ideas were better and stronger, we would prevail in the long run. . . .

I want to emphasize here that I personally never hated the Jews. I considered them to be the enemy of our nation. However, that was precisely the reason to treat them the same way as the other prisoners. I never made a distinction concerning this. Besides, the feeling of hatred is not in me, but I know what hate is, and how it manifests itself. I have seen it and I have felt it.

The original order of 1941 to annihilate all the Jews stated, "All Jews without exception are to be destroyed." It was later changed by Himmler so that those able to work were to be used in the arms factories. This made Auschwitz the assembly point for the Jews to a degree never before known. . . .

When he gave me the order personally in the summer of 1941 to prepare a place for mass killings and then carry it out, I could never have imagined the scale, or what the consequences would be. Of course, this order was something extraordinary, something monstrous. However, the reasoning behind the order of this mass annihilation seemed correct to me. At the time I wasted no thoughts about it. I had received an order; I had to carry it out. I could not allow myself to form an opinion as to whether this mass extermination of the Jews was necessary or not. At the time it was beyond my frame of mind. Since the Führer himself had ordered "The Final Solution of the Jewish Question," there was no second guessing for an old National Socialist, much less an SS officer. "Führer, you order. We obey" was not just a phrase or a slogan. It was meant to be taken seriously.[1]

Since my arrest I have been told repeatedly that I could have refused to obey this order, and even that I could have shot Himmler dead. I do not believe that among the thousands of SS officers there was even one who would have had even a glimmer of such a thought. . . . Of course, many SS officers moaned and groaned about the many harsh orders. Even then, they carried out every order. . . . As leader of the SS, Himmler's person was sacred. His fundamental orders in the name of the Führer were holy. There was no reflection, no interpretation, no explanation about these orders. They were carried out ruthlessly, regardless of the final consequences, even if it meant giving your life for them. Quite a few did that during the war.

It was not in vain that the leadership training of the SS officers held up the Japanese as shining examples of those willing to sacrifice their lives for the state and for the emperor, who was also

their god. SS education was not just a series of useless high school lectures. It went far deeper, and Himmler knew very well what he could demand of his SS.

Outsiders cannot possibly understand that there was not a single SS officer who would refuse to obey orders from Himmler, or perhaps even try to kill him because of a severely harsh order. Whatever the Führer or Himmler ordered was always right. Even democratic England has its saying, "My country, right or wrong," and every patriotic Englishman follows it.

▾ ▾ ▾

Before the mass destruction of the Jews began, all the Russian politruks[2] and political commissars were killed in almost every camp during 1941 and 1942. According to the secret order given by Hitler, the Einsatzgruppe searched for and picked up the Russian politruks and commissars from all the POW camps. They transferred all they found to the nearest concentration camp for liquidation. . . . The first small transports were shot by firing squads of SS soldiers.

While I was on an official trip, my second in command, Camp Commander Fritzsch, experimented with gas for killings. He used a gas called Cyclon B, prussic acid,[3] which was often used as an insecticide in the camp to exterminate lice and vermin. There was always a supply on hand. When I returned Fritzsch reported to me about how he had used the gas. We used it again to kill the next transport.

The gassing was carried out in the basement of Block 11. I viewed the killings wearing a gas mask for protection. Death occurred in the crammed-full cells immediately after the gas was thrown in. Only a brief choking outcry and it was all over. . . .

At the time I really didn't waste any thoughts about the killing of the Russian POWs. It was ordered; I had to carry it out. But I must admit

---

[1] All SS members swore the following oath: "I swear to you Adolf Hitler, as Führer and Chancellor of the Reich, loyalty and bravery. I vow to you and to the authorities appointed by you obedience onto death, so help me God."
[2] Communist Party members.

[3] Cyclon (or Zyclon) B is a blue crystalline substance, whose active ingredient, hydrocyanic acid, sublimates into a gas when it contacts the air. It causes death by combining with the red blood cells and preventing them from carrying oxygen to the body.

openly that the gassings had a calming effect on me, since in the near future the mass annihilation of the Jews was to begin. Up to this point it was not clear to me . . . how the killing of the expected masses was to be done. Perhaps by gas? But how, and what kind of gas? Now we had discovered the gas and the procedure. I was always horrified of death by firing squads, especially when I thought of the huge numbers of women and children who would have to be killed. I had had enough of hostage executions, and the mass killings by firing squad order by Himmler and Heydrich.[4]

Now I was at ease. We were all saved from these bloodbaths, and the victims would be spared until the last moment. That is what I worried about the most when I thought of Eichmann's[5] accounts of the mowing down of the Jews with machine guns and pistols by the Einsatzgruppe. Horrible scenes were supposed to have occurred: people running away even after being shot, the killing of those who were only wounded, especially the women and children. Another thing on my mind was the many suicides among the ranks of the SS Special Action Squads who could no longer mentally endure wading in the bloodbath. Some of them went mad. Most of the members of the Special Action Squads drank a great deal to help get through this horrible work. According to [Captain] Höffle's accounts, the men of Globocnik's[6] extermination section drank tremendous quantities of alcohol.

In the spring of 1942 [January] the first transports of Jews arrived from Upper Silesia. All of them were to be exterminated. They were led from the ramp across the meadow, later named section B-II of Birkenau,[7] to the farmhouse called Bunker I. Aumeier, Palitzsch, and a few other block leaders led them and spoke to them as one would in casual conversation, asking them about their occupations and their schooling in order to fool them. After arriving at the farmhouse they were told to undress. At first they went very quietly into the rooms where they were supposed to be disinfected. At that point some of them became suspicious and started talking about suffocation and extermination. Immediately a panic started. Those still standing outside were quickly driven into the chambers, and the doors were bolted shut. In the next transport those who were nervous or upset were identified and watched closely at all times. As soon as unrest was noticed these troublemakers were inconspicuously led behind the farmhouse and killed with a small-caliber pistol, which could not be heard by the others. . . .

I also watched how some women who suspected or knew what was happening, even with the fear of death all over their faces, still managed enough strength to play with their children and to talk to them lovingly. Once a woman with four children, all holding each other by the hand to help the smallest ones over the rough ground, passed by me very slowly. She stepped very close to me and whispered, pointing to her four children, "How can you murder these beautiful, darling children? Don't you have any heart?"

Another time an old man hissed while passing me, "Germany will pay a bitter penance for the mass murder of the Jews." His eyes glowed with hatred as he spoke. In spite of this he went bravely into the gas chamber without worrying about the others. . . .

Occasionally some women would suddenly start screaming in a terrible way while undressing. They pulled out their hair and acted as if

---

[4]Reinhard Heydrich (1904–1942) was Himmler's chief lieutenant in the SS. He organized the mass execution of Jews in Eastern Europe in 1941.

[5]Adolf Eichmann (1906–1962) was a Nazi bureaucrat originally involved with Jewish emigration. After the Wannsee Conference he was given responsibility for organizing the deportation of approximately three million Jews to the death camps. He fled to Argentina in 1946, but was captured by Israeli agents who took him to Israel, where he was tried and executed in 1962.

[6]Odilio Globocnik was the officer responsible for organizing and training SS units in Eastern Europe.

[7]Birkenau was the German name for the town where a large addition to the Auschwitz complex was built in late 1941 and early 1942.

they had gone crazy. Quickly they were led behind the farmhouse and killed by a bullet in the back of the neck from a small-caliber pistol. . . . As the doors were being shut, I saw a woman trying to shove her children out the chamber, crying out, "Why don't you at least let my precious children live?" There were many heartbreaking scenes like this which affected all who were present.

In the spring of 1942 hundreds of people in the full bloom of life walked beneath the budding fruit trees of the farm into the gas chamber to their death, most of them without a hint of what was going to happen to them. To this day I can still see these pictures of the arrivals, the selections, and the procession to their death. . . .

The mass annihilation with all the accompanying circumstances did not fail to affect those who had to carry it out. They just did not watch what was happening. With very few exceptions all who performed this monstrous "work" had been ordered to this detail. All of us, including myself, were given enough to think about which left a deep impression. Many of the men often approached me during my inspection trips through the killing areas and poured out their depression and anxieties to me, hoping that I could give them some reassurance. During these conversations the question arose again and again, "Is what we have to do here necessary? Is it necessary that hundreds of thousands of women and children have to be annihilated?" And I, who countless times deep inside myself had asked the same question, had to put them off by reminding them that it was Hitler's order. I had to tell them that it was necessary to destroy all the Jews in order to forever free Germany and the future generations from our toughest enemy.

It goes without saying that the Hitler order was a firm fact for all of us, and also that it was the duty of the SS to carry it out. However, secret doubts tormented all of us. Under no circumstances could I reveal my secret doubts to anyone. I had to convince myself to be like a rock when faced with the necessity of carrying out this horribly severe order, and I had to show this in every way, in order to force all those under me to hang on mentally and emotionally. . . .

Hour upon hour I had to witness all that happened. I had to watch day and night, whether it was the dragging and burning of the bodies, the teeth being ripped out, the cutting of the hair,[8] I had to watch all this horror. For hours I had to stand in the horrible, haunting stench while the mass graves were dug open, and the bodies were dragged out and burned. I also had to watch the procession of death itself through the peephole of the gas chamber because the doctors called my attention to it. I had to do all of this because I was the one to whom everyone looked, and because I had to show everybody that I was not only the one who gave the orders and issued the directives, but that I was also willing to be present at whatever task I ordered my men to perform. . . .

And yet, everyone in Auschwitz believed the Kommandant really had a good life. Yes, my family had it good in Auschwitz, every wish that my wife or my children had was fulfilled. The children could live free and easy. My wife had her flower paradise. The prisoners tried to give my wife every consideration and tried to do something nice for the children. By the same token no former prisoner can say that he was treated poorly in any way in our house. My wife would have loved to give a present to every prisoner who performed a service for us. The children constantly begged me for cigarettes for the prisoners. The children especially loved the gardeners. In our entire family there was a deep love for farming and especially for animals. Every Sunday I had to drive with them across all the fields, walk them through the stables, and we could never skip visiting the dog kennels. Their greatest love was for our two horses and our colt. The prisoners who worked in the household were al-

---

[8]Teeth extracted from the corpses were soaked in muriatic acid to remove muscle and bone before the gold fillings were extracted. Some of the gold was distributed to dentists who used it in fillings for SS men and their families; the rest was deposited in the Reichsbank. Hair was used to make felt and thread.

ways dragging in some animal the children kept in the garden. Turtles, martens, cats, or lizards; there was always something new and interesting in the garden. The children splashed around in the summertime in the small pool in the garden or the Sola River. Their greatest pleasure was when daddy went into the water with them. But he had only a little time to share all the joys of childhood.

Today I deeply regret that I didn't spend more time with my family. I always believed that I had to be constantly on duty. Through this exaggerated sense of duty I always had made my life more difficult than it actually was. My wife often urged me, "Don't always think of your duty, think of your family too." But what did my wife know about the things that depressed me? She never found out.[9]

---

[9]In an interview with a court-appointed psychiatrist during the Nuremberg trials in 1946, Höss stated that his wife actually did learn of his participation in the mass executions at the camp, and that afterward, they became estranged and ceased having sexual relations.

## Scientists' Warnings on Atomic Warfare

▼▼▼

## 96 ▼ THE FRANCK REPORT

Spurred by fears that Germany might produce a nuclear weapon and the urgings of some of the world's greatest physicists, including Albert Einstein, in 1939 President Franklin D. Roosevelt approved a massive American effort to produce an atomic bomb. Known as the Manhattan Project after being taken over by the army in 1942, the drive to produce the bomb cost more than $2 billion and employed over one hundred thousand individuals, who worked under the direction of the country's leading scientists and engineers at thirty-seven installations in thirteen states. Their efforts paid off in the spring of 1945 with the manufacture of two types of atomic bombs scientists were convinced would work. By then Germany had surrendered, the Allies had driven the Japanese from most of their conquests, and the Soviet Union had promised to join the war against Japan in the fall of 1945.

At this point, some scientists whose primary incentive had been to defeat the Nazis began to have misgivings about using atomic bombs against Japan. Beginning in April 1945, several prominent physicists, most of whom worked at the Chicago Metallurgical Laboratory, sent letters and petitions to President Roosevelt and, after his death on April 12, to his successor, President Truman, urging them to refrain from using the bomb militarily. These Chicago-based scientists also formed the Committee on the Social and Political Implications of Atomic Energy, chaired by James Franck, a German-born chemist and Nobel laureate (1925) for his work on the bombardment of atoms by electrons. The committee's recommendations, known as the Franck Report, crystallized the groups' fears about atomic warfare. The report was sent to Washington but was challenged by other scientists and ultimately rejected by the group President Truman had formed to advise him on the use of atomic weapons. Truman never read the report before making his decision to drop two atomic bombs on Japan in early August 1945.

The result was the destruction of two cities, Hiroshima and Nagasaki, and the death of more than two hundred thousand individuals, some of whom were instantly vaporized, while others died more slowly of burns, injuries, or radiation sickness. The two bombs also brought World War II to an end. The Japanese surrendered on August 14, 1945, thereby cutting short a conflict that otherwise would have continued to take a dreadful toll on soldiers, sailors, airmen, and civilians.

---

## QUESTIONS FOR ANALYSIS

1. Why, according to the authors of the report, has the defeat of Germany changed their thinking about the use of nuclear weapons?
2. How, according to the report, could nuclear weapons best be limited and controlled in the postwar era?
3. How, according to the report, will the military use of nuclear weapons undermine any postwar agreement on their control and limitation?
4. What is meant when the report states that "only lack of trust" can stand in the way of effective control of nuclear weapons?
5. What kind of future does the report envision in the absence of an agreement to limit nuclear weapons?

Scientists have often before been accused of providing new weapons for the mutual destruction of nations, instead of improving their well-being. It is undoubtedly true that the discovery of flying, for example, has so far brought much more misery than enjoyment and profit to humanity. However, in the past, scientists could disclaim direct responsibility for the use to which mankind had put their disinterested discoveries. We feel compelled to take a more active stand now because the success which we have achieved in the development of nuclear power is fraught with infinitely greater dangers than were all the inventions of the past. All of us, familiar with the present state of nucleonics, live with the vision before our eyes of sudden destruction visited on our own country, of a Pearl Harbor disaster repeated in thousand-fold magnification in every one of our major cities.

In the past, science has often been able to provide also new methods of protection against new weapons of aggression it made possible, but it cannot promise such efficient protection against the destructive use of nuclear power. This protection can come only from the political organization of the world. Among all the arguments calling for an efficient international organization for peace, the existence of nuclear weapons is the most compelling one. *In the absence of an international authority which would make all resort to force in international conflicts impossible, nations could still be diverted from a path which must lead to total mutual destruction, by a specific international agreement barring a nuclear armaments race. . . .*

The consequences of nuclear warfare, and the type of measures which would have to be taken to protect a country from total destruction by nuclear bombing, must be as abhorrent to other nations as to the United States. England, France, and the smaller nations of the European continent, with their congeries of people and industries, would be in a particularly desperate situation in the face of such a threat. Russia and China are the only great nations at present which could survive a nuclear attack. However, even though these countries may value human life less than the peoples of Western Europe and America, and even though Russia, in particular, has an immense space over which its vital industries could be dispersed and a government which can order this dispersion the day it is convinced that such a measure is necessary — there is no doubt that Russia will shudder at the possibility of a sudden disintegration of Moscow and Leningrad and of its new industrial cities in the Urals and Siberia. Therefore, only lack of mutual *trust,* and not lack of *desire* for agreement, can stand in the path of an efficient agreement for the prevention of nuclear warfare. The achievement of such an agreement will thus essentially depend on the integrity of intentions and readiness to sacrifice the necessary fraction of one's own sovereignty, by all the parties to the agreement.

From this point of view, the way in which the nuclear weapons now being secretly developed in this country are first revealed to the world appears to be of great, perhaps fateful importance. . . . Although important tactical results undoubtedly can be achieved by a sudden introduction of nuclear weapons, we nevertheless think that the question of the use of the very first available atomic bombs in the Japanese war should be weighed very carefully, not only by military authorities, but by the highest political leadership of this country. If we consider international agreement on total prevention of nuclear warfare as the paramount objective, and believe that it can be achieved, this kind of introduction of atomic weapons to the world may easily destroy all our chances of success. Russia, and even allied countries which bear less mistrust of our ways and intentions, as well as neutral countries may be deeply shocked. It may be very difficult to persuade the world that a nation which was capable of secretly preparing and suddenly releasing a weapon as indiscriminate as the rocket bomb and a million times more destructive, is to be trusted in its proclaimed desire of having such weapons abolished by international agreement.

Thus, from the "optimistic" point of view — looking forward to an international agreement on the prevention of nuclear warfare — the military advantages and the saving of American lives achieved by the sudden use of atomic bombs against Japan may be outweighed by the ensuing loss of confidence and by a wave of horror and repulsion sweeping over the rest of the world and perhaps even dividing public opinion at home.

*From this point of view, a demonstration of the new weapon might best be made, before the eyes of representatives of all the United Nations, on the desert or a barren island.* The best possible atmosphere for the achievement of an international agreement could be achieved if America could say to the world, "You see what sort of a weapon we had but did not use. We are ready to renounce its use in the future if other nations join us in this renunciation and agree to the establishment of an efficient international control."

After such a demonstration the weapon might perhaps be used against Japan if the sanction of the United Nations (and of public opinion at home) were obtained, perhaps after a preliminary ultimatum to Japan to surrender or at least to evacuate certain regions as an alternative to their total destruction. This may sound fantastic, but in nuclear weapons we have something entirely new in order of magnitude of destructive power, and if we want to capitalize fully on the advantage their possession gives us, we must use new and imaginative methods.

It must be stressed that if one takes the pessimistic point of view and discounts the possibility of an effective international control over nuclear weapons at the present time, then the advisability of an early use of nuclear bombs against Japan becomes even more doubtful — quite independently of any humanitarian considerations. If an international agreement is not concluded immediately after the first demonstration, this will mean a flying start toward an unlimited armaments race. If this race is inevitable, we have every reason to delay its beginning as long as possible in order to increase our head start still further. . . .

Thus it is to our interest to delay the beginning of the armaments race. . . . The benefit to the nation, and the saving of American lives in the future, achieved by renouncing an early demonstration of nuclear bombs and letting the other nations come into the race only reluctantly, on the basis of guesswork and without definite knowledge that the "thing does work," may far outweigh the advantages to be gained by the immediate use of the first and comparatively inefficient bombs in the war against Japan. . . .

One may point out that scientists themselves have initiated the development of this "secret weapon" and it is therefore strange that they should be reluctant to try it out on the enemy as soon as it is available. The answer to this question was given above — the compelling reason for creating this weapon with such speed was our fear that Germany had the technical skill necessary to develop such a weapon, and that the German government had no moral restraints regarding its use.

Another argument which could be quoted in favor of using atomic bombs as soon as they are available is that so much taxpayers' money has been invested in these Projects that the Congress and the American public will demand a return for their money. The attitude of American public opinion . . . in the matter of the use of poison gas against Japan, shows that one can expect the American public to understand that it is sometimes desirable to keep a weapon in readiness for use only in extreme emergency; and as soon as the potentialities of nuclear weapons are revealed to the American people, one can be sure that they will support all attempts to make the use of such weapons impossible.

Once this is achieved, the large installations and the accumulation of explosive material at present earmarked for potential military use will become available for important peace time developments, including power production, large engineering undertakings, and mass production of radioactive materials. In this way, the money spent on wartime development of nucleonics may become a boon for the peacetime development of [the] national economy.

## "The Face of War Is the Face of Death"

▼▼▼

### 97 ▼ Henry L. Stimson, "THE DECISION TO USE THE ATOMIC BOMB"

President Truman, who as a senator from Missouri and as vice president under Roosevelt did not even know about the Manhattan Project, learned of the atomic bomb in a meeting with Secretary of War Henry L. Stimson on April 25, 1945, two weeks after President Roosevelt's death. His first response was to appoint a small committee, known as the Interim Committee, to advise him on the use of atomic weapons in the war and the immediate postwar era. Its members included Stimson and seven others: George Harrison, an insurance executive who was a special assistant to Stimson; James Byrnes, a presidential advisor and soon secretary of state; Ralph Bard, undersecretary of the navy; William Clayton, assistant secretary of state; Vannevar Bush, president of the Carnegie Institution in Washington; Karl Compton, president of the Massachusetts Institute of Technology; and James Conant, president of Harvard University. They were advised by a Scientific Panel, made up of four persons who had played leading roles in the Manhattan Project: Enrico Fermi of Columbia University; Arthur H. Compton of the University of Chicago; Ernest Lawrence of the University of California at Berkeley; and Robert Oppenheimer, director of the atomic energy research project at Los Alamos, New Mexico.

The chair of the Interim Committee and the author of the excerpt that follows was Stimson. Born in 1867 in New York City and a graduate of Harvard College and Yale Law School, Stimson had a distinguished career as a lawyer and public servant. Having served as secretary of war under President Taft and secretary of state under President Hoover, he was named secretary of war by Roosevelt in 1940, despite being a Republican. In 1947, after his retirement from public service and less than three years before his death in 1950, he published the article "The Decision to Use the Atomic Bomb" in *Harper's Magazine.* It focused on the work of the Interim Committee and the reasons why Stimson advised President Truman to drop the bombs on Japan without warning. Excerpts from the article follow.

---

## QUESTIONS FOR ANALYSIS

1. How did the background and specific purposes of the Manhattan Project affect decision making in 1945?
2. For those who supported the immediate use of the bombs, what specific goals did they hope to achieve?
3. How was the choice of Hiroshima and Nagasaki as targets related to these goals?
4. How seriously does it appear that the views expressed in the Franck Report were considered by the Interim Committee and Stimson? Why did they ultimately reject the report's proposals?
5. What were Stimson's views of the nature of war? How did his views affect his decision to support the immediate use of the atomic bombs?

## [GOALS OF THE MANHATTAN PROJECT]

The policy adopted and steadily pursued by President Roosevelt and his advisers was a simple one. It was to spare no effort in securing the earliest possible successful development of an atomic weapon. The reasons for this policy were equally simple. The original experimental achievement of atomic fission had occurred in Germany in 1938, and it was known that the Germans had continued their experiments. In 1941 and 1942 they were believed to be ahead of us, and it was vital that they should not be the first to bring atomic weapons into the field of battle. Furthermore, if we should be the first to develop the weapon, we should have a great new instrument for shortening the war and minimizing destruction. At no time, from 1941 to 1945, did I ever hear it suggested by the President, or by any other responsible member of government, that atomic energy should not be used in the war. All of us of course understood the terrible responsibility involved in our attempt to unlock the doors to such a devastating weapon; President Roosevelt particularly spoke to me many times of his own awareness of the catastrophic potentialities of our work. But we were at war, and the work must be done. . . .

## [RECOMMENDATIONS OF THE INTERIM COMMITTEE AND THE SECRETARY OF WAR]

The discussions of the committee ranged over the whole field of atomic energy, in its political, military, and scientific aspects. . . . The committee's work included the drafting of the statements which were published immediately after the first bombs were dropped, the drafting of a bill for the domestic control of atomic energy, and recommendations looking toward the international control of atomic energy. . . . At a meeting with the Interim Committee and the Scientific Panel on May 31, 1945 I urged all those present to feel free to express themselves on any phase of the subject, scientific or political. Both General Marshall[1] and I at this meeting expressed the view that atomic energy could not be considered simply in terms of military weapons but must also be considered in terms of a new relationship of man to the universe.

On June 1, after its discussions with the Scientific Panel, the Interim Committee unanimously adopted the following recommendations:

(1) The bomb should be used against Japan as soon as possible.
(2) It should be used on a dual target — that is, a military installation or war plant surrounded by or adjacent to houses and other buildings most susceptible to damage, and
(3) It should be used without prior warning [of the nature of the weapon]. One member of the committee, Mr. Bard,[2] later changed his view and dissented from recommendation.

In reaching these conclusions the Interim Committee carefully considered such alternatives as a detailed advance warning or a demonstration in some uninhabited area. Both of these suggestions were discarded as impractical. They were not regarded as likely to be effective in compelling a surrender of Japan, and both of them involved serious risks. Even the New Mexico test would not give final proof that any given bomb was certain to explode when dropped from an airplane. Quite apart from the generally unfamiliar nature of atomic explosives, there was the whole problem of exploding a bomb at a predetermined height in the air by a complicated mechanism which could not be tested in the static test of New Mexico. Nothing would have been more damaging to our effort to obtain surrender than a warning or a demonstration followed by a dud — and this was a real possibility. Furthermore, we had no bombs to waste. It was vital that a sufficient effect be quickly obtained with the few we had. . . .

The committee's function was, of course, entirely advisory. The ultimate responsibility for the recommendation to the President rested upon me, and I have no desire to veil it. The conclusions of the committee were similar to my own, although I reached mine independently. I felt that to extract a genuine surrender from the Emperor and his military advisers, they must be administered a tremendous shock which would carry convincing proof of our power to destroy the Empire. Such an effective shock would save many times the number of lives, both American and Japanese, that it would cost.

The facts upon which my reasoning was based and steps taken to carry it out now follow.

The principal political, social, and military objective of the United States in the summer of 1945 was the prompt and complete surrender of Japan. Only the complete destruction of her military power could open the way to lasting peace. . . .

In the middle of July 1945, the intelligence section of the War Department General Staff estimated Japanese military strength as follows: in the home islands, slightly under 2,000,000; in Korea, Manchuria, China proper, and Formosa, slightly over 2,000,000; in French Indo-China, Thailand, and Burma, over 200,000; in the East Indies area, including the Philippines, over 500,000; in the by-passed Pacific islands, over 100,000. The total strength of the Japanese Army was estimated at about 5,000,000 men.

---

[1]George C. Marshall, Army Chief of Staff, 1939–1945.
[2]Undersecretary of the navy and a member of the Interim Committee. He was the single member of the Interim Committee to oppose its recommendations.

These estimates later proved to be in very close agreement with official Japanese figures. . . .

As we understood it in July, there was a very strong possibility that the Japanese government might determine upon resistance to the end, in all the areas of the Far East under its control. In such an event the Allies would be faced with the enormous task of destroying an armed force of five million men and five thousand suicide aircraft, belonging to a race which had already amply demonstrated its ability to fight literally to the death.

The strategic plans of our armed forces for the defeat of Japan, as they stood in July, had been prepared without reliance upon the atomic bomb, which had not yet been tested in New Mexico. We were planning an intensified sea and air blockade, and greatly intensified strategic air bombing, through the summer and early fall, to be followed on November 1 by an invasion of the southern island of Kyushu. This would be followed in turn by an invasion of the main island of Honshu in the spring of 1946. The total U.S. military and naval force involved in this grand design was of the order of 5,000,000 men; if all those indirectly concerned are included, it was larger still.

We estimated that if we should be forced to carry this plan to its conclusion, the major fighting would not end until the latter part of 1946, at the earliest. I was informed that such operations might be expected to cost over a million casualties to American forces alone. Additional large losses might be expected among our allies, and, of course, if our campaign were successful and if we could judge by previous experience, enemy casualties would be much larger than our own.

It was already clear in July that even before the invasion we should be able to inflict enormously severe damage on the Japanese homeland by the combined application of "conventional" sea and air power. The critical question was whether this kind of action would induce surrender. It therefore became necessary to consider very carefully the probable state of mind of the enemy, and to assess with accuracy the line of conduct which might end his will to resist.

---

▷   After Japan on July 28 rejected the Potsdam ultimatum, which gave their leaders the choice of immediate surrender or the "utter destruction of the Japanese homeland," plans went forward for using the atomic bombs.

---

Because of the importance of the atomic mission against Japan, the detailed plans were brought to me by the military staff for approval. With President Truman's warm support I struck off the list of suggested targets the city of Kyoto. Although it was a target of considerable military importance, it had been the ancient capital of Japan and was a shrine of Japanese art and culture. We determined that it should be spared. I approved four other targets including the cities of Hiroshima and Nagasaki.

Hiroshima was bombed on August 6, and Nagasaki on August 9. These two cities were active working parts of the Japanese war effort. One was an army center; the other was naval and industrial. Hiroshima was the headquarters of the Japanese Army defending southern Japan and was a major military storage and assembly point. Nagasaki was a major seaport and it contained several large industrial plants of great wartime importance. We believed that our attacks had struck cities which must certainly be important to the Japanese military leaders, both Army and Navy, and we waited for a result. We waited one day.

## FINAL REFLECTIONS

. . . As I look back over the five years of my service as Secretary of War, I see too many stern and heartrending decisions to be willing to pretend that war is anything else than what it is. The face of war is the face of death; death is an inevitable part of every order that a wartime leader gives. The decision to use the atomic bomb was a decision that brought death to over a hundred thousand Japanese. No explanation can change that fact and I do not wish to gloss it over. But this deliberate, premeditated destruction was our least abhorrent choice. The destruction of Hiroshima and Nagasaki put an end to the Japanese war. It stopped the fire raids and the strangling blockade; it ended the ghastly specter of a clash of great land armies.

In this last great action of the Second World War we were given final proof that war is death. War in the twentieth century has grown steadily more barbarous, more destructive, more debased in all its aspects. Now, with the release of atomic energy, man's ability to destroy himself is very nearly complete. The bombs dropped on Hiroshima and Nagasaki ended a war. They also made it wholly clear that we must never have another war. This is the lesson men and leaders everywhere must learn, and I believe that when they learn it they will find a way to lasting peace. There is no other choice.

# Chapter 12

## Anticolonialism, Nationalism, and Revolution in Africa, Asia, and Latin America

During the nineteenth century the industrialized nations of Europe and the United States — "the West" — achieved unprecedented global dominance. For India and most of Africa and Southeast Asia, this meant colonial status and outright political control by the Western nations. For China and many states in the Middle East and Latin America, it meant the subordination of their economic interests to those of the West and erosion of their political sovereignty. The great majority of people in Europe and the United States viewed these developments as just and inevitable. To them, their global primacy confirmed their intellectual and moral superiority to black-, yellow-, and brown-skinned people, whom the English writer Rudyard Kipling depicted in his poem "The White Man's Burden" as "half devil and half child."

In the first half of the twentieth century, however, Africans, Asians, and Latin Americans challenged the West's ascendancy and self-proclaimed superiority. In areas ruled by the West as colonies, anticolonial movements gained followers, coalesced into organized parties, and demanded more political power and ultimate independence. Anticolonialism was strongest in India, where opposition to more than a century of British rule escalated from polite requests by educated Indians for greater political responsibility to nationwide boycotts and mass demonstrations for independence. Despite

French, British, and Dutch repression in Southeast Asia, dozens of political parties and secret organizations worked for the peaceful end or violent overthrow of colonial regimes. In Africa, although colonized only in the late 1800s and despite its ethnic and linguistic diversity, articulate and forceful proponents of Pan-Africanism, anticolonialism, and nationalism also emerged. In the Arab Middle East, where nationalist aspirations after World War I were dashed by the mandate system and the continuation of the British protectorate in Egypt, opponents of Anglo-French political control worked for the independence of Egypt, Iraq, Lebanon, and Syria.

While nationalism in colonial areas was directed against foreign rule, in parts of Asia and Latin America where states were independent but nonetheless subservient to U.S. and European interests, it focused on overcoming economic dependency and political weakness. In Turkey this meant a sharp break from its past and implementation of an aggressive program of secularization and modernization under Mustafa Kemal Ataturk, the father of modern Turkey. In China it resulted in a struggle to rebuild the country and end foreign interference in the face of warlordism, civil war between Nationalists and Communists, and the Japanese invasions of Manchuria in 1931 and China itself in 1937. In Latin America it inspired leaders to pursue new, vigorous plans for economic development after the Great Depression of the 1930s eroded world demand for their agricultural and mineral exports. This intensified political struggles between entrenched elites and populist leaders who promised the masses social reforms.

When World War II ended in 1945, many Western leaders thought they could return to the world they had dominated before 1939. In the immediate postwar years, the Dutch, French, and British all used force to maintain their empires but soon realized the futility of their efforts. Asian and African demands for independence proved irresistible, something for which developments in the first half of the twentieth century were largely responsible.

▼▼▼

# Political and Religious Currents in the Middle East

The aftermath of World War I brought political disaster to the Middle East. The Turks, who had fought on Germany's side, were forced in 1920 to accept the humiliating Treaty of Sèvres, which stripped Turkey of its Arab territories, limited the Turkish army to fifty thousand men, gave France, Britain, and Italy control of its finances, and proposed to cede parts of Turkey itself to Italy, Greece, and the new states of Kurdistan and Armenia. The weak sultan, overwhelmed by problems of lawlessness, army desertions, and inflation, meekly accepted the treaty and offered no resistance when the Greeks landed troops in western Anatolia in May 1919.

While the Turks felt despair, their former subjects, the Arabs, experienced bitter disappointment, even though they had been on the winning side in the war. Promised self-rule if they joined the Anglo-French alliance and rebelled against their Ottoman overlords, they learned in 1919 that the British and French had agreed in 1916 to divide Arab lands between themselves, and that this, rather than the promises of Arab independence, would determine the postwar settlement. In 1920 Iraq, Syria, Palestine, Lebanon, and Jordan all became British or French mandates, a status that differed from old-style colonialism in name only.

Arabs were also incensed by the continuation of the British protectorate in Egypt and by the British commitment to honor their promises made during the war to support the establishment of a national home for the Jewish people in Palestine. Farther east, another major Islamic state, Persia, under the decrepit rule of the Qajar Dynasty, also seemed on the verge of becoming a British protectorate.

Efforts to reverse the region's bleak prospects following World War I were most successful in Turkey and Iran. Under Mustafa Kemal, the Turks rallied to drive out the Greeks and smash the nascent Armenian state between 1919 and 1922. In 1922, the Turks abolished the sultanate, and in 1923 the European powers agreed to replace the Treaty of Sèvres with the Treaty of Lausanne, which recognized the integrity and independence of the new Turkish republic. Mustafa Kemal now had his opportunity to transform Turkey into a modern secular state. In Iran, which barely avoided becoming a British protectorate in 1919, Colonel Reza Khan (1878–1944) was named shah in 1925 and, like his hero, Kemal, sought to regenerate his country through economic development, educational reform, and Westernization.

Arab efforts to achieve independence and prevent Jewish immigration to Palestine were less successful. Of the twenty Arab states that stretched from Morocco in the west to Iraq in the east, only relatively backward Saudi Arabia and Yemen were truly independent in the interwar years. Egypt and Iraq attained limited self-rule, but the presence of British troops and continuing British influence over foreign and military affairs was a source of ongoing friction and anger in both countries. The drive for independence was even more frustrating in French-controlled Lebanon and Syria. In the 1930s the French reneged on promises to relinquish their authority, and Lebanon remained a mandate until 1943 and Syria until 1945. Arabs throughout the Middle East were also angered by mounting Jewish migration to Palestine, especially in the 1930s, when U.S. immigration restrictions and mounting anti-Semitism in Europe created a mass of new immigrants.

While confronting these immediate postwar diplomatic and political problems, the people and leaders of the region faced other fundamental issues. What could be done to end poverty and illiteracy? How could the teachings and expectations of Islam be reconciled with the realities and demands of modernization? Was modernization itself desirable, and, if so, how was it to be achieved? Was the goal of Arab nationalism the expulsion of the British and French and the stifling of Zionism or was it the attainment of a single united Arab state? Questions such as these were not new to the people of the Middle East. But in the face of the changes that swept through the region in the first half of the twentieth century, finding answers to them became more urgent and more difficult.

# Secularism and Nationalism in Republican Turkey

▼▼▼

## 98 ▼ Mustafa Kemal,
## SPEECH TO THE CONGRESS OF THE PEOPLE'S REPUBLICAN PARTY

The archsymbol of aggressive secularism and nationalism in the Muslim world in the interwar years was Mustafa Kemal (1881–1938), who first achieved prominence as a Turkish military hero during World War I and went on to serve as first president of the Turkish republic. Disgusted by the Ottoman sultan's acquiescence to the Greek occupation of the Turkish port of Smyrna (Izmir) in 1919, Kemal assumed leadership of a resistance movement against both the sultan's government and the Allies. He led his supporters to victory over the Greeks and forced the annulment of the punitive Sèvres Treaty in 1923. One year earlier, in 1922, Kemal had convened a national assembly, which deposed the sultan and set the stage for a decade and a half of revolutionary change. Exercising his broad powers as president, he sought to transform Turkey into a modern secular nation-state. To accomplish this, he broke the power of Islam over education and the legal system, encouraged industrialization, accorded women full legal rights, mandated the use of a new Turkish alphabet, and ordered Turks to adopt Western-style dress. Directing all Turks to adopt hereditary family names, he took for himself the name *Ataturk,* or "Great Turk."

Having consolidated his authority, Kemal decided in 1927 to review his accomplishments and impress upon his subjects the need for continued support. He chose as the occasion the 1927 meeting of the People's Republican Party, which had been founded by Kemal and was Turkey's only legal political party. Here he delivered an extraordinary speech. Having worked on it for three months (in the process exhausting dozens of secretaries), he delivered it over a period of six days.

In these excerpts, he discusses Turkey's past and future, explains his reasons for abolishing the caliphate, the ancient office by virtue of which Turkish sultans had been the theoretical rulers of all Muslims, and justifies his suppression of the Progressive Republican Party, which despite its name was a party of conservatives who opposed Kemal's plans for Turkey's modernization.

---

## QUESTIONS FOR ANALYSIS

1. What, according to Kemal, were the "erroneous ideas" that had guided the Ottoman state in the past?
2. Why does Kemal argue that nation-states, not empires, are the most desirable form of political organization?
3. What is Kemal's view of the West?
4. What are his views of Islam?
5. What arguments does Kemal offer against the continuation of the caliphate?
6. How does Kemal justify his suppression of the Progressive Republicans? What, in his view, were the positive results of this step?

## [NATIONALISM AND EMPIRE]

We turn our minds to the times when the Ottoman state in Istanbul . . . was master of the crown and the throne of the Byzantine Empire. Among the Ottoman rulers there were some who endeavored to form a gigantic empire by seizing Germany and Western Europe. One of these rulers hoped to unite the whole Islamic world in one body, to lead it and govern it. For this purpose he obtained control of Syria and Egypt and assumed the title of Caliph.[1] Another Sultan pursued the twofold aim, on the one hand of gaining the mastery over Europe, and on the other of subjecting the Islamic world to his authority and government. The continuous counterattacks from the West, the discontent and insurrections in the Muslim world, as well as the dissensions between the various elements which this policy

had artificially brought together within certain limits, had the ultimate result of burying the Ottoman Empire, in the same way as many others, under the pall of history. . . .

To unite different nations under one common name, to give these different elements equal rights, subject them to the same conditions and thus to found a mighty State is a brilliant and attractive political ideal; but it is a misleading one. It is an unrealizable aim to attempt to unite in one tribe the various races existing on the earth, thereby abolishing all boundaries. Herein lies a truth which the centuries that have gone by and the men who have lived during these centuries have clearly shown in dark and sanguinary events.

There is nothing in history to show how the policy of Panislamism[2] could have succeeded or how it could have found a basis for its realiza-

---

[1]The reference is to Selim I, who conquered Egypt and Syria in 1515–1516; it is doubtful that he actually considered himself caliph, that is, leader and protector of all Muslims.

[2]The program of uniting all Muslims under one government or ruler.

tion on this earth. As regards the result of the ambition to organize a State which should be governed by the idea of world-supremacy and include the whole of humanity without distinction of race, history does not afford examples of this. For us, there can be no question of the lust of conquest. . . .

The political system which we regard as clear and fully realizable is national policy. . . . This is borne out in history and is the expression of science, reason, and common sense.

In order that our nation should be able to live a happy, strenuous, and permanent life, it is necessary that the State should pursue an exclusively national policy and that this policy should be in perfect agreement with our internal organization and be based on it. When I speak of national policy, I mean it in this sense: To work within our national boundaries for the real happiness and welfare of the nation and the country by, above all, relying on our own strength in order to retain our existence. But not to lead the people to follow fictitious aims, of whatever nature, which could only bring them misfortune, and expect from the civilized world civilized human treatment, friendship based on mutuality. . . .

## [THE ISSUE OF THE CALIPHATE]

I must call attention to the fact that Hodja Shukri, as well as the politicians who pushed forward his person and signature, had intended to substitute the sovereign bearing the title of Sultan or Padishah by a monarch with the title of Caliph.[3] The only difference was that, instead of speaking of a monarch of this or that country or nation, they now spoke of a monarch whose authority extended over a population of three hundred million souls belonging to manifold nations and dwelling in different continents of

the world. Into the hands of this great monarch, whose authority was to extend over the whole of Islam, they placed as the only power that of the Turkish people, that is to say, only from 10 to 15 millions of these three hundred million subjects. The monarch designated under the title of Caliph was to guide the affairs of these Muslim peoples and to secure the execution of the religious prescriptions which would best correspond to their worldly interests. He was to defend the rights of all Muslims and concentrate all the affairs of the Muslim world in his hands with effective authority. . . .

If the Caliph and Caliphate, as they maintained, were to be invested with a dignity embracing the whole of Islam, ought they not to have realized in all justice that a crushing burden would be imposed on Turkey, on her existence; her entire resources and all her forces would be placed at the disposal of the Caliph?

According to their declarations, the Caliph-Monarch would have the right of jurisdiction over all Muslims and all Muslim countries, that is to say, over China, India, Afghanistan, Persia, Iraq, Syria, Palestine, Hijaz,[4] Yemen, Assyria, Egypt, Libya, Tunis, Algeria, Morocco, the Sudan. It is well known that this Utopia has never been realized. . . .

I made statements everywhere, that were necessary to dispel the uncertainty and anxiety of the people concerning this question of the Caliphate. . . . I gave the people to understand that neither Turkey nor the handful of men she possesses could be placed at the disposal of the Caliph so that he might fulfill the mission attributed to him, namely, to found a State comprising the whole of Islam. The Turkish nation is incapable of undertaking such an irrational mission.

For centuries our nation was guided under the influence of these erroneous ideas. But what has

---

[3]These events took place in January 1923. After Sultan Mehmed V was deposed as sultan on November 1, 1922, his cousin was designated caliph. Because of their long rule and vast territories, Ottoman sultans by the nineteenth century were viewed by many Muslims as caliphs, that is, "successors" of the prophet Muhammad, with jurisdiction

over all of Islam. Shukri was a *hodja* (or *hojja*), a Turkish religious leader; he hoped that the new Turkish state would continue to support the caliphate even after the sultanate was abolished. In 1924, however, Kemal abolished the caliphate.

[4]Western Arabia.

been the result of it? Everywhere they have lost millions of men. "Do you know," I asked, "how many sons of Anatolia have perished in the scorching deserts of the Yemen? Do you know the losses we have suffered in holding Syria and Iraq and Egypt and in maintaining our position in Africa? And do you see what has come out of it? Do you know? . . .

"New Turkey, the people of New Turkey, have no reason to think of anything else but their own existence and their own welfare. She has nothing more to give away to others." . . .

## [THE SUPPRESSION OF THE PROGRESSIVE REPUBLICANS]

As you know, it was at the time that the members of the opposition had founded a party under the name of "Republican Progressive Party" and published its program. . . .

Could seriousness and sincerity be attributed to the deeds and attitude of people who avoided pronouncing even the word Republic and who tried to suppress the Republic from the very beginning, but who called the party Republican and even Republican Progressive? . . .

Did those who appeared under the same flag, but who wanted to be regarded as progressive Republicans, not follow the deep design of provoking the religious fanaticism of the nation, putting them thus completely against the Republic, progress and reform?

Under the mask of respect for religious ideas and dogmas the new Party addressed itself to the people in the following words:

"We want the re-establishment of the Caliphate; we do not want new laws; we are satisfied with the religious law; we shall protect the Medressas, the Tekkes, the pious institutions, the Softahs, the Sheikhs[5] and their disciples. Be on our side; the party of Mustafa Kemal, having abolished the Caliphate, is breaking Islam into ruins; they will make you into unbelievers. . . ."

Read these sentences, Gentlemen, from a letter written by one of the adherents of this program . . . : "They are attacking the very principles which perpetuate the existence of the Muslim world. . . . The assimilation with the Occident means the destruction of our history, our civilisation. . . ." Gentlemen, facts and events have proved that the program of the Republican Progressive Party has been the work emanating from the brain of traitors. This Party became the refuge and the point of support for reactionary and rebellious elements. . . .

The Government and the Committee found themselves forced to take extraordinary measures. They caused the law regarding the restoration of order to be proclaimed, and the Independence Courts to take action. For a considerable time they kept eight or nine divisions of the army at war strength for the suppression of disorders, and put an end to the injurious organisation which bore the name "Republican Progressive Party."

The result was, of course, the success of the Republic. . . .

There were persons who disseminated and sought to gain credence to the thought that we were making use of the law for Restoration of Order and the Courts of Independence as tools of dictatorship or despotism. . . .

Can anyone be of the opinion that this decision of the High Assembly was intended to hand over to us the means for the carrying on of a dictatorship?

Gentlemen, it was necessary to abolish the fez,[6] which sat on our heads as a sign of ignorance, of fanaticism, of hatred to progress and civilisation, and to adopt in its place the hat, the customary

---

[5]A *medressa* is an advanced school of Islamic learning; a *tekke* is a small teaching mosque usually built over the tomb of a saint; a *softah* is a student in an Islamic school; a *sheikh,* or *shaykh,* is a master of a religious order of Sufis, Muslims who adopted a mystical approach to Islam.

[6]The fez was a brimless hat popular among Turkish men during the nineteenth century; its lack of a brim allowed the wearer to touch his forehead to the ground while kneeling during prayer without removing the hat.

headdress of the whole civilised world, thus showing, among other things, that no difference existed in the manner of thought between the Turkish nation and the whole family of civilised mankind. We did that while the law for the Restoration of Order was still in force. If it had not been in force we should have done so all the same; but one can say with complete truth that the existence of this law made the thing much easier for us. As a matter of fact the application of the law for the Restoration of Order prevented the morale of the nation being poisoned to a great extent by reactionaries.

Gentlemen, while the law regarding the Restoration of Order was in force there took place also the closing of the Tekkes, of the convents, and of the mausoleums, as well as the abolition of all sects[7] and all kinds of titles such as Sheikh, Dervish, . . . Occultist, Magician, Mausoleum Guard, etc.[8]

One will be able to imagine how necessary the carrying through of these measures was, in order to prove that our nation as a whole was no primitive nation, filled with superstitions and prejudices.

Could a civilised nation tolerate a mass of people who let themselves be led by the nose by a herd of Sheikhs, Dedes, Seids, . . . Babas and Emirs,[9] who entrusted their destiny and their lives to chiromancers,[10] magicians, dice-throwers

and amulet sellers? Ought one to conserve in the Turkish State, in the Turkish Republic, elements and institutions such as those which had for centuries given the nation the appearance of being other than it really was? Would one not therewith have committed the greatest, most irreparable error to the cause of progress and reawakening?

If we made use of the law for the Restoration of Order in this manner, it was in order to avoid such a historic error; to show the nation's brow pure and luminous, as it is; to prove that our people think neither in a fanatical nor a reactionary manner.

Gentlemen, at the same time the new laws were worked out and decreed which promise the most fruitful results for the nation on the social and economic plane, and in general in all the forms of the expression of human activity . . . the Citizens' Legal Code, which ensures the liberty of women and stabilises the existence of the family.

Accordingly we made use of all circumstances only from one point of view, which consisted therein: to raise the nation on to that step on which it is justified in standing in the civilised world, to stabilise the Turkish Republic more and more on steadfast foundations . . . and in addition to destroy the spirit of despotism for ever.

---

[7]Islamic religious orders.

[8]A *dervish,* or *darvish,* was a member of an Islamic sect famous for their whirling dances that symbolized the movement of the heavenly spheres; an *occultist* was a Sufi who achieved a state of withdrawal from the world; a *mausoleum guard* guarded the tomb of a saint or holy person.

[9]A *dede* was head of a Sufi order; *seids,* or *sayyids,* were descendants of the prophet Muhammad through his daughter Fatima; *baba* was a popular surname among Sufi preachers; in this context *emir* is an honorary Turkish title.

[10]People who told the future by reading palms.

# The Meaning of Zionism
▼▼▼

## 99 ▼ *Hayyim Nahman Bialik,* SPEECH AT THE INAUGURATION OF THE HEBREW UNIVERSITY OF JERUSALEM, JANUARY 4, 1925

After their exile from Palestine by Roman authorities in 70 C.E., some Jews settled in other parts of the Middle East, while others traveled to North Africa, Europe, and years later to the Americas. Wherever they went they were a tiny minority in predominantly Muslim or Christian societies and frequent victims of persecution. In all these years, they retained a strong attachment to the "Land of Canaan," in modern Palestine, which according to their scriptures God had given them as their promised land after He had chosen them as his "chosen people." Only in the late nineteenth century, however, in the face of mounting European anti-Semitism, especially in Russia, where a majority of Europe's Jews lived, did some Jewish intellectuals and religious leaders conclude that Jews could escape persecution and preserve their traditions only if they had their own state, preferably in Palestine. This Jewish nationalist movement came to be known as Zionism, a term derived from Mount Zion, one of the two major hills overlooking Jerusalem, the capital of the ancient Jewish kingdom and the site of the temple destroyed by the Romans in 70 C.E.

Although the first advocates of Jewish resettlement in Palestine were Russian Jews reacting to anti-Jewish pogroms in the 1880s, *political Zionism,* which specifically advocated the foundation of a Jewish *state,* dates from the late 1890s, when the Vienna-based journalist Theodor Herzl published his book *Der Judenstaat (The Jewish State)* in 1896 and convened the first international Zionist Congress in Basel, Switzerland, in 1897. Despite the indifference and outright opposition to Zionism of many assimilated Jews in Western Europe and despite bitter disputes between secularist and religious Zionists over their vision of a future Jewish state, on the eve of World War I approximately ninety thousand Jews lived in Palestine, almost half of whom were recent immigrants from Europe.

Prospects for Jewish migration to Palestine improved after the British took control of Palestine as a League of Nations mandate after World War I. During the war Britain's foreign secretary, Arthur Balfour, in the "Balfour Declaration," committed his government to facilitating "the establishment in Palestine of a national home for the Jewish people." This was a wartime promise the British chose not to ignore. Under the British mandate, the number of Jews in Palestine increased, especially after the Nazis took control of Germany in 1933. Between 1919 and 1939, the percentage of Jews in Palestine's total population grew from slightly under 10 percent to slightly more than 30 percent. More importantly, Jews purchased land, founded industries, and established a basis for the growth of Jewish culture in the area by founding the Hebrew University of Jerusalem and a technical institute in Haifa in 1925. Despite the bitter opposition of Palestinian Arabs, the Zionists' dreams were slowly becoming a reality. In 1947 the independent state of Israel was born.

The Zionists' hopes and expectations are captured in the following speech delivered by Hayyim Nahman Bialik at the opening of the Hebrew University of Jerusalem in 1925. Born in 1873 in Ukraine, Bialik, after receiving a traditional Jewish education and working briefly as a businessman and as a Hebrew language teacher, became one of the most prominent modern poets and short-story writers in Hebrew and Yiddish. In his work he explored the tensions between the Jews' historical experience, especially their persecution, and the modern world. A strong supporter of Zionism, he received permission to leave the Soviet Union in 1921 and settled in Palestine in 1924. He died in 1934 in Vienna, where he had gone for medical treatment, and was buried in Tel Aviv.

In his 1925 speech he describes the Jewish resettlement of Palestine as a historic turning point not just for the Jews but potentially for all humanity.

---

## QUESTIONS FOR ANALYSIS

1. According to Bialik, why have education and study played such an important role in Jewish history?
2. Why does Bialik feel so strongly about the need of the Jews for their own state?
3. What in particular does he deplore about the Jews' experience during the diaspora?
4. How does Bialik view the Jews' historic contributions to human culture?
5. What kind of vision does Bialik have for an independent Jewish state? Is his vision shaped primarily by religious or secular concerns?

The solemnity and exaltation of this moment can only be desecrated by any sort of exaggeration. . . . I am sure that the eyes of tens of thousands of Israel that are lifted from all parts of the Diaspora to this hill are shining with hope and comfort; their hearts and their flesh are singing a blessing of thanksgiving unto the Living God Who hath preserved us and sustained us and let us live to see this hour. They all realize that at this moment Israel had kindled . . . the first candle of the renaissance of her intellectual life. . . .

For let people say what they may: This peculiar people called Israel has, despite all the vicissitudes which for two thousand years have daily, yea hourly, attempted to expel it from its own milieu and uproot it from its spiritual climate — this people, I assert, has accepted upon its body and soul and burden of eternal allegiance to the Kingdom of the Spirit. Within that Kingdom it recognizes itself as a creative citizen and in that eternal soil it has planted its feet with all its might for all time. All the sordidness of the accursed Galut[1] and all the pain of our people's poverty did not disfigure its fundamental nature. . . . Within the boundaries of the realm of the Spirit the Jewish nation fashioned the bases of its national heritage and its principal national

---

[1]Hebrew for exile.

institutions. These preserved it through millennia of wandering, safeguarded its inner freedom amid outward bondage and have led up to this joyful event. . . . The national school in all its forms — the *heder,* the *yeshivah,* the *bet-midrash*[2] — these have been our securest strongholds throughout our long, hard struggle for existence, and for the right to exist, in the world as a separate and distinct people among the peoples. In times of tempest and wrath we took refuge within the walls of these fortresses, where we polished the only weapon we had left — the Jewish mind — lest it become rusty. . . .

Ladies and Gentlemen! You all know what has become of our old spiritual strongholds in the Diaspora in recent times and I need not dwell upon this theme now. For all their inner strength, and for all the energy the nation had expended upon creating and preserving these centers, they stood not firm on the day of wrath; by the decree of history, they are crumbled and razed to the foundations and our people is left standing empty-handed upon their ruins.[3] This is the very curse of the Galut, that our undertakings do not, indeed cannot, prosper. In every land and in every age we have been sowing a bushel and reaping less than a peck. The winds and hurricanes of history always begin by attacking the creation of Israel and, in a moment, uproot and utterly destroy that which hands and minds have produced over a period of generations. Through cruel and bitter trials and tribulations, through blasted hopes and despair of the soul, through innumerable humiliations, we have slowly arrived at the realization that without a tangible homeland, without private national premises that are entirely ours, we can have no sort of a life, either material or spiritual. Without *Eretz Israel* — Eretz means land, literally land — there is no hope for the rehabilitation of Israel anywhere,

ever. . . . We have come to the conclusion that a people that aspires to a dignified existence must create a culture; it is not enough merely to make use of a culture — a people must create its own, with its own hands and its own implements and materials, and impress it with its own seal. Of course our people in its "diasporas" is creating culture; . . . But as whatever the Jew creates in the Diaspora is always absorbed in the culture of others. . . . The Jewish people is therefore in a painfully false position: Whereas its true function culturally is that of a proletariat — i.e., it produces with the materials and implements of others for others — it is regarded by others, and at times even by itself, as a cultural parasite, possessing nothing of its own. A self-respecting people will never become reconciled to such a lot; it is bound to arise one day and resolve: No more. Better a little that is undisputedly my own than much that is not definitely either mine or somebody else's. Better a dry crust in my own home and on my own table than a stall-fed ox in the home of others and on the table of others. Better one little university but entirely my own, entirely my handiwork from foundations to coping[4] stones, than thousands of temples of learning from which I derive benefit but in which I have no recognized share. Let my food be little and bitter as the olive, if I may but taste in it the delicious flavor of a gift from myself.

It was in this frame of mind that we took refuge in this land. We have not come here to seek wealth, or dominion, or greatness. How much of these can this poor little country give us? We wish to find here only a domain of our own for our physical and intellectual labor. . . . Already at this early hour we experience cultural needs that cannot be postponed and must be satisfied at once. Besides, we are burdened with heavy cares for the cultural fate of our people in the

---

[2]These are schools in the traditional Jewish educational system. *Heder* is the elementary school; *yeshiva* is a higher academy of religious studies; *bet-midrash* is a house of study in which advanced students can pursue independent studies of sacred literature.

[3]The reference is to the destruction of Jewish schools during pogroms.

[4]Stones used to cover a wall.

Diaspora. Nations born only yesterday foolishly imagine that through intellectual parching,[5] by means of a *numerus clausus*,[6] they can do to death an old nation with a past of four thousand years of Torah.[7] We must therefore hasten to light here the first lamp of learning and science and of every sort of intellectual activity is Israel, ere the last lamp grows dark for us in foreign lands. . . .

Ladies and Gentlemen! Thousands of our youth, obeying the call of their hearts, are streaming from the four corners of the earth to this land for the purpose of redeeming it from desolation and ruin. They are prepared to pour all their aspirations and longings and to empty all the strength of their youth into the bosom of this wasteland in order to revive it. They are plowing rocks, draining swamps, and building roads amid singing and rejoicing. These young people know how to raise simple and crude labor — physical labor — to the level of highest sanctity, to the level of religion. It is our task to kindle such a holy fire within the walls of the house which has just been opened.

Let those youths build the Earthly Jerusalem with fire and let them who work within these walls build the Heavenly Jerusalem with fire, and between them let them build and establish our House of Life. Four thousand years ago there gathered in this land . . . some groups of wandering shepherds divided into a number of tribes. They became in time, in consequence of events of apparently no great importance, a people small and poor in its day — the people Israel.

. . . And it was they who in the end provided the foundation for the religious and moral culture of the world. Across the centuries . . . their voice has come down to us to this day, and it is mighty and sublime and filled with the power of God even more than at first, as if it were constantly gaining in strength with increasing remoteness in time. After the proclamation of Cyrus,[8] some tens of thousands of exiles rallied again to this poor, waste country and again formed a poor small community, even poorer and smaller than the first. After only some three hundred years, there arose again in this land a man of Israel, the son of an Israelite carpenter,[9] who conveyed the gospel of salvation to the pagan world and cleared the way for the days of the Messiah. Since then two thousand years have elapsed, and we are all witnesses this day that idols have not yet disappeared from the face of the earth; the place of the old has been taken by new ones, no better than the former. And then came the Balfour Declaration. Israel is assembling in Eretz Israel for a third time. Why should not the miracle be repeated again this time? . . .

Who knows but that the task in which great nations have failed amid the tumult of wealth may be achieved by a poor people in its small country? Who knows but in the end of days this doctrine of responsibility for the fate of humanity may go forth from its house of learning and spread to all the people? Surely not for nothing has the hand of God led this people for four thousand years through the pangs of hell and now brought it back unto its land for the third time.

The Books of Chronicles,[10] the last of the Scriptures, are not the last in the history of Israel. To its two small parts there will be added a third, perhaps more important than the first two, . . . the third will undoubtedly begin with the Proclamation of Balfour and end with a new gospel, the gospel of redemption to the whole of humanity.

---

[5]Parch means to dry up or shrivel.

[6]The reference is to the quota system adopted by universities in Europe to limit Jewish enrollment.

[7]The body of wisdom and law contained in Jewish Scripture and other sacred literature and oral tradition.

[8]Cyrus the Great (599–530 B.C.E.), king of Persia, after conquering Babylonia in 539 B.C.E., freed the Jewish captives in Babylonia and allowed their return to Jerusalem; he also approved the rebuilding of the Jewish temple.

[9]The reference is to Jesus.

[10]The two Books of Chronicles, part of the Jewish Bible, recount history from Adam to the time of Cyrus the Great.

# A Call for Islamic Social and Political Action
▼▼▼
## 100 ▼ *The Muslim Brotherhood,* TOWARD THE LIGHT

Although the commitment to modernization advocated by Mustafa Kemal had supporters throughout the Middle East, it also had staunch opponents. Many Muslims — from all classes of society and across all educational levels — were deeply troubled by the prospect of a secularized, Westernized future and sought instead to establish a true Islamic society guided by the Qur'an and conforming to Islamic law. In the interwar years their hopes were best represented by the Muslim Brotherhood, founded in 1929 by an Egyptian schoolteacher, Hasan al-Banna (1906–1949).

Born in a small town in the Nile Delta, Hasan al-Banna as a student in Cairo after World War I was deeply troubled by the factionalism, social conflict, poverty, and religious indifference he observed in Egypt. He concluded that British colonialism and the widespread acceptance of Western values had caused these ills and that a return to fundamental Islamic teachings would cure them. In 1927 he became a primary schoolteacher in the Sinai town of Ismailia, where he organized religious study groups and committed himself to Islamic renewal. In 1929 he founded the Muslim Brotherhood, an organization dedicated to the realization of an Islamic state in Egypt and other Muslim lands.

In the 1930s the Brotherhood grew into a tightly knit, disciplined organization with a million members from all walks of life and a network of branches made up of numerous secret cells. It built mosques, schools, and small hospitals; sponsored youth programs, social clubs, and cottage industries; and publicized its religious message through preaching and publications. In the 1940s, with a greater commitment to political activism, it clashed with British authorities and the Egyptian government itself. Linked to the assassination of several officials, the Brotherhood was outlawed by the Egyptian government in 1949, and Hasan al-Banna himself was assassinated by Egyptian government agents in the same year.

The Brotherhood regained legal status in Egypt in 1950 and since then has continued to be an important religious and political force in the Arab Middle East. It has branches in Sudan, Syria, and other Arab states, vast financial resources, and an estimated membership of two million. It has accomplished this despite attempts by the Egyptian government to suppress the organization on two occasions in the 1950s and 1960s after members of the Brotherhood were implicated in attempted assassinations and antigovernment conspiracies. The organization also has had to deal with bitter internal divisions between militants and moderates. In Egypt, the Brotherhood officially rejected violence in the 1980s and sought to advance its program by winning elected office and increasing its commitment to social service activities. This moderate policy caused some of its members to defect to more militant groups. Organizations such as Islamic Jihad and Hamas, which are committed to the cause of Palestinian liberation and oppose any compromise with Israel, are both offshoots of the Muslim Brotherhood.

The following excerpt is drawn from a pamphlet issued by the Brotherhood in 1936. Directed to King Faruk of Egypt and other Arab leaders, it summarizes the major goals of the Brotherhood in its early years of existence.

## QUESTIONS FOR ANALYSIS

1. How would you characterize the views of the Brotherhood concerning the purpose and goals of government?
2. According to this document, what was the Brotherhood's conception of the ideal government official?
3. What does the document reveal about the attitude of the Brotherhood toward the West? Are there aspects of Western culture the Brotherhood finds acceptable?
4. What role does the Brotherhood envision for women in Islamic society?
5. What are to be the content and goals of education?
6. What policies does the Brotherhood propose to help the poor?
7. What is there in the statement that might help account for the widespread support of the Brotherhood within Middle Eastern Islamic societies?

After having studied the ideals which ought to inspire a renascent nation on the spiritual level, we wish to offer, in conclusion, some practical suggestions. We will list here only the chapter headings because we know very well that each suggestion will require profound study as well as the special attention of experts; we know also that the needs of the nation are enormous; we do not believe that the fulfilling of the needs and the aspirations of the country will be an easy thing; what is more, we do not think that these goals can be reached in one journey or two. We realize the obstacles which these problems must overcome. The task will require a great deal of patience, a great deal of ability, and a willing tenacity.

But one thing is certain: resolve will lead to success. A dedicated nation, working to accomplish the right, will certainly reach, with God's help, the goals toward which it strives.

The following are the chapter headings for a reform based upon the true spirit of Islam:

I. In the political, judicial, and administrative fields:

1st. To prohibit political parties and to direct the forces of the nation toward the formation of a united front;

2nd. To reform the law in such a way that it will be entirely in accordance with Islamic legal practice;

3rd. To build up the army, to increase the number of youth groups; to instill in youth the spirit of holy struggle, faith, and self-sacrifice;

4th. To strengthen the ties among Islamic countries and more particularly among Arab countries which is a necessary step toward serious examination of the question of the defunct Caliphate;[1]

5th. To propagate an Islamic spirit within the civil administration so that all officials will understand the need for applying the teachings of Islam;

---

[1]The office of caliph, or successor of Muhammad as head of the Muslim community, had been held by the Ottoman sultans but was abolished by Kemal in 1924.

6th. To supervise the personal conduct of officials because the private life and the administrative life of these officials forms an indivisible whole;

7th. To advance the hours of work in summer and in winter so that the accomplishment of religious obligations will be eased and to prevent all useless staying up late at night;

8th. To condemn corruption and influence peddling; to reward only competence and merit;

9th. Government will act in conformity to the law and to Islamic principles; the carrying out of ceremonies, receptions, and official meetings, as well as the administration of prisons and hospitals should not be contrary to Islamic teachings. The scheduling of government services ought to take account of the hours set aside for prayer.

10th. To train and to use Azharis, that is to say, the graduates of Al-Azhar University,[2] for military and civil roles;

II. In the fields of social and everyday practical life:

1st. The people should respect public mores: this ought to be the object of special attention — to strongly condemn attacks upon public mores and morality;

2nd. To find a solution for the problems of women, a solution that will allow her to progress and which will protect her while conforming to Islamic principles. This very important social question should not be ignored because it has become the subject of polemics and of more or less unsupported and exaggerated opinion;

3rd. To root out clandestine or public prostitution and to consider fornication as a reprehensible crime the authors of which should be punished;

4th. To prohibit all games of chance (gaming, lotteries, races, golf);

5th. To stop the use of alcohol and intoxicants — these obliterate the painful consequences of people's evil deeds;

6th. To stop attacks on modesty, to educate women, to provide quality education for female teachers, school pupils, students, and doctors;

7th. To prepare instructional programs for girls; to develop an educational program for girls different than the one for boys;

8th. Male students should not be mixed with female students — any relationship between unmarried men and women is considered to be wrong until it is approved;

9th. To encourage marriage and procreation — to develop legislation to safeguard the family and to solve marriage problems;

10th. To close dance halls; to forbid dancing;

11th. To censor theater productions and films; to be severe in approving films;

12th. To supervise and approve music;

13th. To approve programs, songs, and subjects before they are released, to use radio to encourage national education;

14th. To confiscate malicious articles and books as well as magazines displaying a grotesque character or spreading frivolity;

15th. To carefully organize vacation centers;

16th. To change the hours when public cafes are opened or closed, to watch

---

[2]An educational institution in Cairo specializing in Islamic studies.

the activities of those who habituate them — to direct these people towards wholesome pursuits, to prevent people from spending too much time in these cafes;

17th. To use the cafes as centers to teach reading and writing to illiterates, to seek help in this task from primary school teachers and students;

18th. To combat the bad practices which are prejudicial to the economy and to the morale of the nation, to direct the people toward good customs and praiseworthy projects such as marriage, orphanages, births, and festivals; the government should provide the example for this;

19th. To bring to trial those who break the laws of Islam, who do not fast, who do not pray, and who insult religion;

20th. To transfer village primary schools to the mosque and to carry on all beneficial activities there (selecting officers, matters of health, interested support for young children learning their religious duties, introducing the old to science);

21st. Religious teaching should constitute the essential subject matter to be taught in all educational establishments and faculties;

22nd. To memorize the Qur'an in state schools — this condition will be essential in order to obtain diplomas with a religious or philosophical specialty — in every school students should learn part of the Qur'an;

23rd. To develop a policy designed to raise the level of teaching, to unify the different teaching specialties, to bring together the different branches of culture — emphasis should be put upon teaching morality and physics;

24th. Interested support for teaching the Arabic language in all grades — absolute priority to be given to Arabic over foreign languages (primary teaching);

25th. To study the history of Islam, the nation, and Muslim civilization;

26th. To study the best way to allow people to dress progressively and in an identical manner;

27th. To combat foreign customs (in the realm of vocabulary, customs, dress, nursing) and to Egyptianize all of these (one finds these customs among the well-to-do members of society);

28th. To orient journalism toward wholesome things, to encourage writers and authors, who should study specifically Muslim and Oriental[3] subjects;

29th. To safeguard public health through every kind of publicity — increasing the number of hospitals, doctors, and out-patient clinics;

30th. To call particular attention to the problems of village life (administration, hygiene, water supply, education, recreation, morality).

III. The economic field:

1st. Organization of the zakat tax[4] according to Islamic precepts, using zakat proceeds for welfare projects such as aiding the indigent, the poor, orphans; the zakat should also be used to strengthen the army;

2nd. To prevent the practice of usury, to direct banks to implement this policy; the government should provide an example by giving up the interest fixed by banks for servicing a personal loan or an industrial loan, etc.;

---

[3]As opposed to Western studies.
[4]A fixed share of income or property that all Muslims must pay as a tax or as charity for the welfare of the needy.

3rd.    To facilitate and to increase the number of economic enterprises and to employ the jobless there, to employ for the nation's benefit the skills possessed by the foreigners in these enterprises;

4th.    To protect workers against monopoly companies, to require these companies to obey the law, the public should share in all profits;

5th.    Aid for low-ranking employees and enlargement of their pay, lowering the income of high-ranking employees; . . .

7th.    To encourage agricultural and industrial works, to improve the situation of the peasants and industrial workers;

8th.    To give special attention to the technical and social needs of the workers, to raise their level of life and aid their class;

9th.    Utilization of certain natural resources (unworked land, neglected mines, etc.);

10th.   To give priority to projects whose accomplishment is vital to the country. . . .

# Anticolonialism in India and Southeast Asia

During the late nineteenth century, at a time when many Indians were already in a full-scale debate about their relationship with Great Britain and some were demanding independence, most Southeast Asians were experiencing direct European political control for the first time. Nonetheless, developments in both areas showed some marked similarities in the first half of the twentieth century. Nationalism swept through the Indian population, and despite their many differences in religion, education, and caste status, millions of Indians came to agree that Great Britain should "quit India" and allow Indian self-rule. The British responded with minor concessions but mostly delaying tactics and armed repression. Nationalism also intensified in Southeast Asia, especially in Vietnam and the Dutch East Indies, where force was needed to suppress anticolonial movements in both areas in the 1920s and 1930s.

The reasons for this broad upsurge of anti-European sentiment included religious revivals of Hinduism in India, Buddhism in Burma, and Islam in Southeast Asia, all of which heightened peoples' awareness of their differences from the West; the emergence of Japan, which demonstrated that an Asian nation could become a great power; the carnage of World War I, which raised doubts about the Europeans' "superiority"; and the spread of Western education and political ideologies. Most telling, however, was anger over the disparity between the Europeans' stated good intentions about their colonies' futures and their actual record of economic exploitation, racial prejudice, and opposition to self-rule.

To this was added the extraordinary influence of charismatic leaders such as Mohandas Gandhi, who drew the Indian masses into the nationalist movement; Jawaharlal Nehru, who guided the Indian Congress Party in the 1930s and 1940s; Ho Chi Minh, who built a strong nationalist coalition in Vietnam in the face of French persecution; and Achmed Sukarno, who did the same in Indonesia despite opposition from the Dutch.

World War II was the catalyst for the creation of independent nations throughout the region in the late 1940s and 1950s. But events and leaders of the first half of the twentieth century provided the foundation for the achievement of independence.

# Gandhi's Vision for India
▼▼▼
## 101 ▼ *Mohandas Gandhi, "INDIAN HOME RULE"*

Mohandas Gandhi, the outstanding figure in modern Indian history, was born in 1869 in a village north of Bombay on the Arabian Sea. His father was an important government official who presided over an extended family with strict Hindu religious practices. Gandhi studied law in England, and after failing to establish a legal practice in Bombay, he moved to South Africa in 1893 to serve the area's large Indian population.

In South Africa, he became incensed over the laws that discriminated against Indians, many of whom were indentured servants employed by whites. During his struggle to improve the lot of South Africa's Indian population, Gandhi developed his theory of *satyagraha,* usually translated into English as "soul force." Satyagraha sought social justice, not through violence but through love, a willingness to suffer, and conversion of the oppressor. Central to its strategy was massive nonviolent resistance: Gandhi's followers disobeyed unjust laws and accepted the consequences — even beatings and imprisonment — to reach the hearts of the British and change their thinking.

Gandhi first wrote about his theories of satyagraha in 1908 after meeting with a group of Indian nationalists in England who favored force to oust the British. In response, he composed a pamphlet, "Hind Swaraj," or "Indian Home Rule," in which he explained his theory of nonresistance and his doubts about the benefits of modern civilization. Written in the form of a dialogue between a reader and an editor (Gandhi), "Indian Home Rule" was printed in hundreds of editions and still serves as the best summary of Gandhi's philosophy.

---

## QUESTIONS FOR ANALYSIS

1. What does Gandhi see as the major deficiency of modern civilization?
2. How, according to Gandhi, has civilization specifically affected women?
3. Why does Gandhi have faith that Hindus and Muslims will be able to live in peace in India?
4. What, according to Gandhi, is true civilization, and what is India's role in preserving it?
5. What leads Gandhi to his conviction that love is stronger than force?
6. Why did Gandhi's attack on civilization gain him support among the Indian masses?

7. How does Gandhi's view of the West compare to the comments on Western civilization in the Japanese nationalist treatise "The Way of Subjects" (source 94)?
8. Compare Gandhi's view of progress with that of Condorcet (source 38). On what points do the two men disagree?

## CHAPTER VI

### Civilization

READER: Now you will have to explain what you mean by civilization. . . .

EDITOR: Let us first consider what state of things is described by the word "civilization." Its true test lies in the fact that people living in it make bodily welfare the object of life. We will take some examples: The people of Europe to-day live in better-built houses than they did a hundred years ago. This is considered an emblem of civilization, and this is also a matter to promote bodily happiness. Formerly, they wore skins, and used as their weapons spears. Now, they wear long trousers, and for embellishing their bodies they wear a variety of clothing, and, instead of spears, they carry with them revolvers containing five or more chambers. If people of a certain country, who have hitherto not been in the habit of wearing much clothing, boots, etc., adopt European clothing, they are supposed to have become civilized out of savagery. Formerly, in Europe, people plowed their lands mainly by manual labor. Now, one man can plow a vast tract by means of steam-engines, and can thus amass great wealth. This is called a sign of civilization. Formerly, the fewest men wrote books, that were most valuable. Now, anybody writes and prints anything he likes and poisons people's minds. Formerly, men traveled in wagons; now they fly through the air, in trains at the rate of four hundred and more miles per day. This is considered the height of civilization. It has been stated that, as men progress, they shall be able to travel in airships and reach any part of the world in a few hours. Men will not need the use of their hands and feet. They will press a button, and they will have their clothing by their side. They will press another button, and they will have their newspaper. A third, and a motor-car will be in waiting for them. They will have a variety of delicately dished up food. Everything will be done by machinery. Formerly, when people wanted to fight with one another, they measured between them their bodily strength; now it is possible to take away thousands of lives by one man working behind a gun from a hill. This is civilization. Formerly, men worked in the open air only so much as they liked. Now, thousands of workmen meet together and for the sake of maintenance work in factories or mines. Their condition is worse than that of beasts. They are obliged to work, at the risk of their lives, at most dangerous occupations, for the sake of millionaires. Formerly, men were made slaves under physical compulsion, now they are enslaved by temptation of money and of the luxuries that money can buy. There are now diseases of which people never dreamed before, and an army of doctors is engaged in finding out their cures, and so hospitals have increased. This is a test of civilization. Formerly, special messengers were required and much expense was incurred in order to send letters; today, anyone can abuse his fellow by means of a letter for one penny. True, at the same cost, one can send one's thanks also. Formerly, people had two or three meals consisting of homemade bread and vegetables; now, they require something to eat every two hours, so that they have hardly leisure for anything else. What more need I say? All this you can ascertain from several authoritative books. These are all true tests of civilization. And, if any one speaks to the contrary, know that he is ignorant. This civilization takes note neither of morality nor of religion. . . .

This civilization is irreligion, and it has taken such a hold on the people in Europe that those who are in it appear to be half mad. They lack real physical strength or courage. They keep up their energy by intoxication. They can hardly be happy in solitude. Women, who should be the queens of households, wander in the streets, or they slave away in factories. For the sake of a pittance, half a million women in England alone are laboring under trying circumstances in factories or similar institutions. This awful fact is one of the causes of the daily growing suffragette movement.

This civilization is such that one has only to be patient and it will be self-destroyed.

## CHAPTER X

### *The Condition of India (Continued)*
#### *The Hindus and the Muslims*

READER: But I am impatient to hear your answer to my question. Has the introduction of Islam not unmade the nation?

EDITOR: India cannot cease to be one nation because people belonging to different religions live in it. The introduction of foreigners does not necessarily destroy the nation, they merge in it. A country is one nation only when such a condition obtains in it. That country must have a faculty for assimilation. India has ever been such a country. In reality, there are as many religions as there are individuals, but those who are conscious of the spirit of nationality do not interfere with one another's religion. If they do, they are not fit to be considered a nation. If the Hindus believe that India should be peopled only by Hindus, they are living in dreamland. The Hindus, the Muslims, the Parsees[1] and the Christians who have made India their country are fellow-countrymen, and they will have to live in unity if only for their own interest. In no part of the world are one nationality and one religion

synonymous terms; nor has it ever been so in India.

READER: But what about the inborn enmity between Hindus and Muslims?

EDITOR: That phrase has been invented by our mutual enemy.[2] When the Hindus and Muslims fought against one another, they certainly spoke in that strain. They have long since ceased to fight. How, then, can there be any inborn enmity? Pray remember this too, that we did not cease to fight only after British occupation. The Hindus flourished under Muslim sovereigns and Muslims under the Hindu. Each party recognized that mutual fighting was suicidal, and that neither party would abandon its religion by force of arms. Both parties, therefore, decided to live in peace. With the English advent the quarrels recommenced. . . .

Hindus and Muslims own the same ancestors, and the same blood runs through their veins. Do people become enemies because they change their religion? Is the God of the Muslim different from the God of the Hindu? Religions are different roads converging to the same point. What does it matter that we take different roads, so long as we reach the same goal? Wherein is the cause for quarreling?

## CHAPTER XIII

### *What Is True Civilization?*

READER: You have denounced railways, lawyers and doctors. I can see that you will discard all machinery. What, then, is civilization?

EDITOR: The answer to that question is not difficult. I believe that the civilization India has evolved is not to be beaten in the world. Nothing can equal the seeds sown by our ancestors. Rome went, Greece shared the same fate, the might of the Pharaohs was broken, Japan has become westernized, of China nothing can be said, but India is still, somehow or other, sound

---

[1]Members of the Zoroastrian religion in India who descended from Persian refugees of the seventh and eighth centuries.

[2]The British.

at the foundation. The people of Europe learn their lessons from the writings of the men of Greece or Rome, which exist no longer in their former glory. In trying to learn from them, the Europeans imagine that they will avoid the mistakes of Greece and Rome. Such is their pitiable condition. In the midst of all this, India remains immovable, and that is her glory. It is a charge against India that her people are so uncivilized, ignorant, and stolid, that it is not possible to induce them to adopt any changes. It is a charge really against our merit. What we have tested and found true on the anvil of experience, we dare not change. Many thrust their advice upon India, and she remains steady. This is her beauty; it is the sheet-anchor of our hope.

Civilization is that mode of conduct which points out to man the path of duty. Performance of duty and observance of morality are convertible terms. To observe morality is to attain mastery over our mind and our passions. So doing, we know ourselves. The Gujarati[3] equivalent for civilization means "good conduct."

If this definition be correct, then India, as so many writers have shown, has nothing to learn from anybody else, and this is as it should be.


## CHAPTER XVII

*Passive Resistance*

READER: Is there any historical evidence as to the success of what you have called soul-force or truth-force? No instance seems to have happened of any nation having risen through soul-force. I still think that the evil-doers will not cease doing evil without physical punishment.

EDITOR: . . . The force of love is the same as the force of the soul or truth. We have evidence of its working at every step. The universe would disappear without the existence of that force. But you ask for historical evidence. It is, therefore, necessary to know what history means. . . .

The fact that there are so many men still alive in the world shows that it is based not on the force of arms but on the force of truth or love. Therefore the greatest and most unimpeachable evidence of the success of this force is to be found in the fact that, in spite of the wars of the world, it still lives on.

Thousands, indeed, tens of thousands, depend for their existence on a very active working of this force. Little quarrels of millions of families in their daily lives disappear before the exercise of this force. Hundreds of nations live in peace. History does not and cannot take note of this fact. History is really a record of every interruption of the even working of the force of love or of the soul. . . . Soul-force, being natural, is not noted in history.

READER: According to what you say, it is plain that instances of the kind of passive resistance are not to be found in history. It is necessary to understand this passive resistance more fully. It will be better, therefore, if you enlarge upon it.

EDITOR: Passive resistance is a method of securing rights by personal suffering; it is the reverse of resistance by arms. When I refuse to do a thing that is repugnant to my conscience, I use soul-force. For instance, the government of the day has passed a law which is applicable to me: I do not like it; if, by using violence, I force the government to repeal the law, I am employing what may be termed body-force. If I do not obey the law and accept the penalty for its breach, I use soul-force. It involves sacrifice of self.

Everybody admits that sacrifice of self is infinitely superior to sacrifice of others. Moreover, if this kind of force is used in a cause that is unjust, only the person using it suffers. He does not make others suffer for his mistakes. Men have before now done many things which were subsequently found to have been wrong. No man can claim to be absolutely in the right, or that a particular thing is wrong, because he thinks so, but it is wrong for him so long as that is his

---

[3] An Indian dialect spoken in Gujarat, in northwest India.

deliberate judgment. It is, therefore, meet [proper] that he should not do that which he knows to be wrong, and suffer the consequence whatever it may be. This is the key to the use of soul-force. . . .

READER: From what you say, I deduce that passive resistance is a splendid weapon of the weak but that, when they are strong, they may take up arms.

EDITOR: This is gross ignorance. Passive resistance, that is, soul-force, is matchless. It is superior to the force of arms. How, then, can it be considered only a weapon of the weak? Physical-force men are strangers to the courage that is requisite in a passive resister. Do you believe that a coward can ever disobey a law that he dislikes? Extremists are considered to be advocates of brute-force. Why do they, then, talk about obeying laws? I do not blame them. They can say nothing else. When they succeed in driving out the English, and they themselves become governors, they will want you and me to obey their laws. And that is a fitting thing for their constitution. But a passive resister will say he will not obey a law that is against his conscience, even though he may be blown to pieces at the mouth of a cannon.

What do you think? Wherein is courage required — in blowing others to pieces from behind a cannon or with a smiling face to approach a cannon and to be blown to pieces? Who is the true warrior — he who keeps death always as a bosom-friend or he who controls the death of others? Believe me that a man devoid of courage and manhood can never be a passive resister.

This, however, I will admit: that even a man, weak in body, is capable of offering this resistance. One man can offer it just as well as millions. Both men and women can indulge in it. It does not require the training of an army; it needs no Jiu-jitsu. Control over the mind is alone necessary, and, when that is attained, man is free like the king of the forest, and his very glance withers the enemy.

Passive resistance is an all-sided sword; it can be used anyhow; it blesses him who uses it and him against whom it is used. Without drawing a drop of blood, it produces far-reaching results.

# A Vietnamese Condemnation of French Rule
▼▼▼

## 102 ▼ *Nguyen Thai Hoc,* *LETTER TO THE FRENCH CHAMBER OF DEPUTIES*

After the French seized Vietnam's three southernmost provinces, the region known as Cochin China, in 1862, they extended their authority over Tongking (northern Vietnam) and Annam (central Vietnam) in the mid 1880s. Convinced of their civilizing mission, the French sought to undermine Vietnam's Confucian culture by creating a French-trained Vietnamese elite willing to cooperate with the colonial regime. Although some members of Vietnam's upper class resisted French rule (including the young emperor Duy-tan, whose plot to overthrow the French was uncovered in 1916), most at first sought some sort of compromise between Western culture and Confucianism.

Accommodation and compromise gave way to revolutionary nationalism in the 1920s as a result of Vietnamese anger over continued economic exploitation and political repression, despite the ninety thousand Vietnamese troops and laborers who had helped the French war effort during World War I. The leading nationalist organization was the Viet Nam Quoc Dan Dang (Vietnamese Nationalist Party, or VNQDD), founded in 1927 by Nguyen Thai Hoc, a teacher from Hanoi. As a young man he sought to improve life in Vietnam through moderate reform but became disillusioned with the French and turned to revolution. The VNQDD was modeled on Sun Yat-sen's Nationalist Party and was dedicated to achieving an independent and democratic-socialist Vietnam. In 1929, with the VNQDD membership at about 1,500, its leaders plotted an anti-French insurrection. The uprising, known as the Yen Bay Revolt, was crushed by the French in 1930, and the VNQDD leaders were arrested and executed.

While awaiting his execution, Nguyen Thai Hoc wrote the following letter to France's parliament, the Chamber of Deputies. A defense of his actions and denunciation of French colonialism, the letter was also released to the Vietnamese public.

---

## QUESTIONS FOR ANALYSIS

1. In Nguyen Thai Hoc's view, what are French intentions in Vietnam and what has been the effect of French occupation?
2. How did Nguyen Thai Hoc evolve from a moderate reformer to a revolutionary?
3. If implemented, how would his suggestions to Governor General Varenne have improved the lot of the Vietnamese people?
4. What does the French response to the Yen Bay uprising reveal about the nature of French colonial rule?
5. What do you suppose Nguyen Thai Hoc hoped to accomplish by writing this letter?

Gentlemen:

I, the undersigned, Nguyen Thai Hoc, a Vietnamese citizen, twenty-six years old, chairman and founder of the Vietnamese Nationalist Party, at present arrested and imprisoned at the jail of Yen Bay, Tongking, Indochina, have the great honor to inform you of the following facts:

According to the tenets of justice, everyone has the right to defend his own country when it is invaded by foreigners, and according to the principles of humanity, everyone has the duty to save his compatriots when they are in difficulty or in danger. As for myself, I have assessed the fact that my country has been annexed by you French for more than sixty years. I realize that

under your dictatorial yoke, my compatriots have experienced a very hard life, and my people will without doubt be completely annihilated, by the naked principle of natural selection. Therefore, my right and my duty have compelled me to seek every way to defend my country which has been invaded and occupied, and to save my people who are in great danger.

At the beginning, I had thought to cooperate with the French in Indochina in order to serve my compatriots, my country and my people, particularly in the areas of cultural and economic development. As regards economic development, in 1925 I sent a memorandum to Governor General Varenne,[1] describing to him all our aspirations concerning the protection of local industry and commerce in Indochina. I urged strongly in the same letter the creation of a Superior School of Industrial Development in Tongking. In 1926 I again addressed another letter to the then Governor General of Indochina in which I included some explicit suggestions to relieve the hardships of our poor people. In 1927, for a third time, I sent a letter to the Résident Supérieur[2] in Tongking, requesting permission to publish a weekly magazine with the aim of safeguarding and encouraging local industry and commerce. With regard to the cultural domain, I sent a letter to the Governor General in 1927, requesting (1) the privilege of opening tuition-free schools for the children of the lower classes, particularly children of workers and peasants; (2) freedom to open popular publishing houses and libraries in industrial centers.

It is absolutely ridiculous that every suggestion has been rejected. My letters were without answer; my plans have not been considered; my requests have been ignored; even the articles that I sent to newspapers have been censored and rejected. From the experience of these rejections, I have come to the conclusion that the French have no sincere intention of helping my country or my people. I also concluded that we have to expel France. For this reason, in 1927, I began to organize a revolutionary party, which I named the Vietnamese Nationalist Party, with the aim of overthrowing the dictatorial and oppressive administration in our country. We aspire to create a Republic of Vietnam, composed of persons sincerely concerned with the happiness of the people. My party is a clandestine organization, and in February 1929, it was uncovered by the security police. Among the members of my party, a great number have been arrested. Fifty-two persons have been condemned to forced labor

ranging from two to twenty years. Although many have been detained and many others unjustly condemned, my party has not ceased its activity. Under my guidance, the Party continues to operate and progress towards its aim.

During the Yen Bay uprising someone succeeded in killing some French officers. The authorities accused my party of having organized and perpetrated this revolt. They have accused me of having given the orders for the massacre. In truth, I have never given such orders, and I have presented before the Penal Court of Yen Bay all the evidence showing the inanity of this accusation. Even so, some of the members of my party completely ignorant of that event have been accused of participating in it. The French Indochinese government burned and destroyed their houses. They sent French troops to occupy their villages and stole their rice to divide it among the soldiers. Not just members of my party have been suffering from this injustice — we should rather call this cruelty than injustice — but also many simple peasants, interested only in their daily work in the rice fields, living miserable lives like buffaloes and horses, have been compromised in this reprisal. At the present time, in various areas there are tens of thousands of men, women, and children, persons of all ages, who have been massacred.[3] They died either of hunger or exposure because the French Indochinese government burned their homes. I therefore beseech you in tears to redress this injustice which otherwise will annihilate my people, which will stain French honor, and which will belittle all human values.

I have the honor to inform you that I am responsible for all events happening in my country under the leadership of my party from 1927 until the present. You only need to execute me. I beg your indulgence for all the others who at the present time are imprisoned in various jails.

---

[1] Alexandre Varenne was governor-general of Indochina from 1925 to 1929.

[2] In the French colonial hierarchy the *résident supérieur* of Tongking was administrator for northern Vietnam.

[3] A substantial number of civilian deaths did result from French actions following the revolt, but Nguyen Thai Hoc's estimate of ten thousand deaths is an exaggeration.

I am the only culprit, all the others are innocent. They are innocent because most of them are indeed members of my party, and have joined it only because I have succeeded in convincing them of their duties as citizens of this country, and of the humiliations of a slave with a lost country. Some of them are not even party members. They have been wrongly accused by their enemy or by the security police; or they simply are wrongly accused by their friends who have not been able to bear the tortures inflicted by the security police. I have the honor to repeat once again that you need execute only me. If you are not satisfied with killing one man, I advise you to kill also the members of my family, but I strongly beg your indulgence towards those who are innocent.

Finally, I would like to declare in conclusion: if France wants to stay in peace in Indochina, if France does not want to have increasing troubles with revolutionary movements, she should immediately modify the cruel and inhuman policy now practiced in Indochina. The French should behave like friends to the Vietnamese, instead of being cruel and oppressive masters. They should be attentive to the intellectual and material sufferings of the Vietnamese people, instead of being harsh and tough.

Please, Gentlemen, receive my gratitude.

▼▼▼

# Colonialism and the Beginnings of African Nationalism

Compared with the experience of India, the unfolding of colonialism in Africa resembles watching a film shown at high speed. Europeans arrived in force at the end of the nineteenth century, and after crushing resistance and deciding among themselves who controlled what, they gave serious thought to the policies that would determine the future of their new acquisitions. Not long after these issues had been resolved, World War II was fought, and independence movements swept through Africa. In 1957, when the Gold Coast, a British colony, became the independent nation of Ghana, it sparked a chain of events that resulted in the establishment of dozens of new independent states within a decade and a half.

So brief was Africa's colonial experience, and so rapid was the Europeans' exit, that nationalism in Africa never became the broad popular movement that evolved in India during its long struggle against British rule. Furthermore, African nationalist movements were impeded by the indifference of chiefs, farmers, and petty traders who benefited from European rule, the paucity of Africans with formal education and political experience, the gap between educated city-dwellers and the rural masses, and rivalries among different linguistic and ethnic groups. Nevertheless, Africans in the interwar years continued to fight against colonial rule. They demonstrated against labor conscription, new taxes, and government-mandated land confiscations. They also organized political associations, published journals, wrote books and newspaper editorials, joined independent African Christian churches, attended international meetings, and sent representatives to

European capitals to state their opposition to colonial rule. Despite many obstacles, voices of African nationalism multiplied before World War II, and a growing audience listened to what they had to say.

The results of colonialism went well beyond politics and the birth of African nationalism. Colonialism also fostered population growth, encouraged urbanization, undermined traditional religions, altered gender relationships, introduced new sports and pastimes, and changed how people dressed and what languages they spoke. Most importantly, it forced Africans to consider new ways of looking at themselves and their place in the world. Inevitably many features of old Africa — traditional names, music, art, marriage customs, and systems of inheritance — were weakened or lost. Whether such changes have been beneficial or harmful for Africa is still debated today. There was less debate among Africans who actually lived under colonialism. They, with few exceptions, found their colonial experience unsettling, dispiriting, and demeaning.

# Eagles into Chickens
▼▼▼

## 103 ▼ *James Aggrey, PARABLE OF THE EAGLE*

The experience of colonialism was dispiriting for Africans because so much of what took place was predicated on the system's underlying racism. Colonialism's message, stated or unstated, was that Africans were incapable of governing themselves, or at least incapable of governing themselves effectively; nor were they capable of managing a modern economy or even creating a viable culture and social order. For all these tasks they needed Europeans, whose moral and intellectual superiority supposedly justified their political and cultural dominance. Furthermore, Africans were told that in order to succeed under colonialism — to become clerks or civil servants in the colonial administration or to become "assimilated" (an *evolué,* or "evolved one") in French Africa — they would have to shed their African identity and adopt the ideas, views, work habits, dress, and customs of Europeans. This was the price Africans would have to pay to overcome their backwardness.

Sadly, many Africans accepted their presumed inferiority, and came to doubt their capacity for self-rule and true "civilization." This issue is addressed in the following parable told by James Aggrey, an educator and clergyman who was one of the most prominent Africans of his day. Born in 1875 in the Gold Coast, a British colony, and educated in a Protestant mission school, Aggrey converted to Christianity, and at age twenty-three traveled to the United States to study for the ministry. He remained in the United States for twenty years, studying economics and agriculture, speaking out against racial prejudice, and working among the poor blacks of South Carolina. He returned to Africa in 1918 and died in 1927. His "Parable of the Eagle," a powerful indictment of colonialism's psychological effects, was written in the early 1920s.

## QUESTIONS FOR ANALYSIS

1. According to the lesson of Aggrey's parable, what psychological damage results from colonialism?
2. What possible implications does the parable have for colonial policies?

A certain man went through a forest seeking any bird of interest he might find. He caught a young eagle, brought it home and put it among his fowls and ducks and turkeys, and gave it chickens' food to eat even though it was an eagle, the king of birds.

Five years later a naturalist came to see him and, after passing through his garden, said: "That bird is an eagle, not a chicken."

"Yes," said its owner, "but I have trained it to be a chicken. It is no longer an eagle, it is a chicken, even though it measures fifteen feet from tip to tip of its wings."

"No," said the naturalist, "it is an eagle still: it has the heart of an eagle, and I will make it soar high up to the heavens."

"No," said the owner, "it is a chicken, and it will never fly."

They agreed to test it. The naturalist picked up the eagle, held it up, and said with great intensity: "Eagle, thou art an eagle; thou dost belong to the sky and not to this earth; stretch forth thy wings and fly."

The eagle turned this way and that, and then, looking down, saw the chickens eating their food, and down he jumped.

The owner said: "I told you it was a chicken."

"No," said the naturalist, "it is an eagle. Give it another chance tomorrow."

So the next day he took it to the top of the house and said: "Eagle, thou art an eagle; stretch forth thy wings and fly." But again the eagle, seeing the chickens feeding, jumped down and fed with them.

Then the owner said: "I told you it was a chicken."

"No," asserted the naturalist, "it is an eagle, and it still has the heart of an eagle; only give it one more chance, and I will make it fly tomorrow."

The next morning he rose early and took the eagle outside the city, away from the houses, to the foot of a high mountain. The sun was just rising, gilding the top of the mountain with gold, and every crag was glistening in the joy of that beautiful morning.

He picked up the eagle and said to it: "Eagle, thou art an eagle; thou dost belong to the sky and not to this earth; stretch forth thy wings and fly!"

The eagle looked around and trembled as if new life were coming to it; but it did not fly. The naturalist then made it look straight at the sun. Suddenly it stretched out its wings and, with the screech of an eagle, it mounted higher and higher and never returned. It was an eagle, though it had been kept and tamed as a chicken!

My people of Africa, we were created in the image of God, but men have made us think that we are chickens, and we still think we are; but we are eagles. Stretch forth your wings and fly! Don't be content with the food of chickens!

# The Value of African Tradition
▼▼▼

## 104 ▼ *Kabaka Daudi Chwa,*
## *"EDUCATION, CIVILIZATION, AND 'FOREIGNIZATION' IN BUGANDA"*

The Great Lakes region of east central Africa, dominated by the kingdom of Buganda, was one of the earliest areas of European missionary activities in the nineteenth century. British Protestant missionaries arrived in the region in 1877, and were followed by French Catholic missionaries in 1879. With the hold of traditional Baganda religion already weakened by conversions to Islam, the missionaries made numerous converts, especially among young courtiers in the entourage of the hereditary Baganda ruler, known as the *kabaka*. In the 1880s, Protestant-Catholic rivalries among the chiefs led to civil war, the weakening of the kabaka's power, and the establishment of a British protectorate in 1894. In 1900 British authorities and the Baganda chiefs signed the Buganda Agreement, which recognized Baganda dominance over other peoples in the Uganda protectorate and maintained the chiefs' traditional powers as a means of carrying out British policy. Uganda itself was divided into twenty chieftaincies, of which ten were Protestant, eight were Catholic, and two were Muslim.

Daudi Chwa (1897–1939) as a two-year-old was named kabaka of Buganda after his father was deposed and exiled for leading a campaign against the British. A convert to Christianity, he was a figurehead ruler, since the British more or less gave his major chiefs a free hand to administer the colony. He did play an active and successful role in opposing the plan to consolidate Uganda, Kenya, and Tanganyika in the 1930s. Toward the end of his life he developed reservations about the effects of colonial rule, especially in the cultural and religious spheres. In 1935, four years before his death in 1939, he published his views in a pamphlet, "Education, Civilization, and 'Foreignization' in Buganda." In it he deplored how Christianity had replaced traditional beliefs and practices.

## QUESTIONS FOR ANALYSIS

1. How would you characterize the traditional system of justice of the Baganda? By what means did it try to deter behavior that was counter to the people's rules and customs?
2. According to the kabaka, in what ways do traditional Baganda moral values resemble those of Christianity?
3. According to the kabaka, what have the Baganda gained and lost as a result of European colonialism?
4. What sort of thinking about the "backwardness" of the Baganda does the kabaka try to counter in his letter?
5. In the kabaka's view, what should be the proper balance between traditional and European beliefs and practices?

Everyone knows that education and civilization were started simultaneously in this country in their respective rudimentary forms by the kind efforts of the members of the various Missionary Societies and have now been enhanced largely due to the assistance rendered by the Protectorate Government.

Naturally, Education and Civilization gained tremendous favour among the Baganda,[1] and as a consequence there are numerous Schools in remote villages in Buganda Kingdom for the Education of the young generation; while every facility and luxury which are the outcome of civilization are today being extended to all the Baganda, who can afford to avail themselves of the same, throughout the country.

Now my fears are that instead of the Baganda acquiring proper and legitimate education and civilization there is possible danger that they may be drifting to 'foreignization.' . . . To be more explicit, what I mean by the word 'foreignisation' is that instead of the Baganda acquiring proper education at the various Schools and of availing themselves of the legitimate amenities of civilization, I am very much afraid the young generation of this country is merely drifting wholesale towards 'foreignization' of their natural instincts and is discarding its native and traditional customs, habits and good breeding. What is at present popularly termed as education and civilization of a Muganda[2] may be nothing more nor less than mere affectation of the foreign customs and habits of the Western Countries which in some instances are only injurious to our own inherent morals and ideals of native life.

I am well aware that it has been said more than once that the Baganda have neither morals nor public opinion. . . . I do not wish to be considered in this article to uphold the Baganda as a Nation of Angels — But what I do maintain is that prior to the advent of the Europeans the Baganda had a very strict moral code of their own which was always enforced by a constant and genuine fear of some evil or incurable or even fatal disease being suffered invariably by the breaker of this moral code. In fact I maintain the Baganda observed most strictly the doctrine of the Ten Commandments in spite of the fact that Christianity and the so-called Christian morals were absolutely unknown to the Baganda. For instance there was a very strong public opinion against the following offences, which are the fundamental principles of the doctrine of the Ten Commandments:

(a) Theft was always punished very severely, invariably by the loss of the right hand of the offender, so as to render him incapable of committing the same offence again.

(b) Adultery was almost unknown among the Baganda and any man found guilty of such offence was always ostracised from Society.

(c) Murder was invariably followed by a very severe vendetta between the members of the family or clan of the victim and those of the offender.

(d) Filial obedience was most honoured among the Baganda and disobedience or disrespect of one's parents was always supposed to be punished by some higher power by the infliction of some horrible or incurable disease upon the offender.

(e) False evidence was looked upon with contempt. The person who bore false evidence and the person against whom it was given were both subjected to a very severe test by forcing them to drink a certain kind of strong drug known as 'Madudu,' which was supposed to result in making one of the parties who was in the wrong unconscious.

In this connection I should like to point out that although polygamy was universally recognized among the Baganda and was never considered as immoral yet prostitution was absolutely unheard of. Civilization, education and freedom are the direct causes of the appalling state of af-

---

[1]The Baganda are the people of the kingdom of Buganda.
[2]Muganda is the word (singular) for an individual living in the kingdom of Buganda.

fairs as regards prostitution and promiscuous relationships between the Baganda men and women. . . . As an illustration of the strictness of the old moral code of the Baganda I should like to point out here one of the most important native custom of looking after the daughters in a Muganda's home. It was one of the worst filial offences for a daughter to become pregnant while living with her parents. As soon as she was discovered in that condition she was at once expelled from her parents' house, and was absolutely cut off from them. She could not eat with them nor would her parents touch her until the child was born and some rites had been gone through which necessitated a great deal of hardship and shame on the part of the girl and her seducer. This custom was intended to stimulate morality among the Baganda girls, since any girl who went astray before she was given in marriage suffered this indignity and was always looked upon with contempt by all her relatives and friends. Furthermore any girl who was given in marriage and was found not to be a virgin merited unspeakable disfavour in the eyes of her parents, relations and friends. All this, however, is of course, no longer the case. The present so-called education and civilization prevailing in this country has completely destroyed this moral code by removing the constant fear just referred to above from the minds of the young generation of the Baganda by the freedom and liberty which are the natural consequences of the present World civilization.

I think it would not be out of place to state here definitely that it is my firm belief that prior to the introduction of Christianity in this country the Baganda could not be classified as the worst type of a heathen tribe of Africa since they never indulged in any of the worst heathen customs or rites such as human sacrifice or torture which are found in other parts of Africa. Whilst on the other hand apart from their ignorance of Christianity and their practice of polygamy I am strongly of opinion that most of the traditional customs and etiquette of the Baganda . . . were quite consistent with the principles of Christianity. In support of this argument it is only neces-

sary to mention a few customs of the Baganda to show that they unconsciously possessed a sense of the modern Christian morality:

(a) It was one of the most important behaviors among the Baganda for one's neighbour to be considered as his own relative and to share with him in his happiness or unhappiness. For instance a Muganda would always invite his neighbour if he killed a chicken or goat to share it with him, whilst in case of any danger or misfortune it was always the duty of the nearest neighbour to render every assistance to the party in danger or distress.

(b) It was the recognized etiquette for a Muganda to salute every one that he met on the road, whether he knew him or not.

(c) When a Muganda was taking his meal and any one passed by, it was always the custom to invite him to share it with him.

(d) It was always the duty of every one who hears an alarm at any time of day or night or a cry for help to go at once and render assistance to the party in distress or danger. . . .

(e) It was the duty of every Muganda, when requested, to assist any traveller in directing him to his destination, or to give him food or water, and even to give him shelter from rain or for the night. . . .

My intention therefore in this article is to emphasize the fact that while boasting of having acquired Western education and civilization in an amazingly short period, we have entirely and completely ignored our native traditional customs. In other words we have 'foreignised' our native existence by acquiring the worst foreign habits and customs of the Western people. I am only too well aware that this is inevitable in all countries where Western civilization has reached, so I have considered it my duty in this article to warn very strongly all members of the young generation of the Baganda that while they are legitimately entitled to strive to acquire education and civilization they should also take a very great care that acquisition of Western Education and Civilization does not automatically destroy their best inherent traditions and customs which, in my own opinion, are quite as good as those found among the Western Civilized countries but which only require developing and remodelling where necessary on the lines and ideas of western civilization.

# White Rule and African Families in South Africa
▼▼▼

## 105 ▼ *Charlotte Maxeke,*
## *SOCIAL CONDITIONS AMONG*
## *BANTU WOMEN AND GIRLS*

Few groups in Africa were affected more by colonialism than women. In the precolonial African village, a division of labor between men and women had existed in which women were responsible for planting, weeding, and harvesting in addition to food preparation and child care, while men cleared the land, built houses, herded cattle, and sometimes helped with field work. Such arrangements broke down in west Africa when cash-crop agriculture was introduced. Men took over the farming of cotton or cocoa, leaving the responsibility for growing food for domestic consumption exclusively to women. Worse disruption took place in southern and eastern Africa where men left their villages for wage-paying jobs in mines or in the cities. This meant long absences of husbands from their families, greater work and domestic responsibilities for women, and frequently the breakdown of family life altogether.

All these issues were of particular concern to the South African woman Charlotte Maxeke, the founder of the African National Congress (ANC) Women's League, social worker, teacher, and leader in the African Methodist Episcopal Church. Born Charlotte Makgomo Manye in 1874, she received her primary and secondary education in South Africa; in her early twenties she toured England, Canada, and the United States with an African choir. She remained in the United States to study at Wilberforce College in Ohio, where she received her Bachelor of Science degree and met and married another South African, Reverend Marshall Maxeke. On her return to South Africa, she co-founded a secondary school with her husband and remained active in ANC and denominational affairs until her death in 1939.

In 1930 she presented her views on the plight of black women and families in a speech delivered to a rally attended by white and black Christian youth.

---

## QUESTIONS FOR ANALYSIS

1. What, according to Maxeke, are the reasons for the Bantu exodus from the countryside to cities?
2. What special challenges and difficulties confront newly arrived blacks in urban areas?
3. How do the problems of men and women in such circumstances differ?
4. What seems to have been the effect of the changes Maxeke describes on children and young people?

> 5. **What solutions does Maxeke propose to solve the problems confronting African women and their families? Are her proposed solutions likely to be successful?**

There are many problems pressing in upon us Bantu,[1] to disturb the peaceful working of our homes. One of the chief is perhaps the stream of Native life into the towns. Men leave their homes, and go into big towns like Johannesburg, where they get a glimpse of a life such as they had never dreamed existed. At the end of their term of employment they receive the wages for which they have worked hard, and which should be used for the sustenance of their families, but the attractive luxuries of civilisation are in many instances too much for them, they waste their hard earned wages, and seem to forget completely the crying need of their family out in the veld.[2]

The wife finds that her husband has apparently forgotten her existence, and she therefore makes her hard and weary way to the town in search of him. When she gets there, and starts looking round for a house of some sort in which to accommodate herself and her children, she meets with the first rebuff. The Location Superintendent[3] informs her that she cannot rent accommodations unless she has a husband. Thus she is driven to the first step on the downward path, for if she would have a roof to cover her children's heads a husband must be found, and so we get these poor women forced by circumstances to consort with men in order to provide shelter for their families. Thus we see that the authorities in enforcing the restrictions in regard to accommodation are often doing Bantu society a grievous harm, for they are forcing its wedded womanhood to the first steps on the downward path of sin and crime.

Many Bantu women live in the cities at a great price, the price of their children; for these women, even when they live with their husbands, are forced in most cases to go out and work, to bring sufficient income into the homes to keep their children alive. The children of these unfortunate people therefore run wild, and as there are not sufficient schools to house them, it is easy for them to live an aimless existence, learning crime of all sorts. . . .

If these circumstances obtain when husband and wife live together in the towns, imagine the case of the woman, whose husband has gone to town and left her, forgetting . . . all his responsibilities. Here we get young women, the flower of the youth of the Bantu, going up to towns in search of their husbands, and . . . living as the reputed wives of other men, because of the location requirements, or becoming housekeepers to men in the locations and towns, and eventually their nominal wives.

In Johannesburg, and other large towns, the male Natives are employed to do domestic work, . . . and a female domestic servant is a rarity. We thus have a very dangerous environment existing for any woman who goes into any kind of domestic service in these towns, and naturally immorality of various kinds ensues, as the inevitable outcome of this situation. Thus we see that the European is by his treatment of the Native . . . only pushing him further and further down in the social scale, forgetting that it was he and his kind who brought these conditions about in South Africa, forgetting his responsibilities to those who labour for him and to whom he introduced the benefits, and evils, of civilisation. . . .

Then we come to the *Land Question*. This is very acute in South Africa, especially from the Bantu point of view.[4] South Africa in terms of available land is shrinking daily owing to in-

---

[1] In this context, blacks of South Africa who spoke languages of the Bantu family and who traditionally had been farmers and herders.
[2] Afrikaans (the Dutch-based language spoken by Afrikaners) for the grasslands of southern and eastern Africa.

[3] A white official in charge of a black township; these townships were areas adjacent to white towns or cities where blacks were legally compelled to live.
[4] The reference is to the Natives Land Act of 1913.

creased population, and to many other economic and climatic causes. Cattle diseases have crept into the country, ruining many a stock farmer, and thus Bantu wealth is gradually decaying. As a result there are more and more workers making their way to the towns and cities such as Johannesburg to earn a living. . . . The majority earn about £3 10s. per month, out of which they must pay 25s. for rent, and 10s. for tram fares, so I leave you to imagine what sort of existence they lead on the remainder.

Here again we come back to the same old problem . . . — that of the woman of the home being obliged to find work in order to supplement her husband's wages, with the children growing up undisciplined and uncared for. . . . We find that in this state of affairs, the woman in despair very often decides that she cannot leave her children uncared for, and she therefore gives up her employment in order to care for them, but is naturally forced into some form of home industry, which, as there is very little choice for her in this direction, more often than not takes the form of the brewing and selling of Skokiaan.[5] Thus the woman starts on a career of crime for herself and her children, a career which often takes her and her children right down the depths of immorality and misery. The woman, poor unfortunate victim of circumstances, goes to prison, and the children are left even more desolate than when their mother left them to earn her living. . . . About ten years ago, there was talk of industrial schools being started for such unfortunate children, but it was only talk, and we are today in the same position, aggravated by the increased numbers steadily streaming in from the rural areas, all undergoing very similar experiences to those I have just outlined. . . .

Many of the Bantu feel and rightly too that the laws of the land are not made for Black and White alike. Take the question of permits for the right to look for work. . . . The poor unfortunate Native, fresh from the country does not know of these rules and regulations, naturally breaks them and is thrown into prison; or if he does happen to know the regulations and obtains a pass[6] for six days, and is obliged to renew it several times, as is of course very often the case, he will find that when he turns up for the third or fourth time for the renewal of his permit, he is put into prison, because he has been unsuccessful in obtaining work. And not only do the Bantu feel that the law for the White and the Black is not similar, but we even find some of them convinced that there are two Gods, one for the White and one for the Black. I had an instance of this in an old Native woman who had suffered much, and could not be convinced that the same God watched over and cared for us all, but felt that the God who gave the Europeans their life of comparative comfort and ease, could not possibly be the same God who allowed his poor Bantu to suffer so. As another instance of the inequalities existing in our social scheme, we have the fact of Natives not being allowed to travel on buses and trams in many towns, except those specially designed for them.

In connection with the difficulty experienced through men being employed almost exclusively in domestic work in the cities, I would mention that this is of course one of the chief reasons for young women, who should rightly be doing that work, going rapidly down in the social life of the community. The solution to the problem seems to me to be to get women into service, and to give them proper accommodation, where they know they are safe. Provide hostels, and club-rooms, and rest rooms for these domestic servants, where they may spend their leisure hours, and I think you will find the problem of the employment of female domestic servants will solve itself, and that a better and happier condition of life will come into being for the Bantu.

---

[5]*Skokiaan* is Afrikaans for "Bantu beer," an alcoholic beverage brewed from sorghum.

[6]To prevent too many unemployed blacks from living in towns, the government required every black to carry a "pass," which showed the name of his or her employer. Those looking for work were granted temporary passes. Without a valid pass, blacks could be fined, arrested, deported to a rural reserve, or forced to accept a low-paying job for a white employer.

▼▼▼

# Latin America in an Era of Economic Challenge and Political Change

A popular slogan among Latin America's politicians and landowners in the late nineteenth and early twentieth centuries was "order and progress," and, to an extent exceptional in the region's turbulent history, they achieved both. Around 1870 Latin America's economy entered a period of export-driven expansion that lasted until the 1920s. The region became a major supplier of wheat, beef, mutton, coffee, raw rubber, nitrates, copper, tin, and a host of other primary products to Europe, and, with little industrialization itself, a major market for European manufactured goods. Land prices soared, and English and U.S. capital flowed into Latin America to finance railroads, banks, and food-processing facilities, and to lend governments money for the construction of roads, bridges, and public buildings.

Latin America's economic boom took place in a climate of relative political stability. In Argentina, Chile, and Brazil this meant republican governments controlled by an oligarchy of landowning families, sometimes in alliance with businessmen in the import-export trade; in Mexico, Peru, Ecuador, and Venezuela it meant rule by a strong man or dictator *(caudillo)*, who also represented the interests of landowners. Dictators and oligarchs alike sought economic growth by maintaining law and order, encouraging foreign investment and free trade, and confiscating land from the Church and Native Americans. Committed to science and progress and convinced of their God-given right to govern, Latin America's ruling elite entered the twentieth century with high expectations.

By the 1930s, however, the old political order and the neocolonial economy on which it was based were both in shambles. By then urbanization, fueled by European immigration, modest industrialization, and an influx of people from the countryside had undermined Latin America's traditional two-class system — an elite of wealthy and powerful landowners and a mass of impoverished peasants and laborers. In Mexico City, Buenos Aires, São Paulo, and other cities, a factory-based working class emerged, and a middle sector made up of professionals, office workers, teachers, writers, and small businessmen expanded. The political strength of these new groups was revealed in Mexico, where discontented members of the middle class in alliance with rural Indians overthrew the dictator Porfirio Díaz in 1910, and in Argentina, where all adult males won the right to vote in 1912.

In most of Latin America, however, the landowning oligarchy held on to power until economic catastrophe struck with the onset of the Great Depression. Demand for Latin America's agricultural products and raw materials plummeted, driving millions into unemployment, and depriving the region of the foreign exchange needed to buy manufactured goods from abroad. Foreign loans and investments from Europe and the United States dried up after the collapse of stock markets and the international banking system. Governments faced insolvency, and capital shortages crippled plans to end the economic slump through industrialization. Latin Americans came to resent European and especially U.S. ownership of tin and copper mines, oil fields, railroads, banks, processing plants, and prime agricultural land. Once welcomed as a means of attracting capital and encouraging growth, foreign ownership now was condemned as a form of imperialist plunder.

As the Great Depression spread economic misery across Latin America, one government after another fell in an epidemic of election swings, revolts, coups, and counter coups. The military seized power in Argentina and Peru in 1930, and Uruguay's constitutional government collapsed in 1933 when the elected president Gabriel Terra established a dictatorship. Dictators seized power in El Salvador, Guatemala, Honduras, and, with the help of the U.S. government, Nicaragua and the Dominican Republic. In Chile, however, the onset of the Depression led to the fall of a dictator, Carlos Ibanez, in 1931. This was followed by a brief constitutional interlude and more military coups before a center-right government under Arturo Alessandri took power in 1932. In Cuba the dictator Gerardo Machado was forced into exile in 1933, but another dictator, Fulgencio Batista, took his place in 1934. Ecuador had no less than fourteen presidents between 1931 and 1940, and Paraguay four different dictators. Only a few states such as Colombia managed to maintain a measure of political stability.

While most of these short-lived regimes had no long-term political impact, in Mexico and Brazil Depression-driven political changes had lasting consequences for the nations themselves and for Latin America as a whole. In Mexico, these changes took place under President Lázaro Cárdenas, who between 1934 and 1940 sought Mexico's revitalization through educational reform, land redistribution, and nationalization of foreign-owned businesses. In Brazil, they were connected with the career of Getúlio Vargas, who seized power in 1930 and dominated Brazilian politics until 1945 and again from 1951 to 1954. By the end of the 1930s his *Estado Novo* (New State), a mixture of dictatorship, repression, anticolonialism, economic planning, nationalism, industrialization, and government-sponsored programs for housing, improved wages, and medical care, provided Latin America with an authoritarian model for entry into the era of mass politics.

# Economic Nationalism in Mexico
▼▼▼

## 106 ▼ *Lázaro Cárdenas, SPEECH TO THE NATION*

Following the overthrow of dictator Porfirio Díaz in 1911, instability and conflict among aspiring leaders marked the first decade of Mexico's revolution, and it was unclear whether the revolutionary movement would survive. In 1917, however, a constitutional convention drafted a new charter for the nation that confirmed the principles of free speech, religious toleration, universal suffrage, the separation of powers, and the inviolability of private property. It also committed the government to social reform and greater control over foreign corporations.

Little changed, however, until the presidency of Lázaro Cárdenas from 1934 to 1940. In a series of bold steps he confiscated millions of acres of land from large estates for redistribution to peasants, introduced free and compulsory elementary education, and sponsored legislation to provide medical and unemployment insurance. His most audacious step, however, was the nationalization of Mexico's oil industry. In 1936 a dispute between unions and the U.S. and British oil companies erupted into a strike, and in the legal battle that followed, seventeen oil companies refused to accept the pro-union ruling of an arbitration board appointed by Cárdenas and the decision of the Mexican Supreme Court that upheld the board's ruling. This refusal led Cárdenas to announce in a radio address to the nation on March 18, 1938, that the government had seized the property of the oil companies. In the following excerpt from his speech, Cárdenas, after recounting the events in the labor dispute, comments on the role of the oil companies in Mexico's economic and social development.

---

## QUESTIONS FOR ANALYSIS

1. In the account of Cárdenas, which actions by the foreign oil companies forced him to nationalize the oil industry?
2. According to Cárdenas, what truth is there in the oil companies' claims that they have benefited Mexico?
3. According to Cárdenas, who is ultimately responsible for the actions of the oil companies?
4. Which political activities of the oil companies does Cárdenas condemn?
5. What hardships does Cárdenas anticipate for the Mexican people as a result of his decision?
6. In what ways is Cárdenas's speech an appeal to Mexican nationalism?

In each and every one of the various attempts of the Executive to arrive at a final solution of the conflict within conciliatory limits . . . the intransigence of the companies was clearly demonstrated.

Their attitude was therefore premeditated and their position deliberately taken, so that the Government, in defense of its own dignity, had to resort to application of the Expropriation Act, as there were no means less drastic or decision less severe that might bring about a solution of the problem. . . .

It has been repeated *ad nauseam* that the oil industry has brought additional capital for the development and progress of the country. This assertion is an exaggeration. For many years throughout the major period of their existence,

oil companies have enjoyed great privileges for development and expansion, including customs and tax exemptions and innumerable prerogatives; it is these factors of special privilege, together with the prodigious productivity of the oil deposits granted them by the Nation often against public will and law, that represent almost the total amount of this so-called capital.

Potential wealth of the Nation; miserably underpaid native labor; tax exemptions; economic privileges; governmental tolerance — these are the factors of the boom of the Mexican oil industry.

Let us now examine the social contributions of the companies. In how many of the villages bordering on the oil fields is there a hospital, or school or social center, or a sanitary water supply, or an athletic field, or even an electric plant fed by the millions of cubic meters of natural gas allowed to go to waste?

What center of oil production, on the other hand, does not have its company police force for the protection of private, selfish, and often illegal interests? These organizations, whether authorized by the Government or not, are charged with innumerable outrages, abuses, and murders, always on behalf of the companies that employ them.

Who is not aware of the irritating discrimination governing construction of the company camps? Comfort for the foreign personnel; misery, drabness, and insalubrity for the Mexicans. Refrigeration and protection against tropical insects for the former; indifference and neglect, medical service and supplies always grudgingly provided, for the latter; lower wages and harder, more exhausting labor for our people.

The tolerance which the companies have abused was born, it is true, in the shadow of the ignorance, betrayals, and weakness of the country's rulers; but the mechanism was set in motion by investors lacking in the necessary moral resources to give something in exchange for the wealth they have been exploiting.

Another inevitable consequence of the presence of the oil companies, strongly characterized by their anti-social tendencies, and even more harmful than all those already mentioned, has been their persistent and improper intervention in national affairs.

The oil companies' support to strong rebel factions against the constituted government in the Huasteca region of Veracruz and in the Isthmus of Tehuantepec during the years 1917 to 1920 is no longer a matter for discussion by anyone. Nor is anyone ignorant of the fact that in later periods and even at the present time, the oil companies have almost openly encouraged the ambitions of elements discontented with the country's government, every time their interests were affected either by taxation or by the modification of their privileges or the withdrawal of the customary tolerance. They have had money,

arms, and munitions for rebellion, money for the anti-patriotic press which defends them, money with which to enrich their unconditional defenders. But for the progress of the country, for establishing an economic equilibrium with their workers through a just compensation of labor, for maintaining hygienic conditions in the districts where they themselves operate, or for conserving the vast riches of the natural petroleum gases from destruction, they have neither money, nor financial possibilities, nor the desire to subtract the necessary funds from the volume of their profits.

Nor is there money with which to meet a responsibility imposed upon them by judicial verdict, for they rely on their pride and their economic power to shield them from the dignity and sovereignty of a Nation which has generously placed in their hands its vast natural resources and now finds itself unable to obtain the satisfaction of the most elementary obligations by ordinary legal means.

As a logical consequence of this brief analysis, it was therefore necessary to adopt a definite and legal measure to end this permanent state of affairs in which the country sees its industrial progress held back by those who hold in their hands the power to erect obstacles as well as the motive power of all activity and who, instead of using it to high and worthy purposes, abuse their economic strength to the point of jeopardizing the very life of a Nation endeavoring to bring about the elevation of its people through its own laws, its own resources, and the free management of its own destinies.

With the only solution to this problem thus placed before it, I ask the entire Nation for moral and material support sufficient to carry out so justified, important, and indispensable a decision. . . .

It is necessary that all groups of the population be imbued with a full optimism and that each citizen, whether in agricultural, industrial, commercial, transportation, or other pursuits, develop a greater activity from this moment on, in order to create new resources which will reveal that the spirit of our people is capable of saving the nation's economy by the efforts of its own citizens.

And, finally, as the fear may arise among the interests now in bitter conflict in the field of international affairs[1] that a deviation of raw materials fundamentally necessary to the struggle in which the most powerful nations are engaged might result from the consummation of this act of national sovereignty and dignity, we wish to state that our petroleum operations will not de-part a single inch from the moral solidarity maintained by Mexico with the democratic nations, whom we wish to assure that the expropriation now decreed has as its only purpose the elimination of obstacles erected by groups who do not understand the evolutionary needs of all peoples and who would themselves have no compunction in selling Mexican oil to the highest bidder, without taking into account the consequences of such action to the popular masses and the nations in conflict.

---

[1]World War II in Europe was still more than a year away, but the Japanese invasion of China was in full swing, Spain was in the midst of its civil war, and Hitler had just annexed Austria.

## Brazilian Mass Politics and the *Estado Novo*
▼▼▼

### 107 ▼ *Getúlio Vargas,*
### *EXCERPTS FROM SPEECHES*
### *AND INTERVIEWS, 1937–1940*

Not without growing opposition from the middle class and the military, wealthy coffee growers from the states of São Paulo and Minas Gerais maintained their grip on Brazilian politics during the "Old Republic" from 1889 to 1930. In 1930, however, with coffee prices in free fall, a disputed election led to a military coup and the installation as president of Getúlio Vargas. The era of the coffee oligarchy was over, and Brazilian politics embarked on a new path.

Born in 1883 into a politically active family of landowners from the state of Rio Grande do Sul, Getúlio Vargas served in the army, studied law, and was Rio Grande do Sul's congressman and governor before joining the national government as finance minister in 1926–1927. In 1930 he ran for president as the candidate of the Liberal Alliance, a coalition of the urban bourgeoisie, intellectuals, some landowners, and reform-minded army officers. He lost the fraud-filled election, and in its wake, his opponents refused to allow his supporters to take their seats in the Congress and probably were responsible for the murder of his vice-presidential running mate. At this point Vargas's supporters in the army deposed the president and named him head of a provisional government.

Having come to power in 1930 with the support of a diverse coalition, Vargas at first proceeded cautiously. He raised tariffs, encouraged industrialization, and sought to prop up the price of coffee. In 1932 he reduced the voting age to eighteen and granted working women the right to vote. In 1934 a new constitution strengthened the executive, gave the government greater control of the economy, and called for the gradual nationalization of foreign-owned businesses. Then in 1935 Vargas began to move toward one-man rule. He banned the Communist and the fascist Integralist parties and in 1937, after canceling national elections, proclaimed a new constitution and assumed dictatorial powers. Brazil, he announced, had entered the era of the *Estado Novo,* the New State.

In the following excerpts from interviews and speeches given between 1937 and 1940, Vargas outlines the general philosophy and goals of his New State.

## QUESTIONS FOR ANALYSIS

1. What according to Vargas were the major flaws of Brazilian politics before he took power?
2. What steps did he take or plan to take in order to rid Brazil of these flaws?
3. Vargas claims his New State is democratic. Do his comments in his various speeches and interviews support such a claim?
4. Some commentators have discerned elements of fascism in Vargas's political philosophy and policies. Do you agree with such an assessment?
5. What specific policies does he propose to appeal to the urban bourgeoisie and working class?

## [INTERVIEW, APRIL 1938]

The movement of November 10th[1] was, without doubt, brought about by the national will. We had need of order and security in order to carry on; conspiring against that was the critical state of political decomposition to which we had arrived. Slowly our public life had been transformed into an arena of sterile struggles where plots, clashing interests of the oligarchy, personal competitions, and differences in personal interests were decided. Men of character without ambition to govern drew away from it nauseated, leaving the field open to political professionals and to demagogic and audacious adventurers. It was thus that communism succeeded in infiltrating and came to be at one time a national danger.[2] Defeated in its violent attempt to seize power, it continued, nevertheless, its work of undermining authority by utilizing as its weapons the other evils that make the situation of the nation so unstable and chaotic: the weakness of political parties, regional jealousies, and dictatorial flights of fancy. Those three evils are in the final analysis simply the result of a single general cause, well formed and known: the sterility and exhaustion of the sources from which the agents of inspiration and renovation of public life ought to come. The political parties had abdicated their social function. . . . Foresight of the danger in which we found ourselves and which was felt by all caused us decisively to favor the political unification of the nation which is precisely why the regime was established on November 10th. The Estado Novo embodies, therefore, the will and ideas which oppose and work against all the factors tending to weaken and dissolve the fatherland — extremism, sabotage, and compromise. It is ready to fight against those evils. It will mobilize all the best that we possess in order to make our nation strong, dignified, and happy.

---

[1]On November 10, 1937, Vargas announced in a radio message to the nation that he had canceled the upcoming presidential elections, dissolved the legislature, and assumed dictatorial powers under a new constitution.

[2]In 1937 a wing of the Communist Party took part in an anti-Vargas revolt that was crushed by the government. Later in the year the government circulated a forged document that supposedly outlined a Communist plan to seize power.

## [SPEECH, JULY 1938]

As Chief of Government, I systematically seek to hear those who are informed, to appreciate the word of the experts, to study and to boldly face the reality of facts. It was thus that, feeling the profound sentiment of the Brazilian people, I did all possible in order to save them from the dangers of extremism, both — from the right as well as from the left — contrary to our sentiments of understanding and Christian tolerance.

I can affirm to you with certainty that the hours of greatest apprehension now have passed.

Through the spirit of good sense and through the persistent intention of reconciling the peace of the people with national dignity, we have given an example for the world to appreciate. Thus we proceed . . . trying to assure to all and to each a greater share of well-being and tranquility within the just equilibrium between the duties and prerogatives of the citizen.

## [INTERVIEW, MARCH 1938]

Among the profound changes brought about by the new regime are: the implementation of direct, universal suffrage, applicable only to specific questions that pertain to all citizens . . . the city as the nuclear base of the political system; the substitution of the principle of the separation of powers[3] by the supremacy of the Executive; the strengthening of the power of the Union; the effective and efficient participation of economic groups, through its own organizations, in the constructive and integrating work of the government.

The new system consecrates a government of authority by instituting as law the legislative decree, by giving to the President of the Republic powers to expedite law-decrees when congress is not in session, by attributing to him the right to dissolve it in special cases, and by taking from the Judiciary the privilege of ultimate interpretation of the constitutionality or unconstitutionality of the laws which involve public interests of great importance. These new powers, placed under the guard of the government, always overcome private interests.

Profoundly nationalistic, the regime insures and consolidates national unity and formally restricts the autonomy of the state[4] by suppressing regional symbols, extending intervention, establishing the supremacy of federal over local laws in the case of concurrent legislation by attributing to the central government the power to requisition at any time the state militias, etc.

The professions are represented in their own and independent chamber with consultative functions in all the projects concerning the national economy, and eventually it will have legislative functions.[5]

Truly we have instituted an essentially democratic regime because it does not base its representation on a system of indications and artificialities but rather on the direct collaboration of the people through their economic forces and their organizations of production and labor. Only thus can our present political structure make known the effective representation of Brazil.

## [SPEECH, JULY 1938]

If you would ask me what is the program of the Estado Novo, I would tell you that its program is to crisscross the nation with railroads, highways, and airlines; to increase production; to provide for the laborer and to encourage agricultural credit; to expand exports, to prepare the armed forces so that they are always ready to face any eventuality; to organize public opinion so that there is, body and soul, one Brazilian thought.

By examining the government's activities, anyone can verify with his own eyes that the basic

---

[3]The separation of the executive, legislative, and judicial powers within government.
[4]In the Old Republic the states of Brazil had exercised extensive political powers, and politicians from two states, São Paulo and Minas Gerais, dominated the federal government.
[5]Economic and professional groups would be represented in addition to districts, provinces, etc.

problems of Brazilian life, without regional distinctions or political preferences, were resolutely attacked: the increase and expansion of industrial and agrarian centers; the creation of new sources of wealth and the improvement of the processes of exporting; . . . the measures taken to raise the standard of living of the masses; financial support to the producing classes; economic assistance to the worker by means of social security, a just salary, a good home, and the guarantee of his rights; the increase in the number of centers of technical, physical, and intellectual training; care for public hygiene and rural sanitation by making possible the remunerative utilization of large areas of soil abandoned or sacrificed because of climatic disturbances; the systematic repudiation of extremist ideologies and their . . . followers; the combating of all agents of dissolution or weakening of the national energies by the reinforcement of Brazilian traditions and sentiments and the prohibition from functioning in this country of any organization with anti-national activities or linked to foreign political interests; finally the preparation of internal and external defense by the rearmament of our brave armed forces and the simultaneous education of the new generations inculcating in them the spirit and love of the fatherland, faith in its destinies and the desire to make it strong and respected.

▼▼▼

# China in an Era of Political Disintegration and Revolution

The overthrow of the Qing Dynasty following China's Revolution of 1911 resulted not in China's long-awaited national revival, but instead in four decades of diplomatic humiliation, invasion, civil war, and immense suffering for the Chinese people. In the aftermath of the revolution, Sun Yat-sen and his dreams of democracy were pushed aside by General Yuan Shikai, who ruled the Chinese "republic" as a dictator between 1912 and 1916 and was planning to have himself declared emperor before he died in 1916. After his death, China was carved up by dozens of generally unscrupulous and irresponsible warlords, military men whose local authority was based on their control of private armies and whose grip on China was not completely broken until after the Communists took power in 1949. With a weak national government, the Chinese had to endure continued Western domination of their coastal cities and could offer only feeble resistance when the Japanese conquered Manchuria in 1931 and invaded China itself in 1937. Massive flooding of the Yellow River and widespread famine in north China in the 1920s deepened the misery of the Chinese people.

   With Confucian certainties shattered and China falling into ruin, Chinese intellectuals of the 1920s and 1930s intensely debated their country's future. The 1920s in particular were years of intellectual experiment and inquiry, in which members of study groups, journalists, poets, writers of fiction, academics, and university students scrutinized what it meant to be Chinese and debated what had to be done to save China from further catastrophe. Most of these intellectuals vehemently rejected traditional Chinese values, customs, philosophy, and education, arguing that only a sharp break from the past would enable China to stand up to Japan and the West. Most of them believed that China needed to model itself on the West, although what specific Western values and institutions should be borrowed was a matter of debate.

In politics, Chinese who despaired of warlord depredation, Western imperialism, and Japanese aggression had two options. Two revolutionary parties emerged — the Nationalist Party, or Guomindang (GMD), and the Chinese Communist Party (CCP), each with its own plan of how to unify, govern, and revive China. The Guomindang, led by Sun Yat-sen until his death in 1925, was theoretically dedicated to Sun's "three principles of the people" — democracy, nationalism, and livelihood. The party came to be identified with the educated, Western-oriented bourgeoisie of China's coastal cities and in practice, under General Chiang Kai-shek (1887–1975), concentrated less on social reform and democracy than on fighting the warlords in the 1920s and the Communists in the 1930s. The Chinese Communist Party, founded in 1921, was dedicated to Marxism-Leninism, with its leadership provided by intellectuals and its major support eventually coming from China's rural masses.

Aided by agents of the Soviet Union, the Guomindang and Communists formed a coalition in 1923 to destroy the warlords. With their forces combined into the National Revolutionary Army, the Guomindang and the Communists launched the Northern Expedition against the warlords in 1926. The alliance lasted only until 1927, when Chiang Kai-shek, buoyed by his early victories and generous financial support from Chinese businessmen, purged the Communists from the army and ordered Guomindang troops in Shanghai to kill Communist leaders who had gathered there. Communist troops and their leaders fled to the countryside, where under the leadership of Mao Zedong (1893–1976), they rebuilt the party into a formidable military and political force. After a long struggle against the Guomindang and Japanese, who invaded China in 1937, the Communists gained control of China in 1949.

## Warlord Rule in China during the 1920s
▼▼▼

## 108 ▼ *THE CORRUPTION AND CRUELTY OF ZHANG ZONGCHANG WHO DESTROYED THE COUNTRY AND DECEIVED THE PEOPLE*

To historians the era of warlord rule in China presents a muddled picture of venal and short-sighted commanders leading private armies back and forth over a landscape of political disintegration and immense human suffering. With no legitimate sanction for their rule and no clear boundaries separating their territories, warlords were continually fighting among themselves and moving in and out of alliances, or "cliques," as their short-term self-interest seemed to dictate. With no constitutional or theoretical limits on their authority, they could tax and abuse their subjects according to their whims or momentary needs. At the national level, China's government in Beijing maintained foreign relations with other states but it ruled China in name only. China's continued existence as a unified state was in jeopardy.

The following account, printed in the Chinese journal *Yijing* in 1936 and based on readers' recollections, tells the story of Zhang Zongchang (1881–1932), a notorious warlord during the 1920s in Shandong Province, in northeast China on the Yellow Sea. Having followed a tortuous path to power in the late 1910s and 1920s, Zhang fled Shandong to Manchuria and then to Japan when threatened with the arrival of Guomindang troops during the Northern Expedition in 1928. He was assassinated by the son of one of his victims when he returned to Shandong in 1932.

Not all warlords were as irresponsible and erratic as Zhang. Some were reasonable men who worked to establish a stable government and sought social reform. Zhang's career does, however, offer insight into the chaos that ruled much of China in the 1920s.

## QUESTIONS FOR ANALYSIS

1. By what process did Zhang come to dominate the Shandong region? What qualities did he have that contributed to his rise to power?
2. As a ruler, what seemed to have been Zhang's major priorities and concerns?
3. In what ways did life deteriorate in Shandong during Zhang's rule? Did anyone benefit from his rule?

Zhang Zongchang, nicknamed "Dog-meat General" and "Lanky General," was from Yi county in Shandong. His father was a trumpet player (hired for funeral processions, etc.) and barber, and his mother was a shamaness.[1] At the age of twelve or thirteen, Zhang started helping his father by playing the cymbals. When he was fifteen or sixteen he went with his mother to Yinkou, and worked as a servant in a gambling house, mixing with pickpockets and thieves. The gentry of the town, annoyed, drove him away. He then fled to Guandong [in Manchuria] to join the "bearded bandits." His mother stayed on at Yinkou, and lived with the proprietor of a bath-house, then with a cobbler, then with a cloth vendor. The cloth vendor, in a fit of jealousy, killed the cobbler, and was sent to jail. Because of this, Zhang's mother was sent into exile. . . .

When the revolution started in 1911, Zhang led about one hundred "bearded bandits" from Guandong to Yantai [in Shandong] to join Commander Hu Ying's[2] army. When Hu resisted the revolutionary forces, Zhang went to Shanghai to join the regiment commander of the revolutionary army. At that time, there was a truce between the North and the South, and the regiment commander resigned, but not before he had made Zhang, who was not only strong but also brave,

---

[1] A person who had the power to contact the spirits of the dead and hence was consulted by others on matters relating to health and business.

[2] Although it is difficult to trace all the twists and turns of Zhang's career from this brief account, it would appear that as a strong supporter of Yuan Shikai, he suffered a setback

after the "second revolution" of 1916 — when warlords and followers of Sun Yat-sen blocked Yuan's efforts to have himself named emperor. After months of freelancing he attracted the attention of Feng Guozhang, who became vice president of China after Yuan's fall and then president in 1917.

the leader of his men. Zhang and his army were then reorganized by Commander Cheng Dechuan of Jiangsu. Now called "Juangfu" troops, they were sent to Fengpei and Xiaoyi to put down bandits, and were under the Division Commander Leng Yuqin. When the Second Revolution started and Leng was defeated, Zhang took over Leng's soldiers and gained even more military power. However, because Zhang was connected with Leng, his troops were soon dissolved by Feng Guozhang, the honorary title "model supervisory regiment" given him was but an empty name. From then on, Zhang made a profession of murdering his revolutionary comrades. The assassination of Shanghai's commander, Chen Qimei, was Zhang's doing. Because of this, Zhang was taken into the confidence of Feng Guozhang. When Feng was the national vice-president, he appointed Zhang as the chief of his personal guards. . . .

Zhang was very brave in battle, but he had no mind for strategy. His soldiers were mostly bandits, and therefore very valiant warriors, which by and large accounted for his success in military ventures. But he also had an advisor who assisted him in military maneuvers, the fortune-teller Tong Huagu. During the Fengtian-Zhili war,[3] Zhang was stationed to the east of the Xifeng pass. One day, Zhang came across Tong and went up to him for advice. Tong told him that his physiognomy[4] revealed that he would achieve great distinction. He also predicted that the next day, when the Zhili troops passed by train, the train would derail, and if Zhang would take this opportunity, he could attack them and win a big victory. The next day, Zhang stationed his troops to wait for the Zhili troops. Just as Tong had predicted, the train derailed, and Zhang routed the enemies. At the time of the battle Tong paced back and forth on top of a hill, his hair untied, his mouth uttering words of magic. After the battle, Zhang asked Tong to step down from the hill, and with utmost deference appointed him as his military advisor. From then on, Zhang followed Tong's words to the letter where military action was concerned.

It turned out that the fortune-teller was rather shrewd. The night that he met Zhang, he hired a few peasants to remove the screws connecting the rails over a bridge, thereby causing the derailment. Because he knew Zhang could easily be fooled, he used a fairy tale as a stepping-stone to a career. At any rate, on account of Zhang's military distinctions, he was finally appointed governor of Shandong. . . .

Not long after Zhang became governor, two phrases were heard all over the cities: "Cut apart to catch light" and "listen to the telephone." The former referred to the human heads which were treated like watermelons, cut in halves to bask in the sun; the latter referred to the same, except the heads were hung from telephones poles, and from afar they seemed to be listening on the telephone. At the same time, at the train stations along the Jiaoji and Jinpu lines, people started to hear the strange expression, "My head is my passport; my ass is my ticket." This was because people were being regularly kicked, beaten up, abused in vile language, and spat in the face by the soldiers. To the sights of the city of Jinan there were also added White Russian[5] soldiers, who were drunkards, ruffians, and rapists. Living in Shandong at this time, one could really feel the truth in the saying, "A man's life is worth less than a chicken's."

Soon after Zhang Zongchang came to his post, he unveiled his ugly nature and started his vile deeds. Under his "steel sword" policy, the once-flourishing academies disappeared, the better students fled, and the provincial assembly was silenced. On the other hand, clever people moved

---

[3]One of the numerous wars between cliques, or factions, of warlords that broke out after the death of Yuan Shikai; this particular war took place in 1920.

[4]Tong supposedly could judge Zhang's character and future by examining his physiognomy, or facial characteristics.

[5]White Russians were opponents of the Soviet Union's new Bolshevik rulers after the Russian Revolution. After the end of the Russian Civil War (1917–1920), between Whites and Reds, some of the defeated White troops made their way to China to serve as mercenaries in warlord armies.

with the current and began buttering Zhang up. Upholding the philosophy that "In an age of chaos, don't miss the chance to loot during the fire," they went after offices. From circuit intendants and county magistrates to bureau chiefs, all positions were refilled with much pomp. Whenever these henchmen went to a local district, their first priority was to extort and exploit, so that they could repay past favors and secure future ones, whereas the people were becoming skinnier daily. Too true was the proverb, "In the official's house, wine and meat are allowed to rot, but on the roads are the bones of those who starved to death."

Zhang Zongchang was a warmonger, by nature fond of disorder. After his arrival in Shandong, there was not even one day of peace. . . .

---

▷ An account of his wars with other warlords and Guomindang troops follows.

---

After each battle, the field was strewn with bodies. The loss of the soldiers required replacement, which in turn required military funds, which resulted in higher taxes. When funds were raised, more soldiers were drafted, and another war was in the making. This cycle was repeated again and again. This was the way Zhang Zongchang ruled the province of Shandong from 1925 to 1928. The white banners of recruitment flew all over the province, and young people were driven straight into their graves. In such a situation, how could the people of Shandong escape hardship and poverty?

## TAXATION

During the less then four years that Zhang Zongchang ruled, there was not one day that he failed to take money from the people. Besides the regular taxes, there were special taxes and blatant extortions. Whenever he needed a sum of money, he would issue an order to several counties for them to come up with the cash. And when he spent the money, well, that was the end of

that. Thus, the people of Shandong were really in deep water and they suffered more than the rest of the nation.

## FLOODING THE MARKET WITH PAPER MONEY

Zhang Zongchang issued the following paper currencies:

1. Banknotes of the Provincial Bank of Shandong
2. Military stamps
3. Co-op certificates

Altogether several tens of millions of dollars were issued, all without any reserve to back them up. When he was losing his battles on the frontiers, these forms of currency came to be regularly discounted and financial chaos resulted. Zhang's soldiers continued to use his paper money for purchases, however, without accepting a discount on the face value. If anyone objected they would use their fists, legs, and foul tongues against their opponents. For this reason, arguments and fights were frequent, and the merchants suffered. There is a story that a store refused to accept military stamps. Zhang gave orders to arrest the owner, who was beaten up and then shot.

## SALVOS AGAINST HEAVEN

In the summer of 1927, there was a severe drought in Shandong. Not a drop of rain fell, and the crops were all dying. Zhang Zongchang ordered a general fast and personally went to the "Dragon King Temple" to pray for rain. But the Dragon King was apparently not impressed, and the drought continued. In a rage, Zhang slapped the Dragon King's face many times. He then went to the Zhangzhuang Arsenal and fired cannon balls into the sky for hours, so as to vent his anger at Heaven. Nevertheless, it still did not rain. . . .

## DRAFTING SOLDIERS

Zhang literally dragged young people from the streets to become his soldiers so that he could send them to the frontiers, using their flesh against the cannon balls of the enemy. Many students were dragged away, and only after negotiations, were released. In order to prevent such incidents, the schools issued each student a cloth tag with his name and the school's seal printed on it. In this way the students were distinguished from the common people.

## CLEARING THE STREETS

Whenever Zhang came out of his office, he would clear the streets, and all traffic was stopped. The main street in front of the governor's office was sprinkled with clean water. In front of this motorcade, he had the showy White Russian cavalry squad. Soldiers were stationed all along the streets, their rifles loaded with real bullets, their backs to the street. All precautions were taken against possible assassins. . . .

# The Maoist Version of Marxism
▼▼▼

## *109 ▼ Mao Zedong,*
## *REPORT ON AN INVESTIGATION OF THE*
## *PEASANT MOVEMENT IN HUNAN and*
## *STRATEGIC PROBLEMS OF CHINA'S*
## *REVOLUTIONARY WAR*

Mao Zedong (1893–1976) was born into a well-to-do peasant family in Hunan Province and as a university student participated in the anti-Qing revolution of 1911. During the next several years, while serving as a library assistant at Beijing University, he embraced Marxism and helped organize the Chinese Communist Party, which was officially founded in 1921. Originally given the task of organizing urban labor unions, Mao gradually came to believe that in China the peasants, whose capacity for class revolution was discounted by orthodox Marxist-Leninists, were the force to lead China to socialism. He summarized his ideas in his "Report on an Investigation of the Peasant Movement in Hunan," written in 1927.

After the break from the Guomindang, the Communists took their small army to the remote and hilly region on the Hunan-Jiangxi border, where in 1931 they proclaimed the Chinese Soviet Republic. In 1934 Chiang Kai-shek's troops surrounded the Communists' forces, but as they moved in for the kill, more than one hundred thousand Communist troops and officials broke out of the Guomindang encirclement and embarked on the Long March. This legendary trek lasted more than a year and covered six thousand miles before a remnant found safety in the remote mountains around Yan'an in northern Shaanxi province. There Mao, now the party's recognized leader, rebuilt his army and readied himself and his followers for what would be fourteen more years of struggle against the Japanese and Guomindang.

Mao was a prolific writer, who from the 1920s until his death in 1976 produced many hundreds of treatises, essays, and even works of poetry. The following excerpts are drawn from two of his most important writings. The first, his *Report on an Investigation of the Peasant Movement in Hunan,* was written in 1927 after he visited Hunan Province to study the activities and accomplishments of peasant associations, groups of peasants who with the help of Communist organizers, had seized land, humiliated or killed landlords, and taken control of their communities. In it Mao expresses his faith in the poor peasantry as the main source of revolution in China. The second excerpt, from his *Strategic Problems of China's Revolutionary War,* was based on a series of lectures presented to the Red Army College in late 1936. In it Mao assessed China's military situation and outlined his strategy for victory over the Guomindang through guerrilla warfare.

## *QUESTIONS FOR ANALYSIS*

1. What specific developments in Hunan Province have reinforced Mao's convictions about the peasantry as a revolutionary force?
2. What criticisms have been made of the Hunan peasant movement, and how does Mao attempt to counter these criticisms?
3. What can be learned from these two writings about Mao's views of the role of the Communist Party in China's revolutionary struggle?
4. According to Mao, what have been the sources of oppression of the Chinese people? Once these sources of oppression are removed what will China look like?
5. According to Mao, what are the four unique characteristics of China's revolutionary war, and how do they affect Mao's military strategy?
6. What are the characteristics of Mao's "active defense" as opposed to "passive defense"?
7. How do Mao's ideas about revolution resemble and differ from those of Marx (source 63)? How do they resemble and differ from those of Lenin (source 91)?

## FROM REPORT ON AN INVESTIGATION OF THE PEASANT MOVEMENT IN HUNAN

During my recent visit to Hunan[1] I made a first-hand investigation of conditions in the five counties of Hsiangtan, Hsianghsiang, Hengshan, Liling and Changsha. . . . I saw and heard of many strange things of which I had hitherto been unaware. . . . All talk directed against the peasant movement must be speedily set right. All the wrong measures taken by the revolutionary authorities concerning the peasant movement must be speedily changed. Only thus can the future of the revolution be benefited. For the present upsurge of the peasant movement is a colossal event. In a very short time, in China's central, southern and northern provinces, several hundred million peasants will rise like a mighty storm, like a hurricane, a force so swift

[1]Hunan, a province of 105,000 sqaure miles in southeast central China, had a population of approximately twenty-eight million in 1936.

and violent that no power, however great, will be able to hold it back. They will smash all the trammels that bind them and rush forward along the road to liberation. They will sweep all the imperialists, warlords, corrupt officials, local tyrants and evil gentry into their graves. Every revolutionary party and every revolutionary comrade will be put to the test, to be accepted or rejected as they decide. There are three alternatives. To march at their head and lead them? To trail behind them, gesticulating and criticizing? Or to stand in their way and oppose them? Every Chinese is free to choose, but events will force you to make the choice quickly. . . .

"Yes, peasant associations are necessary, but they are going rather too far." This is the opinion of the middle-of-the-roaders. But what is the actual situation? True, the peasants are in a sense "unruly" in the countryside. Supreme in authority, the peasant association allows the landlord no say and sweeps away his prestige. This amounts to striking the landlord down to the dust and keeping him there. . . . People swarm into the houses of local tyrants and evil gentry who are against the peasant association, slaughter their pigs and consume their grain. They even loll for a minute or two on the ivory-inlaid beds belonging to the young ladies in the households of the local tyrants and evil gentry. At the slightest provocation they make arrests, crown the arrested with tall paper-hats, and parade them through the villages, saying, "You dirty landlords, now you know who we are!" . . . This is what some people call "going too far," or "exceeding the proper limits in righting a wrong," or "really too much." Such talk may seem plausible, but in fact it is wrong. First, the local tyrants, evil gentry and lawless landlords have themselves driven the peasants to this. For ages they have used their power to tyrannize over the peasants and trample them underfoot; that is why the peasants have reacted so strongly. . . . Secondly, a revolution is not a dinner party, or writing an essay, or painting a picture, or doing embroidery; it cannot be so refined, so leisurely

and gentle, so temperate, kind, courteous, restrained and magnanimous. A revolution is an insurrection, an act of violence by which one class overthrows another. A rural revolution is a revolution by which the peasantry overthrows the power of the feudal landlord class. Without using the greatest force, the peasants cannot possibly overthrow the deep-rooted authority of the landlords which has lasted for thousands of years. . . . To put it bluntly, it is necessary to create terror for a while in every rural area, or otherwise it would be impossible to suppress the activities of the counter-revolutionaries in the countryside or overthrow the authority of the gentry.

▾ ▾ ▾

A man in China is usually subjected to the domination of three systems of authority: (1) the state system, . . . ranging from the national, provincial and county government down to that of the township; (2) the clan system, . . . ranging from the central ancestral temple and its branch temples down to the head of the household; and (3) the supernatural system (religious authority), ranging from the King of Hell down to the town and village gods belonging to the nether world, and from the Emperor of Heaven down to all the various gods and spirits belonging to the celestial world. As for women, in addition to being dominated by these three systems of authority, they are also dominated by the men (the authority of the husband). These four authorities — political, clan, religious and masculine — are the embodiment of the whole feudal-patriarchal system and ideology, and are the four thick ropes binding the Chinese people, particularly the peasants. . . .

The political authority of the landlords is the backbone of all the other systems of authority. With that overturned, the clan authority, the religious authority and the authority of the husband all begin to totter. . . . In many places the peasant associations have taken over the temples of the gods as their offices. Everywhere they advocate the appropriation of temple property in order to start peasant schools and to defray the expenses of the associations, calling it "public revenue from superstition." In Liling County, prohibiting superstitious practices and smashing idols have become quite the vogue. . . .

In places where the power of the peasants is predominant, only the older peasants and the women still believe in the gods, the younger peasants no longer doing so. Since the latter control the associations, the overthrow of religious authority and the eradication of superstition are going on everywhere. As to the authority of the husband, this has always been weaker among the poor peasants because, out of economic necessity, their womenfolk have to do more manual labour than the women of the richer classes and therefore have more say and greater power of decision in family matters. With the increasing bankruptcy of the rural economy in recent years, the basis for men's domination over women has already been weakened. With the rise of the peasant movement, the women in many places have now begun to organize rural women's associations; the opportunity has come for them to lift up their heads, and the authority of the husband is getting shakier every day. In a word, the whole feudal-patriarchal system and ideology is tottering with the growth of the peasants' power.

## STRATEGIC PROBLEMS OF CHINA'S REVOLUTIONARY WAR

What then are the characteristics of China's revolutionary war?

I think there are four.

The first is that China is a vast semi-colonial country which is unevenly developed both politically and economically. . . .

The unevenness of political and economic development in China — the coexistence of a frail capitalist economy and a preponderant semi-feudal economy; the coexistence of a few modern industrial and commercial cities and the boundless expanses of stagnant rural districts; the coexistence of several millions of industrial workers on the one hand and, on the other, hundreds of millions of peasants and handicraftsmen under the old regime; the coexistence of big warlords controlling the Central government and small warlords controlling the provinces; the coexistence of two kinds of reactionary armies, i.e., the so-called Central army under Chiang Kai-shek and the troops of miscellaneous brands under the warlords in the provinces; and the coexistence of a few railway and steamship lines and motor roads on the one hand and, on the other, the vast number of wheel-barrow paths and trails for pedestrians only, many of which are even difficult for them to negotiate. . . .

The second characteristic is the great strength of the enemy.

What is the situation of the Guomindang, the enemy of the Red Army? It is a party that has seized political power and has relatively stabilized it. It has gained the support of the principal counter-revolutionary countries in the world. It has remodeled its army, which has thus become different from any other army in Chinese history and on the whole similar to the armies of the modern states in the world; its army is supplied much more abundantly with arms and other equipment than the Red Army, and is greater in numerical strength than any army in Chinese history, even than the standing army of any country in the world. . . .

The third characteristic is that the Red Army is weak and small. . . .

Our political power is dispersed and isolated in mountainous or remote regions, and is deprived of any outside help. In economic and cultural conditions the revolutionary base areas are more backward than the Guomindang areas. The revolutionary bases embrace only rural districts and small towns. . . .

The fourth characteristic is the Communist Party's leadership and the agrarian revolution.

This characteristic is the inevitable result of the first one. It gives rise to the following two features. On the one hand, China's revolutionary war, though taking place in a period of reaction in China and throughout the capitalist world, can yet be victorious because it is led by the Communist Party and supported by the peasantry. Because we have secured the support of the peasantry, our base areas, though small, possess great political power and stand firmly opposed to the political power of the Guomindang which encompasses a vast area; in a military sense this creates colossal difficulties for the attacking Guomindang troops. The Red Army, though small, has great fighting capacity, because its men under the leadership of the Communist Party have sprung from the agrarian revolution and are fighting for their own interests, and because officers and men are politically united.

On the other hand, our situation contrasts sharply with that of the Guomindang. Opposed to the agrarian revolution, the Guomindang is deprived of the support of the peasantry. Despite the great size of its army it cannot arouse the bulk of the soldiers or many of the lower-rank officers, who used to be small producers, to risk their lives voluntarily for its sake. Officers and men are politically disunited and this reduces its fighting capacity. . . .

Military experts of new and rapidly developing imperialist countries like Germany and Japan positively boast of the advantages of strategic offensive and condemn strategic defensive. Such an idea is fundamentally unsuitable for China's revolutionary war. Such military experts point out that the great shortcoming of defense lies in the fact that, instead of gingering up [enlivening] the people, it demoralizes them. . . . Our

case is different. Under the slogan of safeguarding the revolutionary base areas and safeguarding China, we can rally the greatest majority of the people to fight single-mindedly, because we are the victims of oppression and aggression. . . . Defensive battles in a just war can not only exercise a lulling influence on the politically alien elements but mobilize the backward sections of the masses to join in the war. . . .

In military terms, our warfare consists in the alternate adoption of the defensive and the offensive. It makes no difference to us whether our offensive is regarded as following the defensive or preceding it, because the turning-point comes when we smash the campaigns of "encirclement and annihilation." It remains a defensive until a campaign of "encirclement and annihilation" is smashed, and then it immediately begins as an offensive; they are but two phases of the same thing, as one campaign of "encirclement and annihilation" of the enemy is closely followed by another. Of the two phases, the defensive phase is more complicated and more important than the offensive phase. It involves numerous problems of how to smash the campaign of "encirclement and annihilation." The basic principle is for active defense and against passive defense.

In the civil war, when the Red Army surpasses the enemy in strength, there will no longer be any use for strategic defensive in general. Then our only directive will be strategic offensive. Such a change depends on an overall change in the relative strength of the enemy and ourselves. The only defensive measures that remain will be of a partial character.

# Chapter 13

▼▼▼

# The Global
# Community since 1945

The human experience since the end of World War II in some respects has been unprecedented. Never before have human beings controlled weapons with the destructive capacity of nuclear bombs and warheads. Even with the arms reduction treaties of the 1980s and 1990s, existing nuclear arsenals have the capacity to obliterate human society many times over. Never before have human beings witnessed so many and such revolutionary technological, medical, and scientific discoveries. Humans have walked on the moon, developed powerful computers, transformed agriculture through the Green Revolution, conquered diseases such as polio, and developed television satellites, sophisticated telephone systems, fax machines, and computer networks that allow instantaneous worldwide communication. Never before have human beings lived in a world with so much interaction and interdependency among human societies. International organizations such as the United Nations, international sporting events such as the Olympic Games, and worldwide coordination of activities such as postal services, disease control, whale hunting, and protection of the ozone layer are taken for granted by human beings whose ancestors' world barely extended beyond their agricultural village.

Yet it would be easy to exaggerate the uniqueness of human experiences in the last half century. Technological innovation has been a constant throughout history, and, as countless examples reveal, it has always brought both benefits and disruptions. The proliferation of firearms and artillery after their invention in the 1330s affected global politics and warfare no less profoundly than the development of nuclear weapons. Countless past empires have declined and disappeared, and in each instance their demise created conflicts and uncertainties as taxing as those following the demise of colonial empires after World War II and the breakup of the Soviet Union in the early 1990s. Every recent and contemporary challenge — national rivalries, environmental pressures, religious and ethnic conflicts, epidemics such as AIDS — has precedents.

What distinguishes the contemporary world is the vast power now in human hands and the question of how that power will be used. The miracles of technology, science, and medicine, when combined with the organizational capacities of modern states, give humans the ability to alleviate many age-old afflictions — poverty, hunger, ignorance, and premature death from disease. Nuclear weapons, on the other hand, provide them a means to self-destruct, literally in a flash. Another danger is that human beings will lack the courage or vision to their power to solve the problems looming before them — environmental damage, resource depletion, global poverty, overpopulation — to name only a few. In such a case, human life will continue, but in a way that will mock the hopes of millions who still dream of human progress.

▼▼▼

# The End of a European-Dominated World

Despite World War I's enormous costs and casualties, it brought no fundamental changes to international political relations in the 1920s and 1930s. Europe's prewar empires in Africa and Asia remained intact and even expanded in areas such as the Middle East, where the mandate system established at the Paris Peace Conference gave Great Britain control of Palestine and Iraq and France control of Syria and Lebanon. With the United States withdrawing from international commitments and the new communist regime in the Soviet Union shunned as an outcast, European states, especially Great Britain and France, and later, a resurgent Germany, dominated international diplomacy. Japan was the only non-European state that could boast of Great Power status.

The aftermath of World War II was far different. With their economies ruined and their people exhausted, the European states lost their dominance of world affairs to the United States and the Soviet Union, the two states whose size, industrial might, and military strength largely had been responsible for the defeat of the Axis powers. The unlikely alliance between the democratic, capitalist United States and the totalitarian, communist Soviet Union began to break down, however, in the closing months of World War II and disintegrated completely after hostilities ended. The establishment of pro-Soviet regimes in Eastern and Central Europe and the Soviet Union's annexation of Latvia, Lithuania, Estonia, and parts of Poland confirmed the West's old fears about communist designs for world domination. At the same time, staunch Western opposition to Soviet expansion reinforced the Soviet leaders' convictions that capitalist nations were determined to destroy communism. Out of these mutual fears began the Cold War, the conflict between the Soviet Union and the United States that dominated world diplomacy until the late 1980s.

Another symptom of Europe's diminished international role after World War II was the rapid disintegration of the European colonial empires. This dramatic political change had many causes, including the military and financial exhaustion of postwar Great Britain and France, the expansion and subsequent collapse of Japan's Asian empire, Soviet and U.S. opposition to colonialism, the upsurge of nationalism in the colonies, and the leadership of such men as Jawaharlal Nehru and Mohandas Gandhi in India, Sukarno in Indonesia, Kwame Nkrumah in Ghana, Ho Chi Minh in Vietnam, Jomo Kenyatta in Kenya, and others. By the mid 1960s just short of ninety former European colonies, most of them in Africa and Asia, had become independent.

In the second half of the twentieth century, Europeans, especially Western Europeans, enjoyed high incomes, excellent health care, and exceptional educational opportunities. European states continued to play an important, though secondary, role in world affairs. But the age of European world dominance had ended.

# Cold War Origins: A U.S. Perspective
▼▼▼

## 110 ▼ George Kennan, THE LONG TELEGRAM

Historians have minutely examined the events and issues that led to the Cold War, and much has been written about which side, the Soviet Union or the United States, was to blame for causing it. One thing is certain, however: 1946 was a pivotal year in Soviet-U.S. relations. Until then, despite wartime disagreements over military strategy and emerging differences about the postwar settlement, many statesmen and diplomats sought cooperation, not confrontation, between the two emerging superpowers. During 1946, however, attitudes hardened, and moderates such as the U.S. Secretary of Commerce Henry Wallace and the Soviet career diplomat Maksim Litvinov were removed from office. When negotiations over nuclear arms control failed in June and the Paris foreign ministers' conference over Eastern Europe ended in acrimony in August, leaders on both sides concluded that Soviet-U.S. conflict was inevitable.

Within the U.S. government one document in particular articulated this bleak assessment of Soviet-U.S. relations in 1946. Written in February by the Moscow-based career diplomat George Kennan, what came to be known as the Long Telegram profoundly influenced U.S. policy toward the Soviet Union in the immediate postwar era and throughout the Cold War. Its author, born into a strict Protestant household in Milwaukee in 1904, entered the U.S. Foreign Service directly after graduating from Princeton in 1925. Having mastered Russian through studies at the University of Berlin, he had postings in Moscow, Berlin, and Prague before returning to Moscow in 1944 as a special advisor to the U.S. ambassador to the

Soviet Union, Averell Harriman. In early February 1946 he received a directive from the State Department to analyze a recent speech by Joseph Stalin that Washington considered confrontational and hostile. Kennan, an advocate of a hard line against the Soviet Union, used the opportunity to compose what is arguably the best-known such dispatch in the history of the U.S. Foreign Service. The Long Telegram was read by State Department officials, cabled to U.S. embassies around the world, and made required reading for hundreds of military officers. In 1947 an edited version of the telegram was published as an article by "X" in the journal *Foreign Affairs.*

In 1947 Kennan was appointed head of the State Department's newly created policy planning staff charged with responsibility for mapping out long-range foreign policy strategy. His opposition to the formation of the North Atlantic Treaty Organization, to increased military spending, and to U.S. involvement in the Korean War led to his resignation in 1951. Since then with the exception of brief ambassadorships to the Soviet Union in 1952 and to Yugoslavia between 1961 and 1963, he has devoted himself to research, writing, and university teaching on foreign policy and Soviet affairs.

## QUESTIONS FOR ANALYSIS

1. What views of capitalism and socialism are presented, according to Kennan, in official Soviet propaganda?
2. What does Kennan consider the most notable characteristics of the Russian past?
3. How, according to Kennan, has this past shaped the policies and views of the Soviet government since 1917?
4. In Kennan's view what role does communist ideology play in shaping the Soviet government's policies?
5. According to Kennan, what strengths and weaknesses does the Soviet Union bring to the anticipated conflict with the United States?
6. What, according to Kennan, are the implications of his analysis for U.S. foreign and domestic policies? What must be done to counter the Soviet threat?

## PART 1: BASIC FEATURES OF POST-WAR SOVIET OUTLOOK, AS PUT FORWARD BY OFFICIAL PROPAGANDA MACHINE, ARE AS FOLLOWS

(a) USSR still lives in antagonistic "capitalist encirclement" with which in the long run there can be no permanent peaceful coexistence. . . .

(b) Capitalist world is beset with internal conflicts, inherent in nature of capitalist society. . . . Greatest of them is that between England and US.

(c) Internal conflicts of capitalism inevitably generate wars. Wars thus generated may be of two kinds: intra-capitalist wars between two capitalist states and wars of intervention against socialist world. Smart capitalists, vainly seeking escape from inner conflicts of capitalism, incline toward the latter.

(d) Intervention against USSR, while it would be disastrous to those who understood it, would cause renewed delay in progress of Soviet socialism and must therefore be forestalled at all costs.

(e) Conflicts between capitalist states, though likewise fraught with danger for USSR, nevertheless hold out great possibilities for advancement of socialist cause, particularly if USSR remains militarily powerful, ideologically monolithic and faithful to its present brilliant leadership. . . .

## PART 2: BACKGROUND OF OUTLOOK

At bottom of Kremlin's neurotic view of world affairs is traditional and instinctive Russian sense of insecurity. Originally, this was insecurity of a peaceful agricultural people trying to live on vast exposed plain in neighborhood of fierce nomadic peoples. To this was added, as Russia came into contact with economically advanced West, fear of more competent, more powerful, more highly organized societies in that area. But this latter type of insecurity was one which afflicted Russian rulers rather than Russian people; for Russian rulers have invariably sensed that their rule was relatively archaic in form, fragile and artificial in its psychological foundations, unable to stand comparison or contact with political systems of Western countries. For this reason they have always feared foreign penetration, feared direct contact between Western world and their own, feared what would happen if Russians learned truth about world without or if foreigners learned truth about world within. And they have learned to seek security only in patient but deadly struggle for total destruction of rival power, never in compacts and compromises with it.

It was no coincidence that Marxism, which had smouldered ineffectively for half a century in Western Europe, caught hold and blazed for the first time in Russia. Only in this land which had never known a friendly neighbor or indeed any tolerant equilibrium of separate powers, either internal or international, could a doctrine thrive which viewed economic conflicts of society as insoluble by peaceful means. After establishment of Bolshevist regime, Marxist dogma, rendered even more truculent and intolerant by Lenin's interpretation, became a perfect vehicle for sense of insecurity with which Bolsheviks, even more than previous Russian rulers, were afflicted. In this dogma, with its basic altruism of purpose, they found justification for their instinctive fear of outside world, for the dictatorship without which they did not know how to rule, for cruelties they did not dare not to inflict, for sacrifices they felt bound to demand. In the name of Marxism they sacrificed every single ethical value in their methods and tactics. Today they cannot dispense with it. It is fig leaf of their moral and intellectual respectability. Without it they would stand before history, at best, as only the last of that long succession of cruel and wasteful Russian rulers who have relentlessly forced country on to ever new heights of military power in order to guarantee external security of their internally weak regimes. . . . Thus Soviet leaders are driven [by] necessities of their own past and present position to put forward a dogma which [apparent omission] outside world as evil, hostile and menacing, but as bearing within itself germs of creeping disease and destined to be wracked with growing internal convulsions until it is given final coup de grace by rising power of socialism and yields to new and better world. . . .

## PART 3: PROJECTION OF SOVIET OUTLOOK IN PRACTICAL POLICY ON OFFICIAL LEVEL

We have now seen nature and background of Soviet program. What may we expect by way of its practical implementation? . . .

On official plane we must look for following:

(a) Internal policy devoted to increasing in every way strength and prestige of Soviet state: intensive military-industrialization; maximum development of armed forces; great displays to impress outsiders; continued secretiveness about internal matters, designed to conceal weaknesses and to keep opponents in the dark.

(b) Wherever it is considered timely and promising, efforts will be made to advance official limits of Soviet power. . . .

(c) Russians will participate officially in international organizations where they see opportunity of extending Soviet power or of inhibiting or diluting power of others. . . .

(d) Toward colonial areas and backward or dependent peoples, Soviet policy . . . will be directed toward weakening of power and influence and contacts of advanced Western nations, on theory that insofar as this policy is successful, there will be created a vacuum which will favor Communist-Soviet penetration. . . .

(e) Russians will strive energetically to develop Soviet representation in, and official ties with, countries in which they sense strong possibilities of opposition to Western centers of power. This applies to such widely separated points as Germany, Argentina, Middle Eastern countries, etc.

(f) In international economic matters, Soviet policy will really be dominated by pursuit of autarchy[1] for Soviet Union and Soviet-dominated adjacent areas taken together. . . .

## PART 4: FOLLOWING MAY BE SAID AS TO WHAT WE MAY EXPECT BY WAY OF IMPLEMENTATION OF BASIC SOVIET POLICIES ON UNOFFICIAL, OR SUBTERRANEAN PLANE. . . .

(a) To undermine general political and strategic potential of major Western Powers. Efforts will be made in such countries to disrupt national self-confidence, to hamstring measures of national defense, to increase social and industrial unrest, to stimulate all forms of disunity. All persons with grievances, whether economic or racial, will be urged to seek redress not in mediation and compromise, but in defiant, violent struggle for destruction of other elements of society. Here poor will be set against rich, black against white, young against old, newcomers against established residents, etc. . . .

(c) Where individual governments stand in path of Soviet purposes pressure will be brought for their removal from office. . . .

(d) In foreign countries Communists will, as a rule, work toward destruction of all forms of personal independence — economic, political or moral. Their system can handle only individuals who have been brought into complete dependence on higher power. Thus, persons who are financially independent — such as individual businessmen, estate owners, successful farmers, artisans — and all those who exercise local leadership or have local prestige — such as popular local clergymen or political figures — are anathema.

(e) Everything possible will be done to set major Western Powers against each other. Anti-British talk will be plugged among Americans, anti-American talk among British. Continentals, including Germans, will be taught to abhor both Anglo-Saxon powers.[2] . . .

## PART 5: [PRACTICAL DEDUCTIONS FROM STANDPOINT OF US POLICY]

In summary, we have here a political force committed fanatically to the belief that with US there can be no permanent modus vivendi,[3] that it is desirable and necessary that the internal harmony of our society be disrupted, our traditional way of life be destroyed, the international authority

---

[1]Economic self-sufficiency as a national policy; getting along without goods from other countries.
[2]England and the United States.

[3]Latin for "manner of living"; hence, a temporary agreement in a dispute pending final settlement.

of our state be broken, if Soviet power is to be secure. . . . In addition, it has an elaborate and far-flung apparatus for exertion of its influence in other countries, an apparatus of amazing flexibility and versatility, managed by people whose experience and skill in underground methods are presumably without parallel in history. Finally, it is seemingly inaccessible to considerations of reality in its basic reactions. . . . This is admittedly not a pleasant picture. Problem of how to cope with this force [is] undoubtedly greatest task our diplomacy has ever faced and probably greatest it will ever have to face. . . . But I would like to record my conviction that problem is within our power to solve — and that without recourse to any general military conflict. And in support of this conviction there are certain observations of a more encouraging nature I should like to make:

(1) Soviet power, unlike that of Hitlerite Germany, is neither schematic[4] nor adventuristic. It does not work by fixed plans. It does not take unnecessary risks. Impervious to logic of reason, and it is highly sensitive to logic of force. For this reason it can easily withdraw — and usually does — when strong resistance is encountered at any point. Thus, if the adversary has sufficient force and makes clear his readiness to use it, he rarely has to do so. If situations are properly handled there need be no prestige-engaging showdowns.

(2) Gauged against Western world as a whole, Soviets are still by far the weaker force. Thus, their success will really depend on degree of cohesion, firmness and vigor which Western world can muster. . . .

(3) Success of Soviet system, as form of internal power, is not yet finally proven. . . .

(4) All Soviet propaganda beyond Soviet security sphere is basically negative and destructive.

It should therefore be relatively easy to combat it by any intelligent and really constructive program.

For these reasons I think we may approach calmly and with good heart problem of how to deal with Russia. As to how this approach should be made, I only wish to advance, by way of conclusion, following comments:

(1) Our first step must be to apprehend, and recognize for what it is, the nature of the movement with which we are dealing. We must study it with same courage, detachment, objectivity, and same determination not to be emotionally provoked or unseated by it, with which doctor studies unruly and unreasonable individual.

(2) We must see that our public is educated to realities of Russian situation. . . .

(3) Much depends on health and vigor of our own society. World communism is like malignant parasite which feeds only on diseased tissue. This is point at which domestic and foreign policies meet. Every courageous and incisive measure to solve internal problems of our own society, to improve self-confidence, discipline, morale and community spirit of our own people, is a diplomatic victory over Moscow worth a thousand diplomatic notes and joint communiqués. . . .

(4) We must formulate and put forward for other nations a much more positive and constructive picture of sort of world we would like to see than we have put forward in past. . . .

(5) Finally we must have courage and self-confidence to cling to our own methods and conceptions of human society. After all, the greatest danger that can befall us in coping with this problem of Soviet communism is that we shall allow ourselves to become like those with whom we are coping.

---

[4]In this context, having a definite outline or plan to follow.

# Cold War Origins: A Soviet Perspective
▼▼▼

## 111 ▼ *Nikolai Novikov,*
## *TELEGRAM, SEPTEMBER 27, 1946*

According to some scholars there is a Soviet version of the Long Telegram: a cable sent to Moscow from Washington in September 1946 by the recently appointed Soviet ambassador to the United States, Nikolai Novikov. Trained in the early 1930s at Leningrad State University in Middle Eastern economics and languages, Novikov abandoned plans for an academic career when he was drafted into the foreign service because of his knowledge of the Middle East. In 1941 he was named ambassador to Egypt, where he also served as liaison to the Yugoslav and Greek governments in exile, both of which were located in Cairo. Early in 1945 he was posted to Washington D.C., where he was named deputy chief of the Soviet mission; in April he became Soviet ambassador to the United States. He resigned from the foreign service in 1947 and returned to the Soviet Union, where he lived in obscurity. He published a memoir of his foreign service career in 1989.

We have little information about the background of Novikov's telegram, which was unknown to scholars until a Soviet official revealed it to a group of Soviet and U.S. historians attending a meeting on the origins of the Cold War in Washington in 1990. According to Novikov's memoir, while he and the Soviet foreign minister Vyacheslav Molotov (1890–1986) were attending the Paris foreign minsters' conference in August 1946, Molotov requested that he write an analysis of U.S. foreign policy goals. Also according to Novikov, Molotov examined an early outline of the document in Paris and made several suggestions about improvements. This information lends credence to the theory that Molotov, who favored a hard line against the West, wanted Novikov's report to present a dark and perhaps exaggerated picture of U.S. foreign policy goals to strengthen his hand against rivals who favored caution and compromise.

We know that Molotov read Novikov's completed cable. The passages underlined in the following excerpt were passages that Molotov himself underlined on the original document. What happened next is unclear. Did Molotov show the telegram to Stalin and other high-ranking officials? Did Novikov's telegram contribute to the atmosphere of confrontation building in 1946? The answer to both questions is probably "yes," but until historians gain access to Soviet archives, no one will know how important a role Novikov's telegram played in the Cold War's murky beginnings.

---

## QUESTIONS FOR ANALYSIS

1. What specific evidence does Novikov cite to prove his assertion that the goal of U.S. foreign policy is world domination?
2. In his view, how does the United States propose to achieve its goal?

3. What is his evaluation of U.S. strengths and weaknesses?
4. How does he view the prospects of Anglo-American cooperation? Is this something the Soviet Union should fear? Why or why not?
5. How does Novikov's analysis compare with Kennan's description in the *Long Telegram* (source 110) of the "Postwar Soviet Outlook, as Put Forward by Official Propaganda Machine"?
6. What insights does your answer to question 5 provide about the reasons Novikov's memorandum was written?

The enormous relative weight of the USSR in international affairs in general and in the European countries in particular, the independence of its foreign policy, and the economic and political assistance that it provides to neighboring countries, both allies and former enemies, has led to the growth of the political influence of the Soviet Union in these countries and to the further strengthening of democratic tendencies in them.

Such a situation in Eastern and Southeastern Europe cannot help but be regarded by the American imperialists as an obstacle in the path of the expansionist policy of the United States. . . .

One of the stages in the achievement of dominance over the world by the United States is its understanding with England concerning the partial division of the world on the basis of mutual concessions. The basic lines of the secret agreement between the United States and England regarding the division of the world consist, as shown by facts, in their agreement on the inclusion of Japan and China in the sphere of influence of the United States in the Far East, while the United States, for its part, has agreed not to hinder England either in resolving the Indian problem or in strengthening its influence in Siam and Indonesia. . . .

The American policy in China is striving for the complete economic and political submission of China to the control of American monopolistic capital. Following this policy, the American government does not shrink even from interference in the internal affairs of China. At the present time in China, there are more than 50,000 American soldiers. . . .

China is gradually being transformed into a bridgehead for the American armed forces. American air bases are located all over its territory. . . . The measures carried out in northern China by the American army show that it intends to stay there for a long time.

In Japan, despite the presence there of only a small contingent of American troops, control is in the hands of the Americans. . . .

Measures taken by the American occupational authorities in the area of domestic policy and intended to support reactionary classes and groups, which the United States plans to use in the struggle against the Soviet Union, also meet with a sympathetic attitude on the part of England. . . .

▾ ▾ ▾

Obvious indications of the U.S. effort to establish world dominance are also to be found in the increase in military potential in peacetime and in the establishment of a large number of naval and air bases both in the United States and beyond its borders.

In the summer of 1946, for the first time in the history of the country, Congress passed a law on the establishment of a peacetime army, not on a volunteer basis but on the basis of universal military service. The size of the army, which is supposed to amount to about one million persons as of July 1, 1947, was also increased significantly. The size of the navy at the conclusion of the war decreased quite insignificantly in comparison with war-time. At the present time, the American navy occupies first place in the world, leaving England's navy far behind, to say nothing of those of other countries.

Expenditures on the army and navy have risen colossally, amounting to 13 billion dollars according to the budget for 1946–47 (about 40 percent of the total budget of 36 million dollars). This is more than ten times greater than corresponding expenditures in the budget for 1938, which did not amount to even one billion dollars. . . .

The establishment of American bases on islands that are often 10,000 to 12,000 kilometers from the territory of the United States and are on the other side of the Atlantic and Pacific oceans clearly indicates the offensive nature of the strategic concepts of the commands of the U.S. army and navy. This interpretation is also confirmed by the fact that the American navy is intensively studying the naval approaches to the boundaries of Europe. For this purpose, American naval vessels in the course of 1946 visited the ports of Norway, Denmark, Sweden, Turkey, and Greece. In addition, the American navy is constantly operating in the Mediterranean Sea.

All of these facts show clearly that a decisive role in the realization of plans for world dominance by the United States is played by its armed forces.

▼ ▼ ▼

In recent years American capital has penetrated very intensively into the economy of the Near Eastern countries, in particular into the oil industry. At present there are American oil concessions in all of the Near Eastern countries that have oil deposits (Iraq, Bahrain, Kuwait, Egypt, and Saudi Arabia). American capital, which made its first appearance in the oil industry of the Near East only in 1927, now controls about 42 percent of all proven reserves in the Near East, excluding Iran. . . .

In expanding in the Near East, American capital has English capital as its greatest and most stubborn competitor. The fierce competition between them is the chief factor preventing England and the United States from reaching an understanding on the division of spheres of influence in the Near East, a division that can occur only at the expense of direct British interests in this region. . . .

The irregular nature of relations between England and the United States in the Near East is manifested in part also in the great activity of the American naval fleet in the eastern part of the Mediterranean Sea. Such activity cannot help but be in conflict with the basic interests of the British Empire. These actions on the part of the U.S. fleet undoubtedly are also linked with American oil and other economic interests in the Near East. . . .

. . . The strengthening of U.S. positions in the Near East and the establishment of conditions for basing the American navy at one or more points on the Mediterranean Sea will therefore signify the emergence of a new threat to the security of the southern regions of the Soviet Union.

The ruling circles of the United States obviously have a sympathetic attitude toward the idea of a military alliance with England, but at the present time the matter has not yet culminated in an official alliance. Churchill's speech in Fulton[1] calling for the conclusion of an Anglo-American military alliance for the purpose of establishing joint domination over the world was therefore not supported officially by Truman or Byrnes,[2] although Truman by his presence [during the "Iron Curtain" speech] did indirectly sanction Churchill's appeal.

Even if the United States does not go so far as to conclude a military alliance with England just now, in practice they still maintain very close contact on military questions. The combined Anglo-American headquarters in Washington continues to exist, despite the fact that over a year has passed since the end of the war. . . .

▼ ▼ ▼

---

[1]The reference is to Winston Churchill's Iron Curtain Speech, delivered at Westminster College in Fulton, Missouri, in March 1946.

[2]James Byrnes (1879–1972), secretary of state from 1945 to 1947.

One of the most important elements in the general policy of the United States, which is directed toward limiting the international role of the USSR in the postwar world, is the policy with regard to Germany. In Germany, the United States is taking measures to strengthen reactionary forces for the purpose of opposing democratic reconstruction. Furthermore, it displays special insistence on accompanying this policy with completely inadequate measures for the demilitarization of Germany. . . . Instead, the United States is considering the possibility of terminating the Allied occupation of German territory before the main tasks of the occupation — the demilitarization and democratization of Germany — have been implemented. This would create the prerequisites for the revival of an imperialist Germany, which the United States plans to use in a future war on its side. One cannot help seeing that such a policy has a clearly outlined anti-Soviet edge and constitutes a serious danger to the cause of peace.

The numerous and extremely hostile statements by American government, political, and military figures with regard to the Soviet Union and its foreign policy are very characteristic of the current relationship between the ruling circles of the United States and the USSR. These statements are echoed in an even more unrestrained tone by the overwhelming majority of the American press organs. Talk about a "third war," meaning a war against the Soviet Union, and even a direct call for this war — with the threat of using the atomic bomb — such is the content of the statements on relations with the Soviet Union by reactionaries at public meetings and in the press. . . .

The basic goal of this anti-Soviet campaign of American "public opinion" is to exert political pressure on the Soviet Union and compel it to make concessions. Another, no less important goal of the campaign is the attempt to create an atmosphere of war psychosis among the masses, who are weary of war, thus making it easier for the U.S. government to carry out measures for the maintenance of high military potential. . . .

Of course, all of these measures for maintaining a high military potential are not goals in themselves. They are only intended to prepare the conditions for winning world supremacy in a new war, the date for which, to be sure, cannot be determined now by anyone, but which is contemplated by the most bellicose circles of American imperialism.

Careful note should be taken of the fact that the preparation by the United States for a future war is being conducted with the prospect of war against the Soviet Union, which in the eyes of American imperialists is the main obstacle in the path of the United States to world domination. This is indicated by facts such as the tactical training of the American army for war with the Soviet Union as the future opponent, the siting of American strategic bases in regions from which it is possible to launch strikes on Soviet territory, intensified training and strengthening of Arctic regions as close approaches to the USSR, and attempts to prepare Germany and Japan to use those countries in a war against the USSR.

# Great Britain Lets Go of India

▼▼▼

## 112 ▼ DEBATE IN THE HOUSE OF COMMONS, MARCH 1947

A turning point in the dismantling of Europe's Asian and African empires took place when the Indian people gained independence from Great Britain and the new states of India and Pakistan were created in August 1947. After the greatest imperial power released its hold on its largest colony — the "jewel in the crown" of its empire — nationalist leaders throughout Asia and Africa demanded equal treatment, and European politicians found it more difficult to justify their continued colonial rule.

British and Indian leaders had debated the timing and framework of Indian independence for decades, but World War II brought the issue to a head. Many Indians, still embittered by the meager benefits they had received for their sacrifices in World War I, showed little enthusiasm for the British cause in World War II, especially after the British viceroy announced that India was at war with Germany in September 1939 without even consulting Indian leaders. In 1942, after Japan's lightning conquest of Southeast Asia, the British government sent Sir Stafford Cripps to Delhi to offer India dominion status after the war if India would support the war against Japan. Negotiations broke down, however, leading Gandhi to launch the "Quit India" movement, his last nationwide passive resistance campaign against British rule. Anti-British feeling intensified in 1943 when a disastrous famine took between one million and three million lives, and the pro-Japanese Indian National Army was organized by Subhas Bose and declared war on Great Britain.

A shift in postwar British politics also affected India's future. The 1945 elections initiated six years of rule by the Labour Party, which had less enthusiasm for the idea of empire than the Conservatives. In the face of mounting restiveness in India, Prime Minister Clement Attlee dispatched a three-person cabinet mission to India in early 1946 charged with preserving Indian unity in the face of Hindu-Muslim enmity and arranging for India's independence as soon as possible. Although the Hindus and Muslims could not reconcile their differences, on February 20, 1947, the Labour government went ahead and announced British rule would end in India no later than June 1948.

This led to an emotional two-day debate in Parliament in which Churchill's Conservatives and some Liberals argued that independence should be delayed. Labour had a strong majority, however, and in March 1947 Parliament approved its plan. At midnight on August 14–15, 1947, predominantly Hindu India and predominantly Muslim Pakistan became independent states.

The following excerpts are from the parliamentary debates of March 4 and 5, 1947. All the speakers are opposing a proposal of Sir John Anderson, a Liberal representing the Scottish universities, that Great Britain should promise independence by June 1948 but withdraw the offer and require further negotiations if a suitable Hindu-Muslim agreement could not be achieved.

---

## QUESTIONS FOR ANALYSIS

1. How did the members of Parliament disagree about the benefits and harm of British colonial rule in India?
2. Some speakers who believed British colonialism had benefited India still supported independence. Why?
3. The critics of British rule in India supported immediate independence. What was their line of argument?
4. According to the speakers, what military and economic realities make it impractical to continue British rule in India?
5. How do the speakers view developments in India as part of broader historical trends?
6. Most of the speakers were members of the Labour Party and thus sympathetic to socialism. What examples of socialist perspectives can you find in their speeches?

Mr. Clement Davies[1] (Montgomery) It is an old adage now, that "the old order changeth, yielding place to new," but there has been a more rapid change from the old to the new in our time than ever before. We have witnessed great changes in each one of the five Continents, and for many of those changes this country and its people have been directly or indirectly responsible. . . . In all the lands where the British flag flies, we have taught the peoples the rule of law and the value of justice impartially administered. We have extended knowledge, and tried to inculcate understanding and toleration.

Our declared objects were twofold — first, the betterment of the conditions of the people and the improvement of their standard of life; and, second, to teach them the ways of good administration and gradually train them to undertake responsibility so that one day we could hand over to them the full burden of their own self-government. Our teachings and our methods have had widespread effect, and we should rejoice that so many peoples in the world today are awake,

and aware of their own individualities, and have a desire to express their own personalities and their traditions, and to live their own mode of life. . . . Our association with India during two centuries has been, on the whole — with mistakes, as we will admit — an honorable one. So far as we were able we brought peace to this great sub-continent; we have introduced not only a system of law and order, but also a system of administration of justice, fair and impartial, which has won their respect. . . . We have tried to inculcate into them the feeling that although they are composed of different races, with different languages, customs, and religions, they are really part of one great people of India.

The standard of life, pathetically low as it is, has improved so that during the last 30 years there has been an increase in the population of 100 million and they now number 400 million people. We have brought to them schools, universities, and teachers, and we have not only introduced the Indians into the Civil Service but have gradually handed over to them, in the Prov-

---

[1] A London lawyer (1884–1962) who was a Liberal member of Parliament from 1929 until the time of his death.

inces and even in the Central Government, the administration and government of their own land and their own people. . . . Then in 1946, there was the offer of complete independence, with the right again, if they so chose, of contracting in and coming back within the British Commonwealth of Nations.[2]

I agree that these offers were made subject to the condition that the Indian peoples themselves would co-operate to form a Central Government and draw up not only their own Constitution, but the method of framing it. Unfortunately, the leaders of the two main parties in India have failed to agree upon the formation of even a Constituent Assembly, and have failed, therefore, to agree upon a form of Constitution. . . .

What are the possible courses that could be pursued? . . . The first of the courses would be to restore power into our own hands so that we might not only have the responsibility but the full means of exercising that responsibility. I believe that that is not only impossible but unthinkable at this present stage. . . . Secondly, can we continue, as we do at present, to wait until an agreement is reached for the formation of a Central Government with a full Constitution, capable of acting on behalf of the whole of India? The present state of affairs there and the deterioration which has already set in — and which has worsened — have shown us that we cannot long continue on that course.

The third course is the step taken by His Majesty's Government — the declaration made by the Government that we cannot and do not intend in the slightest degree to go back upon our word, that we do not intend to damp the hopes of the Indian peoples but rather to raise them, and that we cannot possibly go on indefinitely as we have been going on during these past months; that not only shall they have the power they now really possess but after June 1948, the full responsibility for government of their own peoples in India. . . .

MR. SORENSEN[3] (LEYTON, WEST) I have considerable sympathy with the hon. and gallant Member for Ayr Burghs (Sir T. Moore),[4] because, politically, he has been dead for some time and does not know it. His ideas were extraordinarily reminiscent of 50 years ago, and I do not propose, therefore, to deal with so unpleasant and decadent a subject. When he drew attention to the service we have rendered to India — and we have undoubtedly rendered service — he overlooked the fact that India has had an existence extending for some thousands of years before the British occupation, and that during that period she managed to run schools, establish a chain of rest houses, preserve an economy, and reach a high level of civilization, when the inhabitants of these islands were in a condition of barbarism and savagery. One has only to discuss such matters with a few representative Indians to realize that they can draw up a fairly powerful indictment of the evil we have taken to India as well as the good. . . .

Whatever may have been the origin of the various problems in India, or the degree of culpability which may be attached to this or that party or person, a situation now confronts us which demands decision. . . . That is why, in my estimation, the Government are perfectly right to fix a date for the transference of power. . . . Responsibility is ultimately an Indian matter. Acute problems have existed in India for centuries, and they have not been solved under our domination. Untouchability, the appalling subjugation of women, the division of the castes, the incipi-

---

[2]The British Commonwealth of Nations was founded by Parliament in 1931 through the Statute of Westminster. It is a free association of nations comprised of Great Britain and a number of its former dependencies which have chosen to maintain ties of friendship and practical cooperation and acknowledge the British monarch as symbolic head of their association. Since 1946 it has been known as the Commonwealth of Nations.

[3]Reginald Sorensen (1884–1971) was a clergyman who served in Parliament as a member of the Labour Party from 1929 to 1931 and from 1939 to 1954.
[4]Lieutenant-Colonel Thomas Moore (1888–1971) was a Conservative member of Parliament from 1929 to 1962. He had just spoken against the government's plan for Indian independence.

ent or actual conflict between Muslim and Hindu — all those and many others exist.

I do not forget what is to me the most terrible of all India's problems, the appalling poverty. It has not been solved by us, although we have had our opportunity. On the contrary, in some respects we have increased that problem, because, despite the contributions that we have made to India's welfare, we have taken a great deal of wealth from India in order that we ourselves might enjoy a relatively higher standard of life. Can it be denied that we have benefited in the past substantially by the ignorant, sweated labor of the Indian people? We have not solved those social problems. The Indians may not solve them either. There are many problems that the Western world cannot solve, but at least, those problems are India's responsibility. Indians are more likely, because they are intimate with their own problems, to know how to find their way through those labyrinths than we, who are, to the Indian but aliens and foreigners.

Here I submit a point which surely will receive the endorsement of most hon. Members of this House. It is that even a benevolent autocracy can be no substitute for democracy and liberty. . . .

I would therefore put two points to the House tonight. Are we really asked by hon. Members on the other side to engage in a gamble, first by continuing as we are and trying to control India indefinitely, with the probability that we should not succeed and that all over India there would be rebellion, chaos, and breakdown? Secondly, are we to try to reconquer India and in doing so, to impose upon ourselves an economic burden which we could not possibly afford? How many men would be required to keep India quiet if the great majority of the Indians were determined to defy our power? I guarantee that the number would not be fewer than a million men, with all

the necessary resources and munitions of war. Are we to do this at a time when we are crying out for manpower in this country, when in the mines, the textile industry, and elsewhere we want every man we can possibly secure? There are already 1,500,000 men under arms. To talk about facing the possibility of governing and policing India and keeping India under proper supervision out of our own resources is not only nonsense, but would provide the last straw that breaks the camel's back. . . .

FLIGHT-LIEUTENANT CRAWLEY[5] (BUCKINGHAM) Right hon. and hon. Members opposite, who envisage our staying in India, must have some idea of what type of rule we should maintain. A fact about the Indian services which they seem to ignore is that they are largely Indianized. Can they really expect the Services, Indianized to the extent of 80 or 90 percent, to carry out their policy any longer? Is it not true that in any situation that is likely to arise in India now, if the British remain without a definite date being given for withdrawal, every single Indian member of the Services, will, in the mind of all politically conscious Indians become a political collaborator? We have seen that in Palestine where Arab hates Arab and Jew hates Jew if they think they are collaborating with the British.[6] How could we get the Indianized part of the Services to carry out a policy which, in the view of all political Indians, is anti-Indian? The only conceivable way in which we could stay even for seven years in India would be by instituting a type of rule which we in this country abhor more than any other — a purely dictatorial rule based upon all the things we detest most, such as an informative police, not for an emergency measure, but for a long period and imprisonment without trial. . . .

---

[5] Aidan Crawley (1908–1992) was an educator and journalist who served in the Royal Air Force during World War II. He was a Labour member of Parliament from 1945 to 1951.

[6] The British were attempting to extricate themselves from Palestine, which they had received as a mandate after World War I and was the scene of bitter Arab-Jewish rivalry.

MR. HAROLD DAVIES[7] (LEEK) . . . I believe that India is the pivot of the Pacific Ocean area. All the peoples of Asia are on the move. Can we in this House, by wishful thinking, sweep aside this natural desire for independence, freedom, and nationalism that has grown in Asia from Karachi to Peking,[8] from Karachi to Indonesia and Indo-China? That is all part of that movement, and we must recognize it. I am not a Utopian. I know that the changeover will not be easy. But there is no hon. Member opposite who has given any concrete, practical alternative to the decision, which has been made by my right hon. Friends. What alternative can we give?

This little old country is tottering and wounded as a result of the wars inherent in the capitalist system. Can we, today, carry out vast commitments from one end of the world to another? Is it not time that we said to those for whom we have spoken so long, "The time has come when you shall have your independence. That time has come; the moment is here"? I should like to recall what Macaulay[9] said:

> Many politicians of our times are in the habit of laying it down as a self-evident proposition, that no people ought to be free until they are fit to use their freedom. This maxim is worthy of the fool in the old story who resolved not to go into the water until he had learned to swim.

India must learn now to build up democracy. . . .

---

[7]Harold Davies (1904–1984) was an author and educator who served in Parliament as a member of the Labour Party from 1959 to 1964.
[8]Karachi, a port city on the Arabian Sea, was soon to become Pakistan's first capital city. *Peking* is a variant spelling of *Beijing*.
[9]Thomas B. Macaulay (1800–1859) was an English essayist, historian, and statesman.

▼▼▼

# New Nations and Their Challenges

As one colony after another achieved independence in the 1950s and 1960s, euphoria swept across Africa and Asia. All the indignities of colonialism and all the ways it had branded colonial peoples with the mark of inferiority could now be forgotten. With a unity of purpose forged in the struggle against colonial rule and with constitutions guaranteeing parliamentary government and basic freedoms, leaders and common people alike were ready to show the world they could govern themselves effectively. Their economic outlook was no less optimistic. With the heavy hand of the colonial master lifted from their economies, they anticipated rapid economic development and the alleviation of poverty.

A few new states have achieved their dreams. For the most part, however, they have experienced more difficulties and disappointments than anyone could have imagined at the time of independence. Many were nations in name only, with boundaries drawn by European administrators during the colonial era without regard for cultural affinities, ethnic groupings, religious traditions, and economic viability. After independence, shallow national loyalties were undermined by regionalism and ethnic conflict, and soon civil wars and military coups began to take their toll on democratic governments. The norm became one-party dictatorships, which at their best were controlled by nationalist leaders with the interests of their countrymen at heart, but at their worst were dominated by venal, short-sighted, even genocidal leaders who enriched themselves and their henchmen while their nation's economies crumbled. In some cases, lawlessness, random violence, and warlordism overwhelmed even the dictators; in Mozambique in the 1980s and Liberia and Somalia in the 1990s central governments virtually disappeared. The dismal political record of most former colonies makes India's political achievement particularly remarkable. More than fifty years after independence, it remains the world's most populous constitutional democracy despite religious tensions and formidable social problems.

The economic records of the new states differ widely, but in only a few cases can it be said that the general population's standard of living has improved since independence. Taiwan and South Korea, former colonies of Japan, and Singapore, Malaysia, and Hong Kong, former colonies of Great Britain, have become major industrial, commercial, and financial powers. But the "Asian Tigers'" spectacular success has been unique. In states such as India agricultural and industrial output has grown impressively, but population has grown even faster. In 1941 India's population was 319 million; in 1998 it was 980 million, a figure that does not include Pakistan's 132 million or Bangladesh's 126 million. As a result, per capita income in 1998 was only $430, and job creation and government support for schools and health care have failed to keep pace with the country's demographic explosion. Oil-rich states in the Persian Gulf, the Middle East, and parts of Africa have generated huge revenues from oil sales but have failed to develop the balanced economies needed to improve their people's standard of living or provide a foundation for lasting economic growth.

Postcolonial sub-Saharan Africa has experienced the worst economic problems. The average annual growth of its per capita gross national product since 1965 has only been 0.2 percent, compared with 1.8 percent growth for Latin America, the Middle East, and North Africa, 1.9 percent for South Asia, and 5.3 percent for East Asia. Per capita food production in the past three decades has declined. Able to feed itself in the 1950s, sub-Saharan Africa is now dependent on large-scale food imports and vulnerable to catastrophic famines. Declining economic prospects in the countryside have forced millions into cities that are ill equipped to provide jobs, housing, schools, electricity, clean water, and health care. Poverty breeds lawlessness, which in a vicious cycle thwarts economic development.

Pessimists see no immediate solution to the problems of the new states of Africa and South and Southeast Asia, and view them as a continuing, growing source of environmental degradation, disease, lawlessness, and suffering. Optimists point to declining rates of population growth and other hopeful signs: the end of civil wars in Angola and Mozambique; economic growth in Southeast Asia; signs of economic stabilization in Ghana, Ethiopia, the Ivory Coast, and Uganda; and successful democratic elections in a dozen African countries during the 1990s. Which of these views proves correct will go far in determining the contours of humanity's experience in the twenty-first century.

# The Challenge of Ethnic Tensions
▼▼▼

## 113 ▼ *C. Odumegwu Ojukwu,*
## *SPEECHES AND WRITINGS*

Problems confronting the newly independent states of sub-Saharan Africa have been daunting: poor communications, low literacy levels, resistance of peasant societies to taxation by distant governments, underdeveloped economies, arbitrary national boundaries, and unrealistically high expectations. Overshadowing everything else, however, has been the persistence of strong local and ethnic loyalties that have led most people to judge national policies by the standard of how they benefit one's region or tribe. In Zaire, rebellion and civil war broke out in January 1960, literally within hours of the formal end of Belgian rule. Newly independent Nigeria held together longer, but it, too, fell victim to civil war in 1967 when the eastern province of Biafra declared its independence.

When Nigeria became independent in 1960, its constitution was the product of protracted deliberations among British administrators and representatives of the colony's major ethnic groups, the Hausa-Fulani, the Yoruba, and the Igbo. It established a central government with a prime minister and legislature and three provinces with extensive powers: the Northern Region, dominated by the Hausa-Fulani; the Western Region, dominated by the Yoruba; and the Eastern Region, dominated the Igbo. In 1966 army officers, mostly Igbos, denouncing corruption and the government's failure to address mounting economic problems, led a coup d'état that created a strong centralized national government at the expense of Nigeria's provinces. This angered the Hausa-Fulani and the Yoruba, who feared that the more highly educated and economically sophisticated Igbo would dominate the new regime. The result was another coup led by Yakuba Gowon, an army officer from the Northern Region, and massacres of Igbo living outside the Eastern Province. The Eastern Province refused to recognize the new government and declared itself the independent Republic of Biafra in May 1967.

The leader of the Biafran independence movement was Chukwuemeka Odumegwu Ojukwu, who was born into a wealthy Igbo family and was educated in England, where he received his master's degree in history from Oxford University. He rose through the ranks of the Nigerian army and in 1967 became head of state and commander-in-chief of newly independent Biafra. Immediately attacked by Nigerian forces, which received aid from both Great Britain and the Soviet Union, Biafra held out until 1970, when Ojukwu capitulated and fled to Guinea. Yakuba Gowon now ruled a reunited Nigeria, which he divided into twelve provinces rather than three to defuse ethnic conflict. Free elections were held in 1999, but otherwise, except for the years between 1979 and 1983, Nigeria has been ruled by military dictators since Biafra's defeat.

The following excerpts are from speeches and writings of General Ojukwu from 1966 to 1969. They reveal his views about Nigerian politics and the meaning of the Biafran independence movement.

## QUESTIONS FOR ANALYSIS

1. In Ojukwu's opinion, how did the British and the Northern Nigerians contribute to the problems of the Nigerian state?
2. What characteristics define the people of Eastern Nigeria, in Ojukwu's view?
3. According to Ojukwu, what have been the major flaws of the Nigerian government since independence? How will the new state of Biafra avoid these shortcomings?
4. What specific reasons does Ojukwu provide for the decision of Eastern Nigerians to secede?
5. What does Ojukwu see as the broader significance of the Biafran independence movement?

## THE BACKGROUND OF A CRISIS

The constitutional arrangements of Nigeria, as imposed upon the people by the erstwhile British rulers, were nothing but an implicit acceptance of the fact that there was no basis for Nigerian unity.

It was Britain, first, that amalgamated the country in 1914, unwilling as the people of the North were.[1] It was Britain that forced a federation of Nigeria, even when the people of the North objected to it very strongly. It was Britain, while keeping Nigeria together, that made it impossible for the people to know themselves and get close to each other, by maintaining an apartheid policy in Northern Nigeria which herded all Southerners into little reserves, barring them from Northern Nigerian schools, and maintaining different systems of justice in a country they claimed to be one.[2]

It was Britain, for her economic interest, that put the various nations in Nigeria side by side and called it a federation, so as to have a large market. . . .

On October 1, 1960, independence was granted to the people of Nigeria in a form of "federation," based on artificially made units. The

Nigerian Constitution installed the North in perpetual dominance over Nigeria. . . . Thus were sown, by design or by default, the seeds of factionalism and hate, of struggle for power at the center, and of the worst types of political chicanery and abuse of power. One of two situations was bound to result from that arrangement: either perpetual domination of the rest of the country by the North, not by consent but by force and fraud, or a dissolution of the federation bond. National independence was followed by successive crises, each leading to near-disintegration of the country. . . .

Nigeria in the end came to be run by compromises made and broken between the Northerners and consenting Southern politicians. This led to interminable violent crises, to corruption and nepotism, and to the arbitrary use of power.

The financial institutions and statutory corporations have been completely misused for the self-aggrandizement of a number of adventurers in positions of power and influence. Under the system, mediocrities were transplanted overnight from situations of obscurity into positions of affluence and corrupt power.

Key projects in the National Development Plan were not pursued with necessary vigor. In-

---

[1] The provinces of Northern and Southern Nigeria were brought under a common administration by Sir Frederick Lugard, the governor-general of Nigeria between 1912 and 1919.

[2] Many Eastern Nigerians had moved to other parts of the country, mainly to pursue business opportunities. Many believed they were treated as second-class citizens, especially in the northern Muslim parts of Nigeria.

stead of these, palaces were constructed for the indulgence of ministers and other holders of public offices — men supposed to serve the interest of the common man. Expensive fleets of flamboyant and luxurious cars were purchased. Taxpayers' money was wasted on unnecessary foreign travel by ministers, each competing with the other only in their unbridled excesses.

This has disrupted the economy, depressed the standard of living of the toiling masses, spiraled prices, and made the rich richer and the poor poorer. Internal squabbles for parochial and clannish patronage took the place of purposeful coordinated service of the people. Land, the basic heritage of the people, was converted into the private estates of rapacious individuals who, thus trampling on the rights of the people, violated their sacred trust under this system. The public service was being increasingly demoralized. Nepotism became rife. Tribalism became the order of the day. In appointments and promotions mere lip service was paid to honesty and hard work.

Under the system, efficiency inevitably declined. All this led inevitably to the complete loss of moral and political authority by the former regime. . . .

Those who were supposed to be our servants became our masters, then our owners. This was not enough. They even strove to become our gods. . . .

## GRIEVANCES OF THE EASTERN NIGERIANS

In the old Federation some of you here will remember quite vividly what the contribution of the people from this area, now known as Biafra, was to the betterment of the areas in which we chose to reside and believed was our country. Socially we gave our best in Nigeria. Politically,

we led the struggle for independence and sustained it. Economically, the hope of Nigeria was embedded deeply in this area and we contributed everything for the common good of Nigeria.

Our people moved from this area to all parts of the old Federation, and particularly to Northern Nigeria. Where there was darkness we gave them light! In Northern Nigeria, where they had no shelter we gave them houses. Where they were sick, as indeed most Northerners are, we brought them health. Where there was backwardness we brought progress. And where there was ignorance we brought them education. As a result of all this, we became people marked out in the various communities in which we lived.

Initially we were marked out as people who were progressive. Next, as people who were successful. Finally as people who should be the object of jealousy — people who were to be hated, and this hatred arose as a result of our success. . . . Nigerians hate us simply because where they failed, the Biafran succeeded. . . . We were relegated to the position of second-class citizens and later to slavery — yes, slavery — because as we worked our masters enjoyed the fruits of our labor.

We reached a stage where the people from this part were fast losing their identity. They hid away the fact that they came from this area. . . .

How many of you looked in dismay at our own sons slowly shaving off their hair and putting on Northern Nigerian robes and passing as Northerners? Some of our senior men in public office considered very seriously whether to go to Mecca[3] or not even though they were not Muslims. It became shameful to be an Eastern Nigerian! Those of you who lived in Lagos[4] would probably remember that if you wanted to be able to ride over the law with impunity, all you had to do was to put on the Northern Nigerian gown and pretend to be a Northerner. . . . You all remember that if a Northern Nigerian ran into your

---

[3]Pilgrimage to Mecca, the home of the prophet Muhammad on the Arabian Peninsula, was a religious act to be performed if possible once in one's life by all Muslims.

[4]Nigeria's capital city.

car and damaged it the police would release the Northerner who was at fault and arrest you whose car was damaged by the careless Northerner. This was the state of affairs in the old Nigeria.

The Northern attitude is the attitude of horse and rider. If you look at the map, this becomes very clear. We were carrying the North physically, economically, and in every other way. For all that we received no thanks. They only got furious if we did not travel fast enough. Then they would kick. But, for every mule there comes a time when it bucks and says, "No, I will carry no more." We have bucked. We will carry Northern Nigeria no more!

## THE NEW BIAFRAN SOCIETY

Born out of the gruesome murders and vandalism of yesterday, Biafra has come to stay as a historical reality. We believe that the future we face and our battle for survival cannot be won by bullets alone, but by brainpower, modern skills, and the determination to live and succeed. . . .

Nepotism and tribalism are twin evils. I believe that these can be avoided if we set about making sure that every appointment in our society is based on one and only one criterion — merit. We should ensure that this term "merit" is no mumbo-jumbo. It should be something that is obvious for everyone to see: that is, when you have given somebody a job, the reason for giving that job to that person in preference to others must be generally clear. There must be an avenue for our people to find out, if they want, the reason why this man got the job as opposed to that other man. If they do not have that avenue, we go back to the same problem.

Tribalism is, perhaps, more deeply rooted. . . . When I first came to this area as the military governor, one of the first things I did was to erase tribe from all public documents. We are all Biafrans. "Where do you come from?" you are asked, and the answer is simple: "I come from Biafra." The government must not emphasize tribal origin if it is trying to stamp out tribalism. . . .

Every effort should be made by future governments to educate our people away from tribalism. I would like to see movement of people across tribal frontiers. The government should encourage people to move from their own areas to be educated elsewhere. Yes, I would even go further to support government measures to encourage intertribal marriages. . . . It is only a gesture, but if the government really believes that tribalism could be wiped out, something like a bounty should be given to that young man who marries across tribe, to show that the government appreciates what he has done. Incidentally, it will not be done in retrospect! — the bounty, I mean. . . .

I see a new breed of men and women, with new moral and spiritual values, building a new society — a renascent and strong Biafra.

I see the realization of all our cherished dreams and aspirations in a revolution which will not only guarantee our basic freedoms but usher in an era of equal opportunity and prosperity for all.

I see the evolution of a new democracy in Biafra as we advance as partners in our country's onward march to her destiny.

When I look into the future, I see Biafra transformed into a fully industrialized nation, wastelands and slums giving way to throbbing industrial centers and cities.

I see towns replanned and relocated in harmony with their surroundings.

I see agriculture mechanized by science and technology, which have already made their mark in the present war.

I see a Republic knit with arteries of roads and highways; a nation of free men and women dedicated to the noble attributes of justice and liberty for which our youth have shed their blood; a people with an art and literature rich and unrivaled.

I am sure all Biafrans share these hopes for our country's future and destiny. . . . We are building a society which will destroy the myth that the black man cannot organize his own society.

We are involved in an indigenous revolution, not borrowed from Mao Zedong or from Whitehall[5] or the White House. We are taking our rightful place in the world as human beings. . . . The black man cannot progress until he can point at a progressive black society. Until a society, a virile society entirely black, is established, the black man, whether he is in America, whether he is in Africa, will never be able to take his place side by side with the white man. We have the unique opportunity today of breaking our chains.

If we fail, the white man, who has been so surprised by our movement, the white man, who has entirely miscalculated every facet of this struggle, will have garnered a new range of knowledge about the potential of the black man and prepared himself to combat us should we ever again rear our ugly head. We owe it, therefore, to Africa not to fail. Africa needs a Biafra. Biafra is the breaking of the chains. . . .

---

[5]The thoroughfare in London where the major offices of the British government are located.

# The Challenge of Religious Conflict
▼▼▼

## 114 ▼ *Girilal Jain, EDITORIALS*

Throughout much of the twentieth century it would not have been unreasonable to conclude that religion was a dying force among the world's peoples. In communist states, avowedly atheist regimes in the Soviet Union, China, and elsewhere sought to obliterate religious belief and practice altogether; in the West, established churches experienced declining membership and attendance; throughout much of the Muslim world and in India, governments embraced aggressively secularist policies as part of their drive to modernize their economies, educational systems, and cultures.

Thus when the people of Iran in 1979 rose up in revolt against the Western-oriented, secularist government of Shah Muhammad Reza and instituted an Islamic republic guided by Muslim values and laws, many considered it an aberration or a sign of some sort of defect within Islam. By the 1990s, however, it was clear that Iran's Islamic revolution was no aberration. Instead it was an indication of religion's continuing vitality and a foreshadowing of its growing importance as a politcal force in many late-twentieth-century states.

The conviction that religious values and teachings should shape, regulate, and inspire all aspects of public and private life — often referred to as *religious fundamentalism* — has been evident in every major faith and in states at every level of economic development. The "religious right" in the United States has flexed its political muscle at the local, state, and national levels throughout the 1980s and 1990s; conservative religious Jews have become a powerful force in Israeli politics; church leaders, Catholic and Lutheran, played a significant role in the breakup of communism in Eastern Europe. But religious fundamentalism has been strongest in former colonial states such as India, where the assertion of traditional religious values has provided a way to affirm cultural identity and independence from foreign, Western-inspired values and ideologies.

Independent India has never been free of religious tensions. Even after Muslims were given their own independent state of Pakistan in 1947, religious pluralism characterized India's population. Today it is composed of approximately 83 percent Hindus, 11 percent Muslims, 2.6 percent Christians, slightly over 1 percent Sikhs, and smaller numbers of Jains, Parsis, and Buddhists. None of these groups has been completely satisfied with India's constitution, which procalimed India a secular state that would show no partiality toward any religious group. Many Hindus believe that the government has bent over backward to protect Muslims and Sikhs, whereas Muslims and Sikhs are convinced that the government has pandered to the demands of Hindus. In the early 1980s religious tensions intensified as Muslims began to proselytize successfully among low-caste Hindus in southern India, Sikhs agitated for an independent Punjab, and Hindus organized their own political party, the *Bharatiya Janata (Indian People's) Party,* or *BJP,* whose goal was the "Hinduization" of India. Founded in 1982, BJP representation in the Indian Parliament rose from 2 in 1984 to 185 in 1996 — 50 more than the Congress Party, which had ruled India in all but four years since independence. In recent national elections the BJP has become India's largest political party, but the short-lived coalition governments it has pieced together have been weak and divided.

An important spokesman for Hindu nationalism and the BJP before his death in 1993 was Girilal Jain, a prominent journalist who had been editor-in-chief of the New Delhi *Times of India* between 1978 and 1988. Born into a poor rural family in 1922 and educated at Delhi University, Jain was jailed by the British during the 1942 Quit India campaign. During the 1980s he was drawn to Hindu nationalism and the BJP. He wrote the following editorials in 1990, when Hindu-Muslim tensions were peaking over the issue of a sixteenth-century mosque built in the city of Ayodhya at the site of a Hindu temple believed to be the birthplace of the Hindu god-king, Ram. Hindus demanded the destruction of the mosque, which was no longer used, so a temple in honor of Ram could be built. In December 1992, after Hindus stormed the mosque and destroyed it, Hindu-Muslim violence took the lives of thousands. The Indian government, with its commitment to religious pluralism and democracy, survived this crisis, but so too did the religious hatreds that caused it.

---

## QUESTIONS FOR ANALYSIS

1. What are the reasons for Jain's disenchantment with India's government?
2. What does Jain mean when he says that the issues that concern the BJP have to do with "civilization," not religion?
3. How does Jain define "the West"? How does he view the West's role in Indian history?
4. Why, according to Jain, is the controversy over the Ayodhya mosque so significant for India's future?

5. According to Jain, why have the Muslims been satisfied to go along with the secularist policies of the Indian state?
6. What is Jain's vision of India's future?

A specter haunts dominant sections of India's political and intellectual elites — the specter of a growing Hindu self-awareness and self-assertion. Till recently these elites had used the bogey of Hindu "communalism"[1] and revivalism as a convenient device to keep themselves in power and to "legitimize" their slavish imitation of the West. Unfortunately for them, the ghost has now materialized.

Millions of Hindus have stood up. It will not be easy to trick them back into acquiescing in an order which has been characterized not so much by its "appeasement of Muslims" as by its alienness, rootlessness and contempt for the land's unique cultural past. Secularism, a euphemism for irreligion and repudiation of the Hindu ethos, and socialism, a euphemism for denigration and humiliation of the business community to the benefit of ever expanding rapacious bureaucracy, . . . have been major planks of this order. Both have lost much of their old glitter and, therefore, capacity to dazzle and mislead.

By the same token, re-Hinduization of the country's political domain has begun. On a surface view, it may be a sheer "accident" that the battle between aroused Hindus and the imitation Indian state, neutral to the restoration of the country's ancient civilization on its own oft-repeated admission, has been joined on the question of the Ram Janambhoomi temple in Ram's city of Ayodhya. But the historic significance of this "accident" should be evident to any-

one familiar with Ram's place in our historic consciousness.

Ram has been the exemplar par excellence for the Hindu public domain. There have been other incarnations of Vishnu in the Hindu view and the tenth (the avatar) is yet to arrive.[2] But there has been no other similar exemplar for Hindu polity. In historic terms, therefore, the proposed temple can be the first step towards that goal. . . .

The Hindu fight is not at all with Muslims; the fight is between Hindus anxious to renew themselves in the spirit of their civilization, and the state, Indian in name and not in spirit and the political and intellectual class trapped in the debris the British managed to bury us under before they left. The proponents of the Western ideology are using Muslims as auxiliaries and it is a pity Muslim "leaders" are allowing themselves to be so used. . . .

Secularist-versus-Hindu-Rashtra[3] controversy is, of course, not new. In fact, it has been with us since the twenties when some of our forebears began to search for a definition of nationalism which could transcend at once the Hindu-Muslim divide and the aggregationist approach whereby India was regarded as a Hindu-Muslim-Sikh-Christian land. But it has acquired an intensity it has not had since partition.

This intensity is the result of a variety of factors which have cumulatively provoked intense anxiety among millions of Hindus regarding their future and simultaneously given a new sense

---

[1]*Communalism* is a system in which rival minority groups are devoted to their own interests rather than those of the whole society; in the context of Indian politics, the term refers to loyalties of religious communities.
[2]Ram, or Rama, the hero of the Indian epic *Ramayana,* is believed to be the seventh avatar, or earthly manifestation, of Vishnu, the second god of the Hindu triad along with Brahma and Shiva. In the *Ramayana,* Vishnu returns to

Earth as Ram to protect human society from the demon king Ravana. To his devotees, Ram exemplifies steadfastness, courage, and valor. It is believed that Vishnu's tenth avatar, Kalkin, will appear in the future, riding a white horse and heralding a cataclysm that will usher in the end of the cosmic age.
[3]Hindi for "state" or "polity."

of strength and confidence to the proponents of Hindu Rashtra. The first part of this story begins, in my view, with the mass conversion of Harijans to Islam in Meenakshipuram in Tamil Nadu in 1981[4] and travels via the rise of Pakistan-backed armed secessionist movements in Punjab and Jammu and Kashmir,[5] and the second part with the spectacular success of the Bharatiya Janata Party (BJP) in the last polls. . . .

India, to put the matter brusquely, has been a battleground between two civilizations (Hindu and Islamic) for well over a thousand years, and three (Hindu, Muslim and Western) for over two hundred years. None of them has ever won a decisive enough and durable enough victory to oblige the other two to assimilate themselves fully into it. So the battle continues. This stalemate lies at the root of the crisis of identity the intelligentsia has faced since the beginning of the freedom movement in the last quarter of the nineteenth century. The intelligentsia is incidentally not a monolithic entity. Though its constituents are not too clearly differentiated, they should broadly be divided into at least two groups.

The more resilient and upwardly mobile section of the intelligentsia must, by definition, seek to come to terms with the ruling power and its mores, and the less successful part of it to look for its roots and seek comfort in its cultural past. This was so during the Muslim period; this was the case during the British Raj;[6] and this rule has not ceased to operate since independence.

Thus in the medieval period of our history there grew up a class of Hindus in and around centers of Muslim power who took to the Persian-Arabic culture and ways of the rulers; similarly under the more securely founded and far better organized and managed Raj there arose a vast number of Hindus who took to the English language, Western ideas, ideals, dress and eating habits; . . . they, their progeny and other recruits to their class have continued to dominate independent India.

They are the self-proclaimed secularists who have sought, and continue to seek, to remake India in the Western image. The image has, of course, been an eclectic one; if they have stuck to the institutional framework inherited from the British, they have been more than willing to take up not only the Soviet model of economic development,[7] but also the Soviet theories on a variety of issues such as the nationalities problem and the nature of imperialism and neo-colonialism.

Behind them has stood, and continues to stand, the awesome intellectual might of the West, which may or may not be anti-India, depending on the exigencies of its interests, but which has to be antipathetic to Hinduism. . . .

Some secularists may be genuinely pro-Muslim, . . . because they find high Islamic culture and the ornate Urdu[8] language attractive. But, by and large, that is not the motivating force in their lives. They are driven, above all, by the fear of what they call regression into their own past which they hate and dread. Most of the exponents of this viewpoint have come and continue to come understandably from the Left, understandably because no other group of Indians can possibly be so alienated from the country's cultural past as the followers of Lenin, Stalin and Mao, who have spared little effort to turn their own countries into cultural wastelands.

As a group, the secularists, especially the Leftists, have not summoned the courage to insist that in order to ensure the survival of the secular Indian state, Muslims should accept one common civil code, and that Article 370 of the Con-

---

[4]Hindus were incensed when large numbers of low-caste Hindus, or Harijans, were converted to Islam in 1981. It was believed the missionary campaign was financed by Saudi Arabians.

[5]The Indian states of Punjab, Jammu, and Kashmir were created at the time of independence. With mixed populations of Hindus, Muslims, and Sikhs, they have been plagued by religious conflict and have been a source of bitter conflict between India and Pakistan.

[6]*Raj* is Hindi for "reign" or "rule."

[7]Beginning in 1951 the government adopted a series of five-year plans for the nation's economic development in imitation of the five-year plans initiated by Stalin in 1928 (see source 92). The plans featured central planning and state ownership of major enterprises.

[8]*Urdu* is the primary language of Pakistan and northern India.

stitution, which concedes special rights to Jammu and Kashmir mainly because it is a Muslim-majority state, should be scrapped. They have contented themselves with vague statements on the need for the majorities to join the mainstream, never drawing attention to the twin fact that, of necessity, Hindus constitute the mainstream and that this mainstream is capable of respecting the identities and rights of the minorities, precisely because it is constituted of Hindus. . . .

The state in independent India has, it is true, sought, broadly speaking, to be neutral in the matter of religion. But this is a surface view of the reality. The Indian state has been far from neutral in civilizational terms. It has been an agency, and a powerful agency, for the spread of Western values and mores. It has willfully sought to replicate Western institutions, the Soviet Union too being essentially part of Western civilization. It could not be otherwise in view of the orientation and aspirations of the dominant elite of which Nehru[9] remains the guiding spirit.

Muslims have found such a state acceptable principally on three counts. First, it has agreed to leave them alone in respect of their personal law (the Shariat). . . . Secondly, it has allowed them to expand their traditional . . . educational system in madrasahs[10] attached to mosques. Above all, it has helped them avoid the necessity to come to terms with Hindu civilization in a predominantly Hindu India. This last count is the crux of the matter. . . .

In the past up to the sixteenth century, great temples have been built in our country by rulers to mark the rise of a new dynasty or to mark a triumph. . . . In the present case, the proposal to build the Rama temple has also to help produce an "army" which can in the first instance achieve the victory the construction can proclaim.

The raising of such an "army" in our democracy, however flawed, involves not only a body of disciplined cadres, which is available in the shape of the RSS,[11] a political organization, which too is available in the Bharatiya Janata Party, but also an aroused citizenry. . . . The Vishwa Hindu Parishad[12] and its allies have fullfilled this need in a manner which is truly spectacular.

The BJP-VHP-RSS leaders have rendered the country another great service. They have brought Hindu interests, if not the Hindu ethos, into the public domain where they legitimately belong. But it would appear that they have not fully grasped the implications of their action. Their talk of pseudo-secularism gives me that feeling. The fight is not against what they call pseudo-secularism; it is against secularism in its proper definition whereby man as animal usurps the place of man as spirit. . . .

In the existing West-dominated political-intellectual milieu, it is understandable that BJP leaders act defensively. But it is time they recognize that defensiveness can cripple them, as it did in the past when they sought respectability in claims of adherence to Gandhian socialism, whatever it might mean, and this time in a context favorable to them. The Nehru order is as much in the throes of death as its progenitor, the Marxist-Leninist-Stalinist order. A new order is waiting to be conceived and born. It needs a mother as well as a mid-wife.

[9]Jawaharlal Nehru (1889–1964), India's first prime minister, was a major target of Jain because of his commitment to socialism and secularism.

[10]*Madrasahs* were advanced schools of learning, or colleges, devoted to Islamic studies.

[11]RSS stands for the *Rashtriya Swayamsevak Sangh,* a mili-

tant Hindu organization founded in 1925 dedicated to the strengthening of Hindu culture.

[12]The *Vishwa Hindu Parishad (VHP),* or World Hindu Society, was founded in 1964. It is dedicated to demolishing mosques built on Hindu holy sites.

# The Challenge of Underdevelopment
▼▼▼

## 115 ▼ *World Bank, WORLD DEVELOPMENT REPORTS: 1978–2000*

In 1500, at the dawn of the modern era, a rough economic equality existed among the world's regions and civilizations. In each one of them a small number of extremely wealthy people existed alongside a vast number of others who grew just enough food or earned just enough money to live from day to day and year to year. But there was no sharp division between "haves" and "have-nots" in the world community.

Today the situation is far different. Although poverty still exists in all industrial nations, the overall standard of living in so-called developed countries has improved dramatically in the past two centuries, especially since the end of World War II. In these societies, located mostly in the Northern Hemisphere, people live longer, healthier, and more productive lives than at any time in human history.

But the world also holds more people living in poverty than ever before. There is no hard and fast definition of poverty, and scholars have expended a great deal of energy discussing the merits of various ways to characterize and measure it. The World Bank in 1994 defined *poverty* as having an income below $720 per year and *absolute,* or *extreme, poverty* as having an income of half that amount. However one defines it, the number of the world's poor is increasing. Utilizing the World Bank's definition, 1.3 billion people, approximately 20 percent of the world's population, live in poverty, compared to 800 million in 1972. Most of these poor people live in the Southern Hemisphere, many of them in former colonies. Poverty is growing in Southwest Asia, North Africa, Latin America, and the Caribbean and especially in sub-Saharan Africa, where approximately one-fourth of the world's poor live.

The following tables provide insight into world economic relationships, the meaning of poverty, and the nature and size of the gap between developed and developing nations. The statistics are provided by the World Bank, also known as the International Bank for Reconstruction and Development, one of many international organizations concerned with alleviating world poverty by encouraging economic development. Founded in 1944, it soon became affiliated with the newly established United Nations. Using funds subscribed by UN members, it advances loans to nations and private businesses for economic development projects. Although most loans at first went for postwar reconstruction, since the 1950s the bank mainly has supported loans for projects in developing areas. Since 1978 it has published annually its *World Development Report,* with articles on development strategies and statistics on economic, demographic, and educational trends. The following information, on twenty-six nations, arranged from the poorest to richest, is drawn from editions published in 1978, 1987, and 1999–2000.

*(See page 502 for Questions for Analysis.)*

*World Bank Statistics*

| Nation | Population (millions) | | Gross National Product per Capita (U.S. $) | | Tractors (per thousand agricultural workers) | | Energy Consumption per Capita (kilograms of oil equivalent) | | Population with Access to Safe Water (percent) | | Prevalence of Malnutrition (percent of population under age 5) |
|---|---|---|---|---|---|---|---|---|---|---|---|
| | 1976 | 1998 | 1976 | 1998 | 1979–81 | 1995–97 | 1971 | 1996 | 1982 | 1997 | 1992–1997 |
| Ethiopia | 28.7 | 61 | 100 | 100 | NA | 0 | 19 | 284 | 4 | 26 | 48 |
| Mozambique | 9.5 | 17 | 170 | 210 | 1 | 1 | 103 | 481 | 9 | 24 | 26 |
| Mali | 5.8 | 11 | 100 | 250 | 0 | — | 16 | 22 | 15 | 48 | 40 |
| Nigeria | 77.1 | 121 | 380 | 300 | 1 | — | 39 | 722 | 36 | 50 | 39 |
| Uganda | 11.9 | 21 | 240 | 385 | 0 | — | 58 | 23 | 34 | 42 | 26 |
| Haiti | 4.7 | 8 | 200 | 410 | 0 | 0 | NA | 268 | 38 | 39 | 28 |
| India | 620.4 | 980 | 150 | 430 | 2 | 5 | 111 | 476 | 54 | 85 | 53 |
| Indonesia | 135.2 | 204 | 240 | 680 | 0 | 1 | 71 | 672 | 39 | 65 | 34 |
| China | 835.8 | 1239 | 410 | 750 | 2 | — | 278 | 902 | NA | 83 | 16 |
| Egypt | 38.1 | 61 | 280 | 1,290 | 4 | 10 | 200 | 638 | 90 | 84 | 15 |
| Guatemala | 6.5 | 11 | 630 | 1,640 | 3 | 2 | 155 | 510 | 58 | 67 | 27 |
| Iran | 34.3 | 64 | 1,930 | 1,770 | 17 | 39 | 714 | 1,491 | 50 | 90 | 16 |
| Thailand | 43 | 61 | 380 | 2,200 | 1 | 7 | 178 | 1,333 | 66 | 89 | NA |
| Colombia | 24.2 | 41 | 630 | 2,600 | 8 | 7 | 444 | 799 | 91 | 75 | 8 |
| Turkey | 41.2 | 63 | 990 | 3,160 | 38 | 57 | 377 | 1,045 | 69 | 67 | 10 |
| Mexico | 62.0 | 96 | 1,090 | 3,970 | 16 | 20 | 653 | 1,525 | 82 | 95 | 14 |
| Brazil | 110 | 166 | 1,140 | 4,570 | 31 | 51 | 361 | 1,012 | 75 | 69 | 6 |
| Chile | 10.5 | 15 | 1,050 | 4,810 | 43 | 44 | 709 | 1,419 | 86 | 91 | 1 |
| Korea, Republic of | 36.0 | 46 | 670 | 7,970 | 1 | 34 | 507 | 3,576 | 83 | 83 | NA |
| Israel | 3.6 | 6 | 3,920 | 15,940 | 294 | 336 | 2,073 | 2,843 | 100 | 99 | NA |
| Canada | 23.2 | 31 | 7,510 | 20,020 | 824 | 1,683 | 6,233 | 7,880 | 97 | 99 | NA |
| United Kingdom | 56.1 | 59 | 4,020 | 21,400 | 726 | 821 | 3,790 | 3,992 | 100 | 100 | NA |
| United States | 215.1 | 270 | 7,890 | 29,340 | 1,230 | 1,452 | 7,633 | 8,051 | 100 | 90 | 1 |
| Singapore | 2.3 | 3.0 | 2,700 | 30,060 | 3 | 16 | 1,396 | 7,835 | 100 | 100 | NA |
| Japan | 112.8 | 126 | 4,910 | 32,380 | 209 | 503 | 2,553 | 4,085 | 99 | 96 | NA |
| Switzerland | 6.4 | 7.0 | 8,880 | 40,080 | 494 | 616 | 2,742 | 3,622 | 100 | 100 | NA |

NA = Data not available.

*World Bank Statistics (continued)*

| Nation | Life Expectancy at Birth (years) | | | | Mortality Rate under Age 5 (per 1,000 live births) | | Adult Literacy (percent) of People Age 15 and above | | | |
|---|---|---|---|---|---|---|---|---|---|---|
| | 1960 | 1975 | Female 1997 | Male 1997 | 1980 | 1997 | 1960 | 1974 | Female 1997 | Male 1997 |
| Ethiopia | 34 | 48 | 44 | 42 | 213 | 175 | NA | 7 | 29 | 41 |
| Mozambique | 38 | 44 | 47 | 44 | 223 | 201 | NA | NA | 25 | 57 |
| Mali | 35 | 38 | 52 | 49 | NA | 235 | 5 | 10 | 28 | 53 |
| Nigeria | 34 | 41 | 55 | 52 | 196 | 122 | 25 | NA | 51 | 69 |
| Uganda | 43 | 50 | 42 | 43 | 180 | 162 | 25 | 25 | 53 | 75 |
| Haiti | 43 | 50 | 56 | 51 | 200 | 125 | 10 | 20 | 53 | 58 |
| India | 42 | 50 | 64 | 62 | 177 | 88 | 24 | 36 | 39 | 67 |
| Indonesia | 40 | 48 | 67 | 63 | 125 | 60 | 47 | 62 | 80 | 91 |
| China | 51 | 62 | 71 | 68 | 65 | 39 | NA | NA | 75 | 91 |
| Egypt | 45 | 52 | 68 | 65 | 175 | 66 | 20 | 40 | 40 | 65 |
| Guatemala | 44 | 53 | 67 | 61 | NA | 55 | 38 | 47 | 59 | 74 |
| Iran | 44 | 51 | 70 | 64 | 126 | 35 | 15 | 50 | 66 | 81 |
| Thailand | 49 | 58 | 72 | 66 | NA | 38 | 68 | 82 | 93 | 97 |
| Colombia | 55 | 61 | 73 | 67 | 58 | 30 | NA | 74 | 91 | 91 |
| Turkey | 49 | 57 | 72 | 67 | 133 | 50 | 40 | 55 | 74 | 92 |
| Mexico | 56 | 63 | 75 | 69 | 74 | 38 | 62 | 76 | 88 | 92 |
| Brazil | 56 | 61 | 71 | 63 | NA | 44 | 61 | 64 | 84 | 84 |
| Chile | 56 | 63 | 78 | 72 | 35 | 13 | 84 | 90 | 95 | 95 |
| Korea, Republic of | 53 | 61 | 76 | 69 | 18 | 11 | 71 | 92 | * | * |
| Israel | 68 | 71 | 79 | 76 | 19 | 8 | 84 | 84 | * | * |
| Canada | 71 | 72 | 82 | 76 | 13 | 8 | NA | 98 | * | * |
| United Kingdom | 70 | 72 | 80 | 75 | 19 | 7 | NA | 98 | * | * |
| United States | 70 | 71 | 79 | 73 | 15 | 8 | 98 | 99 | * | * |
| Singapore | 63 | 70 | 79 | 73 | 13 | 6 | NA | 75 | 87 | * |
| Japan | 67 | 73 | 83 | 77 | 11 | 6 | 98 | 99 | * | * |
| Switzerland | 71 | 72 | 82 | 76 | NA | 11 | NA | 99 | * | * |

*More than 95 percent.
NA = Data not available.

Distribution of Gross National Product[1] (percent)

| | Telephone Main Lines (per 1,000 people) 1997 | Personal Computers (per 1,000 people) 1997 | Agriculture 1965 | Agriculture 1985 | Agriculture 1997 | Industry 1965 | Industry 1985 | Industry 1997 | Manufacturing 1965 | Manufacturing 1985 | Manufacturing 1997 | Service 1965 | Service 1985 | Service 1997 |
|---|---|---|---|---|---|---|---|---|---|---|---|---|---|---|
| Ethiopia | 3 | NA | 58 | 44 | NA | 14 | 16 | NA | 7 | NA | NA | 28 | 39 | NA |
| Mozambique | 4 | 1.6 | NA | 35 | 34 | NA | 11 | 18 | NA | NA | 17 | NA | 53 | 54 |
| Mali | 2 | 0.6 | NA | 50 | 45 | NA | 18 | 21 | NA | 4 | 6 | NA | 32 | 34 |
| Nigeria | 4 | 5.1 | 53 | 36 | 32 | 19 | 32 | 41 | 7 | 9 | 5 | 29 | 32 | 27 |
| Uganda | 2 | 1.4 | 52 | 67[a] | 43 | 13 | 7[a] | 18 | 8 | 5[a] | 9 | 35 | 26[a] | 39 |
| Haiti | 8 | NA | NA | 31[a] | 31 | NA | 38[a] | 20 | NA | 15[a] | NA | NA | 31[a] | 48 |
| India | 19 | 2.1 | 47 | 31 | 25 | 22 | 27 | 30 | 15 | 17 | 19 | 31 | 41 | 45 |
| Indonesia | 25 | 8 | 56 | 24 | 16 | 13 | 36 | 42 | 8 | 14 | 25 | 31 | 41 | 41 |
| China | 56 | 6 | 39 | 33 | 18 | 38 | 47 | 49 | 30 | 37 | 37 | 23 | 20 | 33 |
| Egypt | 56 | 7.3 | 29 | 20 | 17 | 27 | 31 | 33 | NA | NA | 26 | 44 | 49 | 50 |
| Guatemala | 41 | 3 | NA | 18[a] | 21 | NA | 26[a] | 19 | NA | 9[a] | 13 | NA | 51[a] | 60 |
| Iran | 107 | 4 | 26 | 18 | NA | 36 | 32 | NA | 12 | 9 | NA | 38 | 50 | NA |
| Thailand | 80 | 19.8 | 35 | 17 | 11 | 23 | 30 | 40 | 14 | 20 | 29 | 42 | 53 | 49 |
| Colombia | 148 | 33.4 | 30 | 20 | 13 | 25 | 25 | 38 | 18 | 18 | 19 | 46 | 56 | 49 |
| Turkey | 250 | 20.7 | 34 | 18 | 15 | 25 | 36 | 28 | 16 | 25 | 18 | 41 | 46 | 57 |
| Mexico | 96 | 37.3 | 14 | 11 | 5 | 31 | 35 | 27 | 21 | NA | 20 | 63 | 73 | 68 |
| Brazil | 107 | 26 | 19 | 11 | 8 | 33 | 39 | 36 | 26 | 28 | 23 | 45 | 50 | 56 |
| Chile | 180 | 54.1 | 9 | NA | 8 | 40 | NA | 35 | 24 | NA | 17 | 52 | NA | 57 |
| Korea, Republic of | 444 | 150.7 | 39 | 14 | 6 | 26 | 41 | 43 | 19 | 28 | 26 | 35 | 45 | 51 |
| Israel | 450 | 186.1 | NA | NA | NA | NA | NA | NA | NA | NA | NA | NA | NA | NA |
| Canada | 609 | 270.6 | 5 | 3 | NA | 34 | 30 | NA | 23 | 16 | NA | 61 | 67 | NA |
| United Kingdom | 540 | 242.4 | 3 | 2 | 2[b] | 41 | 36 | 32[b] | 30 | 22 | 21[b] | 56 | 62 | 66[b] |
| United States | 644 | 406.7 | 3 | 2 | 2 | 38 | 31 | 27 | 29 | 20 | 18 | 59 | 67 | 64 |
| Singapore | 543 | 399.5 | 3 | 1 | 0 | 24 | 37 | 35 | 15 | 24 | 24 | 73 | 62 | 65 |
| Japan | 479 | 202.4 | 9 | 3 | NA | 43 | 41 | NA | 32 | 30 | NA | 48 | 56 | NA |
| Switzerland | 661 | 394.9 | NA | NA | NA | NA | NA | NA | NA | NA | NA | NA | NA | NA |

[1] *Agriculture* includes growing of crops and raising livestock in addition to forestry, hunting, and fishing; in countries with a high level of subsistence farming, much agricultural production is either not exchanged or not exchanged for money and hence is not reflected in the statistics. *Industry* includes mining, manufacturing, construction, and electricity, gas, and water supply; *manufacturing,* the most dynamic part of most nations' economies, is listed separately. The service sector includes all other forms of economic activity, including wholesale and retail trade, transport, government activity, financial services, professional services, and personal services in the areas of education, health care, and real estate. It also includes bank service charges and import duties. Percentages often add up to more than 100%. This results from the difficulty in collecting accurate data for many countries.

[a] 1989, [b] 1995, NA = Data not available.

## QUESTIONS FOR ANALYSIS

1. In what areas have the low-income nations made progress in recent decades?
2. Is the gap between rich and poor nations getting larger or smaller? Cite examples.
3. What do these statistics suggest about changes in the nature of a nation's economic activity as it becomes more developed economically?
4. What do these statistics reveal about the conditions that have slowed down the development in poorer nations?
5. How useful are the various types of data in determining a nation's development and economic prospects?

▼▼▼

# Women in the Modern World

During the twentieth century, political leaders of industrialized nations, revolutionaries such as Lenin and Mao, and nationalist heroes as different as Mustafa Kemal and Gandhi have all supported the ideal of women's equality with men. The 1945 charter of the United Nations is committed to the same purpose, and the United Nations Universal Declaration of Human Rights of 1948 reaffirms the goal of ending all forms of gender-based discrimination.

It would be an understatement to say that progress toward gender equality has been uneven. With some exceptions, women have attained legal equality with men and in democracies have won basic political rights such as the right to vote. Educational and vocational opportunities for women have expanded. Nonetheless, even in developed industrial countries, women typically earn less than men and are underrepresented in managerial positions. Although prime ministers Margaret Thatcher of Britain, Golda Meir of Israel, Indira Gandhi of India, and Benazir Bhutto of Pakistan are four notable exceptions in recent history, politics is overwhelmingly dominated by men, as are professions in fields such as engineering and science.

In developing nations, attainment of gender equality has been especially difficult. In these societies, the small pool of educated women has hindered the development of feminist movements, and advocates for women's rights are relatively few. Fundamentalist religious movements in the Islamic world and elsewhere have sought to keep women in traditional roles. Even in nations such as China and India, which have adopted strong antidiscrimination laws, it has proved difficult to modify, let alone eradicate, centuries-old educational patterns, work stereotypes, marriage customs, and notions of female inferiority.

# Women and Islamic Fundamentalism
▼▼▼

*116 ▼  Zand Dokht,*
*"THE REVOLUTION*
*THAT FAILED WOMEN"*

Although the Pahlavi rulers of Iran, Reza Shah (r. 1925–1941) and Muhammad Reza Shah (r. 1941–1979), gave women political rights, allowed them to abandon the veil for Western-style dress, and encouraged female literacy and higher education, in the 1970s millions of Iranian women shared the growing disgust with the Pahlavi government's autocracy, corruption, and secularism. Women played an important role in the massive demonstrations that preceded Reza Shah's downfall in 1979 and led to his replacement by an Islamic fundamentalist regime under Ayatollah Ruholla Khomeini (1902–1989). True to its Islamic principles, Khomeini's government quickly revoked Pahlavi legislation concerning women and the family and reinstated traditional Islamic practices.

Iranian women who had taken advanatge of educational opportunities and had benefited professionally during the Pahlavi years opposed the Islamic republic's effort to turn back the clock. In 1979 representatives from various women's organizations founded the Women's Solidarity Committee, an organization dedicated to the protection of women's rights in Iran. Although subsequently banned in Iran itself, Iranian women in England maintained a branch of the organization in London. Known as the Iranian Women's Solidarity Group, in the 1980s it published pamphlets and newsletters on issues pertaining to women in Iran. The following selection, written by a Solidarity Committee member, Zand Dokht, appeared in one of its publications in 1981.

---

## QUESTIONS FOR ANALYSIS

1. In what specific ways did the Islamic Revolution in Iran affect women?
2. According to the author, how do Iran's new leaders envision a woman's role in society?
3. How does the author explain the fact that so many Iranian women supported the revolution that toppled the shah?
4. Why, in the author's view, did the shahs' reforms fail to satisfy numerous Iranian women?

When Khomeini created his Islamic Republic in 1979, he relied on the institution of the family, on support from the women, the merchants, and the private system of landownership. The new Islamic constitution declared women's primary position as mothers. The black veil, symbol of the position of women under Islam, was made compulsory. Guards were posted outside government offices to enforce it, and women were sacked from their jobs without compensation for refusing to wear the veil. The chairman of the Employment Office, in an interview with the government's women's magazine said, "We can account for 100,000 women government employees being sacked as they resisted the order of the revolutionary government when it was demanded of them to put the veil on."

Schools were segregated, which meant that women were barred from some technical schools, even from some religious schools, and young girls' education in the villages was halted. Lowering the marriage age for girls to 13, reinstating polygamy and *Sighen* [temporary wives], the two major pillars of Islam, meant that women did not need education and jobs, they only needed to find husbands.

The Ayatollahs in their numerous public prayers, which grew to be the only possible national activity, continuously gave sermons on the advantages of marriage, family, and children being brought up on their mother's lap. They preached that society would be pure, trouble free, criminal-less (look at the youth problem in the West) if everybody married young, and if men married as many times as possible (to save the unprotected women who might otherwise become prostitutes). The government created a marriage bank at a time when half the working population was unemployed, whereby men were given huge sums — around £3,500 — to get married. Another *masterpiece* of the revolutionary Islamic government was to create a system of arranged marriages in prisons, between men and women prisoners, to "protect" women after they leave prison.

Because abortion and contraception are now unobtainable, marriage means frequent pregnancy. If you are 13 when you get married, it is likely that you will have six children by the time you are 20. This, in a country where half the total population are already under 16, is a tragedy for future generations.

Religious morality demands that all pleasures and entertainments be banned. Wine, music, dancing, chess, women's parts in theater, cinema, and television — you name it, Khomeini banned it. He even segregated the mountains and the seas, for male and female climbers and swimmers.

But compulsory morality, compulsory marriage, and the compulsory wearing of the veil did not create the Holy Society that Khomeini was after; but public lashings, stonings, chopping off hands, and daily group executions sank Iran into the age of Barbarism.

Perhaps nowhere else in the world have women been murdered for walking in the street open-faced. The question of the veil is the most important issue of women's liberation in Muslim countries. The veil, a long engulfing black robe, is the extension of the four walls of the home, where women belong. The veil is the historical symbol of woman's oppression, seclusion, denial of her social participation and equal rights with men. It is a cover which defaces and objectifies women. To wear or not to wear the veil, for Muslim women is "the right to choose." . . .

Why do women, workers, and unemployed, support this regime which has done everything in its power to attack their rights and interests? The power of Islam in our culture and tradition has been seriously underestimated . . . and it was through this ideology that Khomeini directed his revolutionary government. The clergy dealt with everyday problems and spoke out on human relationships, sexuality, security, and protection of the family and the spiritual needs of human beings. It was easy for people to identify with these issues and support the clergy, although nobody knew what they were later to do. When Khomeini asked for sacrifices — "we haven't made the Revolution in order to eat chicken or dress better" — women (so great in the art of sacrifice) and workers accepted these antimaterialist ideas. . . .

Women's attraction to Khomeini's ideas was not based simply on his Islamic politics, but also on the way he criticized the treatment of women — as secretaries and media sex objects — under the Shah's regime. Women were genuinely unsatisfied and looking for change. Some educated Iranian women went back to Iran from America and Europe to aid the clergy with the same messages, and became the government's spokeswomen. They put on the veil willingly, defended

Islamic virtues and spiritual values while drawing from their own experiences in the West. They said it was cold and lonely, Western women were only in pursuit of careers and self-sufficiency, and that their polygamous sexual relationships had not brought them liberation, but confusion and exploitation. These women joined ranks with an already growing force of Muslim women, to retrieve the tradition of true/happy Muslim women — in defense of patriarchy.

The mosque is not just a place of prayer, it is also a social club for women. It provides a warm, safe room for women to meet, chat, or listen to a sermon, and there are traditional women-only parties and picnics in gardens or holy places. Take away these traditional and religious customs from women as the Shah — with his capitalist and imperialist reforms, irrelevant to women's needs — tried to do and a huge vacuum is left. Khomeini stepped in to fill that vacuum. The reason why Khomeini won was that the Shah's social-economic program for women was dictatorial, bureaucratic, inadequate (especially in terms of health education) and therefore irrelevant to women's needs. What little the Shah's reform brought to women was just a token gesture. Women dissatisfied with the Shah's reform felt that they had benefited little from him and would not miss it if it was taken away.

## An African Perspective on Female Circumcision
▼▼▼

## 117 ▼ Association of African Women for Research and Development, *A STATEMENT ON GENITAL MUTILATION*

*Female circumcision* is a term referring to a variety of ritual procedures ranging from the drawing of blood, to clitoridectomy (the removal of the clitoris), to infibulation (the removal of the clitoris, the labia minora, and most of the labia majora, the remaining sides of which are joined together to leave a small opening). The operation, which in different societies takes place anytime from shortly after birth to the onset of puberty, is usually performed by midwives or village women without benefit of anesthesia or antibiotics. No accurate statistics on the prevalence of the practice exist. It is most prevalent in sub-Saharan Africa, especially in the Sudan region, but it is also practiced in New Guinea, Australia, Malaysia, Brazil, Mexico, Peru, India, Egypt, and the southern and eastern parts of the Arabian Peninsula. Presumably instituted to guard virginity and dull a woman's sexual desires, female circumcision has come under harsh criticism both from within the societies in which it exists and from outsiders, especially Westerners. Efforts to suppress the practice, which in Africa go back to the colonial era, however, have had little effect among peoples who consider the custom part of their ethnic and religious heritage and a necessary rite of passage into womanhood.

Denunciations of female circumcision by Westerners and Western-inspired campaigns to end the practice have frequently backfired, especially in Africa. Even Africans who oppose the practice consider Western interference insensitive and misguided. The following statement was issued in 1980 by the Association of African Women for Research and Development (AAWORD), which was founded in 1977 and is based in Dakar, Senegal.

---

## QUESTIONS FOR ANALYSIS

1. What is the basis of the authors' assertion that critics of female circumcision are guilty of "latent racism"?
2. How have Western criticisms of female circumcision hindered the efforts of African critics to limit the practice?
3. According to the authors, what would be an appropriate Western approach to the issue of female circumcision?
4. How might an ardent Western critic of female circumcision in Africa counter the arguments contained in the AAWORD statement?

In the last few years, Western public opinion has been shocked to find out that in the middle of the 20th Century thousands of women and children have been "savagely mutilated" because of "barbarous customs from another age." The good conscience of Western society has once again been shaken. Something must be done to help these people, to show public disapproval of such acts.

There have been press conferences, documentary films, headlines in the newspapers, information days, open letters, action groups — all this to mobilize public opinion and put pressure on governments of the countries where genital mutilation is still practised.

This new crusade of the West has been led out of the moral and cultural prejudices of Judaeo-Christian Western society: aggressiveness, ignorance or even contempt, paternalism and activism are the elements which have infuriated and then shocked many people of good will. In trying to reach their own public, the new crusaders have fallen back on sensationalism, and have become insensitive to the dignity of the very women they want to "save." They are totally unconscious of the latent racism which such a campaign evokes in countries where ethnocentric prejudice is so deep-rooted. And in their conviction that this is a "just cause," they have forgotten that these women from a different race and a different culture are also *human beings,* and that solidarity can only exist alongside self-affirmation and mutual respect.

*This campaign has aroused three kinds of reaction in Africa:*

1. the highly conservative, which stresses the right of cultural difference and the defence of traditional values and practices whose supposed aim is to protect and elevate women; this view denies Westerners the right to interfere in problems related to culture;
2. which, while condemning genital mutilation for health reasons, considers it premature to open the issue to public debate;
3. which concentrates on the aggressive nature of the campaign and considers that the fanaticism of the new crusaders only serves to draw attention away from the fundamental problems of the economic exploitation and oppression of developing countries, which contribute to the continuation of such practices.

Although all these reactions rightly criticize the campaign against genital mutilation as imperialist and paternalist, they remain passive and defensive. As is the case with many other issues, we refuse here to confront our cultural heritage and to criticize it constructively. We seem to prefer to draw a veil of modesty over certain traditional practices, whatever the consequences may be. However, it is time that Africans realized they must take a position on all problems which concern their society, and to take steps to end any practice which debases human beings.

AAWORD, whose aim is to carry out research which leads to the liberation of African people and women in particular, *firmly condemns* genital mutilation and all other practices — traditional or modern — which oppress women and justify exploiting them economically or socially, as a serious violation of the fundamental rights of women.

AAWORD intends to undertake research on the consequences of genital mutilation for the physical and mental health of women. The results of these studies could be used as the basis of an information and educational campaign, and could help to bring about legislation on all aspects of this problem.

However, as far as AAWORD is concerned, the fight against genital mutilation, although necessary, should not take on such proportions that the wood cannot be seen for the trees. Young girls and women who are mutilated in Africa are usually among those who cannot even satisfy their basic needs and who have to struggle daily for survival. This is due to the exploitation of developing countries, manifested especially through the impoverishment of the poorest social classes. In the context of the present world economic crisis, tradition, with all of its constraints, becomes more than ever a form of security for the peoples of the Third World, and especially for the "wretched of the earth." For these people, the modern world, which is primarily Western and bourgeois, can only represent aggression at all levels — political, economic, social and cultural. It is unable to propose viable alternatives for them.

Moreover, to fight against genital mutilation without placing it in the context of ignorance, obscurantism, exploitation, poverty, etc., without questioning the structures and social relations which perpetuate this situation, is like "refusing to see the sun in the middle of the day." This, however, is precisely the approach taken by many Westerners, and is highly suspect, especially since Westerners necessarily profit from the exploitation of the peoples and women of Africa, whether directly or indirectly.

Feminists from developed countries — at least those who are sincerely concerned about this situation rather than those who use it only for their personal prestige — should understand this other aspect of the problem. They must accept that it is a problem for *African women,* and that no change is possible without the conscious participation of African women. They must avoid ill-timed interference, maternalism, ethnocentrism and misuse of power. These are attitudes which can only widen the gap between the Western feminist movement and that of the Third World.

African women must stop being reserved and shake themselves out of their political lethargy. They must make themselves heard on all national and international problems, defining their priorities and their special role in the context of social and national demands.

On the question of such traditional practices as genital mutilation, African women must no longer equivocate or react only to Western interference. They must speak out in favour of the total eradication of all these practices, and they must lead information and education campaigns to this end within their own countries and on a continental level.

# A Chinese Woman's Life Story
▼▼▼

## 118 ▼ Ming, RECOLLECTIONS

The following memoir is one of several interviews of Chinese women carried out by Denyse Verschuur Base, a scholar who was trained in law and sociology at the University of Paris and taught sociology at the University of Utrecht in the Netherlands. In 1991, under the auspices of the Academy of Social Sciences in Beijing, she recorded the recollections of some two dozen Chinese women of varying backgrounds about their life experiences. Ming (not her real name) was a twenty-six-year-old teacher at the time of the interview.

Ming lived under a Communist regime that since taking power in 1949 had dedicated itself to the liberation of women from the bonds of patriarchy and Confucian tradition. The constitution of 1950 guaranteed equality between women and men, and the Marriage Law of the same year gave women the right to choose their own husbands and to divorce. Girls were given access to education, no longer had their feet bound, and were brought into the workplace in unprecedented numbers.

At the time of Ming's birth, 1965, China was experiencing a breathing space between two periods of upheaval. The Great Leap Forward, Mao's effort to increase Chinese agricultural and industrial productivity through mass mobilization of ideologically committed workers, had ended in 1960. The Great Cultural Revolution, Mao's effort to reinvigorate the revolution by purging China of "reactionaries" and "bourgeois elements," would begin in 1966. Ming was eleven years old in 1976 when Mao died and thirteen in 1978 when China officially de-emphasized Maoist ideology in favor of economic development. From then on, she lived in a China that was increasingly open to foreign investment and private enterprise. As Ming's memoir reveals, it was also a China in which many old attitudes and practices survived, even in the face of major political and economic transformations.

---

## QUESTIONS FOR ANALYSIS

1. How did Ming's mother respond to her abusive husband's treatment? What was her explanation for not seeking a divorce? What factors other than those stated might have played a role?
2. What do Ming's recollections reveal about changes that took place in China concerning women and families during her lifetime?
3. Ming emphasizes that traditional attitudes about family and women have persisted in the countryside more than in the cities. What might explain this phenomenon?
4. Why is Ming pessimistic about women's future in China?

I was born in the countryside in 1965, I have a young sister and an even younger brother. . . .

I find it difficult to talk about my youth because my family lived under very difficult conditions. My mother suffered a number of consequences. She is now 45 and my father is 50. When my mother was 19, she had her first child. My parents' marriage was arranged by their parents. My father is, in my opinion, the standard type of man you find in the countryside. He thinks that women should listen to men, and he does not respect them in the least. My mother was often beaten by my father. She didn't defend herself. For us children, our mother's submission was very painful.

My mother did not dare resist my father. Often, my father's mother and my aunts would comfort my mother, because she would go see them to tell them about her situation. But then she was brought back home to us, and it always happened again; there was no other means of pressure. All of my father's family advised my father not to beat my mother and not to argue with her. No one ever thought of the possibility of a divorce.

The family tried to comfort my mother every time, but it always happened again and again.

My mother had been educated until the beginning of high school. But in spite of her level, she never thought of divorcing. In the countryside it was very difficult. Even today, women do not think of divorcing, nor does the family. It is still difficult to divorce in the countryside. One day I asked my mother why she did not divorce. I said to her, "You can get a divorce, the law permits it," but my mother answered: "It is because of you, I do not want my children to be separated. Otherwise, I would have divorced long ago." Indeed, in case of divorce, the children are often separated. In our case, there might have been two children in my mother's care and one in my father's. Even when my mother would go to see the director of my father's work unit and explained the case to him, the whole committee would say, "It will get better, don't worry, it will most certainly get better!" But no one would have

ever proposed the possibility of getting a divorce. . . .

At the time, it was the parents who arranged the marriage. It was like that in all families. Even now, it is almost always the parents who arrange the marriage of their children. Only rarely do young people get married having themselves chosen their partner. The difference between the time of my parents and today is that one could not refuse the choice of the parents; even if one did not get along with the chosen partner, one was still obliged to accept. Now it is possible to refuse, and it is mainly the girls who refuse. . . .

I was admitted to high school because of my teachers. Once, my father came to get me there. It was the first time he had done it. He wanted to introduce me to a boy, to arrange my marriage. It was the son of a friend. He had already discussed it with the father. . . .

At the time, I was 17 years old and I was in a boarding school, but my father wanted to take me back home to arrange my marriage. I absolutely wanted to finish high school. My father did not want me to. As I was among the top three students in my class, a teacher tried to persuade my father to let me finish my studies. Up to that time, my father was paying for part of my studying, and from then on, he refused to continue paying. I was in total despair; at that time, I absolutely hated my father, and I was forced to go back to the countryside.

So then I helped my mother. She was working very hard. She encouraged me to try for the entrance exam to university the next year, and I succeeded thanks to her. I respect my mother a lot. My father, on the other hand, was trying to blackmail me. He would say, "If you agree to get married, you can go to university. If you don't, you can't." I knew very well that if I got married, I would never go to university. For me, university was also the chance to go to the city. And I knew that if I got married, I would remain in the countryside all my life. It was at that moment that I decided that I would definitely enter university, and I would be doing it partly for my mother who was working so hard in the fields, planting and harvesting fruits and vegetables. . . .

In the village, my mother is part of a women's association. She helps people who have problems. My sister and my brother still live at home. My mother has already proposed a fiancé to my sister. She wanted someone who did not live too far away, so that they could take care of her later. My sister was in despair. After a long hesitation, I decided to discuss it with my mother. I felt very awkward to be opposing my mother. My sister also respects my mother a great deal. We are so very aware of the fact that she had so many problems and that she endured so much suffering in her life. My mother understood, and she accepted the refusal of her daughter. But generally, in the countryside, it is still the parents who look for partners for their children, and it is still rare for young people to go against the choice of their parents. As for those who would like to look for their partner freely, without any other intervening factor than their own choice, this is very, very rare. . . .

Still today, married women generally live with their husbands' family. And yet things are changing, and more and more men now live with their wives' families, although this arrangement remains exceptional. There are still many more women than there are men living with their in-laws. . . .

Nowadays in the countryside, when people get married, it is the state that dictates when they can have a child. There are production quotas. You might have the right to have a child in two or four years' time; it is up to the state to decide. If the state, the family planning agent, has decided that there can be five children for this village this year, it will look up when people got married and allow five couples to have a child. If a child is conceived outside of the family plan, in theory abortion is obligatory. But some par-

ents have a child outside of the plan and do not declare it. Then the child has no identity card, and the parents have to pay a fine.

If people want a second child, for example, a son after a girl (sons are still preferred to daughters), here again, there will be a fine. The parents must pay up to 700 yuan per year. And the child will not have the right to an identity card until he is 14 years old. At that age he will be getting an identity card. This system is changing because it leads to all sorts of problems. For example, in the region where I come from, if one has a child out of plan, and if the parents are managers, they can lose their position as managers, and the premiums and salaries are diminished. It is still very carefully monitored, and the fines depend on the salaries. . . .

Infanticide of little girls is still quite common in the countryside. One can read about it in the local papers. It happens mainly in the poorer areas, which are also the most backward. The people have no choice. And I agree with them. If the government gave cash premiums to all those who did not have any children, then there would be many less children, because in the countryside children represent help, a workforce. Also, when the children get married, there is a larger income in the family, and when the parents get old, it is better to be dependent on several children than on just one. . . .

The latest changes have brought certain advantages to women. They can study and have a job. But in the countryside, there are only very few women who are lucky enough to study as I did; they rarely get more than a few years of primary school. From a job opportunity point of view, very often only the youngest are given jobs in local industries. I think that changes have come about since 1911. Already in 1912, and also in 1919,[1] there were women's movements, women's demonstrations and claims. Around

---

[1]The Revolution of 1911 resulted in the downfall of the Qing Dynasty and the end of China's imperial age; 1912 saw the founding of the Republic of China; 1919 was the year of the May 4 Movement, which began as a student protest against post–World War I treaty arrangements and grew into a broad movement for China's revival through democracy and science.

1900, the director of the University of Beida in Beijing decided that women would have access to university equal to that of men.

But as for the rest, the spirit of Confucius is still present. The three constraints borne by women, according to Confucius, still exist: to look for a husband, to stay a widow, and to be faithful. The greatest crime was, and still is, to remarry. The greatest honor, or rather the greatest constraint, was thus to have only one man, to devote oneself to one man. And the woman was to respect the parents of her husband, while the man was permitted to look for several women. . . .

Currently, the tendency in China is to send women back home, to give maternity leave for four years, and to give women part-time jobs as much as possible, which means, of course, that women have less and less opportunity to have a career. The purpose of maternity leave for four years is to try to exclude women from the labor market. There are too many people in the factories. According to the law, only three months' maternity leave is to be given. But it is the management of the factories who want to eliminate the surplus of workers.

Unfortunately, I have the feeling that women will be given less and less authority and fewer rights. Before 1966,[2] a certain number of women had held very important positions. Now there are fewer and fewer such women. It is a fact that changes have been made in these last years, but not all changes have been in the best interest of women.

---

[2]The year in which the Great Cultural Revolution began.

---

▼▼▼

# Struggles for Racial Equality

*Racism* is the belief that inherited physical variations among groups of human beings relating to skin color, facial features, and hair texture are outward manifestations of more meaningful differences in behavior patterns, intellect, creativity, and personality traits. Such a belief usually leads to the conclusion that a hierarchy exists among human races, with some superior to others.

Although modern anthropologists and scientists reject the theory that genetic differences among human races affect intelligence or social behavior, in the past racism has been used on many occasions to justify the oppression and exploitation of "inferior peoples" by their self-proclaimed betters. In the last five hundred years, stated or tacit racism has contributed to the transatlantic slave trade, Western colonialism, the Nazi assault on the Jews, the near destruction of Native American culture, Japanese expansionism, and legally sanctioned discrimination in the United States, South Africa, and other societies.

Since World War II, despite the universal revulsion against the Nazis' racist crimes, the end of colonialism in Africa and Asia, and the weight of scientific evidence against its premises, racism continues to distort human relationships in much of the world. Thus an important theme in recent history has been the struggle of oppressed peoples, especially in Africa and the United States, to end racial prejudice and gain full acceptance and equality. Victories have been won, but many battles are still being fought, and it is still unclear if human beings are capable of building a world in which a person's skin color truly does not matter.

# Apartheid's Bitter Fruits
▼▼▼

## 119 ▼ Nelson Mandela,
## THE RIVONIA TRIAL SPEECH
## TO THE COURT

Blacks in South Africa have been victims of racism since the Dutch founded the
first permanent white settlement at Cape Town in the seventeenth century. After
South Africa was granted independence from Great Britain in 1910, in 1913 blacks
formed the African National Congress (ANC) to foster unity among blacks and to
work for political rights. At first the ANC sought to reach its goals through petitions and appeals to white politicians, but following the implementation of apartheid after World War II, it sponsored Gandhi-inspired campaigns of passive
resistance and supported strikes by black labor unions. Violence often resulted,
leading to more government repression and further steps to stifle black political
activity.

Predictably, some blacks abandoned moderation for sabotage and terrorism.
Among them was Nelson Mandela (b. 1918), the son of a tribal chieftain, who
became a lawyer and an ANC activist in the 1940s. After the ANC was outlawed
in 1960 and after he organized a three-day stay-at-home protest in 1961, Mandela
went into hiding. While avoiding a nationwide manhunt, he helped found *Umkonto
we Sizwe* ("Spear of the Nation"), a branch of the ANC that carried out bombings
in several South African cities. Arrested in 1963, he, along with other ANC leaders, was convicted of treason and sent to the notorious prison on Robben Island
in the Atlantic Ocean forty miles from the coast.

Mandela remained a prisoner until 1990, when he reassumed leadership of the
ANC after having been freed by the South African president, F. W. de Klerk.
Prodded by de Klerk and pressured by the ANC and the international community, in 1991 the South African legislature repealed the foundation statutes of the
apartheid era. In 1994 white rule ended when national elections were held for a
new parliament. The ANC won 252 of 400 seats, and Mandela was installed as
South Africa's president in May 1994. Later in the year Nelson Mandela, a man
who spent twenty-seven years in prison, and F. W. de Klerk, a man who came out
of the ranks of those who imprisoned him, were declared co-winners of the Nobel
Peace Prize. Their steps toward ending apartheid and all the bitterness, suffering, and fear that went with it gave hope that other human beings could resolve
similar deep-rooted conflicts in other parts of the world.

The following excerpt comes from a speech delivered by Nelson Mandela on
April 20, 1964, in which he opened his defense against charges of treason before
an all-white court.

---

## QUESTIONS FOR ANALYSIS

1. Why did Mandela decide that the ANC must resort to violence to achieve
   its goals?

2. What distinction does he draw between sabotage and terrorism?
3. Why were Mandela and other ANC leaders attracted to communism?
4. What aspects of apartheid does Mandela find most degrading?
5. According to Mandela, how does apartheid affect the daily lives of the Africans?

In my youth . . . I listened to the elders of my tribe telling stories of the old days. Amongst the tales they related to me were those of wars fought by our ancestors in defense of the fatherland. . . . I hoped then that life might offer me the opportunity to serve my people and make my own humble contribution to their freedom struggle. This is what has motivated me in all that I have done in relation to the charges made against me in this case. . . .

I have already mentioned that I was one of the persons who helped to form Umkonto. I, and the others who started the organization, did so for two reasons. Firstly, we believed that as a result of Government policy, violence by the African people had become inevitable, and that unless responsible leadership was given to canalize and control the feelings of our people, there would be outbreaks of terrorism which would produce an intensity of bitterness and hostility between the various races of this country which is not produced even by war. Secondly, we felt that without violence there would be no way open to the African people to succeed in their struggle against the principle of White supremacy. All lawful modes of expressing opposition to this principle had been closed by legislation, and we were placed in a position in which we had either to accept a permanent state of inferiority, or to defy the Government. . . .

But the violence which we chose to adopt was not terrorism. We who formed Umkonto were all members of the African National Congress, and had behind us the ANC tradition of non-violence and negotiation as a means of solving political disputes. We believed that South Af-

rica belonged to all the people who lived in it, and not to one group, be it Black or White. We did not want an interracial war, and tried to avoid it to the last minute. . . .

The African National Congress was formed in 1912 to defend the rights of the African people which had been seriously curtailed by the South Africa Act, and which were then being threatened by the Native Land Act.[1] For thirty-seven years — that is until 1949 — it adhered strictly to a constitutional struggle. It put forward demands and resolutions; it sent delegations to the Government in the belief that African grievances could be settled through peaceful discussion and that Africans could advance gradually to full political rights. But White Governments remained unmoved, and the rights of Africans became less instead of becoming greater. . . .

Even after 1949, the ANC remained determined to avoid violence. At this time, however, there was a change from the strictly constitutional means of protest which had been employed in the past. The change was embodied in a decision which was taken to protest against apartheid legislation by peaceful, but unlawful, demonstrations against certain laws. Pursuant to this policy the ANC launched the Defiance Campaign, in which I was placed in charge of volunteers. This campaign was based on the principles of passive resistance. More than 8,500 people defied apartheid laws and went to jail. Yet there was not a single instance of violence in the course of this campaign on the part of any defier. . . .

During the Defiance Campaign, the Public Safety Act and the Criminal Law Amendment Act were passed. These statutes provided harsher

---

[1]The South Africa Act was approved by the British in 1909 and enacted in 1910; it established the Union of South Africa out of the four colonies of Transvaal, the Orange Free State, Natal, and the Cape Colony. The Native Land Act (1913) was a South African law restricting the areas where nonwhites could own land.

penalties for offenses committed by way of protests against laws. Despite this, the protests continued and the ANC adhered to its policy of non-violence.

In 1960 there was the shooting at Sharpeville,[2] which resulted in the proclamation of a state of emergency and the declaration of the ANC as an unlawful organization. My colleagues and I, after careful consideration, decided that we would not obey this decree. The African people were not part of the Government and did not make the laws by which they were governed. We believed in the words of the Universal Declaration of Human Rights,[3] that "the will of the people shall be the basis of authority of the Government," and for us to accept the banning was equivalent to accepting the silencing of the Africans for all time. The ANC refused to dissolve, but instead went underground. . . .

It must not be forgotten that by this time violence had, in fact, become a feature of the South African political scene. . . . Each disturbance pointed clearly to the inevitable growth among Africans of the belief that violence was the only way out — it showed that a Government which uses force to maintain its rule teaches the oppressed to use force to oppose it. . . .

The avoidance of civil war had dominated our thinking for many years, but when we decided to adopt violence as part of our policy, we realized that we might one day have to face the prospect of such a war. . . . We did not want to be committed to civil war, but we wanted to be ready if it became inevitable.

Four forms of violence were possible. There is sabotage, there is guerrilla warfare, there is terrorism, and there is open revolution. We chose to adopt the first method and to exhaust it before taking any other decision.

In the light of our political background the choice was a logical one. Sabotage did not involve loss of life, and it offered the best hope for future race relations. Bitterness would be kept to a minimum and, if the policy bore fruit, democratic government could become a reality. . . .

Attacks on the economic life lines of the country were to be linked with sabotage on Government buildings and other symbols of apartheid. These attacks would serve as a source of inspiration to our people. In addition, they would provide an outlet for those people who were urging the adoption of violent methods and would enable us to give concrete proof to our followers that we had adopted a stronger line and were fighting back against Government violence. . . .

Another of the allegations made by the State is that the aims and objects of the ANC and the Communist Party are the same. I wish to deal with this and with my own political position, because I must assume that the State may try to argue from certain Exhibits that I tried to introduce Marxism into the ANC. . . .

It is true that there has often been close cooperation between the ANC and the Communist Party. But cooperation is merely proof of a common goal — in this case the removal of White supremacy — and is not proof of a complete community of interests. . . .

It is perhaps difficult for White South Africans, with an ingrained prejudice against communism, to understand why experienced African politicians so readily accept communists as their friends. But to us the reason is obvious. Theoretical differences amongst those fighting against oppression is a luxury we cannot afford at this stage. What is more, for many decades communists were the only political group in South Africa who were prepared to treat Africans as human beings and their equals; who were prepared to eat with us; talk with us, live with us, and work with us. They were the only political group which was prepared to work with the Africans for the attainment of political rights and a stake in society. Because of this, there are many Africans who, today, tend to equate freedom with communism. . . .

---

[2]The Sharpeville Massacre took place in 1960 when police killed 69 and wounded 178 antiapartheid demonstrators.

[3]The Universal Declaration of Human Rights was adopted by the United Nations on December 10, 1948.

It is not only in internal politics that we count communists as amongst those who support our cause. In the international field, communist countries have always come to our aid. In the United Nations and other Councils of the world the communist bloc has supported the Afro-Asian struggle against colonialism and often seems to be more sympathetic to our plight than some of the Western powers. Although there is a universal condemnation of apartheid, the communist bloc speaks out against it with a louder voice than most of the White world. . . .

Our fight is against real, and not imaginary, hardships or, to use the language of the State prosecutor, "so-called hardships." Basically, we fight against two features which are the hallmarks of African life in South Africa and which are entrenched by legislation which we seek to have repealed. These features are poverty and lack of human dignity. . . .

South Africa is the richest country in Africa, and could be one of the richest countries in the world. But it is a land of extremes and remarkable contrasts. The Whites enjoy what may well be the highest standard of living in the world, whilst Africans live in poverty and misery. Forty percent of the Africans live in hopelessly overcrowded and, in some cases, drought-stricken Reserves, where soil erosion and the overworking of the soil makes it impossible for them to live properly off the land. Thirty percent are laborers, labor tenants, and squatters on White farms and work and live under conditions similar to those of the serfs of the Middle Ages. The other 30 percent live in towns where they have developed economic and social habits which bring them closer in many respects to White standards. Yet most Africans, even in this group, are impoverished by low incomes and high cost of living.

The complaint of Africans, however, is not only that they are poor and the Whites are rich, but that the laws which are made by the Whites are designed to preserve this situation. There are two ways to break out of poverty. The first is by formal education, and the second is by the worker acquiring a greater skill at his work and thus

higher wages. As far as Africans are concerned, both these avenues of advancement are deliberately curtailed by legislation. . . .

The lack of human dignity experienced by Africans is the direct result of the policy of White supremacy. White supremacy implies Black inferiority. Legislation designed to preserve White supremacy entrenches this notion. Menial tasks in South Africa are invariably performed by Africans. When anything has to be carried or cleaned the White man will look around for an African to do it for him, whether the African is employed by him or not. Because of this sort of attitude, Whites tend to regard Africans as a separate breed. They do not look upon them as people with families of their own; they do not realize that they have emotions — that they fall in love like White people do; that they want to be with their wives and children like White people want to be with theirs; that they want to earn enough money to support their families properly, to feed and clothe them and send them to school. And what "houseboy" or "garden-boy" or laborer can ever hope to do this? . . .

Poverty and the breakdown of family life have secondary effects. Children wander about the streets of the townships because they have no schools to go to, or no money to enable them to go to school, or no parents at home to see that they go to school, because both parents (if there be two) have to work to keep the family alive. This leads to a breakdown in moral standards, to an alarming rise in illegitimacy, and to growing violence which erupts, not only politically, but everywhere. Life in the townships is dangerous. There is not a day that goes by without somebody being stabbed or assaulted. . . .

During my lifetime I have dedicated myself to this struggle of the African people. I have fought against White domination, and I have fought against Black domination. I have cherished the ideal of a democratic and free society in which all persons live together in harmony and with equal opportunities. It is an ideal which I hope to live for and to achieve. But if needs be, it is an ideal for which I am prepared to die.

# A Cry for Justice in the United States
▼▼▼

## 120 ▼ *Martin Luther King, Jr.,*
## *LETTER FROM A BIRMINGHAM JAIL*

On December 1, 1955, in Montgomery, Alabama, Mrs. Rosa Parks, an elderly black seamstress who was sitting in the back of a bus in the "colored section," refused to give up her seat to a white man who had to stand. She was arrested and fined, and in response, a young pastor at the Dexter Avenue Baptist Church organized a boycott of the Montgomery bus system by the city's blacks. The U.S. civil rights movement had begun, and with it, the young pastor, Martin Luther King, Jr., emerged as its leader. Until his assassination in 1968, Reverend King's bravery, moral vision, and moving words inspired millions of followers and forced the nation to confront the implications of its long history of racial prejudice and oppression.

Martin Luther King, Jr., was born in Atlanta on January 15, 1929, the son of the Reverend Martin Luther King and Mrs. Alberta Williams King. Educated at Morehouse College, Crozier Theological Seminary, and Boston University, where he received a doctorate in philosophy, King served as a pastor in Montgomery and then became co-pastor with his father of the Ebenezer Baptist Church in Atlanta. After the Montgomery bus boycott he became president of the Southern Christian Leadership Council and organized voter registration drives in Georgia, Alabama, and Virginia. King's "I Have a Dream" speech at the March on Washington in 1963 provided the civil rights movement with one of its most memorable moments. In the mid 1960s King extended his activities to the cities of the North and spoke out against the Vietnam War. In 1968 he traveled to Memphis, Tennessee, to support a strike by sanitation workers. There, he was assassinated, a crime for which James Earl Ray, a small-town thief and an escaped prisoner from the Missouri state penitentiary, was tried and convicted.

King wrote "Letter from a Birmingham Jail" in April 1963, while he was serving a brief jail sentence for participating in civil rights demonstrations in Birmingham. It was an open letter to eight prominent Alabama clergymen who had criticized his leadership and strategy in the civil rights movement.

---

## QUESTIONS FOR ANALYSIS

1. According to King, what specific criticisms have been made of his civil rights campaign in Birmingham? What alternatives have King's critics recommended?
2. How does King respond to these criticisms?
3. King describes his method as "nonviolent direct action." What does he mean by this?
4. According to King, what are the main obstacles preventing blacks from achieving their goals in the civil rights movement?

5. **King sees similarities between the U.S. civil rights movement and the efforts of Asians and Africans to throw off the bonds of imperialism. Is his analogy valid? Why or why not?**

MY DEAR FELLOW CLERGYMEN,

While confined here in the Birmingham city jail, I came across your recent statement calling our present activities "unwise and untimely." Seldom, if ever, do I pause to answer criticism of my work and ideas. If I sought to answer all of the criticisms that cross my desk, my secretaries would be engaged in little else in the course of the day, and I would have no time for constructive work. But since I feel that you are men of genuine good will and your criticisms are sincerely set forth, I would like to answer your statement in what I hope will be patient and reasonable terms. . . .

You may well ask, "Why direct action? Why sit-ins, marches, etc.? Isn't negotiation a better path?" You are exactly right in your call for negotiation. Indeed, this is the purpose of direct action. Nonviolent direct action seeks to create such a crisis and establish such creative tension that a community that has constantly refused to negotiate is forced to confront the issue. It seeks so to dramatize the issue that it can no longer be ignored. I just referred to the creation of tension as a part of the work of the nonviolent resister. This may sound rather shocking. But I must confess that I am not afraid of the word *tension*. I have earnestly worked and preached against violent tension, but there is a type of constructive nonviolent tension that is necessary for growth. Just as Socrates felt that it was necessary to create a tension in the mind so that individuals could rise from the bondage of myths and half-truths to the unfettered realm of creative analysis and

objective appraisal, we must see the need of having nonviolent gadflies[1] to create the kind of tension in society that will help men to rise from the dark depths of prejudice and racism to the majestic heights of understanding and brotherhood. So the purpose of the direct action is to create a situation so crisis-packed that it will inevitably open the door to negotiation. . . .

One of the basic points in your statement is that our acts are untimely. Some have asked, "Why didn't you give the new administration time to act?" The only answer that I can give to this inquiry is that the new administration must be prodded about as much as the outgoing one before it acts. . . .

We all know through painful experience that freedom is never voluntarily given by the oppressor; it must be demanded by the oppressed. Frankly, I have never yet engaged in a direct action movement that was "well-timed," according to the timetable of those who have not suffered unduly from the disease of segregation. For years now I have heard the word "Wait!" It rings in the ear of every Negro with a piercing familiarity. This "Wait" has almost always meant "Never." It has been a tranquilizing thalidomide,[2] relieving the emotional stress for a moment, only to give birth to an ill-formed infant of frustration. . . .

We have waited for more than 340 years for our constitutional and God-given rights. The nations of Asia and Africa are moving with jet-like speed toward the goal of political independence, and we still creep at horse and buggy pace toward the gaining of a cup of coffee at a

---

[1]Any of various flies, such as horseflies, that bite or annoy livestock; in human relations, an intentionally annoying person who stimulates or provokes others by persistent irritating criticism. The philosopher Socrates (ca. 469–399 B.C.E.) considered himself a "gadfly" among his fellow Athenians.

[2]In 1961 the drug thalidomide, used to treat nausea during pregnancy, was found to be associated with a syndrome of congenital malformations, especially of the arms. About ten thousand babies were affected worldwide.

lunch counter. I guess it is easy for those who have never felt the stinging darts of segregation to say, "Wait." But when you have seen vicious mobs lynch your mothers and fathers at will and drown your sisters and brothers at whim; when you have seen hate-filled policemen curse, kick, brutalize and even kill your black brothers and sisters with impunity; when you see the vast majority of your twenty million Negro brothers smothering in an airtight cage of poverty in the midst of an affluent society; when you suddenly find your tongue twisted and your speech stammering as you seek to explain to your six-year-old daughter why she can't go to the public amusement park that has just been advertised on television, and see tears welling up in her little eyes when she is told that Funtown is closed to colored children, and see the depressing clouds of inferiority begin to form in her little mental sky, and see her begin to distort her little personality by unconsciously developing a bitterness toward white people; when you have to concoct an answer for a five-year-old son asking in agonizing pathos: "Daddy, why do white people treat colored people so mean?"; when you take a cross-country drive and find it necessary to sleep night after night in the uncomfortable corners of your automobile because no motel will accept you; when you are humiliated day in and day out by nagging signs reading "white" and "colored"; when your first name becomes "nigger" and your middle name becomes "boy" (however old you are) and your last name becomes "John," and when your wife and mother are never given the respected title "Mrs."; when you are harried by day and haunted by night by the fact that you are a Negro, living constantly at tiptoe stance never quite knowing what to expect next, and plagued with inner fears and outer resentments; when you are forever fighting a degenerating

sense of "nobodiness"; then you will understand why we find it difficult to wait. There comes a time when the cup of endurance runs over, and men are no longer willing to be plunged into an abyss of injustice where they experience the blackness of corroding despair. I hope, sirs, you can understand our legitimate and unavoidable impatience.

You express a great deal of anxiety over our willingness to break laws. This is certainly a legitimate concern. Since we so diligently urge people to obey the Supreme Court's decision of 1954[3] outlawing segregation in the public schools, it is rather strange and paradoxical to find us consciously breaking laws. One may well ask, "How can you advocate breaking some laws and obeying others?" The answer is found in the fact that there are two types of laws: there are *just* and there are *unjust* laws. I would agree with Saint Augustine[4] that "Any unjust law is no law at all."

Now what is the difference between the two? How does one determine when a law is just or unjust? A just law is a man-made code that squares with the moral law or the law of God. An unjust law is a code that is out of harmony with the moral law. To put it in the terms of Saint Thomas Aquinas,[5] an unjust law is a human law that is not rooted in eternal and natural law. Any law that uplifts human personality is just. Any law that degrades human personality is unjust. All segregation statutes are unjust because segregation distorts the soul and damages the personality. It gives the segregator a false sense of superiority, and the segregated a false sense of inferiority.

Let me give another explanation. An unjust law is a code inflicted upon a minority which that minority had no part in enacting or creating because they did not have the unhampered

---

[3] *Brown* v. *Board of Education* was a famous Supreme Court decision that grew out of a suit brought by Oliver Brown against the Topeka, Kansas, Board of Education when his daughter was denied permission to attend an all-white school in her neighborhood. The court ruled that segregation at all levels of public schooling was illegal.

[4] St. Augustine of Hippo (354–430 C.E.), a North African bishop and theologian, was a seminal figure in the history of Christian thought.
[5] Aquinas (1225[?]–1274), a Dominican friar, was a leading medieval Catholic theologian.

right to vote. Who can say that the legislature of Alabama which set up the segregation laws was democratically elected? Throughout the state of Alabama all types of conniving methods are used to prevent Negroes from becoming registered voters and there are some counties without a single Negro registered to vote despite the fact that the Negro constitutes a majority of the population. Can any law set up in such a state be considered democratically structured? . . .

You spoke of our activity in Birmingham as extreme. At first I was rather disappointed that fellow clergymen would see my nonviolent efforts as those of the extremist. I started thinking about the fact that I stand in the middle of two opposing forces in the Negro community. One is a force of complacency made up of Negroes who, as a result of long years of oppression, have been so completely drained of self-respect and a sense of "somebodiness" that they have adjusted to segregation, and, of a few Negroes in the middle class who, because of a degree of academic and economic security, and because at points they profit by segregation, have unconsciously become insensitive to the problems of the masses. The other force is one of bitterness and hatred, and comes perilously close to advocating violence. It is expressed in the various black nationalist groups that are springing up over the nation, the largest and best known being Elijah Muhammad's Muslim movement.[6] This movement is nourished by the contemporary frustration over the continued existence of racial discrimination. It is made up of people who have lost faith in America, who have absolutely repudiated Christianity, and who have concluded that the white man is an incurable "devil." I have tried to stand between these two forces, saying that we need not follow the "do-nothingism" of the complacent or the hatred and despair of the black

nationalist. There is the more excellent way of love and nonviolent protest. . . .

I have no fear about the outcome of our struggle in Birmingham, even if our motives are presently misunderstood. We will reach the goal of freedom in Birmingham and all over the nation, because the goal of America is freedom. Abused and scorned though we may be, our destiny is tied up with the destiny of America. Before the Pilgrims landed at Plymouth we were here. Before the pen of Jefferson etched across the pages of history the majestic words of the Declaration of Independence, we were here. For more than two centuries our foreparents labored in this country without wages; they made cotton king; and they built the homes of their masters in the midst of brutal injustice and shameful humiliation — and yet out of a bottomless vitality they continued to thrive and develop. If the inexpressible cruelties of slavery could not stop us, the opposition we now face will surely fail. We will win our freedom because the sacred heritage of our nation and the eternal will of God are embodied in our echoing demands. . . .

I hope this letter finds you strong in the faith. I also hope that circumstances will soon make it possible for me to meet each of you, not as an integrationist or a civil rights leader, but as a fellow clergyman and a Christian brother. Let us all hope that the dark clouds of racial prejudice will soon pass away and the deep fog of misunderstanding will be lifted from our fear-drenched communities and in some not too distant tomorrow the radiant stars of love and brotherhood will shine over our great nation with all of their scintillating beauty.

Yours for the cause of Peace and Brotherhood,

MARTIN LUTHER KING, JR.

---

[6]Founded in Detroit in the early 1930s, the Black Muslims in 1934 came under the leadership of Elijah Muhammad, a Georgian originally named Elijah Poole. He moved the organization's headquarters to Chicago, where he preached black self-reliance and separatism from white society. At the time of his death in 1975, Black Muslim membership numbered between 150,000 and 200,000.

▼▼▼

# Another New Era:
# The Failure of Communism
# and the End of the Cold War

In the mid twentieth century global political relationships entered an era of moral and ideological absolutes. On one side was the communist world composed of the Soviet Union, its Eastern European satellites, and China, where communists took power in 1949. Characterized by authoritarian, one-party governments and centralized economic planning, these states proclaimed their commitment to the triumph of Marxism and the demise of capitalism throughout the world. On the other side was a bloc of states led by the United States, which called itself the "free world" and set its goal as the defense of capitalism and the spread of liberal democracy. For more than forty years these two blocs organized themselves into formidable military alliances, built up huge nuclear arsenals, supported giant intelligence establishments, and competed for support among nonaligned nations. For both sides the dualisms of the Cold War — communism versus capitalism, the United States versus the Soviet Union, NATO versus the Warsaw Pact — gave clarity, direction, and meaning to international politics.

In reality, the conflict between the free and communist worlds was never completely about ideology. From the very start of the Cold War, the United States and its allies propped up dictators when it served their purposes of containing communism. And as early as the 1950s cracks and fissures began to appear in both coalitions. Anti-Soviet revolts took place in Eastern Europe in 1956 and 1968, and the diplomatic relations between China and the Soviet Union cooled in the mid 1960s. Also in the mid 1960s the prospering, stable democracies of Western Europe, inspired by the independent course of France's leader, Charles de Gaulle, no longer unquestioningly accepted U.S. policies on issues of military deployment in Europe and U.S. involvement in Vietnam.

There were times when the Cold War appeared on the verge of ending, but on each occasion old tensions returned. In the mid 1950s talk of peaceful coexistence gave way to renewed acrimony after the downing of a U.S. spy plane on Soviet soil in 1960, the building of the Berlin Wall in 1961, and the Cuban missile crisis of 1962. Relations between the United States and the Soviet Union improved once more in the 1970s, when the two powers signed treaties on arms limitation and access to Berlin. Soviet–U.S. relations deteriorated, however, after the Soviet invasion of Afghanistan in 1979 and the resulting U.S. boycott of the 1980 Moscow Olympics. In 1980 President Ronald Reagan branded the Soviet Union an "evil empire"; sent U.S. troops to Grenada to overthrow a Marxist government; provided arms to forces trying to overthrow communist regimes in Afghanistan, Nicaragua, and Angola; and sponsored a rapid arms build-up in the United States. Soviet suspicions of the United States deepened, and U.S. leaders showed no sign that they expected anything other than continuing Soviet–U.S. conflict.

By 1991, however, the Cold War was over. In one state after another in Soviet-controlled Eastern Europe, communist regimes either collapsed or were voted out of power and replaced by constitutional democracies. Within the Soviet Union, reforms initiated by Premier Mikhail Gorbachev in 1985 began with policies of *glasnost* (openness) and *perestroika* (restructuring) as a means to rejuvenate Soviet society. But his efforts to save communism by democratization and economic liberalization set in motion forces he could not control, and by the end of 1991, both communist rule and the Soviet Union itself ceased to exist.

Meanwhile changes no less profound were taking place in the world's other major communist state, China. After the death of Mao Zedong in 1976, China, under the leadership of Deng Xiaoping, de-emphasized ideology and egalitarianism in favor of pragmatism and economic development. Deng approved the opening of small private businesses, fostered a market economy in agriculture, opened China to foreign investment, supported scientific and technological education, and encouraged Chinese exports of manufactured goods. The results were spectacular, with annual economic growth rates of 12 percent in the early 1990s. China remained authoritarian and officially communist, but with its commitment to "market socialism," it was far different from the isolated, ideology-driven China of previous decades.

Thus the world's people greet the new millennium with few sure guidelines or certainties. Powerful twentieth-century ideologies such as nationalism and communism have been discredited. Faith in religion and science alike has been shaken. A world dominated by great powers has been replaced by a world with no clearly delineated international structure or guiding principles. Even the viability of the nation-state has been called into question. Free market capitalism is now ascendant, but how long this will continue remains unclear. Only one thing is certain about the twenty-first century: as the stunning demise of communism and the Soviet Union reveals, anything is possible.

## China's New Course
▼▼▼

### 121 ▼ Deng Xiaoping, SPEECHES AND WRITINGS

Of all the events that have taken place in the closing decades of the twentieth century, China's full entry into the global economy and its decision to commit itself to economic development may in the long run prove to be the most significant. Since its emergence as a unified empire in the third century B.C.E., China for many centuries was the world's most successful state in terms of size, wealth, technological sophistication, and the continuity of its political institutions. This was easy to forget in the nineteenth and twentieth centuries, when China became a pawn of the Western powers and a victim of political disintegration, military defeat, and deepening poverty. In the 1980s, however, China's leaders set a new course for their country, which, if successful, might well restore China to its preeminence in Asia, if not its primacy among the world's powers.

The man responsible for launching China on its new course was Deng Xiaoping, whose life spanned almost all of the twentieth century. Born into the family of a well-off landowner in 1904, Deng studied in China and then in France after World War I. Having run out of funds, he worked in a factory before returning to China by way of the Soviet Union, where he studied in 1925–1926. Once in China he joined the Communist Party and became one of Mao's most loyal followers in the struggle against the Japanese and the Guomindang.

After 1949 Deng became a member of the politburo and party secretary general, with responsibilities for overseeing economic development in southwest China. He supported the strategy of developing China's economy by following the Stalinist model of investment in heavy industry, agricultural collectivization, and centralized planning. This was scrapped in 1958 when Mao instituted the Great Leap Forward. In a little more than two years, some twenty-four thousand People's Communes were established, each containing approximately thirty thousand people who performed industrial and agricultural work, received political indoctrination, and participated in various social experiments. The Great Leap Forward was an economic disaster, and in its wake, Deng and other moderates were responsible for dismantling the communes and reintroducing centralized planning.

This made Deng a prime candidate for vilification after Mao launched the Great Cultural Revolution in 1966. Designed to revive revolutionary fervor and rescue China from materialism and Soviet-style bureaucratization, the revolution unleashed the energies of millions of young people who were urged to rise up and smash "bourgeois" elements throughout society. Deng fell from power, was paraded through the streets in a dunce cap, and put to work in a mess hall and a tractor repair shop. As the intensity of the Cultural Revolution faded, Deng was reinstated as a party official, and after Mao's death he led the moderates in their struggle with the radical faction led by Mao's widow, Jiang Qing. Deng's faction won, and in December 1978, the Central Committee of the Chinese Communist Party officially abandoned Mao's emphasis on ideology and class struggle in favor of a moderate, pragmatic policy designed to achieve the Four Modernizations in agriculture, industry, science and technology, and the military.

To encourage economic growth, the government fostered free markets, competition, and private incentives. Although Deng claimed that China had entered its "second revolution," it was an economic revolution only. Reformers who demanded the "Fifth Modernization" — democracy — were arrested and silenced in 1979. When millions of Chinese demonstrated for democracy in the spring of 1989, the government crushed the demonstrators in Beijing with soldiers and tanks, thus assuring the continuation of the party dictatorship. After 1989 Deng withdrew from public life and died in early 1997. The following excerpts are from speeches and interviews given by Deng between 1983 and 1986.

---

## QUESTIONS FOR ANALYSIS

1. According to Deng, what had been the shortcomings of China's economic development planning under Mao Zedong?
2. According to Deng, how is China's new economic policy truly Marxist and truly socialist?

3. How does Deng view China's role in the world? What implications will China's new economic priorities have for its foreign policy?
4. What is Deng's rationale for opposing democracy in China?
5. What similarities and differences do you see between Deng's economic program for China and Stalin's plans for the Soviet Union in the late 1920s and 1930s (see source 92)?

## MAOISM'S FLAWS

After the founding of the People's Republic, in the rural areas we initiated agrarian reform and launched a movement for the co-operative transformation of agriculture,[1] while in the cities we conducted the socialist transformation of capitalist industry and commerce.[2] We were successful in both. However, from 1957 on, China was plagued by "Left" ideology, which gradually became dominant. During the Great Leap Forward in 1958, people rushed headlong into mass action to establish people's communes. They placed lopsided emphasis on making the communes large in size and collective in nature, urging everyone to "eat from the same big pot," and by so doing brought disaster upon the nation. We won't even mention the "cultural revolution." . . . During the 20 years from 1958 to 1978 the income of peasants and workers rose only a little, and consequently their standard of living remained very low. The development of the productive forces was sluggish during those years. In 1978 per capita GNP was less than $250. . . .

Comrade Mao Zedong was a great leader, and it was under his leadership that the Chinese revolution triumphed. But he made the grave mistake of neglecting the development of the productive forces. I do not mean he didn't want to develop them. The point is, not all of the methods he used were correct. For instance, the people's communes were established in defiance of the laws governing socio-economic development. The most important lesson we have learned, among a great many others, is that we must be clear about what socialism is and how to build it.

The fundamental principle of Marxism is that the productive forces must be developed. The goal for Marxists is to realize communism, which must be built on the basis of highly developed productive forces. What is a communist society? It is a society in which there is vast material wealth and in which the principle of from each according to his ability, to each according to his needs is applied. . . .

Our experience in the 20 years from 1958 to 1978 teaches us that poverty is not socialism, that socialism means eliminating poverty. Unless you are developing the productive forces and raising people's living standards, you cannot say that you are building socialism.

After the Third Plenary Session[3] we proceeded to explore ways of building socialism in China. Finally we decided to develop the productive forces and gradually expand the economy. The first goal we set was to achieve comparative prosperity by the end of the century. . . . So taking population increase into consideration, we planned to quadruple our GNP, which meant that per capita GNP would grow from $250 to $800 or $1,000. We shall lead a much better life when we reach this level, although it is still

---

[1]Following the communist victory in 1949 large estates were confiscated from landlords and redistributed to the peasantry. But in the early 1950s agriculture became collectivized under state control and peasants essentially became paid agricultural laborers who turned their crops over to the government in return for wages.

[2]During the 1950s private businesses involved in manu-

facturing and finance were phased out of existence and became state enterprises.

[3]The Third Plenary Session of Eleventh Central Committee of the Chinese Communist Party, held in December 1978, approved the Four Modernizations Program favored by Deng.

much lower than that of the developed countries. That is why we call it comparative prosperity. When we attain that level, China's GNP will have reached $1,000 billion, representing increased national strength. And the most populous nation in the world will have shaken off poverty and be able to make a greater contribution to mankind. With a GNP of $1,000 billion as a springboard, within 30 or 50 more years — 50, to be more accurate — China may reach its second goal, to approach the level of the developed countries. How are we to go about achieving these goals? . . . We began our reform in the countryside. The main point of the rural reform has been to bring the peasants' initiative into full play by introducing the responsibility system and discarding the system whereby everybody ate from the same big pot. Why did we start in the countryside? Because that is where 80 per cent of China's population lives. If we didn't raise living standards in the countryside, the society would be unstable. Industry, commerce and other sectors of the economy cannot develop on the basis of the poverty of 80 per cent of the population. After three years of practice the rural reform has proved successful. I can say with assurance it is a good policy. The countryside has assumed a new look. The living standards of 90 per cent of the rural population have been raised. . . .

After our success in rural reform we embarked on urban reform. Urban reform is more complicated and risky. This is especially true in China, because we have no experience in this regard. Also, China has traditionally been a very closed society, so that people lack information about what's going on elsewhere.

Although some problems have arisen in the process, we are confident that we can handle them. . . . We are sure it will be successful.

It is our hope that businessmen and economists in other countries will appreciate that to help China develop will benefit the world. China's foreign trade volume makes up a very small portion of the world's total. If we succeed in quadrupling the GNP, the volume of our foreign trade will increase considerably, promoting China's economic relations with other countries and expanding its market. Therefore, judged from the perspective of world politics and economics, China's development will benefit world peace and the world economy. . . .

## TRUE SOCIALISM

Our modernization programme is a socialist programme, not anything else. All our policies for carrying out reform, opening to the outside world and invigorating the domestic economy are designed to develop the socialist economy. We allow the development of individual economy, of joint ventures with both Chinese and foreign investment and of enterprises wholly owned by foreign businessmen, but socialist public ownership will always remain predominant. The aim of socialism is to make all our people prosperous, not to create polarization. If our policies led to polarization, it would mean that we had failed; if a new bourgeoisie emerged, it would mean that we had strayed from the right path. In encouraging some regions to become prosperous first, we intend that they should help the economically backward ones to develop. Similarly, in encouraging some people to become prosperous first, we intend that they should help others who are still in poverty to become better off, so that there will be common prosperity rather than polarization. A limit should be placed on the wealth of people who become prosperous first, through the income tax, for example. In addition, we should encourage them to contribute money to run schools and build roads, although we definitely shouldn't set quotas for them. We should encourage these people to make donations, but it's better not to give such donations too much publicity.

In short, predominance of public ownership and common prosperity are the two fundamental socialist principles that we must adhere to. We shall firmly put them into practice. And ultimately we shall move on to communism.

## SPECIAL ECONOMIC ZONES

In establishing special economic zones[4] and implementing an open policy, we must make it clear that our guideline is just that — to open and not to close.

I was impressed by the prosperity of the Shenzhen[5] Special Economic Zone during my stay there. The pace of construction in Shenzhen is rapid. It is particularly fast in Shekou, because the authorities there are permitted to make their own spending decisions up to a limit of U.S. $5 million. Their slogan is "time is money, efficiency is life." In Shenzhen, it doesn't take long to erect a tall building; the workers complete a storey in a couple of days. The construction workers there are from inland cities. Their high efficiency is due to the "contracted responsibility system," under which they are paid according to their performance, and to a fair system of rewards and penalties.

A special economic zone is a medium for introducing technology, management and knowledge. It is also a window for our foreign policy. Through the special economic zone we can import foreign technology, obtain knowledge and learn management, which is also a kind of knowledge. . . . Public order in Shenzhen is reportedly better than before, and people who slipped off to Hongkong have begun to return. One reason is that there are more job opportunities and people's incomes and living standards are rising, all of which proves that cultural and ideological progress is based on material progress.

## CHINA'S FOREIGN RELATIONS

While invigorating the domestic economy, we have also formulated a policy of opening to the outside world. Reviewing our history, we have concluded that one of the most important reasons for China's long years of stagnation and backwardness was its policy of closing the country to outside contact. Our experience shows that China cannot rebuild itself with its doors closed to the outside and that it cannot develop in isolation from the rest of the world. It goes without saying that a large country like China cannot depend on others for its development; it must depend mainly on itself, on its own efforts. Nevertheless, while holding to self-reliance, we should open our country to the outside world to obtain such aid as foreign investment capital and technology. . . .

## CHINA'S POLITICAL FUTURE

The recent student unrest[6] is not going to lead to any major disturbances. But because of its nature it must be taken very seriously. Firm measures must be taken against any student who creates trouble at Tiananmen Square. . . . In the beginning, we mainly used persuasion, which is as it should be in dealing with student demonstrators. But if any of them disturb public order or violate the law, they must be dealt with unhesitatingly. Persuasion includes application of the law. When a disturbance breaks out in a place, it's because the leaders there didn't take a firm, clear-cut stand. This is not a problem that has arisen in just one or two places or in just the last couple of years; it is the result of failure over the past several years to take a firm, clear-cut stand against bourgeois liberalization. It is essential to adhere firmly to the Four Cardinal Principles;[7] otherwise bourgeois liberalization will spread unchecked — and that has been the root cause of the problem. . . .

In developing our democracy, we cannot simply copy bourgeois democracy, or introduce the system of a balance of three powers. I have often

---

[4]The Special Economic Zones (SEZ) were restricted areas where foreign firms could set up businesses and house foreign personnel.
[5]A district next to Hong Kong.
[6]Deng made these remarks in December 1986, when student demonstrations and speechmaking on behalf of the Pro-Democracy Movement had been going on in Tiananmen Square in Beijing for several years.
[7]Issued by Deng in 1979, the Four Cardinal Principles were (1) the socialist path, (2) the dictatorship of the proletariat, (3) party leadership, and (4) Marxism-Leninism-Mao Zedong thought.

criticized people in power in the United States, saying that actually they have three governments. Of course, the American bourgeoisie uses this system in dealing with other countries, but when it comes to internal affairs, the three branches often pull in different directions, and that makes trouble. We cannot adopt such a system. . . .

Without leadership by the Communist Party and without socialism, there is no future for China. This truth has been demonstrated in the past, and it will be demonstrated again in future. When we succeed in raising China's per capita GNP to $4,000 and everyone is prosperous, that will better demonstrate the superiority of socialism over capitalism, it will point the way for three quarters of the world's population and it will provide further proof of the correctness of Marxism. Therefore, we must confidently keep to the socialist road and uphold the Four Cardinal Principles.

We cannot do without dictatorship. We must not only affirm the need for it but exercise it when necessary. Of course, we must be cautious about resorting to dictatorial means and make as few arrests as possible. But if some people attempt to provoke bloodshed, what are we going to do about it? We should first expose their plot and then do our best to avoid shedding blood, even if that means some of our own people get hurt. However, ringleaders who have violated the law must be sentenced according to law. Unless we are prepared to do that, it will be impossible to put an end to disturbances. If we take no action and back down, we shall only have more trouble down the road.

The struggle against bourgeois liberalization is also indispensable. We should not be afraid that it will damage our reputation abroad. China must take its own road and build socialism with Chinese characteristics — that is the only way China can have a future. We must show foreigners that China's political situation is stable. If our country were plunged into disorder and our nation reduced to a heap of loose sand, how could we ever prosper? The reason the imperialists were able to bully us in the past was precisely that we were a heap of loose sand.

# A Plan to Save Communism in the Soviet Union
▼▼▼
## 122 ▼ *Mikhail Gorbachev, PERESTROIKA*

Throughout the 1970s and early 1980s the Soviet Union was one of the world's two superpowers, with an enormous army, a huge industrial establishment, an impressive record of technological achievement, and a seemingly unshakable authoritarian government. No one saw any reason why it would not continue as the United States's great rival in world affairs. In reality, industrial and agricultural production were stagnating, the people's morale was plummeting, and the fossilized bureaucracy was mired in old policies and theories that no longer worked. Against this background Mikhail Gorbachev became general secretary of the Communist Party in March 1985 and began the task of rejuvenating Soviet communism by introducing policies based on *glasnost,* or openness, and *perestroika,* or restructuring.

Gorbachev, who was fifty-four years old when he took power, was born of peasant parents and had studied law and agricultural economics. After filling a variety of positions in the Communist Party, he became a member of the politburo in 1979. After serving as Soviet leader for two years, he published a book, *Perestroika* (1987), from which the following excerpt is taken. In it he describes his goals for Soviet communism. To his sorrow and the world's shock he fell from power in 1991, with his reforms having led not to communism's reform but its demise and not to the Soviet Union's revival but its dismemberment.

---

*QUESTIONS FOR ANALYSIS*

1. What developments in the Soviet Union led Gorbachev to the conclusion that Soviet society and government were in need of reform?
2. In Gorbachev's analysis, what caused Soviet society to "lose its momentum"?
3. In Gorbachev's view, how will the "individual" in Soviet society be affected by his reforms?
4. To what extent is perestroika democratic?
5. What similarities and differences do you see between Gorbachev's statements about perestroika and Deng's comments about the needs of China (source 121)?

Russia, where a great Revolution took place seventy years ago, is an ancient country with a unique history filled with searchings, accomplishments, and tragic events. It has given the world many discoveries and outstanding personalities.

However, the Soviet Union is a young state without analogues in history or in the modern world. Over the past seven decades — a short span in the history of human civilization — our country has traveled a path equal to centuries. One of the mightiest powers in the world rose up to replace the backward semi-colonial and semi-feudal Russian Empire. . . .

At some stage — this became particularly clear in the latter half of the seventies — something happened that was at first sight inexplicable. The country began to lose momentum. Economic failures became more frequent. Difficulties began to accumulate and deteriorate, and unresolved problems to multiply. Elements of what we call stagnation and other phenomena alien to socialism began to appear in the life of society. A kind of "braking mechanism" affecting social and economic development formed. And all this happened at a time when scientific and technological revolution opened up new prospects for economic and social progress. . . .

Analyzing the situation, we first discovered a slowing economic growth. In the last fifteen years the national income growth rates had declined by more than a half and by the beginning of the eighties had fallen to a level close to economic stagnation. A country that was once quickly closing on the world's advanced nations began to lose one position after another. . . .

It became typical of many of our economic executives to think not of how to build up the national assets, but of how to put more material, labor, and working time into an item to sell it at a higher price. Consequently, for all our "gross output," there was a shortage of goods. We spent, in fact we are still spending, far more on raw materials, energy, and other resources per unit of output than other developed nations. Our country's wealth in terms of natural and manpower resources has spoilt, one may even say corrupted, us. . . .

The presentation of a "problem-free" reality backfired: a breach had formed between word and deed, which bred public passivity and disbelief in the slogans being proclaimed. It was only natural that this situation resulted in a credibility gap: everything that was proclaimed from the rostrums and printed in newspapers and textbooks was put in question. Decay began in public morals; the great feeling of solidarity with each other that was forged during the heroic times of the Revolution, the first five-year plans, the Great Patriotic War,[1] and postwar rehabilitation was weakening; alcoholism, drug addiction, and crime were growing; and the penetration of the stereotypes of mass culture alien to us, which bred vulgarity and low tastes and brought about ideological barrenness, increased.

Political flirtation and mass distribution of awards, titles, and bonuses often replaced genuine concern for the people, for their living and working conditions, for a favorable social atmosphere. An atmosphere emerged of "everything goes," and fewer and fewer demands were made on discipline and responsibility. Attempts were made to cover it all up with pompous campaigns and undertakings and celebrations of numerous anniversaries centrally and locally. The world of day-to-day realities and the world of feigned prosperity were diverging more and more. . . .

An unbiased and honest approach led us to the only logical conclusion that the country was verging on crisis. This conclusion was announced at the April 1985 Plenary Meeting of the Central Committee,[2] which inaugurated the new strategy of perestroika and formulated its basic principles. . . .

By saying all this I want to make the reader understand that the energy for revolutionary change has been accumulating amid our people and in the Party for some time. And the ideas of perestroika have been prompted not just by pragmatic interests and considerations but also by our troubled conscience, by the indomitable commitment to ideals which we inherited from the Revolution and as a result of a theoretical quest which gave us a better knowledge of society and reinforced our determination to go ahead.

Today our main job is to lift the individual spiritually, respecting his inner world and giv-ing him moral strength. We are seeking to make the whole intellectual potential of society and all the potentialities of culture work to mold a socially active person, spiritually rich, just, and conscientious. An individual must know and feel that his contribution is needed, that his dignity is not being infringed upon, that he is being treated with trust and respect. When an individual sees all this, he is capable of accomplishing much.

Of course, perestroika somehow affects everybody; it jolts many out of their customary state of calm and satisfaction at the existing way of life. Here I think it is appropriate to draw your attention to one specific feature of socialism. I have in mind the high degree of social protection in our society. On the one hand, it is, doubtless, a benefit and a major achievement of ours. On the other, it makes some people spongers.

There is virtually no unemployment. The state has assumed concern for ensuring employment. Even a person dismissed for laziness or a breach of labor discipline must be given another job. Also, wage-leveling has become a regular feature of our everyday life: even if a person is a bad worker, he gets enough to live fairly comfortably. The children of an outright parasite will not be left to the mercy of fate. We have enormous sums of money concentrated in the social funds from which people receive financial assistance. The same funds provide subsidies for the upkeep of kindergartens, orphanages, Young Pioneer[3] houses, and other institutions related to children's creativity and sport. Health care is free, and so is education. People are protected from the vicissitudes of life, and we are proud of this.

But we also see that dishonest people try to exploit these advantages of socialism; they know only their rights, but they do not want to know their duties: they work poorly, shirk, and drink hard. There are quite a few people who have

---

[1] World War II.
[2] The Central Committee of the Communist Party, the body that sets broad policy for the Soviet government.

[3] A youth organization sponsored by the Soviet regime.

adapted the existing laws and practices to their own selfish interests. They give little to society, but nevertheless managed to get from it all that is possible and what even seems impossible; they have lived on unearned incomes.

The policy of restructuring puts everything in its place. We are fully restoring the principle of socialism. "From each according to his ability, to each according to his work," and we seek to affirm social justice for all, equal rights for all, one law for all, one kind of discipline for all, and high responsibilities for each. Perestroika raises the level of social responsibility and expectation. . . .

It is essential to learn to adjust policy in keeping with the way it is received by the masses, and to ensure feedback, absorbing the ideas, opinions, and advice coming from the people. The masses suggest a lot of useful and interesting things which are not always clearly perceived "from the top." That is why we must prevent at all costs an arrogant attitude to what people are saying. In the final account the most important thing for the success of perestroika is the people's attitude to it.

Thus, not only theory but the reality of the processes under way made us embark on the program for all-round democratic changes in public life which we presented at the January 1987 Plenary Meeting of the CPSU[4] Central Committee.

The Plenary Meeting encouraged extensive efforts to strengthen the democratic basis of Soviet society, to develop self-government and extend glasnost, that is openness, in the entire management network. We see now how stimulating that impulse was for the nation. Democratic changes have been taking place at every work collective, at every state and public organization, and within the Party. More glasnost, genuine control from "below," and greater initiative and enterprise at work are now part and parcel of our life. . . .

The adoption of fundamental principles for a radical change in economic management was a big step forward in the program of perestroika. Now perestroika concerns virtually every main aspect of public life. . . .

Perestroika means overcoming the stagnation process, breaking down the braking mechanism, creating a dependable and effective mechanism for the acceleration of social and economic progress and giving it greater dynamism.

Perestroika means mass initiative. It is the comprehensive development of democracy, socialist self-government, encouragement of initiative and creative endeavor, improved order and discipline, more glasnost, criticism, and self-criticism in all spheres of our society. It is utmost respect for the individual and consideration for personal dignity.

Perestroika is the all-round intensification of the Soviet economy, the revival and development of the principles of democratic centralism in running the national economy, the universal introduction of economic methods, the renunciation of management by injunction and by administrative methods, and the overall encouragement of innovation and socialist enterprise.

Perestroika means a resolute shift to scientific methods, an ability to provide a solid scientific basis for every new initiative. It means the combination of the achievements of the scientific and technological revolution with a planned economy.

Perestroika means priority development of the social sphere aimed at ever better satisfaction of the Soviet people's requirements for good living and working conditions, for good rest and recreation, education, and health care. It means unceasing concern for cultural and spiritual wealth, for the culture of every individual and society as a whole.

Perestroika means the elimination from society of the distortions of socialist ethics, the consistent implementation of the principles of social

---

[4]Communist Party of the Soviet Union.

justice. It means the unity of words and deeds, rights and duties. It is the elevation of honest, highly-qualified labor, the overcoming of leveling tendencies in pay and consumerism.

I stress once again: perestroika is not some kind of illumination or revelation. To restructure our life means to understand the objective necessity for renovation and acceleration. And that necessity emerged in the heart of our society. The es-sence of perestroika lies in the fact that it *unites socialism with democracy* and revives the Leninist concept of socialist construction both in theory and in practice. Such is the essence of perestroika, which accounts for its genuine revolutionary spirit and its all-embracing scope.

The goal is worth the effort. And we are sure that our effort will be a worthy contribution to humanity's social progress.

▼▼▼

# The Earth's Future: Two Perspectives

A striking feature of the late twentieth century has been rising environmental consciousness. Environmental movements have proliferated, and governments, international agencies, and individuals have made ambitious efforts to deal with a wide range of environmental issues, including habitat loss, overpopulation, re-source depletion, solid waste disposal, air and water purity, global warming, and ozone loss. Such efforts have mainly taken place in the industrialized nations of the West, where the roots of modern environmentalism go back to the eighteenth century. As early as the 1750s British, French, and Dutch administrators sought to protect the soil, forests, and species of newly discovered tropical islands in the Caribbean and Indian Ocean by limiting economic development. In the early 1800s the Englishmen Thomas Malthus (1766–1834) and David Ricardo (1772–1823) warned of catastrophic famine without curbs on population growth. And from the 1890s onward conservationists in the United States, Canada, and Eu-rope have sought to protect natural areas from potentially ruinous economic development.

None of these earlier movements, however, generated anything close to the near universal support for environmentalism in the late twentieth century. Be-ginning in the 1960s people in the industrialized nations of North America and Europe saw frightening population projections, learned of the dangers of pesti-cides from Rachel Carson's *Silent Spring,* stopped swimming and fishing in dying lakes and rivers, listened to daily smog reports on the radio, and looked in horror at television images of dead or dying fish, birds, and mammals washing up on California's oil-smeared coast after the Santa Barbara oil spill of 1969. The Arab oil embargo of 1973 and the quadrupling of oil prices in 1974 by the Organization of Petroleum Exporting Countries (OPEC) reinforced the idea that self-restraint and environmental awareness must replace mindless consumption and uncon-trolled economic growth.

The United States, Canada, Western Europe, and Japan responded quickly to the perceived environmental crisis. Governments required industries to meet tough environmental standards, encouraged recycling, allocated large sums to clean up polluted rivers and lakes, fostered the development of alternative en-ergy sources, and outlawed the manufacture and use of hundreds of potentially dangerous compounds. School boards mandate the teaching of environmental topics in the classroom, and manufacturers seek to gain customers by promoting their products as "environment friendly." Public opinion polls in these richer nations show strong support for environmental protection.

Nonetheless, since the late 1980s a sense of unease has become evident among many environmental activists. Evidence of environmental ruination in China and the former Soviet Union and the inability or unwillingness of weak governments in developing nations to halt population growth, pollution, and habitat destruction have been sobering reminders that successful environmental campaigns in developed nations are just one small part of a difficult global struggle to save the planet. Environmentalists worry about complacency, antienvironmental lobbying efforts, and support for causes such as the "wise-use" movement, which considers government efforts to maintain environmental quality as unnecessary and burdensome bureaucratic hindrances to economic growth. Most disturbing of all has been the growing body of literature claiming that the scientific basis of environmentalism is flawed. Environmentalists and their supporters in the scientific community have, so this literature claims, misinterpreted data, ignored damaging facts, and relied on unproven theories. They have created environmental crises where none existed.

During the 1990s, environmentalists and their critics both came to believe that environmentalism was at a turning point. Both sides made strenuous efforts to win the battle for public opinion and political support. Occasionally representatives of the two sides have agreed to participate in public forums in which contending philosophies and theories could be debated. One such occasion took place in New York City in October 1992 under the auspices of Columbia University's School of International and Public Affairs. It brought together Norman Myers, who represented the environmentalist position, and Julian Simon, a critic of the environmentalists. Excerpts from these two men's opening statements follow. Although these relatively brief statements cannot do justice to the nuances and complexities of each man's arguments, they do provide a concise summary of their disagreements and two radically different visions of the Earth's future.

# "There's Plenty of Good News"
▼▼▼

## 123 ▼ *Julian Simon,*
## *OPENING STATEMENT FROM 1992*
## *DEBATE AT COLUMBIA UNIVERSITY*

Born in Newark, New Jersey, in 1932, Julian Simon received his bachelor's degree from Harvard and his master of business administration and doctorate degrees from the University of Chicago. He held several jobs in the private sector before becoming a professor of business administration. His main interest is the effect of population changes on the environment and economic growth. Beginning in 1977 with his book *The Economics of Population Growth,* he has argued in numerous books and articles that humanity has a bright future and that population growth will contribute to it in the long run. Simon currently teaches at the University of Maryland.

---

## QUESTIONS FOR ANALYSIS

1. In what specific economic and social areas are "things getting better," according to Simon?
2. Simon claims resource scarcity has decreased over time. How does he support his claim, and how valid are his arguments?
3. What are the flaws in Malthusian theory, according to Simon?
4. In another context Simon has written that the main problem confronting humanity is not scarcity but the lack of human freedom. Why do you suppose freedom plays such an important part in Simon's hopes for the future?

---

The gloom-and-doom about a "crisis" of our environment is all wrong on the scientific facts. Even the Environmental Protection Agency acknowledges that U.S. air and our water have been getting cleaner rather than dirtier in the past few decades. Every agricultural economist knows that the world's population has been eating ever better since World War II. Every resource economist knows that all natural resources have been getting more available rather than more scarce, as shown by their falling prices over the decades and centuries. And every demographer knows that the death rate has been falling all over the world — life expectancy almost tripling in the rich countries in the past two centuries, and almost doubling in the poor countries in just the past four decades.

The picture also is now clear that population growth does not hinder economic development. In the 1980s there was a complete reversal in the consensus of thinking of population economists about the effects of more people. In 1986, the National Research Council and the National Academy of Sciences completely overturned their "official" view away from the earlier worried view expressed in 1971. They noted the absence of any statistical evidence of a negative connection between population increase and economic growth. And they said that "The scarcity of ex-

haustible resources is at most a minor restraint on economic growth." . . .

For proper understanding of the important aspects of an economy, we should look at the long-run trends. But the short-run comparisons — between the sexes, age groups, races, political groups, which are usually purely relative — make more news. To repeat, just about every important long-run measure of human welfare shows improvement over the decades and centuries, in the United States as well as in the rest of the world. And there is no persuasive reason to believe that these trends will not continue indefinitely. . . .

Would I bet on it? For sure. I'll bet a week's or month's pay — anything I win goes to pay for more research — that just about any trend pertaining to material human welfare will improve rather than get worse. You pick the comparison and the year. First come, first served. Material welfare, not emotional or spiritual or sexual or social. Not ozone but cancers. Not greenhouse warming but agriculture and standard of living. And I'll be happy to bet with Norman Myers about many of the trends that he thinks are going to be bad in the future.

Take a look at . . . a graph of human life expectancy at birth, which slowly crept up from the low 20s thousands of years ago to the high

20s about 1750. Then in about 1750, life expectancy in the richest countries suddenly took off and tripled in about two centuries. In just the past two centuries, the length of life you could expect for your baby or yourself in the advanced countries jumped from less than thirty years to perhaps seventy-five years. What greater event has humanity witnessed?

Then starting well after World War II, the length of life you could expect in the poor countries has leaped upward by perhaps fifteen or even twenty years since the 1950s, caused by advances in agriculture, sanitation, and medicine. . . .

It is this decrease in the death rate that is the cause of there being a larger world population nowadays than in former times.

The most important and amazing demographic fact — the greatest human achievement in history, in my view — is this decrease in the world's death rate. . . .

Let's put it differently. In the nineteenth century, the planet Earth could sustain only 1 billion people. Ten thousand years ago, only 4 million could keep themselves alive. Now, more than 5 billion people are living longer and more healthily than ever before, on average. The increase in the world's population represents our victory over death.

I would expect lovers of humanity to jump with joy at this triumph of human mind and organization over the raw killing forces of nature. Instead, many lament that there are so many people alive to enjoy the gift of life. Some even express regret over the fall in the death rate.

Throughout history, the supply of natural resources always has worried people. Yet the data clearly show that natural resource scarcity — as measured by the economically meaningful indicator of cost or price — has been decreasing rather than increasing in the long run for all raw materials, with only temporary exceptions from time to time. That is, resource availability has been increasing. Consider copper, which is representative of all the metals. . . . The cost of a ton is only about a tenth now of what it was 200 years ago.

This trend of falling prices of copper has been going on for a very long time. In the eighteenth century B.C.E. in Babylonia under Hammurabi — almost 4,000 years ago — the price of copper was about 1,000 times its price in the United States now relative to wages. At the time of the Roman Empire, the price was about 100 times the present price. . . . Everything that we buy — pens, shirts, tires — has been getting cheaper over the years because we know how to make them cheaper. But, extraordinarily, natural resources have been getting cheaper even faster than consumer goods.

So by any measure, natural resources have been getting more available rather than more scarce.

Regarding oil, the price rise since the 1970s does not stem from an increase in the cost of world supply. The production cost per barrel in the Persian Gulf still is perhaps 50 cents per barrel. Concerning energy in general, there is no reason to believe that the supply of energy is finite, or that the price of energy will not continue its long-run decrease forever. I realize that it sounds weird to say that the supply of energy is not finite or limited, but I'll be delighted to give you a whole routine on this in the question period if you ask.[1]

Food is an especially important resource. The evidence is particularly strong for food that we are on a benign trend, despite rising population. The long-run price of food relative to wages is now only perhaps a tenth of what it was two centuries ago. Even relative to consumer products the price of grain is down, due to increased productivity.

---

[1]Simon argues that every "energy crisis" in the past (the deforestation of eighteenth-century England, anticipated coal shortages in the nineteenth century, a huge jump in the price of whale oil in the 1840s) has led to higher prices, which in turn "provided incentive for enterprising people to discover and produce substitutes" (Myers and Simon, *Scarcity or Abundance: A Debate on the Environment* [1994], p. 197). Human ingenuity and inventiveness has and will continue to overcome short-term shortages.

There is only one important resource which has shown a trend of increasing scarcity rather than increasing abundance. That resource is the most important of all — human beings. Yes, there are more people on Earth now than ever before. But if we measure the scarcity of people the same way that we measure the scarcity of other economic goods — by how much we must pay to obtain their services — we see that wages and salaries have been going up all over the world, in poor countries as well as in rich countries. The amount that you must pay to obtain the services of a barber or a cook has risen in India, just as the price of a barber or cook — or economist — has risen in the United States over the decades. This increase in the price of people's services is a clear indication that people are becoming more scarce even though there are more of us.

About pollution now: The evidence with respect to air indicates that pollutants have been declining, especially the main pollutant, particulates. With respect to water, the proportion of monitoring sites in the United States with water of good drinkability has increased since the data began in 1961.

Species extinction is a key issue for the environmental movement. It is the subject of magazine stories with titles like "Playing Dice with Megadeath," whose subtitle is: "The odds are good that we will exterminate half the world's species within the next century."

The issue came to scientific prominence in 1979 with my debate opponent Norman Myers's book *The Sinking Ark.* It then was brought to an international public and onto the U.S. policy agenda by the 1980 *Global 2000 Report to the President.* "Hundreds of thousands of species — perhaps as many as 20 percent of all species on earth — will be irretrievably lost as their habitats vanish, especially in tropical forests," the report said.

The actual data on the observed rates of species extinction are wildly at variance with Myers's and following statements, and do not provide support for the various policies suggested to deal with the purported dangers. . . .

With respect to population growth: A dozen competent statistical studies, starting in 1967 with an analysis by Nobel Prize winner Simon Kuznets, agree that there is no negative statistical relationship between economic growth and population growth. There is strong reason to believe that more poeple have a positive effect in the long run.

Now we need some theory to explain how it can be that economic welfare grows along with population, rather than humanity being reduced to misery and poverty as population grows.

The Malthusian theory of increasing scarcity, based on supposedly fixed resources — the theory that the doomsayers rely upon — runs exactly contrary to the data over the long sweep of history. Therefore it makes sense to prefer another theory.

The theory that fits the facts very well is this: More people, and increased income, cause problems in the short run. Short-run scarcity raises prices. This presents opportunity, and prompts the search for solutions. In a free society, solutions are eventually found. And in the long run the new developments leave us better off than if the problems had not arisen.

When we take a long-run view, the picture is different, and considerably more complex, from the simple short-run view of more people implying lower average income. In the very long run, more people almost surely imply more available resources and a higher income for everyone.

I suggest you test this proposition as follows: Do you think that our standard of living would be as high as it is now if the population had never grown from about 4 million human beings perhaps 10,000 years ago? I don't think we'd now have electric light or gas heat or autos or penicillin or travel to the Moon or our present life expectancy of over seventy years at birth in rich countries — in comparison to the life expectancy of twenty to twenty-five years at birth in earlier eras — if population had not grown to its present numbers. If population had never grown, instead of the pleasant lunch you had, you would have been out chasing rabbits and digging roots.

# "Environmental Degradation Is Overtaking the Planet"

▼▼▼

## 124 ▼ Norman Myers, *OPENING STATEMENT FROM 1992 DEBATE AT COLUMBIA UNIVERSITY*

Norman Myers was born in Whitewell, England in 1934, and after receiving his bachelor's degree from Oxford, he received his doctorate from the University of California at Berkeley. His research has focused mainly on the preservation of animal species, especially in Africa, but he has also published books on the ecology of tropical rain forests and the relationship between environmental degradation and international conflict. Myers has held visiting professorships at several universities and has served as an advisor for the World Bank and the World Wildlife Federation.

### QUESTIONS FOR ANALYSIS

1. What is the basis of Myers's pessimism about the state of the Earth? Who or what does he blame for the current crisis?
2. In what specific areas does Myers present data or informed opinion that he believes undermines Simon's (see source 123) arguments?
3. Are there any areas where Myers and Simon share common ground?
4. Which man has presented the stronger case?

I believe that, by contrast with Julian Simon, we are at a watershed in human history because of the grand-scale environmental degradation that is overtaking our planet in conjunction with excessive population growth and consumerism. Unless we change these trends and patterns, we are going to have a tough time of it. And not only us, but dozens and hundreds of human generations into the future. In fact, in the case of mass extinction of species, as many as 200,000 generations to come will be impoverished because of what we are doing during the present few decades. . . .

What do I mean when I speak of prospective environmental ruin worldwide? Let me give you a few quick statistics, all of them supported by reports from the World Bank, United Nations agencies, the Rockefeller Foundation, and organizations of similar reputable sort. Soil erosion: during the past year we have lost 25 billion tons of topsoil around the world — and it's as severe in parts of Indiana as in India. This lost topsoil has cost us 9 million tons of grain, enough to make up the diets of well over 200 million people who are "undernourished" (the jargon term for people who are semi-starving). Also during the past year we have lost 150,000 square kilometers of tropical forest, taking with them a host of watershed services. The economic costs are sizable: in the Ganges Valley alone in India, deforestation in the Himalayan foothills causes downstream flooding that imposes costs that, according to the Government of India, amount to well over $1 billion per year. During the past year, too, desertification has totaled 60,000 square kilometers, taking out agricultural lands with potential food output worth $42 billion.

Also during the past year, we have lost tens of thousands of species, again with an economic cost. When you visit your neighborhood pharmacy, there is one chance in two that the product on the counter before you would not be there if it were not for startpoint materials from wild plants and animals. The commercial value of these products is more than $40 billion a year. Think, then, of what we are losing when we hear of tens of thousands of species disappearing every year.

In the past year too, we have depleted the ozone layer still further. We have taken a solid step toward a greenhouse-affected world. And at the same time our Earth has taken on board another 93 million people, equivalent to more than a "new Mexico" — and this at a time when our Earth is straining under the burden of its present population of 5.5 billion people. . . .

Professor Simon has made much play with a statement by the National Academy of Sciences in 1986, proposing that population growth and environmental degradation were not really problems at all. Let me tell you of another statement issued by the National Academy of Sciences in May 1992, in conjunction with the British Royal Society in London. . . . The statement goes like this — . . .

> If current predictions of population growth prove accurate and patterns of human activity on the planet remain unchanged, science and technology may not be able to prevent either irreversible degradation of the environment or continued poverty for much of the world. . . . Unrestrained resource consumption for energy production and other uses . . . could lead to catastrophic outcomes for the global environment. Some of the environmental changes may produce irreversible damage to the Earth's capacity to sustain life. The overall pace of environmental change has unquestionably been accelerated by the recent expansion of the hu-

man population. . . . The future of our planet is in the balance.

Let's move on to consider biodiversity and mass extinction of species. The issue is on this evening's agenda as one of the critical points for our debate. It is all the more important, I suggest, because mass extinction is a unique environmental problem: it is irreversible. All our other environmental problems can be turned around if we want to spend enough time and money. We can push back the deserts. We can replant tropical forests. We can wait until topsoil is restored, the ozone layer is replenished, and global climate is stabilized. True, these recoveries will take a few centuries. But no doubt about it, all these problems can be fixed up. Mass extinction of species is different. When a species is gone, it's gone for good. . . .

What is the evidence for the mass extinction under way? Consider a 1992 book by Professor Edward O. Wilson of Harvard University, *The Diversity of Life.* Wilson has calculated, using analytic models which are thoroughly established in the biological field, that we are now losing, very roughly reckoned, at least 30,000 species every year. That is 120,000 times the natural background rate of the prehistoric past. Professor Wilson's estimate is paralleled by those of a dozen other eminent scientists in this country, and by my own estimate as well. We all come up with very similar figures. Fifteen leading scientists in the United States have banded together into what they call the Club of Earth. It is a group open only to biologists who are members of both the National Academy and the American Academy, meaning they are scientists whose professional credentials are beyond question. They have all come up with the same basic conclusion as concerns the figure of 30,000 species every year becoming extinct per year. . . .

Let's move on to the population factor, and the question of how far we may have too many people on Earth already. . . . Technologists will say, with justification, that from 1950 right through 1984, we did a marvelous job. Thanks to the Green

Revolution, each year we produced more food at a rate of increase that was greater than the rate of population growth. For all of those three and a half decades, we had more food per person worldwide, on average. But since 1985, there has been a leveling off in grain production. The increase per year has averaged only 0.7 percent, by contrast with those thirty-five years when it was around 3 percent. Meantime population growth remains almost 2 percent. So the upshot is that food availability per person worldwide has been declining for eight long, lean years.

Fortunately, there's some better news on the population front. It concerns family planning. Some people, and you have put yourself among them, Julian, have referred to family planning as an imperialist imposition on people in the developing world. Today, 90 percent of all people in the developing world live in countries that have declared their population growth rates are too high — and they want to bring them down as quickly as they can. They are clamoring for family planning support from whatever nations in the world will supply it. This applies especially to the 300 million couples who have decided they want no more children, but lack access to birth-control facilities. . . .

A final point: our changing relationship to nature. We are now in control of the Earth. We are no longer a part of nature, we are apart from nature. Or so we like to think — even though we still have to breathe and eat and perform all kinds of other biological functions. With regard to our fellow species, we have reached the point where we have tried to play Noah, and we are finding that our Arks have been far too small (otherwise we would be saving those 30,000 species disappearing every year). Each time we assign a pile of dollars to save one species, we are automatically denying those same dollars to other species. There simply are not enough funds to go around, not by a long way. We don't make this dreadful choice deliberately. But the choice is built into a situation where we have insufficient funds to save all species. Essentially, then, we are deciding which species we shall save and which species we shall put over the side of the boat. Having goofed at playing Noah, we are now playing God. This is a fundamental change in our entire relationship to nature.

A final key question arises from my remarks, ladies and gentlemen. I believe we have to ask ourselves not only how much do we want to spend to save tropical forests or to save species or to grow more food, and so on. The basic question at a crisis stage in human history is this: What sort of a world do we want to live in? What sort of a world do we want to pass on to future generations — not just our children and grandchildren, but hundreds and thousands of generations? In other words, What kind of people do we want to be? That is a question that is not answered by citing reams of statistics from the marketplace.

# Sources

## Prologue

(1) Cecil, Jane, ed. and trans., *Select Documents Illustrating the Four Voyages of Columbus*, 2 vols. (London: The Hakluyt Society, 1930–1933), 1:2–18. Reprinted by permission of David Higham Association, London. (2) Anonymous, Woodcut of 1511.

## Part One ▾ *The World in the Era of Western Expansion: 1500–1650*

## Chapter 1

Source 1: William Hazlitt, ed. and trans., *The Table Talk of Martin Luther* (London: H. G. Bohn, 1857), pp. 25–27, 117, 198, 205–206, 219, 294, 298, 300, 357, 359. Source 2: From Hans J. Schroeder, *Canons and Decrees of the Council of Trent* (St. Louis, MO: B. Herder, 1941), pp. 42–43, 273, 276–278, 175–176, 152–153, 253–254, 215–216. Source 3: (1) Lucas Cranach, *Two Kinds of Preaching: Evangelical and Papal,* © Staatliche Museen zu Berlin Preussischer Kulturbesitz. Kupferstichkabinett. (2) Mattias Gerung, *Allegory: The Pope and Sultan in a 2-way Cart.* Courtesy of The British Museum. Source 4: Charles Gibson, ed., *The Spanish Tradition in America* (New York: Harper & Row, 1968), pp. 113–120. Source 5: Bartolemé de Las Casa, *In Defense of the Indians,* ed. and trans. by Stafford Poole (DeKalb, IL: Northern Illinois Press, 1992). Copyright © 1974 Northern Illinois University Press. Used with permission of the publisher. Source 6: Katherine Usher Henderson and Barbara F. McManus, *Half Humankind: Contexts and Texts of the Controversy about Women in England* (Champaign, IL: University of Illinois Press, 1985), pp. 336–342. Copyright © 1985. Used by permission of University of Illinois Press. Source 7: (1) Anton Woensam, *Allegory of a Wise Woman,* in Max Geisberg, ed., *The German Single Leaf Woodcut 1500–1650* (New York: Hacker Art Books, 1974), vol. 4, p. 1511. Used with permission of the publisher. (2) Erhard Schön, *No More Precious Treasure Is on the Earth Than a Gentle Wife Who Longs for Honor,* Courtesy of Schlossmuseum Gotha, Gotha, Germany. Source 8: Merry E. Wiesner, "Midwives and Their Duties: from *Birth, Death, and Pleasures of Life: Working Women in Nuremberg, 1480–1620.* University of Wisconsin PhD Dissertation, 1977–1978, pp. 65–71. Reprinted by permission of the author. Source 9: Reprinted from *The Complete Essays of Montaigne,* translated by Donald M. Frame with the permission of the publishers, Stanford University Press. © 1958 by the Board of Trustees of the Leland Stanford Junior University. Source 10: Excerpts from *Discoveries and Opinions of Galileo* by Galileo Galilei. Copyright © 1957 by Stillman Drake. Used by permission of Doubleday, a division of Random House, Inc.

## Chapter 2

Source 11: Leo Africanus, *The History and Description of Africa,* ed. by Robert Brown (London: The Hakluyt Society, 1896), vol. 3, pp. 823–827, 832–834. Source 12: *The Book of Duarte Barbosa: An Account of the Countries Bordering the Indian Ocean,* 2 vols. (London: The Hakluyt Society, 1918, 1921). Source 13: Basil Davidson, trans., *The African Past* (London: Curis Brown, Ltd., 1964). Source 14: George McCall Theal, ed. and trans. *Records of South-Eastern Africa* (London: F.W. Clowes for the Government of the Cape Colony, 1898), vol. 7, pp. 293–300. Source 15: (1) *A Benin-Portuguese Saltcellar,* © Copyright The British Museum, London. (2) *A Benin Wall Plaque*: Multiple Figures, Edo Peoples, Benin Kingdom, Nigeria, Photograph by Franko Khoury, courtesy of The National Museum of African Art, Eliot Elisofon Photographic Archives, Smithsonian Institution. Source 16: James Lockhart, ed. and trans., *We People Here: Nahuatl Accounts of the Conquest of Mexico.* University of California Press, 1993. Reprinted by permission of the University of California Press. Source 17: Mi 'kmaq elder's speech, in Crestian Le Clercq, *New Relation of Gaspesia,* William Ganong, trans. (Toronto: The Champlain Society, 1910), pp. 103–106. Source 18: John H. Parry and R obery Keith, "Exploitation vs. Amerindian Rights in the Encomienda System" from *New Iberian World,* vol. 5 (New York: Times Books, 1984), pp. 308–312. Source 19: Antonio Vazquez de Espinosa, *Compendium and Description of the West Indies* (Washington, DC: Smithsonian Institution, 1942), pp. 621–625, 629, 631–634. Source 20: James Lockhart, Francis Berdan, and Arthur Anderson, eds., "Deliberations of the Tlaxcalan Municipal Council" from *The Tlaxcalan Actas* (Salt Lake City: University of Utah Press, 1986), 80–84. Reprinted by permission of the University of Utah Press.

## Chapter 3

Source 21: Ogier Ghiselin de Busbecq, *The Life and Letters of Ogier Ghiselin de Busbecq* (London: Kegan Paul, 1881), pp. 113–120 (passim), 153–155, 218–220, 254. Source 22: From Fr. Paul Simon: *A Chronicle of the Carmelites in Persia and the Papal Mission of the XVIIth and XVIIIth Centuries* (London: Eyre and Spottiswoode, 1939), I, pp. 158–161, 162. Source 23: David Price, trans., *Memoirs of the Emperor Jahanguir Written by Himself* (London: Oriental Translation Society, 1928), pp. 8–12, 13–20, 33–36, 51–53, 65–66. Source 24: John J. Saunders, ed., *The Muslim World on the Eve of Europe's Expansion* (Englewood Cliffs, NJ: Prentice-Hall, 1966), pp. 41–43. Source 25: Abul Fazl, *The Ain-i-Akari,* ed. and trans. by H. S. Jarrett (Calcutta, India: Baptist Mission Press, 1868–1894), vol. 3, pp. 8, 114–119, 159–160, 225–232, 279, 284, 285–286, 291–292. Source 26: C. T. Foster and F. H. Blackburne Daniell, eds., *The Life and Letters of Ogier Ghiselin de Busbecq,* 2 vols.

(London: The Hakluyt Society, 1881), vol. 1, pp. 152–156, 219–221. **Source 27:** Poems by Nanak from *The Sacred Writings of the Sikhs,* translated by Trilochan Singh, Bhai Jodh Singh, Kapar Singh, Bawa Harkishen Singh, Kushwant Singh. (London: Allen & Unwin, 1960), pp. 76–79. Part of *UNESCO Collection of Representative Works: Indian Series.*

## Chapter 4

**Source 28:** From *Self and Society and Ming Thought,* by Theodore de Bary, ed. (New York: Columbia University Press, 1970), pp. 352–361. © 1970 Columbia University Press. Reprinted with the permission of the publisher. **Source 29:** David J. Lu, *Japan: A Documentary History* (Armonk, NY: M. E. Sharpe, 1997), pp. 258–261. Reprinted by permission of the author. **Source 30:** Extracts of Wang Dao-k'un, Biography of Zhu Jiefu and Gentleman Wang. Reprinted with the permission of The Free Press, A Division of Simon & Schuster from *Chinese Civilization and Society: A Sourcebook* by Patricia Buckley Ebrey. Copyright © 1981 by The Free Press. **Source 31:** (1) Zhang Hung, *Landscape of Shixie Hill,* Collection of the National Palace Museum, Taiwan, Republic of China. (2) Sheng Maoye, *Scholars Gazing at a Waterfall,* © Bildarchiv Prussischer Kulturbesitz, Berlin. Staatliche Museen zu Berlin-PreuBischer Kulturbesitz. Museum fur Ostasiatische Kunst. Foto/Jahr: Petra Stüning/1991. **Source 32:** Lien, Memorial to Emperor Ming Xizong is reprinted with the permission of The Free Press, a Division of Simon & Schuster, from *Chinese Civilization and Society: A Sourcebook,* 2nd ed. by Patricia Buckley Ebrey (New York: The Free Press, 1993), pp. 263–266. Copyright © 1993 by Patricia Buckley Ebrey. **Source 33:** Ryusaka Tasunoda, William Theodore de Bary, Donald Keene, and others, *Sources of Japanese Tradition* (New York: Columbia University Press, 1958), pp. 117–200. **Source 34:** David John Lu, *Sources of Japanese History* (New York: McGraw-Hill, 1974), vol. 1, pp. 207–209. **Source 35:** *Records of the Relations between Siam and Foreign Countries in the Seventeenth Century* (Bangkok: Council of the Vajiranana National Library, 1916), vol. 2, pp. 10–14, 17–18.

## Part II ▾ A World of Transformation and Tradition, from the Mid Seventeenth to Early Nineteenth Century

## Chapter 5

**Source 36:** James Spedding, R. L. Ellis, and Douglas Heath, eds., *The Works of Francis Bacon* (New York: Hurd and Houghton, 1864), vol. 10, pp. 67–69, 72–75, 131–132, 140–142. **Source 37:** Sébastien Le Clerc, *The Royal Academy and Its Protectors* and *Dissection at the Jardin des Plantes.* Courtesy of The Bancroft Library, University of California

at Berkeley. **Source 38:** Marquis de Condorcet, *Esquisse d'un tableau historique des progrès de l'esprit humain,* in *Oeuvres de Condorcet,* vol. 6 (Paris: Firmin Didot Frères, 1847), pp. 186–187, 223–225, 229–321, 237–244, 250–251, 255–256, 263–266, 272–276. **Source 39:** Jean-Baptiste Colbert, *Lettres, instructions et mémoires de Colbert* (Paris: Imprimerie Nationale, 1870) vol. 6, pp. 262–266; vol. 7, pp. 233–256. **Source 40:** Adam Smith, *An Inquiry into the Nature and Causes of the Wealth of Nations* (Hartford, CT: Cooke and Hale, 1818); vol. 7, pp. 10–12, 40, 43, 299–304, 316, 317, 319, 330, 331. **Source 41:** Blinoff, *Life and Thought in Old Russia* (University Park: Pennsylvania State University Press, 1961), pp. 49–50; Eugene Schuyler, *Peter the Great,* vol. 2, pp. 176–177; L. Jay Oliva, *Peter the Great* (Englewood Cliffs, NJ: Prentice-Hall, 1970), p. 50; George Vernadsky et al., *A Source Book for Russian History from Early Times to 1917,* vol. 2 (New Haven and London: Yale University Press, 1972), pp. 347, 329, 357. **Source 42:** From *On the Corruption of Morals in Russia* from M. M. Shcherbatov, A. Lenten, trans. and ed. Copyright © 1969 Cambridge University Press. Reprinted with the permission of Cambridge University Press. **Source 43:** *The Statutes: Revised Edition* (London: Eyre and Spottiswoode, 1871), vol. 1, pp. 10–12. **Source 44:** J. B. Buchez and P.-C. Roux, *Histoire parlementaire de la revolution française* (Paris: Librarie Paulin, 1834), vol. 1, pp. 335–354, trans. by J. Overfield. **Source 45:** From *Women in Revolutionary Paris, 1789–1795.* Copyright 1979 by the Board of Trustees of the University of Illinois. Used with the permission of the University of Illinois Press. **Source 46:** Thomas Paine, *The Political Writings of Thomas Paine* (New York: Solomon King, 1830), vol. 1, pp. 21, 22, 25, 28, 29, 31, 33–35, 40–47. **Source 47:** From Simón Bolívar, *Selected Writings,* ed. Harold A. Bierck, trans. Lewis Berrand (New York: Colonial Press, 1951), pp. 103–122.

## Chapter 6

**Source 48:** Paul Edwards, ed. and trans., *Equiano's Travels* (Oxford Heinemann Educational Books, 1967), pp. 25–42. **Source 49:** J. Awnsham and J. Churchill, *Collections of Voyages and Travels,* 3rd ed. (8 vols.) (London: H. Lintot, 1744–1747), pp. 459, 460, trans. by J. Overfield. **Source 50:** Lucien Peytraud, *L'esclavage aux Antilles Françaises avant 1789* (Paris: Hachette & Cie, 1897), pp. 193–203, trans. by J. Overfield. **Source 51:** Mehmed Pasha, "The Book of Council . . . ," in Mehmed Pasha, *The Book of Counsel for Viziers and Governors,* ed. and trans. Walter L. Wright, Jr. Copyright © 1935 by Princeton University Press. Reprinted by permission of Princeton University Press. **Source 52:** François Bernier, *Travels in the Mogul Empire,* ed. Archibald Constable (London: Oxford University Press, 1891), pp. 205–209, 220–225, 230–231. **Source 53:** J. O'Kinealy, "Translation of an Arabic Pamphlet on the History and Doctrines of the Wahhabis, Written by 'Abdullah,

Grandson of 'Abdul Wahhab, the Founder of the Wahhabis," *Journal of the Asiatic Society of Bengal,* vol. 43 (1874), pp. 68–82. **Source 54:** Usman dan Fodio, "The Book of Differences," from M. Hiskett, "Kitab al-farq: A Work on the Habe Kingdoms Attributed to Uthmann dan Fodio," in *Bulletin of the School of Oriental and African Studies,* vol. 23 (1960); "Concerning the Government of Our Country," from Tanbih al-ikhwan, translation in Thomas Hodgkin, *Nigerian Perpectives* (Oxford: Oxford University Press, 1975), pp. 244, 245; "Light of Intellectuals," from *Nur al-albab,* in Hodgkin, pp. 254–255; "Dispatch to the Folk of the Sudan, from A. D. H. Bivar, "The Whatiqat ahl al-Sudan: A Manifesto of the Fulani Jihad," in *The Journal of African History,* vol. 2 (1961).

## Chapter 7

**Source 55:** From *Emperor of China: Self-Portrait of K'ang-hsi* by Jonathan D. Spence. (New York: Random House, 1974), pp. 29–30, 32–34, 40, 50, 51, 67, 68, 72–75, 79–82. Copyright © 1974 by Jonathan D. Spence. Reprinted by permission of Alfred A. Knopf, a Division of Random House, Inc. **Source 56:** J. O. P. Brand, *Annals and Memoirs of the Court of Peking* (Boston: Houghton Mifflin, 1914), pp. 325–331. **Source 57:** Mitsui Takafusa, "Some Observations on Merchants," from "Some Observations on Merchants, a translation of Mitsui Takafusa's *Choni Koken Roku,"* ed. and trans. E. S. Crawcour in *Transactions of the Asiatic Society of Japan,* Third series, vol. 8 (Tokyo, 1961), pp. 39–41, 49, 56, 57, 77, 78, 82, 103, 121. Reprinted by permission of the Asiatic Society of Japan. **Source 58:** Excerpted from *The Japanese Discovery of Europe, 1720–1830,* Revised Edition, by Donald Keene with the permission of the publishers, Stanford University Press. © 1952 and 1969 by Donald Keene. **Source 59:** Robert McNab, *Historical Records of New Zealand* (Wellington, New Zealand: Government Printing Office, 1908), vol. 1, pp. 417–421. **Source 60:** *House of Common Parliamentary Papers* (London: Her Majesty's Printing Office, 1839), enclosures no. 2 in "Copies of Extracts of Dispatches Relative to the Massacre of Various Aborigines of Australia in the Year 1838 and Respecting the Trial of Their Murderers," pp. 6–13.

## *Part Three ▾ The World in the Age of Western Dominance: 1800–1914*

## Chapter 8

**Source 61:** "Report from the Committee on the Bill to Regulate the Labour of Children in the Mills and the Factories of the United Kingdom," *British Sessional Papers,* vol. 15 (London, 1832), pp. 195, 196; "Second Report of the Commission of Inquiry into the Employment of Children in Factories," *British Sessional Papers,* vol. 21, pt. D-3 (London, 1833), pp. 26–28; "First Report of the Commission

of Inquiry into the Employment of Children in Mines," *British Sessional Papers,* vol. 16 (London, 1842), pp. 149, 230, 258, 263–264. **Source 62:** Samuel Smiles, *Self-Help* (New York: Harper, 1897), pp. 21–23, 298–299, 302, 305; *Thrift* (London: John Murray, 1875), pp. 30–40. **Source 63:** Karl Marx and Friedrich Engels, *The Manifesto of the Communist Party,* authorized English trans. by Samuel Moore (London: W. Reeves, 1888). **Source 64:** Sarah Stickney Ellis, *Wives of England* (London: 1843), pp. 70, 76–77, 78, 101–102, 102–105. **Source 65:** Gerda Lerner, ed., *The Female Experience: An American Documentation* (Indianapolis, IN: Bobbs Merrill, 1977), pp. 343–347. **Source 66:** Louis L. Synder, ed., *Documents of German History* (New Brunswick, NJ: Rutgers University Press, 1958), pp. 259–262. Copyright © 1958 by Rutgers, the State University. Reprinted by permission of Rutgers University Press. **Source 67:** Ralph Austen, ed., *Modern Imperialism* (Lexington, MA: D. C. Heath, 1969), pp. 70–73. Copyright © 1969. Used by permission. **Source 68:** (1–3) Mrs. Ernest (Mary Frances) Ames, *An ABC for Baby Patriots* (London: Dean & Son, 1899), pp. "E," "I," "W." Courtesy of de Grummond Children's Literature Collection, University of Southern Mississippi. (4) From *The Kipling Reader* (London: Macmillan, 1908), illus. by J. MacFarlane. By permission of the Houghton Library, Harvard University. (5) Masthead from *The Missionary News,* March 15, 1866. Courtesy of the Art Archive. (6) Lipton Teas ad from *Illustrated London News,* vol. XVI, no. 3058, November 27, 1897. Courtesy of The Illustrated London News Picture Library. **Source 69:** Gottfried Menzel, The United States of North America, with Special Reference to German Emigration. From Edith Abbott, *Historical Aspects of the Immigration Problem* (Chicago: University of Chicago Press, 1926), pp. 136–142. Reprinted by permission of the Ayer Company. **Source 70:** *Congressional Record,* Fifty-Fourth Congress, First Session, vol. XXVIII (Washington, DC: United States Government Printing Office, 1896), pp. 2817–2820.

## Chapter 9

**Source 71:** Edward Hertslet, ed., *The Map of Africa by Treaty,* 2nd ed. (Her Majesty's Stationery Office, 1896), vol. 1, pp. 467–468. **Source 72:** Margery Perham, ed., *Ten Africans.* Copyright © 1936 by Faber & Faber, Ltd. Used with permission. **Source 73:** From C. G. K. Gwasa and John Iliffe, *Records of the Maji-Maji Rising.* (Nairobi: East African Publishing House, 1967), pp. 4–8 (Historical Association of Tanzania, Paper Number 4). **Source 74:** E. A. Van Dyck, *Report upon the Capitulations of the Ottoman Empire since the Year 1150* (Washington, DC: United States Government Printing Office, 1881, 1882), Part 1, pp. 106–108. **Source 75:** Edward G. Brown, *The Persian Revolution of 1905.* Copyright © 1966 by Frank Cass & Co. Used with permission. **Source 76:** A. Sarrov, *La Jeune-turquie et la révolution* (Paris: Bergier-Leviault, 1912), pp. 40–42, trans. as "Young Turks" in Rondo Cameron, ed. and trans., *Civilization Since Waterloo* (Arlington Heights, IL: Harlan Davidson, 1971), pp. 245–246. Reprinted with permission. **Source 77:** Sylvia Haim, *Arab Nationalism: An Anthology* (Berkeley: University of California Press, 1962), pp. 83–88. Selection and translation of text are made by her and copyrighted to her. **Source 78:** Rammohun Roy, *The English Works of Raja Rammohun Roy* (Allahabad, India: Panini Office, 1906), pp. 471–474. **Source 79:** G. V. Joshi, *Writings and Speeches* (Poonah: Arya Bhushan Press, 1912), pp. 674, 675, 680–682, 688, 689.

## Chapter 10

**Source 80:** Dun J. Li, *China in Transition* (New York: Van Nostrand, 1969), pp. 64–67. Used by permission of Wadsworth Publishing Company. **Source 81:** Dun J. Li, *China in Transition* (New York: Van Nostrand, 1969), pp. 64–67. Used by permission of Wadsworth Publishing Company. **Source 82:** Reprinted from *Prescriptions for Saving China: Selected Writings of Sun Yat-sen,* edited by Julie Lee Wei, Ramon H. Myers, and Donald G. Gillin, with the permission of the publisher, Hoover Institution Press. Translation copyright 1994 by the Board of Trustees of the Leland Stanford Junior University. **Source 83:** Charles Terry, "Sakuma Shozan and His Seiken-Roku," unpublished master's thesis, Columbia University, 1951, in Ryusaka Tsumoda, W. T. de Bary, and Doanld Keene, *Sources of Japanese Tradition* (New York: Columbia University Press, 1958), pp. 611–613. Copyright © Columbia University Press 1966. Used by permission. **Source 84:** David John Lu, *Sources of Japanese History* (New York: McGraw-Hill, 1974), vol. 2, pp. 42–45. **Source 85:** (1) *The Black Ship,* Kurofune-Kan [Black Ship Museum], Kashiwazaki, Japan. Courtesy of Yokohama Archives of History.(2) Anonymous, 1853, Japan. "Visit of American Ships in Shimoda Harbor, Kaei VI (1853) with Commodore Perry, Officers and Men, etc." Handscroll in colors on paper. Gift of Mrs. Walter F. Dillingham (Given in Memory of Alice Perry Grew), 1960. HAA 2732.1. Courtesy of Honolulu Academy of Arts. (3) Kobayashi Kyochika, *Fukuchi Gen'ichiro.* In Julia Meech-Pekarik, *The World of Meiji Print* (New York: John Weatherill, 1986). Courtesy of the Metropolitan Museum of Art. (4) Kanagaki Robun, *Hiking through the West.* (5) Honda Kinkichiro, *"Monkey Show Dressing Room,"* and (6) Kobayashi Kyochika, *"Hands Dance, Feet Stomp, Call Out Hurray!"* (New York: John Weatherill, 1986). Used with permission. (Prints for 1 and 3–6 Courtesy of the Library of Congress.) **Source 86:** Chomchai Prachom, *Chulalongkorn the Great* (Tokyo: Center for East Asian Cultural Studies, 1965), pp. 52–56, 90–95. Copyright © 1965 by the Center for East Asian Cultural Studies. Used with permission. **Source 87:** From *We the Vietnamese: Voices from Vietnam* by Francis Sully and Donald Kirk, © 1971 Praeger Publishers. Reprinted by permission of Henry Holt and Company, LLC.

## Part Four ▾ Global Society and Its Challenges in the Twentieth Century

Chapter 11

**Source 88:** (1) B. Hennerberg: *The Departure,* in *World War I and European Society: A Sourcebook,* by Marilyn Shevin-Coetzee and Frans Coetzee (Lexington, MA: D. C. Heath, 1995) p. 6. Copyright © 1995. Used by permission of D. C. Heath & Co. (2) Advertisement card from Golden Dawn Cigarettes, (3) Australian recruitment poster, and (4) French poster encouraging purchase of war bonds, Courtesy of Imperial War Museum, London. **Source 89:** Wilfred Owen, *Poems,* ed. by Siegfried Sassoon (London: Chatto and Windus, 1920). **Source 90:** (1) C. R. W. Nevinson, *The Harvest of Battle,* Courtesy of Imperial War Museum, London. (2) Otto Dix, *The War II/2: Shock Troop Advancing under Gas Attack.* (1924). Etching, aquatint and drypoint, printed in black, plate: 7-9/16 x 11-5/16: (19.3 x 28.2 cm.). Courtesy of The Museum of Modern Art, New York. Gift of Abby Aldrich Rockefeller. Photograph © 1997 The Museum of Modern Art, New York. **Source 91:** V. L. Lenin, *Collected Works,* vol. 5, (London: Lawrence and Wishart, 1973), pp. 352–353, 375–376, 399–401, 413–414, 425, 454, 463–467. **Source 92:** Joseph Stalin, "The Tasks of Business Executives" (Speech at the First All-Union Conference of Managers of Soviet Industry, February 1931), in *Problems of Leninism* (Moscow, 1940), pp. 359–360, 365–366. **Source 93:** Adolf Hitler, *Mein Kampf* (Munich: F. Eher Nachfolger, 1927), trans. by J. Overfield. **Source 94:** Otto D. Tolischus, *Tokyo Record* (New York: Harcourt Brace, 1943), pp. 405–407, 411–415, 421–426. **Source 95:** From Rudolf Höss, *Death Dealer, The Memoirs of the SS Kommandant at Auschwitz,* ed. Steven Paskuly (Amherst, NY: Prometheus Books). Copyright 1992. Reprinted by permission of the publisher. **Source 96:** Michael B. Stoff, Jonathan Fanton, and R. Hal Williams, *The Manhattan Project: A Documentary Introduction to the Atomic Age* (Philadelphia: Temple University Press, 1991), pp. 140, 143–145. **Source 97:** Copyright © 1947 by *Harper's Magazine.* All rights reserved. Reproduced from the February issue by special permission.

## Chapter 12

**Source 98:** Mustafa Kemal, *A Speech Delivered by Ghazi Mustapha Kemal* (Leipzig: F. F. Koehler, 1929), pp. 376–379, 589–594, 717, 721–722. **Source 99:** *The Zionist Idea* by Arthur Hertzberg, copyright © 1959 by Arthur Hertzberg. Used by permission of Doubleday, a division of Random House, Inc. **Source 100:** Hasan al-Banna, "Towards the Light," in Robert Langdon, *The Emergence of the Middle East* © 1970. Reprinted with permission of Wadsworth, a division of Thomson Learning. **Source 101:** Mohandas Gandhi, *Indian Home Rule* (Madras, India: Ganesh & Co., 1922), pp. 30–35, 47–50, 63, 64, 85, 68, 90, 91. Copyright © 1922. Used by permission of Ganesh & Co. **Source 102:** Harry Benda and John Larkin, *The World of*

*Southeast Asia* (New York: Harper & Row, 1967), pp. 182–185. Copyright © 1967 by Harper & Row, Publishers. Reprinted by permission of the authors. **Source 103:** James Aggrey, "Parable of the Eagle," in Edward W. Smith, *Aggrey of Africa.* Copyright © 1929 by SCM Press. Used by permission. **Source 104:** Donald A. Low, *The Mind of Buganda* (Berkeley: University of California Press, 1971), pp. 104–108. Reprinted by permission of the University of California Press. **Source 105:** Thomas Karis and Gwendolen M. Carter, eds., *From Protest to Challenge: A Documentary History of South Africa, 1882–1964*, vol. 1 (Stanford, CA: Hoover Institution Press, 1972), pp. 344–346. **Source 106:** Benjamin Keen, ed. and trans., *Readings in Latin American Civilization* (Boston: Houghton Mifflin, 1955), pp. 362–364. **Source 107:** Bradford E. Burns, *A Documentary History of Brazil* (New York: Knopf, 1966), pp. 347–353. **Source 108:** Reprinted with the permission of The Free Press, a Division of Simon & Schuster, from *Chinese Civilization: A Sourcebook*, 2nd ed., by Patricia Buckley Ebrey. Copyright © 1993 by Patricia Buckley Ebrey. **Source 109:** Mao Zedong, *Selected Works of Mao Tse-tung* (Beijing: Foreign Languages Press, 1965), pp. 89–90, 92–96, 103–105.

## Chapter 13

**Source 110:** George Kennan, "The Long Telegram" in Kenneth Jensen, ed., *Origins of the Cold War*, The Novikov, Kennan and Robert's "Long Telegrams of 1946" (Washington, DC: The United States Institute of Peace, 1991), pp. 3–31, *passim*. Reprinted by permission of the United States Institute of Peace. **Source 111:** Nikolai Novikov, "Telegram September 27, 1946" in Kenneth Jensen, ed., *Origins of the Cold War*, Novikov, Kennan and Robert's "Long Telegrams of 1946" (Washington, DC: The United States Institute of Peace, 1991), pp. 3–31, *passim*. Reprinted by permission of the United States Institute of Peace. **Source 112:** *Parliamentary Debates*, 5th ser., vol. 434 (London: His Majesty's Printing Office, 1947). **Source 113:** Excerpts from *Biafra: Volume 1, Selected Speeches; Volume 2, Random Thoughts* by C. Odumegwu Ojukwa. Copyright © 1969 by Chukwuemka Odumegwa Ojukwu. Reprinted by permis-

sion of HarperCollins Publishers, Inc. **Source 114:** Girilal Jain, "On Hindu Rashtra," from Koenrad Elst, *Ayodya and After* (New Delhi: Crescent Printing Works, 1991). Reprinted by permission of the author. **Source 115:** World Bank, *World Development Report: 1972, 1978, 1984, 1998, 1999–2000* (New York: Oxford University Press, 1972, 1978, 1984, 1998, 1999). **Source 116:** Miranda Davies, ed., *Third World, Second Sex* (London: Zed Press, 1983), pp. 152–159. Copyright © 1983. Used by permission of Zed Books, Ltd. **Source 117:** Association of African Women for Research and Development, "A Statement on Genital Mutilation," from Miranda Davies, ed., *Third World, Second Sex* (London: Zed Press, 1983), pp. 217–220. Reprinted by permission of Zed Books, Ltd. **Source 118:** Ming, "Biographical Recollections," in Denyse Vershuur-Basse, *Chinese Women Speak,* Elizabeth Rauch-Nolan, trans. Copyright © 1996 by Praeger Publishers. Reproduced with permission of Greenwood Publishing Group, Inc., Westport, CT. **Source 119:** Nelson Mandela, *No Easy Walk to Freedom,* ed. Ruth First (New York: Basic Books, 1965), pp. 163–168, 180–181, 184–189. Copyright © 1965. Used by permission of Heinemann Educational Books, Ltd. **Source 120:** "Letter from a Birmingham Jail," From Martin Luther King, Jr., *Why We Can't Wait* (New York: Harper and Row, 1963). Reprinted by arrangement with the Heirs to the Estate of Martin Luther King, Jr., c/o Writers House, Inc. as agent for the proprietor. Copyright 1963 by Martin Luther King, Jr., copyright renewed 1991 by Coretta Scott King. **Source 121:** Deng Xiaoping, *Fundamental Issues in Present-Day China* (Beijing: Foreign Languages Press, 1987), pp. 105–109, 42–44, 69–72, 101–102, 162–163. Pergamon Press. **Source 122:** Excerpts (pp. 18, 19, 21–25, 30–36) from *Perestroika* by Mikhail Gorbachev. Copyright © 1987 by Mikhail Gorbachev. Reprinted by permission of HarperCollins Publishers, Inc. **Sources 123 and 124:** From *Scarcity or Abundance? A Debate on the Environment*, by Norman Myers and Julian L. Simon. Copyright © 1994 by Norman Myers, Julian Simon, and the Columbia University School of International and Public Affairs. Reprinted by permission of W. W. Norton & Company, Inc.